Cases in Strategic Management

Cases in Strategic Management

SECOND EDITION

Edited by

Colin M. Clarke-Hill and
Keith W. Glaister

PITMAN PUBLISHING
128 Long Acre, London WC2E 9AN

A Division of Pearson Professional Limited

First published in Great Britain in 1991
Second edition 1995

© C.M. Clarke-Hill and K.W. Glaister 1991
© Pearson Professional Limited 1995
© Cases 6 and 7 J.L. Thompson 1995

British Library Cataloguing in Publication Data
A CIP catalogue record for this book can be obtained from the British Library

ISBN 0 273 60380 9

10 9 8 7 6 5 4 3 2 1

Typeset by Mathematical Composition Setters Ltd.
Printed and bound in Great Britain by Page Bros.

The Publishers' policy is to use paper manufactured from sustainable forests.

CONTENTS

List of Contributors ix

Preface xi

Acknowledgements xiii

Section 1 THE STRATEGIC MANAGEMENT PROCESS AND THE CASE METHOD

Chapter 1 Introduction to the strategic management process 3
K.W. Glaister, University of Leeds

Chapter 2 Strategic management case analysis 25
K.W. Glaister, University of Leeds

Chapter 3 Financial analysis for case studies 33
K.W. Glaister and H. Short, University of Leeds

Section 2 RETAILING

Case 1 Asda Group Plc (A) 55
K.W. Glaister, University of Leeds

Case 2 Asda Group Plc (B) 75
K.W. Glaister, University of Leeds

Case 3 Argyll Group Plc 90
C.M. Clarke-Hill, University of Huddersfield and
T.M. Robinson, University of Teeside

Case 4 Burton and Next – the changing high street 108
C.M. Clarke-Hill, University of Huddersfield

Section 3 NOT-FOR-PROFIT ORGANIZATIONS

Case 5 Cromarty Courthouse Museum 123
G. Watson, Ross and Cromarty District Council

Case 6 London Zoo 132
J.L. Thompson, University of Huddersfield

Case 7 The National Trust 141
J.L. Thompson, University of Huddersfield

Case 8   Kirklees Metropolitan Council:
          corporate strategy in a local authority   150
          S. Davies, University of Leeds, and D. Griffiths, Kirklees MC

Section 4   SERVICES

Case 9   Abbey National Plc   177
          D. Thwaites, University of Leeds, and J.P. Dewhirst,
          Elmwood Design Ltd

Case 10   The *Caisses d'Epargne* (French savings banks)   197
          B. Moingeon and B. Ramanantsoa, Groupe HEC,
          Jouy-en-Josas, France

Case 11   Corporate strategies within the newly privatized
          water plcs   224
          S.G. Ogden, University of Leeds

Section 5   CONSUMER PRODUCTS

Case 12   The European food industry and Groupe BSN   239
          J.R. Anchor and C.M. Clarke-Hill, University of
          Huddersfield

Case 13   Glaxo Holdings Plc   268
          J. Fernie, University of Abertay Dundee

Case 14   Kwik-Fit Holdings   279
          J.G. Gallagher and R.S. Scott, Napier University

Case 15   Chrysalis Group   304
          J. Day, University of Huddersfield

Section 6   INDUSTRIAL PRODUCTS

Case 16   Volkswagen Group   335
          I.D. Turner, Henley Management College

Case 17   Fisons Plc   352
          J.R. Anchor, University of Huddersfield

Case 18   Redland Plc   368
          B. Kenny and E C. Lea, University of Huddersfield

Case 19   ICI and Hanson – a contrast in styles   396
          J.R. Anchor, University of Huddersfield

Section 7   TRANSPORT AND DISTRIBUTION

Case 20   Stagecoach Holdings Plc   423
           G.M. Sharkey and J.G. Gallagher, Napier University

Case 21   Christian Salvesen Plc   444
           C.M. Clarke-Hill, University of Huddersfield

Case 22   Virgin Atlantic Airways   460
           K.W. Glaister, University of Leeds

Case 23   NFC Plc   481
           C.M. Clarke-Hill, University of Huddersfield

Case 24   Distribution in the UK: an industry note   506
           *A.E. Whiteing and C.G. Bamford, University of
           Huddersfield*

Questions relating to the cases   515

Index   525

LIST OF CONTRIBUTORS

EDITORS

Colin M. Clarke-Hill   Senior Lecturer in Business Policy, School of Business, University of Huddersfield.

Keith W. Glaister   Senior Lecturer in Strategic Management, School of Business and Economic Studies, University of Leeds.

CONTRIBUTORS

John R. Anchor   Senior Lecturer in Business Economics, School of Business, University of Huddersfield.

Colin G. Bamford   Head of Department, Department of Transport and Logistics, University of Huddersfield.

Stuart Davies   Lecturer in Strategic Management, School of Business and Economic Studies, University of Leeds.

John Day   Senior Lecturer in Economics, School of Business, University of Huddersfield.

J.P. Dewhirst   Group Financial Director, Elmwood Design Ltd.

John Fernie   Senior Lecturer in Marketing, Dundee Business School, University of Abertay Dundee.

James G. Gallagher   Lecturer in Business Policy, Napier Business School, Napier University.

David Griffiths   Head of Corporate Development, Kirklees Metropolitan Council.

Brian Kenny   Reader in Business, School of Business, University of Huddersfield.

Edward C. Lea   Professor and Dean of School, School of Business, University of Huddersfield.

Bertrand Moingeon   Assistant Professor, Department of Strategy and Business Policy, HEC Graduate School of Management, Paris.

Stuart G. Ogden   Senior Lecturer in Accounting, School of Business and Economic Studies, University of Leeds.

Bernard Ramanantsoa   Professor, Department of Strategy and Business Policy, and Dean of Faculty and Research, HEC Graduate School of Management, Paris

Terry M. Robinson	Principal Lecturer in Marketing, Teeside Business School, University of Teeside.
Robert S. Scott	Lecturer in Business Policy, Napier Business School, Napier University.
Grace M. Sharkey	Senior Lecturer in Business Studies, Napier Business School, Napier University.
Helen Short	Lecturer in Accounting and Finance, School of Business and Economic Studies, University of Leeds.
John L. Thompson	Head of Management Strategy, School of Accounting, Law and Management, University of Huddersfield.
Des Thwaites	Senior Lecturer in Marketing, School of Business and Economic Studies, University of Leeds.
Ian D. Turner	Lead Tutor in Strategy, Henley Management College.
Graham Watson	Museum Development Officer, Ross and Cromarty District Council.
Tony L. Whiteing	Senior Research Fellow, Department of Transport and Logistics, University of Huddersfield.

PREFACE

The teaching of strategic management – and associated courses such as business policy and corporate strategy – has traditionally been reliant on the use of case studies. An ongoing problem faced by teachers delivering such courses is the lack of up-to-date case material based on UK and European companies. The collection of new cases presented in this volume is an attempt to redress this problem. This book contains 23 new cases on commercial and non-commercial organizations facing a variety of strategic issues and one comprehensive industry note. The majority of the cases have been successfully proven either in class discussions or for examination purposes with final year undergraduate and MBA students. The wide range of issues addressed by the cases should enable them to be successfully adopted on most strategic management teaching programmes at the undergraduate, post-experience and MBA levels.

The cases are grouped under industry headings and cover large multinational companies, medium sized UK-based firms, and a number of not-for-profit organizations. Each of the cases is accompanied by a set of indicative questions, which encompass the significant issues found in each case and should be a helpful guide to both tutors and students in their analysis. An *Instructor's Manual* is available from the publisher to those tutors who adopt the book. This guide develops perspectives on the questions relating to the cases and is designed to assist tutors in conducting case analysis in the classroom.

Usually students begin a course in strategic management with little background knowledge of the subject matter or experience of the case method. The three chapters in Section 1 are designed to introduce the student to the nature of the subject and to the analysis of cases. Taken together these chapters should enable the student to use the case book effectively. The intention of Chapter 1 is to help the student set the subject matter in context. We would stress that this chapter is not intended to be a substitute for a thorough grounding in the subject of strategic management which the student is encouraged to obtain from wider reading. The nature of case analysis and the demands placed on students by the case study method are discussed in Chapter 2. This chapter provides a framework of analysis and is designed to give students confidence in their approach to learning by the case method.

A particular aspect of case analysis that students sometimes find troublesome is the financial appraisal of a company. This aspect of analysis is often treated very briefly in textbooks on strategic management. To redress this balance a guide to the financial analysis of case material is provided in Chapter 3. While this should adequately serve the needs of the majority of students, those wanting more detailed information should consult relevant accounting texts.

We would stress that although each case reflects real issues faced by the organizations under consideration, the cases have been written for the purposes of student instruction and are not intended to illustrate either effective or ineffective management of a business. The current management of the organizations discussed in the cases cannot be held responsible for any of the views expressed by the case authors.

The number and range of cases presented in this volume has been made possible by the efforts of our co-contributors. We would like to thank them all for providing such high quality material for publication. Finally, we would like to thank Penelope Woolf, our editor at Pitman, who encouraged us to provide a completely new set of cases for this book.

Colin M. Clarke-Hill and Keith W. Glaister

ACKNOWLEDGEMENTS

The editors and publisher wish to thank the following for permission to reproduce copyright material: Datastream International; *The Local Government Chronicle*; *The Huddersfield Daily Examiner*; The Macmillan Press Ltd; The Free Press; Extel Research Products; J.R. Wriglesworth, UBS Ltd; MCB University Press; The Braybrooke Press Ltd; *Building Magazine*.

SECTION 1

The strategic management process and the case method

Chapter 1   Introduction to the strategic management process
             K.W. Glaister, University of Leeds

Chapter 2   Strategic management case analysis
             K.W. Glaister, University of Leeds

Chapter 3   Financial analysis for case studies
             K.W. Glaister and H. Short, University of Leeds

Introduction to the strategic management process

Keith W. Glaister

INTRODUCTION

Strategic management is concerned with determining the future direction of an organization and implementing decisions aimed at achieving the organization's objectives. The strategic management process is applicable to many different kinds of organizations both commercial and non-commercial. It is, therefore, applicable to large multi-business enterprises as well as to small owner-managed companies, and equally to not-for-profit organizations such as charities and to public sector concerns such as local authorities. While the strategic management process is applicable to all kinds of organizations, this is not to argue that all of the tools and techniques of strategic analysis are equally applicable to both commercial and non-commercial organizations, while some will he pertinent to both, others will be more appropriate to one form of organization than to the other. Nevertheless, it remains the case that the fundamental principles behind the strategic management process, as set out in this chapter, are applicable to both sets of organizations.

Strategic management considers the organization as a whole and one of its primary benefits is that it provides the organization with consistency of action. A sound strategic management process helps ensure that all parts of the organization are working towards the same ends. Top management of an organization must manage strategically. Organizations are subject to change which means that managers cannot rely on decisions based on established rules or long-standing operating procedures. Change renders ineffective past approaches to competition. The concepts and processes of strategic management provide a way of dealing with such change.

The purpose of this chapter is to provide an overview of the strategic management process. The chapter presents a normative strategic planning model and discusses traditional concepts of strategy formulation and implementation. The next section considers the levels and types of strategies found in organizations. There then follows a model of the strategic management process, which concentrates in particular on the concept of strategy formulation. To assist in the understanding of the strategic management process a number of key terms are set out in Table 1.

LEVELS AND TYPES OF STRATEGY

The responsibility for strategic management will fall to different individuals depending on the size of the organization. In a small business the owner will perform the role

Table 1 Glossary of terms

Corporate strategy	Defines the business in which the organization will compete, determines the long-run objectives of the organization and identifies the courses of action and allocation of resources necessary to achieve these objectives.
Business strategy	Focuses on how to compete in a given business, determines the competitive approach of companies which have a single product or the strategies for each strategic business unit of a multi-product organization.
Functional strategy	Relates to the functional areas of a business and is concerned with the process of implementing business strategies.
Mission	Identifies the reason for the organization's existence. Often includes a description of the organization's products or services and a definition of its markets.
Objectives	A statement of what the organization wishes to achieve.
External environment	Everything outside the organization that has an impact on its business.
Strength	An activity within an organization that is performed particularly well.
Weakness	An activity within an organization that is performed badly and limits its success.
Opportunity	Trends and events in the external environment that could benefit the organization.
Threat	Trends and events in the external environment that are potentially harmful to an organization's competitive position.

of the chief executive and will be responsible for the various facets of the strategic management process. As the business grows, the strategic management role will be assigned to a number of managers at different levels. In large organizations top management assume responsibility for the entire process with middle management concerned with the implementation of programmes to successfully achieve the strategy objectives.

For a large, multi-divisional business, it is possible to identify three levels of strategy: corporate strategy, business strategy and functional strategy, as shown in Figure 1.

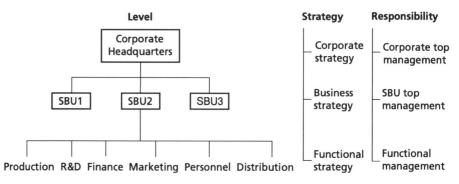

Fig. 1   The levels of strategy.

Corporate strategy

Corporate strategy considers the organization as a whole and identifies the most favourable portfolio of businesses for the firm to be engaged in. Corporate strategy is concerned with the identification of objectives for the organization and the best way that these may be achieved in terms of the strategic orientation of the company. In general, corporate strategies are concerned with either growth, stability or retrenchment.

Business strategy

Business strategy is concerned with the way in which the particular divisions of the organization successfully cope with the industry environment in which they operate. It is usual for a division to be organized as a strategic business unit (SBU), which is an operating unit that has a single product line that is sold to a clearly defined market segment and with identifiable external competitors. It is usual for top management to treat an SBU as a semi-autonomous unit. The managers of the SBU are then free to set their own business strategy under the umbrella of the corporate strategy set by the top management. Business strategies may take the form of cost leadership or differentiation for the industry as a whole, or focus on a particular segment of the industry in terms of either cost or differentiation.

Functional strategy

The main aim of functional strategy is to obtain the maximum productivity from resources. Given the constraints set by the corporate and business strategies, functional departments must develop strategies in which their activities and skills are harnessed for the improvement of performance.

Within a large organization such as the multi-divisional type illustrated on the left-hand side of Figure 1, the three levels of strategy form a hierarchy. Although the three types of strategy involve different levels of management each making different types of decisions, the strategies should be consistent with one another and be well integrated if the whole organization is to be successful. If corporate, business and functional strategies do not fit, the organization will soon encounter serious difficulties.

A STRATEGIC MANAGEMENT MODEL

Strategic management focuses on the total enterprise. It looks beyond everyday operating concerns and concentrates on the organization's long-term development. As noted, strategic decision-making is the major responsibility of the top management of the business. Strategic decisions faced by top management include whether to expand current operations or to retrench on some operations, whether to diversify into new businesses and whether to merge with another firm.

To appreciate how managers take such decisions it is necessary to have an understanding of the strategic management process. This process involves three basic elements: strategy formulation, strategy implementation and strategy evaluation, each element of which includes a number of action steps. Figure 2 shows the elements of the strategic management process and the main sets of activity undertaken at each stage.

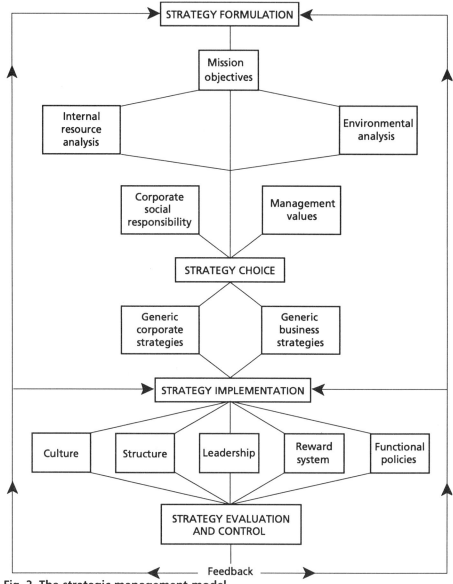

Fig. 2 The strategic management model.

Figure 2 shows that the first component of the process is defining the mission and major objectives of the organization. Figure 2 also indicates that in the strategy formulation stage, top management assesses the external environment facing the company to identify opportunities and threats and to undertake an internal audit of the organization in order to determine company strengths and weaknesses. The significant strategic factors arising from this external and internal appraisal are summarized with the acronym SWOT, which stands for Strengths, Weaknesses, Opportunities and Threats. The identification of the SWOT elements and their relative importance allows the management to determine the strategy of the organization.

It is not enough simply to formulate strategies – management must ensure that the strategy is successfully implemented. This occurs through the management ensuring the correct allocation of resources within the organization and is facilitated through functional policies. The company must also establish the appropriate corporate culture and organizational structure, appoint suitable managers to lead the organization and provide relevant reward systems in order to bring the strategy to successful fruition. Finally, in order to assess the success of the strategy, company performance is monitored and evaluated. As Figure 2 shows, information is fed back into the strategic management process in order to ensure adequate control.

Although Figure 2 sets out the strategic management process as a set of logical steps in sequence, starting with strategy formulation and ending with strategy evaluation, this is a false impression because the strategic management process is a continuous activity which never really ends. If the monitoring of the strategy indicates that expected performance is not being achieved – for example because a competitor has introduced a new product which has taken away sales from the company – this will require a change in corporate objectives and strategy. It is necessary, therefore, to monitor and evaluate internal and external factors on a continuous basis and to be prepared to change strategy accordingly.

Having provided an outline of the strategic management process the following sections consider in more detail the various components of the model shown in Figure 2.

STRATEGY FORMULATION

Formulation of the mission statement

The corporate mission is the purpose or reason for the organization's existence. The management writer Peter Drucker (1974) has observed that: 'A business is not defined by its name, statutes or articles of incorporation. It is defined by the business mission. Only a clear definition of the mission and purpose of the organization makes possible clear and realistic business objectives.'

The mission statement answers the basic question: 'What business are we in?' Defining the mission of an organization is important because it sets the boundaries of its operations and prevents the organization from overlooking related fields of endeavour. A mission statement is not designed to express concrete ends, but to provide motivation, general direction, an image and a philosophy to guide the enterprise. The mission statement should reveal the organization's self-concept, its principal product or service and the primary customer need that the firm wishes to satisfy.

Setting objectives

Objectives are the long-term results that an organization seeks to achieve in pursuing its basic mission. Business organisations pursue a variety of different objectives. Many, however, are expressed in financial terms, for example the desire to attain a particular return on capital employed or growth in earnings per share. Increasingly, though, organizations have set non-financial objectives such as concern for employee welfare or to be at the leading edge of technological advance.

A common view is that objectives should be:

- *measurable*, so it will be possible to know whether or not the organization has achieved the objective;
- *communicable*, so all concerned know what they are;
- *realistic*, in terms of what the environment will allow.

An objective to attain 20 per cent return on capital employed, for example, is both measurable and communicable; the extent to which it is realistic will depend on the nature of opportunities and threats facing the firm and the ability of management to cope with the environmental factors.

Although many writers have agreed that objectives are not helpful unless they are measurable and capable of being achieved, others have taken the view that successful companies do not have to state precise, clear objectives. It is thus argued that it is possible for some objectives to be important to a firm but difficult to quantify or express in measurable terms. Some companies, for example, may set an objective of being the leader in technological development within their industry. Such an objective would be extremely difficult to express in a measurable way. Also, senior management may actively resist the announcement of precise and explicit objectives largely because competitors may learn too much about the intentions of the organization. Despite this difference of view, it is generally conceded that objectives are vital to organizational success. For instance, they provide direction, aid in evaluation, allow coordination and are necessary for the effective planning, organizing and controlling of activities.

The process that leads to the determination of strategic objectives is conditioned by various stakeholders both inside and outside the organization. The management at various levels in the organization will influence the nature of the objectives set but of particular importance will be the top management of the firm. Other influences come from the employees (particularly where the workforce is unionized), the shareholders (especially institutional shareholders with large equity stakes in the company), the customers, the suppliers, the government and various social interest groups.

Strategic position

A key stage of the strategy formulation process is for managers to appreciate the relative standing of the firm. This calls for an assessment of the external environment in which the firm operates as well as an appraisal of the firm's internal position.

External analysis

The variables in the external environment form the context within which the organization exists. Although the external environment consists of everything outside the organization the focus of assessment is on the external factors which have an impact on the organization. It is useful to distinguish two features of the external environment: the *broad environment*, which constitutes the general environmental influences that all firms must cope with, and the *competitive environment*, which comprises the specific features of the industry – or task – environment within which the firm operates.

Broad environmental factors include many general forces but it is usual to consider them in the following major categories.

Economic forces

There are a number of aspects of the economic environment that will impact on the firm. The underlying rate of economic growth and the phase of the economic cycle – recession, depression, recovery or boom – will affect the level of demand facing the firm. The level and composition of unemployment may affect both demand for the firm's products and the availability of labour input. Also of significance will be the government's attempts to control the economy. A policy of high interest rates, for example, may make it extremely difficult for businesses to finance their operations from borrowed funds.

Socio-cultural forces

Socio-cultural factors shape the way people live, work and consume. In recent years, for example, there has been a trend towards married couples delaying the birth of their first child, a greater participation of married women in the labour force and an increased incidence of divorce. There has also been a change in lifestyles towards 'healthy' living associated with people taking more exercise and reducing the consumption of certain types of food. Individuals are now more aware of the natural environment and are increasingly concerned about the environmental impact of productive activity. These types of changes create new kinds of consumers and consequently a need for different types of goods and services.

Demographic factors

The absolute size of the population as well as its growth rate and composition are central issues to strategists. In the UK the relative decline in the number of school leavers affected firms selling to the teenage market, while the employment practices of a large number of organizations have been revised in order to draw potential employees from a wider pool of prospective workers. At the same time the 'greying' of the population, represented by a higher proportion of the population above retirement age, often with significant spending power arising from a combination of occupational pension income and the ending of mortgage commitments, has stimulated the demand for various types of goods and services.

Political and governmental

Central and local government set the legal framework within which organizations must operate. Competition policy, for example, may determine whether one firm may take over another in the pursuit of its strategy of external growth. The government is a major customer of some organizations, so when a different political party forms a new government with a revised set of public spending priorities, this is likely to affect a large number of firms. At the international level the change in relationships between countries will also affect the prospects for many firms.

Technological factors

Technological developments, for example in computing, robotics, communications and pharmaceuticals, can dramatically affect an organization's products and processes as well as those of its competitors. Technological developments can create new markets, change the relative cost position of competitors in an industry and cause existing products and services to become obsolete.

The broad factors outlined above provide the general framework within which firms must operate. For firms in a particular industry the conditions determined by these factors are substantially the same. An evaluation of the competitive environment also involves, however, a consideration of the various forces that shape the industry (or industries) in which the firm operates. Probably the best known approach to industry analysis has been provided by Porter (1980), who distinguishes five basic forces that govern competition in an industry, and which are illustrated in Figure 3.

The threat of new entrants

The ease of entry to an industry is a key indicator of its competitiveness. From an individual firm's viewpoint the greater the barriers to entry the less the threat from new competitors and the more secure its position. In the case of a monopoly, for example, there must be effective barriers to entry in order that the situation of a single supplier persists.

A number of factors give rise to entry barriers including the following:

- *Economies of scale*. Where established firms have a large market share and are producing at a high volume of output they will have lower long-run average costs than those of potential entrants who can expect only a small market share and so will be producing at low volumes of output. The lower cost position of the established firms will thus deter entry.
- *Absolute capital cost requirements*. The greater the level of capital expenditure required to enter an industry the fewer the number of firms likely to enter.
- *Product differentiation*. This creates unique features for the goods of established firms and leads to brand loyalty on the part of consumers which new firms may find difficult to overcome.

The bargaining power of buyers

In general the more powerful are buyers the greater is their ability to hold down prices, so reducing industry profitability. There are a number of determinants of bargaining power including:

- the concentration and size of buyers;

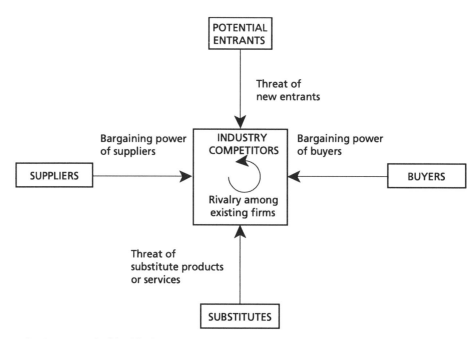

Fig. 3 Forces behind industry competition.
Source: Porter, M.E. (1980) *Competitive Strategy*, New York, Free Press. Reproduced with permission.

- the importance of purchases to the buyer in cost terms;
- the costs of switching between suppliers;
- the degree of standardization of products.

The bargaining power of suppliers

Suppliers by increasing their prices to firms in the industry also have the ability to squeeze industry profits. There are a number of factors leading to supplier power including the following:

- if the supplier group is dominated by a few companies and is more concentrated than the industry it sells to;
- there are no substitute products for sale to the industry;
- the industry is not an important customer of the supplier group;
- the supplier's product is an important input to the buyer's business.

Porter points out that labour must also be recognized as a supplier and one that exerts power in many industries.

Essentially, the power of buyers and suppliers results in an influence over margins: the greater their power the more likely it is that margins will be low.

The threat of substitutes

The availability of substitute products will affect the demand for the products of the industry. For an individual firm the main issue is the extent to which there is a danger that substitutes may encroach on its activities.

The threat of competitive rivalry

The extent of rivalry among existing firms is a function of numerous factors including the following:

- the number of competitors and their relative sizes, i.e. the degree of concentration;
- the rate of industry growth – with slow growing industries often experiencing an intensification of competition;
- the degree of product differentiation – the lower the extent of product differentiation the more intense tends to be price competition;
- the height of exit barriers – where firms find it difficult to leave the industry, for example because they have specialized assets with low liquidation values, they may remain in the industry, thus leading to an intensification of competition.

The tactical moves employed by firms to seek an advantage over their competitors Porter refers to as 'jockeying for position'. This normally takes the form of policies towards pricing, promotion, product innovation and service level. Any initiative by one firm in any of these areas is likely to provoke a competitive reaction from other firms in the industry. The extent of this retaliation will determine the degree to which firms in an industry are mutually dependent. The greater the degree of retaliation between the firms the more active and volatile will be the competitive rivalry.

The analysis of the external environment should allow management to identify a number of opportunities and threats facing the company. Opportunities are external circumstances, events or situations that could significantly benefit an organization. Threats are external factors, forces or situations that might potentially create problems or harm the organization.

Strategic
groups

An industry does not consist of a homogeneous set of firms all competing with each other in the same way. Firms within an industry differ in size, products, production technologies, resources, skills, culture and numerous other attributes. These individual differences mean that the structural forces of the industry do not have the same effect on all firms. Moreover, all firms in an industry do not compete with each other, rather each industry often has several clusters of closely competitive firms.

Strategic groups are clusters of firms that compete with each other and where each member of the cluster follows the same basic strategy, but a strategy that is different from the one followed by companies in other strategic groups. The purpose of strategic group analysis is to refine understanding of the nature of competition in an industry. It also aids in identifying more specific opportunities and threats in the industry. Thus it should be recognized that a firm's immediate competitors are those rivals in its own strategic group and that they may pose the most significant threats to the firm's profitability. Also each strategic group can have a different standing with respect to Porter's five competitive forces, which can vary in intensity between different strategic groups within the same industry. For instance, companies in high volume production strategic groups may be in a much stronger position with respect to industry suppliers than companies in low volume production strategic groups. Some strategic groups are therefore more attractive than others for they face greater opportunities and have a lower level of threats.

Managers must judge whether their company would be better off located in a different strategic group. Where the environment of another strategic group is more benign, the possibility of moving into that group can be considered an opportunity. Mobility barriers mean, however, that the movement between strategic groups is not cost-free. Entry barriers to a strategic group and exit barriers from a strategic group must be overcome. The existence of entry barriers implies that the firms within a strategic group may be protected to some extent from the threat of entry from firms based in other strategic groups. The greater are entry barriers the lower the threat of entry will be from firms in other strategic groups and the more freedom firms within the protected group will have to raise prices and earn higher profits without attracting entry.

Internal analysis

The basic idea behind an internal analysis is to undertake an objective assessment of the organization's current status. It is an attempt to identify those things which the organization does particularly well together with those things it does poorly. Clearly, the internal analysis consists of an evaluation of those variables that are within the organization itself and form the context within which work is done. They include the corporation's structure and culture.

Corporate
resources

Corporate resources are those assets that form the input for the production of an organization's goods or services. These resources include the personnel and managerial talent, financial assets and physical plant and facilities. The skills, abilities and expertise of the workforce and management within the functional areas are also important assets of the company.

It is necessary to review the skills and resources within the functional areas of the business. The following list is illustrative of the nature of the questions that should be asked when undertaking an internal audit:

- *Production.* What is the nature of the manufacturing process and is it appropriate for meeting current competition? Is it flexible enough to be adapted to meet future competition? What is the quality of the manufacturing management? Is the plant and equipment appropriate? Does it embody the latest technology?
- *R&D.* What is the nature and depth of the R&D capability? Are R&D efforts well planned, directed and controlled? Have enough new products been generated by the R&D process? Is the R&D effort based on customer needs as revealed by market research?
- *Marketing.* What is the nature of the marketing capability? What is the extent of the marketing effort? To what degree is the firm marketing oriented?
- *Finance.* What is the financial standing of the firm and what is the quality of financial management? The firm's financial position is an extremely important indicator of its competitive position. In order to appreciate this aspect of the internal analysis fully, Chapter 3 shows how to undertake a financial appraisal of the firm.
- *Personnel.* Does the company have the right people with the right skills in the right place? Does the firm offer competitive rates of pay and conditions of employment? What is the industrial relations record of the firm? Does management keep the workforce informed about developments within the organization?

As well as evaluating the functional areas of the business it is also useful to consider in general the way in which the company's resources have been used. An assessment should be made of the extent to which the resources have been used in an effective and efficient manner. Effectiveness relates to whether the resources have been deployed in the best possible way, i.e. 'doing the right thing', while efficiency measures how well the resources have been utilized, i.e. 'doing things right'. An organization should seek to make both effective and efficient use of its resources – it will serve the firm no useful purpose, for example, to be the most efficient producer of a product that no one wants, i.e. a combination of efficiency and ineffectiveness.

Corporate structure

Corporate structure refers to the way in which a firm is organized in terms of authority, communication and work flow. Corporate structure is often referred to as the 'chain of command' and may be illustrated by way of an organization chart, such as that shown in Figure 1. As the firm grows the organizational structure will change. A small firm or one with a narrow product range is likely to have a functional structure, i.e. the organization is based on the primary tasks it has to carry out such as production, finance, marketing and personnel. As the operations of the firm become larger or more diversified the firm is likely to develop a multi-divisional structure. Here the organization is subdivided into units which are usually responsible for defined market or product areas of the enterprise – the strategic business units shown in Figure 1. The SBUs themselves are usually split up into functional management areas. Other types of structural forms exist, in particular the holding company structure which is representative of an enterprise operating a portfolio of virtually autonomous business units, and the matrix structure which is a mixture, usually taking the form of product and geographical divisions or functional and divisional structures operating in tandem.

Each of these structural types has its own set of advantages and disadvantages.

What is important from the viewpoint of the internal analysis is that the structure of the organization supports and does not hinder the strategy being pursued.

Corporate culture

Corporate culture is the pattern of beliefs, expectations and values shared by the organization's members. In a firm norms of behaviour will emerge which are expected to be followed by the managerial hierarchy and the employees. The shared values and expectations of the organization will have a number of features and will establish, for example, the degree of autonomy given to individuals to exercise responsibility, initiative and innovation. Corporate culture has therefore a major role to play in providing a guide to behaviour within the organization stemming from the established behavioural norms.

The internal analysis should provide for the firm a list of organizational strengths and weaknesses. The internal analysis can be used to arrive at the distinctive competencies of the firm, i.e. the identification of those particular strengths that give the company an edge over its competitors. Distinctive competencies represent the unique strengths of a company and are the bedrock of its competitive advantage which enables it to outperform its competitors. There will be an attempt made by competitors to imitate these distinctive competencies, which if successful will eliminate the company's competitive advantage. It is therefore necessary for the company to continually seek to upgrade the source of its distinctive competencies in order sustain its competitive advantage.

There are two complementary sources of distinctive competence: a company's resources and its capabilities. *Resources* are the physical, human, financial, technological and organizational assets of the firm. Some resources are tangible, for example land, buildings, plant and equipment, while others are intangible, for example patents, brand names and reputation. *Capabilities* are a company's skills at coordinating its resources and putting them to productive use. These skills are located in an organization's routines, that is in the way a company makes decisions and manages its internal processes. Capabilities are intangible, they are not the personal skills of individuals but are bound up in the way individuals interact, cooperate and make decisions within the context of an organization. For a company to have a distinctive competence, at a minimum it must possess a unique and valuable resource and the capabilities necessary to exploit that resource. Alternatively it must have some unique capability to manage common resources . A company's distinctive competence will be strongest where it possesses both unique resources and unique capabilities to manage those resources. The resource-based view of strategy formulation stresses this perspective (see Grant, 1991).

THE SWOT MATRIX

The next stage in the strategic management process is to bring the external analysis and the internal analysis together in a SWOT matrix, illustrated in Figure 4. Strategy should arise from matching company strengths to environmental opportunities. SWOT analysis enables an organization to exploit future opportunities while combating threats, and to do so through strategies founded on its strengths and distinctive competencies.

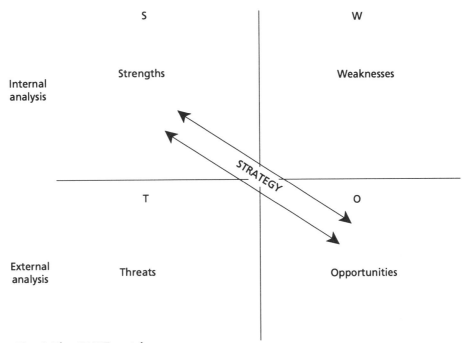

Fig. 4 The SWOT matrix.

Corporate social responsibility

When selecting a strategy on the basis of economic criteria, a company is also making a choice that will inevitably have wider social consequences. For example, if a large company that is a major employer in a small community decides to retrench its activity and close down a plant employing many hundreds of workers, this will have a fundamental social impact on the local community. Also, the choice of certain production technologies and processes may have a significant impact on the wider community if they generate particular kinds of environmental pollution and waste products which are hazardous to dispose of. The choice of strategy may therefore be conditioned by the desire of the management of the organization to act in a socially responsible manner.

There are a number of reasons for companies deciding to act in a socially responsible manner. There may be strongly held belief within the company that this is the correct way for a company to behave. The Body Shop, for example, expresses concern for the natural environment and is not prepared to sell products which have been tested on animals. Less altruistically, it may be in a company's own self-interests to behave in a certain way in order to maintain the support of key stakeholders. It is not necessarily easy for a company to decide which social issues to respond to; however, a comparison of the social impact of the strategy against its economic return will allow the company to identify strategies with positive or negative social consequences.

Management values

The nature of the personal value systems of the strategic managers of an organization will partly determine the choice of strategy. Values embody what their holders view as desirable and affect the perception of situations. While managers may not consciously set their values as they make decisions, those values will nevertheless greatly impact on the decisions at the subconscious level. Groups of managers will differ in their attitudes towards such things as risk taking, concern for short-run and long-run objectives and concern for profitability. Hence some managers are strong proponents of strategies that take a long-term view and that aim at building a presence in new businesses, while others in contrast stress the efficient exploitation of existing businesses and avoid the development of new ones. It should be clear, therefore, that managers do not dispassionately assess what strategy to adopt, rather the choice of strategy is fundamentally affected by the personal philosophy of the managers concerned.

DETERMINATION OF STRATEGY

A strategy is a means to an end. An organization's strategy describes its method for achieving its strategic objectives. This step in the strategic management process includes the identification, evaluation and selection of alternative strategies.

As already noted, it is possible to identify three different levels of strategy: corporate strategy, business strategy and functional strategy. The nature of the strategy alternatives available at each level is now briefly considered, on the assumption that the organization under discussion is multi-divisional in structure having several SBUs as illustrated in Figure 1.

CORPORATE STRATEGY ALTERNATIVES

The corporate strategy to be pursued will be determined by the organization's mission, objectives and results of the external and internal analysis as summarized in the SWOT matrix. The broad strategy alternatives can be classified as being concerned with growth, stability or retrenchment.

Growth

The direction in which growth maybe pursued was first presented by Ansoff (1968), in terms of a growth vector matrix, shown in Figure 5. Ansoff gave the alternatives of market penetration, market development, product development and diversification.

Market penetration

In following this strategy the firm continues to operate in the same markets offering the same products. By winning a larger share of its markets with existing products, growth is achieved. Unless the markets themselves are growing, this strategy necessarily involves taking business away from competitors. This is a low-risk strategy for management because the firm can build on knowledge and experience gained in its markets. A further advantage is that this strategy requires no investment in new products.

Market development

This strategy involves taking the firm into new markets with existing products. This strategy will be followed when existing markets offer few prospects for growth compared with new markets. This is a higher-risk strategy for managers because they will have

Product Market	Present	New
Present	Market penetration	Product development
New	Market development	Diversification

Fig. 5 Growth vector components.
Adapted from Ansoff, H.I. (1968) *Corporate Strategy*, Harmondsworth, Penguin.

less knowledge of the characteristics of the new markets, hence they may fail to correctly anticipate competitor reaction, and may underestimate the brand loyalty of established products.

Product development

With this strategy the firm remains in its present markets but develops new products for these markets. Growth will occur if the new products yield additional sales and market share. This strategy is likely to be successful where there is low brand loyalty and/or short product life cycles. Although this strategy is low risk, in that the firm continues to operate in existing markets, there is a risk associated with the development of new products.

Diversification

A strategy of diversification involves the company moving away from its present markets and present products and, as such, may involve greater risk for the firm than the other strategies so far identified. Diversification strategy broadly consists of two types: related diversification and unrelated diversification.

Related diversification represents development beyond present markets and products but is still within the broad dimensions of the industry or where there exists a connection to existing businesses such as in related technology or skills, for example in production or marketing.

Integration strategies are usually considered as part of related diversification. *Backward integration* occurs when the firm gains control over inputs to its existing businesses. *Forward integration* occurs when the firm gains control of distributors or retailers of its existing products or services. *Horizontal integration* occurs when the firm acquires control over competitors in the same line of business.

Unrelated (or conglomerate) diversification occurs where the firm enters a new business totally outside the scope of its existing operations. The new business has no close relationship or common thread to present markets or products.

In considering these alternatives for growth the organization often has a choice as to the manner in which they may be achieved. In principle, many of the growth strategy alternatives may be followed either by internal (i.e. organic) expansion, or else by acquiring or merging with another firm. Growth by acquisition has three main advantages over organic growth: acquisition allows a faster rate of growth; there is immediate access to factor inputs and markets; and there is the advantage of purchasing a tried and working business.

Stability

Where the organization is satisfied with its performance, in that it is achieving corporate objectives while it either does not recognize or wish to respond to opportunities and faces no significant threats, there will be no desire to change fundamentally the strategic direction of the company. Under these circumstances a stability strategy may be followed which has two broad alternatives: a holding strategy and a harvesting strategy.

With a *holding strategy* the company continues at its present rate of development. The aim is to retain current market share. Although growth is not pursued as such, this will occur if the size of the market grows. The current level of resource input and managerial effort will not be increased which means that the functional strategies will continue as previously implemented and at previous levels of expenditure. Where a firm has the dominant market share it may seek to take advantage of this position and generate cash for future business expansion. This is termed a *harvesting strategy* and is usually associated with cost cutting and price increases to generate extra profits.

Retrenchment

Circumstances may be such that the firm will find it appropriate to reduce the overall scale of its operations or to withdraw its commitment to a particular market. Broadly there are three possible strategies for the firm to follow: liquidation, divestment and turnaround.

Liquidation will occur when a firm withdraws from a declining market. The firm should seek to reinvest the resources so released in new product market areas to take the place of those that are being phased out.

Divestment is a strategy of selling off an SBU. This will occur when changes in the environment reveal threats towards the present position of the SBU so that it can no longer perform effectively. Divestment will also occur if the SBU no longer fits into the business portfolio of the organization. Thus divestment has occurred when diversified conglomerates have shed peripheral businesses in order to shrink back to their core business concerns.

Turnaround strategy is necessary when a business is failing and approaching bankruptcy. The aim is to improve the competitive standing of the business in order to achieve a satisfactory level of performance. A number of operational strategies are required to achieve this but part of the solution may be liquidation of assets and divestment of parts of the business.

The international dimension

International expansion involves establishing significant market interests and operations outside a company's home country. Foreign markets provide additional sales opportunities for a firm that may be constrained by the relatively small size of its domestic market and reduces the firm's dependence on a single national market. Firms usually begin the process of internationalization by exporting goods and services to foreign markets. There are though a number of other methods by which firms may achieve international expansion: licensing, franchising, entering into a joint venture with a foreign partner and establishing a wholly owned subsidiary abroad. Each method of entering an overseas market has advantages and disadvantages that must be carefully assessed.

One of the major strategic choices faced by multinational companies (MNCs, i.e. companies that transact business in two or more countries), is whether to pursue a multi-domestic strategy or a global strategy. A multi-domestic strategy – the traditional way in which international companies compete – is based on the assumption that there are considerable differences between national markets in terms of consumer tastes and preferences, underlying competitive conditions, operating conditions and the socio-economic, political and legal structures of nations. In order to deal with these differences a company may pursue a multi-domestic strategy, whereby manufacturing, marketing and other key decisions are decentralized to the national subsidiaries. Thus each national subsidiary would have its own manufacturing facilities, its own marketing function, etc. The features of the products produced would then vary among nations in line with the tastes and preferences of local consumers. The management of each national subsidiary pursues a business level strategy independent of that in other countries. In other words there is no attempt on the part of the corporate management of the MNC to coordinate strategy between the national subsidiaries.

In contrast, a global strategy is based on the assumption that consumer tastes and preferences differ little between countries. The MNC then seeks to market a standardized product in each country and to manufacture that product in a limited number of geographic locations, determined by the most favourable mix of factor costs and skills, in order to realize significant economies of scale. A global strategy also allows the MNC to integrate competitive moves across nations; for instance, it may use profits generated in one country to attack a competitor in another country.

BUSINESS STRATEGY ALTERNATIVES

Business strategy focuses on deciding how an SBU can most effectively compete in a particular business or industry once the organization has decided how the business is going to be managed, what results it expects and the amount of resources it should receive. Porter (1980, 1985) argues that the business unit should adopt a competitive position which will allow it to defend itself against the five forces in the industry environment, shown in Figure 3. To achieve this three broad generic strategies are proposed by Porter: overall cost leadership, differentiation and focus, which are illustrated in Figure 6.

Overall cost leadership requires the business unit to achieve lower costs than other competitors in the industry while maintaining product or service quality. This strategy requires aggressive construction of efficient scale facilities, vigorous pursuit of cost reductions from experience curve effects, tight cost and overhead control, avoidance

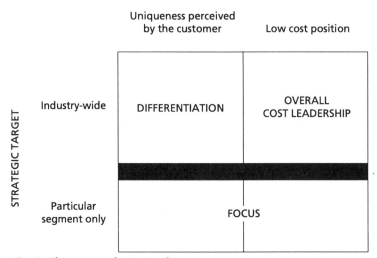

Fig. 6 Three generic strategies.
Source: Porter, M.E. (1980) *Competitive Strategy*, New York, Free Press. Reproduced with permission.

of marginal customer accounts and cost minimization in the functional areas.

Differentiation is based on creating something unique as far as customers in the industry are concerned. This entails achieving industry-wide recognition of different and superior products and services compared to competitors, such as superior customer service, superior technology or a superior dealer network.

With a *focus strategy*, a particular buyer group or segment of the market is selected as the basis for competition rather than the whole industry. Within the targeted segment the business may attempt to compete on a low cost or differentiation basis.

Porter argues that sometimes a firm can pursue more than one generic strategy though this is rarely successful. Rather the firm must adopt one of the generic strategies in order to outperform competitors.

FUNCTIONAL STRATEGIES

Functional strategy is concerned with the formulation of strategies in each of the functional areas of the organization – production, marketing, finance, etc. – which, when properly implemented, should achieve the business strategy. Clearly, there will be a large array of possible combinations of strategies in and between the functional areas. The essential point in devising such strategies, however is that they should be seen as the means of successfully carrying out the business strategy.

STRATEGY CHOICE

At this stage of the strategic management process the *feasible* strategic alternatives must be identified and the best alternative selected. The internal and external analysis will place limitations on the feasible strategic alternatives. The financial analysis could reveal, for example, a problem of capital funding which could severely limit an organization's options for expansion.

The evaluation and final selection of feasible strategies involves the integration of the mission, objectives, external analysis and internal analysis. The strategy chosen must offer the organization the best chance of achieving its mission and objectives through actions that are compatible with its tolerance of risks and value structure. Once the grand strategy has been identified additional sub-strategies must be chosen to support it.

STRATEGY IMPLEMENTATION

Once the strategy has been decided upon, the second stage in the strategic management process is strategy implementation. This is the action stage of the strategic management process. The implementation process covers the entire range of managerial activities including such matters as motivation, compensation and control processes. Except when significant corporation-wide changes are needed, such as a completely new structure or a shift in cultural norms within the organization, the implementation of strategy is typically conducted by middle and lower managers with a review by top management.

Strategy implementation can be considered under two broad headings: organizational factors and functional policies.

Organizational factors

The organization must adopt the correct corporate culture and structure, appoint appropriate leaders and establish suitable reward systems.

Corporate culture
Corporate culture is clearly important in ensuring that strategic management is effective. As environmental conditions change and new strategies are pursued by management the prevailing corporate culture may no longer be appropriate. In such circumstances it is necessary to pursue cultural change within the organization in order to produce a fit or match between culture and strategy.

Structure
The structure of the organization must be assessed and dealt with as part of the implementation process. It is often argued that the structure should follow the strategy in that the organizational structure should be changed as strategy alters in order to accomplish best the strategic objectives.

Although an organization's structure can always be altered, doing so may impose high costs. A reorganization, for example, might result in substantial hiring and training costs for newly created jobs. Thus from a practical standpoint, an organization's current structure may impose certain restrictions on how a strategy may be implemented.

Leadership style
Leadership skills are a critical component in the implementation of strategy. Leaders need to inspire commitment to the strategies on the part of personnel throughout the organization. Effective leaders are therefore a significant factor in ensuring that successful implementation is accomplished. It is important to guarantee that the leadership style fits the strategy in that different management characteristics appear

to be relevant depending on the objectives being pursued by a given strategy. So, for example, where the strategy is one of unrelated diversification this should be headed by managers with a high propensity for risk-taking.

Reward systems An important means of achieving cooperation from personnel in implementing the strategy is the adoption of an appropriate reward system. Monetary rewards can take various forms such as graded pay levels, bonus payments and profit-sharing schemes. Where production and sales targets are met, for example, bonuses may be awarded. Non-monetary rewards such as promotion and increased status are also important. It is necessary to create systems that reward performance that is consistent with the firm's strategy and the long-term objectives of the strategy. If growth of profits is the objective, for instance, then profit-sharing schemes are likely to be more appropriate than rewards based on short-term sales targets.

Functional policies

Flowing from chosen strategies, policies provide guidance for decision-making throughout the organization. Policies are usually established for situations that are repetitive or recurring in the life of the strategy and are most often stated in terms of functional activities, for example, training practices within the personnel function. Policies are thus broad guidelines which serve to link the formulation of strategy with its implementation. Each of the functional areas of the business – R&D, production, finance, marketing, logistics, etc. – will be set goals to achieve and will follow procedures in order to meet successfully the strategic objectives.

STRATEGY EVALUATION

In the final stage of the strategic management process results are monitored so that actual performance can be compared with desired performance. Managers at all levels in the organization should use the performance information to take corrective action and resolve problems.

The broad-scale results are monitored and evaluated by top management by means of periodic reports dealing with key performance indicators such as return on investment, net profits and earnings per share. The results of these reports indicate the kind of action that top management needs to take. To help managers identify those areas with performance problems, companies are sometimes structured with profit centres, investment centres, cost centres and revenue centres. For evaluation and control to be effective, managers must obtain clear, prompt and unbiased feedback. The evaluation and control mechanisms can pinpoint weaknesses in previously implemented strategic plans. Figure 2 indicates the feedback loop in the strategic management process from strategy evaluation to both strategy formulation and strategy implementation, stimulating the process to start again.

Strategic evaluation also involves the firm in reviewing the internal and external factors that represent the underpinnings of its current strategy. The firm must determine whether the same strengths, weaknesses, opportunities and threats still exist or if a new set of internal and external forces has emerged. This is a critical stage in the strategic management process. To be successful firms must anticipate and adapt to change quickly and effectively. Management should devise a series of contingency plans that can be put into action quickly if environmental circumstances change unexpectedly.

DIFFERENT PERSPECTIVES OF THE STRATEGY PROCESS

This chapter has emphasized the rational planning approach to the strategic management process that views strategy as a plan to be explicitly formulated before being implemented. This approach focuses on *deliberate* strategies. It should be noted that some strategy writers reject this approach and take the view that strategies can emerge from within the organization without any formal plan. Mintzberg (1990), for instance, has criticized the basis of the strategic management process as set out in this chapter. Even in the absence of the intent to create a deliberate strategy, Mintzberg argues that strategies can emerge from the grassroots of an organization and only in retrospect is the strategy of the organization identified from the pattern of actions taken. This approach therefore views strategy as a pattern in the stream of organizational activities, and focuses on *emergent* strategies. In practice, however, it is probably the case that the final realized strategies of most organizations are some combination of both intended (or planned) strategies and emergent (or unplanned) strategies.

SUMMARY

The strategic management process is concerned with determining the future direction of an organization and implementing decisions aimed at achieving its objectives. The strategic management process consists of three major interrelated sub-processes: strategy formulation, strategy implementation and strategy evaluation.

Strategy formulation is concerned with establishing the organization's mission and strategic objectives. It is further concerned with an assessment of the strengths, weaknesses, opportunities and threats facing the organization. This involves an examination of the external environment as well as internal analysis of the organization. The SWOT assessment leads to the identification of appropriate strategies from which the management must choose the one that will best achieve the organization's mission and objectives.

The next task is to implement the strategy. Strategies formulated but not implemented serve no purpose. Resources must be allocated within the organization and functional policies established to encourage work toward the stated objectives. Strategic implementation activities impact on all managers and employees in an organization and they are essentially operational in nature. To implement the strategy successfully, the organization must adopt the appropriate culture and structure, employ managers with leadership qualities which match the nature of the strategy and introduce relevant reward systems.

In the strategy evaluation phase managers continuously monitor and evaluate performance and activities on the basis of measurable results and audits of key areas. If results and activities fail to measure up to the plans, managers must take appropriate corrective action.

Although these sub-processes have been described as though they are carried out in sequence, in practice the entire strategic management process is dynamic and iterative by nature, as indicated by the feedback loop shown in Figure 2.

REFERENCES

Ansoff, H.I. (1968) *Corporate Strategy*. Harmondsworth, Penguin.

Drucker, P. (1974) *Management: Tasks, Responsibilities and Practices*. New York, Harper & Row.

Grant, R.M. (1991) 'The resource-based theory of competitive advantage: implications for strategy formulation.' *California Management Review*, Spring, pp. 114–35.

Mintzberg, H. (1990) 'The design school: reconsidering the basic premises of strategic management', *Strategic Management Journal*, Vol. 11, pp. 171–95.

Porter, M. (1980) *Competitive Strategy: Techniques for Analysing Industries and Competitors*. New York, The Free Press.

Porter, M. (1985) *Competitive Advantage: Creating and Sustaining Superior Performance*. New York, The Free Press.

FURTHER READING

This chapter only presents the basic ideas behind the strategic management process. These ideas are more fully elaborated in text books on strategic management. Two useful UK texts are:

Johnson, G. and K. Scholes (1993) *Exploring Corporate Strategy*. London, Prentice Hall International.

Thompson, J.L. (1993) *Strategic Management: Awareness and Change*. London, Chapman & Hall.

A text with a European perspective which includes a number of key articles dealing with various facets of the strategic management process is:

De Wit, B. and R. Meyer (1994) *Strategy: Process, Content, Context*. St Paul, Minn., West Publishing Co.

The strategic direction of the company and the formulation of competitive strategy is examined fully in:

Lowes, B., C. Pass and S. Sanderson (1994) *Companies and Markets*. Oxford, Blackwell.

The international dimensions of strategic management are covered in a series of papers reproduced in:

Vernon-Wortzel, H. and L.H. Wortzel (1991) *Global Strategic Management: The Essentials*. New York, Wiley.

CHAPTER 2

Strategic management case analysis

Keith W. Glaister

INTRODUCTION

The purpose of this chapter is to provide some guidance for those students who are not familiar with the analysis of case studies and the case method of teaching. Case analysis is a widely used method in the teaching of strategic management and has been so for many years. One of the basic objectives of the case method is to add realism to the study of strategic management through the examination of actual situations in real organizations. A case study is essentially a written description of an organization. Cases vary in content and length but usually contain information on the development of the business, the external environment in which the firm operates and its internal situation. Strategic management case studies thus tend to be multi-faceted – they provide information on a wide range of issues relating to the business. In essence the student's role in case analysis is to diagnose and size up the situation described in the case and to arrive at appropriate responses to the case questions. To do this the student is required to provide a detailed analysis of the case material.

Case analysis is useful to students for a number of reasons. Your analytical and judgement skills will be developed through case analysis. The application of theories and concepts to real-world situations through case analysis assists in the development of complex thinking skills and to an appreciation that several perspectives to a problem may exist. Your ability to ask the right kind of questions about an organization and its relationship to the environment will be developed through case analysis. The wide variety of situations depicted in the cases provide the student with a broad base of experience from which to develop managerial insights. Through participation in case analysis your written and oral communication skills will be enhanced. Skills that lead to a clear and persuasive oral delivery and a succinct and forceful writing style require extensive practice. The class presentations and written assignments that are associated with the case method of teaching will facilitate the development of these skills.

The success of the case method of teaching largely depends on the contribution students make in class. The case method of teaching is significantly different from the traditional lecture approach, where little or no preparation is required of the student prior to the lecture. Also, unlike a lecture class, where in the main the student is a receptive but passive observer, the case method requires the student to become much more actively involved in the learning process. A willingness on the part of students to participate in the classroom discussion is thus fundamental to the case method learning experience. The challenge of assuming greater responsibility for his or her own learning is something that the student of strategic management must recognize and accept.

Cases deal with actual business situations and provide the student with an opportunity to appreciate the nature of decisions which are of long-term importance to the organization. Often, however, students find case analysis quite demanding. One difficulty which is frequently experienced is the unstructured nature of the problems faced by strategic managers. This is reflected in the mass of information which the case presents to students and which they are expected to analyse. Further, students often argue that they do not have enough information and request more in order to analyse better the firm's position or before making a recommendation for action.

The view taken here is that the analysis and decision-making should be based on the information given in the case. The main reason for this is that a manager never has all of the information necessary to make a decision and since case analysis represents the situation facing the corporate manager, the student should be expected to come to some reasoned conclusions and make recommendations based on less than complete information. Students must, therefore, work with the information they have and make reasonable assumptions.

The essential task in all case study work is an in-depth analysis of the situation presented. The total dimensions of the case will not be grasped if the case is read only once. Usually the significance of much of the information presented does not become clear until a detailed analysis is undertaken. The following sections provide a guide to enable the student to undertake such an analysis in order to be well prepared both for class discussions and written submissions.

It should be stressed that the cases in this book are not intended to be examples of correct or incorrect, good or bad management. Similarly, the analysis of a case does not assume that this will result in the 'right' answers being found or the recommendation of the 'correct' course of action. Rather the framework of analysis is presented in order to ensure that the relevant factors will have been considered thus leading to a better diagnosis of the situation with appropriate recommendations for action.

QUESTIONS RELATING TO THE CASE

The nature of questions asked on strategic management cases will vary between tutors and the nature of the information contained in particular cases. A set of questions is provided for each case in this book and these questions range from the specific to the general. With issue specific questions the analysis must be tailored to the actual questions asked and it clearly is not possible to provide a guide here. Instead this chapter concentrates on providing an overview analysis of a case. It is still useful to follow the overview guidelines even when asked to consider specific questions because this is often the best way of coming to terms with the details of the case before the specific issues are addressed. The overview approach should also help the student to appreciate the integrated nature of most case studies in strategic management. Failure to recognize this integration is likely to result in faulty analysis and poor recommendations.

GUIDELINES FOR CASE ANALYSIS

In order to analyse a case effectively it is helpful to have a model around which to structure one's thinking. The main elements of one such model are summarized in Table 2. The steps outlined in Table 2 basically follow the stages of the strategic management process outlined in Chapter 1.

Although designed to be of help to students it is recognized that this method of working will not suit everyone. Indeed, there are a number of different approaches to case preparation and each student must develop his or her own method of approach – there is no 'best' way. At a minimum, however, the model presented here can act as a guide. Students may be required to analyse a case for the purpose of class discussion and/or for written submission. Some advice relating specifically to each of these purposes is provided in later sections. First, however, some of the general issues of case analysis are considered:

- It is recommended that you read the case through once relatively quickly. This is designed to do little more than provide an overview of the case. No analysis should be undertaken on this first reading. After a short break the case should be read again rather more slowly. You should now consider the nature of the information provided and how it might be used. You should recognize that a case study provides a mix of information which ranges from the highly relevant to the hardly relevant at all, so you will need to sift the information in order to be able to devote time

Table 2 The case preparation process

1. Read the case through quickly to obtain an overview of the nature of the organization and its environment. Don't worry too much about the details of the case at this stage.

2. Read the case again more slowly. Attempt to identify and evaluate the organization's mission, objectives and strategy. The case itself may not state these clearly, but you need to attempt to determine this for yourself. Put the case aside for a while.

3. Read the case again. This time sift carefully through the material and identify the key strategic factors facing the organization. Where appropriate use relevant concepts and tools of analysis to investigate the organization. Consider the resource capability of the firm and list the internal strengths and weaknesses. Perform a financial analysis. Also consider the environment facing the company and identify opportunities and threats.

4. Rank each of the strengths, weaknesses, opportunities and threats in order of importance. From this analysis determine the alternative strategies open to the firm. These strategies should resolve the problem(s) or issue(s) of the case. Also list a set of objectives for the firm.

5. Evaluate each of the alternative strategies bearing in mind the internal and external factors affecting the company, its mission and the objectives you have set. After considering the pros and cons of each alternative make a choice on which one to recommend as the best course of action for the firm to take.

6. Make suggestions as to how the company can implement your chosen strategy. There are four critical areas to effective strategy implementation – organization structure, corporate culture, human resources (especially leadership from top management) and organization rewards. You should ensure that there is consistency among these four factors and the newly developed strategy.

7. Suggest feedback and control systems to ensure that the recommended strategy is carried out as planned.

to the relevant aspects of the information presented. This is similar to the situation faced by the manager of an organization who must also separate the relevant and useful information from the rest. If possible you should now put the case aside for a few hours before coming back to it in order to undertake a more detailed analysis.

- The SWOT analysis should not just be presented as a series of concise statements – it must be used. Its real value lies in the implications that arise from it. An evaluation should be made of the key issues facing the company and the priorities set for dealing with them. The strengths of the company should be used for taking advantage of the opportunities presented to it. At the same time weaknesses must be overcome and threats minimized. The logic of a recommended course of action lies in the coherent underpinning provided by the SWOT analysis.

- An important aspect of the internal analysis of the company is a consideration of its financial position. The following chapter discusses in some detail how to do this. Some care must be taken when presenting this information in written form, and it is probably best to provide a table of results in an appendix. A written summary of the key financial strengths and weaknesses arising from the ratio calculations should be incorporated into the main body of your assignment paper. It is not usually necessary to go through an account of how the ratios are calculated or an elaboration of their meaning.

- In both oral and written work avoid making broad generalizations. It is far better to be specific, yet a failure to do so is one of the biggest shortcomings of students' case analyses. For instance, instead of stating 'The firm's liquidity position is poor', it is better to say 'The firm's current ratio fell from over 2.9 in 1993 to just over 1.0 in 1994. There was also a decline in the acid test ratio from 1.2 to 0.5 over the same period. This clearly indicates a weakness in the firm's financial position.' It is particularly important to attempt to be specific with respect to recommendations for future action. So instead of simply stating that the company should follow a particular type of strategy, for example growth, explain the nature of the strategy, why it is to be followed, how the strategy is to be implemented, when and where. Also avoid recommending a course of action beyond a company's means. Suggest only what you can argue is feasible and attempt to be realistic.

- In moving from an evaluation of the firm's position to suggesting courses of action to take, some attempt should be made to be creative. A number of ideas should be generated and the pros and cons of particular recommendations should be considered. It has already been noted that there is no 'correct' answer to a question such as 'What should the firm do next?' The action which the firm itself actually took can be the subject of heated debate, even amongst the management of the organization. What is required of the student, however, is a defensible and justifiable course of action. Since there is no single best solution to a case the justification for any recommendations made is particularly important.

- Clear indication should be given as to how the organization can implement the chosen strategy. In particular the organizational design and major resource requirements should be specified. This is an area often neglected by students. The formulation of strategy becomes vacuous, however, without specific recommendations on implementation. Again these recommendations should be specific. If, for instance, the firm needs to raise finance to fund the recommended strategy, you should indicate whether this will come from internal sources (retained profit), debt or the issue of new shares. If it is to come from increased borrowing it should be made clear that this is feasible given the firm's level of gearing and interest cover. Another issue associated with implementation is that of leadership. It is necessary to specify whether the current leadership skills match up to the needs of the strategy or whether changes in top management are required.

- Above all your analysis should demonstrate appropriate use of the tools and techniques of strategic analysis. Each case study provides an opportunity to demonstrate your understanding of how and when to use the strategic management concepts presented on the course.

Oral case analysis

The case method of teaching involves a classroom situation where students are expected to do most of the talking. The tutor's role is mainly to ask questions and encourage student interaction regarding ideas, analysis and recommendations. Obviously there is an onus on the student to be well prepared in order to become involved in the class discussion. You will gain little by attending a class for a case that you have not read and you will be unable to contribute meaningfully to the discussion. The basic message is that a case assignment requires conscientious preparation before the class. You should be able to answer basic questions concerning the strengths, weaknesses, opportunities and threats facing the organization, and the nature of its existing strategies and objectives. In addition you should be able to recommend future strategies and indicate how they may be implemented. At the same time you should be prepared to provide a justification for these answers.

The outcome of the class discussions for the student will largely depend on the effort that is made. Discussing strategic management cases in class can be an exacting and challenging experience which many students find intimidating. It can, however, also be an enjoyable and rewarding experience for the well prepared student who is willing to participate. Unless you are prepared to participate in the discussion you will not obtain feedback on any ideas and views you may have. More than this, if you put nothing into the discussions or are reluctant to offer any comments then not only are you failing to benefit from case analysis but your fellow students will be deprived of another perspective and will have to suffer a dampening effect on what could develop into a lively debate. It should be clear, therefore, that a case session in which the student chooses not to participate is of little use to the student concerned or his or her classmates.

You should also expect that your class tutor will question the basis of your analysis. The tutor may offer alternative views, play the devil's advocate, at times take the lead in the discussion and solicit the views of other students. You should not expect your tutor to passively accept your analysis, rather you must be prepared to defend your diagnosis.

Case discussion provides a number of useful benefits. Cases require the student to make decisions about the issues presented and to defend these decisions to a group of peers. This situation is similar to that faced by many managers who, during the course of decision-making, have to persuade their peers and superiors that their analyses and solutions are the best. This requires both communications and human relations skills. Case discussions provide students with the opportunity to develop these skills. In adopting a particular line of reasoning or making a specific recommendation you may be criticized by others who take a different view. You should not be afraid to face such criticism. It is better to look upon the case discussion as an opportunity to learn what such criticism is like and how to deal with it. Since there is no one right answer to a case, discussion and criticism should help you to develop skills in justifying a position. You should also be prepared to challenge the opinions and interpretation of others during the discussion. This should be done with tact and should not be seen as an opportunity to belittle another student.

Rather than encouraging a general discussion the tutor may require particular students or groups of students to present a case analysis to the rest of the class. The group method is partly designed to teach people how to work successfully in teams. Before the group meets, each member individually should go through the steps of analysis outlined above. When meeting with your team members an effort should be made to distribute the workload of analysis and presentation fairly. For the group to achieve its tasks successfully it is necessary to maintain an effective level of cooperation and interaction among the group members. Sufficient time must be budgeted to coordinate the activities of the group and to allow the tasks assigned to individuals in the group to be completed. The individual efforts of the members of the group will, however, need to be brought together into a coherent piece of work. In order to assess the work of individual team members your tutor may ask you to undertake some form of peer group evaluation. This is designed to identify the work contribution in that part of the preparation that largely goes unseen by the tutor.

Where you are required to make a case presentation to the rest of the class, you should look upon this as an opportunity to practise making formal presentations, a skill which is frequently required in many organizations. In making such presentations you should attempt to catch and hold the interest of the class. Some suggestions for gaining and holding attention are:

- Avoid reading from a prepared script. You should become familiar enough with your material only to rely on a brief set of notes. Familiarity with the material should also allow you to make frequent eye contact with your audience. Obviously you should speak clearly and distinctly and do not rush through the presentation.
- Use visual aids such as OHP transparencies and handouts to illustrate your discussion so enabling the audience to follow better what you are trying to convey. Avoid cluttering transparencies with too much detail; they should be used to draw out the main points and should therefore only contain the key items.
- If you are talking for more than about five minutes, actively attempt to involve your listeners directly. Do not be afraid, for example, to pose a question to the group. Wait for a reply and be prepared to discuss any issues raised.
- You will probably have to work to a time constraint. You should therefore practise and time your presentation. Only attempt to deliver that amount of material that can be comfortably fitted into the allotted time.

Written case analysis

In addition to preparing a case for class discussion, you may be required to provide a written case analysis. Preparing a written case analysis is similar to preparing a case for class discussion except that written reports are generally more structured and more detailed. The following procedures may assist you in this task.

- Be clear about the nature of the assignment and consider carefully what is required of you. If you are asked to 'evaluate' or 'appraise' particular issues this requires some critical analysis on your part.

- Adhere to instructions which specify length and particular formats for answering the questions. Typically a written analysis should not follow the formal essay style but should be more in the way of a report. Sub-headings and divisions should be used wherever possible, so that a logic to the case analysis is evident. You should attempt to present your tutor with the results of your thinking in a form which is easy to follow and reflects the quality of your effort.

- Make use of charts, diagrams and tables where appropriate. As already noted the financial ratio analysis should be presented in tabular form in an appendix. This avoids a tedious recital of financial results and saves space in the main body of your paper. In a similar fashion an organizational chart can be used to convey a good deal of information in a limited space.

- Refrain from reviewing or rehashing the entire case background – the golden rule of a written case analysis is to avoid simply repeating the facts presented in the case. Your tutor will be familiar with the case and does not require an extensive summary of the details. What is of crucial interest is your *analysis* of the material. If you find that your report repeats case material without manipulating it or presenting new insights you are probably not providing an analysis of the issues. Only interpretation, analysis and reasoned proposals will gain credit, since these are your own work.

- Be clear about you recommendations and conclusions. Remember that they should be specific. Do not, for example, write 'The company should undertake more marketing.' Instead argue that 'The director of marketing should organize market research in order to identify new market segments for current products.'

- A rather obvious point, but one that experience shows it is necessary to make, be sure to eliminate spelling errors and check the grammar carefully. A well constructed set of arguments can lose their impact if spelling and grammar are poor.

CONCLUSIONS

This chapter has presented a framework for the analysis of strategic management case studies and offered some guidelines for the preparation of cases for class discussion and written submission. The basic rule is to be analytical and present your ideas in a clear, lucid and straightforward manner. You will benefit most from the case method if you avoid being a silent observer. Attempt to overcome any shyness you may feel and try to contribute fully to the discussion. Although often daunting for students, case preparation and presentation, while challenging, can also be one of the most rewarding aspects of the strategic management course.

FURTHER READING

A number of strategic management textbooks set out the principles of the case method of teaching and provide useful advice for students who are unfamiliar with the analysis of case studies. Any of the following would be a useful supplement to this chapter.

David, F.R. (1991) *Strategic Management*. New York, Merrill. See 'Case analysis,' pp. 369–80.

Dess, G.G. and A. Miller (1993) *Strategic Management*. New York, McGraw-Hill. See Chapter 12, 'Analysing strategic situations and cases,' pp. 354–77.

Higgins, J.M. and J.W. Vincze (1989) *Strategic Management: Text and Cases*. Orlando, Fla., Dryden Press. See 'Appendix 1: Introduction to the case method,' pp. 1132–54.

Thompson, A.A. Jr. and A.J. Strickland III (1992) *Strategic Management: Concepts and Cases*. Homewood, Ill., Irwin. 'A guide to case analysis,' pp. 278–88.

Wheelan T.L. and J.D. Hunger (1992) *Strategic Management and Business Policy*. Reading, Mass., Addison-Wesley. Chapter 14, 'Suggestions for case analysis,' pp. 401–20.

Financial analysis for case studies

Keith W. Glaister and Helen Short

INTRODUCTION

The assessment of the financial position of a firm constitutes an important aspect of the internal analysis which must be carried out to determine the strengths and weaknesses of the organization. The overall performance of the firm will ultimately be measured in financial terms and a financial analysis will indicate the extent to which the firm is meeting some of its key objectives. A financial analysis will also reveal some of the constraints on the firm in terms of formulating particular strategic objectives and plans. A firm's financial position can eliminate some strategies as feasible alternatives – for example, a firm may not be generating enough cash to fund a strategy of growth. Also financial factors often result in existing strategies being altered and implementation plans being changed.

It is usual for a case study in strategic management to provide financial information relating to the firm under consideration and which students are expected to analyse. The purpose of this chapter is to set out the basic tools required to undertake this analysis. Most of the information on which the financial analysis is based is provided in the organization's profit and loss account and balance sheet. The profit and loss account summarizes the revenue and expenses of the business for an accounting period, usually a year. The balance sheet provides a summary of the assets and liabilities of the business at the end of the accounting period. The profit and loss account and balance sheets for 1992 and 1993 for Northern Foods plc are shown in Tables 3 and 4. Northern Foods plc is a large food manufacturer. They produce a wide range of chilled foods under the 'own labels' of major retailers and brands including Ski, Eden Vale and Pork Farms. They also manufacture grocery products including Fox's biscuits. The financial information on Northern Foods will be used to illustrate this chapter. The tables show the *consolidated* accounts for Northern Foods. A parent or holding company is required to publish consolidated accounts which present the affairs of a group of companies (the holding company and its subsidiary companies) as if they were a single entity.

OVERVIEW ANALYSIS

To place a detailed financial analysis in context it is necessary first to consider trends in key figures over a number of years. Generally, the most interesting trends will include figures for sales, profit, net assets and dividends. The overall trend should be noted and the percentage annual increase or decrease in each should be calculated. The five year record, 1989 to 1993, for Northern Foods is shown in Table 5.

Table 3 Northern Foods plc: Consolidated profit and loss account for the year ended 31 March 1993

	1993 £m	1992 £m
Turnover	2,026.1	1,444.2
Cost of sales	(1,484.1)	(1,056.4)
Gross profit	542.0	387.8
Distribution costs	(259.2)	(181.2)
Administrative costs	(105.8)	(71.7)
Other operating costs	2.7	2.6
Income from interest in associated undertaking	1.1	—
Operating profit	180.8	137.5
Investment income	3.0	1.9
Interest payable	(26.8)	(9.7)
Allocated to profit sharing	(3.8)	(3.5)
Profit on ordinary activities before taxation	153.2	126.2
Taxation on ordinary activities	(38.8)	(32.7)
Profit on ordinary activities after taxation	114.4	93.5
Dividends	(48.2)	(41.6)
Retained profit for the year	66.2	51.9

The reported figures in Table 5 show that, over the period 1989 to 1993, there were substantial increases in turnover, profit before tax and ordinary share dividends and a significant increase in net assets, which suggests a healthy company. Care should be taken, however, when interpreting trends over time when inflation has occurred. In order to assess the true underlying performance of a company the reported figures should be converted to real or constant pound figures to eliminate the effects of inflation. One way of adjusting for inflation is to deflate the reported figures by an inflation index which reflects changes in the prices of the goods and services for the industry to which the firm belongs.[1] As Northern Foods is predominantly a food manufacturer, the producer price index for the output of food manufacturing is the appropriate index to use.[2] This and other indices are published

---

1. The Retail Price Index reflects increases/decreases in the retail price of a basket of goods and services purchased by consumers and is therefore a suitable index to use when the firm in question operates in the consumer goods and services industries. For firms operating in the manufacturing industries, producer price indices which reflect changes in output prices for individual industries are the appropriate indices to use.

2. Strictly speaking, the producer price index for the output of food manufacturing should only be used to adjust the turnover figures. Other appropriate indices should be applied to profits, dividends and net assets. However, as this is an extremely complicated procedure to carry out and involves many subjective judgements regarding, for example, the nature of costs, fixed assets, etc., for simplicity, the producer price index has been applied to all figures.

Table 4 Northern Foods plc: Balance Sheet as at 31 March 1993

	1993 £m		1992 £m
Fixed assets			
Tangible fixed assets	598.3		560.2
Investments	4.4		—
	602.7		560.2
Current assets			
Stocks	72.6	73.1	
Debtors	239.0	227.2	
Cash at bank and in hand	26.0	45.8	
	337.6	346.1	
Creditors: Amounts falling due within one year	495.2	558.3	
Net current liabilities	(157.6)		(212.2)
Total assets less current liabilities (net assets)	445.1		348.0
Creditors: Amounts falling due after more than one year			
Convertible subordinated bonds 2008	91.3	—	
Others	2.2	9.0	
	93.5		9.0
Provisions for liabilities and charges	30.5		62.0
Capital and reserves			
Called-up share capital	142.9	70.6	
Share premium account	9.2	0.2	
Revaluation reserve	12.0	12.1	
Other reserves	4.1	4.1	
Profit and loss account	152.9	190.0	
Shareholders' funds	321.1		277.0
	445.1		348.0

Other information:		
Number of ordinary shares in issue (weighted average for year, adjusted for capitalization issue)	569,372,505	488,147,704
Share price (at 31 March)	267.00p	270.00p
Share price (at 31 December)	234.00p	265.00p
Dividend per share	8.40p	7.87p
Number of employees	30,219	27,002

in the *Monthly Digest of Statistics*. The annual average of the index of food manufacturing producer prices over the 1980–93 period is shown in Table 6.

As the five-year record for Northern Foods dates back to 1989, the reported figures
for subsequent years are converted into 1989 pounds. This is accomplished by dividing
the 1989 index shown in Table 6 by the index for the year of the reported figure
and multiplying it by the reported figure. The result is the inflation adjusted figure.

Table 5 Northern Foods plc: five-year record (£m)

	Turnover		Profit before tax		Ordinary share dividend		Net assets	
	Reported figure	Inflation adjusted	Reported figure	Inflation adjusted	Reported figure	Inflation adjusted	Reported figure	Inflation adjusted
1989	1,041.3	1,041.3	85.3	85.3	24.9	24.9	314.0	314.0
1990	1,094.4	1,043.0	90.2	86.0	27.8	26.5	324.4	309.2
1991	1,187.0	1,083.5	105.4	96.2	32.2	29.4	324.9	296.6
1992	1,444.2	1,268.5	126.2	110.8	41.6	36.5	348.0	305.7
1993	2,026.1	1,695.2	153.2	128.2	48.2	40.3	445.1	372.4
% change 1989–93	94.57	62.80	79.60	50.29	93.57	61.85	41.75	18.60

Table 6 Producer price index – output of manufacturing industry: annual average

1980	64.3
1981	69.4
1982	74.3
1983	77.6
1984	81.9
1985	84.3
1986	86.6
1987	88.7
1988	91.7
1989	95.3
1990	100.0
1991	104.4
1992	108.5
1993	113.9

Index: 1990 = 100.0
Source: Department of Industry

Taking the reported turnover figure for 1991 as an example:

$$\frac{1989 \text{ Index}}{1991 \text{ Index}} \times \text{Turnover } 1991 = \frac{95.3}{104.4} \times 1,187.0 = 1,083.5$$

The inflation adjusted five-year performance record for Northern Foods is shown in Table 5. After adjusting for inflation, it is clear that Northern Foods has experienced substantial growth in sales, profits and dividends. In real terms, net assets actually decreased up until 1991, thereafter substantial increases have been made, largely as the result of acquisitions. A reduction in net assets may be an indication of a company which is shrinking, perhaps selling off subsidiaries or not renewing fixed assets.

As part of the overall analysis it is also interesting to note the movements in the firm's share price compared to the movement in the Financial Times Stock Exchange 100 Index (FTSE 100) and the index for the sector to which the firm belongs. Such a comparison for Northern Foods is shown in Figure 7, for the period 1989–93.

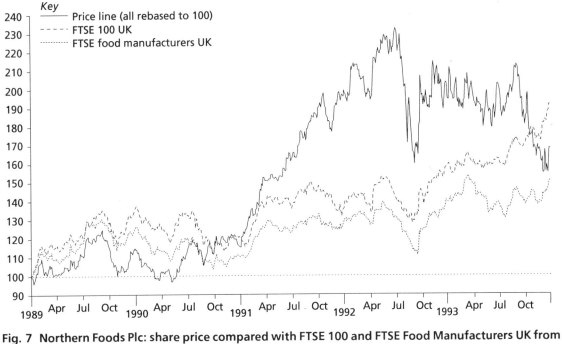

Fig. 7 Northern Foods Plc: share price compared with FTSE 100 and FTSE Food Manufacturers UK from 4/1/89 to 28/12/93 (all rebased to 100 at 4/1/89).

Source: Extel Financial Limited.

Figure 7 shows that for the period from the beginning of 1989 to the middle of 1990, Northern Foods share price under-performed both the FTSE 100 Index and the food manufacturing sector index. Towards the end of 1990 until September 1993, there was a dramatic rise in Northern Foods' share price such that it substantially outperformed both its sector and the FTSE 100 Index. This performance is particularly notable, as during this time the food manufacturing sector index was below the FTSE 100 Index. However, towards the end of 1993, the company's share price fell considerably, such that by the end of 1993, Northern Foods were performing less well than the FTSE 100 but were still outperforming the food manufacturing sector average.

RATIO ANALYSIS

Ratio analysis is an extensively used method of assessing the financial position of a firm. It is aimed at characterizing the firm in a few basic dimensions which affect the financial standing of a firm. This technique can be used in two ways:

1 to analyse trends over a number of years and to examine the way in which performance may have changed over time – this is known as *times-series analysis*;

2 for comparison with the industry average or with competitors at a single point in time. This comparison allows a judgement to be made about the firm's position within the industry. This is know as *cross-sectional analysis*.

It must be stressed that in order to interpret the meaning of a ratio it is necessary to have some basis of comparison. Comparisons should be made using either times-

Table 7 Summary of key financial ratios

Ratio	Formula	Meaning
Liquidity ratios		
Current/working capital ratio	$\dfrac{\text{Current assets}}{\text{Current liabilities}}$	Indicates the extent to which a firm can meet its short-term liabilities from its current assets without having to raise finance by borrowing, issuing more shares or selling fixed assets.
Acid test/quick ratio	$\dfrac{\text{Current assets} - \text{Stocks}}{\text{Current liabilities}}$	Measures the firm's ability to meet its short-term liabilities from its current assets without having to rely on the sale of its stock.
Gearing ratios		
Debt ratio	$\dfrac{\text{Total borrowings}}{\text{Capital employed}} \times 100\%$	Measures the proportion of capital employed which is financed by borrowed funds.
Debt-to-equity ratio	$\dfrac{\text{Total borrowings}}{\text{Shareholders' funds}} \times 100\%$	Measures the amount of borrowing as a percentage of shareholders' funds.
Interest cover	$\dfrac{\text{Profit before interest and tax}}{\text{Interest payable}}$	Measures how many times interest payments are covered by operating profits.
Activity ratios		
Net asset turnover	$\dfrac{\text{Sales}}{\text{Net assets}}$	Measures how efficiently the net assets are used to generate sales: measures the sales revenue generated by each £1 of net assets.
Fixed asset turnover	$\dfrac{\text{Sales}}{\text{Fixed assets}}$	Measures the sales revenue generated by each £1 of fixed assets.
Stock turnover	$\dfrac{\text{Sales}}{\text{Stocks}}$	Measures the number of times that stocks of finished goods were sold during the year.
Debtor turnover	$\dfrac{\text{Sales}}{\text{Debtors}}$	Measures the number of times debtors are cycled during the year.
Average collection period	$\dfrac{\text{Debtors}}{\text{Sales}} \times 365 \text{ days}$	Indicates the number of days credit the firm gives to customers.
Profitability ratios		
Return on capital employed	$\dfrac{\text{Operating profit}}{\text{Capital employed}} \times 100\%$	Measures the performance of the firm regardless of the method of financing.
Return on equity	$\dfrac{\text{Profit after tax}}{\text{Shareholders' funds}} \times 100\%$	Measures the profitability of the shareholders' investment in the firm.
Operating profit margin	$\dfrac{\text{Operating profit}}{\text{Sales}} \times 100\%$	Shows how much £1 of sales earns as operating profit.
Net profit margin	$\dfrac{\text{Profit after tax}}{\text{Sales}} \times 100\%$	Shows how much £1 of sales earns as profit available for shareholders.
Stock market ratios		
Earnings per share	$\dfrac{\text{Profit after tax}}{\text{Number of ordinary shares in issue}}$	Measures the earnings generated for each ordinary share.

Table 7 *Continued*

Ratio	Formula	Meaning
Price/earnings ratio	$\dfrac{\text{Market price per share}}{\text{Earnings per share}}$	Shows the esteem in which the market holds the company, the higher the ratio the more highly rated the share.
Net dividend yield	$\dfrac{\text{Dividend per share}}{\text{Market price per share}} \times 100\%$	Indicates the net dividend rate of return to ordinary shareholders.
Dividend cover	$\dfrac{\text{Earnings per share}}{\text{Dividends per share}}$	Shows how many times earnings cover the amount paid out in dividends.

series analysis, or by using cross-sectional analysis. The use of a single ratio on its own is virtually meaningless.

No single ratio provides sufficient information for evaluating the financial condition and performance of a firm. Reasonable judgements can only be made when groups of ratios are evaluated. There are five basic groups of ratios which may be considered: liquidity ratios, gearing ratios, activity ratios, profitability ratios and stock market ratios. The main ratios within each of these five groups are set out in Table 7 above. It must be noted that there are many different accounting ratios which may be calculated and, in many cases, a variety of different methods for calculating each ratio. The key to ratio analysis is consistency – in order to make valid comparisons, each particular ratio must be calculated using the chosen formula both for the firm across time and for the industry or competitors. The calculations of these ratios for Northern Foods and the food manufacturing sector are shown in Table 8.[3] Each of these groups of ratios are considered below.

Liquidity ratios

The *current ratio* indicates the extent to which the claims of short-term creditors are covered by assets convertible into cash; in other words, it is a crude measure of the firm's ability to meet its current obligations. A large ratio is not necessarily a good sign for the firm as it may indicate that the organization is not making the most efficient use of its assets. On the other hand, a high current ratio is not necessarily a bad sign as it may indicate that the firm is maintaining a high ratio as an insurance against future uncertainty.

Many textbooks cite a 'rule of thumb' measure for the current ratio of 2, that is, the firm should have twice as many current assets as current liabilities. Such advice is best ignored as the optimum ratio will vary from industry to industry and will depend on the environment in which the firm operates and the structure of its assets and liabilities. The more volatile industries will typically carry higher current ratios than those more stable industries. Food retailing companies, such as Sainsbury and

---

3. The food manufacturing sector average ratios have been calculated from sector accounts data extracted from Datastream. The sector ratios are calculated using the formulae presented in Table 7 and in a manner that is consistent with Northern Foods balance sheet structure. For example, many companies in the food manufacturing sector, such as Cadbury Schweppes, include brand valuations as intangible assets in the balance sheet, whereas Northern Foods does not. To ensure consistency between Northern Foods and the sector ratios, intangible assets have been deducted from capital employed when calculating sector ratios. In many cases, the sector ratios have been directly extracted from Datastream, but where Datastream's formulae differs from that presented here, ratios have been recalculated to ensure consistency.

Table 8 Financial ratios for Northern Foods plc

Ratio		1993	1992	Food manufacturing industry average 1992–93
Current ratio	$\dfrac{337.6}{495.2}$	0.68	0.62	1.24
Acid test	$\dfrac{337.6 - 72.6}{495.2}$	0.53	0.49	0.80
Debt ratio: (including short-term debt)	$\dfrac{146.5 + 91.9}{445.1 + 146.5} \times 100\%$	40.30%	41.68%	29.69%
(long-term debt only)	$\dfrac{91.9}{445.1} \times 100\%$	20.65%	1.58%	21.06%
Debt-to-equity ratio: (including short-term debt)	$\dfrac{146.5 + 91.9}{321.1} \times 100\%$	74.24%	88.38%	60.32%
(long-term debt only)	$\dfrac{91.9}{321.1} \times 100\%$	28.62%	1.99%	38.09%
Interest cover	$\dfrac{153.2 + 26.8}{26.8}$	6.72	14.01	6.19
Net asset turnover	$\dfrac{2,026.1}{445.1}$	4.55	4.15	2.78
Fixed asset turnover	$\dfrac{2,026.1}{598.3}$	3.39	2.58	3.90
Stock turnover	$\dfrac{2,026.1}{72.6}$	27.91	19.76	9.48
Debtor turnover	$\dfrac{2,026.1}{239.0}$	8.48	6.36	7.73
Average collection period	$\dfrac{239.0}{2,026.1} \times 365 \text{ days}$	43.06 days	57.42 days	47.21 days
Return on capital employed: (including short-term debt)	$\dfrac{180.8}{445.1 + 146.5} \times 100\%$	30.56%	23.41%	21.92%
(long-term debt only)	$\dfrac{180.8}{445.1} \times 100\%$	40.62%	39.51%	24.61%
Return on equity	$\dfrac{114.4}{321.1} \times 100\%$	35.63%	33.75%	23.21
Operating profit margin	$\dfrac{180.8}{2,026.1} \times 100\%$	8.92%	9.52%	8.12

Table 8 *Continued*

Ratio		1993	1992	Food manufacturing industry average 1992–93
Net profit margin	$\dfrac{114.4}{2,026.1} \times 100\%$	5.65%	6.47%	4.38
Earnings per share	$\dfrac{114,400,000}{569,372,505}$	20.09p	19.15p	N/A
Price/earnings ratio	$\dfrac{234.00}{20.09}$	11.65	13.84	15.25
Net dividend yield	$\dfrac{8.40}{234.00} \times 100\%$	3.59	2.97	N/A
Dividend cover	$\dfrac{20.09}{8.40}$	2.39	2.43	2.25
Sales per employee	$\dfrac{2,026.1m}{30,219}$	67,047	53,485	89,420
Operating profit per employee	$\dfrac{180.8m}{30,219}$	5,983	5,092	7,252
Capital employed per employee	$\dfrac{445.1m + 146.5m}{30,219}$	19,577	21,750	33,091

Tesco, have relatively low current ratios as they rarely carry debtors. In addition, the ability of the firm to raise additional funds should a liquidity problem arise will have an effect on the size of the liquidity ratios. Large quoted firms are more likely to be able to raise additional funds at short notice than are smaller unquoted firms and hence the larger firms are likely to carry lower liquidity ratios.

The current ratio for Northern Foods appears to be very low at 0.68 in 1993, having risen marginally from 0.62 in 1992. These figures indicate that Northern Foods would be unable to meet its current liabilities by liquidating its current assets if the need arose. A comparison with the average for the food manufacturing sector, which is 1.24, shows that the company's current ratio is some way below the industry norm and suggests that Northern Foods may indeed have some problems in respect of liquidity. However, in order to present a fuller explanation of the liquidity situation, it is useful to look at the components of current liabilities, details of which may be found in the notes to the accounts. The relevant information is reproduced in Table 9. Inspection of Table 9 reveals that Northern Foods has a sizeable proportion of its total debt in the form of short-term debt which is responsible for its large current liabilities figure.

The *acid test or quick ratio* is a more stringent test of a company's liquidity position than that provided by the current ratio. Stocks and work-in-progress are excluded from the figure for current assets on the basis that they are the least liquid of current assets. The firm, if forced to sell stocks to meet current obligations, may have to

Table 9 Analysis of current and long-term liabilities for Northern Foods

	1993 £m		1992 £m	
Total borrowings falling due in one year:				
Bank overdrafts	—		3.7	
Bank loans	53.9		144.0	
Bills payable	91.9		83.1	
Other loans	0.7		8.5	
		146.5		239.3
Other creditors falling due in one year		348.7		319.0
Creditors: amounts falling due in one year		495.2		558.3
Total borrowings falling due after one year:				
Bank loans	0.3		4.9	
Finance leases	0.3		0.6	
Convertible bonds	91.3		—	
		91.9		5.5
Other creditors falling due after more than one year		1.6		3.5
Creditors: amounts falling due after more than one year		93.5		9.0

sell at a loss and in extreme cases may not be able to find a buyer at all, for example if stocks are obsolete.

The acid test ratio for Northern Foods increased slightly from 0.49 in 1992 to 0.53 in 1993. As with the current ratio, this is somewhat below the industry average of 0.80. However, before jumping to conclusions regarding the liquidity position of Northern Foods, it is important to remember that poor short-term liquidity as presented in the ratios is not necessarily a serious problem if a firm is able to borrow funds relatively quickly should the need arise. Therefore, it is important to assess the overall borrowing capacity of the firm by evaluating the gearing ratios.

Gearing ratios

Gearing ratios measure the financial contributions of the owners of the business through shareholders' funds compared to the financing provided from outside the firm from borrowed funds. The gearing ratios are an indication of the organization's financial risk as debt has to be serviced in the form of interest payments. If the firm's shareholders are providing only a small proportion of the total financing, gearing will be high. Highly geared firms face greater risk as there is increased risk of liquidation if fixed interest payments cannot be met in any year. An advantage of low gearing is that it provides scope to increase borrowing when potentially profitable projects are available to the company. Companies with low gearing should find it easier to borrow and may find that it is possible to borrow more cheaply (that is, at lower rates of interest) than if gearing is already high. The US term for gearing is 'leverage' as this reflects the fact that using capital with a committed interest charge (i.e. borrowed funds) will amplify either profits or losses in relation to the equity of ordinary shareholders.

In the UK, many companies tend to borrow short term – usually by means of a bank overdraft – and roll forward such debt. They in effect use short-term debt on a long-term basis. It is, therefore, legitimate to include both short-term and long-term debt when calculating gearing ratios for UK companies. Information on short-term and long-term borrowings is usually found in the notes to the accounts and is reproduced for Northern Foods in Table 9.

There are a number of debt ratios or measures of gearing. Two of the main ones are considered here. The *debt ratio* measures the firm's percentage of total funds provided in the form of borrowed funds. This ratio is important because creditors' claims must be repaid before any profit can be taken out of the business by its shareholders. Clearly, high gearing reflects a commitment to an interest charge which has to be met annually. Lenders prefer moderate debt ratios because the lower the ratio the greater the cushion against their losses in the event of liquidation. Shareholders often prefer a high ratio in order to magnify earnings through the leverage affect. Also shareholders may prefer that the company takes on more debt rather than increasing the level of equity funding as the latter may mean relinquishing some control of the firm. However, as noted above, too much debt increases the risk of loss of control through liquidation.

Northern Foods' debt ratio including short-term borrowings was 40.30 per cent in 1993, falling from 41.68 per cent in 1992. As can be seen from Table 9, the structure of debt changed substantially over the two years, with short-term borrowings being reduced and long-term borrowings increased. Overall, the level of total debt decreased. This illustrates the importance of including short-term debt in the debt ratio – the debt ratio for 1992 and 1993 is 1.58 per cent and 20.65 per cent respectively if short-term borrowings are excluded from the calculation. This may lead to interpretation that debt levels are increasing, whereas, in fact, total borrowings have decreased.

The *debt to equity* ratio shows the relative proportion of funding provided to the firm by debtholders and shareholders. For Northern Foods, debtholders provided 74.24 per cent of shareholders' funds in 1993 compared with 88.38 per cent in the previous year. If short-term borrowings are excluded from the calculation, the debt ratio is 28.62 per cent for 1993 and 1.99 per cent for 1992. Overall, these figures indicate that Northern Foods relies heavily on borrowed funds but is moving away from its reliance on short-term borrowing to long-term funds.

Interest cover measures the number of times that interest payments could be covered by operating income and indicates the ease with which the firm can meet its annual interest commitments. Obviously, the higher the ratio the greater the margin of safety for both the debtholders and the shareholders. A relatively low ratio would provide information that additional debt may be difficult to secure.

Interest cover is calculated as profit before interest and tax divided by interest payable. In order to calculate profit before interest and tax, we need to take the figure in the profit and loss account for profit on ordinary activities before tax (which is after interest) and add back interest payable. Northern Foods' interest cover for 1993 is 6.72, having fallen from 14.01 in 1992. Whilst the 1993 figure for interest cover suggests that the company is able to easily meet its annual interest payments from its earnings and is in line with the industry average, the fall from the 1992 level warrants some explanation, given that the total level of borrowing decreased over the period. The reason for this apparent anomaly is that, in historic terms, the debt levels were exceptionally high at 31 March 1992. However, the increase in borrowings in the 1992 reporting year largely took place at the end of the reporting period with the result that the interest payable for 1992 does not fully reflect this rise. This illustrates the need to examine the calculated ratios carefully and to dig deep for explanations to apparent inconsistencies in the figures.

Activity ratios

Activity ratios indicate how efficiently management is using the resources of the firm. By comparing sales revenue/turnover with the resources used to generate such revenue, it is possible to measure how efficiently the firm is being operated.

The *net asset turnover ratio* measures how efficiently management is using the net assets at its disposal to generate sales. Industry figures for net asset turnover will vary depending on capital intensity. Highly capital intensive sectors, such as machine tool manufacture, will have relatively low ratios because of large investments in assets. In contrast, many service sector industries, such as advertising, operate with relatively few tangible assets (their main assets being their employees which do not appear on the balance sheet) and hence have high net asset turnover ratios.

Northern Foods had a net asset turnover of 4.55 for 1993 compared to an industry average of 2.78. A relatively high net asset turnover may indicate that the company is using its net assets more efficiently to generate sales than is its competitors. However, caution must be exercised in this case, as Northern Foods have much lower net assets figures than do its competitors, due to its relatively large amounts of short-term borrowings.

Fixed asset turnover is a measure of the efficiency of use of plant and equipment. As with net asset turnover, this ratio will also vary across industries depending on the extent of capital intensity. Northern Foods' fixed asset turnover has increased to 3.39 from 2.58 in the period 1992 to 1993. This indicates that the company is improving the efficiency in which it uses its plant and equipment, although the ratio is still slightly below that of the industry average. However, the ratio is dependent on the methods used to value fixed assets – at market value or at historic cost – and will differ from company to company.

Stock turnover measures how many times the company's stock is turned over each year and is an indication of management's efficiency to control investment in stock. The faster stock is turned over (or sold) the faster will be sales and the faster cash will flow into the company. Strictly speaking, this ratio should be calculated by dividing the cost of goods sold by stock. However, most companies do not provide such detailed information in their accounts (cost of sales figures are not the same as cost of goods sold) and hence the sales/turnover figure is usually used as a compromise.

The stock turnover figure will vary widely from industry to industry depending on the nature of the stock under consideration. The stock of relatively small inexpensive items is likely to turnover much faster than are stocks of large expensive items. For example, shipbuilding would be associated with low stock turnover ratios whereas food retailing would be associated with high stock turnover ratios. In general, the higher the stock turnover ratio the better. A low stock turnover ratio compared to the industry average may indicate overstocking. The holdings of large amounts of stock which is slow moving is a drain on the company's working capital resources and may result in cash flow problems. It is particularly dangerous for companies in certain industries where stock may become obsolete in a short period of time or where perishable goods are involved.

Northern Foods' stock turnover ratio has increased from 19.76 in 1992 to 27.91 in 1993. As stock levels themselves have not substantially decreased, this is the result of the large increase in turnover from 1992 to 1993. The company's stock turnover ratio compares extremely favourably with the industry average which is only 9.48. However, a higher than average figure is to be expected as Northern Foods manufactures perishable goods (dairy products) which require a high turnover rate.

Debtor turnover shows the number of times debtors are turned over in a year. A high ratio could indicate a loss of sales because the company has too restrictive a credit policy in comparison with its competitors. Alternatively, a low ratio indicates that too much working capital is being tied up with debtors and that credit control is poor, increasing the risk of bad debts. Northern Foods debtor turnover ratio has increased from 6.36 to 8.48 over the 1992–93 period. The meaning of the debtor turnover ratio is perhaps easier to understand if it is considered in terms of the *average collection period*. This shows the number of days credit the firm gives to its customers. A high debt turnover is equivalent to a short collection period. Northern Foods had an average collection period of approximately 43 days in 1993 compared to 57 days in 1992. This suggests that the company is tightening up its credit policy by allowing fewer days of credit.

Profitability ratios

Profitability measures indicate how effectively the total firm is being managed and in many ways constitute the most important set of ratios. Business success is largely viewed in terms of profits and profitability is the ultimate measure of management's performance.

The *return on capital employed* ratio expresses operating profit as a percentage of the assets employed in the business and measures how effectively the company's assets have been managed. It is useful at this stage to indicate how capital employed is measured. One method is to calculate capital employed as total long-term capital and equal to shareholders' funds plus minority interests plus long-term liabilities. This definition makes capital employed equal to net assets which equal total assets minus current liabilities.

It should be noted that this method of calculating capital employed, as being equal to net assets, excludes short-term sources of finance such as bank overdrafts. Care must be taken, therefore, when making inter-company comparisons of profitability. A company which finances its activities from an overdraft will appear to be earning a higher rate of return on capital employed than a competitor which uses long-term bank loans. These particular problems arise in the case of Northern Foods, which, as stated earlier, employs large amounts of short-term borrowings. An alternative method of calculating capital employed is to include all short-term liabilities (making it equal to total assets) or to add only short-term borrowings (excluding trade creditors, etc.) to the net assets figure.

Excluding short-term borrowings from capital employed, Northern Food's return on capital employed is 40.62 per cent in 1993. Compared to the industry average of 24.61 per cent, Northern Foods' return looks extremely favourable. However, if short-term borrowings are included in capital employed, the ratio is 30.56 per cent in 1993, having increased from 23.41 per cent in 1992. This is still better than the industry average of 21.92 per cent but to a much lesser degree.

Return on equity measures the rate of return on the shareholders' capital. To ensure that the numerator and denominator of the ratio are consistent, profit should be calculated as profit after interest and tax, that is calculating profit which is attributable to ordinary shareholders. This figure measures the amount of profit available to shareholders after paying any interest and charges to other stakeholders such as debtholders. Northern Foods' return on equity has increased over the period to 35.63 per cent in 1993 and once again compares favourably with the industry average of 23.21 per cent. Overall, the return on equity ratio indicates that Northern Foods offers a higher return to its shareholders than does the industry on average.

Operating profit margin indicates how successfully the company has anticipated changes in the market-place and how effective its marketing and pricing strategies have been. There are three main factors which affect the operating profit margin – the price of the goods sold, the cost of sales and the mix of products sold. Northern Foods' operating profit ratio has fallen slightly from 9.52 per cent in 1992 to 8.92 per cent, but is still somewhat better than the industry average of 8.12 per cent. The *net profit margin* is a more specific ratio of profitability than is the operating profit margin and shows company efficiency after all expenses and taxes have been paid. As with the operating profit margin, Northern Foods' net profit margin is decreasing but is still better than the industry average.

Some care should be taken over the interpretation of the level of profitability margins. Low margins are often associated with inefficiency and poor quality management. Within a particular industry, however, a company may choose a policy of low profit margins as part of a strategy designed to increase market share by cutting selling prices. Low margins may also be due to high development costs associated with new products introduced to gain market share. High margins relative to competitors or improving margins are usually taken as indicators of efficiency and good management. However, if a firm dominates a particular market, it will be able to achieve high margins even with relatively poor quality management.

Pyramid of ratios

It is often difficult to determine the causes of a firm's poor profitability record. Although return on capital employed provides a good measure of the overall performance of a company it is a broad measure which encapsulates the effects of many diverse influences which serve to reduce its ability to identify problem areas. To an extent this limitation can be reduced by breaking down the ratio into a number of elements, in effect working through a pyramid of ratios, which makes it possible to see how the various measures interact to determine the overall profitability of the firm.

Starting with the measure for the return on capital employed and recalling that capital employed is equal to net assets, then:

$$\frac{\text{Operating profit}}{\text{Net assets}} = \frac{\text{Operating profit}}{\text{Sales}} \times \frac{\text{Sales}}{\text{Net assets}}$$

which may be expressed as:

Return on capital employed = Operating profit margin × Net asset turnover.

Operating profit margin is a measure of marketing effectiveness while net asset turnover is a measure of production effectiveness. Broken down in this way, the resulting ratios show that improvements or deterioration in profitability may be traced to marketing effectiveness or production effectiveness. This can be investigated further by breaking down the net asset turnover ratio. As net assets are equal to fixed assets plus working capital, the net asset turnover ratio may be split by calculating separately:

$$\frac{\text{Sales}}{\text{Fixed assets}} \quad \text{and} \quad \frac{\text{Sales}}{\text{Working capital}}$$

where Working capital = Current assets – Current liabilities.

A pyramid of ratios is shown in Figure 8. The higher level ratios may be analysed in terms of the lower level ratios. Thus the company's overall results can be studied in even greater detail by splitting the accounting ratios as shown in the figure providing that the information is available.

Stock market ratios

A useful analysis is to express some of the information in the financial statements on a per share basis. This enables the performance of the firm to be judged from the equity holder's perspective. Note that the number of ordinary shares and the share price do not constitute part of the profit and loss account or balance sheet. The number of ordinary shares in issue is usually given as part of the notes to the accounts. The share price must be obtained from published information on the stock market, for example the financial pages of the newspapers. The way in which *The Financial Times* presents stock market information on companies is shown in Figure 9. By studying the share information page in *The Financial Times* it is possible to

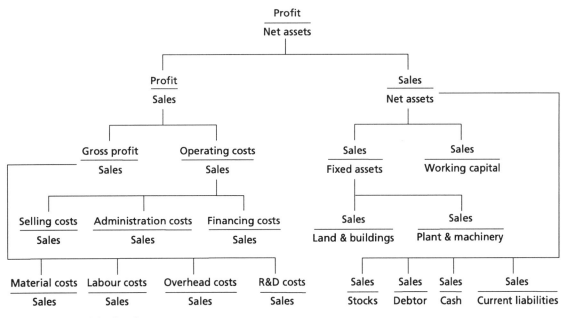

Fig. 8 A pyramid of ratios.

Price
The price listed in this column is the previous day's closing price. This closing price usually reflects the mid-price of the best bid and offer prices. This is only an indication of the actual price which you will pay or receive when buying or selling the shares. The symbol *xd* after the price indicates that the stock is currently ex-dividend which means that buyers are no longer eligible to receive the current dividend.

Industry sector
Listed shares are listed by industry sector to allow easy comparison of directly competitive companies. Examples of industry sectors include food retailing, household goods, chemicals, etc.

Market capitalization
This is calculated as share price multiplied by the number of shares in issue.

Price/earnings ratio
This is calculated as the market price of the share divided by the company's most recent twelve months' earnings per share.

FOOD MANUFACTURERS

	Notes	Price	+ or −	1994 high	low	Mkt Cap£m	Yld Gr's	P/E
Acatos & Hutch	†N☐	280xd	+1	368	265	92.4	3.8	11.2
Albert Fisher	♣gN☐	47xa	......	*74	46	332.6	10.0	10.4
Assoc Brit Foods	sN☐	537	+3	607	499	2,411	3.5	10.4
Avonmore I£	♣☐	133	......	165	113	99.4	3.5	9.4
For BSN see Danone								
Banks (SC)	♣†	263	......	270	220	22.6	4.3	10.0
Bar (AG)	†N	349	−1	358	305	66.0	2.4	22.4
Bensons Crisps	♣N	57	......	*72	56	10.5	6.2	18.9
Booker	♣N☐	405	+2	481	378	865.1	6.7	14.4
Bols Wessanen		£13⅝	−13/32	£16⅛	£13 7/32	1,101	3.3	12.5
Borthwicks	N☐	53½xd	......	56½	48	30.9	3.0	22.9
Cadbury Schweppes	♣N☐	433	+8	*545	407	3,606	4.2	14.7
Canadian Pizza	♣W☐	101	......	225	101	17.4	7.3	φ
Carr's Mill	♣†N	194	......	232	143	13.3	2.9	φ
Cranswick	♣N	151xd	......	*167	130	20.3	6.8	12.6
Dalepak	‡N	94	......	154	90	10.9	6.6	27.4
Dalgety	♣†N☐	436	......	543	389	1,001	5.9	12.7
Daniels (S)	N	57	......	87	50	4.73	0.7	−
Danone FFr		£95 11/16	+13/32	£114 31/32	£91 11/16	6,200	2.9	φ
Devro Int'l	WN☐	230	......	294	219	310.5	3.4	15.5
Everest	♣N	61	......	101	60	15.5	7.6	11.6
Finlay (J)	N☐	76xd	......	85	68	75.8	6.8	14.2
Global	♣♣N☐	15	......	20½	14	18.1	4.2	13.7
Golden Vale I£	N	55¼	−¼	121	54½	90.7	4.7	5.5
Grand Central	♣☐	40	......	68	40	15.8	−	−
Greencore I£	♣†N☐	342xd	+4	379	325	286.4	3.6	10.2
Hazlewood	qN☐	128xd	......	194	119	297.2	6.5	7.8
Hillsdown	N☐	162	......	196½	151	1,122	6.8	13.0
Hobson	N☐	20	−½	28	16	78.1	−	−
IAWS A I£	♣†	80	......	88	76	30.7	3.6	11.5
JLI	N☐	96xd	−1	111	93	39.8	6.2	φ
John Lusty	♣☐	8	......	14½	6½	7.96	−	−
Kakuzi KSh	h	185xc	+12	245	173	36.3	0.5	63.7
Kays Food	☐	5	......	5½	5	4.00	−	−
Kerry Group A	N	305	+5	325	250	476.0	1.1	14.8
Linton Park	N	375xd	......	400	313	64.2	5.0	φ
Matthews (B)	N☐	108	+3	113	85	134.0	2.9	17.2
Moran		54	......	54	40	7.22	−	−
Nestle' (Reg) SFr	♣	£528⅛	−1⅛	£653⅞	£511⅞	20,430	2.2	φ
Nichols (Vimto)	♣N☐	208	+3	246	205	82.2	3.5	13.9
Northern	N☐	204xd	−1	271½	197	1,171	5.4	9.9
Northumbrian	♣☐	13	......	*14	9	7.99	−	−
Pascoe's		40	......	*46	31	6.12	−	−
Perkins	N☐	64	......	81	63	79.0	8.7	10.7

Price movements
This column tells you how much the price of the share has fallen or risen on the previous day's closing price.

High/low for current year
This shows the highest and lowest price achieved by the share since the beginning of the year.

Gross dividend yield
This shows the percentage return on the share before income tax is deducted at the rate of 20 per cent and is calculated by dividing the gross dividend by the current share price.

Fig. 9 *Financial Times* share statistics.

Many daily newspapers carry full details of stock market information and provide the reader with a great deal of information in order to monitor the performance and prospects of a company's shares. The example above, taken from the *Financial Times* of Thursday 14 July 1994, illustrates the information on a group of firms in the food manufacturing sector. This type of information is provided Tuesday to Saturday. On a Monday, the *Financial Times* includes information which changes less often: dividends, dividend cover, dividend payment dates, the last ex-dividend date and the week's percentage change in stock.

derive a guide to what constitutes an acceptable price earnings ratio, dividend yield and dividend cover for a particular industrial group.

Earnings per share (EPS) measures how much profit attributable to ordinary share-holders is being earned for each ordinary share. Northern Foods' earnings per share has risen from 19.15p per share in 1992 to 20.09p in 1993. Note that industry or competitor comparisons of earnings per share are not valid as the figures depend on the number of shares in issue which naturally differ substantially between companies.

The price/earnings (PE) ratio is a representation of the esteem in which the stock market holds the company and is one of the most widely quoted ratios. It shows the relationship between the company's share price and its EPS and indicates how many years' worth of earnings the share price represents. If the market price of the share rises for a given EPS, then so will the PE ratio, and vice versa. Therefore, the PE ratio will change from day to day as the share price fluctuates on the stock market. In general the higher the PE ratio the more highly the stock market rates the company. A relatively high PE ratio is likely to be associated with higher than average prospects of a future growth in earnings, whilst a relatively low PE ratio is suggestive of lower than average growth prospects.

Care must be taken in calculating PE ratios. Whilst it is possible to calculate a PE ratio as market price of the share at the year end divided by earnings per share, this measure would be rather meaningless. This is because, at the accounting year end of, for example, 31 March 1993, the market price would not reflect the current year's earnings of 20.09p per share. Northern Foods did not release information regarding earnings for the 1993 year until June 1993. A more meaningful calcula-tion is to take a market price some time after the earnings information has been released. In this case, the share price at the 31 December 1993 has been used and hence the PE ratio at that date has been calculated.

Northern Foods' PE ratio fell from 13.84 in 1992 to 11.65 in 1993 compared to the sector PE ratio of 15.25. This suggests that the market considers Northern Foods to have fewer growth opportunities than other companies within the sector. Indeed, as was seen from Figure 7, the market performance of the food manu-facturing sector as a whole is improving whilst that of Northern Foods is declining.

Net dividend yield shows how much income, in the form of dividends, as a per-centage of the share price the shares offer the shareholder. The yield will vary inversely with the share price and the PE ratio if the dividend per share remains the same. Hence a relatively high PE ratio will be associated with a relatively low yield. A high yield in general will suggest that the market believes there is a risk that the company may reduce or fail to pay a dividend in the future. Dividends are paid to shareholders net of basic rate tax. Where the tax element is added back to the divi-dend paid, this is known as the gross dividend yield and the return to the share-holder on the price paid for the shares is the gross dividend yield. Northern Foods' net dividend yield has increased over the period from 2.97 to 3.59.

Dividend cover indicates the ease with which the firm can meet dividend payments from earnings. The higher the dividend cover, the more secure are the shareholders' dividends. A dividend ratio of less than one is a worrying sign as it means that divi-dends are greater than earnings and are therefore being paid out of reserves – essen-tially eating into shareholders' funds. Northern Foods have maintained their dividend cover at over two times during the period. It may be noted that in general there is a potential conflict between management's wish to retain profit for further investment and shareholders' desire for increased dividend payments.

Other ratios

The ratios which have been discussed are not an exhaustive list and various other measures are possible. In some businesses, particularly retailing, it may be useful to consider sales and costs on a 'per square foot' basis. For many businesses key financial statistics such as sales, costs, assets and profits may be usefully analysed on a 'per employee' basis. Some ratios based on the number of employees in Northern Foods are shown in Table 8. Sales, operating profits and capital employed per employee are all lower than the sector averages which may suggest that Northern Foods is more labour intensive than its competitors.

ANALYSIS OF CASH FLOW STATEMENTS

It should be noted that further insight into the financial policies of a company can be obtained from an analysis of its cash flow statement. Indeed, it may be argued that the cash flow statement is the most important document in terms of evaluating the performance and the strategic strength of a company. The level of profits reported by a company are largely dependent on the accounting policies adopted and companies are able to enhance profits using 'creative accounting'. However, cash is virtually impossible to 'create' out of thin air (without resorting to fraud!) and it is therefore a more objective measure of the company's performance. The generation of cash is vitally important – a company cannot survive for any reasonable period of time without cash. The cash flow statement sets out movements in cash during the accounting year. It allows the user to make an assessment of whether the operating activities of the firm are generating or consuming cash. Major strategic changes can be examined by looking at the cash consumed or generated by acquisitions, capital expenditure, investments and asset disposals. Finally, it shows how the firm is financing any cash shortfall or using surplus cash.

The cash flow statements for 1992 and 1993 for Northern Foods are presented in Table 10. The net cash inflow from operating activities indicates that the company is generating increasing amounts of cash from its operating activities. It is vital that a company is able to generate cash from its core operating activities as it signals management's ability to develop and implement a strategy necessary for the company to compete effectively in its markets.

The sections in the cash flow statement dealing with returns on investments and servicing of finance, taxation and investing activities reveal whether cash is being absorbed or generated from non-operating activities. Of particular interest are the amount of funds generated or absorbed by its investing activities in terms of acquisitions or sales of subsidiaries and the purchase and disposal of fixed assets. It is clear from Table 10 that Northern Foods made major acquisitions in 1992 which accounted for the large proportion of its net cash outflow before financing. As can be seen, acquisitions can be a major drain on a company's resources and it is important that the acquisitions undertaken are able, over time, to generate substantial operating cash flows.

Table 10 Northern Foods: Cash flow statement for the year ended 31 March 1993

	1993 £m		1992 £m	
Net cash inflow from operating activities		195.9		154.3
Returns on investments and servicing of finance:				
Interest received	3.0		2.4	
Interest paid	(26.2)		(12.4)	
Interest element of finance lease payments	(0.2)		(0.2)	
Dividends paid	(44.2)		(34.4)	
Net cash outflow from returns on investments and servicing of finance		(67.6)		(44.6)
Taxation:				
UK corporation tax paid	(23.6)		(20.8)	
Overseas tax paid	(0.2)		(0.4)	
Tax paid		(23.8)		(21.2)
Investing activities:				
Acquisitions	(23.0)		(351.8)	
Purchase of shares in associated undertaking	(8.5)		—	
Cash balances of acquisitions	(1.3)		(30.3)	
Purchase of tangible fixed assets	(92.7)		(88.9)	
Sales of plant and machinery	4.8		6.9	
Net cash outflow from investing activities		(120.7)		(464.1)
Net cash outflow before financing		(16.2)		(375.6)
Financing:				
Issue of subordinated bonds	91.3			—
Costs of subordinated bonds	(2.5)			
New short-term loans	3.7		10.8	
Repayment of amounts borrowed	(40.5)		(6.3)	
Capital element of finance lease payments	(0.5)		(1.0)	
Issue of ordinary share capital	6.0		236.9	
Costs of share issues	(0.3)		(6.5)	
Net cash inflow from financing		57.2		233.9
Increase/(decrease) in cash and cash equivalents		41.0		(141.7)

Overall, for Northern Foods the net cash flow from operating and non-operating activities is negative, although that outflow has fallen considerably in 1993 from the 1992 level. This cash outflow has to be financed, by taking on additional loans, issuing new shares, depleting cash reserves or increasing its overdraft. If there is a cash inflow from operating and non-operating activities, the company may increase its cash reserves or repay borrowings. For 1992, Northern Foods financed the large cash outflow largely by issuing new shares and substantially increasing its overdraft (as reflected in the decrease in cash and cash equivalents). In 1993, a much reduced cash outflow was financed largely by issuing new long-term debt (subordinated bonds), part of which was used to repay short-term bank loans. Overall, Northern Foods' cash position at the end of 1993 was much healthier than that at the end of 1992.

CONCLUSIONS

Financial analysis provides an important tool for assessing the strengths and weaknesses of an organization within its industry. Care should be taken, however, in interpreting the results of financial analysis for the following reasons:

- The view provided by financial analysis is based on historic data. Although the underlying trends provided by the analysis may be noteworthy, this does not automatically imply that such trends will continue into the future.
- Accounting policies may vary between firms, for example in the way they account for depreciation or value fixed assets such as land and buildings.
- Further complications arise when conducting financial analysis on consolidated accounts. Consolidated accounts aggregate the assets, liabilities and profits or losses of companies within a group and this aggregation must be borne in mind when interpreting ratios. For example, when interpreting liquidity ratios, it should be remembered that it is unlikely that all creditors have equal rights to claim against the consolidated assets – the creditors of an individual company in the group will normally be able only to claim against that company and not the group as a whole.

It is also important to recognize that the financial position of a firm is the outcome of a large number of factors. These factors include management decisions with respect to finance, marketing, production and research and development, but also actions by competitors, suppliers and customers as well as underlying trends in the broad environment faced by the firm. Financial analysis should, therefore, be used with judgement and caution.

FURTHER READING

The following is an excellent, clearly written text which links strategy, financial and stock market analysis. It explains how to carry out a comprehensive analysis of a company linking all three perspectives:

Ellis, J. and D. Williams (1993) *Corporate Strategy and Financial Analysis*. London, Pitman.

SECTION 2

Retailing

Case 1   Asda Group Plc (A)
              K.W. Glaister, University of Leeds

Case 2   Asda Group Plc (B)
              K.W. Glaister, University of Leeds

Case 3   Argyll Group Plc
              C.M. Clarke Hill and T.M. Robinson, University of Huddersfield

Case 4   Burton and Next – the changing high street
              C.M. Clarke Hill, University of Huddersfield

Asda Group Plc (A)[1]

Keith W. Glaister

INTRODUCTION

Asda invented the modern supermarket in the UK – a 25,000 square foot ware-house stocking around 20,000 grocery lines, located on the edge of population centres and with plenty of surface car parking space. Asda grew substantially to rank as the UK's fourth largest food retailer and the number one superstore operator in Scotland and the North of England. Asda pioneered the move to edge-of-town, one-stop family shopping, with trouble-free parking and large superstores providing a wide range of customer services from in-store restaurants to cash point machines. By the 1990s Asda operated more superstores than any other food retailer, with over 200 stores nationwide. From the beginning Asda's trading philosophy was to operate a national pricing policy of permanently reduced prices on branded goods, i.e. all offering 'Asda Price', which became synonymous with good prices.

The development of Asda stores in the seven years to 1991 is shown in Table 1.1, with the regional distribution of stores in 1990 shown in Table 1.2.

The origins of the Asda group were quite removed from the superstore concept and lie in the efforts of English dairy farmers to protect themselves from falling milk prices after the First World War. A Yorkshire dairy farmer named J.W. Hindell led a number of his fellow farmers in the creation of Hindell's Dairy Farmers Limited, a 1920 partnership whose purpose was to acquire or build both wholesale and retail outlets for their milk, in that way securing a steady market and a floor price. During the next 25 years, Hindell's assembled a wide variety of dairy businesses, involved in everything from the raising of dairy cattle to the processing and distribution of milk and dairy products, as well as the promotion of numerous cafes, retail milk shops and bakeries. By the time of the Second World World War, Hindell's with its headquarters in Leeds, had extended its interests across the Midlands and diversified into meat packing and the quarrying of lime. The partnership became a public company in March 1949, as Associated Dairies and Farm Stores Limited, with eight dairies, two bakeries and 42 shops. The name was changed to Associated Dairies in 1963.

Noel Stockdale, who had joined the company in 1946, was made vice-chairman in 1962 at the age of 41, when profits were around £300,000. Stockdale, who had succeeded his father as vice-chairman, became chairman in 1969. In 1965 the parent company created a subsidiary called Asda Stores Limited and bought two large US-owned stores, one in Nottingham and the other in Leeds. Within a year Stockdale

---

1. I would like to thank Amanda Donaldson-Briggs for her assistance in helping to prepare material for this case.

Table 1.1 Asda stores

	No. of stores	Total area ('000 sq. ft)	Sales (incl. VAT) £m
1991	204	8,160	4,425.0
1990	199	7,795	3,526.0
1989	129	4,975	2,694.0
1988	120	4,431	2,436.0
1987	111	3,892	2,156.0
1986	104	3,555	2,074.0
1985	101	3,406	1,884.4

Table 1.2 Asda stores by region, 1990

Scotland	25
Wales	9
North	20
North West	34
Yorkshire & Humberside	26
West Midlands	16
East Midlands	14
East Anglia	5
South West	13
South East	27
Greater London	10
Total	199

had moved the stores from losses into profits through the adoption of strict financial control techniques 'borrowed' from the dairy operation. The stores were a little before their time – both were even larger than the superstores of the mid-1980s and both had car parking space. Associated Dairies had come up with a merchandising concept entirely new to England, and the stores were an immediate success. This success encouraged Associated Dairies to expand the large discount store formula into other areas of the North. The company opened extremely large, rather spartan stores in abandoned warehouses or mills, offering to the public a limited selection of produce at the lowest possible prices.

By 1978 when Associated Dairies (Asda) went public, it had 60 superstores, The company experienced fast growth in the late 1970s and early 1980s. In the ten-year period to 1983 turnover rose from £158.2m to £1,519m and pre-tax profits increased from £7.4m to £77.4m. The combination of rapid geographical expansion and volume growth in existing stores was so impressive that by the early 1980s Asda ranked third in the supermarket league in market share terms, behind Sainsbury and Tesco.

Towards the end of the 1970s Asda embarked on a diversification strategy into the non-food sector in a bid for even greater growth and improved profit margins, initially diversifying into carpet and furniture retailing. In 1977 Asda bought Wades Department Stores, occupying about 70 prime trading positions on the high street and employing about 1,300 people. In 1978 Asda bought Allied Retailers comprising Allied Carpets, Ukay Furniture and Williams Furnishing (the latter operation was merged with Wades in 1980). In the wake of the recession which followed these acquisitions there was hefty price discounting in the furniture sector and increased competition. In 1982 Asda closed the Ukay Furnishing interests at a cost of £3.3m

Table 1.3 Asda Group: ten-year record

	1982	1983	1984	1985	1986	1987	1988	1989	1990	1991
Sales and profits										
Turnover (£m)	1,306.1	1,519.1	1,755.2	1,934.2	2,516.6	2,667.1	2,462.4	2,708.6	3,550.2	4,468.1
Profit before tax (£m)	60.8	77.4	104.6	119.0	169.5	192.0	215.3	246.6	175.8	168.3
Earnings per ord.share (p)	5.2	6.9	7.4	7.8	10.1	11.21	12.10	13.82	10.13	10.01
Dividends per ord.share (p)	1.7	2.3	3.0	2.8	3.2	3.50	4.10	4.80	4.80	4.80
Balance sheet (£m)										
Fixed assets	217.6	253.6	312.9	412.9	651.7	858.6	890.0	1,300.3	2,179.1	2,239.5
Stocks	85.1	94.2	103.2	112.3	184.8	212.4	174.3	208.8	362.3	379.1
Debtors	30.3	35.4	45.6	34.6	40.9	60.9	73.3	79.4	124.9	156.5
Investments	0.3	0.4	0.3	53.7	0.4	14.2	367.5	263.6	2.2	2.5
Cash, etc.	53.7	89.1	82.2	67.5	36.3	54.7	27.5	2.9	40.8	82.8
Creditors: due within one year	152.8	207.8	231.8	315.4	404.3	391.4	393.0	471.3	994.5	1,082.8
Total assets less current liabilities	234.2	264.9	312.4	365.6	509.8	809.4	1,139.6	1,383.7	1,714.8	1,777.6
Creditors: due after one year	33.2	35.5	244.5	77.7	82.4	296.3	281.8	442.9	636.2	567.5
Capital and reserves	201.0	229.4	67.9	287.9	427.4	513.1	857.8	940.8	1,078.6	1,210.1

on top of £1.1m losses. Allied Carpets, with some 63 carpet stores, was one of the largest carpet retailers in Europe, but only showed £260,000 operating profit in 1982. Wades furnishing was just over breakeven, but with 71 outlets it had a significant presence in the market. With the end of recession, however, came recovery in the carpets business. In 1983 Allied Carpets' contribution significantly increased to £1.4m while Wades Department Stores pushed up profits to £839,000.

In January 1985 Asda announced the sale of Wades Department Stores in a management buy-out. Chairman Noel Stockdale was quoted as saying, 'We do not see a lot of future in them. We are expanding Allied Carpets with the acquisition of sites and if we kept Wades we would be buying similar sites so we decided to grasp the nettle' (*The Guardian*, 10 January 1985). The group planned to open eight new Allied stores in 1985, in addition to eight new superstore openings.

The financial record of the Asda Group in the ten years to 1991 is shown in Table 1.3.

ASDA IN THE FIRST HALF OF THE 1980s

For a time during the late 1970s and early 1980s – when it was becoming fashionable for the whole family to do one major shopping trip per month to a large out-of-town superstore, Asda was in vogue. The rest of the market-place did not stand idly by, however. With Asda's success as a model, the established grocery chains began building similar superstores at out-of-town locations and Asda had a fight on its hands. Tesco ran its superstore strategy in parallel with a redevelopment of its high street sites, and Sainsbury never abandoned the high street, moving to edge-of-town rather than out-of-town sites where it felt it needed the extra room. While Tesco and Sainsbury developed their superstore strategies in the late 1970s and early 1980s in the southern half of Britain, Asda was ruling supreme in the north. The recession in the early 1980s prompted Asda to begin a drive south to take on Tesco and Sainsbury on their home grounds. Unfortunately, Asda failed to recognize that consumer tastes were changing. Shoppers wanted pleasant surroundings as well as low prices, and they soon obtained both in the more luxurious superstores opened by Asda's rivals. As a result, by the early 1980s the Asda format of high volume, low price and no frills had come to seem dated and unappealing. Asda's superstores had become less 'super' than the rest. Asda's rather stark stores, which eschewed modern design concepts, were out of place with consumers who were being wooed by design-led retailers such as Next and Habitat. At the same time as Asda's drive south was beginning to falter, both Tesco and Sainsbury were making inroads into its traditional northern territory.

Asda by early 1985 was in a state of flux. Its superstore development programme in the south-east was floundering, its older stores were in urgent need of some design-led refurbishment, it needed a more efficient distribution system, and its product range needed broadening. Such was the diagnosis of John Hardman when he became managing director of Asda Stores in June 1984.

John Hardman was born in Liverpool, went on to study economics at Liverpool University, and afterwards qualified as an accountant. He spent his formative years in business overseas. He worked for the US conglomerate RCA Corporation from 1967 to 1980, and later as director of Thorn Colour Tubes' European, African and Far Eastern operations. He then returned to the UK to work for the RCA subsidiary

Oriel Foods where he came into contact with John Fletcher, a graduate of Oxford University and Harvard Business School. Hardman had not been with Oriel very long before it was acquired by Argyll, and he found himself dismissed. Fletcher had moved onto Asda in April 1981, and in August 1982, was appointed managing director of the Asda chain of stores, now comprising 96 supermarkets. Fletcher invited Hardman to join him at Asda and in 1981 he became finance director of Asda Stores. The two worked together closely for a long period. Keen to improve Asda's profitability while building brand share, Fletcher was determined to offer the consumer the best possible deal, both on price and quality. At the beginning of the 1980s there was a very heavy programme of new store openings and considerable investment in the build-up of the fresh food business. However, non-foods also became an important part of the Asda package. A market in the non-food sector that grew quietly for Asda in the early 1980s was clothing, most of which was sold under the Asdale label. Here Asda waived its strict policy of backing brands, largely because there were few brands in the market, and instead promoted the house label, which provided Asda with control and consistency. Despite its success the Asdale label was relatively underdeveloped. Also Asda's venture into non-foods was not wholly successful at this time. There was a much publicized exit from the large electrical appliances business, although Asda did find success with smaller appliances such as microwave ovens.

In a surprise move Fletcher was dismissed by Stockdale in May 1984. It was alleged that Hardman helped engineer Fletcher's dismissal in order that he could then move into the vacant seat. In May 1984 Hardman was appointed to the main board and was made managing director of the supermarket chain.

Hardman believed that the market had moved ahead of Asda and would soon leave Asda floundering in its wake. In the mid 1970s, Asda had been significantly cheaper than Tesco or Sainsbury, but this was no longer the case. Asda could not cut gross margins further to compete, nor could it bolster profits from own-brand products. The lack of own-brand products, particularly in the convenience food area, was acknowledged by Asda management as a prime factor in Asda no longer being ahead of consumer trends. During the early 1980s Asda held back from going into own-label in a big way for fear of upsetting its image as a fair dealer with the brand suppliers and the major retailer that 'backs the brands'. The key thing about brands is that the customer can compare prices, but Asda rather lost its reputation for being the cheapest. Sainsbury's set the trend in own-brand labelling, with its own label perceived to be at a premium versus most brands. There is a huge economic advantage of own labels – providing about 20 per cent gross margins. Asda had a long way to go to catch up with Sainsbury's and Tesco's own-label ranges. In 1985 over 50 per cent of Sainsbury's businesses was own label and with Tesco more than 40 per cent but Asda had only developed 10 per cent of its food range as own-brand. By early 1986 Asda's market share had fallen from the third place position it held for so long behind Sainsbury (11.9 per cent) and Tesco (11.6 per cent) to fourth place (7.1 per cent), having been overtaken by Dee Corporation (7.4 per cent), following a run of acquisitions. Behind Asda came Argyll (5.5 per cent).

Hardman therefore proposed a radical repositioning of the Asda chain, which included the following improvements:

1 A completely new look for all of the stores, replacing their stacked carton, industrial brown decor with a new, appetising green colour, dramatic lighting, dropped ceilings, and imaginative display racks.

2 The chain would introduce its own 'Asda Brand' line of foods, since private-label merchandising generally yields substantially higher gross margins (25 per cent compared with an average 12 per cent on branded goods). The concept behind Asda's own-brand goods was to improve customer choice, to allow for innovation, to control the product offer and to strengthen the company's identity and image. First introduced in 1986, with a target of 1,500 items, by the early 1990s there were over 8,000 Asda Brand products spanning food and non-food lines. These changes required the company to revise its promotion strategy, the 'Asda Price' image no longer being appropriate.

3 The stores were to adopt the EPOS system – electronic point of sale registers – to provide more efficient records and inventory control.

4 The company would build a centralized network of distribution warehouses, eliminating the scores of trucks that arrived each day at store loading docks.

5 Asda would push toward the more affluent population in the South of England and the London area, where relatively few superstores had yet been built.

In October 1984 Asda opened its one hundredth store in Charlton, south-east London, this being only its fourth London site. Hardman confirmed the group would like to run about 30 superstores in the London area. By the mid 1980s in the North East there was one superstore for every 110,000 people. In the South East there was one for every 375,000 and in London the figure was one for 400,000. Local authorities in the South tended to be worried about the impact of superstores on local shops and the prospect of a single developer acquiring precious acres in one go, and often refused planning permission. Competition for sites meant that prices were high, for example Asda paid in excess of £20m for a site in Watford. But experience showed that superstores were so popular with shoppers that it was almost impossible to pay too much for a good site, and hardly worth bothering about a second-rate one. The cost of a typical site could be £8m, with the cost of actually building the store anything between £6m and £8m. So the total bill for setting up a store with 25,000 square feet of selling area plus 700 car parking spaces could top £15m.

ASDA-MFI MERGER: 'A MERGER FOR THE 1990s'

The then largest merger in British retailing history was announced in April 1985 between Asda and the furniture group MFI, one of the country's most profitable retailers. Asda offered £615m for MFI in an agreed bid, in shares (15 Asda for every 8 MFI). The merger was described as a 'merger for the 1990s', a means of putting Asda in shape to cope with the expected saturation of the UK retail food market by the middle of the following decade. MFI was the leading UK furniture retailer, trading out of 127 large edge-of-town stores and specializing in self-assembly kitchen and bedroom furniture.

The stockbroker Scrimgeour Kemp-Gee, advisors to both companies, suggested to Asda chairman Stockdale that a merger of the two businesses made excellent sense. The stockbroker argued that the two companies were a very good fit, having close similarities in the way they do business:

- both built their businesses in dominating edge-of-town sites;
- both laid stress on providing customers with what they perceive as value – good quality for a fair price;

- both were exceptionally skilled at promotional advertising;
- each was acknowledged to have a very strong management team in a business which, by common consent, has not always attracted the brightest and best.

A rationale for the merger was also seen in the fact that key directors in both companies were all aged around 40. The key advisor at Scrimgeour argued that people of 40 tend to have a wide vision of the next decade, forming a longer timescale on which to operate. It was also claimed they were more ambitious people than those of 60 thinking about retirement.

Stockdale commented that the merged group would be 'well positioned both to maximize organic growth and to capitalize on the opportunities for the further physical expansion that the next decade will present' (*The Standard*, 15 April 1985). Stockdale pointed out that the food-based superstores and the self-assembly furniture centres had many of the same physical characteristics and operating philosophies. Stockdale became chairman of the merged group and MFI chairman Derek Hunt joined the Asda board and headed the household furnishing division, comprising Asda's Allied Carpet business as well as MFI itself. Derek Hunt started his working life as a policeman, subsequently became a management trainee at BHS and then moved to supermarket chain Elmo, which was acquired by Fine Fare. He joined MFI in 1972 and became chairman in September 1984.

It was argued that MFI was a logical choice for Asda, given its out-of-town operations and products based on high volume and low margins. Started in the early 1960s selling mail-order camping gear and low-cost furniture that came unassembled, it was floated on the stock market in 1971. MFI pulled out of mail order in 1974 because of delivery problems and, finding itself unable to afford conventional high street locations, was forced to go to out-of-town greenfield sites. Critics maintained that no one would drive to such stores – but they did. MFI uncovered a segment of the market that was largely untapped by conventional retailers. Consumers who chose furniture often had to wait weeks for delivery: MFI offered it instantly via 'flat packs' that could be carried home by car and assembled within hours. The MFI formula worked despite scepticism about quality both from within the trade and from consumers. In 1985, however, MFI felt itself being stalked as a possible takeover target – so it decided it made more sense to enter into a friendly marriage with Asda rather than await an unwanted takeover.

After the merger the company was by market capitalization (of just over £1,900m) Britain's fourth largest retailing group, just marginally behind Great Universal Stores, with Marks & Spencer and J. Sainsbury as the two largest. Before the acquisition Asda had 25 per cent of its business outside food but after the merger it was approaching 50 per cent. In November 1985, the name of the group was changed to Asda-MFI.

The financial results announced in 1985 were lacklustre. Although the full year figures of £119m before tax for Asda and of £46.1m before merger costs for MFI represented progress over the previous year, both partners suffered self-inflicted damage in the second half. MFI had an ill-judged range of kitchens which failed to sell well, Asda ran a disastrous in-store promotional lottery (a hitch over printing the lottery tickets and the fact that none of Asda's customers won any money meant that the promotion flopped, and led Asda to suing its sales promotion agency), while tighter market conditions at large were compounded by the miners' strike and higher mortgage rates.

ASDADRIVE

In 1984 Asda was approached by Graeme Miller, a former managing director of FSO Cars, an importer of Polish made cars and marketing director of Mazda Cars UK, and Mr John Kiayman, a non-executive director of Marketing, Motivation and Management, with the idea of establishing a motor dealership. After two years of research and planning, in April 1986 Asda-MFI announced it was entering the retail motor trade with the launch of Asdadrive, a joint venture with Asda owning 75 per cent of the equity, and Miller as managing director and Kiayman as chief executive. The venture was intended to embrace the sale of new cars supplied by many main manufacturers, credit finance, servicing, repairs and the acceptance of used cars as trade-ins. This represented the first venture by a stores chain into multi-franchising car retailing. The venture was initially launched at six of Asda's sites with the intention to extend the concept to about 70 of Asda's 104 superstores. Each Asdadrive showroom was to display a specific manufacturer's range of cars on a site next to the superstore to allow ease of access to potential customers. The premise of the venture was that, despite the fierce competition in the motor trade, adequate profits could be made by applying the group's skills in high volume low-cost retailing, with strong emphasis on standards of service and modest margins on each aspect of the business. Although competition was already severe and heavy discounting rife, it was believed there was fertile ground for a retailing group whose expertise was specifically geared to high turnover on low margins.

Although Asda expected the majority of its car customers to be private buyers, it installed a fleet manager at each outlet to seek company business. About half of all new car sales are made to fleets. The Asdadrive concept was, however, pitched strongly at women, who accounted for two-thirds of Asda's customers. Basically Asdadrive was to sell new cars at discounted, but non-negotiable, prices. The company would take trade-ins, but these would be disposed of through British Car Auctions, which was to provide non-negotiable valuations. Commenting on the Asdadrive scheme John Hardman said, 'I think we can make an awful lot of money out of this' (*Daily Mail*, 6 June 1985).

In the year or so following the merger, Asda-MFI's share price under-performed the market by around 25 per cent with superficially at least two growth stocks having been turned into one dullard. Asda Stores were contributing over 60 per cent of operating profit, Associated Fresh Foods 7 per cent, MFI 28 per cent and Allied Carpets 5 per cent. At the AGM in 1986 Derek Hunt said that Asda was hell bent on driving forward its business. He reiterated that one of the aims of the strategy was to increase stores in the South. Net of closures there had been just three new store openings over the preceding two years. Also, Asda Store's profit growth was inhibited by the revamp in the superstores needed to catch up with the competitors. Asda had, though, been very successful in introducing own-brand food in an attempt to improve margins with the company ahead of target with 2,500 own-brand labels now likely to be in the stores by the end of 1987. This was described by Hardman as the most rapid and comprehensive introduction of own-labels by any retailer. Half the £5m it would cost Asda to launch these labels had already been borne.

MFI's problems were rather different from those of Asda. Furniture retailing is a volatile business and in the preceding year demand had been flat. MFI was still stuck with its 'pile it high, sell it cheap' image of the late 1970s. It had 40 per cent of the flat-pack market which had reached a plateau. While MFI claimed to have raised quality and design, the message had not got across to the consumer. Hunt also admitted that the MFI management would have been coming under a great deal of pressure from investors had they not engineered the merger with Asda. It was the contact with the Asda management that made the MFI team look closely at the MFI business. Following the AGM, Stockdale retired from the company, a move that had been announced several months earlier. On his retirement Stockdale was succeeded as chairman by David Donne, chairman of Steetley and formerly chairman of Dalgety. Derek Hunt, chairman of MFI, became chief executive and a deputy chairman of the group. John Hardman was to continue as managing director of Asda Stores as well as becoming a deputy chairman of the group.

In May 1987, the Asda-MFI board announced that the Asdadrive venture would cease. The existing outlets were closed and the expansion plans shelved. Asda announced that the project would have taken up too much of its management's valuable time just when the company was going through a major refurbishment and expansion programme of its core business. The profits generated by Asdadrive were also seen as too low to justify that sort of management involvement.

THE BIG DIVORCE

In July 1987, Asda-MFI startled the City with an announcement of one of the most ambitious restructuring and refocusing plans ever attempted by a major public company. All parts of the group not directly related to the Asda superstores were to be sold, and the cash raised used to finance the even more rapid expansion of Asda in the South of England. The disposals meant that the post of chief executive disappeared. Derek Hunt who held that post decided to stay with MFI and 'take his chances' with whoever decided to buy. Chairman David Donne in announcing the news stressed that the board decision was unanimous, and that there had been no disagreement with Hunt about the future direction of the group, or on the need in future to concentrate all the management efforts on wringing the best possible results out of superstores. John Hardman, managing director of Asda Stores, was appointed to the same position at group level. Anticipated sales from the various businesses would provide Asda with more than £800m to spend on expansion. The proposed disposal marked a 180 degree turn in corporate strategy, away from retail diversification and back towards sole reliance on Asda's superstores. Commenting on the sell-off, Donne declared that 'They will grow faster separately than they will together.' There had been no serious consideration of demerging MFI and Allied into a separate company because Asda wanted to maximize the cash proceeds of the disposal. The stock market reacted favourably to the plan, with Asda-MFI shares adding 22p to 221p, giving a market capitalization of £2.5bn.

Asda had decided to focus on a three-year development plan for the superstores which involved spending almost £1bn. The lion's share would go on a fast-expanding, store opening programme as Asda moved back into gear to catch up with the opening rates of competitors such as Sainsbury and Tesco. This would intensify the tough battle for good sites in the South East as the main Asda thrust went into expanding in the most affluent part of the country. Asda had clearly lost impetus in the openings race. In the three years to 1987, only 11 new stores were opened. Key competitors opened at least three times as many.

In August 1987, Asda sold most of its Associated Fresh Foods business for £84m cash. The dairy division was sold to a management buy-out team for £65m. The cheese business was sold to a Unilever subsidiary for £15m. Asda retained Associated Fresh Foods' meat operations in West Yorkshire, because virtually all its output went to Asda stores.

In October 1987 it was announced that a management buy-out of MFI from Asda had been agreed, which ranked as the largest UK management buy-out to that date. According to the terms, the MFI management paid about £505m to Asda, which in turn paid £52m for a 25 per cent stake in the furniture retailer. At the same time MFI bought Hygena, the privately held kitchen and bedroom manufacturer, which accounted for 45 per cent of MFI sales, paying £215m. Asda was effectively paying £52m for a quarter of a company that had been put together for £720m. The end result, however, was that Asda ended up with £450m in cash but realized a significant loss on its two and a half year investment. The deal went ahead despite the stock market crash of October 1987. Following the radical changes in the shape of the group, John Hardman succeeded David Donne as chairman of the group in January 1988. Donne remained on the board as deputy chairman.

In light of the instability of the stock market, the Asda board decided to retain the Allied Carpets business and to concentrate on developing its fullest potential. At one time it looked as if Asda would obtain £120m from the Allied sale with six potential buyers interested in the company. This came down to a short list of three which included a proposed MBO, but as the equity market collapsed so did the buyers' valuation of Allied. It is thought that Asda was eventually offered £80m for the carpet retailer but rejected it. Following its other disposals Asda was now carrying about £300m of cash, which was available to fund Asda's massive investment programme over the next three years.

Asda appointed a new managing director to Allied, Richard Harker, who moved from Woolworth. He set about assessing the potential of the company. In terms of priorities, Harker put 'getting a grip on the business' at the top, with forward planning a close second. Organic growth coupled with a more marketing oriented management was to be the basis of the new business strategy.

Turnover and operating profit by activity and the average number of employees by activity for the Asda Group over the 1987–1991 period are shown in Tables 1.4 and 1.5.

While the annual results announced in July 1988 showed a 12.1 per cent rise in pre-tax profits, and interim results announced in January 1989 indicated that Asda's investment programme was paying off, with pre-tax profits rising by 15 per cent, some analysts were worried that Asda was failing to match the gains being achieved by competitors such as Tesco and Sainsbury. A problem for Asda was that it had moved away from a business based on price to a business purporting to be based on quality and range. For some, however, Asda did not impress in these areas and was seen as lacking a strong retailing formula. By mid 1989 Asda hoped to have a total of about 130 stores, just half the number of Sainsbury, and with the market leader expanding at the rate of 20 stores a year. Asda did not appear to have any different formula for overtaking the rest in terms of sales, profits or margins. Moreover with Sainsbury, Tesco and Argyll (Safeway) all chasing customers, volume growth

Table 1.4 Turnover and operating profit by activity[1] £m

	1987		1988		1989		1990		1991	
	Turnover	Operating profit	Turnover	Operating profit	Turnover	Operating profit	Turnover	Operating profit	Turnover	Operating profit
Asda Stores	2,023.5	122.9	2,281.6	152.7	2,521.4	176.1	3,300.2	206.0	4,142.6	250.6
Allied Maples	118.7	9.6	151.8	10.5	169.8	13.8	218.4	6.7	205.9	1.6
Gazeley	—	—	29.0	5.4	17.4	9.5	31.6	12.4	119.6	10.2
	2,142.2	132.5	2,462.4	168.6	2,708.6	199.4	3,550.2	225.1	4,468.1	262.4

1. Continuing businesses.

Table 1.5 Average number of employers by activity

	1987	1988		1989		1990		1991	
	Employees	Employees	Full-time equivalents	Employees	Full-time equivalents	Employees	Full-time equivalents	Employees	Full-time equivalents
Asda Stores	35,611	42,840	25,858	48,181	28,914	59,918	36,249	71,242	41,450
Allied Maples	1,760	2,148	2,061	2,231	2,101	3,088	2,872	2,777	2,556
Gazeley	—	47	47	53	53	75	75	90	90
	37,371	45,035	27,966	50,465	31,068	63,081	39,196	74,109	44,096

was slow. From the autumn of 1988 and into 1989 Asda shares under-performed those of Sainsbury, Tesco and Argyll by almost 15 per cent, and the market as a whole by more than a quarter over the year.

THE QUANTUM LEAP

In April 1989 it was announced that a consortium of bidders, under the name of Isosceles, was attempting to buy Gateway, and had agreed to sell Asda 62 of the group's larger superstores for £705m if the bid succeeded. This news provoked a mixed response from analysts with some believing it would prove a good deal for Asda in the longer term while others expressed concern over the quality of some of the superstores Asda might acquire, as well as the proposed price to be paid (in a bid about a year earlier by Barker and Dobson, Asda had proposed to pay Barker and Dobson £250m for Gateway's 76 largest stores). The acquisition of Gateway's superstores would catapult Asda from fifth to third place in the league of British food retailers, behind Sainsbury and Tesco. They would add £60m profits and £1bn of sales to Asda. John Hardman was quoted as saying that 'An opportunity like this won't come round again. We will be able to achieve four years' work in one hit' (*The Times*, 19 April 1989). A feature of the acquisition was that Asda would double its stores exposure in the south to 21, where the group had been struggling for years to find the right locations at the right price to make a significant breakthrough. Hardman believed that there was scope for squeezing considerably more profits out of Gateway stores which were achieving average profit margins of just under 5 per cent compared with nearly 7 per cent at Asda. In July 1989, in the wake of the successful Isosceles bid for Gateway, Asda eventually acquired 60 superstores for £705m. This purchase in a single stroke increased Asda's selling area by 50 per cent from 5 million to 7.5 million square feet, and further solidified its position as the largest operator of superstores in the UK. Stock in the stores, valued at around £40m, was bought separately. Asda did not take up the option of buying the £25m Huntingdon warehouse. Critics believe it may have wanted to 'wriggle out' of more but was worried about its credibility, especially under bid threat. Asda was left short of cash following the decision by MFI (of which Asda owned 25 per cent) to shelve its flotation planned for March. Asda hoped to reap £150m, but instead it had to inject £8m. The Gateway deal and the continuation of the stores development programme was financed by a combination of £750m in new debt and an issue of £150m worth of convertible capital bonds to shareholders. These could be converted into equity at any time in the following fifteen years.

During the first half of 1989 there were several rumours that Asda was a potential takeover target with significant market trading in its shares. In May 1989 it was announced that First City Financial Corporation, the Vancouver-based investment company, had acquired a 2 to 4 per cent stake in Asda. FCFC was controlled by the Canadian Belzberg family. The immensely wealthy Belzsbergs had a record as prominent takeover specialists and corporate raiders.

In late April 1989, it was announced that the Asda Group was paying £29m to acquire the bulk of the stores owned by Gillow, the furniture and carpet retailer. Gillow was the product of a management buy-out, which abandoned plans to return the market in 1988 after poor trading results. Asda acquired 48 of Gillow's 87 stores and the brand names of 'Maples' and 'Waring and Gillow', two old-established names in the furniture business. The stores being sold to Asda made an operating profit of £2m in 1987–88. Richard Harker, chief executive of Allied Carpets, said there were many benefits to be derived from putting the Allied Carpets business together with that of Gillow.

'GEORGE'

In late April 1989, it was announced that George Davies, who was ousted as chairman and chief executive of Next in December 1988, and who was credited with revolutionizing fashion retailing in classy high street shops, was to return to retailing with a joint venture company that would take over the selection of men's, women's and children's clothing products sold in Asda Stores. The partnership was to be controlled by Davies and his wife with 60 per cent of the partnership, the senior managers in the partnership holding 20 per cent and with a 20 per cent stake being held by Asda. The plan was for the newly formed George Davies Partnership to provide buying and range consultancy services to Asda's clothing and footwear divisions. The non-food division was to be redesigned by Davies and his team and given a new brand name. Davies was joined in the partnership by a number of his ex-colleagues at Next. Taking overall charge of everything from designing new products and sourcing them to marketing them in the Asda stores, Davies's partnership was to receive 25 per cent of any profits it generated from these businesses over and above the returns projected in Asda's business plans. Davies preferred the partnership arrangement to becoming an employee of Asda, because this gave him independence. The initial arrangement was scheduled to run for five years. Davies argued that Asda had a strong niche in out-of-town clothes retailing which could be developed much more quickly by entrusting it to specialist control. Asda stores of around 40,000 sq. ft devoted approximately 6,000 sq. ft to clothing and footwear. Whilst sales per square foot were obviously less than in the food departments, profitability was comparable.

The 'George' clothes retailing concept was launched in Asda stores in February 1990, controlling more than 500,000 sq. ft of selling space in 120 stores. Some City observers were rather sceptical, fearing that even Davies's undoubted retail skills might struggle to make a significant impact on Asda, arguing that customers do not go to buy food and clothes at the same time. However, Davies designed special packaging to try to overcome consumer resistance to the idea, providing wrapping stations where customers could help themselves to large 'flight bags', in which to hang the clothes. These clip on the side of the trolley and keep the clothes away from the food. Asda expected the Davies formula to boost its clothing sales by between 20 per cent and 30 per cent by the end of 1991. The design team's brief was to launch a range of clothing of the quality of Marks & Spencer, but less expensive than most of the high street retail chains. The only group not catered for were teenagers, who tended not to shop at Asda. Davies said that his new venture was able to produce quality clothes cheaply because of good sourcing, low overheads and low margins. Davies argued that his collection would not alienate traditional Asda shoppers, but would introduce them to better designed, quality clothes.

In the company report and accounts published in July 1989, Hardman wrote, 'I am pleased that results for the year ended 29 April 1989 provide further evidence of the successful implementation of the strategy instigated in 1985.' The chairman's statement also said, '1989/90 will end with all key objectives of the strategic plan accomplished and Asda once more at the leading edge of retail development as the UK's major superstore operator.' The results showed a rise in pre-tax profits of 14.5 per cent. In announcing the results Hardman said the group was nearing the end of a five-year programme to revive Asda from a poor position in the mid 1980s. Although Asda had lost its consumer franchise and its direction, it was now ready for the tough competition of the 1990s. During that programme costs had risen sharply; even so, Hardman said the group had continued to increase profits. In order to devote more time to group strategy, early in 1989 Hardman passed the position of chief executive of Asda Stores to Graham Stow, who was supported by his two joint managing directors, Tony Campbell and Bill Bailey.

By 1989 Asda had 4,000 own-brand products, achieved in just three years. This meant that the choice offered to customers was greatly extended. In introducing Asda Brand, Asda were careful not to restrict the availability of leading brands, but sought to complement them. Thus Asda Brand was introduced in order either to match leading brands in quality, but at a lower price, or increasingly to offer high quality products unique to Asda.

Speculation increased at the end of August 1989 that Asda had become a bid target as the share price continued to nudge towards its peak. Rumour was that Tengelmann, the German supermarket chain, had linked with Kohlberg Kravis Roberts, the American buy-out specialist, with a view to making a bid. The Belzberg family, still with about 4 per cent of Asda, could prove willing sellers at the right price. Other stories claimed that the bidder could be Dairy Farm International of Hong Kong. With Gateway now removed from the quoted arena Asda appeared the most vulnerable of the food retailers.

In September 1989, to reflect recent acquisitions, Allied Carpet Stores changed its name to the Allied Maples Group.

At an EGM on Thursday 12 October 1989 shareholders voted through the £705m acquisition of 60 superstores from Isosceles, the new owner of Gateway. Two days after shareholders approved the acquisition, Asda's broker Cazenove issued a forecast warning of a sharp downturn in the expected profits of Asda. Some institutional investors expressed disquiet and claimed that there was no firm indication of a profits shortfall given by the company in advance of the shareholders' meeting. Asda denied this, pointing out that at the annual general meeting in September 1989, Hardman told shareholders that the government's high interest rate policy was taking its toll on the company. During the spring and summer there had been a slowdown in clothing, footwear and household sales. This had also impacted on Allied and the associated company MFI. Reasons given by Cazenove for the projected profits shortfall were that there was no immediate benefits from the new distribution network for fresh foods, nor would there be any contribution from the 25 per cent stake in MFI. Allied Carpets' profits were expected to be flat and it was noted that the non-food operations overall were having a difficult time. Following the shareholders' approval of the Gateway deal Asda's share price fell by more than 25 per cent to 140p, although this was in part due to the general collapse of share prices following the crash on Wall Street on Friday, 13 October 1989.

THE BURWOOD HOUSE GROUP

In December 1989 Asda announced a property deal with British Aerospace subsidiary Arlington, to form a joint venture into which 34 Asda superstores (a fifth of its retail space) were to be injected, together with an Asda town centre shopping scheme and nine Arlington retail development sites. The joint company paid £375m for the Asda stores, and £75m for Arlington's developments. The superstores were leased back to Asda at a commercial rent. The benefits to Asda's interest bill from the deal initially exceeded the extra rents by £10m in a full year. Asda liberated £275m in cash from the deal, and showed a £173m surplus over the book value of its properties. The 50/50 joint venture was named the Burwood House Group.

At the beginning of December 1989 Asda issued a warning that its interim pre-tax profits would be 25 per cent lower than the £109m made in the first half of the previous year. It also warned that pre-tax profits for the full year would be significantly below the previous year's. Announcing the news Hardman said he was disappointed, but added: 'We are all over 21, and there is no use crying about it' (*Financial Times*, 5 December 1989). He blamed the downturn on difficult trading conditions for non-food items, such as clothing and footwear, and the carpet and furniture retail business of its Allied Maples subsidiary and its MFI furniture group associate. He also said that efficiency levels in the group's new fresh food distribution system had been lower than planned and that the late completion of the acquisition of 60 Gateway superstores would hit second half profits. The Gateway stores would not now be converted to Asda stores until well after Christmas, and would not cover their funding costs in the current year. Hardman said the board remained confident of the strategic direction of the business and looked forward to a good recovery from the current year's difficult trading conditions. Analysts claimed that Asda's senior management was relatively inexperienced, and that the new nationwide food distribution network appeared in management terms to have been a disaster. Also, they argued that the directors appeared to have taken their eye off the trading ball in their expenditure of £705m on the Gateway superstores, which themselves were not shining examples of the best in British supermarketing, with a downmarket image that may take longer to shake off than Asda was prepared to admit. Further, stresses at the top of the company were not helped by the fact that Asda was losing market share to Kwik Save in its heartland in the North of England. There was a continuing loss of sentiment in Asda's shares which almost halved in price in the space of four months. This not only reflected the problems spelled out by Hardman but a more fundamental concern about the entire direction being taken by the group.

When the interim results were announced in mid December 1989, the actual fall in pre-tax profits was 24 per cent to £83.5m, a little less than the 25 per cent drop the company estimated. Hardman reiterated that annual profits would be significantly lower than the previous year's. The first half had been hit by two main problems: the group's new central distribution system had not been able to supply stores with sufficient fresh foods and this had knocked about £20m off sales. The other difficulty was that sales of non-food items were affected by the squeeze on consumer spending. Also Allied Maples saw operating profits fall and Asda's stake in MFI contributed a loss.

In mid January 1990 three senior directors of Asda Stores were sacked – the joint managing director Bill Baily, management information systems director Mike Palmer and food director Keith Clarke. Clarke and Palmer had been with Asda for about four years, as divisional and later full board directors. Baily had been in his job for eight months. The company's chief executive, Graham Stow, said the dismissals were designed to strengthen the management team. An unnamed source said: 'Keith Clarke was responsible for introducing Asda's own-brand range almost single-handed. How can you say that removing him strengthens the management?' The new joint managing director, responsible for buying and marketing, was Richard Harker, chief executive of Allied Maples. Four other new directors were promoted from within Asda Stores.

There was City speculation that the sudden sacking of the three directors of Asda Stores was caused by a serious breakdown in Asda's distribution systems over Christmas, the most crucial time of year for all retail groups. Apparently the three directors were all members of a working party which set up the new systems brought in for Asda's switch to centralized distribution. Rumours circulating in the City said Asda's distribution to stores in the build-up to Christmas had been disrupted with deliveries of some lines bearing no relation to what had been ordered.

In May 1990 Asda announced that it was selling three sites with outline planning permission to build superstores to Tesco for £54.75m. Asda argued it did not need the sites in Shoreham (Sussex), Hillingdon (Middlesex) and Ashford (Kent), because its acquisition of Gateway's superstores gave it more than enough to do. Others pointed out that the sale was motivated by balance sheet rather than commercial considerations, pointing out the need for Asda to shrink its debt, and Asda had, according to its own figures, only 6 per cent market share in the South.

Table 1.6 Asda Group: Consolidated profit and loss account
(52 weeks ended 27 April 1991)

	£m	
	1991	*1990*
Turnover	4,468.1	3,550.2
Operating costs	4,205.7	3,325.1
Operating profit	262.4	225.1
Exceptional charges	——	12.5
Share of losses of associated undertakings	(4.1)	(2.4)
Net interest paid	(90)	(34.4)
Profit before taxation	168.3	175.8
Taxation	49.6	56.0
Profit after taxation	118.7	119.8
Minority interests	0.3	0.2
Profit before extraordinary items	118.4	119.6
Extraordinary items	—	86.7
Profit	118.4	206.3
Dividends	56.4	56.4
Retained profit	62.0	149.9
Earnings per ordinary share	10.01p	10.13p
Dividends per ordinary share	4.8p	4.8p

Announcing the full year results in July 1990, Hardman reported a sharp fall in annual pre-tax profits as the company was hit by high interest charges, weak furniture sales and distribution disruptions. Hardman said that although the results were disappointing Asda had entered the current year in a healthier strategic position following the acquisition of the Gateway superstores and the introduction of a new distribution system. Increased borrowings, stemming largely from the £705m Asda paid for the Gateway stores, resulted in an interest charge of £29.9m. This compared with interest receivable of £34.5m in the previous year. Difficulties in setting up Asda's new distribution system also undermined profits to the tune of £16m. But Hardman said these problems had been resolved, claiming Asda now had the latest state-of-the-art distribution system.

The consolidated profit and loss accounts and balance sheets for the Asda Group in 1990 and 1991 are shown in Tables 1.6 and 1.7.

Asda was the last of the major UK food retailers to move to centralized distribution and the only one to build a complete network from scratch. In just two years, eight strategically placed distribution centres were designed, built and commissioned, at a cost of £170m. By the beginning of 1991 they were intended to handle 80 per cent of all Asda food deliveries and all its clothing. Without the network Asda's acquisition of the Gateway stores would have been impossible, as would

Table 1.7 Asda Group: Balance sheets (at 27 April 1991)

	£m	
	1991	*1990*
Fixed assets		
Tangible assets	2,136.0	2,071.1
Investments	103.5	108.0
	2,239.5	2,179.1
Current assets		
Stocks	379.1	362.3
Debtors	156.5	124.9
Investments	2.5	2.2
Cash at bank etc.	82.8	40.8
	620.9	530.2
Creditors: amounts due within the year		
Borrowings	(460.7)	(351.5)
Other creditors	(622.1)	(643.0)
Total assets less current liabilities	1,777.6	1,714.8
Creditors: amounts falling due after more than one year		
Borrowings	(496.9)	(555.3)
Other creditors	(0.8)	(10.8)
Provision for liabilities and charges	(69.8)	(70.1)
	(567.5)	(636.2)
Capital and reserves		
Shareholders' funds	1,136.9	1,074.3
Minority interests	0.2	4.3
Convertible capital bonds	73.0	—
	1,210.1	1,078.6

the rapid expansion of own-label goods and product range. The cost and speed of installation were heavily criticized, especially following the disastrous start-up difficulties in 1989 which saw some stores with empty produce shelves. However, the late entry into the game had enabled Asda to construct the most advanced distribution system in the country. Control and management of stock means a wider product range is possible, perishable goods are fresher and reach the stores more quickly. New stores can be built without the need for massive warehouse facilities and a large proportion of the space in existing stores previously given over to warehousing can be utilized for extra sales area.

In September 1990 it was reported that Asda saw the cloud of the Canadian Belzberg family's stake lift as it was placed with institutions at 106p per share. At the time of the announcement, market makers were offering the shares at around 111p. The 64 million shares were sold without difficulty. The Canadian stake represented 5.46 per cent of Asda's issued ordinary stock. The Belzbergs are estimated to have paid an average price of 178p per share to build up their holding. After deducting the broker's turn, the Canadian arbitrageurs suffered a loss of about £48m in a stock which their buying once pushed up to 220p. Analysts commented that the disposal was more a reflection of potential bidders' reluctance to come forward than of Asda's long-term prospects, and the fact that institutions were prepared to buy the stock at 106p was a vote of confidence.

In October 1990 Asda issued a £70m convertible capital bond dated 2005 in a bid to reduce its heavy borrowings. The subordinated bonds would be convertible into redeemable preference shares and would be exchangeable into ordinary stock. The issue effectively completed the equity portion of the Gateway acquisition financing. The bond issue enabled some reduction in the gearing level.

'A COMPANY IN DECLINE'

In April 1991, the brokers Hoare Govett, which had forecast lower profits for Asda in 1992/93, cut its estimate for that year still further. The broker argued that a slower stores opening programme in 1991/92 combined with increased competition from its rivals and larger interest payments were eroding Asda's profitability. Hoare Govett described Asda as 'a company in decline'.

Also in April 1991 major institutional shareholders in Asda called for the roles of chairman and chief executive, held by Hardman, to be separated, and pushed for more non-executive directors. One institutional shareholder is reported as saying, 'the poor earnings performance throws into doubt the legitimacy of having a joint chairman and chief executive. Given the size of the group, there should also be more than two non-executives' (*Daily Telegraph*, 4 May 1991). Asda's non-executives at this time were, Kenneth Morton, director of Kleinwort Benson, and Sir Godfrey Messervy, non-executive chairman of Costain, the engineering and construction group. Another major shareholder was quoted as saying, 'Time is running out for the management to prove it can improve profits and get to grips with the superstores.'

In the first six months of 1991, Tesco, Sainsbury and Argyll, who between them had 40 per cent of the UK grocery market, raised around £1.5bn, largely through rights issues, to fund a building programme which would increase their joint capacity by 10 per cent in each of the following three years. This rate of expansion would clearly put pressure on both Asda and Gateway, with a further fifth of the market between them, who were heavily in debt. With a rights issue effectively denied it by the low standing of the shares, Asda with £800m of debt looked to be boxed in. Some observers also thought that institutions would not be prepared to support a cash call with the current management still in place. Analysts believed that Asda's debt burden had led it to curtail its expansion programme and thus impair its ability to generate the level of earnings growth of Tesco and Sainsbury – who were also hitting Asda's trade by opening stores nearby.

Towards the end of May 1991, Asda announced that it was preparing to split Hardman's dual role of chairman and chief executive and that a search was on for a new chairman, while Hardman would retain the job of chief executive. A spokesman for Asda stated that this change was something that Hardman had had in mind for some time. Hardman was employed on a three-year rolling contract, earning in 1990 £231,000, down from £266,000 the year before.

In June 1991, John Hardman resigned as chairman and chief executive of Asda Group, after pressure both from the board and institutional investors. At the same time Graham Stow, chief executive of Asda Stores, also resigned. It was believed that the resignations would clear the way for a rights issue. It was apparent that Asda has made a number of costly errors in the recent past, and thus badly needed to raise cash through a rights issue. The group's advisors appear to have concluded that the institutions would simply not stump up the cash if it was to be handed over to the same management team. With net debt of £900m at the last half year, analysts had been arguing for some time that a rights issue was needed, claiming that Asda was undercapitalized in relation to the strategic needs of the business. Sir Godfrey Messervy, aged 66, took over as chairman. He said he was turning his attention to strengthening the non-executive presence on the board, as well as ensuring that a new chief executive was promptly recruited.

In early July 1991, the day before Asda's final results were announced for 1990/91, Sir Geoffrey Messervy temporarily had to stand down as chairman after a minor heart attack. His position was filled by Kenneth Morton, Asda's only remaining non-executive director. This meant Asda announced its final results without a group chairman or chief executive, or a chief executive of the stores division.

Asda announced a 'disappointing' set of annual results in July 1991, and gave little indication of how its debt burden could be driven down, but suggested that it was not looking to raise money through selling or leasing properties. Asda Stores, reflecting the first full year's contribution from the ex-Gateway outlets, lifted operating profits from £206m to £251m. During the year 37 stores were converted to the Asda format and a further 20 would be completed by November. Although the first 20 stores to be refurbished produced increases in trading profit of 20–30 per cent, some of the original stores appeared to have been neglected. Asda identified a sickly group of 49 stores which between them suffered a 9 per cent decline in sales volume in the year because of uninspired layout, inadequate space devoted to food and under-investment. While food proved relatively immune to the retail recession, Asda's non-food activities, with the notable exception of the clothing range designed by George Davies, did not. Earnings per share slipped marginally to 10.01p (from 10.13p). The final dividend was held at 2.95p for an unchanged 4.8p total. Asda said that this reflected the board's confidence in the inherent strength of the business.

Asda said the search for a new chief executive was progressing well, but it was likely to be some weeks before an appointment could be made. Industry insiders, however, were reported as saying that Asda had been forced to look overseas for the right candidate after several top managers from rival UK food groups turned down the post.

Asda Group Plc (B)[1]

Keith W. Glaister

'Asda's mission is to become the UK's leading value for money grocer with an exceptional range of fresh foods together with those clothing, home and leisure products, that meet the everyday needs of our target customers.' Archie J. Norman, Chief Executive.

At Asda's annual general meeting in September 1991, Sir Godfrey Messervy, chairman, told shareholders that the effects of the recession coupled with the company's high level of operational gearing would have a significant impact on pre-tax profits and forecast a one-third cut in the interim dividend. In light of this news the share price dropped by 29 per cent to 67 pence, in recognition of the dismal prospects for Asda. The only reason that the shares did not fall further was because there was a bout of bid speculation. The rumour machine identified a number of potential bidders – Carrefour of France, the privately owned German discounter Aldi, the German retailing group Tengelmann and Britain's Kwik Save.

Following the AGM, Patrick Gillam, deputy chairman of Standard Chartered and former managing director of British Petroleum, was appointed chairman of the Asda Group, replacing Sir Godfrey Messervy. At the same time Frank Knight, formerly deputy chief executive of United Biscuits, became a non-executive director of Asda Group.

As the end of September 1991 approached it became clear that Asda had fallen badly out of favour with the City. The company's failure to find a new chief executive to replace John Hardman who resigned the previous June irritated institutional investors, who perceived the company to be drifting without direction at a time when it urgently needed a clear strategy. Moreover, speculation that Asda would seek a rights issue to reduce its mountain of debt threw up further uncertainty, which the company declined to dispel.

Some analysts began to speculate whether Asda would be around in its present form for much longer. It was believed that several institutions privately hoped for a takeover by a continental competitor, believing this would be in the best interests of employees, consumers and, of course, the funds they managed. The institutions by and large blamed Asda's management for the state the company was in. Other observers recognized, however, that Asda's problems had not emerged overnight and argued that institutional shareholders should also share some responsibility for allowing them to persist. One industry analyst stated: 'Asda has stood still for years in a market in which you cannot afford to stand still for a month.'

Although Asda was the first chain to see the potential for edge-of-town superstores, it steadily lost ground to its ferocious rivals, Sainsbury, Tesco and Safeway, which all seized upon the benefits of centralized distribution systems, the development of own-label products and computerized point-of-sale equipment. The institutions

---

1. I would like to thank Amanda Donaldson-Briggs for her assistance in helping to prepare material for this case.

appeared not to complain when Asda expanded away from its heartland in the North of England to compete head-on with Tesco and Sainsbury in the South and wasted management effort on briefly diversifying into home furnishings. Nor was there much opposition when the company paid £705m to buy 60 Gateway stores in 1989, largely the cause of Asda's debt problem. Institutional discontent was partly responsible for Mr Hardman's departure. This left the company rudderless, however, while Asda's rivals took the initiative by tapping the equity market in a series of rights issues.

For their part the institutions argued that it is not their job to run a company; they can only ensure that the composition of the board is such that effective management can be implemented, and that ultimately it is up to the management to manage. While the institutions can highlight problems and prevent the worst of excesses, they can propose few, if any, constructive solutions. The nature of institutional shareholdings militates against investors taking early action. Because institutional investors have to watch many companies at the same time, interventions by the institutions often come too late. Collective action is not forthcoming until the problems are well recognized.

The institutions were now suggesting that Asda recruit a credible chief executive, sort out its strained balance sheet, retrench to its core business and trading area, and develop and communicate an effective strategy for the future. One institutional view was that either Asda should be soundly financed with a quality management team in place or it would be better for all concerned if it became part of wider group with stronger finances.

At the end of September 1991, Asda announced the terms of a £357m rights issue. Asda launched the new shares at 35 pence in the ratio of 9 for 10 The market's immediate reaction was to mark Asda shares sharply lower, down to an all-time low of 43 pence, before they steadied to close a net 9.5 pence down at 45.5 pence. At the same time Asda announced that it was urgently renegotiating borrowing arrangements with its banks. In the absence of such refinancing Asda said it might breach its banking covenants, with £600m of debt becoming due for repayment within the following year. Asda's total outstanding debt was £931.1m. The 9 for 10 issue at 35 pence per share was underwritten by Asda's merchant bank S.G. Warburg, but was dependent on the company renegotiating its short-term borrowing facilities.

The new chairman, Patrick Gillam, blamed Asda's financial problems on the financing of its £705m acquisition of 60 Gateway superstores from Isosceles. 'The company got itself into financing difficulties through failing to tackle its debt. But the underlying business is good, it is generating cash,' he said (*Daily Telegraph*, 1 October 1991). Asda was due to repay £300m of its almost £1 billion of borrowings during 1992. Some £128m was due for repayment in October 1991, with a further £290m due in November 1991, and a further £133m to be paid to holders of the company's 4.75 per cent convertible bonds in April 1992. The risk for Asda was that if these facilities were not continued or refinanced a shortage of working capital would result. Asda was on course to breach its loan covenants within weeks.

THE 'NORMAN WISDOM'

In mid October 1991, it was announced that Archie Norman, finance director of the Kingfisher retailing chain – which included Woolworth, B&Q and Comet – had been offered the job of chief executive of Asda. The company had been without a chief executive ever since John Hardman left the group the previous June. On joining

Asda, Norman was paid an annual salary of £325,000 and options on 4.4m shares at 38.5p per share. Norman's contract was terminable on three years' notice.

Norman said he found the offer 'irresistible', and that he would implement significant changes in the running of the company. 'There is a clear need for a new direction; no change is just not an option,' he said. 'The business cannot stand still' (*Financial Time*, 17 October 1991). In fact the company a week earlier had already embarked on a streamlining initiative to save £8m a year, which would lead to the loss of about 400 head office jobs.

Some analysts remained sceptical that Asda would be able to find a new formula for tackling the strategic dilemmas of competing with the fast-expanding Sainsbury, Tesco and Safeway chains. Norman dismissed such talk as 'misguided' and criticized what he called the 'black propaganda' suggesting that Asda was in terminal decline. 'There is no evidence to suggest that Asda is anything other than a secure business, with more than £4bn of sales, and a healthy record of profits,' he said (*Financial Times*, 17 October 1991).

The announcement of Norman's appointment coincided with the approval by shareholders of Asda's proposed £357m rights issue. Around the same time a syndicate of about 30 banks agreed to amend Asda's borrowing facilities. Eventually Asda was able to achieve a new £300m syndicated bank facility, with softer covenants, more competitive interest rates and involving fewer banks.

Asda's choice of Archie Norman as its group chief executive won exceptional acclaim in the financial world. The appointment virtually assured the success of the rights issue which closed on 8 November. Although only 37, during his five years with Kingfisher Norman came to be recognized in the investment world as 'incisive' – by which was meant he is one who goes straight to the point and sees the answers others cannot. He was known for demanding and getting the highest standards from those who work for him. Norman went to Charterhouse, a public school which has a strong representation in the higher echelons of the City, then on to Cambridge followed by study at Harvard, where he acquired his MBA. After a short spell at Citibank he joined the American management consultants McKinsey & Co. at 23, becoming one of their youngest ever partners. It was his work there that brought him in touch with Kingfisher in 1986. He was invited to join the Kingfisher main board with responsibility for finance, strategy and property. At Kingfisher, Norman enhanced his reputation as part of the management team which turned the company into one of the most efficient and tightly run in the retail sector.

In accepting the job of chief executive with Asda, from one perspective Norman was taking a big gamble with his thus far spotless business reputation. From another perspective he had little to lose. He had become the youngest chief executive of a FTSE 100 company and, as some observers argued, he could not go wrong. If he should fail he could say it was all a hopeless situation and nothing could be done. While if he were to succeed he could cash in his share options and retire at an early age, or move on and become chairman of a major company. When Norman arrived at Asda in December 1991, he called it 'Day Zero'. Everything from the past was to be forgotten. The Daimlers of the top management were withdrawn, along with the directors' car park at Asda House in Leeds.

There were a number of key issues facing Norman on his appointment: Asda's strategy, portfolio, product offering and distribution network, as well as deciding what to do with its home furnishings subsidiary, Allied Maples, and its 25 per cent investment in MFI. Another concern was how to restore staff morale which had received a battering as a result of the 400 or so job losses which the company announced shortly before Norman's appointment. Norman had to deal with all these problems in the face of a recession while competing against formidable adversaries – its big three rivals Sainsbury, Tesco and Safeway. While the latter three had raised £1.4bn to invest in expansion, Asda's rights issue process could only be used to reduce its borrowing total.

With the arrival of rivals from mainland Europe, such as Aldi and Netto, who provided cheaper goods in discount stores, Asda began to consider the possibility of a discount pilot scheme in one of the poorer areas it served. A strategic review team at Asda was studying how to match the products on its shelves to different areas' spending levels. Asda's target had been to offer a superstore service at all of its sites. It was now recognizing that there were substantial differences in the general nature of some of its areas. Group corporate affairs director Paul Dowling said that while Asda was looking at whether it was appropriate to provide the same type of service in all areas, that was a long way from going down the road of a discount chain. It would, however, be going down the road of offering less upmarket goods at cheaper prices.

The rights issue, which looked to be on the brink of disaster before Archie Norman agreed to join the company, was completed at the beginning of November 1991, with shareholders taking up 93.5 per cent of the £357m issue. The extent of the take-up of the rights issue signalled a clear vote of confidence by shareholders in Archie Norman. The success of the rights issue was a tribute to his reputation because Norman was still working out his notice with Kingfisher and was not yet in a position to set out a future strategy for Asda.

Archie Norman took up his appointment with Asda in early December 1991, and quickly moved to announce the appointment of a new finance director, Phil Cox, who came to Asda after nearly two years as chief executive of the troubled recruitment and financial services company Burns-Anderson, where Cox's main task was disposing of most of the financial services operations. Before that Cox was in retailing – though not food – most recently with the clothing retailer Horne Brothers. Cox replaced Ron Scott, who had been in the post since 1988, and was closely identified with Asda's recent troubles, including the financing of the purchase in 1989 of the Gateway superstores which had left Asda heavily debt laden as interest rates soared.

Asda's interim results, announced in January 1992, showed a loss of £68.8m. This was in line with expectations, as Asda continued to suffer from falling operating profits, a mounting interest bill and a string of exceptional charges relating to reorganization costs and property write-downs, including a provisional £39m for the Gazeley property pull-out from city centre retail developments associated with the weak property market. Asda accepted that it had paid too much for the 60 superstores it bought from Gateway for £705m in 1989 – implying that a current asset revaluation would include a further write-down in the year-end accounts. Announcing the interim results, Archie Norman said that a full-scale strategic review of the whole group had been launched and that there were no sacred cows within the company, implying that if he could raise the right price, he would sell sizeable chunks of the business to bring down gearing. 'We are not coming in a swashbuckling way and saying that we have the magic formula for Asda. What we have to do is look at the assets of the business and see whether there is potential for doing something better with them,' he said (*Financial Times*, 16 January 1992). Norman added, 'It is essential to make Asda's core business work.' One part of the business that was performing very well was the fashion operation run by George Davies, with clothing sales up 25 per cent. This was at least in part because it had a very real sense of direction. Norman expressed dismay, however, at the 'lousy' way Asda used its sales information. 'I cannot tell you whether our canned vegetables are profitable or our toys. But the systems that we now have in place give us the opportunity to do that. Such improvements are an obvious priority,' he said.

Another priority was to restore credibility with its customers by improving Asda's pricing position. Already the company had taken several initiatives on the price front. It had frozen the price of 30,000 items in the run up to Christmas 1991, and then introduced a range of 200 lower priced products at its under-performing stores. New price discounts were announced for the superstores in January 1992, with the launch of an extra value promotion featuring hundreds of products at 'substantial' reductions. Norman said: 'We must have a clear image differentiation from our competitors, and that is for good prices across a wide range of goods.' While this would bring in much needed cash flow, however, it would not help the company's thin margins.

In January 1992, it was announced that Asda was demanding immediate payment of £80m from British Aerospace (BAe), as a result of a property partnership that had turned sour when the market collapsed. The dispute arose from a £450m joint venture deal in December 1989 between Asda and BAe's property arm Arlington. The two firms set up a new company, Burwood House, each with a 50 per cent interest. Asda injected into Burwood 34 of its superstores, valued at £375m. Arlington put in £75m of development properties. A 'one-way' indemnity for Asda was included in the deal. The agreement protected Asda from a drop in the value of Burwood's assets by specifying that Arlington would have to make up the whole of the shortfall. An independent valuation of the properties in December 1990 concluded that the properties were worth £80m less than they were a year earlier. BAe was contesting the sum involved and also argued that since it owned half the joint development, it should get back half any amount it had to pay out. However, in February 1992 it was reported that BAe had paid £79m to resolve the dispute.

Also in February, 1992, Asda announced a reshuffle of its senior management, with the aim of producing a more focused retailing structure. Archie Norman, group chief executive, was to assume a more direct role in running the core retail business by taking on the additional post of chief executive of Asda Stores. This position had been held jointly by Richard Harker and Tony Campbell, who became retail director and trading director respectively. Asda now had a single management board responsible for all its businesses. Asda was to appoint a new marketing director and a new personnel director in March. When making these announcements Norman stressed that he wanted to return to Asda's 'traditional strengths', which he defined as real value for money, a clear consumer image and tight cost control. It was also reported that Asda had hired McKinsey, the management consultancy, to assess its financial options and review its product offering. It was believed that Asda was researching several possible trading formulas and was especially concerned to develop a viable format for 49 of its older stores which had been significantly under-performimg its competitors. Asda was also working with Anderson Consulting to maximize the effectiveness of information technology and introduce direct product profitability (DPP) techniques, such systems already being common among Asda's competitors. Following a close review of its relations with all its professional advisors, in March 1992 Asda announced that Warburgs had been removed as financial advisors, partly as a result of its involvement in advising Asda's rivals Sainsbury and Isosceles (which runs the Gateway chain). Morgan Grenfell was appointed as Asda's new financial advisors.

Also in March 1992, Asda announced that it was freezing the pay of its 65,000 employees, including directors, from 1 June 1992 until 1 June 1993, in a bid to cut costs. The GMB union said it was disappointed but recognized Asda's position.

'REAPPRAISAL AND RENEWAL'

Asda's annual report and accounts issued in the summer of 1992 was headed 'Reappraisal and Renewal'. In the report Archie Norman set out a three-year recovery programme for Asda with the ultimate objective to create the basis for sustainable growth in shareholder value. The following are key extracts from the programme set out by Archie Norman:

(i) REAPPRAISAL

We are convinced that traditional Asda virtues can be applied effectively to the Group's large superstore network and that the results will be a re-energized and simplified company closer to its customers and traditional markets.

The Key Issues:

Price Competitiveness   The heritage of the Asda Brand lies in the strength of its image for consistent value for money across a wide range of goods in lively exciting stores. The shift in Asda Stores' strategy during the 1980s towards a higher added-value proposition increased our costs rapidly. The resultant pressure on profits required substantial improvements in gross margin to achieve acceptable results. Although range enhancement, introduction of own-label and the launch of central distribution contributed 'genuine' margin gain there was a progressive decline in Asda's price competitiveness. As a result the business has walked away from its historic brand values and lost support, particularly in less well off areas.

Potential in Fresh Foods   The significant amount of space allocated to non-food and its positioning at the entrance to stores has limited the space available for fresh food compared to the competition. As a result the visual impact of fresh food has been impaired. So, despite very substantial improvements in the quality of fruit, vegetables and other fresh foods stocked, Asda has so far failed to convince consumers that its fresh food offer matches that of its superstore competitors.

The Scope for Clothing, Home and Leisure   The markets for Asda's traditional non-food products changed dramatically during the 1980s. The decade was marked by the development of specialist out-of-town DIY superstores, garden centres and electrical retailers. The role of clothing, home and leisure ranges in our stores therefore needs repositioning to exploit those markets which fit comfortably alongside a grocery retailing business.

We are thus successfully developing sales in markets such as stationery and cards, where growth rates and profit contribution are well above the norm.

We have been generally more successful in clothing. The 'George' range has helped to create a brighter, more 'cheerful' ambience at the entrance to our stores. There remains scope to target ranges more precisely to specific store catchments.

Need for Efficiency and Productivity   In recent years the business has become substantially more complex in its store design and head office organization. This has inevitably increased its cost base. The restoration of greater price competitiveness makes essential a return to the company's traditional highly efficient attitude to costs.

The under exploited potential

- The substantial strengths of the business will form the basis of Asda's renewal.
- Sales of more than £4 billion, with substantial market shares in Scotland and the North.
- 8 million square feet of selling space in 206 superstores with an average size of 40,000 square feet.
- A highly efficient, modern composite distribution system.
- A systems infrastructure linking all stores on line to support EPOS, EFTPOS, stock replenishment and management information systems.
- Operating management skills.

(ii) RENEWAL

The new management team is energetically implementing a ten-point plan. The cornerstone of this plan is our commitment to value for money and everyday low prices. All our activities will be coordinated to achieve this.

We will concentrate on meeting the weekly shopping needs of ordinary working people and their families.

We will pay particular attention to satisfying the needs of the majority of people who live around stores better than our competition.

We will re-establish our price reputation.   Product ranging and pricing will be matched to the requirements of our customers in particular catchment areas. We have already introduced a substantial range of 'good quality basic value' lines and intend to develop these further. We plan never to be undersold by other superstores on frequently purchased staples and leading brands.

We will develop new formats.   The main business will be revitalized by substantially changing our stores. This is a major programme which will involve a significant increase in food space, a radical improvement in the quality and presentation of fresh foods, and refocusing our clothing, home and leisure offer on products that appeal to our target customers. Our first pilot conversion will open this in Autumn 1992. In addition an experimental discount format, trading as 'DALES', is being piloted in selected non-core stores. Dales is strongly differentiated from other discount operators by:

- A tight range of approximately 7,500 lines (compared to over 22,000 in a typical super-store) focused on items most frequently purchased by family shoppers. Most other discount operators meet only a selection of needs.
- A superior range of fruit and vegetables and other fresh foods, unmatched by any other discount operator in the UK.
- Low operating costs throughout the store and the supply chain. Dales uses pallet displays and warehouse racking to minimize store labour costs.

We will drive change through the store portfolio.   Capital investment will result in more improvements in existing stores than in any previous year. The refurbishment programme will over the next three years fully update at least two-thirds of our stores.

We will compete through productivity improvements.   We intend to put in place a progressive programme of cost reductions. Over 1,000 positions have been eliminated in the stores and at headquarters and there is a wage freeze in place across the Group. Management will continue to apply relentless pressure for increased efficiency as an essential means of securing the future for both employees and shareholders.

We will pursue innovation in packaged groceries and drinks. Asda Brand will continue to play an important role in markets such as toiletries, beers and wines, where we have traditional strength. In addition we will put particular emphasis upon developing positions of strength in volume and growth markets relevant to our target customers.

We will exploit our investment in Logistics. The heavy investment of recent years has given us an excellent configuration of state-of-the-art distribution centres. During the coming year, we will improve store replenishment and continue to reduce working capital.

We will focus information technology on profit generation. We have developed direct product profitability systems which will support both strategic and day-to-day decision-making. Improved systems will support improvements in store productivity management and our ability to flex individual stores to better meet the needs of their immediate catchment areas.

We will reposition and redevelop Clothing, Home and Leisure ranges. Product ranges will be reviewed so as to be consistent with the weekly food shopping trip. Our 'George' range, sourced through The George Davies Partnership, will focus upon leisure clothing and in particular children's clothes, where there is significant market share potential. Home and Leisure products will operate with less space and stockholding.

We will focus on fresh foods. We believe that fresh foods are crucial to gaining a higher share of our customers' food spend and to attracting new customers. The three-year programme of refurbishment of our core superstores will, wherever possible, position fresh foods more prominently in the store as well as increasing total space allocation. We will exploit our leadership position in in-store bakeries where our quality reputation is high.

A relentless pressure on costs and efficiency will enable us to re-establish Asda's reputation for consistent value for money. We will rebuild our business by an increasing commitment to the principles of our 'virtuous circle'. [See Figure 2.1.]

Allied Maples
Allied is the UK's leading carpet and upholstery business. However, Allied has diversified away from its core markets and this, together with its over-expansion, has left it vulnerable to weakened demand and escalating occupancy costs. We will therefore refocus the business upon its core markets of carpets, beds and upholstery, where Allied's position as the market leader is reflected in the relative strength of its returns from carpets as opposed to its more recently developed product markets. Costs are being sharply reduced. In May we announced the decision to close 17 unprofitable stores and in recent weeks numbers employed have been reduced by 13%.

Gazeley
At the half year we announced Gazeley's withdrawal from town centre retail and office developments.

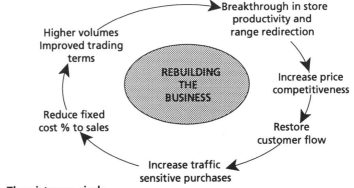

Fig. 2.1 The virtuous circle.

Gazeley will now concentrate upon:

- providing a property management role for the Group, including project managing the record programme of change in Asda;
- further exploiting the potential of Magna Park and its distribution park expertise, when further expansion will confirm its status as one of Europe's leading distribution parks.

In July 1992, the MFI Furniture Group, of which Asda owned 25 per cent was floated on the stock exchange. Asda's interest in MFI was sold, for which it received net cash of £73m. In October, 1992, Asda sold two development sites and one store for £57m as part of an effort to reduce its large debt burden.

In January 1993, Asda announced a rights issue of £347m (a 3-for-10 offer at 53p a share), the cash being raised to be allocated across the group in order to refocus the stores portfolio and drive earnings forward. Observers commented that there was so much to be done at Asda it was difficult to see how even the tightest of controls would be sufficient to squeeze out the cash flow necessary to implement the required changes. Although refurbishment could be funded out of cash flow, there would have been insufficient finance available for the resiting and rebuilding element of the programme. The development of the Dales chain would also have been curtailed. Faced with this dilemma, the choice was either to shrink the group or seek the additional funds from shareholders. Norman had chosen the latter route, which not only left the recovery programme intact but also allowed him to accelerate parts of it. While the rights issue could be seen in terms of laying the foundations for a more stable and broadly based medium-term future, it was unlikely to lead to any significant improvement in the group's short-term fortunes. While the new stores would help to improve sales and net margins, Asda still had a long way to go. Sales at £10 per sq. ft were considerably short of sales of £19 per sq. ft achieved by Sainsbury. The need to rebuild the balance sheet was largely caused by Asda's acquisition of 60 Gateway stores from Isosceles in 1989 for £705m. According to Archie Norman the final cost of the acquisition, which he said should never have been made, was about £1bn, after adding the costs of integration and refurbishment. Much of the cash raised from the rights issue would be invested in rebuilding and recycling the Asda stores in the company's 'heartland' in the Yorkshire region. Archie Norman said: 'We are very much concentrating on our Northern stronghold' (*Yorkshire Post*, 29 January 1993).

The City welcomed the rights issue with Asda shares rising 5p to 68p, compared with the 53p issue price for the new shares. This response indicated that the main shareholders were happy with the progress made so far by Norman, and approved of his strategy for the future. Without the rights issue, Asda would only have been able to spend £130m in 1994 out of its projected cash flow. Yet there was a not-to-be missed opportunity to 'recycle' its old stores, something which had been neglected under the former management – some stores had been unchanged for 15 years. The plan involved resiting 15 of the oldest stores, rebuilding between five and ten stores on existing sites, and adding stores in catchment areas where its brand was strong but where it was under-represented. Just how fast Asda would be able to go with the greenfield developments depended on site acquisition as Asda had virtually no land bank left. Renewing an Asda store would cost £2m. A complete rebuild would cost about £9m. The movement of a store to a nearby greenfield site would cost from £12m to £32m, depending on land costs. The pay-off from refurbishment was impressive, however, with expectations of sales rising 20 per cent. A further use of the money would be to expand the Dales format, based on selling only a third of the lines typically sold in an Asda store, but with an even stronger emphasis on fresh foods. By early 1993, Asda had opened four Dales sites at previously under-performing Asda stores with a resulting uplift in sales close to 50 per cent. Asda was now looking to acquire and rent new sites.

In April 1993, Asda announced its intention to close its loss-making meat factory, Lofthouse Foods, based in Wakefield, with the loss of 1,300 jobs. Local MP Bill O'Brien said: 'While Asda is claiming that Lofthouse is a victim of over capacity shop stewards at the factory claim that it is a victim of asset stripping' (*Yorkshire Post*, 26 April 1993). Asda's corporate affairs director, Paul Dowling, said Lofthouse was not making profits and was operating in a declining market where there was large over-capacity. Lofthouse Foods, formally known as Farm Stores, set up in Wakefield in 1928 and was one of the largest single-plant food manufacturers in Europe. It had been Asda's biggest single supplier of meat products, pizzas and savoury snack foods since 1965, and produced more than 250,000 pizzas each week and nearly 10 million pies a year.

In September 1993, it was revealed that members of Asda's management team would receive substantial share bonuses it they successfully turned the company around, with Archie Norman eligible for a £2m bonus, and other executive directors entitled to share options which could, over a five-year period, be worth about £1m each. Defending the bonus scheme, Asda chairman Patrick Gillam said it was put in place by non-executive directors to get people to work for Asda. Half the bonuses will be paid if the share price is at least £1 in 1998, and the other half if earnings per share (excluding extraordinary items) have increased by a compound 15 per cent over that period. The stock market value of the company was £420m when it was put in place so to benefit, the directors would have to increase the company's value by more than seven times, to over £2bn, and generate excellent cash flow. Against that progress, the bonus would be equal to three-tenths of one per cent of the increase in the group's value. 'These people took some very fundamental risks with their careers. If they are successful, the proportion of what they gain is small – and if they are not successful they get nowt,' said Mr Gillam (*Yorkshire Post*, 23 September 1993).

At the AGM in July 1993, Archie Norman warned that superstore expansion in the retail grocery industry could not continue without damaging profitability. 'The halcyon days of grocery retailing are over,' he said, 'and 1991 will probably be seen as the *annus mirabilis*' (*The Guardian*, 3 July 1993). Norman forecast that price would become an increasingly important aspect of competition as saturation approached. 'The industry is not going to be able to sustain the level of new openings without having an effect on margins,' he said.

In the report and accounts for 1993, Asda chairman Patrick Gillam explained how the platform for recovery had been created and how the process of renewal would continue. In the previous year Asda had concentrated on improving Asda's appeal to its traditional customers. This was epitomized by the relaunch of 'Asda Price' and the establishment of Asda as the lowest priced national superstore chain. Asda management believed that the present decade would see considerable structural changes in food retailing. Capital investment by the industry on yet more selling space was set to continue at record levels. This meant that in more and more towns shoppers were faced with a growing choice of superstores, now supplemented by the rapid expansion of new discount chains. Furthermore in a low growth, low inflation economy, consumers were unlikely to return to the free spending ways of the late 1980s. In this situation Asda's management believed that the successful retailers would be those who create and sustain a reputation for value for money.

Asda hoped to renew 40 stores during 1993 and intended to start reinvesting in its heartland with new store openings at Huddersfield and Burnley and rebuilt stores at Colne and Chadderton, as well as extensive improvements benefiting the majority of stores.

Under the heading 'Renewing the Organization' in Asda's 1993 Report and Accounts, Archie Norman made the following points:

Behind almost every substantial business failure is organizational weakness and Asda up until last year was no exception. We had too many layers of management, narrow functional attitudes and a controlling bureaucratic head office culture. The business was no longer effective in understanding and responding to its customers' needs. We have therefore embarked upon a comprehensive programme of change in our organization, people and in the way we work together.

Organizational renewal means not just changing people and structures but changing habits and ingrained behaviour. Such a programme takes time and initially results in a high level of uncertainty and insecurity. We are now, however, well down the road, results are encouraging and the business is gaining in confidence.

- The restructuring and recruitment of the top management team is substantially complete so that the business has strong leadership dedicated to the task of renewal.
- There is a common sense of values and direction amongst the management group built around the idea of a business focused on our type of customer and their shopping needs.
- The mind set of the business has been very much shifted towards the stores with much more focus on active selling within the stores.
- The style of management in the stores is becoming less authoritarian, more sensitive and respectful of colleagues at all levels.
- Levels of management have been reduced in most areas of the business with total head count in the centre down to 1,360 from more than 2,000 two years ago.
- Productivity has improved so that sales per full-time equivalent employee have increased by 13% in the last year.
- Communication is improving at all levels. In recent months for instance more than 2,000 managers have attended conferences or briefings on new trading developments.

It is our objective to create a totally different type of retail organization. We are a large company with £4.5 billion of turnover and 65,000 employees. But we want Asda to feel like a small business based on not many more than 200 stores, each one of which will be known well to all senior management and be very actively traded. Within the stores we believe that a more involving, and in some cases, caring approach to our colleagues will make Asda both a better place to work and a higher productivity business. Almost without exception, each store is a major employer and focal point within its local community. We therefore want to encourage it to develop a common sense of identity, purpose and responsibility. At this stage of our programme we are only establishing the foundations of this new organization. But already both in the centre and in our pioneering 'Renewal' experimental stores we have demonstrated the value of this new approach in releasing skills, ability and enthusiasm. During the next phase we will be accelerating the programme of change. This process will involve widespread dissemination of the new management practices, a greater commitment to management development and a singular focus on the stores, selling and customer service.

In the year to mid 1993 Asda re-established its position as the lowest priced national superstore retailer. The new 'Asda Price' brand positioning was based on an advertising campaign of high potency and recall. This was synonymous with the early growth of the business. Customers understood this to mean unbeatable value, not just price, as well as consistently high quality. Asda restored this guarantee.

In December 1993, Asda sold the loss-making Allied Carpets. Maples, the furniture operation, also making a loss, was expected to be sold soon after to a group of managers. Allied was absorbed into Carpetland, which was formed in 1991 to buy a string of outlets from the bankrupt Lowndes Queensway. As part of the transaction Asda took a 40 per cent stake in Carpetland. The enlarged business was renamed Allied, and managers expected it to be floated on the stock exchange within three years. Severing ties with Allied and Maples required Asda to write off about £70m, reflecting the book value of the investment it had made in the businesses. In addition Asda charged £53.3m against its profit and loss account to reflect goodwill involved with Allied's purchases of other companies over the previous 15 years.

The financial position of the Asda Group in 1992 and 1993 is shown in Tables 2.1, 2.2 and 2.3. The Asda Group board of directors in 1993 is shown in Table 2.4.

Table 2.1 Asda Group Plc: Consolidated profit and loss account
(52 weeks ended 1 May 1993 (1992: 53 weeks)

	1993 £m	1992 £m
Sales	4,991.8	4,904.1
Value added tax	378.0	375.0
Turnover	4,613.8	4,529.1
Operating costs	4,423.8	4,349.1
Operating profit	190.0	180.0
Share of profits of associated undertakings	1.2	2.1
Net interest payable	(50.8)	(95.3)
Profit before taxation and exceptional items	140.4	86.8
Exceptional items	1.7	(451.6)
Profit/(loss) on ordinary activities before taxation	142.1	(364.8)
Taxation	(35.6)	20.8
Profit/(loss) before extraordinary items	106.5	(344.0)
Extraordinary items	50.0	—
Profit/(loss) for the financial year	156.5	(344.0)
Dividends	(43.0)	(46.8)
Retained profit/(deficit)	113.5	(390.8)
Earnings/(loss) per ordinary share	Pence	Pence
Basic	4.35	(17.55)
Before exceptional charges	3.85	2.73
Dividend per ordinary share	1.60	2.10

Table 2.2 Asda Group Plc: Balance sheets (at 1 May 1993)

	Group	
	1993 *£m*	*1992* *£m*
Fixed assets		
Tangible assets	1,932.5	2,003.6
Investments	103.7	104.5
	2,036.2	2,108.1
Current assets		
Stocks	313.1	307.3
Debtors	137.9	117.8
Investments	371.4	0.4
Cash at bank and in hand	10.6	38.4
	833.0	463.9
Creditors: amounts falling due within one year		
Borrowings	(49.6)	(282.7)
Other creditors	(674.2)	(553.9)
	(732.8)	(836.6)
Net current assets/(liabilities)	109.2	(372.7)
Total assets less current liabilities	2,145.4	1,735.4
Creditors: amounts falling due after more than one year		
Borrowings	(408.8)	(433.9)
Other creditors	(0.3)	(0.7)
Provisions for liabilities and charges	(168.6)	(193.5)
	1,567.7	1,107.3
Capital and reserves		
Called-up share capital	724.6	557.4
Share premium account	302.4	122.7
Revaluation reserve	88.9	86.6
Profit and loss account	451.8	340.6
	1,567.7	1,107.3

Table 2.3 Asda Group Plc: Turnover[1] and segmental[2] analysis

	1993 £m	1992 £m
Turnover		
Asda	4,396.3	4,308.3
Allied Maples	205.4	218.0
Gazeley	12.1	2.8
	4,613.8	4,529.1
Profit		
Asda	196.1	185.6
Allied Maples	(7.9)	(9.8)
Gazeley	1.8	4.2
Operating profit	190.0	180.0
Share of profits of associated undertakings	1.2	2.1
Net interest payable	(50.8)	(95.3)
Profit before taxation and exceptional items	140.4	86.8
Exceptional credits/(charges)		
Asda	7.7	(382.8)
Allied Maples	(6.0)	(29.7)
Gazeley	—	(39.1)
	1.7	(451.6)
Profit/(Loss) on ordinary activities before taxation	142.1	(364.8)
Net assets		
Asda	1,483.0	1,636.5
Allied Maples	43.7	38.8
Gazeley	56.1	62.7
	1,582.8	1,738.0
Investments in associated undertakings	103.7	104.5
Unallocated net liabilities[3]	(118.8)	(735.2)
Total net assets	1,567.7	1,107.3

1. Turnover comprises the value of sales excluding value added tax.
2. The group operates in three principal areas of activity categorized as follows:

    Asda   – retail of food, clothing, home and leisure products
    Allied Maples – retail of furniture and carpets
    Gazeley   – property development.

3. Unallocated net liabilities comprise balances in respect of investments, dividends and borrowings.

Table 2.4 Asda board of directors 1993

Chairman – Patrick Gillam, 60, appointed September 1991 following retirement from the Board of the British Petroleum Company plc, where he was a Managing Director for ten years. He is Chairman of Standard Chartered plc and Non-Executive Director of Commercial Union plc.

Group Chief Executive – Archie Norman, 39, appointed in December 1991. Formerly a partner at McKinsey and Co. and Group Finance Director of Kingfisher plc. Currently a Non-Executive Director of British Rail.

Marketing Director – Allan Leighton, 40, appointed in March 1992. Previously eighteen years with the Mars Corporation, where he was most recently Sales Director, Pedigree Petfoods.

Finance Director – Phil Cox, 43, appointed in January 1992. Formerly Group Chief Executive of Burns Anderson plc and Finance Director of Horne Brothers plc.

Trading Director – Tony Campbell, 43, appointed in 1987, having joined Asda in 1985, following senior management positions with other leading food retailers.

Retail Director – Peter Monaghan, 45, appointed in August 1992. Previously Operations Director of DIY retailer B&Q.

Company Secretary and Corporate Counsel – Denise Jagger, 34, appointed in January 1993. Formerly a solicitor with Slaughter and May and a Partner with Booth & Co.

Non-Executive Directors:

Susan Ellen, 44, appointed in September 1992. Managing Director of BUPA Health Services, which runs all BUPA Hospitals and Healthcare.

David O'Brien, 51, appointed in July 1992. Chief Executive of National & Provincial Building Society and Chairman of Pagoda Limited, a management consultancy company.

Sir Godfrey Messervy, 68, appointed in 1986. Formerly Chairman and Chief Executive of Lucas Group and Chairman of Costain Group plc.

Frank Knight, 56, appointed a Director in September 1991 and Deputy Chairman in July 1992. Chairman of Field Group plc, Deputy Chairman of Berisford International plc, Non-Executive Director of Ocean Group plc and London International Group plc.

Rt. Hon. Francis Maude, 39, appointed in July 1992. Formerly Financial Secretary to the Treasury, and currently a Director and Head of Privatization at Morgan Stanley International, London.

Argyll Group Plc

C.M. Clarke-Hill and T.M. Robinson

INTRODUCTION

The decade of the 1980s saw many significant changes in the UK economy. Many companies, in every sector of the economy and particularly in retailing, rose from obscurity to gain national or international prominence. Among them was the Argyll Group. Since 1978, Argyll, through a series of astute acquisitions, had become the third largest food retailer in the UK by 1992, with sales of over £5bn and a market capitalization (December 1992) of £4.45bn. By 1992, Argyll Group operated throughout the UK from 819 stores that had a combined sales area of 8.44 million square feet. In addition to supermarkets, Argyll also had interests in the cash and carry and specialist frozen food distribution sectors. In the fourteen years since 1978, Argyll's pre-tax profit had risen from zero to £365m.

GROWTH AND DEVELOPMENT OF THE COMPANY

The origins of Argyll can be traced back to the early 1970s when a management team, comprising James Gulliver, Alistair Grant and David Webster became responsible for the development of Oriel Foods which was acquired by the RCA Corporation in 1974. Following three years of success, they left Oriel/RCA to lay the foundations of the current Argyll company. These foundations were laid on a pattern of acquiring under-performing companies and rebuilding their businesses. The Argyll team's first move into the food industry came in April 1978 when they took control of Morgan Edwards, a loss-making listed grocery distributor based in Shrewsbury. Many of Morgan Edwards' underperforming Supavalu stores were closed, Edwards' discounting policy was reversed and controls on costs and margins were tightened. Much of the restructuring and debt reduction of the Morgan Edwards business was funded by the sale of their non-retail businesses whilst at the same time a compatible business (Paddys based in the North Midlands) was acquired to give the embryonic retail group some economies of scale.

Early in 1979, another heavily geared and loss-making company, also quoted on the stock exchange, came under the team's management control, namely Louis C. Edwards & Sons (Manchester), a meat processing and wholesaling company with retail butchers shops. A strategy similar to that followed at Morgan Edwards was observed; the loss-making processing and wholesaling operations were disposed of or closed and margins in the butchers shops rebuilt. In the same year two successful biscuit manufacturers, Yorkshire Biscuits and Furniss & Co., were acquired for £3 million.

In 1980, Louis Edwards acquired Cordon Bleu, a freezer chain with 46 outlets in the North West Midlands, as well as Dalgety Frozen Foods with its 33 strong chain of freezer centres in the South East. It was at this point the Argyll Group itself was formed with the merger of Louis Edwards and Morgan Edwards.

Further acquisitions came in the early 1980s with Freezer Fare and Bonimart, both of which were integrated with Cordon Bleu to create a chain of more than 130 freezer centres. Following closely was the enlargement of the biscuit activities by the acquisition of Patersons Scottish Shortbread which was integrated with Yorkshire Biscuits and Furniss.

A key development in the expansion of Argyll came in February 1981 with the purchase of Oriel Foods from the RCA Corporation. A number of similarities existed in the way in which Oriel Foods had developed and that of Argyll itself – culturally and structurally the two businesses were compatible. The purchase of Oriel for £19.5 million represented 80 per cent of Argyll's then stock market valuation. The Oriel acquisition contributed £4.5 million in profits and £22.1 million in net tangible assets. More significantly perhaps, Argyll inherited a strong senior management team many of whom were former colleagues. Oriel's retail and wholesale operations, Lo Cost discount stores, Mojo cash and carry and Snowking frozen foods fitted neatly with Argyll. The acquisition provided Argyll with scope for rationalizing its overheads, integrating distribution and increasing its purchasing power.

The Lo Cost brand gave Argyll an effective retailing presence complementing its Supavalu stores. Argyll merged these two brands under the Lo Cost fascia, an exercise that was to be repeated five years later with the merger of Safeway.

The Oriel acquisition also brought into Argyll food manufacturing capacity in the shape of edible oil processing, and tea and coffee businesses. Although these interests did not fit in with its existing operations, Argyll was able to manage this diversity efficiently.

Argyll's strategic aim at this time was to create a substantial retailing and wholesale distribution business. The internal development of the existing businesses, whilst satisfactory, did not facilitate Argyll's effective competition with the industry leaders at the time. In 1981 Argyll's total sales were £102 million. In September 1981 the company took a 20 per cent stake in Linfood Holdings, a wholesale, retail and cash and carry group, now known as Gateway, with sales of £1 billion. In October of that year Argyll launched its first contested takeover valuing Linfood at £91 million against its own stock market value of £46 million. Argyll's stake in Linfood rose to 30 per cent and this was followed a month later by a referral to the Monopolies and Mergers Commission. Argyll was unwilling to finance the cost of its shareholding in Linfood while the investigation continued and subsequently withdrew its bid.

In January 1982 Argyll purchased 67 Pricerite stores for a consideration of £3 million.

In the spring of 1982, Cavenham Foods put its Allied Suppliers business up for sale. Allied Suppliers was one of the UK's largest grocery retailers trading under such brands as Galbraith and Templeton in Scotland, as well as Presto and Lipton in England. Its portfolio consisted of 923 stores with sales of £847 million and a market share of 4.6 per cent with its regional strength in Scotland and North East England. Argyll and Cavenham agreed terms in May 1982 valuing Allied Suppliers at £101 million. Argyll funded the deal by the issue of 95 million shares which raised £81 million with the balance in cash. After this acquisition Argyll's gearing reached 100 per cent. The Allied purchase gave Argyll the critical mass to compete effectively in the UK food retailing industry however, a number of strategic problems still remained to be solved (details of which are documented in the strategy section below). A further acquisition was made in 1984 when Argyll took over the Hintons supermarket group for £27.5 million.

A parallel development at Argyll was the creation of an alcoholic beverages distribution business involving the distillation and distribution of scotch whisky, rum as well the wholesaling and retailing of wines and spirits in the UK. A strategic acquisition in the USA was also completed with the purchase for £24.6 million of Barton Brands of Chicago, a manufacturer of bourbon, gin and rum, and a distributor of imported beers wines and spirits.

In 1987, Argyll disposed of its drinks businesses and food manufacturing interests to concentrate on grocery retailing. In the same year, Argyll purchased Safeway Stores, a subsidiary of a USA company of the same name, for £651m. Safeway had a strong brand name in the UK and was renowned for its innovation and the quality of its retailing operations. It had a UK market share of 3.4 per cent with sales in 1986 in excess of £1 billion and pre-tax profits of £43.8 million. Safeway traded from 133 stores with an aggregate selling area of 2.0 million square feet. Its geographical coverage was as follows:

- 86 stores in London and the South;
- 25 stores in the Midlands and the North;
- 22 stores in Scotland.

The modern company was thus created.

At the beginning of the 1990s Argyll, along with Ahold of the Netherlands and Casino of France, formed the European Retail Alliance in order to co-operate in areas such as marketing, distribution, production and information technology. This alliance involved a £35 million investment in cross-shareholding among the three groups. In addition to the ERA a buying organization based in Switzerland entitled Associated Marketing Services was created involving the three ERA members and nine other European food retailing companies.

Table 3.1 gives a five-year summary of Argyll's financial history. More detailed accounts for 1990–93 are provided in Appendix 3.1.

STRATEGY AND STYLE

By 1992, of the original three founding members of Argyll only Grant (now Sir Alistair Grant) and David Webster remained. James Gulliver, Argyll's first chairman, left in 1986 after losing a bitterly fought contested takeover for Distillers plc. It was Gulliver's vision and entrepreneurial skill that had created the Argyll group, and when he left, his natural successor Grant assumed control of Argyll. It was Grant's strategy that steered Argyll deeper into food retailing, masterminding the takeover of Safeway and dismantling Gulliver's ventures into international drinks and food manufacturing.

The grocery retailing industry in the UK was dominated by the large multiples, with J. Sainsbury, Tesco and Argyll the top three players. 'The pecking order,' said Grant, 'was not written in stone. Back in 1979 Asda was the most profitable retailer

Table 3.1 Argyll Group Plc – five-year summary financial history 1988–92

Profit and loss account	1992 £m	1991 £m	1990 £m	1989 £m	1988 £m
Net sales	4,729.2	4,496.1	3,920.0	3,500.9	3,236.3
Operating profit	331.0	285.3	224.6	187.8	161.9
Net interest received	33.5	5.5	19.0	20.7	13.7
Profit before taxation	364.5	290.8	243.6	208.5	175.6
Exceptional item	—	—	(16.1)	(29.8)	(43.5)
Profit before taxation	364.5	290.8	227.5	178.7	132.1
Taxation	(102.1)	(81.4)	(68.3)	(53.6)	(54.9)
Profit after taxation	262.4	209.4	159.2	125.1	77.2
Extraordinary item	78.3	—	4.1	—	22.4
Profit for the financial year	340.7	209.4	163.3	125.1	99.6

Balance sheet	1992 £m	1991 £m	1990 £m	1989 £m	1988 £m
Fixed assets	1,751.7	1,389.7	1,117.8	818.2	597.6
Net current liabilities	(132.4)	(356.7)	(314.0)	(186.4)	(61.8)
Total assets less current liabilities	1,619.3	1,033.0	803.8	631.8	535.8
Creditors (due after one year)	157.6	207.4	114.3	109.9	90.9
Deferred taxation	15.4	10.2	6.4	5.8	4.5
Total shareholders' funds	1,446.3	815.4	683.1	516.1	440.4
Total capital employed	1,619.3	1,033.0	803.8	631.8	535.8
Net cash/(borrowings)	199.2	(165.7)	(11.3)	59.8	130.4

	1992 pence	1991 pence	1990 pence	1989 pence	1988 pence
Earnings per share:					
– before exceptional item	24.2	21.6	18.0	15.7	12.8
– after exceptional item	24.2	21.6	16.8	13.5	8.9
Dividend per share:					
– net	9.75	8.49	7.07	6.05	5.17
– gross	13.0	11.32	9.44	8.07	6.96
Net tangible assets per share	129.9	83.8	70.5	55.1	47.7
Share price range[1]					
– high	432.0	315.0	250.8	251.8	209.8
– low	273.0	234.9	193.2	159.1	154.2

1. Share prices are as at 31 December taken from the Extel Card for Argyll Plc, except for 1992 where price was taken as at 31 December from the FT listings.

Source: Company accounts.

followed by Tesco and then Sainsbury.' By 1992 that position was reversed, and Argyll had emerged as a major player. (Appendix 3.2 shows the key financial ratios of these three retailers along with the ratios for the food retailing industry as a whole.) Grant said that he took no pleasure in seeing rivals lose money and strongly refuted the idea that running supermarkets was like 'owning a toll bridge where you cannot possibly fail'. Argyll's success, he contended, was 'not simply achieved by financial sleight of hand. Since we bought Allied Suppliers in 1982, we have overtaken Waitrose, Kwik Save, Gateway, Morrison and Asda. What is more we have raised the net assets of the business from £117m to £1.5bn.' Grant likens Argyll to a 'horse that wins hurdle races. The acquisitions are the hurdles, but you actually win the race by the speed you gallop between the hurdles.' Argyll started 1993 five percentage points behind Sainsbury and Tesco, but Grant believed that Argyll was capable of narrowing the gap.

It was Grant's view that Argyll had at least a decade of growth ahead of it in its supermarket business. 'What warms our heart is that Safeway stores still only cover 40 per cent of the population compared with 60 per cent for Sainsbury.' This growth was likely to be concentrated in the South East of England where Safeway was relatively weak but, paradoxically, where it was most profitable. Grant's strategy was to intensify the battle with Sainsbury on Sainsbury's home territory. Over the next three years to 1995–96, in many South East towns where only two superstores compete for the consumer's grocery shopping basket, Argyll intended to add a third – Safeway.

The corporate strategy and the retailing strategy at Argyll are inextricably linked. Since the takeover of Safeway, it had always been the objective of the company to create a distinct Safeway culture that differentiated it from its rivals. Argyll's strategy had always been based around a central 'recipe of success'. Acquisitions allowed the firm to grow quickly to achieve critical mass and to obtain a good geographic spread of stores. Strong management attended to margin improvement and operating efficiency while the infrastructure that was created allowed the management to attend to the cost base and marketing to facilitate brand growth in the three retail market areas Argyll traded in. The Safeway strategy was central to Arygll's success. Table 3.2 shows the breakdown of sales turnover and operating profit by class of business for the period 1989–92.

Table 3.2 Sales turnover and operating profit by class of business 1989–92

		1992	1991	1990	1989
Sales turnover:					
– Safeway	£m	3,905.0	3,496.6	2,805.8	2,071.0
– Other food activities[1]	£m	1,134.3	1,260.9	1,337.5	1,625.4
– Total (inc. VAT)	£m	5,039.3	4,757.5	4,143.3	3,696.4
Operating profit:					
– Safeway	£m	275.3	222.5	158.8	105.6
– Margin (ex VAT)	%	7.5	6.7	6.0	5.4
– Other food activities[1]	£m	51.9	59.0	61.7	79.9
– Margin (ex VAT)	%	4.9	5.0	4.9	5.2
– Property and other income	£m	3.8	3.8	4.1	2.3
– Total for the year	£m	331.0	285.3	224.6	187.8

1. 'Other food activities' includes stores other than Safeway as well as food retailing and the group's wholesale activities.

The Safeway business

The acquisition of Safeway brought Argyll into the premier league of UK food retailing. The group had acquired an excellent brand, an innovative management team and an excellent portfolio of stores. Argyll's primary objective was to place its Presto brand into the new stores group it now controlled and expand Safeway's selling area from 2 million sq. ft to 6 million sq. ft. This would be primarily achieved by

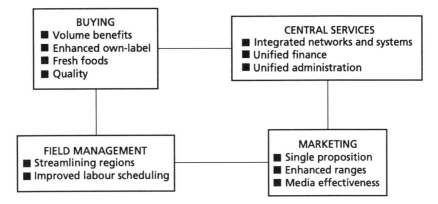

Figure 3.1 Operational benefits.

converting 100 of Presto's largest stores into Safeways and by adding capacity by building new stores.

The acquisition now meant that Argyll had three sets of everything. Rationalization was uppermost in the minds of Argyll's senior managers. Safeway and Presto's distribution systems were merged and Safeway practices were introduced into Presto's store operations. In 1987, a typical Safeway store's sales per square foot was 55 per cent higher and its operating profitability some 76 per cent greater than a typical Presto unit. This was largely explained by the different sales mix at Safeway, concentrated as it was on fresh produce. Other areas of commonality were also addressed, namely marketing and central administration. Argyll saw the relationship as an interlocking cycle involving four key components – Buying, Central services, Marketing and Field management, as illustrated in Fig. 3.1.

Argyll, as a result of the Safeway acquisition progressively built its corporate and retailing strategy around its newly acquired store brand. By 1992, 85 per cent of Argyll's profits came from the Safeway business. The larger Presto stores were progressively refurbished and converted to become Safeway units, and along with new store opening, the average sales area for a Safeway store rose to 20,000 sq. ft. The Presto brand was scaled down in terms of store size, operating a medium sized outlet at around 5,000 sq. ft. The discount shops, Lo Cost were in the small category of about 3,000 sq. ft. The store profile meant that the Safeway marque competed directly with Sainsbury, Tesco and Asda and the Lo Cost brand with Kwik Save, whose shopping basket profile was very similar. Argyll was one of the few food retailers in the UK to operate a dual branding strategy. The Co-op, Gateway and recently Asda, with the Dales brand, are attempting such a dual branding strategy.

Linking the Safeway and Presto operations permitted Argyll the economies of scale and scope it needed to be an efficient national operator. It allowed Argyll's other store chain Lo Cost to be operated separately as it was more geographically focused in the North of England and Scotland. The store conversion and infrastructure programme cost the group some £1 billion. By 1991, the conversion programme had run its course. Further growth in stores had now to be new openings.

Argyll had thus operated a concurrent strategy of store conversion, new openings and store closures. Much of the finance for this programme came from cash flow and borrowings. In 1991, the group raised £386m net of costs in a 1-for-6 rights issue. This new capital was to be used to fund the next phase in the company's development plan that envisaged some 20 new store openings a year. The cost of each new store amounted to about £1.5m for the site and about £10m for the building cost. Each new store took on average 55 weeks to complete. All the major retailing groups have ambitious store opening programmes.

Table 3.3 depicts the scale of the Safeway store development programme since the acquisition was made and the Presto conversion programme completed.

Table 3.3 Safeway store development 1989–91[1]

	1987	1988	1989	1990	1991
Sales area (000 sq. ft)	2,006	2,873	4,265	5,436	6,001
– net increase (%)	3.1	43.2	48.5	27.5	10.6
New stores opened	2	21	19	23	18
Average size (000 sq. ft)	29	23	29	30	28
Presto transfers and conversions	—	22	51	34	9
Average size (000 sq. ft)	—	18	18	17	18
Size analysis:					
– over 20,000 sq. ft	27	49	82	110	130
– 10–20,000 sq. ft	75	94	124	146	152
– under 10,000 sq. ft	31	33	34	35	28
Number of stores	133	176	240	291	310
Average size of all stores (000 sq. ft)	15	16	18	19	19

1. By 1992 the planned conversion of Presto stores to Safeway stores was completed and Argyll Plc added a further 17 new Safeway stores to their portfolio, increasing the sales area by a further 642,000 square feet. The group planned a further 25 new Safeway store openings in 1993.

Source: Company reports.

The Argyll retailing strategy of creating a Safeway culture differentiated from its rivals involved an apparent value-added approach consisting of the creation in the stores of added service provision along with strong own-label presence and quality fresh produce displayed in an attractive manner. This included bakeries, post offices, dry-cleaning services, cafés and, in some stores, crèches. In keeping with its rivals, Argyll's new sites had retail petrol for its customers. Safeway's other distinguishing feature was its close links with its customers through the customers' panel. Safeway operated between 15,000 to 20,000 lines and serviced around 6 million customers per week. By March 1992 the following specialist departments were evident in the Safeway stores: Delicatessens 317, Bakeries 275, Petrol Stations 31, Pharmacies 53, Coffee Shops 49, Post Offices 10 and Dry Cleaners 10.

The international alliance that Argyll formed with its partners Ahold and Casino had begun to reap some early benefits. Fifty Casino own-label recipes were transferred to the Safeway brand in the UK. Other buying economies from the AMS grouping were expected to filter through in the near term as the Alliance strategy matures.

In keeping with the overall strategy of the group, Argyll had invested heavily in scanning technology, becoming the first national player to achieve 100 per cent scanned sales. This would effectively allow further savings to be made in logistics and distribution systems. A new enlarged division was created in 1992 to make the advantages of scanned data more strategic in nature and help deliver a further enhanced quality of service to Safeway customers in the area of fresh produce. Improved stock-holding from scanned data had improved inventory control.

Other food activities

The bulk of the group's sales and profits came from the Safeway business. This did not mean that Argyll had neglected the Presto and Lo Cost operations. The section of the business not involved in Safeway included the Snowking and Mojo cash and carry and a small retail liquor and wholesale drinks business. In 1991, Argyll divested itself of the drinks businesses and finally severed the link with the past strategy of the former chairman, James Gulliver.

The Presto conversion had depressed sales turnover in this part of the group. No new stores were planned to be opened under the Presto fascia, and only two new shops were commissioned under the Lo Cost marque in 1990–91. The group planned to change this strategy in 1993/94 and strengthen its position in the mid-sized and discount end of the retail market. Five Presto stores and ten Lo Cost stores were planned to be built in 1993 and further store openings were likely as the discount brand was strengthened to meet the challenge from Kwik Save, Asda's Dales brand and the continental new entrants into the UK grocery market, namely Aldi and Netto. Table 3.4 shows the stores profile of the Argyll Group.

Table 3.4 Stores profile for the Argyll Group 1988–92

		1992	1991	1990	1989	1988
Safeway						
– Number of stores		322	310	291	240	176
– Sales area	(000 sq. ft)	6,424	6,011	5,436	4,265	2,873
– Average size	(sq. ft)	20,000	19,400	18,680	17,771	16,324
Presto						
– Number of stores		212	215	227	270	488
– Sales area	(000 sq. ft)	1,132	1,157	1,356	2,041	3,520
– Average size	(sq. ft)	5,300	5,400	5,970	7,560	7,213
Lo Cost						
– Number of stores		285	298	320	353	288
– Sales area	(000 sq. ft)	888	913	935	1,003	801
– Average size	(sq. ft)	3,100	3,100	2,921	2,841	2,780
Total						
– Number of stores		819	823	838	863	952
– Sales area	(000 sq. ft)	8,444	8,081	7,727	7,309	7,194

THE RETAIL GROCERY INDUSTRY/MARKET

Introduction

To fully grasp the issues and the dynamics of the UK retail grocery market it is necessary to focus on the supplier side (the food industry), as well as the retailers.

The food industry by the early 1990s had undergone a number of important structural changes at the domestic as well as the European level. The industry, through merger and acquisition, had sharply increased in concentration and progressively the smaller, under-resourced competitors had become increasingly vulnerable due to the rising costs of branding. At the European level, the industry witnessed a sharp increase in European merger and acquisition activity, the formation of cross-border marketing and distribution agreements, and attempts by the large groups to create pan-European brands. The European food groups were increasingly challenged by the large US food groups that saw growth prospects in the European market as opportunities for their global development. This opportunity was in part due to the opening up of the Eastern European markets.

Structural change on the retail side was no less significant. At the domestic level, the UK saw a polarization of the retail environment, increasing retailer concentration thus raising their power over suppliers, increasing sophistication in interactions with suppliers, and the creation of very efficient distribution and logistical systems that made UK retailers among the most profitable retailers in Europe. At the European level, cross-border expansion and the formation of pan-European retailing alliances were among the most significant structural changes.

The UK grocery market

The UK retail grocery sector in 1978 had some 71,000 retail outlets spread between the multiples, the cooperatives and the independents. By 1990, this total figure had fallen to 42,446. Market share by value for the multiples rose from 52 per cent to 75 per cent during that period, with corresponding falls for the cooperatives and the independent sectors. This market share gain was primarily at the expense of the small shopkeeper. While the number of store units had fallen during the period, the average size of trading unit had risen, so by 1990, the UK grocery market had an aggregate 58.4 million square feet of sales space. This represented about 5,838 square feet per 1,000 of the population. In 1978, average operating margins were around 1.8 per cent, with Tesco as market leader. Asda was the most profitable retailer in the sector with pre-tax margins of 4.9 per cent. By 1992, the positions had changed markedly, with Sainsbury as market leader both in market share as well as profitability terms.

The 1980s was a decade of mergers and acquisitions that saw the development of the 'super group'. Kingfisher, Dixons, Burton, Tesco, Sainsbury, Argyll and Marks & Spencer, to name but a few, were all M&A players, either in the domestic market or in the cross-border sector. The significant point behind the 1980s was that the leading food retailers moved away from being merchants to now become fully responsible for product development, supply chain management and distribution. Their enhanced margins reflected this increased role which they relished. Previously, food retailers were subsidiaries of companies that operated in the food business; now the main grocery retailers were fully focused food retailers.

The multiples saw their market share grow to such an extent that by 1990, 7,200 of the largest stores were responsible for nearly 85 per cent of total sales in a market valued at £40bn. In keeping with this concentration of retailer power, town centre landscapes changed. The large multiples sited their large new superstores in new edge-of-town sites or in suburban centres, each new store being in excess of 25,000 sq. ft, with parking for several hundred cars and facilities for the motorist like petrol. The grocery retailers had branched out into petrol retailing, challenging the established players like Shell and Esso. Table 3.5 below gives the market share positions of the main players in the UK grocery market for the years 1987–91.

Table 3.5 UK grocery market share 1987–91

	1987 %	1988 %	1989 %	1990 %	1991 %
J. Sainsbury	13.9	14.3	14.5	16.0	16.7
Tesco	13.5	14.3	14.9	15.3	16.2
Safeway	9.9	10.9	11.0	11.0	11.3
Asda	7.6	7.8	7.9	10.5	10.5
Gateway	11.5	11.8	11.2	8.0	7.3
Kwik Save	3.0	3.0	3.5	3.9	4.4
Waitrose	2.7	2.6	2.6	2.5	2.5
Morrison	1.6	1.7	1.9	2.2	2.3
Iceland	0.5	0.6	1.8	1.9	1.9
Other multiples	7.7	5.2	5.0	1.0	3.2
Cooperatives	12.1	11.7	11.3	11.0	10.7
Independents	14.6	11.4	14.0	13.7	13.0

Source: Verdict, IGD Research Services.

Trends and other issues

The UK recession of the early 1990s was acute, and had seriously affected a number of industrial sectors. Poor retail sales, low consumer confidence and high real interest rates had their effects on the retail sector. The food sector was one of the few areas of the economy that had been largely unaffected by the recession, but concerns about the sector's continued growth were present among some analysts, although most agreed that there was at least ten more years of growth and expansion in this sector. The sector in the long run was likely to be affected by the recession and tougher market conditions if the economy continued in its depressed state into 1993 and beyond.

Financial results by the top groups in this sector had shown little increase in volume on a like-for-like basis. Sales volume rises had been generated from new store openings and from geographic expansion. This trend was likely to continue for the foreseeable future, as all the main players had ambitious new store opening programmes. J. Sainsbury, for instance, had earmarked £800m a year for new stores.

New stores, larger stores and more stores all contributed to increasing benefits of scale, and along with changing sales mixes towards the higher margin fresh produce and ready prepared dishes and other services, enabled store groups to maintain their margins. Absolute scale economies would be likely to plateau as stores reached optimum size and advantages from infrastructure and information technology investment peaked.

While consumer confidence and the continuing poor performance of the economy brought their own problems to the food retailers, other more pressing issues continued to dominate the sector. This was to be the market entry of the continental groups Aldi and Netto into the UK at the discount end of the market, and the small-scale emergence of the warehouse idea from the USA. The warehouse idea was the ultimate 'pile it high and sell it cheap' concept. Other competitive threats from the continent of Europe in the form of the French groups Leclerc and Continent and the German group Tengleman were not to be dismissed. A likely entry strategy into the UK market by a large European player would be through the acquisition of one of the weaker UK groups. Likely candidates were the troubled Gateway group and possibly Asda. Both firms have struggled in the recession due to high debt gearing and poor sales performances.

UK grocery's high margins were potentially attractive to relatively low margin but powerful European groups. European food retailers believed that their UK rivals were less competitive and that the UK was a 'soft' market. As Peter Martin of the Belgium group Delhaize put it:

> We would like to be as profitable as Sainsbury, but unlike British stores we have to operate in a highly competitive market. We have more competition in Belgium, both from other supermarkets and independent shops. The result is a tradition of low prices.

Sergio Dias, a Carrefour executive, agreed with this statement:

> There is more emphasis on convenience stores in the UK, while in France we have many more hypermarkets which deliberately pursue a low margin policy.

A number of factors could be said to contribute to higher margins in the UK than elsewhere in Europe. Distribution and logistical systems, widespread use of scan data, complex supplier relationships, own-brand development and the demise of the independent are major contributory factors. Many mainland European groups are still family owned and are not listed companies and thus enjoy less market pressure on them than their UK rivals. A further reason could be that while UK customers want value for money, they are less price driven than their European cousins. UK store groups have responded to this customer characteristic by developing the appropriate strategy.

The competitive battleground has been enlarged, as grocery retailers have attempted to increase their service package and draw in more customers. By 1997, it has been estimated that UK grocery retailers will command around 20 per cent of the retail petrol market. Supermarket petrol retailing offers the customer petrol from a basic filling station at prices of 10–15 pence a gallon cheaper than at existing branded petrol stations. In 1992, Tesco operated 151 petrol stations with plans to build a further 20, Safeway operated 37 stations with plans for 20 or so new sites, and J. Sainsbury had 100 petrol stations in service with plans for a further 100 units. Market leaders Esso and Shell are potentially threatened.

Retailer alliances

The continued long-term organic growth in national markets is believed to be limited. Growth via the merger and acquisition route is also seen as being restricted due to competition regulation at both the domestic and the EC level. This means that grocery retailers have turned to alliances and have formed international buying groups as an alternative growth method strategy. These alliances operate on a voluntary basis, and some involve cross-shareholding, the objective of which is to allow for operational, buying and marketing synergies to accrue to member firms. Table 3.6 shows the extent of such alliances, and excludes the European Retail Alliance which is discussed separately later.

Table 3.6 Major pan-European buying groups

Buying group	Location	Members	Purchasing power in Europe (est. $US)
Intercoop	Denmark	Coop(I), Coop(CH), CWS(UK), EKA(SF), FDB(DK), FNCC(F), KF(S), Konsum(A), NKL(NI), SOK(SF)	51.8bn
Deuro-Buying	Switzerland	Asda(UK), Carrefour(F), Makro(NI), Metro(D)	39.6bn
CEM (Cooperation Européenne de Marketing)	Belgium	Conad(I), Crai(I), Edeka(D), UDA(E), Booker(UK)[3]	34.3bn
Difra	France	Ariaud(F), Casino(F), Catteau(F), Co-op Normandie-Picardie(F), Delhaize(B), Montlaur(F), Rallye(F), SCA Monoprix(F), Zanin(I)	22.6bn
Eurogroup	Germany[1]	GIB(B), HOKI(Dk), Rewe(D), Vendex(NI)	23.7bn
Intergroup Trading	Netherlands	Despar(I), Spar(A), Spar(B), Spar(D), Spar(E), Spar(UK), Spar(NI)	20.7bn[2]
EMD (European Marketing Distribution)	Switzerland	Selex(I), Markant(NI), Markant(D), Selex(E), Sodadip(F), Uniarme(P), ZEV(A)	15% of European food market

1. Two additional purchasing offices in Italy and Spain.
2. Specializes in purchase of fresh fruit and vegetables. Worldwide figure.
3. Joined January 1992.

Source: Euromonitor (1991), Burt (1991).

THE EUROPEAN RETAIL ALLIANCE

Argyll, Casino and Ahold were the founding members of the European Retail Alliance (ERA), which they set up at the end of 1989. This alliance, while being voluntary, includes an element of cross-shareholdings between each of the members. The ERA is linked to another operational organization, Associated Marketing Services (AMS), which in turn has another nine retailing members affiliated to it. Table 3.7 shows the membership and its geographic coverage.

The AMS with its 11 members controls 13,439 retail outlets, visited weekly by 50 million customers, services more than 130 million consumers and has an estimated combined purchasing power of about 11 per cent of the European food market.

The relationship between the individual retailer and the AMS is managed by a designated senior executive in each company. These coordinators meet formally on

Table 3.7 Membership of the Associated Marketing Services Group

Group member	Country of domicile	Number of stores
Ahold	Netherlands	945
Allkauf	Germany	235
Argyll	UK	853
Casino	France	3,223
Dansk Supermarked[1]	Denmark	250
Hagen Gruppen	Norway	264
ICA	Sweden	3,100
Kesko	Finland	3,445
Mercadonna	Spain	125
Migros	Switzerland	541
Rinacente	Italy	696
Superquinn	Republic of Ireland	12

1. Dansk Supermarked left the AMS in 1992.

Source: AMS (1991).

a four-week routine cycle, or more frequently if necessary. In addition to the activities of the coordinators, relationships exist at the product buyer level among the retailers so as to pool experience and to discuss matters relating to supplier selection, promotions, quality specifications, physical distribution, new product launches and the development of fighting brands. The AMS has identified a number of areas of mutual benefit to member firms and their suppliers. The possible areas of opportunity AMS has identified were as follows:

- development of existing business;
- coordination of supplies;
- coordination of promotional support;
- introduction and market testing of new products;
- standardization of product and packaging;
- introduction of suppliers to new markets;
- coordination of distribution;
- development of merchandising and promotional presentation materials;
- coordination of own-brand development;
- material sourcing for own-brand suppliers;
- assistance in production and distribution;
- operation of stockholding;
- management of temporary supply shortages;
- a forum for retailer/supplier issues.

The AMS itself works through marketing coordinators assigned by participating companies to work on behalf of the alliance on a full-time basis. These coordinators in turn have direct access to the marketing and buying executives of the member firms and work closely with and through them.

Trends in tastes, lifestyles and choices for the European consumer appear to be converging and own-brand retailers wish to reflect this trend in much the same way as the branded producer. A number of illustrations of this can be evidenced from recent successes of the AMS. In October 1991 the AMS announced the launch of a pan-European kitchen towel through all AMS stores, with the exception of Migros. This low priced product provided on its wrapping product information in the languages of the AMS members. Ten million packs were produced in the first year of supply. In addition to the paper towel, the AMS, in conjunction with a French baby care products manufacturer, launched a baby's disposable nappy under a unified brand name throughout its stores. The manufacturer put in dedicated production capacity for the production of this product. Other areas of cooperation will be developed in future. Orange juice, light bulbs, dry cells and food brand and recipe exchanges are planned. An executive at the AMS summed this development as follows:

> For a long time, manufacturers we spoke to said it was impossible to create a common product for Europe. Now we have demonstrated what top brand suppliers were not able to do.

The driving forces for such buying alliances are that they spread the risk of development and accelerated learning can potentially overcome very real mobility barriers. As one executive from the AMS put it:

> The purpose of the company (AMS) is to work with manufacturers and suppliers of branded, non-branded and own-label goods and services to identify opportunities to improve the efficiency of the supply chain, to reduce the cost of goods and services, and to share in the benefits from this cooperation.

ENDPIECE

Towards the end of 1992, Argyll Group acquired nine stores in Northern England from the Jackson Grandway Group and converted one into a Safeway store and the other eight into the Presto format.

On 18 December 1992, Tesco announced the acquisition of a controlling interest in the French grocery retailer Catteau for a consideration of FFr 1.47bn. Catteau controlled 90 stores in northern France and is a member of the buying alliance Difra. This was Tesco's first foreign acquisition, but is its move into Europe the beginnings of a trend for the big UK food retailers? How will the other big two respond?

Towards the end of 1992, J. Sainsbury announced that it was to launch an aggressive package of price cuts early in the new year (1993). The announcement raised fears that a damaging price war could follow.

REFERENCES

Argyll Plc (1991) *The Argyll Story*. UK, Argyll Plc.

Burt, S. (1991) 'Trends in the internationalization of grocery retailing: the European experience', *International Review of Retail, Distribution and Consumer Research*, Vol. 1, No. 4, pp. 487–515.

Euromonitor (1991) *Europe's Major Retailers 1991*. London, Euromonitor.

APPENDIX 3.1
ARGYLL GROUP PLC: DETAILED ACCOUNTS

Table 3.8 Argyll Group Plc – Profit and loss accounts 1990–92 (year ended 31 March)

	1992 £m	1991 £m	1990 £m
Sales turnover	5,039.3	4,757.5	4,143.3
Value added tax	(310.1)	(261.4)	(223.3)
Turnover ex value added tax	4,729.2	4,496.1	3,920.0
Cost of sales	(3,662.8)	(3,551.6)	(3,121.0)
Gross profit	1,066.4	944.5	799.0
Net operating expenses	(735.4)	(655.2)	(574.4)
Operating profit	331.0	285.3	224.6
Investment income	2.5	2.6	—
Net interest receivable	31.0	2.9	19.0
Profit on ordinary activities before taxation and exceptional item	364.5	290.8	243.6
Exceptional item	—	—	(16.1)
Profit on ordinary activities before taxation	364.5	290.8	227.5
Taxation	(102.1)	(81.4)	(68.3)
Profit before extraordinary item	262.4	209.4	159.2
Extraordinary item	78.3[1]	—	4.1
Profit for the financial year	340.7	209.4	163.3
Dividends	(108.3)	(82.5)	(68.6)
Retained profit for the year	232.4	126.9	94.7
Retained profit, beginning of year	404.7	277.8	183.1
Retained profit, end of year	637.1	404.7	277.8

1. 'Extraordinary item' comprises £100m received by the company from Guinness Plc in settlement of a claim resulting from the failure of the company's bid for the Distillers Company Plc in April 1986, net of £1.9m in costs and £19.8m in taxation.

Table 3.9 Argyll Group Plc – Balance sheets 1990–92 (year ended 31 March)

	1992 £m	1991 £m	1990 £m
Fixed assets			
Tangible fixed assets	1,684.3	1,324.7	1,047.9
Investments	67.4	65.0	69.9
Total fixed assets	1,751.7	1,389.7	1,117.8
Current assets			
Stocks	262.9	308.2	283.1
Debtors	150.4	117.6	90.8
Investments and deposits	516.5	122.0	229.9
Cash at bank and in hand	78.0	92.0	
Total current assets	1,007.8	639.8	603.8
Current liabilities (due within one year)			
Bank overdrafts	(63.8)	(73.5)	(59.4)
Loans	(173.9)	(98.8)	(67.5)
Other creditors	(902.5)	(824.2)	(790.9)
Net current assets/(liabilities)	(132.4)	(356.7)	(314.0)
Total assets less current liabilities	1,619.3	1,033.0	803.8
Creditors (due after one year)			
Loans	(157.6)	(207.4)	(114.3)
Deferred taxation	(15.1)	(10.2)	(6.4)
Net worth	1,446.3	815.4	683.1
Capital and reserves			
Called-up share capital	278.3	237.3	236.3
Share premium account	530.9	173.4	168.8
Profit and loss account	637.1	404.7	277.8
Total shareholders' funds	1,446.3	815.4	683.1

APPENDIX 3.2
KEY RATIOS – ARGYLL, THE INDUSTRY AND KEY COMPETITORS

Table 3.10 Argyll Group

No.	Description	2/4/88	1/4/89	31/3/90	30/3/91	28/3/92
701	Return on s'holders equity %	23.49	24.37	23.61	25.56	17.96
707	Return on capital employed %	29.63	24.49	25.78	25.89	20.63
713	Operating profit margin %	4.43	4.48	5.24	6.27	6.91
716	Pre-tax profit margin %	4.85	5.11	5.80	6.47	7.62
717	Net profit margin %	3.15	3.32	3.77	4.30	5.17
725	Stock ratio (days)	27.68	27.45	26.36	25.02	20.29
727	Debtors' ratio (days)	4.83	5.62	6.97	7.78	9.51
729	Creditors' ratio (days)	55.38	61.21	61.98	58.11	57.66
741	Working capital ratio	0.88	0.75	0.64	0.62	0.86
762	Sales per employee	54,379	55,225	60,625	68,021	72,053
763	Operating profit per employee	2,408	2,474	3,175	4,268	4,982
764	Capital employed/ employee	9,170	11,857	14,160	17,955	27,945
792	Cash earnings per share	14.97	17.34	21.19	26.34	30.24

Source: Datastream, output from Program 190. Reproduced with permission.

Table 3.11 Food retailing – UK

No.	Description	10/6/87	24/6/88	7/7/89	7/7/90	11/7/91
701	Return on s'holders equity %	19.60	18.13	19.72	18.56	17.42
707	Return on capital employed %	23.26	21.46	21.27	20.46	19.76
713	Operating profit margin %	4.76	4.85	5.39	5.62	5.92
716	Pre-tax profit margin %	5.04	5.27	5.62	5.55	5.62
717	Net profit margin %	3.30	3.46	3.74	3.63	3.74
725	Stock ratio (days)	24.94	22.07	22.41	22.55	21.67
727	Debtors' ratio (days)	6.73	7.82	8.78	8.76	8.94
729	Creditors' ratio (days)	48.84	44.45	48.37	50.34	48.57
741	Working capital ratio	0.70	0.83	0.67	0.60	0.66
762	Sales per employee	59,632	66,210	65,054	69,658	74,747
763	Operating profit per employee	2,841	3,209	3,509	3,913	4,421
764	Capital employed/ employee	13,903	17,533	19,288	22,108	25,243

Source: Datastream, output from Program 190. Reproduced with permission.

Table 3.12 J. Sainsbury

No.	Description	19/3/88	18/3/89	17/3/90	16/3/91	14/3/92
701	Return on s'holders equity %	18.71	19.82	20.48	20.81	16.42
707	Return on capital employed %	22.28	20.46	21.90	22.90	21.43
713	Operating profit margin %	5.67	6.12	6.30	6.92	7.11
716	Pre-tax profit margin %	5.85	5.95	6.05	6.47	7.26
717	Net profit margin %	3.96	4.01	4.04	4.38	4.98
725	Stock ratio (days)	18.25	18.45	16.24	16.85	15.20
727	Debtors' ratio (days)	2.42	6.28	5.00	5.43	3.39
729	Creditors' ratio (days)	45.72	46.90	44.78	45.20	42.73
741	Working capital ratio	0.37	0.36	0.42	0.41	0.55
762	Sales per employee	58,004	64,101	69,303	71,690	77,099
763	Operating profit per employee	3,290	3,921	4,369	4,964	5,482
764	Capital employed/ employee	17,628	22,488	23,567	24,861	30,454
792	Cash earnings per share	17.02	20.12	25.33	30.64	30.96

Source: Datastream, output from Program 190. Reproduced with permission.

Table 3.13 Tesco

No.	Description	27/2/88	25/2/89	24/2/90	23/2/91	29/2/92
701	Return on s'holders equity %	16.65	17.03	17.40	13.04	15.45
707	Return on capital employed %	19.54	21.80	22.34	17.42	19.05
713	Operating profit margin %	4.95	5.57	5.86	6.27	6.76
716	Pre-tax profit margin %	5.44	5.62	6.05	6.57	7.68
717	Net profit margin %	3.53	3.72	3.93	4.27	5.14
725	Stock ratio (days)	15.86	14.87	14.38	13.31	11.40
727	Debtors' ratio (days)	3.52	2.12	1.43	1.53	1.89
729	Creditors' ratio (days)	37.37	43.03	45.18	44.16	45.36
741	Working capital ratio	0.50	0.48	0.34	0.68	0.60
762	Sales per employee	57,802	62,356	64,908	72,371	81,548
763	Operating profit per employee	2,858	3,475	3,807	4,539	5,509
764	Capital employed/ employee	17,220	18,430	20,064	30,794	36,349
792	Cash earnings per share	14.26	15.94	19.45	24.47	26.53

Source: Datastream, output from Program 190. Reproduced with permission.

Burton and Next – the changing high street

C.M. Clarke-Hill

INTRODUCTION

Overview of the UK retail market

The boom period of the mid 1980s, often termed the 'Lawson Boom' after the then Chancellor of the Exchequer Nigel Lawson, gave way to one of the longest periods of economic recession in the UK since the 1930s. This recessionary period began towards the end of 1989 and by March 1994 the first signs of confirmation that the UK economy was beginning to emerge from the worst aspects of that recession was evident. Manufacturing output was slowly rising, unemployment falling and retail sales, after a very patchy Christmas 1993 period, began to show signs of growth.

In the first quarter of 1994 the following overall trends were apparent from the published macro-economic figures:

- *Employment.* The number of people out of work and claiming benefit in February 1994 stood at the seasonally adjusted figure of 2,751,800, or 9.8 per cent of the workforce. In 1993, most of the new jobs that were created were mainly part time and mostly for women. The trend towards part-time employment in the retailing sector continued, and these types of jobs were being created at the fastest rate over the period 1991–93. It was estimated that by the end of the decade, that there would be more economically active women in the labour force than men.
- *Average earnings.* The first small rise in average earnings was observed for the first time since February 1992. The underlying increase in earnings in the 12 months to January 1994 was 3.25 per cent.
- *Retail sales volumes.* Following a sharp fall in the period 1991–92, retail sales began an upward trend. The Christmas 1993 period and the early part of 1994 saw retail sales fairly flat. The food sector and the mail-order sector were the only parts of the retail trade that showed significant rises. While retail volumes were shown to be rising, retail values were still flat. There was evidence of heavy discounting and/or out-of-season promotion activity driving the market. Retailers were fighting for every consumer pound.

In the March 1993 budget, the Chancellor announced that VAT would be imposed on fuel, power and light in a two-staged increase. In April 1994, gas, electricity and domestic fuel would attract a VAT rate of 8 per cent, rising to the full rate of 17.5 per cent by April 1995. Further taxation changes were announced by the UK government in the autumn of 1993, which would raise the taxation level of ordinary households by an estimated £1,000 a year by 1995. This rise in taxation was designed to offset an increasing public sector deficit, and the government was of the opinion that the tax rises would not jeopardize the recovery. In tandem with the taxation increases, the government systematically reduced interest charges in a series of steps, to the level where bank base rate stood at 5.25 per cent at the end of February 1994. This level contrasted with the very high bank base rates of the early 1990s that reversed the 'Lawson Boom' of the 1980s.

The recession in the UK produced a number of very serious effects for retailing companies like Next and Burton. As interest rates rose, manufacturing output fell and unemployment and job security suffered, affecting consumer confidence. Many householders, urged to purchase their homes in the 1980s, saw their property values fall sharply as interest rates rose. People who had borrowed heavily to fund their house purchase were particularly badly affected. The recession reversed the trend of sharply rising house prices and the housing market collapsed leaving many householders with 'negative equity', a position where a householder's mortgage debt is worth more than the market value of the house. Repossessions and falling mobility aggravated an already poor set of market conditions.

The problems of the property market were not only confined to the housing sector. Commercial property companies were particularly badly affected. A number of spectacular failures of property companies were reported, the most notable being Olympia and York, the developer of Canary Wharf. The 'Lawson Boom' and the optimism of the Thatcher decade fuelled an office building spree in advance of an expected demand that never materialized. Large office buildings remained unlet, and rents collapsed.

The 1980s boom increased the number of shops that retail companies controlled, and these retailers paid premium prices and rents for their sites. The recession saw many store groups financially over-stretched with rising costs and falling sales. Prices were unable to match these costs, and discounting and out-of-season sales were the tactics used by many retailers to reduce stocks and maintain volumes. This state of affairs was particularly severe on fashion retailers like Next, Burton, Storehouse and Sears, to name only four. As profits collapsed, managements at these groups were forced into rethinking their business policies and strategies. It was ironic that in the mid to late 1980s, the retail groups Next, Burton and Storehouse were seen as dynamic, design orientated and fashion leaders in the British high street. These firms expanded by acquisition and often diversified their interests thus complicating their businesses. Acquisition was a key strategy to increase retail space quickly, but as this strategy was often predicated against high corporate debt, the recessionary effects were particularly poignant.

Retail landscapes were changed in the 1980s. The food retailers built more and larger superstores on the edge of town, retail parks and retail zones were being created outside towns, and in many parts of the UK, town centres were affected. In Dudley, for instance, the development of the Merry Hill shopping centre reduced the town centre to vacant and boarded up shops as the established retailers like Marks & Spencer, BhS, Burton and Next moved to the new facility. Their vacant shops were taken up by discounters and short-stay lets. This out-of-town move by retailers was seen by government as potentially problematical. Planning permission guidelines were replaced by PPG 13 in March 1994 that addressed the need to reduce car journeys and, with PPG 6, wished to create 'a suitable balance in providing for retail development between town centres and out of town retail facilities'. Developments would be vetoed unless there was evidence that the result of the development would not undermine the vitality and viability of the town centre. (See *Financial Times*, 30 March 1994, p. 20.)

Employment changes in the high street

Retailer organizations which were forced to review their operations in the difficult market conditions in the early 1990s looked at their cost base first. Apart from the usual and company-specific reorganizations and restructuring, a more general trend was observable. Personnel costs in service-based businesses like retailing are an important source of cost in the retail value chain. Shop groups reconsidered their employment policies in an attempt to rebuild their margins. Retail groups like Allied Maples, Burton, Sock Shop and BhS began to adopt a policy of employing more workers on part-time contracts. They did this by switching full-time workers to part-time contracts with increased hourly rates to compensate for loss of earnings. Both Sock Shop and the Burton Group announced such moves in January 1993. Sock Shop redeployed its 400 full-timers to part-time status; Burton similarly announced that nearly 1,000 full-time jobs would be lost and up to 3,000 part-time jobs would be created.

There were several incentives for employers to switch employees' contracts in this way. It could create genuine increases in flexibility, allowing more staff in the shops at busy or peak times. It could also be popular with some employees. However, cost saving was the main factor for this shift in employment pattern for most retailers. An employee who worked less than 15 hours per week, or earned less that £56, did not have to be covered for National Insurance. When that threshold was reached, then National Insurance was paid on all hours worked. Moreover, any employee who worked for less than 16 hours a week did not qualify for employment protection or for any of the statutory benefits that were granted under employment legislation. It was for these reasons that this trend towards part-time workers seemed likely to continue in the retail sector. However, a recent House of Lords ruling on the subject has reversed some of these issues. Certain statutory rights previously denied to part-time workers could after all apply because of employment legislation at the EU level in the form of the European Union's working time directive. Aspects of the Social Chapter of the Maastricht Treaty, which the UK government had negotiated an opt-out of, may after all be binding on the UK. However, the earnings threshold and the National Insurance rules still applied as did rules on maternity benefits for part-time workers, but any major changes in part-time employment rules would affect retail companies.

Changes in retail employment were further mirrored by changes in shopping behaviour in the 1990s. Sunday opening, while against the law in some sectors in England and Wales, has become increasingly popular with the public. Changes in legislation now mean that Sunday opening for all classes of retail business has been legalized and the law simplified. Large retail shops will be allowed to open for six hours on Sunday from 10 a.m. to 4 p.m.

John Hoerner, the Burton chief executive, justified his company's employment policy as follows:

> There is no question about the fact that as social trends change, and more and more people work and so want to shop outside traditional shopping hours, there will be more part-time workers.

THE BURTON GROUP PLC

The Burton Group is one of the UK's largest store groups, operating, 1,800 shops in a variety of target markets in the men's and women's clothing sector. Burton had always followed a strategy of differentiation, catering for a wide market in clothing and fashion. Collectively, Burton's trading divisions cover 95 per cent of the British population with its 1,800 shops. This differentiation through trading format and brand has meant that Burton's customers were often not aware of the size of the company and did not readily associate the different trading formats and brands as belonging to the Burton Group. Table 4.1 shows the Burton store profile.

The Burton Group's fortunes have improved dramatically since it was nearly over-taken by debts that had accumulated as a result of ill-judged property speculation and over-expansion in the 1980s. The company had two rights issues, first in 1991 and then in 1993, designed to restore the health of the company's balance sheet.

Table 4.1 The Burton Group market profile for 1993–94

Division	Target market SEG[1]	Target age (years)	Solus shops	Shops in shops
Burtons Formal/casual menswear	C1–C2	25–45	377	38
Dorothy Perkins Womenswear	C1–C2	20–45	433	108
Evans Womenswear size 16+	C1,C2,D	20–55	209	88
IS Value discount retailer	C2,D,E	20–55	46	3
Principles for Men Formal/casual menswear	A,B,C1	25–35	119	57
Principles for Women Formal/casual womenswear	A,B,C1	30–40	115	80
Top Man Young menswear	C1,C2	15–25	177	53
Top Shop Young womenswear	All	15–20	157	90
Debenhams Men/women/children/home	A,B,C1,C2	25–65	86	25

1. Target market classified by the National Readership Survey socio-economic grouping (SEG).

Source: Burton Group.

Gearing was sharply reduced to the 23 per cent it stood at in August 1993. Table 4.2 gives a five-year trading summary of the Burton Group.

The Burton Group had suffered pre-tax losses for three years, and it was not until 1993 that the Group turned in a pre-tax profit. Much of this turnaround was due to Burton's American-born chief executive, John Hoerner.

Hoerner had succeeded Laurence Cooklin, Burton's chief executive, who resigned from the group in February 1992. That year, a number of significant changes were made in Burton's senior management group designed to strengthen the team and to turn Burton's around. This task fell to John Hoerner. One of his first tasks was to conduct a major review of the Burton Group's businesses, from trading formats, target markets and sales promotion through to management structure and employment policies.

Hoerner created a group management board that consisted of the top 17 executives within Burton's. This board was made responsible for the operations of the group and played an important part in the planning and strategic activity for the company. The management board met every two weeks to ensure that a common approach to the business was shared. The establishment of the management board was seen as an essential step towards recovery. In the words of one Burton executive:

> We needed a mechanism that would enable the separate businesses to cooperate for the good of themselves and the Group overall. The Burton Group has no *raison d'être* unless it can create synergy and get more out of the divisions than would be possible if they were stand-alone businesses.

In May 1992, the Multiples Sector and Services Sector were dismantled and brought together as one central group function, and a new post of group operations director

Table 4.2 Burton Plc: Five-year trading history 1989–93

	1993 £m	1992 £m	1991 £m	1990 £m	1989 £m
Turnover	1,893.1	1,764.6	1,661.1	1,788.7	1,808.0
Retail profit	60.9	35.3	46.2	194.8	255.3
Other income	6.4	1.4	(2.2)	2.3	3.2
Interest and similar charges	(29.2)	(27.3)	(32.8)	(51.0)	(41.7)
Profit before exceptional items	38.1	9.4	11.2	146.1	216.8
Exceptional items	(19.6)	(10.2)	(192.6)	(170.9)	—
Profit/(loss) before taxation	18.5	(0.8)	(181.4)	(24.8)	216.8
Taxation	(4.6)	10.2	16.0	37.2	71.6
Profit/(loss) after taxation	13.9	9.4	(165.4)	12.4	145.2
Dividends	(28.0)	(22.4)	(22.4)	(33.6)	(51.2)
Retained earnings/(deficits)	(14.1)	(13.0)	(187.8)	(21.2)	94.0
Shareholders' funds	853.1	701.1	714.1	741.3	708.9
Earnings/(loss) per share					
– after exceptional items (pence)	1.1	0.8	(23.9)	1.9	21.8
– before exceptional items (pence)	2.3	0.8	1.6	15.7	21.8
Dividends per share (pence)	2.0	2.0	2.6	5.0	7.7

Source: Company accounts.

was created. The managing directors of all the retail divisions reported directly to Hoerner as chief executive officer.

The priority in 1992 was to develop highly defined trading strategies for each division that made strategic sense within the division itself, but which covered all the major market sectors targeted by Burton's, and to minimize internal competition among the competing brands.

The 1992 strategy was based around the following points:

- sharing strengths;
- service redefined;
- domination of the sector;
- concept development;
- retail fundamentals;
- getting the price right.

These key elements in the strategy were to be centred around a focus on presentation and to optimize the assets at the company's disposal. Hoerner's view was that Burton had to focus on 'retail basics' and trade their way out of trouble.

Hoerner's approach was designed to reverse the poor results of the past and to change the Burton culture. This accent on change was to return to the retail fundamentals and the old retailer adage that 'retail is detail'. Burton's response to the 1980s recession was a mixture of panic and poor detail. Merchandise quality was upgraded, clear ticketing on the merchandise was instituted and fewer mark-downs and mark-ups were to occur. Customers instinctively knew the price/value relationship of the clothes they purchase. If a shop was perceived as not knowing the price/value relationship correctly then customers would not purchase. Mark-downs were costly, and sales out of season could seriously damage a store's image. Presentation, marketing, pricing and basic retailer detail needed to be reinforced at Burton. This Hoerner implemented in 1992.

While 1992 was a year of far-reaching change for the Burton Group, the strategy still had to deliver on reduced costs and improved market share. Burton Group tested and later instituted a programme of new developments in the form of new retail formats and concepts. This development programme led to the creation of IS, the youth targeted discount store. This activity was the visible side to the Hoerner strategy – the presentation and marketing of the Burton brands. Behind the scenes Burton was actively working on new policies and programmes to deliver a more cost-effective operation.

The 1993 strategy was designed to build on the 1992 policies. The recession in the UK high street was deepening and Hoerner described trading conditions as the 'worst retailing recession since the Second World War'. Apart from the strategy of 'retail basics', Hoerner saw the need to reduce overheads and implement new ways of operating. In January 1993, new employment policies were instituted and carried out during the year, designed to reduce the cost base of the business but still maintain customer service. On the marketing side, some change in format was carried out, and certain product categories were deleted and a greater focusing on target groups was implemented. Burton stopped selling men's suits and franchised this activity out to its main supplier. New merchandising and new shop format strategies which had been implemented in the Multiples division now resulted in an increasing market share by 0.5 per cent to 12.8 per cent of the UK clothing market.

Away from the retail side of the business, the Burton Group continued to withdraw from some areas of the property market. Its property developments in the US were sold, and its stake in the Luton retail park was also disposed of. The remaining sections of the property portfolio was dramatically slimmed down which had a direct effect on the Burton financial position.

Hoerner's strategy was now firmly focused on the long term, and there was continuation of the 1992 strategy into 1993 and 1994. This long-term view was based on the following three areas:

- *Best practice:* the policy of reducing costs, improving efficiency and attention to retail basics;
- *Townprint:* a comprehensive and fundamental analysis of space allocation in all the sites where Burton Group trades in. The objective was to enhance the productivity of the trading assets, before any modernization of stores is undertaken. This approach was also designed to align shops more closely together across the trading estate and to respond to the changing patterns of development in the high street;
- *Modernization programme:* divisions developed new trading formats. Some were ready to be rolled out, other divisions were still at the planning stage. Modernization of the retail estate was seen as a precondition for recovery and for developing competitive advantage in the high street. In 1993, 120 stores were modernized and converted to new designs.

A full account of this policy is given in the Burton Group Review 1993 booklet that accompanies the 1993 annual report of accounts.

The UK high street was still in recession in April 1994. The upturn was still slow in coming, retail sales still showed no sign of a recovery. The Burton Group had made a number of key strategic decisions and to an extent had begun its personal recovery. The share price at one time stood at an all-time low of 29 pence, but had recovered by the end of 1993 to stand at 87.5 pence, a threefold rise. At the time of writing, 1 April 1994, the Burton share price stood at 55.5 pence. Commentators on the Group believed that the real problems at Burton continued to be in its Multiples division, and Hoerner's strategy, while showing signs of working, still had to be proved to be successful.

Tables 4.3 to 4.5 set out in detail the financial picture of the Burton Group over the years 1991–93.

Table 4.3 Burton Group Plc: Turnover and trading profit analysis 1991–93

	Turnover			Trading profit		
	1993 £m	1992 £m	1991 £m	1993 £m	1992 £m	1991 £m
Fashion multiples	1,007.0	959.0	946.3	7.3	6.1	17.1
Stores	854.4	772.9	678.2	57.7	31.7	26.0
Continuing businesses	1,861.4	1,731.9	1,624.5	65.0	37.8	43.1
Businesses sold	—	—	36.6	—	—	3.1
Other businesses	31.7	32.7	—	(4.1)	(2.5)	—
Turnover and retail profit	1,893.1	1,764.6	1,661.1	60.9	35.3	46.2
Other income				6.4	1.4	(2.2)
Interest and similar charges				(29.2)	(27.3)	(32.8)
Profit before exceptional costs				38.1	9.4	11.2
Exceptional costs				(19.6)	(10.2)	(24.6)
Profit/(loss) before taxation				18.5	(0.8)	(13.4)

Source: Company accounts 1992–93.

Table 4.4 Burton Group Plc: Consolidated Profit and loss accounts 1991–93 (for the year ended 29 August)

	1993 £m	1992 £m	1991 £m
Turnover	1,893.1	1,764.6	1,661.1
Cost of sales:			
Ongoing	(1,735.3)	(1,625.2)	(1,509.9)
Exceptional[1]	(14.6)	—	—
Total cost of sales	(1,749.9)	(1,625.2)	(1,509.9)
Gross profit	143.2	139.4	151.2
Distribution costs	(36.8)	(36.5)	(36.8)
Administrative expenses	(60.1)	(67.6)	(68.2)
Trading profit	46.3	35.3	46.2
Exceptional items[2]	(5.0)	(10.2)	(24.6)
Other income	6.4	1.4	(2.2)
Interest and other charges	(29.2)	(27.3)	(32.8)
Profit/(loss) before taxation	18.5	(0.8)	(13.4)
Taxation	(4.6)	10.2	—
Profit on ordinary activities After taxation	13.9	9.4	(13.4)
Extraordinary items[3]	—	—	(152.0)
Profit for the financial year	13.9	9.4	(165.4)
Dividends	(28.0)	(22.4)	(22.4)
Transfer from retained earnings	(14.1)	(13.0)	(187.8)

1. Exceptional cost –   1993   Costs associated with the 'Best Practice' programme for redundancy and other costs taken as a cost of sales.
2. Exceptional items –   1991   Rationalization and reorganization costs.
   1992   Provision for write-down withdrawal from property development.
   1993   Loss on the sale of Champion Sport solus branches.
3. Extraordinary items – 1991   Write-down on withdrawal from property development and loss on the disposal of the Financial Services Division.

Source: Burton Group Report and Accounts 1992–93.

Table 4.5 Burton Group Plc: Consolidated balance sheets 1991–93 (for the year ended 29 August)

	1993 £m	1992 £m	1991 £m
Fixed assets			
Tangible assets	903.2	959.5	1049.6
Current assets			
Stocks	279.6	300.6	231.7
Debtors	105.5	100.3	155.1
Assets held for sale	122.4	101.1	55.4
Cash in hand and at bank	80.5	69.5	116.9
	588.0	571.5	559.1
Creditors (due within one year)			
Funding debt	24.3	201.0	237.7
Other creditors	363.9	379.9	426.5
	388.2	580.9	664.2
Net current assets/(liabilities)	199.8	(9.4)	(105.1)
Total assets less current liabilities	1,103.0	950.1	944.5
Creditors (due after one year)			
Funding debt	249.9	247.5	186.9
Provisions for liabilities and charges	—	1.5	43.5
Net worth	853.1	701.1	714.1
Capital and reserves			
Called-up share capital	140.3	335.1	335.1
Capital redemption reserve	223.4	—	—
Share premium account	251.1	113.6	113.6
Revaluation reserve	80.4	80.4	80.4
Retained earnings	157.9	172.0	185.0
Total shareholders' funds	853.1	701.1	714.1

Source: Company Report and Accounts 1992–93.

NEXT PLC

Next is a retail clothing company that grew out of the traditional menswear retailer J. Hepworth in the early 1980s. Under the leadership of George Davies, Next Plc expanded rapidly in the mid 1980s to become a business with a turnover of over £1 billion. This was achieved as much by acquisition as by organic growth. Davis was a retail manger with a flair for design. Davies and Next were to dominate the high street in the 1980s and bring affordable design style to the mass market. Next's competitive advantage was based around a highly focused niche approach to retailing that was to extend from menswear to womenswear and later to childrenswear and furnishing accessories. This concept extension was also applied to home shopping with the Next Directory. Next, like many other retail groups expanded their business by acquisition, funding this corporate development with external debt. In the autumn of 1988 Davies resigned after a board room battle and was replaced by David Jones, the ex-chief executive of Grattans, one of Next's large acquisitions in the mid 1980s. A new chairman, Lord Wolfson, was appointed to Next Plc in 1990. Table 4.6 gives a five-year trading history of the company, 1989–93.

Table 4.6 Next Plc: Five-year trading history 1989–93

	1993 £m	1992 £m	1991 £m	1990 £m	1989 £m
Turnover	484.7	462.0	877.9	1,028.3	1,210.1
Profit before interest	30.5	11.1	7.2	38.9	91.8
Net interest income/(expense)	5.7	1.2	(14.4)	(12.5)	(21.7)
Profit/(loss) before exceptional items	36.2	12.3	(7.2)	26.4	70.1
Exceptional items	2.7	—	(33.5)	(73.1)	(7.8)
Profit/(loss) before taxation	38.9	12.3	(40.7)	(46.7)	62.3
Taxation	(2.2)	(0.9)	(9.3)	15.8	(22.5)
Profit/(loss) after taxation	36.7	11.4	(50.0)	(30.9)	39.8
Extraordinary items	—	—	(395.2)	(132.4)	(47.6)
Dividends	(9.3)	(2.8)	(2.6)	(17.4)	(27.3)
Profit/(loss) transferred to reserves	27.4	8.6	(477.8)	(180.7)	(35.1)
Shareholders' funds	198.6	168.5	160.0	384.7	374.5
Dividend per share (pence)	2.5	0.75	0.7	4.7	7.4
Earnings per share (pence)	9.9	3.1	(13.6)	(8.4)	10.7
Number of shops	305	318	361		
Selling space (000 sq. ft)	937	966	1,077		

Source: Next Plc Annual Report and Accounts, 1992–93.

By the end of 1989, Next's financial problems were beginning to be apparent to the new team at the company. The recession, the end of the 'Lawson Boom' and falling consumer confidence, helped conspire against the company. Next's retail profits of 1989 halved in 1990, as margins and sales volumes collapsed. This situation got worse in 1991, when Next posted record after-tax losses of over £475 million. During the period 1989–93, Next had accumulated losses of over two-thirds of a billion pounds. Next suffered yet more as its share price collapsed to about 17 pence a share. The management had to do something to avert a disaster of epic proportions.

The Next management team began to address these problems early. Much of the after-tax losses on the Next profit and loss account was a result of extensive provisions for extraordinary and exceptional items that arose from a policy of retrenchment that was to be followed by the management team.

In 1990–91, Next followed a strategy of asset disposals designed to simplify the business and raise funds to pay for a £160m convertible bond that was due to mature in early 1992. In the period covered by the case, Next withdrew or reduced its commitment from the following activities:

- property development;
- disposed of its foreign manufacturing subsidiaries;
- reduced the company's third-party credit financing operation at Club 24;
- disposed of the Grattan mail-order company to the German mail-order house Otto;
- closed a large number of shops;
- sold its jewellery business to a management buy-out.

The disposals and allied retrenchment policies brought much needed cash into the business. Next at one time during this period was closing three shops a week to offset the debt faced by the company. The management at Next used this retrenchment to simplify the business into two main divisions – Next Retail and Next Directory. The object behind this policy was that after the balance sheet was rebuilt and margins restored, Next would follow a cautious growth phase. Included in this plan was an expansion into the North American market. During the period 1991–93, Next opened a small number of stores in selected cities on the American eastern seaboard. These stores were operated as a joint venture with an American partner.

Next Plc's management believed that its policies of the early 1990s had positioned the company very clearly to benefit from any upturn in retail spending in the mid 1990s, and that it had made the appropriate decisions early in the recessionary cycle to avoid the problems that other retailers were facing in the mid 1990s. Next Plc was well on the way to recovery.

Tables 4.7 to 4.11 set out a detailed financial record for Next Plc for the period 1991–93.

Table 4.7 Next Plc: Turnover, operating profit and net assets by sector 1991–93

	Turnover			Operating profit			Net assets		
	1991 £m	1992 £m	1993 £m	1991 £m	1992 £m	1993 £m	1991 £m	1992 £m	1993 £m
Business sector:									
Next Retail	273.3	282.1	332.9	(2.3)	6.4	24.4	79.8	51.2	38.3
Directory	87.5	88.1	90.8	2.6	4.0	6.4	44.8	48.0	44.8
Other activities	25.7	22.7	19.2	2.6	0.7	(0.3)	32.7	42.6	24.0
	386.5	392.9	442.9	2.9	11.1	30.5	157.3	141.8	107.1
Club 24	90.1	69.1	41.8	(4.9)	—	—	8.5	8.5	25.7
Discont. businesses	401.3	—	—	9.2	—	—	—	—	—
Total	877.9	462.0	484.7	7.2	11.1	30.5	165.8	150.3	132.8
Interest bearing assets/(liabilities)							(5.8)	18.2	65.8
Total net assets							160.0	168.5	198.6

Table 4.8 Next Plc: Turnover, operating profit and net assets by geographical area 1991–93

	Turnover			Operating profit			Net assets		
	1991 £m	1992 £m	1993 £m	1991 £m	1992 £m	1993 £m	1991 £m	1992 £m	1993 £m
Geographical location:									
United Kingdom	865.0	454.2	480.9	7.1	11.2	31.4	165.8	148.7	131.9
Rest of Europe	7.2	—	—	(1.3)	0.1	(0.3)	1.5	0.1	(0.3)
North America	5.7	7.8	3.8	1.4	(0.2)	(0.6)	(1.5)	1.5	1.2
	877.9	462.0	484.7	7.2	11.1	30.5	165.8	150.3	132.8
Interest bearing assets/(liabilities)							(5.8)	18.2	65.8
Total net assets							160.0	168.5	198.6

Table 4.9 Next Plc: Staff costs and number of people employed at Next 1991–93

	1991	1992	1993
Next Retail	6,826	5,912	6,382
Next Directory	788	849	818
Other activities	1,616	1,111	1,163
Discontinued businesses	5,521	—	—
Total employed	14,751	7,872	8,363
	£m	£m	£m
Total staff costs	136.3	64.6	84.5

Table 4.10 Next Plc: Profit and loss account 1991–93 (for the year ended 31 January)

	1993 £m	1992 £m	1991 £m
Turnover	484.7	462.0	877.9
Cost of sales	(378.1)	(411.1)	(745.2)
Gross profit	106.6	50.9	132.7
Distribution costs	(18.0)	(15.2)	(42.3)
Administrative expenses	(56.6)	(46.8)	(83.4)
Income from associated businesses	1.5	0.2	0.2
Club 24 operating profit/(loss)	(3.0)	22.0	—
Operating profit	30.5	11.1	7.2
Net interest receivable/(payable)	5.7	1.2	(14.4)
Profit before exceptional items	36.2	12.3	(7.2)
Exceptional items	2.7	—	(33.5)
Profit on ordinary activities before taxation	38.9	12.3	(40.7)
Taxation	(2.2)	(0.9)	(9.3)
Profit on ordinary activities after taxation	36.7	11.4	(50.0)
Extraordinary items[1]	—	—	(395.2)
Profit/(loss) for the financial year	36.7	11.4	(445.2)
Dividends	(9.3)	(2.8)	(2.6)
Profit/(loss) transferred to reserves	27.4	8.6	(447.8)
Earnings per share (pence)	9.93	3.08	(13.58)

1. Extraordinary items 1991:

	£m
Profit/(loss) on the sale of discontinued businesses:	
Grattan	(298.8)
Property development	(50.0)
Overseas manufacturing	(9.7)
Others	(17.9)
Provision against investment in BSB Ltd	(17.5)
Deferred tax asset written off	(1.3)
Total extraordinary items for 1991	(395.2)

Source: Company Accounts 1991 to 1993.

Table 4.11 Next Plc: Consolidated balance sheets 1991–93
(for the year ended 31 January)

	1993 £m	1992 £m	1991 £m
Fixed assets			
Tangible assets	90.1	113.9	213.8
Investments	6.2	8.6	15.3
	96.3	122.5	229.1
Current assets			
Stocks	61.5	53.2	130.1
Debtors	141.6	218.6	649.4
Cash at bank and in hand	17.9	114.3	54.9
	221.0	386.1	834.4
Current liabilities			
Creditors: amounts due within one year	105.2	312.9	685.5
Net current assets/(liabilities)	115.8	73.2	148.9
Total assets less current liabilities	212.1	195.7	378.0
Creditors: amounts due after one year	1.0	3.1	109.5
Provisions for liabilities and charges	12.5	24.1	108.5
Net worth	198.6	168.5	160.0
Capital and reserves			
Called-up share capital	38.1	38.0	38.0
Share premium account	1.3	—	0.8
Revaluation reserve	21.7	21.9	22.6
Other reserves	(6.8)	(6.8)	249.4
Profit and loss account	144.3	115.4	(150.8)
Shareholders' funds	198.6	168.5	160.0

Source: Company Accounts 1991 to 1993.

ENDPIECE

This case has set out the fortunes of two UK clothing retailers and their strategies during the early 1990s. The issues described in this case are unlikely to change for the remaining part of 1994 and well into 1995. Both companies face considerable difficulties in the tough trading environment of the UK high street. Next and Burton, along with all other non-food retailers, will continue to compete vigorously for the consumer pound, and will have to develop appropriate strategies for success in such a tough trading environment.

SECTION 3

Not-for-profit organizations

Case 5   Cromarty Courthouse Museum
          G. Watson, Ross and Cromarty District Council

Case 6   London Zoo
          J.L. Thompson, University of Huddersfield

Case 7   The National Trust
          J.L. Thompson, University of Huddersfield

Case 8   Kirklees Metropolitan Council: corporate strategy in a local
          authority
          S. Davies, University of Leeds, and D. Griffiths, Kirklees MC

Cromarty Courthouse Museum

Graham Watson

INTRODUCTION

Cromarty Courthouse is a new museum, opened in 1991, which preserves and interprets the story of the town of Cromarty. The Cromarty Courthouse Trust was founded in 1989 with a view to setting up a museum. The Trust have entered their fifth year of existence so could be said to have completed their start-up phase and should be entering a period of growth. On the other hand, the successful completion of the start-up phase provides the Trustees with an opportunity to review the mission of the organization and to set long-term goals other than start-up and survival. This is a difficult task in a period of both economic and local government instability.

THE COURTHOUSE MUSEUM PROJECT

In 1989 the Trustees got together with a view to setting up a museum. The members of the Trust were aware that they wanted to collect objects connected with the history of the Burgh of Cromarty and display them to locals and visitors. This would preserve some of the unique history of the community, a goal the Trustees believed had merit. They also had a strong belief that the history of the town was unique enough, and the story interesting enough, to attract visitors to the town, thus improving the economy. These were the beliefs that drove the initial impetus to set up the Courthouse. A Trust Deed was signed which embodied these aims: 'To establish a museum or heritage centre within the Cromarty Courthouse'. The Trustees also registered under the Museum and Galleries Commission Scheme of Registration as a Trust seeking to 'preserve and interpret the history and material culture of (Cromarty)', (Museums and Galleries Commission, 1990: 1).

The local authority, Ross and Cromarty District Council, had a policy of enabling and supporting communities to set up and manage their own facilities. In the heritage field this meant that local groups were encouraged to set up a variety of ways of involvement in their heritage, culminating in a grant supported museum, which was defined as a registered museum with professional curatorial staff. The council also had a Tourism Development Policy, which designated Cromarty as a priority area for investment. This meant that a partnership between the Trust and the District Council was a logical way forward. The Council's Museum Development Officer was invited to assist the Trust and the project was launched.

From the outset it was apparent that the project had considerable potential. The Courthouse itself preserved much of its original fabric intact, in particular a period eighteenth-century courtroom. The building was the heart of a spectacularly well preserved example of an eighteenth-century Scottish burgh. The reason for this became clear as the research for the project progressed. Cromarty had seen a period of great prosperity and expansion in the latter part of the eighteenth century, based on the rich farmland of the interior of the area and trade with England and Europe. However, the period of prosperity had ended in the nineteenth century. The houses of the merchants and fisherfolk had never been replaced and stood as monuments to happier times. The town's lowest ebb was reached in the 1970s when the population fell to its lowest point. Just at that time the economy of the Cromarty Firth was revitalized by the policy of the then Highlands and Islands Development Board and the local government agencies to invest in the Cromarty Firth as an industrial base for the Highlands. An oil fabrication yard was set up at Nigg, across the Firth from Cromarty, and many workers bought and renovated the smaller houses in the town. The new prosperity attracted other incomers and the population began to grow again. The central area of the town was designated a planning control area thus ensuring the preservation of its unique character.

It was felt by all concerned with the project that if visitors to the Highlands could be made aware of this architectural and historical wealth, they would be attracted to spend time and money in the town. The problem was that Cromarty sits at the end of a peninsula some twenty miles from the main north/south artery of the A9. Although it is not unusual for heritage to be used to maintain or extend the length of time a tourist spends in a particular location, it was a new venture for the Highlands to create and maintain a new market, and it was believed that the story was strong enough to merit such interpretation to hold the visitor. However, if it was to have the strength to attract visitors the length of the Black Isle to Cromarty it was believed that it needed a unique selling point. In the case of the Courthouse this was to be the method of interpretation used in one of the major exhibits – the reconstruction, using animatronic figures, of a trial that had actually taken place in the courtroom. This was to be coupled with a new level of quality of presentation for the Highlands, exemplified by the wearing of period costume by the staff of the Courthouse. Although they were not to be in character, as this was felt to be inappropriate for the scale of the project, they would be noticeably different for the customer and indicate a level of service that would be comparable with other tourist developments they might have visited elsewhere. Thus the expectation of service would be one comparable with other parts of the country rather than competing with other Highland attractions. Although challenging this was an important decision for the Trustees and defined much of the future development of the project.

The first major step was to commission a study to examine in detail the cost of the project and to determine what the returns might be. Funding was available for this from the Highlands and Islands Development Board and Development Services of Ross and Cromarty District Council. By its nature this funding was designed to examine the business viability of projects, thus the study concentrated on the financial rather than the social and cultural aspects of the enterprise. The study suggested that the project was viable in that the returns on the public sector investment would be thirteen direct and indirect jobs and, eventually, some 40,000 visitors a year would be attracted to Cromarty. This was deemed sufficient to give approval for a public sector investment totalling £270,000.

This approval allowed the project to proceed with the fundraising stage. This was paralleled with a six-month period of detailed research by a full-time researcher. This post was a local appointment as were others to be throughout the project. The local base of the project was a fundamental principle for the Trustees and for the major sponsors. The success of this stage allowed progress to the final phase, the scriptwriting, design and fitting out of the Courthouse.

An important facet was the public support for the project. As a museum it was recognized that the Courthouse would have to undertake activities not geared to generating profit. The local authority agreed an annual subsidy formula based on one-third of the agreed running costs of the Courthouse on condition that the council set a series of targets for the museum to meet, reviewable on a yearly basis. Although essential to the research and care of the collection side of the project, this subsidy meant that the council became major external stakeholders in the project.

The product which was available to the visitor in March 1991 was made up of a number of parts. The marketing of the product was based on Cromarty itself as a half-day visit from Inverness, with the Courthouse as a 'must visit' element of the package. This was the result of Tourist Board research on visitor needs in the Highlands. At the Courthouse the visitor was met by a member of staff in period costume who both welcomed the visitor, made them familiar with the elements of the visit, and took the entrance fee of £1.90 (now £2.70). After some traditional introductory displays putting Cromarty into its geographical and historical setting, the visitor met Sir Thomas Urquhart, an animatronic reconstruction of one of the town's earlier lairds and a noted eccentric of his day. This figure could be asked to discourse on a number of subjects by the visitor pressing buttons, and this interactive nature made it a popular feature of the displays. The detailed story of the town and its development was presented as a video production, as it was felt that this was, for the visitor, the most comfortable and familiar way of receiving a mass of detailed information. Against expectations and received wisdom visitors tended to watch the whole of the sixteen minute video rather than to dip in. The courtroom scene, now with a mixture of animatronic and static figures, told the story of the trial of one Annie Hossack charged with stealing flax from the local factory where she was employed, the visitors being invited to sit in the jury box to view the trial. The tour ended in the shop. However, part of the entrance fee included a tape tour of Cromarty using walkman-type equipment. This was chosen to both add to the visitor experience and give value for money, and to encourage people to go round the town and use the various retail facilities. The whole visit would take a maximum of one and a half hours plus one hour twenty minutes for the tape tour. The average time spent by visitors in the first six months was one hour twenty minutes. Only about one-third took up the option of the tape tour, although the reports back on it were highly favourable. These factors suggested that the product was well received by visitors, who slightly exceeded the numbers predicted for the first year. The spend per head in the shop also exceeded predictions at £1.20 per visitor.

MANAGEMENT PHILOSOPHY

The Trustees of the Courthouse, and the curator, developed some management policies from the outset while others grew out of the experience of the first few years. Underpinning some of these was the funding package. The Trustees could count on a public subsidy from the District Council of one-third of the agreed running costs. This meant that they were responsible, annually, for raising two-thirds of the running costs, plus any resources needed for projects not agreed by the council or outside the basic annual programme. Thus the business side of the project was seen as important. The Courthouse was seen by all as a small business, albeit one not concerned with profit. Sound business planning, good customer care, a quality product and the importance of marketing underpinned the planning process. However, the Trustees were keen that the Courthouse should not be just a business whose profits were then spent on providing social benefits. They felt that this would divorce the museum from its local context. It was important that the museum belonged to the community of Cromarty, whilst serving the function of a tourist attraction. The museum was to be a source of burgh pride, embodying the social and cultural values of the town. It was a manifestation of the growing strength of the community and its confidence, not just in its past, but in its future. Most importantly it was to be used by local people, and from the outset access for local people was free. To make sure that this role was maintained, and that the usage was not measured by visitor numbers alone, some of the business ratios adopted were designed to demonstrate how the Courthouse was used. Part of the local role was to be the quality and depth of the research work carried out in the Courthouse, and how that research was Transmitted to a non-academic and local audience.

One of the major sponsors, Ross and Cromarty District Council, was also keen on developing museums in its area. It saw museums as institutions whose role revolved round collections of artifacts. The Museum and Galleries Commission Scheme of Museum Registration was used as a basis for making funding decisions. Major funding, including up to one-third of annual running costs, was available to museums which registered under the scheme. Smaller scale funding was available to other heritage organizations on condition that they did not maintain collections. This funding did not include annual revenue grants although one-off grants could continue on a year-to-year basis. The Courthouse, as a museum, now had obligations both to collect objects, and to conserve and preserve them to defined standards. The status of registered museum also gave access to sources of government funding, but the cost element was high. It has been estimated that the cost of collecting and maintaining objects would account for 38 per cent of the running costs of a museum (Lord, Lord and Nicks, 1989: xxiii). Being a museum also created limitations for what was collected and how these objects were used. In some cases this might conflict with local wants. For example, given the cost element of maintaining a collection, and the need to adopt a collecting policy, the Trustees would have to weigh up the need to preserve an item not unique to the town, but important to the community, for example lifeboat equipment, common to many museums, mass-produced by industrial processes and readily available, but important by association to many of the fishing community of the town. The Trustees have three objectives to balance. To be an effective small business, to be a museum, and to be a local cultural centre.

DEVELOPMENT OF THE PROJECT

Although the Courthouse has a clear social role, since it receives only one-third of its running costs from the public sector its function as a small business is critical to its long-term success. Original projections by consultants suggested that the first five years should see a steady growth pattern from 20,000 to 40,000 visitors. However, the period 1991 to 1994 saw Britain fall into a deep recession, which was reflected in visitor figures to the Highlands. Whilst attractions on the main tourist routes maintained their visitor figures, those on the periphery did badly. Three seasons of poor summer weather also served the shoulder seasons and second holiday visits poorly. Secondly, the initial report suggested that there was a large market for school visits. This was doubted by the staff of the project, as government legislation on the local management of schools suggested that resources for educational trips were about to be reduced. In addition, changes to the curriculum suggested that such school visits as were possible would be tied closely into the subject matter being taught, necessitating a lot of work on the part of museums wishing to attract such a market. Leeway for the non-delivery of the initial visitor figures was built into the planning process.

In the event this was justified as the Courthouse failed to meet its targets and, after initial increases, dropped back to an average of about 20,000 visitors per year. Although tourist figures were poor, and school visits almost non-existent, those for the Highland residential market exceeded expectations. Part of the initial marketing was to make Cromarty the destination of a half-day trip, a major segment of the Highland market. The high figures for visitors from the Highlands suggested that the Courthouse had succeeded in this area, although it was seen that this might create longer-term problems. The attraction was offering static displays yet would rely for its income on repeat visitors. The impact on the local community was also considerable. Although given free access, to gauge interest locals had to collect membership cards to get entry, and some 80 per cent of local residents collected the cards and visited the Courthouse in the first year of opening.

Cromarty Courthouse opened to much local acclaim. To date it has won some ten awards for setting new levels of standards in display for a heritage attraction in the Highlands. A key factor was the level of spend on display in relation to the cost of building work. This set standards of interpretation and display for a public sector supported attraction which subsequent developments have had to match. In its first year the Courthouse received the Museum of the Year award. This has been followed by a Europa Nostra award and a recent commendation in the Interpret Britain awards. The Museum also succeeded in gaining recognition as a registered museum under the Museum and Galleries Commission guidelines and was accepted as a full member of the Association of Scottish Visitor Attractions, which has rigorous entry standards largely determined by customer service criteria. The Courthouse was also set targets to meet in return for its grant from the local authority. These targets were concerned with museological and social issues such as the number and quality of temporary exhibitions and events and the standards of collection care.

The equivalent of four full-time jobs were directly created in Cromarty, an employment black-spot as the local oil industry winds down. In addition, some 80,000 visitors were attracted over the first three years, underpinning the local economy. Visitor research suggests that the bulk of these were new visitors, creating a new tourist market. To date much of the reported results must be anecdotal; however, two new tea shops have opened in villages on the Black Isle, on route to the Courthouse. Cromarty was a finalist in the 1993 Tourist Village of the Year competition, gaining a five-minute slot on commercial television in which the Courthouse featured prominently. On a more specific note, visitor numbers in Groam House Museum, and Hugh Miller's Cottage, a National Trust property, both in the Courthouse's visitor area, rose by 74.69 per cent and 22.92 per cent respectively. Both facilities charge, although both added to their attractions around the time the Courthouse opened.

Thus a number of the initial aims of the various sponsors were being met. The Courthouse is recognized as a museum, and it preserves and interprets the history of Cromarty, doing so to recognized national standards. This is at a cost to the public sector of about £20,000 a year. For the public sector sponsors, this is significantly cheaper than a comparable wholly public sector institution could be run. It is a quality attraction recognized on a UK level. It has created a number of direct and indirect jobs locally as well as stimulating the tourist economy and it has made a considerable impact on the research of the human and natural heritage of the area with a number of publications and a recording programme.

However, in 1992–93 the Trustees and their advisors were still faced with the problem that they were not attracting enough visitors to match the full expectations of the original development plan, and had to take action to match outputs to the new projected earnings.

The Trustees had to take a detailed look at the product on offer. Was there a question mark over the product, its place in the market, or in the marketing itself? Given the recognition the Courthouse had received for its product, and having just won a marketing award, and the fact that many of the original objectives were indeed being met, the reduced financial returns were deemed to be the result of the downturn in the market, and its position on the periphery of the tourist routes. Advice on whether this was a correct assumption was sought from a number of business support agencies which confirmed that the Courthouse was aiming at the right market segment, the car-borne AB1 tourist visitor looking for a half-day outing, but that a commercial venture would place itself nearer the existing market. It was still believed that with good marketing the Courthouse would see a steady growth in visitor numbers. Clearly the option of relocating was not open to the Trustees.

A NEW STRATEGY FOR THE COURTHOUSE

The Trustees recognized that the business element remained paramount in the planning process. Although many of the objectives of the organization were non-financial, without income, these could not be met in full. In the summer of 1993, it was accepted that the lower expectations of visitor numbers should be seen as a norm, and the business plan reworked to reflect this. This decision was made on the basis that an upturn in the tourist trade in the Highlands could not be guaranteed, particularly with the projected competition with Europe as a destination once the Eurotunnel opened in 1994. Secondly the schools market projected in the original plan did not exist, and would take a disproportionate amount of the available staff time to develop. It was also recognized that many of the non-financial objectives could be delivered by devoting staff time to them rather than money alone. For example, quality research and interpretation were better delivered by someone familiar with the local area, rather than from someone brought in from outside. In addition, time was recognized as a potential cost-saving factor. Objectives delivered over a longer timescale was seen as a way of reducing the financial drain on the organization. Thus a key factor in the planning process was to maintain professional curatorial staff rather than seeking savings in this area.

With this as the basis for the planning process, the Trustees began to redefine the objectives of the organization. This had to be done in the light of the competing objectives of the various funding organizations and the financial realities of the market-place. It was clear that the Courthouse had gained a place in the quality niche of the tourist market. Since 1991, two other attractions of a similar quality opened in the Highlands. Balnain House, marketing itself as the 'home of Highland music', in Inverness, and Aros, on Skye. The Trustees proposed a remarketing of the Courthouse, possibly in conjunction with other similar organizations, to develop this niche market. The Courthouse's own publicity material would be revamped to aim to appeal to this end of the market. A new attraction in the Easter Ross area, 'The Pilgrimage' had a projected opening date of summer 1994. It proposes to interpret the Burgh of Tain as a major site of medieval and royal pilgrimage in the sixteenth century. James IV visited Tain on a number of occasions, so often that the route he took through the Black Isle and across to Tain is known locally as the 'King's Route'. It passes over the Cromarty Firth at Cromarty, at the site of a modern ferry crossing. The Trustees proposed putting resources into developing this as a tourist route, recognized and promoted by the Scottish Tourist Board. This would make the Courthouse part of a network of attractions and natural heritage that would appeal to the car-borne market. As an alternative tourist route this might attract additional public funding, and the network element of the proposal would increase its attractiveness to the public sector.

The need was perceived to prioritize the various social and community objectives of the organization. This area was recognized as the least focused of the Courthouse's activities and the need to choose a direction was paramount. The Trustees felt that the sponsoring bodies had general concepts of the areas that they wanted to see developed, but no specific agenda beyond the Courthouse's museum function and a desire for a managed, quality approach that took community issues into account. This meant that the Trustees had both the freedom and also the responsibility to decide a direction for themselves.

The museum context was recognized in both the development plan and in the collecting policy. As a new museum, the Courthouse was not tied to large collections, and could limit collecting to what could be afforded. The collecting policy adopted determined the Trustees to collect only what was unique to the history of Cromarty, rather than common items with a connection with Cromarty only by association. These could probably be borrowed when necessary from elsewhere. This, plus regular collecting decisions reflecting the financial implications of acquisition, would retain the costs of collecting within affordable bounds.

The museum's outreach programme was seen as a problem area. Outreach was essential to retain local interest, but was a cost drain to the organization. The vagaries of the tourist market meant that it could not be depended on year on year. Bad weather, or a terrorist attack such as the Lockerbie bombing, could have a real measurable effect on visitor numbers. It was decided that outreach as a core activity should be put one year out of step with the tourist market. Thus the income from the 1992 season would define the level of activity of the 1993 season, and so on. This would also put the Trustees in a strong position to argue with the main funding agencies over the reasons why a particular planned programme might be a decrease on the previous year's activity.

The recognition that there were so many options for community development work led to a major discussion over the primary role of the Courthouse. This revolved around whether the Courthouse should follow the route of an eco-museum, that is a museum concerned with the community and its natural and cultural environment, or a centre of excellence for the study of Highland history. Both of these would allow the museum flexibility in the delivery of services to the local community. Exhibitions, events, collections, education programmes, arts outreach and community involvement could be maintained at similar levels in either of the possible directions. However, the 'eco-museum' context would both widen the scope of the organization and open new sources of public funding for environmental projects. It might also serve to create new audiences for the museum, although their local nature would not increase the revenue of the organization.

The development of the human heritage side of the museum's work would be a development of the museum's existing work. It was recognized in the planning process that the eastern side of Ross and Cromarty had a large number of academics who had either retired to or had family connections with the area. Building on the resources of the museum as a study centre might attract these people to give of their time and knowledge, as well as attracting lay people who wished to develop their skills and interest in local history. The lack of a university in the Highlands was seen as meaning that there was a lack of a focus for detailed historical work. That a new University of the Highlands was being actively progressed by Highlands and Islands Enterprise and the Highland Regional Council meant that the Courthouse would have an opportunity both to influence this development and to gain resources from it in the longer term. This research would then provide a basis for the filtering down of information to a general audience through an outreach programme, and be an added attraction for the tourist market niche to be attracted to the Courthouse in future, research having suggested that the perceived depth of the visitor experience was a factor in the decision to visit a given facility.

The Trustees decided to prioritize the development of the Courthouse as a centre of excellence for the study of Highland history for a number of reasons. Given that there were a number of organizations involved in the Cromarty community, not least a strong community council, the over-arching role of the eco-museum approach was one which was unsuitable for the Courthouse to appropriate. Secondly, the eco-museum approach involved a widening of the role of the museum in a period of retrenchment. And thirdly, although additional public sector funding might at first sight seem attractive, it would mean additional goals to be met and more outside pressure to meet diverse results. Without a guarantee of 100 per cent public funding, this new role could be yet another drain on resources.

The role of a history centre appealed because of its close ties to the original aims of the Trust. It also allowed for a gradual development as funds became available without draining existing resources, and provided an input into the other goal of increasing income from visitors. Lastly, it could be adopted without detailed reference to the existing sponsors as it involved no deviation from the current goals. Involvement by the Courthouse in the natural environment was not ruled out. It was agreed that the Courthouse should act in partnership with other organizations, and, in time, put its own resources into goal achievement in this area. However, it was not appropriate for the Courthouse to take a leading role at this stage in its development. It was hoped that, as a centre of excellence for the study of local history, the Courthouse will be able to build on its position in the market-place; develop its audience and increase its income; fulfil its role as an economic generator for the town and so input to the growing confidence of the community; as well as preserving the past for its own sake, and improving the quality of life of the people of Cromarty.

REFERENCES

Lord, B.G., G. Lord and J. Nicks (1989) *The Cost of Collecting: Collection Management in UK Museums*. London, HMSO.

Museums and Galleries Commission (1991) *A Scheme of Registration For Museums*. London Museums and Galleries Commission.

CASE 6

London Zoo

John L. Thompson

PART A

The Zoological Gardens in Regent's Park, known to most of us as London Zoo, is controlled and administered by the Zoological Society of London. The Society was established in 1826, the Zoo in 1828. The Zoological Society also runs an Institute of Zoology with a worldwide reputation for its work in genetics and veterinary science, and a scientific society for its members. Since 1931 it has run Whipsnade Park, near Dunstable in Bedfordshire, as a complementary collection to London.

The Society was incorporated in 1829 and its charter laid down its primary purpose as 'the advancement of zoology and animal physiology, and the introduction of new and curious subjects of the Animal Kingdom'.

Is this a realistic statement of the zoo's role in the late twentieth century? Does the scientific orientation give clear direction, or is it in any way a constraint? How should the zoo seek to fulfil its objectives? Are the key stakeholders the public who pay to visit, the managers, curators and keepers, many of them scientists by background, or the influential management committee of the council of the Zoological Society? This committee has Sir David Attenborough as a member, and the Council includes politicians and businessmen as well as academics.

London Zoo, of course, is located in a Royal Park, and consequently its activities are affected by the relevant bye-laws. There are, for example, restrictions on advertising. In addition the site includes ten listed buildings amongst the various animal houses. Several of these are described as totally unsuitable for their present purpose, but they cannot be altered substantially. Restoration would cost some £35 million. Several terraces are in poor repair and unused.

Income and expenditure

Internationally major zoos are funded by a mixture of admission charges and grants. London Zoo is 'the only National collection in the world not publically funded on a regular basis'. However, for 150 years the zoo operated quite successfully on admission charges alone. But changing social habits and leisure preferences and inflation have taken a toll. Although visitors are generally increasing in the late 1980s, this follows years of decline. There were 3 million visitors per year during the 1950s, when there was little competition and a general lack of transport restricted the ability of people who lived in and around London to travel widely outside the area. By 1960 the figure had fallen below 2 million, and by the early 1980s it was little over 1 million. In 1975 the Zoo switched from making a surplus of income over expenditure to a deficit. Whilst there were just nine zoos in the whole country during the 1950s there are now over 250 animal attractions open to visitors.

In the 15 months from January 1985 to March 1986 the Zoological Society recorded a surplus of income over expenditure of £984,000 – but only after receiving a £3.5 million grant from the Department of Environment, the first ever. Twelve months later the surplus was £298,000 following a £2 million grant (see Table 6.1).

> Government grants for the 1986–7 period totalled £2.03 million made up of a revenue grant of £2.0 million and a capital grant of £34,300 to match pound for pound what the Society has raised from private sources in 1985/6. Financial support will continue for 1987/8 and will comprise a revenue grant of £2 million and further capital grants to match pound for pound what the Society has raised from private sources in 1986/7, approximately £150,000...
> During the forthcoming financial year, the Society and Government, at Government's expense, are to ask consultants to produce a radical strategy for the options for future management and funding of London Zoo and Whipsnade Park. The study will concentrate on the commercial possibilities whilst maintaining the Society's interests and objectives as laid down in its charter.
> (*Source*: Zoological Society Annual Report)

Although government funding is only a recent contribution it is argued the Society always believed government would fund any major shortfalls. In fact in May 1988 the government granted £10 million as a one-off payment to London Zoo to be used for modernization. The intention is to attract more visitors in order to make the zoo self-financing. The consultants appointed by the Department of the Environment, Peat Marwick McClintock, recommended a facelift with amusement and theme-park type attractions and new animal housing and displays. There is no intention, though, of creating a Disneyland-style amusement park because of the threat of interference with scientific research.

Objectives

The basic dilemma concerns how much zoos are places of entertainment, with customers paramount, and how much they are organizations with primarily educational and scientific purposes. Many visitors pay for relaxation and entertainment, and essentially are only *sympathetic* to the scientific and educational aspects – though this is what they actually fund.

Many visitors are attracted by big animals, as evidenced by the past success of safari parks. But these are costly and dangerous, well researched and 'relatively safe' as far as endangered species go. Many animals, birds and insects that are endangered and in need of protection and research are nothing like as attractive to the public. The Rodriguez fruit bat is an excellent example of this dilemma. Of little interest to the average visitor, it has been the subject of a difficult and (arguably) important breeding programme at London Zoo.

Zoos must give their customers a 'good day out' with a variety of animals, catering, shops and an interested and interesting staff who will talk to people. They must, though, 'act responsibly' and present the animals instructively as well as entertainingly. London Zoo, as the premier national collection must take this seriously, but they can only take it so far. The retail publications are additionally important, and again, a world apart from the scientific publications for zoologists around the world. Getting the balance 'right' is difficult. If London Zoo does wish to change its orientation in any real way marketing will be increasingly important . . . if the zoo does want

Table 6.1 The Zoological Society of London: Income and expenditure (year ended 31 March 1987)

	Income £000	Expenditure £000
London Zoo		
Admission of visitors	2,770.9	
Catering and retail surpluses	449.4	
Miscellaneous income	60.4	
'Friends of the Zoos'	98.5	
	3,379.2	3,767.0
Whipsnade Park		
Admission of visitors	670.6	
Admission of cars	87.5	
Catering and retail surpluses	44.3	
Miscellaneous income	77.8	
	880.2	1,570.3
Education	92.8	158.6
Library	0.4	75.9
Publications	314.0	309.5
Institute of Zoology	595.3	1,416.3
Members' subscriptions	111.0	7.1
Other		21.5
	5,372.9	7,326.2

	£000
Deficit	(1,953.3)
Administration expenses	(78.3)
Income from consultancy/investment	321.0
Operating deficit	(1,710.6)
Department of Environment grant	2,000.0
	289.4
Sale of assets	8.9
	298.3
Transfer to building and equipment fund	235.0

to investigate threatened animals, and needs money for this, it must persuade the public.

London Zoo has, in fact, been criticized for its lack of marketing success in this respect. The zoo is very active in conservation, with a record of successful breeding programmes for endangered species both at Regent's Park and 'on location' around the world. Zoo staff have recently saved mountain gazelles in Saudi Arabia, for example. Critics argue that London Zoo's work is not recognized outside the scientific community because it does not publicize its achievements. These critics also point out that the zoo fails to market its animal collection as well as it might. Comparisons are often made with Chester Zoo, where information displays are used more effectively to explain the work, objectives and successes of the zoo's keepers. Defenders of London Zoo's efforts argue that it is hard to convince visitors of any achievements when most of the animals are caged in, rather than free to roam within protected areas.

But there are other problems and priorities as far as the collection is concerned. London Zoo has no hippos (since the 1960s) and now no bears, which it let go in 1986 because the 'facilities were inappropriate for the necessary husbandry'. Bringing them back will require money. Critics argue the bears went because of financial reasons. The zoo wanted to save money and to highlight shortages. The zoo argue that their overheads were not affected in any major way and that zoological, not financial, considerations were more important.

What animals, then, are appropriate for the 'national collection' to be credible? Visitors perhaps expect particular species in the country's foremost zoo, and whilst there is a huge collection (1,400 mammals, 1,000 birds, 400 reptiles and 170 amphibians), some species are missing and some are thin on the ground. Whipsnade has fewer animals (1,225 mammals, 900 birds, 85 reptiles, just 6 amphibians, all toads), but it is far larger, located in the country, and visitors drive their cars within the park, stopping as they wish, and getting out to view the animals. It is not a safari park concept. Whipsnade covers 600 acres; London Zoo 34.

The Zoological Society see the two zoos as complementary, and because the facilities are more appropriate, concentrate their work with large animals at Whipsnade, smaller animals at London Zoo (see Table 6.2).

There are, of course, people who believe zoos like London should not exist in their current form, arguing that animals are 'suffering the deprivations of captivity in the name of entertainment' (Zoo Check). The zoos themselves strongly counter this and claim that 'without zoos having an ark function in breeding endangered species there would be no animals to put back into the wild' (The National Federation of Zoos). Moreover, they argue, there is an essential need to inform the urban population of the variety of animal life.

Visitors

In 1986/7, 1,199,000 visitors came to London Zoo, 5 per cent fewer than the year before. Adverse weather conditions had caused forecasts below the level actually achieved. Predictions are notoriously difficult because zoos are very much a 'dry weather pleasure'. Most visiting parties are 'families' who typically decide to go only two to three days beforehand.

London Zoo is the 'fourth most popular paid for attraction in England', and a

Table 6.2 Selected larger animals, 1987

	London Zoo	Whipsnade
Hippos	0	2[1]
Rhinos	3 (Black)	14
Elephants	2 (Asian)	3 (Asian and African)
Bears	0	5 (Brown)
Giant pandas	1	0
Lions	4	3
Tigers	4	4
Leopards	2	0
Jaguars	3	5
Cheetahs	2	18
Giraffes	6	3

1. Plus 5 pygmies.

quarter of the visitors are foreign tourists. Eighty-five per cent pay; the other 15 per cent are 'free' children. Seventy per cent of home visitors come from Metropolitan London and a further 20 per cent from the Home Counties.

Whipsnade attracted 350,000 visitors and 37,500 cars in the same year. Ninety per cent paid, and 80 per cent lived within a 35 mile radius.

The 1987/8 targets are 1.3 million and 400,000 respectively.

There are organized education programmes for school visiting parties at both zoos and in 1986/7 London Zoo 'taught' 55,000 children and Whipsnade 14,000. Again this is weather determined and concentrated in the summer months.

Future developments

The Zoological Society has a building and equipment fund of £2.5–4.0 million per year and incurs annual expenditures on maintaining existing houses and exhibitions. New buildings can be donated, and have been in the past. The capital programme, which 'could easily be £25 million per year if money was available', has to be constrained as too much development work at any time would be detrimental to visitors.

London Zoo is currently concentrating its efforts on a new aquarium, to be built on the edge of the site, and with a separate entrance. It will be open in the evenings, and catering will be linked in. There is no major aquarium in the UK, although a number of developments are in progress. Planning issues and funding have slowed down the programme.

Performance measures

Performance measures link to the achievement of objectives. London Zoo measure their financial results, numbers of visitors, profits on retailing and catering, etc., all of which are relatively straightforward. But should they – and if so, how can they – use as measures breakthroughs in breeding, contributions to zoological science (worldwide), the actual (national) collection of animals?

The marketing challenge

For a long time London Zoo had concentrated on expanding the collection, and neglected important revenue-earning areas such as catering and retailing. By the time the need to develop and market these additional activities was properly realized the number of visitors – and t138
he revenue they contributed – had fallen to a level where the investment needed for marketing could not be funded out of current earnings.

Other changes had either been slow or they had been resisted. In 1976, for example, London Zoo opened a new lion terrace. Other leading zoos around the world, led by the influence of the large American zoos, were at this time rethinking their role in terms of conservation needs and animal rights, and were moving lions and similar beasts out to wildlife parks.

From a revenue point of view London Zoo needs to attract more visitors, and more from further afield. External funding is essential to improve the facilities in order that this might happen. In line with this London Zoo must arguably offer a differently constituted 'fun day out'. This potentially must conflict with educational aspects and the 'scientific' decision to concentrate certain collections at Whipsnade. Any changes must not stray too far from the basic charter, and both growth and activities are constrained by Park restrictions. Even if money were freely available only certain types of development will prove feasible. Windsor Safari Park, comprising drive-round and walk-round exhibits, shops and catering, the best collection of marine mammals in the UK and a children's adventure playground, is privately owned and profitable. On its busiest days its revenue amounts to £20,000. But it is not a zoo.

PART B

In April 1991 newspapers first reported that London Zoo might have to close in six months' time, at the end of the summer tourist season, unless new funding was secured. Closure would imply some slaughter of animals, but hopefully many would be transferred to Whipsnade and to other zoos. Admissions, 1.25 million in 1990, a slight increase from 1.22 million in 1989, were below the level required for the zoo to break even. In June 1992 the situation had not improved and the closure was announced formally.

The Director of Zoo Check suggested that good might come out of the crisis – 'if London Zoo is able to move to a new, more appropriate, concept of presenting wildlife.'

Essentially London Zoo, with its present levels of cost and income, has a projected breakeven target of 1.7 million visitors, and on present admission figures needs an annual subsidy in the order of at least £2 million. The press reports indicated that the zoo was looking for an immediate cash injection of £13 million to cover an 'unexpected backlog' of repairs and maintenance, and some £40 million long term. This followed on from the 1988 one-off final government subsidy of £10 million, not all of which had in fact been spent.

The reaction of the Department of the Environment to the initial announcement in 1991 was not sympathetic: 'Clearly the Zoo is not attracting enough visitors.'

The zoo itself launched a public appeal for £12 million, involving a credit card hotline for pledges and collection boxes at the zoo. The numbers of visitors increased immediately after the potential closure announcement.

What, then, had happened since 1988?

The Peat Marwick McClintock Report

Prior to the cash injection of £10 million by the Department of the Environment in 1988 the consultants Peat Marwick McClintock (PMM) had been brought in to advise on the future prospects and strategy for London Zoo.

Their investigations and report established that there is a role for zoos which are 'modern, and professionally presented and managed'. Management at London Zoo, they argued, did not reflect the commercial emphasis which was essential for survival and prosperity without a permanent subsidy. PMM recommended the establishment of a new company, under new management, which would manage both London and Whipsnade Zoos, but not any scientific work their scientists also undertook. The Zoological Society would continue to look after research. Senior managers in the new company 'need not necessarily be zoologists' but they needed to be experienced 'in the real world'.

Subsequently a new company, Zoo Operations Ltd, was set up.

It was also proposed that the Regent's Park site be extended by 10 acres, but, because of considerable hostility and opposition by local residents, this has not happened.

Zoo Operations Ltd (ZOL)

Zoo Operations was established in October 1988 as a wholly-owned subsidiary of the Zoological Society. ZOL's brief was specifically to 'transform the visitor experience' at London Zoo and make it more like the best American zoos. San Diego Zoo in Southern California is regarded as the most successful zoo in the world, and it is also one of the largest with 3,200 animals and 800 species. The animals are separated from the public only by moats, and the zoo is fully landscaped with tropical and subtropical vegetation. Birds are contained in roofed-over natural canyons. There are tour buses, an aerial tramway and a separate, small, children's zoo where tame animals can be petted.

London Zoo was to have a new corporate image, themed restaurants, exotic animal enclosures and electronic penguins and lions. ZOL did not have, as such, any scientific or educational brief. Their aim was to reverse the falling trend in admissions and bring the zoo back into profit in three years.

The managing director of ZOL was an American leisure consultant, who had previously worked in marketing at San Diego Zoo, and who had worked on the Peat Marwick McClintock report. He was not paid a salary. Instead his consultancy company was paid an annual fee to cover him and others he employed. The 1989/90 fee has been reported as almost a quarter of a million pounds.

ZOL incurred an operating loss of £2.8 million in 1989/90. This had to be added to a smaller operating loss recorded for the zoo itself before being reduced by interest payments received on investments, including a fair proportion of the 1988 £10 million grant.

ZOL defended the loss, arguing that it was investing to put in place the necessary structure and systems for long-term viability. A second subsidiary company had been established to attract money from private donors, in order to fund new exhibits to attract more visitors.

The situation in 1992

Donations ensured that London Zoo stayed open throughout 1991, although attendances actually deteriorated again to 1,116,000. This proved critical as London Zoo still depended upon gate income for over 80 per cent of its total revenue. The zoo was only ninth in the popularity table for attractions in and around London. Cost-cutting and rationalization ensured that the zoo broke even financially. However, one-third of the animals and one-third of the keepers had had to go.

Late in 1991 a group of self-styled reformers amongst the fellows of the Zoological Society requested a special general meeting at which they tabled a vote of no confidence in the Council. The outcome of the meeting in January 1992 was a decision to place greater emphasis on conservation and focus on a more limited range of activities and exhibits. The Zoo's Director, Dr David Jones, resigned and left in April.

Admissions were at a disappointingly low level in early summer 1992, and it was perhaps not unexpected when, in June 1992, it was announced that London Zoo would close before Christmas, with some animals destroyed, but most moved elsewhere, including Whipsnade. The zoo's keepers rallied behind a new chief executive, Dr Jo Gipps, previously the head keeper, and clashed with the external governing Council over the way in which London Zoo should present itself, its animals and its achievements. The staff favoured stronger marketing through the media (to attract visitors) and inside the zoo itself. One argument was for bigger and better information cards, placed alongside the animal cages, to provide visitors with much more information. There was general agreement that conservation should be the theme.

The media publicized the demise of the zoo, and it soon became apparent that substantial private funding was the only realistic solution. The government was not going to come to the rescue. Substantial donations from certain private benefactors together with many smaller gifts again saved the zoo. Kuwait, for example, donated £1 million.

Few people really seemed to believe that London Zoo would actually close down completely, but unquestionably it would not survive without change, possibly radical change. Cost reduction, *per se*, was not really an option. This would imply reducing stock, which would precipitate a further fall in visitors and a downward spiral. But a smaller zoo with a new concept, say natural animal habitats, and with less emphasis on caged animals, might prove popular. A variety of possibilities were in fact postulated throughout 1992. One suggestion was that this might take the form of a special theme park with, say, an African rain forest, complete with gorillas, and a Chinese mountain with pandas being simulated or re-created. A children's educational centre, covering all or part of the Regent's Park site, and with sponsorship from toy manufacturers, was also mooted.

Whatever, there was a recognized need that the zoo be perceived as an all-year attraction, not just one for the summer months. Any changes of this magnitude would require funding for new building and to cover the costs of transferring existing animals to Whipsnade and to other locations.

The fundamental marketing problem of four years ago clearly still remained, albeit in the form of a different challenge.

The situation in 1993

Eight months after the closure announcement London Zoo was still open for visitors. Sufficient external funding had been secured and for the moment the zoo was safe. Its future viability depends upon its success in transforming itself into a new concept and in attracting more visitors.

In October 1992 the Council for the Zoological Society had approved new proposals submitted by Dr Jo Gipps. The objectives are to retain the site in Regent's Park and focus on important breeding groups and endangered species. These are to include Asian lions, Sumatran tigers and lowland gorillas. London Zoo is to be developed into a 'world-class animal and breeding centre' but with a children's zoo and educational centre. It is possible that dilapidated terraces will be restored so that bears can be reintroduced.

> There will be less emphasis on the Zoo as a good day out ... We are going to appeal to people's intelligence ... Zoos have no right to exist in the late 20th century unless they can show they are good for animals.

The cost of transformation has been estimated at £21 million spread over ten years. By February 1993 the first £2.5 million had been raised.

Whilst London Zoo survived this period of turmoil Windsor Safari Park closed. Receivers were appointed in January 1992 after dramatic falls in revenue and profit, but they were unable to find a buyer. The Park was closed down in October the same year.

The National Trust

John L. Thompson

INTRODUCTION

The National Trust, in essence, holds countryside and buildings in England, Wales and Northern Ireland 'for the benefit of us all'. Trust properties include woodlands, coastal paths, nature reserves and country parks; sites of archaeological interest; castles and country houses, some associated with famous people such as Sir Winston Churchill and Rudyard Kipling; abbeys and priories; lighthouses; and even whole villages and hamlets. At the end of 1991 these amounted to some 575,000 acres, over 500 miles of coastline and more than 200 houses and gardens which are open to the public. More than 10 million visitors per year are recorded at properties where admission fees are charged, and millions more visit the open countryside free of charge. The most popular property, measured by the number of visitors, was Fountains Abbey and Studley Royal in North Yorkshire.

The National Trust, which is independent of government despite the 'national' in the name, is almost 100 years old. Founded in 1895 by a group of individuals concerned with conservation and preservation of the countryside and important buildings, the National Trust now boasts over 2 million members. The 2 million figure was reached in October 1990. The growth of membership has been dramatic during the 1980s. The first thousand was reached in 1926, increasing to 10,000 in 1946, 100,000 in 1961 and 1 million in 1981. Members pay an annual subscription in return for free entrance to Trust properties and a variety of support publications. Initially the Trust concentrated on looking after land and ancient buildings; country houses have been included since 1934.

The Trust was formally incorporated by Act of Parliament in 1907. It has a constitution and legislation enables it to acquire property and hold it is as either 'inalienable' or 'alienable'. That part which the Trust formally declares 'inalienable', usually the important core of an estate, cannot by law be sold. For this reason it is not valued in the Trust's balance sheet. It has been estimated that the current market value, hypothetically, would exceed £2 billion. Land, however, can, and frequently is, leased to farmers in return for an annual rent.

THE MISSION AND OBJECTIVES

In simple terms, the purpose of the National Trust is the preservation of historic houses and beauty spots in England, Wales and Northern Ireland, keeping them open for the Nation.

The 1907 Act of incorporation states '... promoting the permanent preservation, for the benefit of the Nation, of lands and tenements (including buildings) of beauty or historic interest, and as regards lands, for the preservation (so far as is practicable) of their natural aspect features and animal and plant life'.

Given this mission and the 'inalienable property' constraint the timescale is clearly infinite and in fact the planning period for certain gardens is 100 years.

Conservation and preservation, however, costs money; revenues must be generated. The primary sources are members' subscriptions and the fees paid by non-member visitors, in addition to rents (see Appendix 7.1 for details). This implies accessibility, which could result in damage if there are too many visitors. Light, humidity and the passage of time are all enemies to old properties and their furnishings; so too are curious fingers and thundering feet. *Hence there is an important potential conflict between conservation and access.*

During the late 1980s, for example, gardens were generally more popular with visitors than country houses. Whilst the Trust is generally happy to see more visitors at its various properties – enjoying them and at the same time contributing to their upkeep – occasionally a certain stage is reached where it is felt that more visitors would conflict with the preservation needs of the property 'and the brakes need to be applied'. To prevent over-use and damage the Trust has selectively introduced policies to restrict entry, but these are exceptional rather than general practice. They have taken the form of direct controls (fixed numbers at any one time, say a half hour period) and indirect influence such as reduced marketing, higher admission prices and limited car parking availability. These restrictions have taken precedence over the thought of investing more resources to make the most popular properties even more enjoyable in order to attract increasing numbers of visitors and generate additional revenues. Generally the commercialism of many privately owned estates and houses is avoided by the National Trust. There are no safari or theme parks in the grounds. Activities like practising farmyards, mainly for children, are as far as the Trust is happy to go.

Instead attention has focused on the revenue potential of shops and restaurants (National Trust Enterprises) and publications. Donations and investment income are other significant sources of funds. These are discussed in greater detail later in the case.

In the main the National Trust takes over properties where no one else can or will, mainly the latter, responding to need rather than specifically seeking to acquire identified houses and gardens. The objectives are, therefore, more concerned with the preservation and improvement of properties already owned rather than the acquisition of new ones. There is, though, a clear long-term objective of acquiring some 900 miles of 'threatened' British coastline. This is almost half of the total of 2,000 miles of coastline, and the project, Enterprise Neptune, which itself has been running for 25 years, is over half-way to its target. The rate of coastline acquisition depends upon the success of the support fundraising.

ADMINISTRATION

The Trust has a head office executive staff comprising the Director-General, Angus Stirling, the Deputy Director-General and Directorates for Estates, Finance, Legal

Affairs, Public Affairs, National Trust Enterprises and Personnel. In addition there are 16 regional offices which are directly responsible for the properties in their regions. This executive operates within, and reports to, an elaborate committee structure of honorary non-executives.

The ruling committee is the Council, which is made up of 52 members, half of these nominated by organizations interested in, and appropriate to, the Trust's activities such as the Victoria and Albert Museum, the National Gallery, the Council for British Archaeology, the Royal Agricultural and Royal Horticultural Societies, the Ramblers' Association and various other protection and conservation agencies. The other half are elected by the members and come from all parts of the country. The Council itself has an Executive Committee which appoints, amongst others, a Finance and a Properties Committee and 16 regional committees. The Executive Committee 'reviews and carries out policies required to pursue the principles laid down by Council'. The Council, incidentally, is not bound by decisions taken at the annual general meeting of National Trust members. This has been evidenced recently when the Council did not adopt an AGM decision in favour of banning hunting on National Trust lands. In fairness only a small minority of members actually voted, either for or against.

Since the mid 1980s the senior executives of the Trust have operated with a management board which meets fortnightly. Prior to this, control was more directly hierarchical. These senior managers are responsible to all main committees of non-executives.

Staff in regional offices, guided and constrained by head office staff, will put forward proposals and plans to the various committees for approval. In general the Properties Committee considers property management issues in terms of policy, and issues papers on such subjects as the care of historic buildings, forestry and archaeology, whereas the Finance Committee approves the annual budget and accounts. When an acquisition is recommended by regional staff, the Properties Committee will evaluate the merit of the proposal and the Finance Committee the financial implications. Both pass their recommendations to the Executive Committee for the final decision.

REGIONAL OFFICES

The sixteen regional offices are directly responsible for the maintenance and improvement of existing properties, and they will also be involved in potential new acquisitions. Each property has a managing agent who is charged with drawing up an annual plan or budget for repairs, maintenance and possible investments in, say, a larger car park or better sales kiosk facilities. Revenues from admission charges for non-members and all associated sales of publications and so on are estimated to arrive at a subsidy figure. In the main this subsidy will be provided from general funds, made up of such things as members' subscriptions and profits from retail activities.

A head office committee of senior staff reviews the management and finances of individual properties roughly every five years on a continuing cycle. If any growing deficit or subsidy requirement is seen as being in need of close examination, then a number of options will be considered, such as:

- the potential (if desirable) for attracting more visitors, say by working through tourist authorities;

- additional marketing activity by the Trust itself to target the property at defined market segments or niches;
- new uses for the property, such as rallies, wedding receptions and outdoor concerts;
- higher entry fees; and
- lower staff costs.

The constraint of not threatening conservation by commercialism is ever-present in discussions, but is, apparently, rarely a real issue because of the culture and values held by the Trust's employees both nationally and regionally.

NEW PROJECTS

New projects, such as new exhibition material, better presentations, or better visitor facilities can be financed from a special fund introduced by the Trust's Finance Director. Regions can apply for investment funding if they can demonstrate that the projected return on the capital is likely to exceed a particular target. This fund is seen as a revolving fund, on the grounds that monies should be repaid within a relatively short space of time. Whilst the objective of the investment should primarily be to improve quality in the form of enjoyment from the visit the financial return is utilized as a constraint.

FINANCE

A summary of income and expenditure in 1991 is provided in Appendix 7.1. Table 7.1. also provides a breakdown of the percentages of the various contributions to the Trust's income.

In addition the Trust receives grants from government departments, conservation agencies and individuals, together with legacies, appeal proceeds and the sale of leases. The magnitude of these varies every year, often quite substantially. The National Trust is Britain's leading charity in terms of both total incomes and total voluntary contributions.

Table 7.1 National Trust: Contribution to income

	1991 %	1990 %	1989 %
Subscriptions	43	40	38
Rents (farms etc.)	16	16	17
Admission fees	10	11	12
Investment income	21	22	23
Profit from enterprises[1]	7	7	7
Produce sales	1	2	<2
Gifts	2	2	<2

1. This represents a $7\frac{1}{2}$ per cent margin on the revenues generated.

INVESTMENTS

The National Trust holds and invests substantial funds, the majority of which have been donated over the years to support the upkeep of particular properties. In 1991 over three hundred million pounds was invested, comprising:

- *the capital endowment funds*: endowments tied to specific properties, and required before the properties were acquired by the Trust. This is discussed below. Only the interest, not the capital, from this fund can be spent;
- *the defined purpose funds*: gifts and donations tied to specific repair and maintenance projects and/or specified properties. Both the interest and the capital can be spent;
- *the general fund*: cash which can be used as the Trust chooses. As highlighted earlier this is typically the annual subsidizing of those properties (in reality, most of them) which cannot be self-funded.

Wherever possible investment policies are linked to relevant time horizons. Funds designated for repairs are often earning short-term returns; capital endowment funds are invested for the optimum long-term benefits.

THE ACQUISITION OF NEW PROPERTIES

The National Trust only agrees to take on new properties if an endowment (calculated by a formula) to cover maintenance for the next 50 years is in place. Present owners, conservation agencies and the government through the Department of the Environment and the National Heritage Memorial Fund are the traditional sources of endowment funds.

The National Trust accepts that sometimes they underestimate the funding which will be required, and consequently the endowment covers only a percentage of the 50 years. Wage inflation has proved difficult to forecast over 50 years; depreciation is unpredictable though not markedly relevant; most significant has been the march of scientific knowledge which results in ever higher standards being set by the state, and expected by the public, in hygiene, security and accommodation. Higher targets for maintenance and improvement often prove expensive.

When the National Trust acquires a property it seeks to decorate and furnish it as closely as possible to the way Trust employees believe the original owners would themselves have had it. This requires extensive knowledge of period preferences and tastes, and it can also again prove difficult and expensive. Where the most recent owners have views on the way the property should be presented these are encapsulated into a 'Memorandum of Wishes', but this is not legally binding.

Funds are also boosted continually by donations and legacies, and by fundraising, usually tied to specific appeals. Enterprise Neptune, to cover the cost of acquiring and looking after threatened coastline, has been ongoing for 25 years. As additional funds are raised more can be accomplished in this long-term project. Following storm damage in 1990 there has been a successful Trees and Gardens Storm Disaster Appeal. The Lake District Appeal is another long-term venture to cover the cost of improving paths and preserving facilities, often utilizing volunteer labour. These are just a sample of many special appeals.

MEASURING SUCCESS

Measuring the success of the National Trust is a complex issue, and the various stake-holders and interest groups are likely to have differing views on the most appropriate measures, and on priorities.

- The Trust would argue that the main measure of success is the standard of preservation achieved, though this is clearly and inevitably subjective.

Other measures support the achievement of preservation standards:

- Firstly, the number of members, including those who renew their subscriptions and those who join for the first time. The growth figures would suggest the Trust is successful, and this is logically linked to the next measure.
- The ability to meet public expectations. The National Trust believe that their members and visitors are, in the main, seeking period authenticity – the property presented as it would have been lived in originally – rather than 'museum collections', say covering several generations, or activities for children. Resources are committed to achieving this type of presentation.

  Clearly there is support for the way the National Trust market their properties. Were they to change their policies in any significant way they may well lose existing supporters but at the same time appeal to different market segments.
- The number, and particularly the substance, of complaints. The Trust argue that they treat all complaints seriously.
- The ability to generate new funds and endowments to enable them to take on additional properties where necessary.

In addition the National Trust has to measure the extent of any damage and decay at properties and react accordingly. There is, as highlighted earlier, a penalty for attracting too many visitors.

The Trust also has a number of key financial yardsticks which are measured on a monthly basis. Where figures fall below trigger thresholds remedial actions are implemented.

ENVIRONMENT–VALUES–RESOURCES

The major environmental influences (the Trust's stakeholders), the National Trust's core skills and competences, and the manifest values of the Trust and its employees are listed below.

Stakeholders and interested parties

These include:

- Members and visitors – 'represented' at the AGM and by Committee members.
- Donors of properties. Many are motivated by genuine altruism, a wish to spread the enjoyment of their inheritance. Their wishes are sought and often followed, and visitors often find their interest in a property is enhanced if they know that the donor or a descendant, frequently related to the family which may have owned the property for centuries, is still resident.
- Conservation agencies.
- Ramblers' associations.

- Government. Government provides some financial support and legislates about certain requirements. Increasingly the National Trust may be affected by European legislation.
- Financial benefactors – although in some cases it must be debatable whether the financial support is directed at the specific properties rather than the work of the National Trust as a whole.
- Employees – whose values and orientations, as well as their expertise, are likely to be an important issue when they are appointed.
- The nation itself (as opposed to the state).

Core competences

The National Trust recognize that to be successful they must develop and preserve expertise in a number of areas:

- *Property management*. As well as the general maintenance and upkeep of properties the land resources must be managed effectively, and this includes the commercial lease arrangements with farmers and so on.
- *Expertise in arts, furnishings and in the ways that people historically have lived and kept their properties*. Many National Trust members are themselves experts and connoisseurs.
- *Public relations and marketing* – attracting the most appropriate visitors and providing them with an enjoyable, satisfying visit, and in addition, running the National Trust shops both profitably and in keeping with the desired image of the Trust. Generally high quality merchandise is sold at premium prices.
- *Financial skills*, including the management of a sizeable investment portfolio, together with an understanding of the fundamentals of economics. Yields do rise and fall, but the National Trust is substantially dependent upon the returns from its various investments.

Values

- The National Trust feels that a high moral tone is appropriate for all their activities.
- The themes of preservation and improvement are dominant, but financial accountability and responsibility cannot be overlooked.
- The Trust also seeks to be educational where it is appropriate. Involving children is seen as important, but it is encouraged mostly at specific sites selected for their location, intrinsic interest and the 'resilience of the fabric'.
- Generally Trust staff also share an 'ethos' which combines the feeling of working for a good cause, a degree of identification with its purpose and principles, and a certain readiness (typically shared by people who work for other charities) to accept rewards which may be less than employees of many manufacturing and service businesses would normally receive.

THE FUTURE

Whilst ever the National Trust can cover its ongoing expenses and acquire those new properties which both the Committees and staff feel it should take over, then its policies, which have emerged incrementally over a long period through a democratic, if potentially bureaucratic, organization structure, need not change dramatically.

The dilemma comes when the National Trust cannot meet its expenses from current activities, supplemented by external grants, appeal proceeds and legacies. Membership fees could be increased substantially, but members are under no obligation to pay them. Other than in their first or early years of membership, members frequently and happily regard a proportion of their annual fee as a subsidy. They could save money by paying at individual properties when they visited, but of course they would not receive the Trust's directory, magazines and details of new properties and developments.

Admission charges could be raised, but this is likely to deter visitors, and, in fact, is more likely to be used when a property is too popular and conservation needs are threatened.

Support commercial activities, shops, restaurants, publications and holiday cottages are all capable of growth as long as they do not conflict with the values and culture of the Trust. However, these activities remain relatively small in relation to the Trust's total income.

APPENDIX 7.1
OUTLINE INCOME AND EXPENDITURE, 1991

Income	£000	£000
Membership income	32,979	
Admissions and produce sales	9,014	
Rents from land leases etc.	12,194	
		54,187
Profit from National Trust Enterprises (shops, cottages, catering)	5,340	
Investment income	16,233	
Gifts	1,885	
		23,458
		77,645
Expenditure		
Expenditure on property:		
Property preservation	68,830	
Purchases of new properties	8,930	
Regional offices and staffing	11,905	
Conservation services	3,644	
		93,309
Non-property expenditure:		
Membership and recruitment	5,602	
Publicity and fundraising	4,540	
Administration	4,302	
		14,444
		107,753
Deficit		30,108
Covered by:		
External grants and contributions		10,798
Contribution from National Trust funds		19,310

Note: In addition, the National Trust received £3.0 million in new grants to endow newly acquired properties. In 1989 it received £18.8 million; in 1990 nothing.

Kirklees Metropolitan Council: corporate strategy in a local authority[1]

S. Davies and D. Griffiths

INTRODUCTION

The public sector was subjected to a number of legislative challenges in the 1980s. This case study focuses on how one local authority dealt with strategic issues between 1988 and 1994.

Local government forms a significant part of the public sector. Contained within it are considerable variations in policy and practice, so no one case study can claim to be 'typical'. Nevertheless, what happened in Kirklees Metropolitan Council (KMC) does illustrate the problems and attempted solutions to be found in many of the more dynamic local authorities of recent years. In 1988 a management review of KMC found it to be ill-equipped to meet the challenges facing it. In 1992 KMC was voted (by local authority chief executives) one of the top sixteen best managed local authorities in the country (out of over four hundred). The case study examines how KMC sought to achieve this strategic transformation in a relatively short period of time.

LOCAL GOVERNMENT: THE CHANGING ENVIRONMENT

By 1988 a radical programme of legislative change for local government was in full swing.

> Take Mr Ridley's three new laws (competitive tendering, poll tax, housing) together, add more over the horizon, throw in Mr Kenneth Baker's education bill, and the total represents the biggest shake-up of local government not just since it was re-shaped in the early 1970s but in centuries ... local government will never be the same again.
>
> (*The Economist*, 30 July 1988)

The legislation was designed to make local government more accountable, opening up service providers to competition, increasing efficiency and effectiveness and reducing the cost of government. The overall impact would be to change and probably reduce the role of local government.

---

1. This case study has been written with the full cooperation of Kirklees Metropolitan Council. The text is based on review documents, committee reports, published descriptions of management change in Kirklees MC and the authors' own knowledge of the authority.

Although some of the changes which will take place as a result of the current legislative programme concern particular services or operations, their combined effect will leave few corners of local government untouched. Not least, the role of the local authority will be significantly different, with less emphasis on direct service provision and more on setting the framework within which a range of providers will operate.

(J. Stewart, *Managing Tomorrow*, Local Government Training Board paper, April 1988)

All local authorities now needed to consider how fit they were to face up to legislative pressures and to embrace the role of being 'enablers' as well as (or even instead of) 'providers'. Furthermore, post-1979 Conservative governments believed that all public services could be market-tested (subjected to competition), either by compelling monopoly local authority providers to compete with the private sector or (where no private sector alternative was viable or available) by creating competitive conditions *within* the public services.

Out of the Government's experience of piecemeal action and reaction has come a new coherent view of the role of local government in Britain. It is a minimalist vision of local government, in which the market is relied upon for an increasing range of services previously regarded as appropriate for direct provision by local authorities. Where the private sector cannot provide, there is a commitment to approximating market conditions to guide the remaining public provision.

(S. Leach and G. Stoker (1988), in C. Graham and A. Prosser (eds), *Waiving the Rules*. Open University Press, p. 113)

Legislative changes affecting local government were but one aspect of major change in other parts of the public sector, notably in the privatization of the public utilities (water and electricity) and the reform of the National Health Service where a purchaser/provider split was created by making a distinction between District/Health Authorities (who determined what was required) and NHS Trusts (who delivered the services). By creating competition it was believed that market forces would reduce costs and drive out inefficiency.

Compulsory competitive tendering was introduced to selected activities following the Local Government Act of 1988. This obliged local authorities to open up certain of the services usually delivered by in-house departments (such as building cleaning, parks maintenance, vehicle maintenance, catering and refuse collection) to external competition from private companies through a regulated tendering system. (Building repair and construction had been under a similar regime since 1980.)

The local management of schools, a consequence of the Education Act 1988, obliged local education authorities (normally the education department of the local authority) to devolve most of its budget (often representing 60 per cent of the authority's total budget) to individual schools, and to allow them more autonomy of action, including the ability to 'opt out' of local authority control altogether if they so wished.

The introduction of *significant funding changes* also had a considerable impact on local authorities. About two-thirds of local government spending is financed directly by central government. The other one-third is covered by local taxation, in recent years the rates, then the community charge (the 'poll tax') and currently the council tax. During the 1980s successive Conservative governments sought ways in which to make local authorities more directly accountable to their citizens (i.e. those who pay local taxes) and their customers (those in receipt of services). The notorious and disastrously unsuccessful 'poll tax' is the best known of these. But they also tried to control spending (and the taxation burden on the citizen) by estimating what they thought were appropriate levels of expenditure (calculated through formulae such as the Standard Spending Assessment (SSA)) and then 'capping' (centrally determining the level of local spending, and thus taxation) any local authority which substantially exceeded its SSA. Along with increased accountability, the other principal aim of these measures was of course to reduce the public sector borrowing requirement.

Many local authorities were faced by expenditure crises in the late 1980s. Demands for their services were growing along with the cost of delivering them. Many were determined to deliver services at a level which they knew to be needed (or demanded) locally even if this were at variance with central government's perception. Increasing social and economic legislation coming out of Westminster, much of which was the responsibility of local government to implement and enforce, simply added to their burdens. Caught between this and the threat of capping, most found themselves forced to reduce expenditure voluntarily, bringing with it a deterioration in the quality and quantity of many services and job losses. Others were capped and had to make large-scale and often arbitrary cuts. By 1989 most local authorities were enveloped in a general atmosphere of gloom and apprehension about the future of locally delivered services.

LOCAL AUTHORITIES: HOW THEY WORK

There are two main components to a UK local authority's structure. The first is the *committee structure*. It is through the committees (and their associated sub-committees) that most formal decisions relating to local authority business are taken, though some are reserved to the *full council*, attended by all the elected members (councillors) of the authority (72 in KMC's case). The number and size of the committees will vary from authority to authority. The majority political party (headed by 'the leader') will select the chair for each committee. Places on the committees must in law be allocated pro rata to the balance of the political parties. On some committees (and more commonly on sub-committees) there may be non-elected representatives from relevant voluntary organizations or similar interested bodies. The frequency of committee meetings will vary from authority to authority, but six a year is not uncommon.

Each committee deals with a major area of the local authority's business, for example education, social services, housing, etc. The chief officers (i.e. the heads of departments) of one or more departments present written reports to them. The reports may recommend action, offer alternatives for the elected members to make a decision on a particular issue, or simply be matters for information. What matters are brought for committee decision or comment will depend on the extent that the committee delegates decision-making powers to the chief officer. The 'rules' for this are usually embodied in the council's 'standing orders' or set of procedures. The most common items discussed at committee are those relating to 'policy', finance and contentious operational decisions.

The other main component is the *departmental structure*. This consists of a number of 'departments', 'divisions', 'directorates' or 'services', each responsible for a more or less distinct area of either public service delivery (e.g. education, social services) or support service (e.g. finance, personnel). Each department is headed by a chief officer, some or all of whom make up the authority's management team which is chaired and headed by a chief executive, who frequently also has a departmental role, as, for example, solicitor to the council, or heading up a miscellaneous collection of central support services, often including legal services, public relations and marketing.

Each department may have a number of subdivisions, particularly where it is large and complex (e.g. education) or where there are a number of distinct operations subsumed within it (e.g. leisure services including sports centres, parks, libraries, museums and the arts). It is the chief officer's responsibility to clearly advise the elected members, to facilitate their decision-making and then ensure that their decisions are implemented.

It is, however, inadequate to view the operation of a local authority as being simply about structures. What makes for effective local government decision-making and delivery of public services is the relationship between committees and departments.

Figure 8.1 illustrates how the 'hard' structural relationships within a local authority are 'lubricated' by the 'soft' processual aspects of the council's operations. The *procedures* are the formal rules and guidelines which regulate the relationship between on the one hand the democratically elected policy-makers and decision-makers, and on the other the salaried and waged employees, whose principal task is to implement policy and decisions taken by the elected members. The formal and informal *processes* are those through which decisions are reached, usually depending on a constructive interaction between members (whose priorities may be primarily political) and officers (whose priorities ought to be the efficient and effective delivery

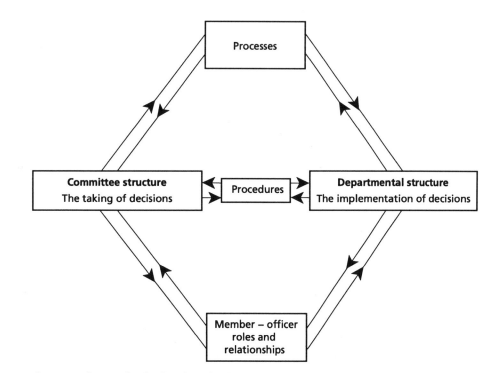

Fig. 8.1 The work of a local authority (After the INLOGOV Report, 1988.)

of identified services). Finally, a key element is the *Member–officer roles and relationships*. Who is actually responsible for what? How much decision-making can be informally delegated? When is it appropriate for members to become deeply involved in operational issues? These and the simple quality of personal relationships between members and officers can be vital ingredients in determining how well the machinery of local government actually works in practice.

KIRKLEES: THE DISTRICT

Kirklees is the seventh most populous of the thirty-six metropolitan districts, with a population of some 375,000. It is the third biggest physically, at 160 square miles. Kirklees includes the West Yorkshire industrial towns of Huddersfield, Dewsbury, Batley and Cleckheaton, as well as several smaller centres and rural areas ranging from wooded valleys to bleak moorland. Kirklees is the largest metropolitan district which is not based on a large city, but has both scattered settlements and numerous urban centres. In the latter are concentrated some of the worst effects of economic

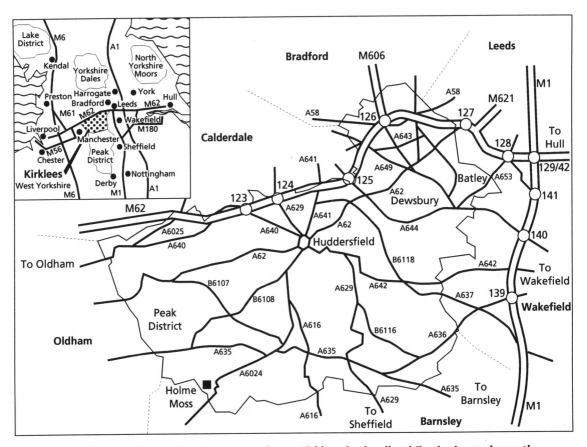

Fig. 8.2 The Kirklees district. The large map shows Kirklees in detail, while the inset shows the district in context.

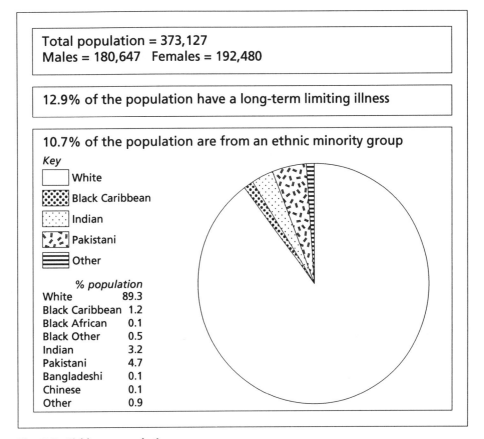

Total population = 373,127
Males = 180,647   Females = 192,480

12.9% of the population have a long-term limiting illness

10.7% of the population are from an ethnic minority group

Key
☐ White
▦ Black Caribbean
⬚ Indian
▨ Pakistani
≣ Other

	% population
White	89.3
Black Caribbean	1.2
Black African	0.1
Black Other	0.5
Indian	3.2
Pakistani	4.7
Bangladeshi	0.1
Chinese	0.1
Other	0.9

Fig. 8.3 Kirklees population.
Source: 1991 Census of Population.

decline and social deprivation in the Yorkshire and Humberside region. (See Figs 8.2 and 8.3.)

KIRKLEES: THE COUNCIL BEFORE 1989

Kirklees Metropolitan Council came into existence in April 1974, as part of a nation-wide reorganization of local government. It replaced eleven existing local authorities, and was constituted as a metropolitan district, adopting unitary status (that is having responsibility for virtually all local government services and functions within its boundaries) after the abolition of the West Yorkshire Metropolitan County Council in April 1986.

Topography, settlement patterns, cultural diversity and the previous existence of a network of small local authorities all conspired to make Kirklees a difficult district to govern effectively. In many ways it resembles a county rather than a metropolitan district, but it does not have a century of local government tradition to help it.

Over a long history, a 'county council culture' typically develops, which emphasizes country-wide issues, encourages loyalty to the county as a whole, and often regards special pleading for a particular locality as 'parochialism'. The mere 15 years of Kirklees' existence has not proved anything like an adequate period of time for such cultural developments and perceptual changes to take place.

(INLOGOV Report, 1988)

The council itself did not create adequate forums for local debate or decision-making within the various parts of the District, which meant that parochial issues had a tendency to dominate its business, driving out more strategic matters. None of this was helped by its being one of the most arbitrary of metropolitan districts in terms of its boundaries. The divided nature of Kirklees was indeed summed up by the fact that its very name was taken from a priory which actually lies just outside the boundaries of the district!

The INLOGOV Report of 1988 described how this perception of Kirklees as a 'divided' authority was only reinforced by the strength of councillors' loyalty to their own towns (or even villages), their antipathy to 'Kirklees' *per se* (shared by large numbers of their constituents), political hostility between parties, severe internal divisions within parties (often along geographical lines), inconsistent relationships between members and officers, and a problematical management team.

The history of the authority during the 1980s had done nothing to help this situation. Perhaps because of the size and diverse nature of the authority neither members nor officers had really come to terms with it and the comfortable reference points remained the smaller, more recognizable and perhaps more manageable pre-1974 authorities. There had also been a number of unfortunate rancorous 'affairs' (some of which reflected role confusion between members and officers) which had done little to build up a sense of trust or purpose within the authority. Since 1984 two chief executives had come and gone and there had been two periods when Kirklees Council was not sure whether or not it wanted a chief executive at all, and during which other chief officers had operated as 'acting chief executives'. Uncertainty was only increased by the fact that no political party had overall control of the Council after May 1986, and although the Labour group continued to lead and to chair the committees, they were deeply divided among themselves over policies and principles.

There were, before 1989, a number of significant weaknesses in the Kirklees decision-making apparatus. Although the number of committees (nine) was by no means unusual, the existence of nearly sixty sub-committees was extraordinary even by local government standards. In addition, there was an overall lack of delegation in the system, from full council to the committees, from the committees to the sub-committees, and (with some exceptions) delegation in general from members to officers. Reports going from one committee to another seriously 'clogged up' the system and slowed down the conduct of business. Other impediments to decision-making included a lack of informal arenas for members and officers to discuss key strategic issues or problems.

By the late 1980s Kirklees Council had a classical departmental structure. There were seven directorates each headed by a director: Education, Social Services, Health and Housing, Highways, Leisure, Technical Services and Finance. The rest of the council's key functions, including legal services, personnel, estates management and economic development, each had their own chief officers but were gathered together in 'the Office of the Chief Executive'. The chief executive, assistant chief executive, directors and chief officers constituted a 17-strong management team 'noted more for its interdepartmental battles and "macho" style than for its corporate leadership', as consultants were to observe. The committee structure of the council reflected the directorate organizational structure. Officer–member relationships were reportedly rather formal and it was alleged that this only thinly veiled considerable distrust between the two.

Consultants who reported on the committee structure in 1989 observed:

> It is rare for us to have come across an Authority in which there is so much overt conflict, so widely acknowledged and expressed. (In our 103 visits to local authorities in 1985, in connection with the Widdicombe research programme, there were only 7 or 8 in which, in our view, the level of internal conflict was so pronounced). Kirklees is clearly by no stretch of the imagination a happy Authority ... One feature of Kirklees which does stand out is the *uncooperative climate of management team meetings* ... In our interviews with chief officers it is rare to find anyone who had a good word for them ('management team meetings are a pain; they're riddled with conflict' was one characteristic comment).

One consequence of this situation had been to make it very difficult to engage in truly corporate activities. The chief executive's main role seemed to be to act as a mediator between squabbling chief officers and as some sort of an 'honest broker' to maintain a semblance of good relations between the elected members and the officers. Under such circumstances Kirklees MC would at best be seen as reactive and simply an umbrella organization for the quasi-independent directorates, who competed with each other for resources and favour rather than worked together to achieve some broader corporate goal.

In all local authorities there is an almost inevitable tension between, on the one hand, a *service committee/department* which typically wants to maximize its policy autonomy, and *central committees/departments* which typically wish to control, constrain or modify in one way or another what the service committee/department wishes to do. In some authorities this tension operates in a healthy and creative way; in Kirklees it was perceived as a problem. None of this was unique to Kirklees. 'However, the *particular* problem in Kirklees is the *combination* of this not uncommon uncertainty and tension *with* the legacy of mistrust and, in some cases, personal antipathy associated with the succession of crises/affairs of the 1980s' (INLOGOV, 1988). Kirklees seemed to be badly in need of both strong political and executive leadership.

The problems were recognized and there was a willingness to tackle them, if only because political priorities were not being transformed into executive action.

> I think the main problem came down to very unhealthy relationships within the authority, and this is sometimes on a personal level, but also the framework was unhealthy ... The trigger was impatience; impatience with the lack of corporate working we saw in the authority (we saw departments fighting each other for status, for position, rather than cooperating, which is what we wanted) and impatience ... with the authority's perceived inability to deliver the policy which elected members set and that made elected members very frustrated; they then got bogged down in minutiae, in detail, which perhaps they should never have done, rather than setting policies, simply because setting policy was a thankless task when it didn't seem to have much effect upon the organization. Now that's a caricature. It's not entirely fair to say that the organization was unresponsive but it wasn't as responsive as it should be and political horizons are notoriously short. So members do need to see, quite properly need to see, as representatives of the local population, they need to see results.
>
> (J. Harman, 'Strategic Management in Focus', Local Government Management Board training video, 1991)

These issues, and their political importance, were the immediate catalyst for change.

John Harman

John Harman, head of mathematics at Barnsley College, was elected to Kirklees Metropolitan Council in 1986, aged 35. Three days after his election he was elected leader of a divided Labour group. Despite having spent the previous five years as an influential elected member on the West Yorkshire Metropolitan County Council (just abolished by Margaret Thatcher's second government), many people did not rate highly his chances of survival. They turned out to be very wrong. Kirklees had acquired someone who came to be widely regarded as its most talented political leader to date.

Kirklees was a 'hung council' in 1986 with no party having an overall majority, but Harman successfully led a minority Labour administration until they regained overall control in May 1990. He was responsible for the appointment of new senior officers who then implemented the restructuring of management along Cabinet lines, while political direction (though not formal decision-making power) lay with a new Policy Board on which opposition parties were not represented.

A political realist, he believes that elected members need to rethink their roles in a local democracy, recognizing that, like it or not, public service provision (and the organization supporting it) has been significantly changed over the last decade. He feels that they need to emphasize their representative and advocacy roles. He also feels that if council members use their platforms to amplify and debate national issues then Labour is seen to be competing with the government machine and is seen as a genuine alternative.

An ambitious politician, he has fought for and failed to win the Colne Valley seat at the past two parliamentary elections. His main interest is not local government but the politics of the environment and international trade. 'The biggest challenge in front of the western political system is can we feed all the people in the world. After that it is the environment.' He has achieved a national reputation for his leadership on these issues.

Harman also enjoys a reputation for having the ability to absorb a briefing quickly, extract the key information from masses of paperwork and ask incisive questions. But, as one journalist has observed, 'his ability to effortlessly convey the impression of a person with something to contribute is probably his greatest strength.'

Source: *Local Government Chronicle*, 5 February 1993.
JH interviewed by Nick Shanagher.

REVOLUTION: SETTING A NEW AGENDA

In July 1988 Robert Hughes took up the post of chief executive of KMC. The following month the University of Birmingham's Institute of Local Government Studies (INLOGOV) were appointed as consultants to the council with the following terms of reference:

> To review the Committee system of Kirklees Council – including structure, terms of references and delegated powers – in order for it to reflect the changing nature of the Council's environment and functions.

In December 1988 they produced an interim report, *Responding to Change: Organizational Principles and the Scope for Choice* and in May 1989, their final report, *Oiling the Wheels: Processes to Support the New Decision-Making Structures*. These reports, which we have already quoted, included both a detailed analysis and appraisal of decision-making within the local authority (including recommendations for changes) and some general observations on KMC in the context of INLOGOV's extensive knowledge of other local authorities.

A large number of recommendations were put forward, but among the more important relating to processual issues were:

- a review be undertaken of the role and purpose of both service and central directorates;
- increased autonomy should be provided for service-providing units within the directorates;
- new organizational arrangements were urgently required in the areas of planning, economic development, environment and highways;

Robert Hughes

From pop singer to council chief executive is a transition calculated to raise a few eyebrows. It was as a teenager in his home city of Birmingham that Robert Valentine Hughes (born 1943) adopted the stage name of 'Bobby Valentine'.

I started with a rock and roll group in the pre-Beatles era. We performed at venues such as dance halls and town halls, and I remember doing all-night rock concerts at Birmingham Town Hall. I moved on eventually to cabaret, mainly as a semi-professional but for a while as a full-time pro. I was never a big star and never had a Top Twenty hit, although I wrote songs that did quite well. It was second division stuff but none the worse for that.

Hughes had left school at 16 and did a variety of jobs, including a spell as an encyclopaedia salesman, but eventually went back to college and university to acquire qualifications in administration and management.

In 1974 he moved into local government as a committee clerk with Birmingham City Council. Then he had four years with West Midlands Metropolitan County Council before returning to the city as a principal assistant to the chief executive and then chief development and promotions officer. His next move was to become Town Clerk and Chief Executive of Great Grimsby Borough Council for three and a half years before he moved to Kirklees in 1988.

On his desk Hughes has a notice proclaiming 'The buck stops here'. It's a motto he tries hard to live up to.

Ultimately, the politicians take the final decisions. But in terms of the bureaucracy the buck stops with me as the chief bureaucrat. I thoroughly enjoy the work. It's a worthwhile job and I believe in the public service and in democratic local government.

When he arrived he says he was impressed by the determination of politicians from all parties to change things and he set out to create the environment and conditions for change.

Source: Huddersfield Daily Examiner, 18 October 1991.
RVH interviewed by Mike Shaw.

- there was a need to generate mutual trust and greater informality between members and officers (reinforced, at the same time, by reform of the existing formal conventions or procedures governing committee business);
- that any formal system of extended delegation to officers be balanced by an informal system (of enhanced information and consultation procedures) strengthening the ability of members to play their local constituency roles effectively;
- that the necessary provisions enabling members to 'refer up' delegated matters be triggered only by the demonstration of a valid and sufficient reason for doing so;
- improvements to the mechanics of the committee system were required, notably in agenda planning and the use of standardized report formats;
- that the council reform its budgetary process, moving from a 'traditional' approach to a 'policy planning' approach.

In May 1989 a two-day member/officer seminar, entitled 'Kirklees: The Future' considered the INLOGOV findings (many of the recommendations from which had already been implemented) and, more importantly, began the process of building a corporate agenda for the future. The seminar's objectives were:

1 To clarify and understand better the challenges and opportunities facing the council.
2 To identify more closely the council's key goals and develop a stronger sense of shared purpose around these.
3 To consider the implications for the council's decision-making processes, organization and management.
4 To make a start in formulating a plan of *action*.

The seminar considered a number of the environmental issues confronting Kirklees, including legislation, demographic, social and economic change, and competitive pressures on front-line services. But while the council had to cope with these, it was determined not to do so passively. It identified three goals of its own which it wished to pursue:

- economic regeneration;
- community regeneration;
- customer care.

Two new regeneration sub-committees had already been set up in response to the INLOGOV recommendations. These would form the focal point for the pursuit of those goals. Crucially, they were not to be tied to departmental interests. There was still a Planning and Economic Development Committee to which the Economic Development Unit reported and which dealt with all the routine operational issues. The Economic Regeneration Sub-Committee was concerned with economic regeneration 'as a *strategic purpose* for the Council as a whole'. Similarly the Community Regeneration Sub-Committee was concerned 'with the *quality of life*' in its broadest sense for Kirklees residents and with '*consultation and communication*'. These were seen as very much strategic issues rather than operational ones, a fact reinforced by the setting up of 'task forces' to look at children's services, community development and poverty, which, almost incidentally, provided a valuable 'vehicle for corporate working, bringing together officers and members across service boundaries'.

A Customer Care Working Party had been set up in January 1989:

> While the regeneration strategies are much concerned with the council as 'enabler' and 'advocate', its core business, for the foreseeable future, will be the delivery of a range of community services. Here the twin pressures of competition and consumer choice make vital an obsession, no less, with responsiveness to the individual customer.

They had already recommended the 'development of a council-wide customer philosophy', the creation of an effective network of access points for council customers, improved communications about council services, quality circles, training programmes and a corporate complaints procedure. By May the priority to be addressed was 'the need to develop an implementation strategy which is owned by each of the directorates'.

Having established these three goals (and agreeing not to exclude other possibles such as equal opportunities or environmental protection) the seminar turned to issues of implementation:

> The council needs clarity about its policies and about the activities to be pursued – and by whom – in pursuit of those policies. For each council activity there need to be explicit targets, performance measures and resource allocations, thus enabling management accountability for results and a process of monitoring and review which feeds back into policy formulation. This management process needs to be underpinned by adequate information, adequate training and clarity about member and officer roles in the process.

Clarifying policies was recognized as particularly important in order to provide clear criteria for the continuous process of decision-making undertaken by members and officers. The clearer the policy framework, the more consistent should be the operational decisions which emerge.

Accountability was another key area for discussion, providing the link between clear policies, devolved management and customer orientation:

The crucial advantage of greater clarity about policies, activities and targets is that it enables a shift to a more devolved management style. In the past the organization has been controlled by centralized financial and establishment controls and bureaucratic hierarchy. This approach does not permit the customer responsiveness which must now be a watchword ... The alternative is to give managers clearer accountability for delivering defined outcomes, but greater flexibility over their use of resources to achieve them. There is then a need for a process of performance management and appraisal ... The key is to translate policies and activities into directorate, sectional and personal goals and action plans, the achievement of which can be monitored and appraised.

The Policy Unit were set the task of consulting with the directorates about clarifying policies and the Customer Care Working Party were given the signal to push on with the implementation of their recommendations. But devolved management was still more of a distant goal than anything approaching reality. The next stage of 'the Kirklees revolution' was therefore to address the authority's management structure.

ALL CHANGE: CREATING NEW STRUCTURES

On 1 August 1989 the chief executive presented members with his blueprint for the future management of the authority. It was needed, he claimed, because of the challenges facing local government in general and the inadequacies of Kirklees MC's own structures and practices in particular.

The old method of delivery of our services, i.e. through 'stand alone' functional directorate and bureaucratic hierarchies, is likely to be inadequate, inflexible and ineffective and a more strategic approach to the management of the organization, with a streamlined management structure, greater delegated responsibility to operational units working within clear guidelines set down by the centre, needs to be developed.

In his analysis of the situation as it existed that summer, Hughes pointed out that 'the budget process is still far from satisfactory' and 'corporate policy-making is frankly almost non-existent'. The chief reason for this he identified as the directorate system where the director's corporate role is regarded as very much subordinate to departmental responsibilities.

Apart from being inadequate to deal with environmental changes the senior management structure had failed to 'deliver the goods'. A review of central services in the office of the chief executive had revealed a number of weaknesses, apparently confirmed by members' own experiences:

1 Lack of corporate leadership by the management team. This was in turn exacerbated by the relatively weak position of the chief executive and the absence in his job description of powers of direction over other directors.
2 Failure to address corporate issues effectively.
3 Little strategic thinking, particularly about the future issues and challenges facing the authority.
4 Failure to resolve conflicts between different priorities and policies.
5 The work of the council was dominated by sectional, or departmental, interests to the detriment of the corporate whole.
6 Failure to deliver on the policy decisions of the elected members, particularly in areas of corporate policy such as equal opportunities, the poverty initiative and environmental protection.

The role of the chief executive

Currently the role of the chief executive in Kirklees is what could almost be termed as the traditional one. He is essentially the 'first amongst equals'. He is chairman of the management team, and Standing Orders contain a requirement for all directors to discharge their responsibilities to his satisfaction. However, there is only one director who has written into his job description a specific injunction which makes him responsible to the chief executive in a management sense. All other directors and chief officers have independent powers and responsibilities through the various committees of the council; some of course have statutory responsibilities as required by law. All have a right to be members of the management team. In a perfect world, of course, consensus is indeed the best way to manage. However, it is clearly apparent that without powers of direction the chief executive cannot be held responsible for either the performance of the management team in particular or the local authority's officers in general. He, therefore, clearly needs these powers if such accountability and responsibility is to be vested in him. This would be a key change forming part of the new management structure and the setting up of an executive board. The Local Government Bill does, of course, require that a head of the paid service be appointed for each local authority and in future this would clearly be the role of the chief executive. Under his new job description the chief executive would also in future be not only chairman of the executive board but all other executive directors would be responsible to him for the discharge of their duties. In other words, in a real sense, the chief executive thereby becomes the leader of the executive board, rather than simply the 'first amongst equals' as has hitherto been the case.

Source: Report of the Chief Executive on 'The Future Management of the Authority', August 1989.

7 Lack of accountability, especially in areas of corporate policy where it was often unclear which directorate was responsible for implementing what. This was in turn exacerbated by an intensely hierarchical and bureaucratic organization with too many layers of management, which confused line management responsibility and accountability.

Possible alternative models for organizational change had been examined over the previous months. 'Many other bodies, in both the public and private sector (including a number of local authorities), have adopted what is termed a *strategic management* approach, and that is the option that is favoured ...' Hughes proposed that an *executive board* be established, consisting of about five *executive directors* and led by the chief executive. The executive directors would be chosen not only for their skill and experience in a particular field but also for their ability to think strategically and act corporately. They would *not* have any direct line management responsibilities but they were to be given a 'bundle' of services for which they had a strategic oversight (see Figs 8.4, 8.5 and 8.6).

The monolithic directorates would no longer be needed and would be broken down into basic functional units of an appropriate size. The directors were to be all made redundant, with the entitlement 'to either take advantage of the council's various retirement and severance packages or to indicate that they wish to apply for any of the new executive director posts'. The new functional units would each have a *head of service* who would report to an executive director only in so far as the executive director would be responsible for assuring the executive board that council policies were being implemented in individual services. To encourage cross-service working the heads of each service in a bundle would meet with the executive director as an *operational board*, although this was not explicit in the chief executive's original proposals.

Finally, it was envisaged that a *policy board* would also be established as a coherent

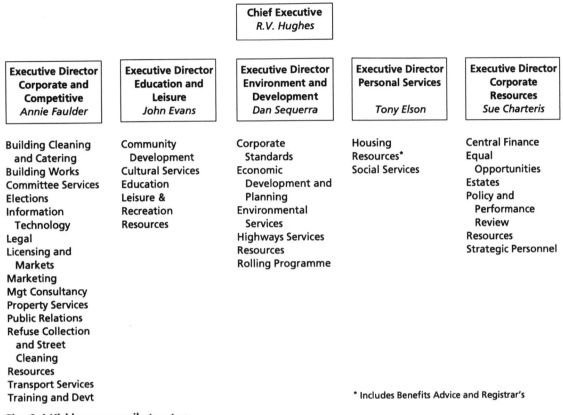

Chief Executive R.V. Hughes				

Executive Director Corporate and Competitive Annie Faulder	**Executive Director Education and Leisure** John Evans	**Executive Director Environment and Development** Dan Sequerra	**Executive Director Personal Services** Tony Elson	**Executive Director Corporate Resources** Sue Charteris
Building Cleaning and Catering Building Works Committee Services Elections Information Technology Legal Licensing and Markets Marketing Mgt Consultancy Property Services Public Relations Refuse Collection and Street Cleaning Resources Transport Services Training and Devt	Community Development Cultural Services Education Leisure & Recreation Resources	Corporate Standards Economic Development and Planning Environmental Services Highways Services Resources Rolling Programme	Housing Resources* Social Services	Central Finance Equal Opportunities Estates Policy and Performance Review Resources Strategic Personnel

* Includes Benefits Advice and Registrar's

Fig. 8.4 Kirklees: council structure.

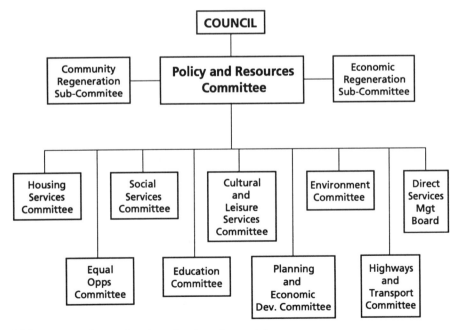

Fig. 8.5 Kirklees: committee structure (major elements).

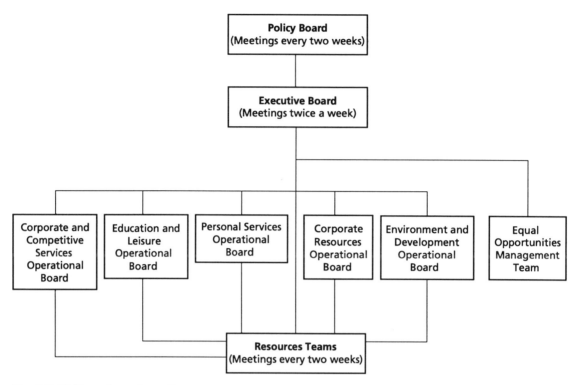

Fig. 8.6 Kirklees: board meetings.

source of political direction (though formally and legally, all executive decisions must still be taken by the all-party committees. The membership of it would be the senior elected members (basically the chairs of committees) (representing the non-executive element) and the executive board. The elected members were of course all from the ruling party. Similar boards of members and heads of service were eventually proposed and created at the 'bundle' level, and, because they mirrored the operational boards, they came to be called *mirror boards*.

The composition of the 'bundles' reflected the newly defined corporate goals of the authority and some attempt at rationalizing the key purposes of local government. Thus the *Executive Director (Personal Services)* had an overview of local personal services for individual needs, including housing, social services and welfare benefits. On the other hand, the *Executive Director (Education and Leisure Services)* had a bundle of multi-site specific services for the community in general, including education, leisure, libraries and community development (a new creation). The *Executive Director (Corporate and Competitive Services)* had the most diverse bundle, including an overview of all the direct service organizations and the direct labour organization, which provided the services subject to CCT and thus were very much in the 'hot seat' of competition. The *Executive Director (Environment and Development Services)* could give some real leadership on environmental and economic regeneration issues while the *Executive Director (Corporate Resources)* could ensure that policy and resources were appropriately synchronized.

The new executive board was approved and implemented very quickly. The assistant chief executive and one of the directors were retained as executive directors while the remaining five directors left the authority. The three executive board vacancies were advertised in October 1989 and the board was eventually complete by the summer of 1990.

The process of deciding on an appropriate new structure of service units took a little longer, but the 32 heads of service were appointed during the following year. In some instances (e.g. Community Development) new service structures had to be established while in many of the others major restructuring occurred to reflect the changes at senior management level. Over something like a two-year period, the initial restructuring of the council was completed, although individual services found that external pressures and budget cuts forced them to consider 'restructuring' as a more or less continuous process rather than an occasional review exercise. As Hughes himself announced to the press: 'We must reorganize the authority so that it can adapt to change at regular intervals and be flexible enough to respond to new challenges and initiatives.'

THE POLICY PROCESS

One key stage in this was the move towards an integrated process of policy and service planning, budgeting and review. Four elements were identified in Kirklees as being 'the building blocks of a strategic management process', and explained in *The Policy Process in Kirklees*, produced in the Policy and Performance Review Unit (see Figs 8.7 and 8.8):

1 A *scan* of the external environment, including demographic, economic and social trends and legislative pressures, together with public perceptions and preferences. In Kirklees this work is coordinated by a corporate 'Research and Information Group', made up of service representatives.
2 A broad statement of the council's own *goals and values*, provided for by 'Our Vision for Kirklees'.
3 *Strategies* for advancing towards goals, taking account of external opportunities and threats, and internal strengths and weaknesses of the organization itself. A strategy realistically identifies how the external environment can be changed and the organization developed, to bring the achievement of goals and values closer. Strategies in Kirklees tend to be issue-based, as in economic regeneration, equal opportunities, marketing and cultural strategies.
4 *Policies* which define more specifically and prescriptively what action is actually to be taken. They will typically involve defined targets, specified clearly enough to measure progress towards implementation. Targets are set for executive directors and heads of service.

The operational requirements must also be met, so further key elements are:

5 Detailed *service plans* which are produced annually and set out what will actually be done, taking account of both policy initiatives and operational requirements. These may include defined *performance standards*.
6 A *budget* process which allocates resources to services, and then to specific activities, to enable the plans to be delivered.
7 A *review* process which as far as possible monitors and appraises performance against plans, so that they can be adjusted in the light of results.

The latter three processes have to be accommodated into some form of operational cycle. Kirklees has over 30 operational services, some of which subdivide into distinct activities. There are also a number of council-wide initiatives to carry forward corporate priorities. For each of the 100 or so activities and initiatives, an annual *service plan* is produced and agreed by the council in March for the coming financial year. The service plan includes in a two-page format:

- description of the activity;
- objectives of the activity;

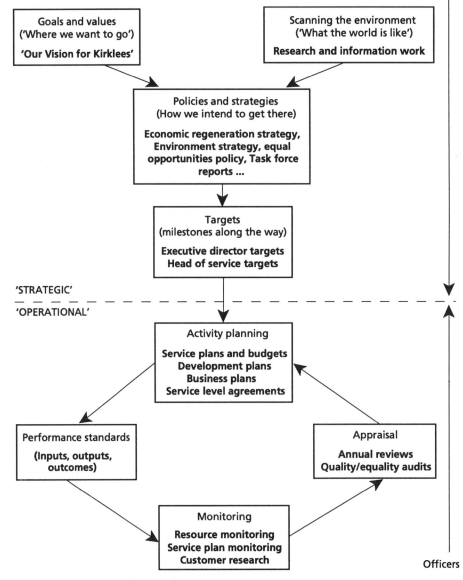

Fig. 8.7 Kirklees: planning, budget, review.

Source: The Policy Process in Kirklees.

Total Net Revenue Budget, 1992/3 = £290 million

Capital Budget, 1992/3 = £30 million

Community Charge, 1992/3 = £249.50

Staff, March 1992 = 19,560

Employees	Full-time	Part-time	Total
Non-Manual	4,389	1,893	6,282
Manual	2,297	5,559	7,856
Teaching	3,904	1,518	5,422
Total	10,590	8,970	19,560

Fig. 8.8 Kirklees: council resources.
Source: Finance Service Corporate Resources.

- prospects for the coming year and later;
- plans for the coming year;
- key measures of performance;
- revenue budget;
- capital budget;
- employee budget.

Monitoring the progress towards achieving these plans is made through reports to appropriate committees on a regular timetable, culminating in an *annual review* document.

Finally, there are other types of plans in use within Kirklees. Some of the public services have much more detailed development plans, typically covering a 3–5-year period. *Business plans* have been required since 1991 for the direct service organizations (e.g. building repairs and grounds maintenance). A number of *planning documents* are produced annually to meet statutory requirements or to obtain government financial allocations, and most are then published for wider circulation. From 1992/93 the council also introduced *service level agreements* which match the requirements of public services with the support services offered internally, and thus link service and business plans.

TURNING POLICY INTO ACTION: CORPORATE INITIATIVES

From 1989 onwards Kirklees MC was characterized by a major upsurge in corporate activity, designed to implement the new sense of purpose created by reviews and member–officer seminars. A selection of these corporate initiatives is documented here.

The Vision

The key goals and themes that had been identified during the INLOGOV review and subsequently were pursued through both new sub-committees and a whole range of working parties and task forces. But the 'new order' still needed to be communicated to the workforce and to others if it were to take root properly. In December 1990, therefore, Harman and Hughes launched 'Our Vision for Kirklees' (see Figs 8.9 and 8.10):

> In order to ensure that everyone in Kirklees is aware of the Council's main policy themes, the Policy and Resources Committee has agreed the following statement. This in turn has been used to develop performance targets for the Chief Executive and Executive Board. 'Our Vision for Kirklees' is being distributed to all employees of the Council and many other organizations within the Community. We hope that it will help to clarify what we are trying to do and how we aim to achieve it. The statement and targets will be reviewed and updated every year.

'Our Vision for Kirklees' stated the corporate aims or goals of Kirklees MC:

> As a Council, we are committed to bringing new life to Kirklees. We aim for a thriving economy, a flourishing, community and a healthy environment.

It also stated the council's core values:

> Building up Kirklees is what we aim to do. Working for quality and equality is how we aim to do it. These are our central values as a Council. By providing high quality services for everybody, we aim to show Kirklees residents that we are the Council of the People, not just for the people.

The goals and values were followed by statements about resources ('... we need to make hard choices, in order to concentrate resources on our highest priorities') and management ('... we shall need a different organizational culture'). Finally, the corporate targets of the executive board for 1991 and the individual executive directors' targets were listed.

'OUR VISION FOR KIRKLEES' Adopted in November 1990, updated October 1991.

Three Corporate Goals:

A THRIVING ECONOMY
– strengthening and broadening the economic base
– infrastructure and physical regeneration
– improving image and quality of life
– education, training and participation

A FLOURISHING COMMUNITY
– working with communities to build up their confidence
– targeting resources on priority neighbourhoods and particular sections of the community

A HEALTHY ENVIRONMENT
– reducing energy use, conserving energy, minimizing energy waste and maximizing the utilization of renewable energy sources
– reducing the polluting effects of transport
– raising environmental awareness

Fig. 8.9 Kirklees: corporate goals.
Source: 'Our Vision for Kirklees'.

Fig. 8.10 Kirklees: core values.
Source: 'Our Vision for Kirklees'.

Although greeted with a measure of cynicism in some quarters, this was the first time that the council had been able to unequivocally announce what its goals and values were. It now also had a document which could be used to 'cascade' these goals and values throughout the workforce and beyond. Some attempt was made to try and get services to directly respond to 'the Vision' and indicate how they were going to engage with it. As a systematic exercise this met with only limited enthusiasm and was not pursued, but three years on it was felt that 'the Vision' had become, in many different ways, a reference point throughout the organization.

> We didn't start with a mission statement; rightly or wrongly, members felt they knew what their mission was; they didn't feel that the organization showed it. We started from feeling we needed to change the culture of the organization to one which was based on devolution of responsibility as far as practical, not taking responsibility away from members but making sure that people within the organization know what their role is, are given responsibility for fulfilling that role, are held responsible in performance terms for it and are accountable, and therefore enabling the staff of the authority to do the job we wanted them to do, not asking them to look over their shoulder the whole time.
>
> (J. Harman, 'Strategic Management in Focus', Local Government Management Board training video, 1991)

The budget process

Another significant innovation was the creation of a number of corporate revenue budgets, designed to 'bend' resource allocation towards strategic priorities. The principle first emerged in 1988/89 with the provision of a 'poverty pool' of £40,000 to support the council's anti-poverty initiatives. By 1992/93 corporate budgets had grown to £3.4 million and were funding a large number of corporate initiatives, including child care, customer care, the environment, a corporate discount card ('the Kirklees Passport'), information technology, research, training and the costs of preparing for competition under CCT. From 1992/93 onwards, in addition, systematic efforts were made to allocate resources to mainstream services on the basis of corporate priorities, and not purely on a historical basis.

Internal communication

Internal communication within this large authority was generally considered to be poor. One small but significant innovation was the 'chief executive's roadshow'. In a series of meetings in town halls every member of the workforce had the opportunity to hear the chief executive (and executive directors) explain what 'the Vision' was all about and how they fitted in. Such direct communication with the workforce was unheard of before this. The introduction of an employee newsletter (*Inside Kirklees*) and a management information bulletin (*Management Matters*) were designed to improve the flow of information. Cross-service working parties on key issues have also helped, bringing together officers who might normally have little contact with colleagues outside their own service. By this means a corporate perspective could be spread among key middle managers in Kirklees.

Management development

There has been full recognition of the fact that change can only be effective if the authority's managers are well prepared to embrace it. A management development programme for heads of service was launched in 1990 and a new emphasis on the importance of comprehensive training for all staff based on training needs analysis was highlighted by the use of corporate budget resources to help it on its way. Other initiatives included the creation of a management development group, the preparation of a 'profile of the Kirklees manager' and a series of management forums usually involving guest speakers and dealing with key managerial issues. Indeed, there was a gentle movement away from the old concept of 'officers' to that of 'managers' being responsible for implementing policies and delivering services.

TURNING POLICY INTO ACTION: THE CHANGE AGENTS

The executive board

The chief executive and the executive directors' role in turning policy into action should not be overlooked. None of them worked for Kirklees prior to 1988 and their enthusiasm for 'the Vision' has been a key driving force. They are also very much the physical embodiment of the 'new order', strongly reminding the rest of the council that Kirklees is now managed significantly differently from how things were before 1989.

The Policy and Performance Review Unit

Of all the 'central' departments this had been the one at the leading edge of not only assisting in policy formulation but also in its implementation. Working closely with the executive board, its officers played a major part in the development of 'the Vision' and provided a lot of the 'organizational glue' at critical points. The unit's mission statement was:

> To assist the council in clarifying its corporate objectives and developing clear policies to achieve these. To take necessary initial steps to secure their implementation, without detracting from the operational responsibility of individual services, and to develop adequate processes to review progress.

But perhaps even more importantly they have often been leading figures in the new cross-service working parties (such as customer care), have drafted (or helped to draft) key strategy documents and have had to assume responsibility for major corporate initiatives (such as 'the Kirklees Passport', a discount scheme for disadvantaged citizens) which had no obvious operational home. They (no more than seven officers) also initiated a major programme of improving the research information available to the authority, through 'factsheets', customer surveys and other methods.

MONITORING AND MEASURING SUCCESS

By 1992 it was possible to realistically evaluate progress towards the ambitious objectives which the authority had set itself in 1989. In a personal appraisal, the head of the Policy and Performance Review Unit identified a number of problem areas. Firstly, it had proved more difficult than supposed to maintain *strategic focus*. Despite their respective strategic remits, both the Community and Economic Regeneration Sub-Committees had allowed themselves to become overly preoccupied with operational issues. However, the Policy Board, he believed, had become a more effective strategic forum. The mirror boards unfortunately had been less successful, partly because the creation of the new boards had not been compensated by any reduction in the public committee structure. As a result there were 'real problems of "meeting fatigue" and over-extended deliberative processes in what was intended to be a "streamlined organization"'.

There were also some doubts among many operational managers about the role of the executive board and the respective roles of executive director, head of service and chair of committee:

> If the essence of strategic management is selectivity, there is a need for consistent messages about what issues are and are not of strategic interest, and in an ever-changing world such messages are hard for the Board to project and for managers to predict. The inevitable result is that the Board is perceived sometimes to be unnecessarily imposing itself on operational decision-making, at other times occupying a detached ivory tower.

An additional aspect of this problem was some measure of inconsistency in approach by key players. Some executive directors, for example, were perceived as being more strategic and less 'hands on' line managers than others.

Some developments that were not envisaged in Hughes' original 'Vision' also created unexpected tensions. Determined to loosen the traditionally strong grip of large finance and personnel departments, it was resolved to devolve all but their most strategic elements. As a result 'Resources' groups were created at 'bundle' level, no doubt helping the executive directors to lead those bundles strategically, but at the same time raising the question of how close to the operational frontline should these vital support functions be placed. Some heads of service felt that one monolithic finance department had been replaced by six only slightly less so.

Chief Executive Hughes has often said that the proof of the pudding must at the end of the day be measurably improved service to the public. While almost everyone involved closely with the council's work is convinced that this has been the case since 1989, actually *demonstrating* it has proved much more difficult. Attempts to establish a 'performance culture' within the authority itself have suffered from a number of 'false starts'. Regular monitoring and performance reports appear to be often resented by managers and regarded as 'boring' (or incomprehensible) by members. Although annual reviews and annual reports have been encouraged, they have not been universally adopted. Nor indeed have attempts at pre-empting government initiatives by introducing local citizens' or customer charters.

Market research has been a more effective tool. Many services have embraced research methods to help improve the quality of their service delivery, and specific initiatives, such as the 'Kirklees Passport', have had the responses of those whom they have supposed to benefit directly tested. However, the most positive step forward has been the introduction in 1991 of a major customer satisfaction survey of council services. This has been the first time that the council has directly tested how well its services are being received by the citizens of Kirklees as a whole, and a repeat survey in 1993 showed a public perception of significantly improved 'customer care' on several measures. So far this sort of technique has been confined to easily identifiable public services, but there is potential to extend them to testing the council's goals and values to ensure that they do actually match the aspirations of its citizens. The Policy and Performance Review Unit took the lead on this work, but the creation of a separate Marketing Unit in 1992 is also indicative of the council's desire to be both responsive to its customers and take the initiative in promoting its services.

A NEW ROLE FOR ELECTED MEMBERS?

In 1991, government tried to stimulate a debate about future forms of internal management in local authorities. Relatively few had actually been inclined to experiment with new systems. Some, like Kirklees, had adopted Cabinet-style government, a single-party policy board holding ultimate political power while the all-party committees administered or monitored day-to-day service delivery, entrusted with making decisions which did not need to be ratified by full council meetings. But there were problems.

Opposition members were obviously unhappy, feeling that they had been completely excluded from sharing in decision-making for the whole community. But Labour's own 'backbench' members also seemed to lack an effective role, while the power of the policy and executive boards had apparently grown at the expense of ordinary elected members.

> Apart from a select group of leading Labour members forming the single-party behind-closed-doors Policy Board, few councillors any longer believe that they have real influence over the council's business.
>
> (Retired opposition politician)

It was certainly clear that further attention needed to be paid to the purpose of elected members in the new-style Kirklees.

During 1991 and 1992 an Internal Management Task Force looked at different models to reform the committee structure. They included one based on 'strategic issues', another on 'service areas' and a third reflecting the structure of the authority at operational board level. Partly as a result of these deliberations, but more directly reflecting Harman's personal vision, was a shake-up of the committee system in 1993, which included the development of *scrutiny commissions*. These enable elected members of all parties (often from the backbenches) to examine issues of public concern, including the work of local 'public' services now run by non-elected bodies (such as the NHS trusts or the public utility companies).

> We are not setting ourselves up to shoot quangos, though it's quite good fun and not to be under-estimated. But what we are trying to do is to represent and give voice to the local communities. If anyone is undertaking public works in the area, with public money, then the public expects you to have some grip on it.
>
> (J. Harman, *Independent on Sunday*, 27 February 1994)

Although the reduction in the numbers of sub-committees (by merging or scrapping them) may be seen as a structural reform to the committee system which the changes of 1988/89 failed to deliver, the main thrust of the 1993 proposals was not about decision-making or managerial structures but about governance.

John Harman strongly believed that elected members needed to reaffirm their role as representatives of the people, rather than get sucked into pseudo-managerial roles, or, as he put it, become 'unpaid bureaucrats'. Public service provision was now very fragmented. Local government, the health service, water, pollution monitoring and training, for example, were all run more or less separately from each other. Many of them were run by management boards which were entirely *appointed* (by central government) rather than *elected* locally. He saw the role of the elected member in local government to be not only the guardian of its citizens' interests where services were provided by the council but also where they were provided by other agencies.

> The key principle is the principle of *community government* to which we are committed, that is to say the council acting as the voice of the communities of Kirklees. It means strengthening the role of the councillor as public representative in asking the questions which the citizen wants answering, and in monitoring and improving the quality of service which the citizen receives, without detracting from his or her roles as decision-maker and local case worker. It means extending the practice of democracy and open government beyond the local authority itself and reaching out to all the agencies and bodies which affect the lives of Kirklees citizens; it means a recognition that the council is not simply a provider or administrator of services, but also the guardian of local democracy and the voice of local people; it claims a fundamental value for local democracy equal to that claimed for national democracy and springing from the needs and aspirations of local people. We want Kirklees continually to improve not only the quality of its service provision and the efficiency of its management of public resources, but also the exercise and theory of local democracy.
>
> (J. Harman, 19 May 1993)

The new scrutiny commissions would hopefully provide an opportunity to involve a wider range of elected members in investigating and, if necessary, challenging those responsible for any of the public services offered to Kirklees citizens. In addition Harman's proposals, adopted by the council, required all major committees to build into their agendas regular sections relating not only to the review of policy and performance but, most importantly, service quality also. Quality reviews were to be undertaken by small, all-party groups of members examining of service delivery at ground level. In taking these steps he believed that these proposals would 'keep Kirklees in the forefront of development of a good local government management'.

WHAT FUTURE?

By 1994 Kirklees Metropolitan Council was a very different sort of organization (at least at its senior management levels) from that which it had been in 1988. The general view from the top was that while there was still much to be done to change the remnants of an old culture, Kirklees should be proud of how it has tackled the enormous challenges to local government over the last previous five years.

In May 1994 the Labour group's programme of change was put in jeopardy. The local elections went badly for them and (somewhat against the national trend) they lost overall control of the council. Although retaining the mayoralty (which gave them a decisive casting vote at the bi-monthly full council meetings) all the committees were deadlocked and no chairs could be appointed. While not hindering the delivery of council services, this did mean that medium and long-term policy-making would be very difficult and the continued existence of a one-party policy board (sitting at the heart of the new approach in Kirklees) was precluded.

As this case study is completed (June 1994) these issues have not been resolved, but it is clear that the evolution of the council has entered a new phase.

SECTION 4

Services

Case 9   Abbey National Plc
              *D. Thwaites, University of Leeds, and J.P. Dewhirst, Elmwood
              Design Ltd*

Case 10   The caisses d'épargne (French savings banks)
              *B. Moingeon and B. Ramanantsoa, Groupe HEC, Jouy-en-Josas,
              France*

Case 11   Corporate strategies within the newly privatized water plcs
              S.G. Ogden, University of Leeds

Abbey National Plc

D. Thwaites and J.P. Dewhirst

INTRODUCTION

Building societies were first established in the latter half of the eighteenth century as Britain experienced a transition from an agriculturally based economy to one in which industrialization played a major role. A consequence of this industrial revolution was the migration of many former agricultural workers to the towns and cities where they encountered social problems such as unemployment, bad housing, poor working conditions and a constant risk of illness. To militate against these difficulties workers formed self-help groups, later to be known as friendly societies, centred around a trade association or chapel. Together with money clubs, which balloted for the right to borrow subscriptions collected during the week, the friendly societies were instrumental in promoting the development of building societies.

Loopholes in existing building society legislation and malpractice by some societies precipitated further controls in 1874 and 1894 which, *inter alia*, increased the power of the Chief Registrar of Friendly Societies to investigate and control the operations of building societies and limited their activities in certain fields of business. Even at this early stage building societies were clearly distinguishable from banks by virtue of their regulatory control, business focus and mutual status (owned by their investors and borrowers). A feature of the development of building societies was the introduction of legislation to accommodate specific events and the lack of a contemporary regulatory framework. Although a new Act became effective in 1962, in the main this consolidated a number of earlier statutes, and the primary legislation, which was over 100 years old, failed to reflect the prevailing business environment. Building societies were tightly constrained by the provisions of the Act and were precluded from offering their members services such as banking, unsecured loans, estate agency, conveyancing and certain insurance schemes.

> The purpose for which a building society may be established under this Act is that of raising by the subscriptions of members a stock or fund for making advances to members out of the funds of the society upon security by way of mortgage of freehold or leasehold estate.
>
> (Section 1(1), Building Societies Act 1962)

Changes in the nature of financial services markets during the early 1980s, coupled with government policy towards greater competition, influenced further legislation in 1986. This provided building societies with scope for the introduction of additional services while retaining a specialist role in the finance of house purchase and the area of personal savings.

Table 9.1 Commercial asset categories and limits

Category	Broad description	Initial limit	1990 limits	1991 limits	1993 limits
Class 1	Loan secured by first mortgage of owner-occupied house	Minimum 90%	Minimum 82.5%	Minimum 80%	Minimum 75%
Class 2	Other loans secured on property, i.e. loans to housing associations, loans to house builders, loans on non-residential property, second mortgage loans on owner-occupied property	Together with Class 3 not more than 10%	Together with Class 3 not more than 17.5%	Together with Class 3 not more than 20%	Together with Class 3 not more than 25%
Class 3	Unsecured loans up to £5,000,[1] acquisition and development of land, investments in subsidiaries and associates	Not more than 5% unsecured lending, and acquisition and development of land not available to societies with commercial assets below £100m	Not more than 7.5%	Not more than 10%	Not more than 15%

1. This limit was increased to £10,000 following the Treasury's Review of Building Society Powers.

Source: L. Drake (1989) *The Building Society Industry in Transition*. London, Macmillan, p. 12.

The *primary* purpose of a building society is to raise funds from individual members for lending on security by mortgage of owner occupied residential property.

(Section 1(1), Building Societies Act 1986)

Under the provisions of the new legislation building societies were still obliged to restrict 90 per cent of their lending to first mortgages on owner-occupied houses. Subsequent changes have reduced this figure to 75 per cent (Table 9.1). In relation to securing funds the Act allowed for the raising of up to 40 per cent of total share, deposit and loan balances from non-retail sources, i.e. the wholesale markets. However, an initial limit of 20 per cent was set under subs. 15. On 1 January 1988 this constraint was removed, although it is still argued that few societies will be able to go above 30 per cent.

In addition to widening the range of services on offer and increasing the scope for lending, the 1986 Act gave new rights to members which facilitated more active participation in their society's activities. It also introduced the Building Societies Commission and an investor protection scheme. Despite the additional powers available some building societies still felt constrained by the legislation and began to investigate the case for abandoning their mutual status and converting to a plc.

INDUSTRY BACKGROUND

The decade preceding the conversion of the Abbey National Building Society to a plc was notable for several important developments which had an influence on the growth of the personal financial services (PFS) market. While the economic outlook towards the end of the the period showed signs of deterioration, the general picture was one of highly favourable conditions which encouraged saving. Asset values, reflected by the FTSE 100 Index, showed a general increase, despite some peaks and troughs. Growth was also apparent in net personal financial wealth and in the percentage of the population owning shares, primarily through privatization.

Additionally, the suppliers of financial services in the UK had specialized in distinct sections of the market and competition was limited. For example, the banks focused on the provision of finance for business and offered money transmission services, whereas building societies were the major source of funding for house purchase and offered a range of deposit and savings products. During the early 1980s these historical patterns of behaviour began to change with a progressive dismantling of the traditional lines of demarcation.

While a number of forces were influential drivers of change in PFS, legislative and regulatory issues coupled with technological developments held particular importance. During June 1980 government policy moved from quantitative limitation towards market force control of credit flows with the removal of the Supplementary Special Deposit arrangements (known colloquially as the 'corset'). This mechanism had limited the scope for banks to develop links with the personal sector and compete for mortgage business. Between 1980 and 1982 they responded positively to this new opportunity and their share of net mortgage lending rose from 8.1 per cent to 35.9 per cent.

The determination of interest rates by building societies was based on recommendations by the Building Societies Association (BSA) and consisted of two elements:

- a recommended rate for investments and mortgages;
- an undertaking by participating societies to provide 28 days' notice of their intention to vary interest rates.

These practices were questioned because they limited the scope for competition and resulted in mortgage rates below market clearing levels. This excess demand allowed building societies to be highly selective and was accompanied by mortgage queues. The differential between the rates for saving and borrowing was also criticized for being too wide, thereby allowing inefficient societies to survive. The demise of the cartel in 1983, together with the removal of regulatory asymmetry in the guise of the 'corset', led to mortgage rates rising to meet the excess demand. The replacement of non-price rationing removed the gap between potential housing demand (due to underlying factors such as incomes and demographics) and effective demand (financed by mortgage lending). Households were therefore able to react to their expectations about the benefits of home ownership (price increases) and alter their gearing to a desired level, encouraged by government tax concessions. A fundamental change in competitive behaviour ensued as customers could at last choose between competing institutions.

Government policies towards financial deregulation and wider home ownership had a positive impact on economic activity, employment and profits in the financial services industry during the 1980s. This was accompanied by the encouragement of share ownership and the privatization of several public utilities, for example telecommunications and water. Consideration of a change in legal structure by Abbey National in 1989 was therefore consistent with the prevailing Thatcherite ethos.

Legislative changes in financial markets allowed the provision of additional services to satisfy the needs of more sophisticated customers but also introduced new systems of control. The Building Societies Act 1986 increased the scope for share dealing, personal equity plans and the provision of personal credit, life and pensions products. Further powers were added in 1988 which facilitated fund management (including unit trusts), ownership of life companies or stockbrokers and the introduction of a wide range of banking services. Appendix 9.1 provides a comprehensive list of the new services. The Financial Services Act 1986, *inter alia*, focused particular attention on the role of the financial intermediary through polarization. Intermediaries were required to indicate whether they were offering advice on the products of a single company (tied agent) or across a broad range of companies (independent).

Technological developments within the PFS market have had a profound effect in relation to the time and cost of handling payments, the ability to create and accommodate expanded customer bases and the removal of traditional constraints on time and place (e.g. automated teller machines, home banking). Technology has also been highly influential in the production and delivery of many new services and the provision of enhanced marketing information systems. While the rapid diffusion of technology within the sector has supported or driven a number of changes, it exhibits both positive and negative aspects. For example, it is suggested that where technology reduces personal contact this also reduces loyalty and the ability to cross and up-sell. Competitive equilibrium has also been disturbed as both entry and exit barriers have been eased. Organizations are no longer precluded from entry or exit through expensive branch networks. Moves towards standardized technology and sharing between institutions restricts the scope of product differentiation while patterns of distribution, branch design and staff roles have seen major modification to incorporate technology.

Although the market for PFS grew rapidly during the 1980s a number of the favourable influences were unlikely to continue into the 1990s and it was suggested that institutions would need to seek alternative sources of profit. As the market expanded new institutions had been attracted to the point that over-capacity existed. In particular the growing maturity of the mortgage market as a result of the near saturation level of owner-occupation was obscured by the dramatic increase in the value of net mortgage advances during the 1980s. The absence of non-price or quota rationing of mortgage funds allowed households to respond to their expectations of property price movements. Higher housing demand increased the demand for mortgages, raising mortgage borrowing in step with house prices. Households also used mortgage finance as a substitute for other forms of personal borrowing through equity extraction. Any constraints on market growth could only exacerbate the trend towards more intense competition. Appendix 9.2 provides a SWOT analysis for the major players in PFS during 1990.

The PFS market in the late 1980s was therefore characterized by discontinuous change and significant environmental turbulence. The dynamics of the housing market changed significantly as deregulation fundamentally altered underlying relationships which helped determine prices. Increases in prices were accompanied by consumer expectations of yet further increases. The same expectations have had an influence in reverse as house prices in real and nominal terms have fallen since the peak of the UK housing boom in 1988.

To be successful in the new environment institutions needed to develop a mode of strategic behaviour appropriate to the levels of turbulence in the environment and to configure the organization in a manner which complemented the chosen mode. It was in this context that the Abbey National Building Society considered a change of legal structure to a plc.

ABBEY NATIONAL

Abbey National Building Society was formed with the merger of the Abbey Road and the National Building Societies on 1 January 1944 and until its conversion to a bank in 1989 remained the second largest society in the UK. During the 1970s Abbey National sought to differentiate itself through extensive TV advertising which promoted the 'Abbey Habit' and by the early 1980s had developed a reputation for product innovation and aggressive marketing which had contributed to the society's dramatic growth (Table 9.2).

In September 1983 Abbey National withdrew from the interest rate cartel of the Building Societies Association, signalling its confidence to compete in an open market. This was one of several proactive moves which typified Abbey National's approach during the 1980s. The main achievements of Abbey National Building Society during the 1980s are listed in Table 9.3.

In 1984 Abbey National appointed Peter Birch as Group Chief Executive. His appointment was atypical within the building society industry as his experience had been gained outside the financial services sector (formerly he worked as Group General Manager of Gillette (UK) Ltd, 1975–81, and as Managing Director, 1981–84) and at 46 years old was relatively young. Mr Birch soon became active in lobbying for the reform of the Building Societies Act 1962 which provided the regulatory framework for the industry. Despite the opportunities brought about by the Building Societies Act 1986 it was apparent that Abbey National was seeking more radical change. On 23 March 1988 Sir Campbell Adamson, Chairman, announced that the board of Abbey National would be asking its members to vote on a proposal that the society convert to a public limited company. The members of the board of directors at this time are listed in Appendix 9.3.

The reasons for the decision were set out in the subsequent Transfer Document issued by the Society in 1989. Conversion was seen as providing the society greater flexibility in its range of services and increased access to capital resources:

> These factors will enable Abbey National to develop more effectively its businesses and enhance its ability to compete with its major competitors in the UK personal financial services market.

The directors recognized that the great majority of the society's income would

Table 9.2 Abbey National expansion 1950–87

As at 31 December	Total assets (£ million) December	Abbey National's share of total building society assets (%)	Number of savers (million)	Number of borrowers (million)	Number of branches[1]
1950	122	9.7	0.4	0.1	54
1960	389	12.3	0.7	0.2	90
1970	1,522	14.1	1.9	0.4	196
1980	8,641	16.1	6.6	0.8	635
1985	19,553	16.2	7.6	1.0	674
1986	23,041	16.4	7.8	1.1	676
1987	26,411	16.5	7.7	1.1	677

1. Figures do not include Cornerstone estate agency branches, the first of which was acquired in January 1987 and which numbered 82 at 31 December 1987.

Source: Abbey National Building Society Transfer Document (1989), London, p. 53.

Table 9.3 Achievements of Abbey National Building Society 1980–88

October 1980	: First society to release survey reports to borrowers.
October 1981	: Installation of on-line counter terminals in branches.
July 1982	: Issue of negotiable bonds.
August 1982	: Introduced a seven-day savings account.
March 1983	: Introduced a savings account with a cheque book.
September 1983	: Directly responsible for the break up of the Building Societies Association interest rate cartel.
February 1985	: Viewdata introduced in branches to give 'instant' insurance quotations.
September 1985	: Launched Five Star, a tiered instant access account.
November 1985	: Launched Abbeylink cash dispenser network.
	First society with multi-account cash dispenser card.
January 1987	: Entered estate agency and unsecured personal loan markets.
February 1987	: Performance related pay scheme for staff implemented.
	: Launched Sterling Asset, a tiered 90-day account with a bonus.
March 1987	: Launched a $1 billion euro certificate of deposit programme.
December 1987	: First society to enter another domestic EC market (Spain).
January 1988	: Commenced sale of Abbey National branded insurance and investment products.
March 1988	: First society to issue US commercial paper.
	: Launched interest bearing current account and high interest cheque account together with £100 cheque guarantee card.
June 1988	: First society to clear its own cheques.
September 1988	: Launched a fixed rate mortgage.
October 1988	: Introduced a unit-linked personal pension.

Source: Abbey National Building Society Transfer Document (1989), London, pp. 53–4.

continue to be derived from its core savings and mortgage businesses. Conversion was identified as the means by which the society's distribution network could be modernized and expanded, including development of the substantial Cornerstone estate agency network.

Abbey National plc would continue the society's expansion into other sectors of the UK personal financial services market including insurance and pensions products and money transmission. There would also be limited development of the society's overseas operations in European Community countries and selective involvement in domestic UK property development.

Diversification was regarded as a prudent strategy to avoid over-dependence on the UK mortgage market and to both retain and increase the existing customer base. Critically the Abbey National board believed that:

> If Abbey National were to remain a building society, its ability to achieve its aims as competition intensifies would be seriously disadvantaged by the constraints of building society legislation. The combination of having to compete against other financial institutions operating at an advantage to building societies and the reliance, enforced by the Act, on the mortgage market as the source of the great majority of its income will, in the long term, have serious effects on the quality and range of services offered to the savers and borrowers of Abbey National.

Table 9.4 Pre-tax return on capital

	1990 %	1991 %	1992 %	Difference (92–90) %
Abbey National	23	22	18	–5
Bank average	11	9	9	–2
Building society average[1]	26	19	18	–8

1. 'Building society average' refers to major UK building societies (Halifax, Alliance & Leicester, and Woolwich) and Abbey National. Bank average is that of the four major clearers (Barclays, NatWest, Lloyds and Midland).
Source: UBS Limited (1993) *Abbey National Plc*. London, UBS Global Research, p. 2.

Although the board pledged that conversion would not affect the essential character of Abbey National and its commitment to good customer relations and service, members opposed to the conversion formed an 'Abbey Members Against Flotation' pressure group. The primary objections to ending mutuality were based on the benefits which would accrue from the status and operation as a building society. One such argument was that loss of building society status would lead to a loss of the traditional friendliness and service of building societies. The pressure group expressed fear that conversion would lead to a concentration on making profits with an adverse shift in the interest rate tariff offered to savers and charged to borrowers. A further objection was that Abbey National could be subject to a potential threat of takeover and the survival of the organization would be determined by market vagaries. Probably more fundamental were the arguments that diversification could be implemented as effectively under the rules of mutuality and that conversion would not necessarily raise significant amounts of capital, net of dissatisfied saver withdrawals.

The conversion of the Abbey National was agreed by its members and the status of a bank was achieved on 12 July 1989. The conversion was regarded as successful and with opportunity for potential capital gains the share issue proved to be oversubscribed. However, several hundred thousand investors failed to receive share certificates or refund cheques on time and burnt remains of certificates were found in a skip at Greenwich. The capital proceeds from the flotation were sufficient to satisfy the capital requirements of Abbey National's new regulator, the Bank of England, and finance the expansion of Abbey National's activities. Despite the recession of the early 1990s profitability has remained high and compares extremely favourably with other major players as illustrated in Table 9.4.

Abbey National's accounts for the year to 31 December 1989 claimed that this represented the largest flotation to be carried out in the UK, both in terms of the amount of money raised and the number of shareholders created.

POST-FLOTATION AND DIVERSIFICATION ACTIVITIES

Abbey National maintained its position as a market leader in the provision of savings and mortgage products to the UK personal sector. The flotation provided capital funding for the extensive refurbishment and improvement of its 680 outlets with 480 branches modernized by the end of 1993 at a cost of £180m. A feature of the refurbishment was the adoption of a more consumer friendly design and layout conducive with the need to sell a broader range of services. Abbey National also undertook a major reorganization of its branch structure with regional administration centres to improve operating efficiency.

Financial services

Abbey National had already taken advantage of the diversification opportunities allowed by the Building Societies Act 1986 before flotation. New products offered by the Abbey National included a cheque account and unsecured loans. This strategy was in line with the contemporary view that customers would respond positively to the concept of 'one-stop' shopping which had developed in the retail sector. Abbey National was able to promote itself as a provider of financial services beyond mortgages and savings in parallel with the media publicity afforded to the flotation process. Abbey National Financial Services Ltd was established in 1987 as an independent intermediary of personal financial products, operating separately from the branch and Cornerstone networks.

Estate agency

Abbey National's headline diversification, in common with other financial institutions, was into estate agency with the launch of its Cornerstone subsidiary in 1987. Flotation proceeds facilitated further capital investment in the Cornerstone network.

The strategic significance of estate agency to building societies had been demonstrated by the entry of other financial institutions. The control of estate agents by other rival organizations was significant as it increased the proportion of house sales in the hands of competitors who could dominate the origination of house loans and achieve profitable insurance sales.

As with other societies Abbey National had entered estate agency as a defensive measure. However, estate agency was also seen as a lucrative profit centre in its own right as well as facilitating a supermarket, one-stop financial shopping outlet which could distribute Abbey National's own financial products in addition to mortgages.

The Cornerstone network had 427 outlets by the end of 1990, although by the end of 1992 these had been rationalized to 355. Despite the investment of additional resources after flotation the depressed housing market conspired against profitability. In March 1993 Abbey National announced its intention to divest the estate agency business disclosing that it had cost the organization £226m over the previous five years with a £20m trading loss during 1992.

Sir Christopher Tugendhat, Chairman, conceded that in addition to ongoing trading losses the acquisition had not achieved the desired level of mortgage business for the parent bank. The scale and cost of entry had been partly determined by the extent to which other financial institutions had sought to acquire estate agents with the price of estate agency businesses having been driven up. Abbey National, however, was not the first institution to announce its subsequent divestment with others, most notably the Prudential in 1990, having already exited with high losses. It was estimated, for example, that Abbey National had spent £160m buying estate agency outlets since 1987; in August 1993 it was announced that the whole network had been sold to two private businessmen for £8m.

Housing development

Abbey National Homes Ltd was established to develop housing for people to either rent or buy. The downturn in the UK housing market had a significant impact upon the company's fortunes; although it did not undertake any new development after 1990 it recorded a trading loss of £13m in 1992, reflecting the fall in property values.

Expansion into Europe

In addition to developing new businesses in the Channel Islands and Gibraltar Abbey National diversified into Europe with mortgage finance subsidiaries in France, Italy and Spain. Abbey National's main investment was its £40m acquisition of Fico France in 1990 which subsequently suffered material trading losses (including £50m in 1992 and provisions of £94m) arising from adverse commercial lending exposure. In the 1992 Annual Review Peter Birch, Chief Executive, commented that:

> We remain committed to building a niche position in Europe and generating a stream of profits for shareholders.

Treasury assets

Abbey National Treasury Services plc was established as a wholesale banking subsidiary to raise funds for the Abbey National Group from the national and international banking sector. This activity was a direct consequence of flotation. Firstly, Abbey National's new status allowed it to derive a higher proportion of its funding from the wholesale sector (as opposed to the traditional retail or personal sector) than building societies. This allowed Abbey National flexibility to obtain funding at preferential rates and volumes if necessary. Secondly, with the growth of the Group, and indeed its stronger capital position, the specialist treasury function provided management of Abbey National's liquid assets and funding requirements.

Rather than acting as an administrative unit the Treasury function operated as an active profit centre. In September 1993 Abbey National announced that it was setting up a joint venture with Baring Brothers, the merchant bank, to sell derivative financial products such as interest rate swaps and options to companies.

By the end of 1992 Treasury Services represented Abbey National's most significant diversification both in terms of size and complexity with a shift from reliance on core product activities. At this time Treasury assets had doubled in comparison to 1990 at £24.8 billion and compared with £42 billion in mortgages.

Scottish Mutual/Abbey National Life

Scottish Mutual Assurance plc was acquired by Abbey National for £285m in January 1992. Its products are sold through independent financial advisers and therefore provides an additional distribution network for Abbey National. The acquisition also allowed the development of Abbey National Life plc on the basis of the experience and expertise within Scottish Mutual. Abbey National Life began trading on 1 February 1993.

The Abbey National Chief Executive's statement for the year to 31 December 1992 reported that:

> Abbey National Life's presence in the Group as a manufacturer of life assurance means that rather than being a distributor, we will be able to design products that match much more closely the needs of our customers. At the same time, we will be able to improve

our earnings stream. By broadening our range of own-brand life assurance products, we are also diversifying profits away from a heavy reliance on the mortgage market.

Although Abbey National Life and Scottish Mutual are separate companies they share key resources such as information technology systems and investment management thereby reducing costs.

THE COMPETITIVE POSITION OF ABBEY NATIONAL

By the end of 1992, three years after conversion from a building society, Abbey National had become a hybrid organization. Abbey National's diversifications could be regarded as the outcome of an opportunistic and experimental strategy of utilizing its available capital. An alternative interpretation is provided in the 1992 Annual Review where the Chairman reported that:

> We have strengthened our core business and developed in areas such as life assurance and treasury. Both of these will reduce our dependency on the UK housing market in the long term.

Abbey National remains the only building society to have converted into a bank. Other large societies have openly expressed their preference for mutuality and have been ambivalent about conversion as a critical success factor. With the exception of diversification into Treasury assets other societies have participated in similar activities to Abbey National with a number entering 'bancassurance' and others also divesting their estate agency subsidiaries.

Performance comparisons between the banks and major building societies are illustrated in Table 9.5. Of particular relevance is that fact that Abbey National has the statutory advantages of a bank (e.g. powers and funding) which places it in a good position to compete against building societies. Additionally, as a former building society it has the cost benefits which enable it to compete against the banks. The ability as a plc to diversify assets away from residential property and land is clearly shown in Table 9.6.

Conversion increased the balance sheet size of Abbey National considerably and it now represents the fourth largest bank in terms of assets (£83.8 billion, December 1993) and the UK's second largest residential mortgage lender, after the Halifax. Abbey National has continued to increase its mortgage market share and during 1993 there were indications that it was gaining market share at the expense of building societies through its 'fixed-rate' mortgage products, financed primarily from wholesale funds. In 1992 Abbey National held approximately a 14 per cent share of the UK mortgage market, although this rose significantly to 23 per cent during the first half of 1993. While building societies have limited the outflows of savings through maintaining relatively high rates for investors, this has left their mortgage rates uncompetitive. Abbey National Group financial summaries for the years 1988 to 1992 are shown in Appendix 9.4.

The members of Abbey National could also reflect upon the increase in value of their shares. From a level of 130p on 12 July 1989 the value had tripled to 397p by 1 March 1993. Strong rises in share prices towards the end of 1993 saw the Abbey National rise even further to 512p by 31 December.

Table 9.5 Bank and building society comparisons

	Assets (£bn)	Capital[2] (£bn)	Before tax profits (£m)	Before tax profits/mean capital (%)	Before tax profits/mean assets (%)	Tier 1 risk asset ratio[3] (%)	Management expenses/ total Income (%)	Interest Income/ total Income (%)
Bank[1]								
Barclays	147.2	6.0	(242)	(3.9)	(0.2)	5.5	64	55
National Westminster	143.2	5.7	405	7.1	0.3	5.2	65	57
Abbey National	71.8	3.2	564	19.1	0.9	9.7	43	79
Midland	61.4	2.4	178	7.2	0.3	5.7	71	52
Lloyds	54.9	3.3	801	25.7	1.4	6.5	62	56
Royal Bank of Scotland	34.5	1.8	21	1.2	0.1	7.0	64	59
TSB	27.6	1.6	43	2.5	0.2	7.6	66	51
Bank of Scotland	28.8	1.3	125	9.9	0.5	5.8	52	67
Building society[1]								
Halifax	71.8	3.2	680	23.5	1.1	10.9	40	80
Nationwide	35.0	1.5	185	13.3	0.6	9.0	48	77
Woolwich	23.3	1.1	149	14.4	0.7	10.2	51	75
Alliance & Leicester	20.5	0.9	123	14.5	0.6	9.3	66	59
Leeds Permanent	18.3	0.9	153	18.5	0.9	10.7	43	76
Cheltenham & Gloucester	16.1	0.8	131	18.9	0.8	11.0	22	84
Bradford & Bingley	13.0	0.7	91	17.2	0.7	10.6	45	76
National & Provincial	12.0	0.6	80	14.7	0.7	9.9	41	79

1. Banks and building societies are presented in order of their asset size; all figures relate to their most recent financial year ends (generally 1992/3).
2. Banks' capital = shareholders' funds plus minority interests (NB excludes debt capital). Building societies' capital = reserves (less revaluation reserves) + subscribed capital + minority interests.
3. Building society risk asset ratios are UBS Limited estimates (residential mortgages weighted 0.5, liquid assets weighted 0.2, and other (non-life) assets weighted 1).

Source: UBS Limited (1993) *Building Societies Research: The Major Players.* London, UBS Global Research, p. 83.

Table 9.6 Commercial assets

Societies presented by size of residential mortgage balances	Advances secured on residential property		Other advances secured on land		Other commercial assets	
	1992 £m	1991 £m	1992 £m	1991 £m	1992 £m	1991 £m
Halifax	51,108	47,868	685	700	396	442
Abbey National plc	40,399	37,867	636	639	3,072	1,180
Nationwide	26,710	26,497	1,374	1,210	207	206
Woolwich	18,563	15,817	537	492	132	145
Leeds Permanent	14,631	13,238	83	47	345	179
Alliance & Leicester	13,462	13,782	653	757	680	590
Cheltenham & Gloucester	12,670	11,721	482	508	14	55
Bradford & Bingley	9,961	9,236	495	296	48	45
National & Provincial	9,826	8,845	208	200	129	115

Source: UBS Limited (1993) *Building Societies Research: The Major Players*. London, UBS Global Research, p. 76.

APPENDIX 9.1
NEW POWERS UNDER THE BUILDING SOCIETIES ACT 1986 (AS AMENDED)

- Money transmission
- Foreign exchange
- Acting as agents
- Managing mortgage investments
- Services relating to acquisition and disposal of investments
- Establishment and management of personal equity plans
- Arranging provision of credit
- Administration of pension schemes
- Arranging provision of insurance
- Unsecured loans (maximum £10,000)
- Estate agency
- Surveying and valuation
- Conveyancing
- Housebuilding and ownership
- Fund management and provision of unit trusts
- Life insurance (through purchase of a company or establishing their own)
- Own up to 15% of a general insurance business
- Leasing, hire purchase, financial planning, executor and trusteeship, safe deposit, etc.
- Own a stockbroker
- Removal and storage services
- Operations in EEC

Source: Building Societies Act 1986 and subsequent amendments.

APPENDIX 9.2
SWOT ANALYSES

The following analyses are taken from Thwaites, D. (1991) 'Forces at work: the market for personal financial services', *International Journal of Bank Marketing*, Vol. 9, No. 6, pp. 32–4.

CLEARING BANKS

Strengths
- Large captive account base
- Branch network/high street presence
- Considered trustworthy
- Estate agents (some) (subject to state of mortgage market)
- Improving sales process
- Increasing current account stock (some)
- Adequate capital for expansion (some)

Opportunities
- Growing PFS markets
- Pensions, life and health

Weaknesses
- Generally under-developed selling skills
- High cost structures
- Plethora of banking products
- Some with lack of experience in administration/processing
- Low PFS product knowledge (some)
- Historic banking cultures
- Inflexible technologies

Threats
- Competition from building societies and life companies with direct salesforce
- Downturn in stock market (but may stimulate savings)
- Increased competition from new entrants at home and from the Continent
- Slow-down in mortgage market

BUILDING SOCIETIES

Strengths
- Large captive account base
- Branch network/high street presence
- Long opening hours
- Friendly image
- Presence in estate agency (though a weakness in downturn)
- Savings activities as springboard to expand into investments

Opportunities
- Growing PFS markets
- Deregulation permitting wider activities
- Life companies desperately seeking distribution outlets
- Links with other players, e.g. retailers, life companies, fund management companies
- Downturn in stock market

Weaknesses
- Lack access to adequate capital for diversification and expansion (some)
- Not yet sales-driven/lack sales process
- Lack depth of management to handle change
- Current dependence on mortgage market

Threats
- Competition from existing participants, e.g. banks' interest on current accounts
- New entrants, e.g. centralized mortgage lenders (Mortgage Corporation)
- Smaller societies vulnerable to merger/takeover
- Slow-down in mortgage market

LIFE MUTUALS*

Strengths
- Technical experience
- Brand names
- Critical mass
- Wide product range
- Salesforce in some cases
- Ties in some cases

Weaknesses
- Generally limited channels of distribution
- Dependence on independent intermediaries
- Rising costs of new business acquisition
- Capital constraints
- Lack of profit motive – sometimes non-commercial

Opportunities
- Smaller mutuals demutualize
- Consolidation
- Links with other players, e.g. retailers

Threats
- Takeover/merger
- Competition from banks, building societies and direct salesforces of proprietary life companies.

*Mutual companies have no shareholders and the profits are owner by the policyholder, for example Scottish Widows, Standard Life, Norwich Union.

PROPRIETARY LIFE COMPANIES*

Strengths
- Technical experience
- Administration capabilities
- Brand names
- Varying quality and coverage of distribution channels
- Critical mass (some)
- Access to capital for expansion
- Wide product range
- Large funds under management
- High stock market rating

Weaknesses
- Industrial branch image (some)
- Weak customer loyalty
- Hard sell image (some)
- Rising costs
- Some heavily dependent on mortgage market
- Dependence on 'with profits' business for profits (older companies)

Opportunities
- Growing PFS markets
- Ties with existing independents
- European markets
- Pensions, PEPs and health

Threats
- Competition from banks and building societies
- Takeover
- Taxation changes
- Downtown in stock market
- Growth in PEP mortgages

* Proprietary companies are owned by shareholders and most of the largest insurance companies (both life and general) are of this type. For example, Prudential, Sun Life, Guardian Royal Exchange.

RETAILERS*

Strengths
- High street presence
- Brand names
- Friendly image
- Opening hours
- Retailing experience
- Large loyal customer base

Opportunities
- Growing PFS market
- Ties or joint venture with product manufacturer
- Cross-sell existing store cardholders
- Access to capital

Weaknesses
- Little or no experience in PFS
- Untested customer loyalty for PFS
- Service quality

Threats
- Competition from traditional suppliers/distributors
- Tighter margins on core business
- Not successful in USA

* For example Marks & Spencer.

INDEPENDENT INTER-MEDIARIES*

Strengths
- Customer loyalty
- Product knowledge
- Extensive product range
- Image of impartiality
- Effective sales process
- Able to claim to give best advice

Opportunities
- Niche specialities, e.g. serving higher net worth customers
- High commissions available from tying to a life company

Weaknesses
- Many lack critical mass
- Cost of compliance
- Practical difficulties of meeting best advice rules
- No captive customer base (though many have strong links with existing customers)

Threats
- Requirements to disclose commissions
- Competition from banks and building societies and direct salesforces of life companies

* Intermediaries who provide advice on financial matters, for example, insurance brokers.

APPENDIX 9.3
ABBEY NATIONAL BOARD OF DIRECTORS 1989

Chairman

- *Sir Campbell Adamson*, aged 66, joined the Board in 1976 and was appointed non-executive Chairman in 1978. He was Director-General of the CBI from 1969 to 1976 and is currently a director of Tarmac PLC. Previously, he was chairman of both Renold plc and Revertex Limited and a non-executive director of Imperial Group Plc, Doulton Limited and Yule Catto & Co. plc.

Deputy Chairmen

- *Jeremy Rowe*, aged 60, joined the Board in 1976 and was appointed non-executive Deputy Chairman in 1978. He was chairman of London Brick plc from 1952 to 1984 and is currently chairman of the Occupational Pensions Board and Family Assurance Society and a director of John Maunders Group plc.

- *Peter Davis*, aged 47, joined the Board in 1982 and was appointed non-executive Deputy Chairman in 1988. He is a Chartered Accountant and was a partner of Price Waterhouse from 1974 to 1980. He was executive deputy chairman of Harris Queensway plc from 1980 to 1987 and is currently group finance director of Sturge Holdings PLC and a director of Avis Europe plc.

Executive Directors

- *Peter Birch*, aged 51, is Group Chief Executive, having joined the Board in 1984. He was group general manager of Gillette (UK) Limited from 1975 to 1981 and managing director from 1981 to 1984. He is a director of Hoskyns Group plc.

- *John Bayliss*, aged 55, is Managing Director, Retail Operations, having joined the Board in 1984.

- *Richard Baglin*, aged 46, is Managing Director, New Business Operations, having joined the Board in June 1988.

- *Charles Villiers*, aged 48, is Managing Director, Corporate Development, having joined the Board in January 1989. He is a chartered accountant and between 1963 and 1972 he was employed first by Arthur Andersen and then by ICFC. He joined the National Westminster Bank Group in 1972, becoming deputy chief executive of County Bank Limited in 1977 and its chairman and chief executive from 1984 to 1986. He was a director of National Westminster Bank PLC from 1985 to 1988 and chairman of County NatWest Limited from 1986 to 1988.

- *John Fry*, aged 52, is Group Services Director, having joined the Board in 1984.

- *James Tyrrell*, aged 47, is Finance Director, having joined the Board in January 1989. He is a chartered accountant and joined the Group in 1982. He was formerly finance director of EMI Records Limited from 1975 to 1978 and managing director of HMV Shops Limited from 1979 to 1982.

Other Directors

- *Sir John Garlick*, KCB, aged 67, joined the Board in 1981. He was Permanent Secretary at the Department of the Environment from 1978 to 1981 and is currently a member of London Docklands Development Corporation.

- *Michael Heap*, aged 54, joined the Board in 1986. He is a Fellow of the Chartered Building Societies Institute and was a branch manager with Abbey National from 1963 to 1985.

- *Sir Myles Humphreys*, aged 63, is the Chairman of the Abbey National Northern Ireland Advisory Board, having joined the Board in 1981. He is a Fellow of the Chartered Institute of Transport and is currently chairman of Northern Ireland Transport Holding Company and a director of Walter Alexander (Belfast) Limited.

- *Dame Jennifer Jenkins*, DBE, aged 68, joined the Board in 1984. She is chairman of The National Trust and was chairman of the Consumers' Association from 1965 to 1976 and a director of J. Sainsbury plc from 1981 to 1986.

- *Martin Llowarch*, aged 53, joined the Board in January 1989. He is a chartered accountant and is a director and chief executive of British Steel plc.

- *Sara Morrison*, aged 54, rejoined the Board in 1987, having formerly been a Director from 1979 to 1986. She is a director of The General Electric Company plc with responsibility for, amongst other matters, employee relations.

- *Hugh Rees*, aged 61, is the Chairman of the Abbey National Welsh Advisory Board and of Abbey Housing Association Limited, having joined the Board in 1976. He is the principal of Hugh Rees & Co., Chartered Surveyors, and was on the Board of the Welsh Development Agency from 1980 to 1985.

- *Sir Edward Singleton*, aged 67, joined the Board in 1981. He is a solicitor and was President of the Law Society in 1974/75. He is also a Fellow of the Chartered Institute of Arbitrators and a Companion of the Institution of Civil Engineers. He was a partner in Macfarlanes from 1954 to 1977.

- *Sir Iain Tennant*, KT, aged 69, is the Chairman of the Abbey National Scottish Advisory Board, having joined the Board in 1981. He is a director of Clydesdale Bank plc and chairman of Grampian Television PLC.

Source: Abbey National Building Society Transfer Document (1989), London, pp. 65–6.

APPENDIX 9.4
ABBEY NATIONAL GROUP FINANCIAL SUMMARY

Profit and loss accounts

	1992 £m	1991 £m	1990 £m	1989 £m	1988 £m
Interest receivable	5,963	5,851	5,915	4,459	3,113
Interest payable	(4,669)	(4,708)	(4,959)	(3,693)	(2,479)
Net interest receivable	1,294	1,143	956	766	634
Other income and charges	335	265	189	174	131
Operating expenses	(706)	(635)	(508)	(425)	(338)
Provisions for loans and advances	(322)	(155)	(55)	(14)	(13)
Exceptional items:					
Reorganization of estate agency business	(138)	—	—	—	—
Sale of unclaimed shares	101	—	—	—	—
Profit on ordinary activities before tax	564	618	582	501	414
Tax on profit on ordinary activities	(247)	(204)	(205)	(178)	(144)
Profit on ordinary activities after tax	317	414	377	323	270
Transfer to non-distributable reserve	(7)	—	—	—	—
Dividends	(151)	(138)	(125)	(75)	—
Retained profit for the year	159	276	252	248	270
Profit on ordinary activities before tax included as a result of acquisitions	30	—	4	1	(10)
Earnings per share	24.2p	31.6p	28.8p		
Pro forma earnings per share				27.3p	24.5p
Dividends per share (pence)					
Net	11.5p	10.5p	9.5p	5.7p	—
Gross equivalent	15.3p	14.0p	12.7p	7.6p	—
Dividend cover (times)	2.1	3.0	3.0	—	—

The statutory accounts for 1989 were drawn up for a nine-month period during which the Company traded from 12 July 1989 (the date of conversion from building society to plc) to 31 December 1989. For comparative purposes pro forma accounts have been produced for the year to 31 December 1989 reflecting the results of the business for the whole of that year.

Pro forma earnings per share for 1988 and 1989 were calculated by adjusting the pro forma consolidated profit after tax assuming the benefit of new share capital raised had been derived from 1 January 1988. Assumed interest rates of 10% for 1988 and 13% for 1989, net of corporation tax were used. The dividend paid in 1989 was a final dividend only, relating to the period following conversion to 31 December 1989. The notional full year dividend was 8.5p net and 11.3p gross equivalent.

Source: Directors' Report and Accounts (1992). London, Abbey National, p. 46.

Balance sheets

	1992 £m	1991 £m	1990 £m	1989 £m	1988 £m
Assets					
Cash and short-term funds	3,819	5,193	4,035	3,587	3,525
Securities and investments	17,186	9,995	6,113	3,237	2,303
Advances secured on residential property	40,399	37,867	34,044	29,126	25,111
Other advances secured on land	636	639	678	352	145
Net investment in finance leases	1,781	729	104	—	—
Other commercial assets	1,076	451	292	269	210
Long-term assurance business	215	—	—	—	—
Long-term investments	1,567	1,249	385	1	1
Tangible fixed assets	518	489	354	254	199
Other assets	1,799	793	491	375	43
Assets of long-term assurance funds	2,816	—	—	—	—
Total assets	71,812	57,405	46,496	37,201	31,537
Liabilities and shareholders' funds					
Retail funds and deposits	33,616	32,711	29,735	26,943	25,316
Non-retail funds and deposits	29,330	19,642	12,440	6,732	4,320
Dividend proposed	101	92	83	75	—
Other liabilities	1,951	1,539	1,297	732	456
Provisions for liabilities and charges	166	61	5	20	12
Subordinated liabilities	648	388	233	245	120
Minority interests	—	1	4	3	1
Liabilities of long-term assurance funds	2,816	—	—	—	—
Total liabilities	68,628	54,434	43,797	34,750	30,225
Share capital	131	131	131	131	—
Share premium	836	834	834	834	—
Reserves	2,217	2,006	1,734	1,486	1,312
Total shareholders' funds	3,184	2,971	2,699	2,451	1,312
Total liabilities and shareholders' funds	71,812	57,405	46,496	37,201	31,537

Source: Directors' Report and Accounts (1992). London, Abbey National, p. 47.

The Caisses d'Epargne (French savings banks)

B. Moingeon and B. Ramanantsoa

I. THE CAISSES D'EPARGNE NETWORK

The *Caisses d'Epargne et de Prévoyance* are currently undergoing a profound transformation. In conformity with the reforms adopted in France in 1990, the network
is being completely restructured. These 'private bodies of public utility' (1935 law),
that in 1983 became non-profit-making credit institutions, are undergoing upheavals
on a scale unknown to them since the first *caisse* was opened in Paris in 1818. Set
up by the philanthropists Benjamin Delessert and the Duc de la Rochefoucauld-
Liancourt, the original vocation of the *Caisses d'Epargne* was to carry out peda-
gogic work. Veritable 'primary schools of capitalism', they were designed to enable
the greatest number of people to make rational use of their money by demonstrating
the virtues of saving. Clients were invited to regularly deposit their savings in a *livret*
(a kind of savings account) The money collected with the aid of this *livret* was managed
by the state (via the Caisse des dépôts et consignations). The effects this state tutel-
age had on the strategy of these institutions are still visible to this day. It wasn't
until the end of the Second World War that a process of diversification was undertaken, albeit one that remained closely controlled by the state.[1] For a very long time,
the role of the *Caisses d'Epargne* was limited to that of a collector of funds, while
the banking functions that determined how those funds were to be used were assured
by the Caisse des dépôts et consignations.

After the reform law of 1983 and the banking law of 1984 (to which the *Caisses
d'Epargne* are attached), a Centre National des Caisses d'Epargne (CENCEP)[2] was
created to bring the French *Caisses d'Epargne* under one roof. Sociétés Régionales
de Financement (SOREFI)[3] were set up to serve as regional banks for the *Caisses
d'Epargne*. The SOREFI were credit institutions (financial corporations), with the
status of private limited companies. They were responsible for managing 'everyday

---

1. It is worth drawing attention to a number of striking changes:
   1950: loans to communities;
   1966: complementary livret and mortgage-account livret;
   1978: écureuil ('squirrel') current account;
   1982: delivery of banking cards.
2. Structure of the capital of the CENCEP: 50 per cent is held by the *caisses*, 35 per cent by the Caisse
des dépôts et consignations and 15 per cent by the SOREFI (regional banks for the *Caisses d'Epargne*).
3. The SOREFI are constituted in equal part between the Caisse des dépôts and the *Caisses d'Epargne*
of the region.

resources': current accounts, vouchers, mortgage accounts, etc. They were set up to decentralize throughout the network the financial functions previously ensured by the Caisse des dépôts et consignations. The latter remained in charge of re-employing funds collected by the *Caisse d'Epargne* on the *livrets*.

Despite the fact that the CENCEP had been set up, the different *Caisses d'Epargne* continued to function in a highly autonomous fashion. Some people even went so far as to compare them to 'little kingdoms' set apart from the rest of the 'banking world'. The director of a *caisse* was appointed by the 'Orientation et Surveillance' Council (COS), which was likewise responsible for how the establishment was run. This Council itself was made up of staff from the *caisse*, local politicians and representatives on behalf of individuals. This last group was the largest (some people saw in this a form of 'patronage'). In reality, the director of a *caisse* had considerable freedom. The Council generally functioned as a recording room 'mastered' by the director. The *caisses* enjoyed close ties with the life of the locality in which they were 'rooted'. After the law Minjoz in 1950, the *caisses* were authorized to use part of the funds collected to make loans to local communes. They also took part in cultural development by acting as patrons, as well as sponsoring the town's sporting associations. Their leaders had always been considered as local dignataries. They often entertained close relations with local politicians (mayors, members of parliament, etc.).

In 1990, the *Caisse d'Epargne* network numbered 186 autonomous entities. Each *caisse* possessed agencies that in many cases resembled administrative bodies rather than local banks (with the exception of those whose internal architecture had evolved during the 1980s). The employees were situated behind a counter and, in some cases, were even separated from the clients by a hygiaphone.

In a sector where competition was increasingly fierce, the network, though it had a certain number of trump cards at its disposal, also had a number of weaknesses. Among its trump cards, one might mention:

- *penetration level*: one French person out of two was a client of a *Caisse d'Epargne*;
- *local implantation*: the *Caisses d'Epargne* network was France's third-ranking network in terms of the number of agencies it possessed;
- *the amount of equity capital available*: with nearly FF50 billion of equity capital, the *Caisses d'Epargne* network ranked second in France and fifteenth in the world.

For almost 150 years, the *livret* was the only product on offer to clients. Half the aggregate amount in 1990 derived from funds collected in this way. Nevertheless, the product was ageing and was no longer as successful as it had been in the past (see Fig. 10.1). It was unable to stand up to competition from other, more profitable ways of placing one's savings. Confronted in this way with a powerful run on financial products at the expense of cash savings (*livrets*), CENCEP leaders decided that the strategy and structure of the network would have to be thought through in depth. Above all, they felt that a marketing effort would have to be made and that restructuring the network was inevitable. To help them in their undertaking, they addressed themselves to the McKinsey consultancy firm.

The conclusions reached by the consultants were clear and reinforced the feelings of the CENCEP leaders. McKinsey showed in particular that sizeable economies would have to be sought and that the *Caisses d'Epargne* would have to be given the opportunity of functioning like fully-fledged banking institutions. This would involve:

- merging the *caisses* (from more than 180 to less than 80), which would reduce

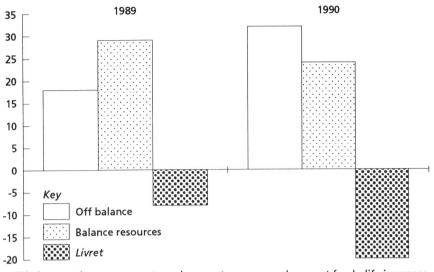

Off balance = short-run monetary placements, common placement funds, life insurance, shares and bonds.

Balance resources = cheque accounts, housing savings, savings bonds and limited accounts, etc.

Fig. 10.1 Flow of collected funds: the *Caisses d'Epargnes* network (in FF billion)

the disparity between the smallest and the largest local *caisse* (1 to 300 → 1 to 6);
- transferring the financial functions of the SOREFI to the new *caisses*;
- homogenizing the group's marketing approach around a new local branch and distribution concept;
- updating its image with a new logo expressing a unique approach.

According to McKinsey, reorganizing the network in this way would, among other things, triple marketing efficiency and improve customer service.

On 27 June 1990, the General Meeting of the CENCEP adopted a restructuring scheme that envisaged regrouping (merging) the *caisses* at a regional level and doing away with the SOREFI. The new entities would be responsible for their own balance sheets, would assure the totality of the banking intermediation function and have full control over their commercial and financial policy. According to the Chairman of the Directoire 'transferring the financial functions carried out by the SOREFI to the new regional *caisses* will not only have an impact on size; it will result in a radical change of dimension and profession. The new *Caisses d'Epargne* are on their way to becoming fully practising banks.'

The law passed on 6 July 1991 confirmed the restructuring scheme adopted at the General Meeting of the CENCEP. In introducing the law, attention was drawn to the nature of the *Caisses d'Epargne* as non-profit-making credit institutions and to the markets in which they can intervene. The legislator notably pointed out that investments in corporate bodies (small and medium-sized companies or common law associations) could not exceed 30 per cent of the total investments in each *Caisse d'Epargne* between then and 1997. He also pointed out that the *caisses*, when allocating resources related to their commercial and banking activities, should give priority to the local, social economy, as support for local communities. A summary of this text is provided in Appendix 10.1.

During the years 1991–92, the network underwent a profound transformation.[4] The various mergers carried out at a regional level led to 186 local *caisses* and 22 regional SOREFI being dismantled and 31 new regional *Caisses d'Epargne* being created (see Appendix 10.4 which includes a map of the *Caisses d'Epargne* in France), a figure much lower than that originally foreseen by McKinsey.

If one studies the chronology of the configuration, different stages can be identified:

- *Stage 1: The geographic scheme is prepared.* Regional concertation commissions are in charge of elaborating a plan defining the network's geographical organization. On the basis of these documents, the CENCEP Surveillance Council opts for a geographic target scheme of 30 or so *caisses*.
- *Stage II: Preparation for the mergers gets underway.* A project leader is appointed for each region. The project leader – who is either a director of one of the *caisses* taking part in the merger, or a member of SOREFI – is chosen by his peers and approved by the CENCEP. He is responsible for preparing the mergers and overseeing the new *caisse*'s organizational works. He also has to coordinate the activities of the *caisses* during the period of transition till the merger has been achieved.

  Each region elaborates a merger plan which it submits to the CENCEP.
- *Stage III: The finishing legal touches are brought to the plans, which are submitted for approval in the course of 1991.* The merger records drawn up under the authority of the project leaders are submitted to the CENCEP Surveillance Council before being approved by the Committee of Financial Institutions.
- *Stage IV: The definitive bodies are set up (late 1991 and 1992).* Members of the 'orientation et surveillance' councils (COS)[5] are elected and definitive trustees appointed.

II. CASE-STUDY OF THE CAISSE D'EPARGNE OF FRANCHE-COMTE

Franche-Comté is a region in the eastern part of France. It includes four departments: Doubs, Haute-Saône, Jura and Territoire de Belfort. It has a population of about 1.1 million. In 1990, there were 11 autonomous *Caisses d'Epargne* in Franche-Comté: Belfort, Besançon, Lure, Luxeuil, Vesoul, Gray, Dole, Champagnole, Lons-Le-Saunier, Saint-Claude and Montbéliard. There was also a regional firm, set up in 1985, which served as a bank for the 11 *caisses*: the SOREFI of Franche-Comté

As in the other regions, a project leader was appointed to prepare the merger and oversee the way in which the new regional *caisse* was organized.

Mr Theuriet, the project leader, and the members of the different work groups (staff from the different organizations affected by the creation of the new *caisse*) reflected on the kind of structure that should be set up. With help from McKinsey

---

4. At the same time as local *caisses* were merged to form regional *caisses*, local agencies were renovated ('a new agency concept based on counselling and the legibility of the offer') and a new logo appeared ('This logo will be the logo of the new *Caisse d'Epargne* and our customers' first tangible symbol of our restructuring' (Declaration of the Chairman of the Directoire at the General Meeting, 1991). With regard to the new agencies and the logo, see Appendixes 10.2 and 10.3 respectively.

5. In each *caisse*, the COS is constituted of 21 members elected by clients, partners and staff. It defines, on proposition or after consultation with the Directoire, the *Caisse d'Epargne*'s broad orientations and oversees their application. It appoints the members of the Directoire and chooses its chairman.

consultants, they set about elaborating a target scheme of organization. The 11 *caisses* of the 'natural' region would be merged, while Franche-Comté's regional financial company (SOREFI) would be absorbed into the new structure. Under this new scheme, the Caisse d'Epargne de Franche-Comté would consist of roughly 500 employees and would be organized on three levels:

- 1 head office;
- 7 commercial groups (representing the Caisse d'Epargne of Franche-Comté locally and coordinating the activities of customer activity centres attached to them);
- 25 customer activity centres made up of several sales outlets (a total of 124 local agencies). As required by the law, the Caisse d'Epargne de Franche-Comté would be administered by a Directoire under the control of an 'Orientation et Surveillance' Council. The main mission of the head office would be to elaborate the *Caisse d'Epargne's* strategy, to define norms and procedures for *caisse* as a whole and to see that they were respected. It would provide the commercial groups with the necessary support, both on a functional level and in the form of shared resources. It would have a total staff of 130 people.

Preparing and setting up the new structure took six months, work being completed in early October 1991. Officially, everyone congratulated each other on the speed with which the plan had been carried out. Mr Theuriet nevertheless wondered whether the 'steamroller' he had set in motion with the aid of McKinsey would not, in the long run, come up against barriers. The apparent facility of 'his' reform was worrying him. He wondered about its practicality in terms of culture and identity. He noticed with anxiety that the studies carried out to elaborate the target scheme of organization did not provide an answer to this question. It was at this point that management researchers sought authorization to study the setting up of the new *caisse*. Mr Theuriet seized the opportunity, proposing that they analyse the problems likely to crop up once the new structure had been set up. Appendixes 10.5 to 10.8 provide the following information: extracts from interviews carried out with members of the new Caisse d'Epargne de Franche-Comté, the results of a staff survey, various statistical data on staffing at the Caisse d'Epargne de Franche-Comté's head office, along with details concerning the structure of this *caisse* (notably the description of the organization chart proposed by Mr Theuriet).

APPENDIX 10.1
LAW PASSED ON 10 JULY 1991

In his introduction, the legislator has made a point of stressing the *Caisses d'Epargne*'s nature as non-profit-making credit institutions, as well as the markets in which they are allowed to intervene.

On this last point, the text states that jobs in corporate institutions (small and medium-sized companies or common law associations) cannot exceed 30 per cent of jobs in each *Caisse d'Epargne* between now and 1997. It also points out that the *caisses,* when allocating resources related to their commercial and banking activities, should give priority to the local, social economy, as support for local communities.

1. Dispositions concerning the way in which the network is organized

The notion of network is reinforced

The *Caisses d'Epargne et de prévoyance* are affiliated by law to the Centre National des *Caisses d'Epargne et de Prévoyance* (CENCEP). Likewise affiliated to the CENCEP, under the conditions laid down by decree by the Conseil d'Etat (state council), are those credit institutions which are controlled by the *Caisses d'Epargne et de prévoyance,* and those whose activities are necessary in order for the institutions in the network to function properly, notably the institutions formed in association with the *Caisse des dépôts et consignations* (state). The SOREFI will be dismantled, at the latest, one year after the present law has been passed.

The devolution of SOREFI's capital assets is established by agreement between the CENCEP and the Caisse des dépôts, or, in default of this, by decree. The CENCEP remains owned by the *Caisses d'Epargne* which have at least a 65 per cent stake and the Caisse des dépôts which has at least a 35 per cent stake.

The CENCEP is administered by a *Directoire* and controlled by a *conseil de surveillance.* The surveillance council is made up, in addition to representatives from the Caisses d'Epargne and the Caisses des dépôts, two members of parliament and a senator.

The members and the chairman of the *Directoire* are appointed by the Ordinary General Meeting on a proposal from the surveillance council. The statutes of the Centre National and the nomination of the chairman of the *Directoire* are submitted for approval to the Minister of Finance and the Economy.

A college made up of chairmen from *caisse* councils is instituted as part of the CENCEP, which will be consulted on reforms concerning the network. Each year, the CENCEP sends parliament a report on the activities of the network and the use made of the funds collected. The CENCEP appoints a censor to each *Caisse d'Epargne.*

2. Details concerning the organization of the *Caisses d'Epargne*

(a) The *Directoire*
The *Caisses d'Epargne* are administered by a *Directoire* of two to five members, appointed for a duration of five years (renewable), and subject to approval by the CENCEP.

(b) Consultative councils
In the *Caisses d'Epargne* comprised of several departments, at least one consultative council must be instituted for each department.

The members of the council are elected on a proportional representation basis for six years. They must meet at least twice a year, on the initiative of the 'Orientation et Surveillance' council.

(c) 'Orientation et surveillance' councils (COS)
The COS is composed of 17, 21 or 25 members elected for six years and distributed as follows:

- members elected on a proportional representation basis by mayors, and from among members of municipal, departmental and regional councils. A local member of parliament can be chairman of the COS provided he or she does not hold more than two electoral mandates and provided he or she exercises neither the function of chairman of local or regional councils nor of mayor of a commune of 100,000 inhabitants or more;
- members elected by and from among staff of the *Caisse d'Epargne*;
- members representing the account holders, elected on a one-round basis from among each consultative council or group of consultative councils;
- two members elected to complete the representation of account holders among the account holders with a corporate identity.

Members representing the account holders have a majority of seats on the 'orientation et surveillance' council, the other seats being shared equally between the two remaining colleges (elected members, staff).

APPENDIX 10.2
A NEW TYPE OF AGENCY

The *Caisse d'Epargne* innovates in the field of banking distribution with a new local agency concept based on counselling and the legibility of the offer. On the outside, the transparent glass window-front, the 'totem' and the new logo are the distinctive signs of a new agency.

The interior architecture gives the consumer an all-round view of the way in which the sales space is organized; the signal system allows him or her to pick out easily the zones corresponding to the different categories of service and the types of relation on offer.

(CENCEP, *La Caisse d'Epargne: une mutation réussie*, October 1991)

APPENDIX 10.3
THE NEW ÉCUREUIL ('SQUIRREL') DESIGN

1950

1960

1965

1968

1975

1983

CAISSE D'EPARGNE
1991

Fig. 10.2 The evolution of the *Caisses d'Epargne* logo.

The evolution of the *Caisse d'Epargne* logo is mapped out in Fig. 10.2 above.

> The old squirrel design, the animal in silhouette, was designed to be monolithic and reassuring, as a reflection of a vocation dedicated to promoting people's savings.
>   The new design, made up of moving lines on a square, is a sign of force and is comprised of several elements. Its more elaborate structure symbolizes the wide range of activities and products on offer from the Caisse d'Epargne. Its 'high-tech' style is suggestive of technical accomplishment, competence and modernity. The red for commercial dynamism is married to the institution's grey.
>   (CENCEP, *La Caisse d'Epargne: une mutation réussie*, October 1991)

APPENDIX 10.4
THE *CAISSES D'EPARGNE* NETWORK

Figure 10.3 details the *Caisses d'Epargne* network at the end of 1990, and the target scheme for 1992–93. Note that the target scheme may have several half-way stages for some regions which are not shown in Fig. 10.3.

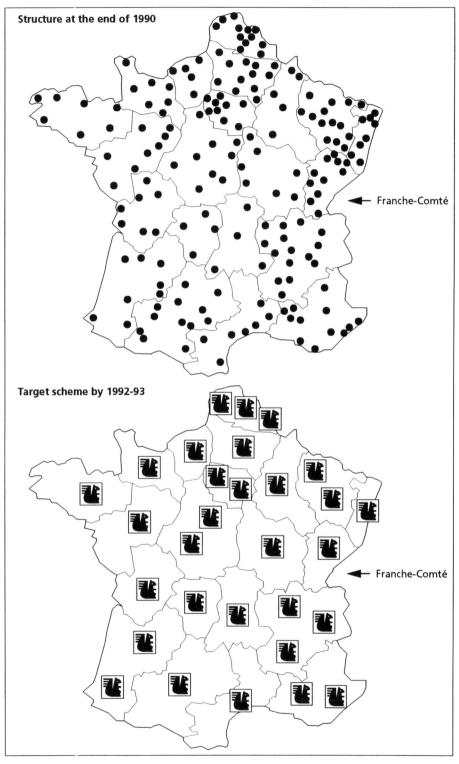

Fig. 10.3 The *Caisses d'Epargne* network.

APPENDIX 10.5
EXTRACTS FROM INTERVIEWS WITH STAFF OF THE NEW *CAISSE D'EPARGNE* OF FRANCHE-COMTE

The way people feel about the new structures

1 'The restructuration, I think, was a good thing globally, but it was not thought through. In my opinion people in the field were not sufficiently involved' (24 years' seniority).

2 'I get the impression that there was a bit of a shake-up at the top of the ladder. If some lost out when duties were redistributed, you bet they must have made enough before.'

3 'Now things look a bit fairer. Some people are probably slightly ill at ease. For employees at our level, this restructuring is a good thing.'

4 'At group level some directors try to rebuild their regional fiefs. After 20 or 30 years of unchallenged leadership, suddenly having a boss above them, it's probably hard to swallow.'

5 'In the new *caisse* the key functions are: first of all, the Directoire, then the Finance and Accounts departments' (former *Caisse d'Epargne* employee).

6 'The main task of the *Caisse d'Epargne* was to collect funds for the Caisse des dépôts et consignations (state). Now this won't do anymore. We simply have to be commercially as active as the other banks' (former SOREFI employee).

7 'The tensions in this establishment are due to the young age of SOREFI people. They feel that we, the veterans, the pillars of it all, stop them from operating smoothly and just put the brakes at every opportunity.'

8 'People from the old *caisses* have lost the comfort of stable, well-paid jobs and daily routine. They resent putting themselves in question, they are used to a cool rhythm, you know. And of course not worried about the health of the business, about results' (former SOREFI employee, three years' seniority).

9 'According to me people who come from a *Caisse d'Epargne* and have joined the network years ago, are forced to change their cushy habits and to put themselves into question' (former SOREFI employee).

10 'SOREFI was a small team of 50. At the new *caisse*, even though we still have the same boss, some of the friendliness, the warmth, has gone, all the things that you only find in small offices, like the strict minimum in terms of procedure and a more informal style.'

11 'We, at the SOREFI, unlike people at the *caisses*, thought in terms of a bank, we already had that culture.'

12 'SOREFI was the *caisses*' bank, so we already functioned like a bank'.

13 'Ask anyone from SOREFI, they'll tell you we've lost some of our efficiency. Now things are more sluggish. This is partly due to the size factor, but people always feel, and, sometimes even I say that our difficulties are due to the fact that we and the *caisses* have different working methods. We, SOREFI people, constantly complain that things are going too slow, too inefficiently.'

14 'We have to learn to live together, and often find that problems are due to our different cultures, both professional and general. So we have different ways of doing things, and, ultimately, it tells on the working relations, on the internal functioning of departments.'

15 'In the Caisse d'Epargne of Besançon we used to have our own rhythm, a rapport with clients, which maybe other local *caisses* did not enjoy in terms of volume or variety of

clients. But the main difference is with SOREFI people. Sometimes there are tensions. We don't have the same way of handling business and customer relations. All is not wrong of course, but what to do [silence].'

16 'The SOREFI people don't have a clue about what makes the *Caisses d'Epargne* network what it is. How can I explain this to you? [silence]. Well, in a way they are more abrupt and cutting. They have never been in contact with clients. So they'll handle clients and the business they bring in a cool, detached way. Whereas we may agree with them, but we feel "this may not be the best way to handle a client". We know what a client is, how he or she feels, what he or she is looking for, what he hopes to get. But they will simply make a decision, pat, and that's the end of it, surgical, it's just banking practice, impersonal and cold' (21 years' seniority).

17 'What we, the veterans most dread is to see *Caisse d'Epargne* turn into just another bank.'

18 'I've been 28 years in a *Caisse d'Epargne*, quite a time. I have always felt strongly for *Caisses d'Epargne*. [silence] I shall do my level best to ensure things work out. I am 100% devoted to *Caisses d'Epargne*, and as far as I know, all the veterans feel the same way.'

19 'The head-office brings together people of all horizons: the former local *caisses*, SOREFI, new recruits. But with *Caisse d'Epargne* colleagues, things are different, there is undeniably a common way of thinking, things are smoother, less complicated. Outsiders simply don't belong to the network. Some people at first thought they could just boss us because they handled our money with Caisse des dépôts et consignations (state). What they forget is that we have experience. We don't just do things, we feel them.'

20 'For us, you see, joining the *Caisse d'Epargne* was like joining a large family, and we had to learn the ropes. The others [SOREFI people], they are the younger types with degrees. They are used to juggle with funds. It's easy to play generous with money that's not your own. They never worked hard to build up the funds, never worried about making a business profitable' (23 years' seniority, holder of a technical diploma).

21 'Now that we work with the *caisses* people, the whole thing has changed. The mindset is different. In SOREFI, we were small, efficient-minded teams. We knew our objectives. In the *Caisses d'Epargne*, I get the feeling people are kind of fatalistic. They operate like civil servants.'

22 'SOREFI brought together people from different banks, different social backgrounds, to this extent we were less modelled than the *caisses* by the institution-side of *Caisse d'Epargne*. That enabled us to adapt quickly to the shakeup that followed the McKinsey report. They practically came up with conclusions we had already arrived at.'

23 'The *Caisse d'Epargne* spirit has disappeared. It may develop in due time' (20 years' seniority).

24 'We used to have a yearly meeting for all Besançon *caisse* employees. It was an occasion to take stock of the situation.'

25 'SOREFI people used to have a party when the Beaujolais Nouveau came out. We didn't have this sort of thing in Besançon, but I think next year our bosses are going to make a kitty and give us a treat.'

26 'In SOREFI we always had a party for the Beaujolais Nouveau. It was a custom, we suggested to do it again this year, I think it will go on.'

27 'What mattered in the *caisses* used to be seniority. I think this will create a problem for some people.'

28 'In the new *caisse*, people won't be able to get on just because they are the son of a director or a manager. Those days are over' (21 years' seniority).

29 'The reshuffle, no doubt means you have to put yourself into question. One has to get one's bearings, I have to get my bearings. It's not always easy.'

30 'When I was with the Caisse d'Epargne de Besançon, I had much more freedom than here. You can't take a piss without filling out a report.'

31 'I almost went under the weather. You need to put yourself into question, people at the top don't always understand the human consequences. In the Caisse d'Epargne de Besançon I used to take my own decisions, act according to day-to-day requirements. Things become inefficient when they get too heavy. Some find it hard to adapt. Its no easy task.'

32 'The way I see it is that we are in an institution in which senior employees behave as if the rest of us were a their service. Now they are not sure anymore what their purpose is although they are convinced their role is essential' (a recent recruit).

33 'The number of people appointed to "Group" structures is twice what was originally planned. There were supposed to be two or three people for each Group manager. Now they are almost ten. There are always good reasons, one can always find good reasons for this.'

34 'At head-office, the "Orientation et Surveillance" Council (COS) chairman and the members of the Directoire as well as the heads of departments have red wall-to-wall carpets, and the COS chairman and members of the Directoire are the only ones who have curtains in their office. When a department manager moves offices, if the carpeting is not red, he gets it changed, even if it's new. All department heads want red carpets.'

35 'There is a whole debate on salary policy that means that the problem of the fairness of salaries is never really discussed. There is no way of finding out who lives in a building belonging to the *Caisse d'Epargne* and who does not' (recent recruit).

36 'For the *Caisse d'Epargne* people, the notion of devolution means noting. It's a serious shortcoming. They don't have objectives. They work hard but never wonder "what's the purpose of it?" At the *Caisse d'Epargne* there is a drama where managerial culture is concerned' (former SOREFI employee, five years' seniority).

37 'Former *caisse* people don't have a culture of the written word. They reject it. They find it hard to read the documents we circulate about new procedures. They also refuse to put themselves into question. Former *Caisse d'Epargne* people positively fear self-questioning. *Caisse d'Epargne* is an organization which occults its own dysfunctions' (former SOREFI, four years' seniority).

Caisse d'Epargne and other banks

38 'One of my brothers-in-law is a farmer. When he married my sister in 1975 they got loans to pay their share to the seven brothers and sisters. One for the house and one to build a warehouse. All this over 15 years. Crédit Agricole [a French bank] never bothered about whether they could repay that much. For them what mattered was to invest their money and peddle their new products. They have a different approach. Their cashiers and sales agents are paid on a commission, not here' (more than 20 years' seniority).

39 'Selling is their [Crédit Agricole employees] business not ours, at *Caisses d'Epargne*, the values are different.'

40 'We act as consultants, we make sure we don't burden clients with debts. Crédit Agricole makes no bones about it. We will always respect the clients we deal with more than certain other banks' (a management and sales officer with 23 years' seniority).

41 'The *Caisse d'Epargne*'s view of things is not that of a banker. In my view our relationship with clients is a highly distinctive one. Our clients don't walk into a *Caisse d'Epargne* as they walk into a bank' (17 years' seniority).

42 'I believe people genuinely like the relationship with the *Caisse d'Epargne*. They are hostile to the transformation into a bank with cards and distributors. They find it hard to accept.'

43 'The *Caisse d'Epargne* should not end up just like any other bank. Never! I've been here for ten years and I can assure you that we don't have the same aims as a bank. We don't try and sell at all cost. That's why we have a good relationship with our clients.'

44 'The *Caisse d'Epargne* is lagging way behind other banks. This is partly due to the government which prevented diversification. The *Caisse d'Epargne* should affirm itself as a bank in the strong sense of the term. It's a matter of survival' (former SOREFI).

45 'In the past, the *Caisses d'Epargne* were social. It was our predecessors who created the public baths and gardens.'

46 'I fear that the restructuring will destroy whatever it was that made the *Caisse d'Epargne*. One should not forget that at first we had a social mission. But now, I fear that by wanting to become a bank just like the other banks we will go further and further away from that mission. And that surely is a very unfortunate thing' (18 years' seniority).

47 'At the moment, we are fighting to be a bank. The image we want to convey is that of a bank' (former SOREFI, two years' seniority).

48 'We still have our *livret*. It's not doing very well, in fact very badly, but still we have kept our damned *livret* and that's a good thing. It's unique to the *Caisse d'Epargne*. We have been around for 150 years. That kind of experience matters a lot, it makes us as strong a bank as any other, I think' (23 years' seniority).

49 'People at *Caisse d'Epargne* are sentimentally very attached to the *livret*. It's the basis of the *Caisse d'Epargne*.'

50 'The *livret*'s very important. It's thanks to the *livret* that we are here today. One shouldn't forget this' (16 years' seniority).

51 'Even if some criticize it, the *livret* remains what makes the *caisses* different, what makes us different from the banks. The *livret*, it's a way of thinking. And it's security too' (18 years' seniority).

52 'We have a psychological complex of inferiority relative to the other banking establishments.'

53 'The *Caisse d'Epargne* spirit is: only provide clients with what they want. There is a kind of hostility to all that would go against the client's interest. That's the social vocation of the *Caisse d'Epargne*.'

54 'You never leave the *Caisse d'Epargne*. No one ever leaves the *Caisse d'Epargne*.'

55 'To help us in certain things where we were a little weak, we found employees from other banks who came and worked with us. But I know of no employee from a *Caisse d'Epargne* who has left us to work in other banks.'

56 'With the restructuring, we risk loosing what made the *Caisses d'Epargne* network specific. It is nothing short of the family bank' (more than 20 years' seniority).

57 'Our problem at the *Caisse d'Epargne* is that we no longer have any basic objective like contributing to the development of popular savings.'

58 'Salaries at the *Caisse d'Epargne* are about a third higher than at other banks.'

59 'At *Caisse d'Epargne*, people generally think that: we are here to stay. *Caisse d'Epargne* will go on for ever' (former SOREFI, two years' seniority).

60 'The *Caisse d'Epargne* has such big stocks that it takes about five or six years to use them up. All they had to do to survive was to sit tight.'

61 'Clients used to trust us, trust the *Caisse d'Epargne*, and I feel that this is being lost, may be because personal contact is disappearing. And it is disappearing because we are more and more interested in objectives, quantity rather than quality, and it may not be the best way of improving our image' (27 years' seniority).

Opinions about management

62 'One third of the people here at the head office don't know the clients. They never worked behind a counter, never attended to them on the day before Christmas. And that's why now they've decided to give us the afternoon before Christmas off. Totally unheard of in the Caisse d'Epargne of Besançon!'

63 'At the *Caisse d'Epargne*, you started behind the counter and, in time, ended up as boss, except for the last generation when it was the father and then the son. But now, we are managed by people with no field experience.'

64 'At the *Caisse d'Epargne*, you can start at the bottom of the ladder and end up at the top. With the restructuring, I'm not sure that things will still work out this way' (18 years' seniority).

65 'Our bosses always made it a point to save. At SOREFI, there was a lot of cash, they were use to [silence]. Whereas here at the *Caisse d'Epargne*, we are used to tightening our belts and work hard for proper results.'

66 'Here at head office there are too few veterans. Not enough people who know the field, people with experience' (former Caisse of Besançon, 26 years' seniority).

67 'For me, the important thing is competence. To be competent, contrary to what people at the *caisse* believe, is not to be old' (former SOREFI).

68 'The budget used to be managed much more carefully before. Now we get the feeling that money is spent too quickly, too fast. We never saw that before.'

69 'Each *caisse* used to be ruled by a little king. When I joined the *Caisse d'Epargne*, I was struck by the importance attached to hierarchy, to the exterior signs of power' (former Caisse of Montbéliard, six years' seniority)

70 'One must recognize that the *caisses* had problems, especially with the bosses. Some of the directors acted like dictators, quite a problem at times.'

71 'SOREFI people, who are not field people, are not able to assess staff requirements. They rarely seek advice but we assert ourselves. I think that they will respect us by and by. The fact is that we, in Besançon, have done things that no one has tried before.'

72 'The SOREFI people have seized power. That's what I'd call carrying out a robbery on the *Caisses d'Epargne*, at least the Franche-Comté *Caisses d'Epargne*. They fill all the management posts and that's it. No one stepped forward from the *Caisses d'Epargne*. *Caisse d'Epargne* people never used to step forward, we were used to being appointed. You did your job properly and you were appointed.'

73 'We, the former SOREFI staff, have practically all ended up at the *caisse*'s head office. Some people accuse us of having got the upper hand. For me, it's just a question of competence.'

74 'When we reorganized work, some people who used to be fit for their job in their little *Caisses d'Epargne* found that they may no longer be fit for their new job in the new, enlarged

caisse. Some people actually lost their jobs because of this, lost their jobs because they were not able to perform the tasks required of them.'

75 'The Finance Ministry, Caisse des dépôts et consignations and CENCEP, everybody knew what the McKinsey report would recommend. But they knew they had to use a consultancy firm to make us swallow the pill on that, otherwise, politically, it would have been impossible.'

76 'All the old bosses have lost their power. That's obvious. Most of them have received nice golden handshakes because they were close to retirement. That enabled them to leave, if not with their head high, at least with a fat wallet. Some of those who stayed behind were given honorary posts.'

77 'Now Group managers actually form part of a concern called the Caisse d'Epargne de Franche-Comté to which they belong as a mere part.'

78 'We have some 40 per cent job mobility. When, from being under-manager of a small *caisse* you become manager of a client network – which boils down to manager of a sales team – you definitely change jobs.'

79 'For major decisions, Mr Theuriet consults the "Orientation et Surveillance" Council [COS]. To say that Mr Theuriet decides everything, is perhaps a little too much. But it's true that at the COS, things are put to us in such a way that we are bound to agree, but still, we are asked to give an opinion' (employee elected to the COS).

80 'The "Orientation et Surveillance" Council is a monitoring and watchdog body. As its name shows, it only validates general guidelines and is supposed to monitor what goes on in the company. But in most "technical" establishments, the power of elected members can be neutralized by using a professional jargon. For example, you would never believe that farmers actually have anything to do with the management of Crédit Agricole. Well, in our case it's the same thing.'

81 'I think that Mr Theuriet controls the company, he is the company. Well, the company is made of its staff, but he is the leader. It seems that, even if not everyone agrees with this or that policy, this or that implementation, this or that thing, everyone has a great deal of respect for Mr Theuriet, a certain admiration' (former SOREFI, two years' seniority).

82 'I think that if Mr Theuriet had to leave today, the whole thing would collapse. The restructuring has a lot to do with him. You feel that he is the one in command' (former SOREFI three years' seniority).

83 'Mr Theuriet pays a lot of attention to the grassroots. As a union representative, I see this clearly. What's nice about him is that it's possible to have direct contact and say whatever you have to say' (former Caisse de Besançon).

84 'Theuriet's a guy who's up to the task, that's obvious. SOREFI has been the driving force of restructuring. That's why you find them in the good posts. There was a lack of dynamism on the part of *Caisses d'Epargne*, that's possible too' (former Caisse de Besançon).

85 'People acknowledge Theuriet as the leader of the company because he was able to put his foot down at the right moment. He set things right in certain Groups' (former Caisse de Champagnole).

86 'Our boss is the humanist type although he belongs to the modern tradition. He has the company spirit. He said "what we want to find are the errors, not the culprits". He frequently had a chance to sack people, but he never did it.'

87 'The image attached to Mr Theuriet is one of a competent, congenial man, both inside and outside the firm. Everybody recognizes that he has a lot of charisma. He also enjoyed a national standing. When we go to meetings at the national level, people tell us "you are lucky, you have Mr Theuriet"' (former SOREFI).

APPENDIX 10.6
SURVEY CARRIED OUT AMONG THE STAFF OF THE *CAISSES D'EPARGNE* NETWORK

**National results (1,100 people questioned)
and results specific to the Franche-Comté (100 people questioned)**

1. In your opinion, the *Caisse d'Epargne* today has which kind of public image:

	Static	Not very active	Fairly active	Dynamic
National network	3%	28%	60%	7%
Franche-Comté	2%	35%	61%	1%

2. What effect do you think restructuring has had on the *Caisse d'Epargne's* image:

	National network	Franche-Comté		
		Under 40s	40s+	Total
Very positive	16%	6%	10%	7%
Fairly positive	49%	49%	35%	44%
Fairly negative	10%	19%	45%	29%
Very negative	1%	0%	0%	0%
Has changed nothing	34%	24%	3%	17%

3. If you wished to define the *Caisse d'Epargne's* position in the banking world today what would you say?

	National network	Franche-Comté		
		Under 40s	40s+	Total
● The *Caisse d'Epargne* is just like any other bank	22%	24%	6%	18%
● The *Caisse d'Epargne* is a financial institution with a special status	44%	34%	65%	44%
● The nature of client relations at the *Caisse d'Epargne* makes it different from other banks	31%	42%	29%	38%

4. **If you wished to define the position that the *Caisse d'Epargne* will have in the banking world of tomorrow, what would you say?**

	National network	Franche-Comté Under 40s	40s+	Total
● The *Caisse d'Epargne* is just like any other bank	34%	37%	26%	34%
● The *Caisse d'Epargne* is a financial institution with a special status	4%	4%	0%	3%
● The nature of client relations at the *Caisse d'Epargne* makes it different from other banks	59%	57%	74%	62%

5. **Which of the following institutions, in your opinion, are our two main competitors (two answers maximum):**

	National network	Franche-Comté
● Crédit Agricole	87%	85%
● Banques Populaires	7%	23%
● BNP, Société Générale, Crédit Lyonnais	17%	8%
● La Poste	52%	45%
● Crédit Mutuel	35%	37%

6. **Should the fact that the *Caisse d'Epargne* are organized as a network and have a common logo result, in your opinion, in:**

	Not at all	Not really	On the whole	Absolutely
● The same form of client relations:				
National network	6%	8%	41%	44%
Franche-Comté	2%	9%	42%	46%
● The same company values for all staff:				
National network	2%	3%	35%	60%
Franche-Comté	1%	2%	37%	60%
● The same products and services throughout France:				
National network	1%	3%	25%	71%
Franche-Comté	0%	2%	24%	74%
● The same sign systems and sales outlets:				
National network	1%	2%	28%	68%
Franche-Comté	2%	2%	26%	70%

7. **The fact that the regional *Caisses d'Epargne* are today organized as a network is:**

	National network	Franche-Comté
● A necessity forced on it by the law	8%	7%
● An opportunity to face up to competition	88%	91%
● A damper on growth for regional *caisses*	3%	1%

8. The *Caisse d'Epargne* is one of the oldest financial institutions in France. Is the public aware of this fact?

	National network	Franche-Comté
Yes	84%	81%
No	16%	19%

9. The fact that the *Caisse d'Epargne* is one of the oldest financial institutions in France is:

	National network	Franche-Comté Seniority up to 10 years	Seniority 10 and over	Seniority total
• Basically a good thing for the *Caisse d'Epargne*'s image	67%	47%	69%	62%
• Basically a bad thing for the *Caisse d'Epargne*'s image	13%	23%	6%	11%
• Makes no difference	19%	30%	23%	26%

10. Respondent's institution of origin prior to restructuring

	National network	Franche-Comté
• A *Caisse d'Epargne*	86%	72%
• A SOREFI	4%	12%
• A subsidiary	1%	1%
• Other	9%	14%

APPENDIX 10.7
STATISTICAL DATA

Tables 10.1 and 10.2 provide a variety of statistical data concerning the staff at the head office of the new Caisse d'Epargne de Franche-Comté.

Table 10.1 Origins of staff

Institution of origin	Number of agents	%	Seniority
Sorefi	41	29.71	4.80
Besançon	42	30.43	14.29
Montbéliard	10	7.25	14.90
Champagnole	2	1.45	13.50
Dole	2	1.45	22.50
Jura Centre	6	4.35	19.67
Haut Jura	1	0.72	12.00
Belfort	9	6.52	5.89
Gray	3	2.17	19.00
Luxeuil	1	0.72	32.00
Vesoul	1	0.72	9.00
External	20	14.49	0.70

Table 10.2 Qualifications of staff

Institution of origin	No diploma		CSEs & O-levels		A-levels		BA, BSc		MA, MSc		Age
	Staff	Age	Staff	Age	Staff	Age	Staff	Age	Staff	Age	
Sorefi	0		4	34.50	9	26.78	9	30.56	19	33.37	31.30
Besançon	9	44.67	11	41.36	7	37.43	11	31.00	4	37.75	38.44
Montbéliard	2	43.00	2	44.00	0		4	38.25	2	32.00	39.31
Champagnole	0		0		0		1	44.00	1	35.00	39.50
Dole	0		1	54.00	1	31.00	0		0		42.50
Jura Centre	3	46.67	3	39.33	0		0		0		43.00
Haut Jura	0		0		0		1	34.00	0		34.00
Belfort	2	28.50	1	42.00	0		1	24.00	5	31.6	31.53
Gray	0		1	46.00	0		1	35.00	1	43.00	41.33
Luxeuil	0		1	50.00	0		0		0		50.00
Vesoul	0		0		0		1	33.00	0		33.00
External	0		1	39.00	3	32.00	7	32.71	9	33.33	34.26
Total	16	42.81	25	41.20	20	31.50	36	32.44	41	38.78	36.35

APPENDIX 10.8
DETAILED STRUCTURE OF THE CAISSE D'EPARGNE DE FRANCHE-COMTE

The organization charts provided in Figs 10.4 to 10.14 describe the structure of the new Caisse d'Epargne de Franche-Comté. Information about people with positions involving high responsibilities is also given. This information concerns:

- institution of origin (local *Caisse d'Epargne* (CE), SOREFI or external recruitment (EXTERNAL));
- age;
- sex;
- training level and diplomas;
- seniority (date of arrival in the *Caisses d'Epargne* network).

Figure 10.15 provides a detailed map of group and customer activity centre offices from the new *caisse*. The destinations of the managing directors of the former local *Caisses d'Epargne* of Franche-Comté are listed below:

- Belfort: group director, Belfort
- Besançon: member of the Directoire, Company Secretary
- Lure: arranged retirement
- Luxeuil: standard retirement
- Vesoul: arranged retirement
- Gray: group director, Lons-Le-Saunier, Haut Jura
- Dole: group director, Dole, Champagnole and Jura Nord
- Champagnole: customer activities director
- Lons-Le-Saunier: development director (head office)
- Saint-Claude: arranged retirement
- Montbéliard: arranged retirement.

The former functions of the new group managing directors were as follows:

- Besançon: development director, SOREFI
- Haute-Saône: development manager, CE Belfort
- Pontarlier, Haut-Doubs: sector manager, CE Besançon
- Pays de Montbéliard: member of a SOREFI in another region
- Lons-Le-Saunier, Haut-Jura (Jura Sud): managing director, CE Gray
- Dole, Champagnole and Jura Nord: managing director, CE Dole
- Belfort: managing director, CE Belfort.

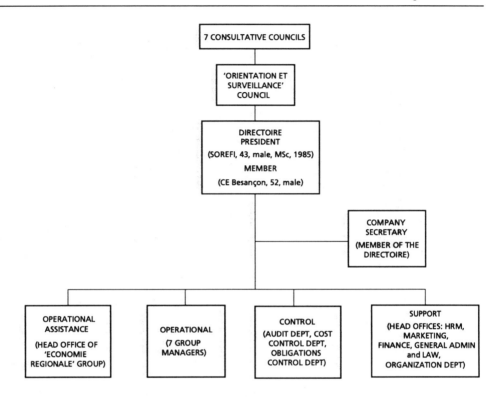

Fig. 10.4 Structure of global organization.

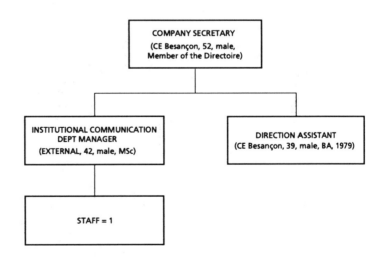

Fig. 10.5 Company secretariat organization chart.

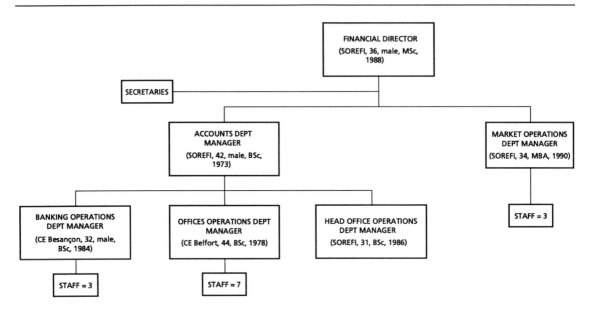

Fig. 10.6 Finance and accounts department organization chart.

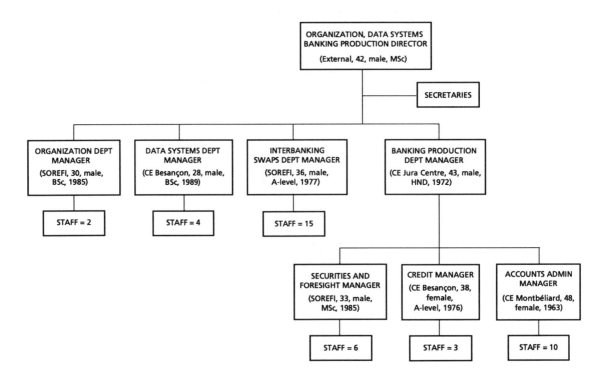

Fig. 10.7 Organization, data systems and banking production department organization chart.

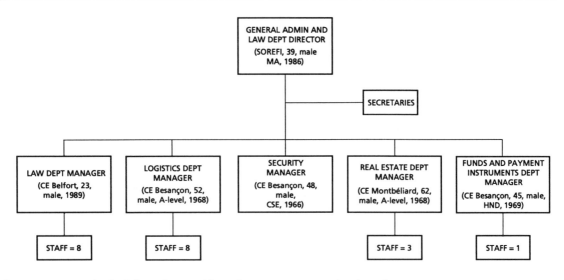

Fig .10.8 General administration and law department organization chart.

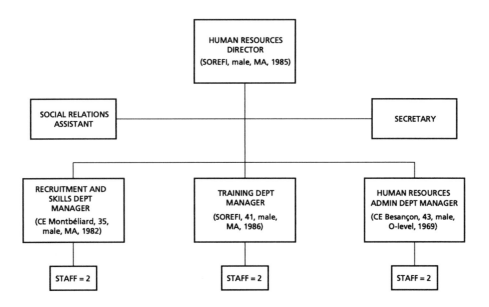

Fig. 10.9 Human resources management department organization chart.

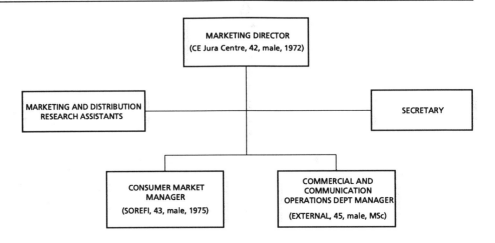

Fig. 10.10 Marketing department organization chart.

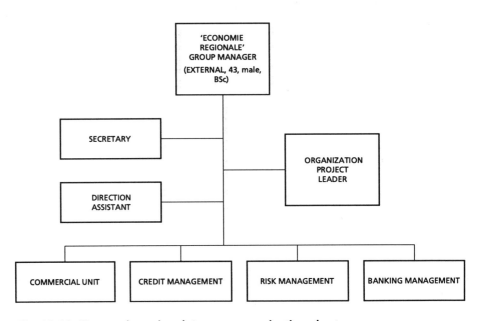

Fig. 10.11 'Economie regionale' group organization chart.

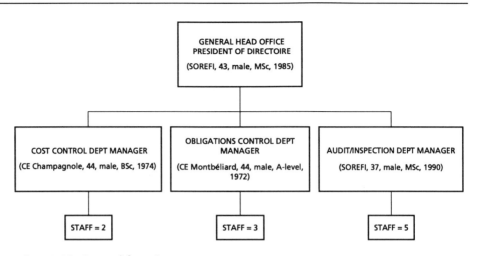

Fig. 10.12 Control functions.

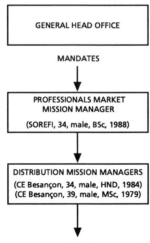

Fig. 10.13 Distribution and professionals market missions.

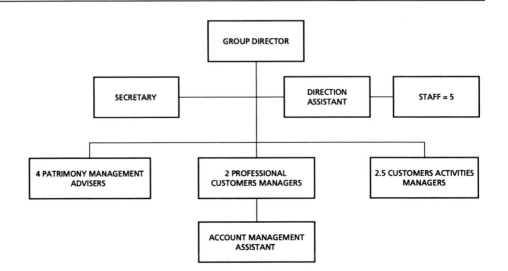

Fig. 10.14 Group functions.

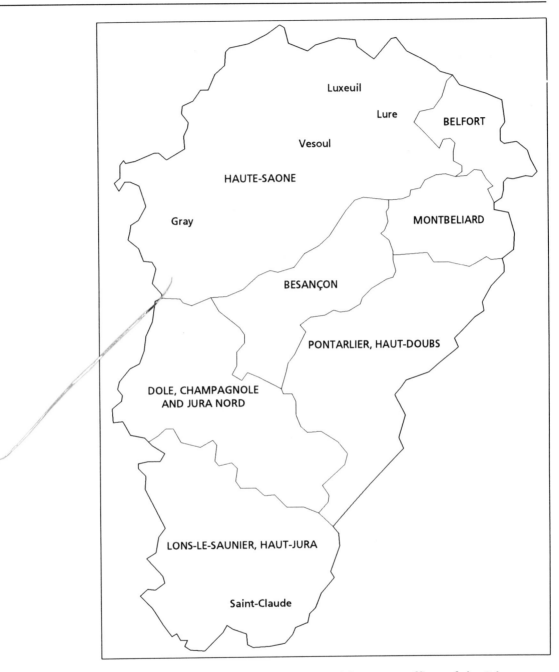

Fig. 10.15 Map of group and customer activity centre offices of the Caisse d'Epargne de Franche-Comté.

Corporate strategies within the newly privatized water plcs

S.G. Ogden

In 1989 the ten English and Welsh Regional Water Authorities were privatized. The Water Authorities – Anglia, Northumbria, North West, Severn Trent, Southern, South West, Thames, Wessex, Yorkshire and Welsh Water – are substantial organizations. They vary in size from Thames, the largest with a turnover in 1989 of £558 million and a workforce of 8,977, to South West, the smallest with a turnover in 1989 of £106.3 million and a workforce of 1,876. They are primarily concerned with providing water supply and sewerage services.[1] Their transfer from the public to the private sector of the economy was part of a wider programme of privatization which, the government argued, was expected to bring greater efficiency and improvements in the production of goods and standards of services as a consequence of more competition and easier access to capital markets (White Paper on Water Privatization, 1986). All the new Water plcs faced pressures as a consequence of their privatization to develop corporate strategies that were distinctly different from those they had previously embraced as public sector Water Authorities. Prior to privatization the Water Authorities were preoccupied with meeting government imposed financial targets and performance aims for reducing operating costs. With privatization management was now charged with pursuing improvements in corporate performance that would be measured primarily in terms of profitability. The government expected privatization, despite the fact that the provision of water services would continue to be subject to economic regulation, to 'lead to improved standards, greater efficiency, and a better allocation of resources within the water industry', but government also believed that privatization would encourage the Water plcs 'to compete effectively in fields where they can do so' and said that it 'would like to see the Water plcs expand their entrepreneurial activities, such as the provision of consultancy services, particularly overseas' (White Paper on Water Privatization, 1986, paras 39, 78, 64). Investors and shareholders also anticipated that the Water plcs would be able to take profitable advantage of market opportunities outside the regulated business of providing water services.

PRIVATIZATION AND THE REGULATION OF THE CORE BUSINESS OF PROVIDING WATER SERVICES

In the water industry the opportunities for competition are extremely limited and consequently privatization has left the monopoly character of the industry

---

1. In 1989 there were also 29 statutory water companies supplying water only, which were already privately owned. These were reduced in numbers by mergers to 25 by 1992.

unaltered.[2] This has resulted in a continued need for economic regulation,[3] and responsibility for this has been vested in the new Office of Water Services (Ofwat) and its Director General. The primary duty of the Director General is to ensure that the functions of water and sewerage undertakers are properly carried out, and that companies are able (in particular by securing reasonable returns on their capital) to finance the proper carrying out of their functions (s. 7, Water Act 1989). Subject to this duty the Director General is also charged with protecting customers, promoting efficiency and economy, and facilitating competition. The main focus of economic regulation is through price control. Charges are regulated by a pricing formula which is based on the retail price index plus a 'K' factor. The K factor is assessed separately for each Water plc by the Director General on the basis of investment requirements, operating costs and revenues, and an efficiency target. Although this pricing formula provides incentives to management to reduce costs as a means of enhancing profitability, the main pressure on management to be more efficient will emanate from 'yardstick' competition which allows the Director General to make comparative judgements using the performance achieved by the best companies as a yardstick to assess the others in reviewing the 'K' factor in the pricing formula. The initial K factors were set at the time of privatization, and the Director General has announced that he will conduct a Periodic Review of K factors, and charges, in 1994. Given that profit levels have been higher than planned, due to higher than expected revenue, greater than anticipated achievement of cost savings and what is now seen as a somewhat generous initial setting of K factors, everyone in the industry has expected the regulatory review of K factors to result in much tougher limits on prices and lower returns on capital, a view confirmed by the Director General's recent announcements on his approach to the Periodic Review (Ofwat, November 1993). While mindful of the need for profits to be sufficient to attract and retain capital in the business, the Director General believes that 'profitability can now be lower than that enjoyed by companies so far' and that 'maintaining the viability of the companies does not require the same expectation of profit as was necessary to float them' (Ofwat, December 1993, p. 3).

While the main focus for management has been the core utility business, particularly managing the large investment programmes[4] and pursuing efficiency improvements, corporate strategies have been developed to take advantage of business opportunities beyond the regulated activity of providing water services. This has generally proceeded in two stages: initially each company has reorganized its business, since

---

2. Although there was more potential to introduce market competition into gas and British Telecom, two other privatized utilities, the government did little to achieve this, a fact which attracted much critical attention.

3. In addition to these new regulatory arrangements the Water plcs continued to be subject to a variety of other regulatory bodies which had operated previously: the Secretary of State for Environment has responsibility for regulating drinking water quality which is monitored by the Drinking Water Inspectorate; Her Majesty's Inspectorate of Pollution has responsibility for monitoring sewage sludge disposal; and the National Rivers Authority, a new agency established to carry out statutory functions previously performed by the Water Authorities, is now responsible for environmental regulations including the management of water resources and control of water pollution as well as duties in respect of flood defence, fisheries, recreation and navigation. In addition Water plcs are subject to regulations originating from EC directives and legislation.

4. The total capital investment for the industry for the period 1989–90 to 1994–95 is £17,922 million (1991–92 prices). This has largely been the result of the need to improve service levels and meet new compliance standards on drinking water, bathing water and sewage treatment.

the ways in which it was previously constituted under the old public sector Water Authority were no longer appropriate; subsequently each company has engaged in diversification activity. While most of the companies have followed a similar pattern as regards the first, differences are emerging as regards the latter.

BEGINNINGS

Although it might well have been argued that, given their existing resources and expertise and the fact that their experience was confined to one industry, the Water plcs should remain exclusively focused on their core business of providing water and sewerage services, they nevertheless have pursued a number of initiatives, including diversification, to develop and expand their business activities.

There are a number of reasons for this. First, and perhaps most importantly, is the acknowledged limits to growth in the core business of providing water and sewerage services. Each company mentioned in its share prospectus that it would seek to develop significant earnings from other businesses. For example North West's prospectus stated that the 'removal of HM Government constraints will bring new opportunities, both nationally and internationally, which the Board intends to pursue vigorously.' One senior manager when interviewed described the position as follows:

> We believe the core business of water services will reach a point over the next year or so where its growth in terms of its contribution to profits, earnings per share and so on will stop. It will plateau: we will go ex growth. And if the overall company is to develop, it's got to identify and grow an alternative source of income and profits. Obviously at the present time the contribution (of the non-regulated businesses) to overall group profitability is very small. The core business is the 'cash cow', and we have got to get to a situation we believe by the end of the decade where the overall contribution to group profit from the non-regulated parts of the business is equal to or even greater than the regulated business, and that's a tremendous challenge.

The need to develop alternative sources of revenue and profits has been reinforced by the anticipated harsher financial climate generally expected to emanate from the Director General's 1994 review of the K factor and the prices that water customers may be charged. A second reason for pursuing diversification is the extent to which the companies have the means to do so: all the companies have relatively low gearings,[5] with consequent substantial potential borrowing capacity at their disposal. Although the availability of financial resources is not sufficient reason in itself, the opportunity this offers to diversify their activities has been coupled with strong City expectations that the Water plcs should use them to do so.

As well as external expectations that newly privatized companies, especially large ones, should use their resources profitably in taking advantage of market opportunities to grow their businesses, there were also internal expectations held by senior managers that diversification activity could have a beneficial impact on what they regarded as the prevailing 'organizational culture'. Senior managers were anxious to change corporate cultures since the transfer to the private sector through privatization entailed a profound transformation of organizational rationale. In seeking to foster in managers and employees new values of customer care, innovation, flexibility, enterprise and competitiveness, corporate management have sought a shift in the

---

5. Gearing in the industry is on average around 10 per cent.

Table 11.1 Composition of boards of privatized Water plcs

Background of board members:	Chairmen			Board members (excluding non-executive directors)			Non-executive directors		
	Private	Public	Water	Private	Public	Water	Private	Public	Water
Date of appointment to board of Water Authority plc									
1974–1982	2	1	1	—	1	—	4	1	—
1982–1987	5	1	—	3	3	3	11	7	1
1987–1990	—	—	—	12	4	12	19	—	—
Total		10			38			43	

Source: Prospectus of water share offers.

Table 11.2 Origins of board members of Water plcs in 1993[1]

	Private sector	Water industry	Public sector	Total
Anglia	4(2)	4(2)	2(1)	10(5)
Northumbria	2	3	3(1)	8[2](1)
North West	10(4)	1(1)	—	11(5)
Severn Trent	9(1)	2(1)	1(1)	12(3)
Southern	6(3)	3(1)	—	9(4)
South West	8(3)	2(1)	2	9(4)
Thames	5	2	1	8
Welsh	5(1)	2(1)	—	7(2)
Wessex	7(3)	2	1(1)	10(4)
Yorkshire	3	3(1)	3	9(1)
Total	59(17)	24(8)	13(4)	96(29)
	61%(59%)	25%(28%)	14%(13%)	100%(100%)

1. Figures in brackets refer to the number of new appointments made since 1990.
2. There are three other new directors whose origin is not yet ascertained.

Water Authority culture from one based exclusively on engineering and operating demands and notions of public service to one which gives greater salience to business priorities and customer needs. Considerable impetus had already been given to this desired cultural change in the years immediately preceding privatization by the new more commercially oriented boards appointed by the Secretary of State in 1983 which had deliberately set out to give a much greater emphasis to running the Water Authorities as businesses. This was reflected in the composition of the boards themselves where new directors increasingly have come from private sector backgrounds. Table 11.1 shows that at the time of privatization 79 per cent of the non-executive directors and 40 per cent of the executive directors had come from the private sector. Table 11.2 shows that since privatization 59 per cent of the new appointments to the boards of the Water plcs have come from the private sector, and that overall 61 per cent of all board members have private sector backgrounds. Diversification, it was hoped, particularly into related activities, would facilitate amongst managers in the core business of water services a closer engagement with private sector values and priorities and create the possibility of management interchanges.

Lastly, account needs to be taken of the extent to which senior corporate executives are keen to confirm their status as enterprising private sector players, and to differentiate their company from the others in terms of its successful corporate strategy. The pursuit of diversification through acquisition and joint venture as a stage upon which to demonstrate successful management competence has attracted considerable scrutiny from audiences of City analysts[6] and investors. One City analyst, a specialist on the water companies, commented in interview as follows:

> Broadly speaking what's happened to date is that these companies have got themselves on a good or bad rating with regard to the rest of the companies in the sector. I mean, my view is it's been a perception of what the management is like and a lot of that has been drawn on how the management have handled their moves into a non-regulated business. So I think there's a kind of feeling that the regulated business is low risk and most of them without a doubt can manage that pretty well – it's what they've done forever. Some will do better than others, but we haven't had enough evidence yet as to who was doing it significantly better than others So the management have been judged on other things that have been more easy to sort of say: 'That looked like a good or bad move'. And what it has been so far is how investors, how the City has perceived their moves into non-regulated businesses, the acquisitions they have tried to make or the joint ventures they have got involved with. All of these things, the market is happier with, because it understands that.

In reacting to these pressures the Water plcs have undertaken a variety of initiatives which may be considered in terms of diversification. This may be defined as 'the entry of a firm or business unit into new lines of activity, either by processes of internal business development or acquisition, which entail changes in its administrative structure, systems, and other management processes' (Ramamujan and Varadarajan, 1989). Within this broader framework developments may be discussed in terms of redesigning the business and major initiatives.

REDESIGNING THE BUSINESS

All the companies have reorganized their corporate structure. The pattern normally followed has been to establish a group holding company with a number of subsidiary companies, one of which is the appointed business licensed by the regulator, the Director General of Ofwat, to provide water and sewerage services. One advantage of this realignment has been the opportunity to relocate various activities previously done by the Water Authority but not now deemed essential to providing water services, outside appointed business and thus beyond the realm of Ofwat's regulation. However, the Director General has imposed constraints on how far this process may be taken by laying down guidelines which define the activities to be regarded as within the appointed business and specify the information to be provided on transactions between the appointed business and other associated companies within the group to ensure that transfer pricing arrangements do not involve any cross-subsidy between the appointed business and other parts of the group (Ofwat, 1993).

Characteristic of the realignment process has been the emergence of new 'enterprise'

---

6. This may be gauged for example by the increasing number of City analysts preparing and publishing reports on diversification by the water companies.

companies based wholly or primarily on managers, employees and expertise previously employed by the Water Authority. Typical examples (see Table 11.3) include scientific services, plumbing services and property companies. So, for instance, Southern Water has relocated its laboratories in a new company, Southern Science, established Southern Watercare to carry out plumbing operations and two companies, Bowsprit Property Development and Bowsprit Holdings, to develop its property interests. Some of the new businesses that have emerged from these initiatives have been further supported or complemented by acquisitions, although these have generally to date been small in scale. Again using the example of Southern Water it acquired M.W. Longley, heating and ventilation contractors, to boost its plumbing services, and is now contemplating combining these operations with its in-house pipe-laying and maintenance services to form a new company, Pipeworks Ltd, which is intended to provide a comprehensive service in the fields of pipe and sewer laying, pipe surveys, renovation, replacement and plumbing services.

Although all the Water plcs have followed a similar pattern, some more than others have explored the possibilities for transferring activities previously done in-house into new businesses operating outside the regulated appointed business. This is particularly true of Yorkshire which is currently engaged in a major initiative to separate out its maintenance support and administration functions from what it has redefined as its 'core' business in water services. Southern has already set up a relatively large number of new companies, but although supported in several instances by acquisitions, albeit small in scale, the bulk of the turnover of these new companies continues to be generated by the appointed business. The latter point is relevant to all the companies, with contributions to turnover and profit excluding internal transfers of business still relatively small (see Table 11.4). However, a different experience is provided by Wessex Water. Although initially it restructured rapidly along the pattern adopted by Southern, it reversed this process in 1991 by taking back into the core business of Wessex Water Services a number of companies, including Laboratory Services, EMIT (its engineering function), Wessex Watercare and Westwick Construction, that had begun operating separately under the umbrella of the new business ventures division, Wessex Water Commercial. This structural rethink was partly prompted by the large new joint venture with Waste Management International (see below), but also by the poor profit performance of Wessex Water Commercial, the very limited development of new customers beyond the core business together with poor market conditions, and the European Community public procurement directive which requires all work offered to subsidiary companies to be simultaneously offered to other interested parties. Consequently, by taking back, for example, EMIT into the core business, Wessex Water has guaranteed that its engineering work is done by in-house personnel.

In contrast some of the larger companies such as Severn Trent, Thames and North West have leaned more towards a policy of 'keeping the utility intact'. This is evident, for example, in the area of pipe network maintenance and mains laying activities. While all the companies use contractors for some of this work, the larger companies have decided to retain in-house a bigger proportion of this activity, and have not followed the example of Southern and Yorkshire in relocating their in-house facilities in separate enterprise companies to compete with contractors for business in the water industry and from other customers. The main considerations affecting the balance struck between retaining in-house facilities and outsourcing revolve around the different valuations of the attractiveness of the cost considerations measured

Table 11.3 Subsidiary companies (SC) and associated undertakings (AU) of the ten new Water plcs

Water plc	Water supply and sewerage services	Design, consultancy and construction activities	Technical and scientific services	Water related business (e.g. plumbing services, pipe-laying, and design and manufacture of equipment)	Environmental and waste treatment services	Other
Yorkshire	Yorkshire Water Services Ltd (SC)	Babcock Water Engineering Ltd (AU)	AL control (SC) Lab Services (SC) IT (SC)	Waterlink (SC) Leeds Pipeline Services (SC)	Y.W. Enterprises Ltd (SC) (includes Yorkshire Environmental, Global, Dramwell, Tidywaste, Esmil) Fospar (SC)	White Rose Property investments Ltd (SC) Yorkshire Windpower Ltd (AU) Yorkshire Cable Communications Ltd (AU) Ridings Insurance Company Ltd (SC)
Wessex	Wessex Water Services Ltd (SC)	Wessex Water Commercial Ltd (SC) (includes Wessex Water Technologies and Wessex Water International) Wimpey Wessex Ltd (AU)			Wessex Waste Management Ltd (AU)	Wessex Water BV (SC) Brunel Insurance (AU)
Southern	Southern Water Services Ltd (SC)	Southern Projects Ltd (SC) McDowells Ltd (SC) Aquaclear Ltd (SC) Coastal Waste Water Consultants Ltd (SC)	Southern Science Ltd (SC) T Southern Ltd (SC) Tynemarch Systems Engineering Ltd (SC)	Southern Watercare Ltd (SC) M.W. Longley Ltd (SC) Hazeley Down Mineral Water Co. Ltd (SC)	Ecoclear Ltd (SC) Greenhill Enterprises Ltd (SC) Clinical Waste Ltd (SC)	Sectron Systems Ltd (SC) Topmark Vehicle Contents Ltd Paperstream Ltd (SC) Waterline Insurance Co. Ltd (SC) Bowsprit Property Developments Ltd (SC) Bowsprit Holdings Ltd (SC) Mark Rawling Ltd
North West Water Group	North West Water Ltd	North West Water International Ltd (SC) Water Engineering Ltd (SC) CIDA Hydroquimica SA, Spain (AU) WRc (Process Engineering Ltd) (AU)	North West Australia Pty Ltd (SC) North West Water Malaysia (SC) US Water Inc. (SC)	Wallace and Tiernan Ltd (SC) (also in USA and Germany) Edwards and Jones Ltd (SC) Ceramesh Ltd (SC) Jones Environmental (Ireland) Ltd Envirex Inc., USA (SC) General Fitter Company Inc., USA (SC) Asdor Ltd, Germany (SC) Consolidated Electric Company, USA (SC)		NWW Properties Ltd (SC) Lakeland Smolt Ltd

Northumbrian Water Group	Northumbrian Water Ltd	Entec Europe Wallace Whittle and Partners Simon Engineering plc	Amtec Europe Imass Ltd	Montec International Ltd Renovex Technology Ltd	Northumbrian Environmental Management Ltd Hydrogeologie GmbH Analytical and Environmental Services Ltd	Kelda Contract Hire NWG Leasing (Holdings) Ltd Northumbrian Spring Natural Mineral Water Northumbrian Water Estates Coquetdale Property Investment
Anglian Water	Anglian Water Services Ltd (SC)	Anglian Water Process Engineering (SC) Anglian Water International	Anglian Water Engineering and Business Systems Ltd (SC) Anglian H & G (AU)	Purac-Rosewater Ltd (SC) Plumbsure Ltd (SC) Aquafine Engineering Services Ltd (SC)	Alpheus Environmental Ltd	Rutland Insurance Co. Ltd (SC) Anglian Water Commercial Developments Ltd (SC)
Thames Water	Thames Water Utilities (SC)	PWT (SC) (includes 29 separate companies) Thames Water International (SC) UTAG (SC) Binnie Thames Water Ltd (AU)		Thames Water Products and Services (SC) Metro Rod plc (SC) Subterra Holdings Ltd (AU)	Thames Water Environmental Services (SC) Thames Waste Management Ltd (SC) Morgan Collis Group Ltd (SC) Brophy Group plc (AU)	Isis Insurance Company Ltd (SC) Kennet Properties Ltd (SC) Thames Water Properties Ltd (SC) Thames Water Developments Ltd (SC)
Severn Trent	Severn Trent Water Ltd (SC) East Worcester Water plc (SC)	Severn Trent Water International (SC) Charles Haswell Ltd (SC) Acer Engineering Ltd (AU)	Severn Trent Systems Ltd (SC) Severn Trent Laboratories (SC)	Fusion Meters Ltd (SC) Jabay Ltd (SC) Capital Controls Ltd (SC) Minworth System Ltd (AU)	Biffa Waste Services Ltd (SC) Wastedrive Ltd (SC) ST Environmental Services Inc., USA (SC)	Paperflow Services Ltd (SC) Derwent Insurance Ltd (SC) Severn Trent Property Ltd (SC) (plus 3 others) Associated undertakings in property development Grafham Carbon (AU) Biogas Generation Ltd (AU)
Welsh Water plc	Dwr Cymru	Welsh Water International (SC) Acer (SC) Wallace Evans (SC)	Watertec Welsh Water information Technology Services (SC)	Beacon Pipeline Services (SC) Daniel Pipelines (SC)	Welsh Water Industrial Services	Welsh Water Transport Services (SC) Hamdden Ltd (SC) Brecon Insurance Company Ltd (SC) Pen y Fan Properties Ltd
South West Water plc	South West Water Services Ltd (SC)	J.J. Brent Ltd (SC) Pell Frischmann Water Ltd (AU)	PHOX Systems Ltd (SC)	Copa Products Ltd (SC)	Peninsula Waste Technology Ltd (SC) Haul-Waste Ltd (SC) Rugged Environmental Technology Systems Ltd	Peninsula Insurance Ltd (SC) Peninsula Properties (Exeter) Ltd (SC) Rydon Properties Ltd (SC)

Table 11.4 Contribution of the appointed business and other non-appointed businesses to group turnover and operating profit

	Turnover[1] (£m)		Profit (£m)	
	Appointed business	Non-appointed business	Appointed business	Non-appointed business
Anglian Water	554.2 (95%)	29 (5%)	216 (102%)	–4.4 (-2%)
Northumbrian WaterGroup	186.1 (74%)	66 (26%)	60.8 (87%)	8.9 (13%)
North West Water Group	692.3 (79%)	185.6 (21%)	284.8 (99%)	3.4 (1%)
Severn Trent	735.8 (86%)	120.5 (14%)	293 (97%)	9.6 (3%)
Southern Water	298.9 (94%)	20.3 (6%)	111 (93%)	8.4 (7%)
South West Water	184.1 (95%)	10.3 (5%)	83.2 (100.5%)	–0.4 (–5%)
Thames Water	802.9 (77%)	239.9 (23%)	281 (99.5%)	1.1 (0.5%)
Welsh Water	355.9 (93%)	26.5 (7%)	136.6 (88%)	19.4[2] (12%)
Wessex Water	193.6 (84%)	36.2 (16%)	78.4 (92%)	7.1 (8%)
Yorkshire Water	454.2 (94%)	27.4 (6%)	146.2 (98%)	2.6 (2%)

1. Adjusted for the elimination of inter-company transactions.
2. This includes £17 million profit on disposal of the shares in South Wales Electricity plcs.

Source: Annual Reports.

against the increase in risk of poor quality of work and standards of performance. The latter consideration may be illustrated in these comments from a senior manager interviewed from one of the larger companies:

> We decided that we wished to keep in-house that part of the mains servicing activity which was planned on a short-term horizon. It was very much more the responsive reactive work which by nature was far more customer sensitive ... we want to keep that in-house really because these people represent a significant element of the workforce who actually come into direct contact with the public. They can have a considerable influence on our customer service image and performance. I believe that was a very critical consideration in all this.

Different considerations have influenced another realignment initiative. Where previous in-house resources and expertise have been deemed insufficient to merit stand-alone enterprises, joint ventures have been launched with other companies or acquisitions made with a view to creating stronger units better able to take advantage of perceived business opportunities in targeted markets. Typically engineering consultancy has featured prominently in this kind of development, both as a response to the substantial increases in capital expenditure programmes which all the Water plcs have experienced, and to the opportunity to offer design and consultancy services to third parties. Examples include Yorkshire Water's decision to transfer its engineering division into a new 50/50 joint venture company, Babcock Water Engineering Ltd, which it set up with Babcock International; and Welsh Water's acquisition of Wallace Evans, a firm of consulting engineers (see Table 11.3).

MAJOR INITIATIVES

In contrast to the realignments indicated above larger-scale acquisitions and in some instances joint ventures have been undertaken, but all the companies have so far largely restricted themselves to activities which are associated in some way or other with their core business.[7] These have mainly centred on moves into the area of waste management and international water business (see Table 11.3). Although still on a relatively small scale (see Table 11.4) this aspect of the companies' corporate strategy is becoming increasingly important. Waste management has been a growing area of activity throughout the 1980s as environmental issues received more attention and concern was expressed about the standards of waste management. Although it is estimated that 75 per cent of the market is currently catered for by small operators, it is expected that more stringent environmental legislation and the higher technical standards required of operators to effectively cope with waste disposal will favour larger companies. Moreover, with producers of waste under the 1990 Environmental Protection Act incurring from 1992 a duty of care, which entails the responsibility to ensure that waste is being disposed of properly, in accordance with the law, there will be a tendency to favour large reputable disposal companies in order to minimize the risk of liability. Although there are differences in some of the operational and technical skills required, there are sufficient similarities with the waste water business, particularly in the areas of liquid waste treatment and incineration, to make waste management attractive to the water companies. Moreover the Water plcs are expecting to achieve competitive advantage on the basis of reputations for dealing competently with waste products acquired through performing well in the regulated business of providing water and sewerage services. One senior manager interviewed typically commented as follows:

> We're absolutely committed to serving our customers in water services, and that has a number of benefits ... in the business sector, if we're recognized as being customer focused and providing an excellent service, there are actually business opportunities to be had, serving our business and industrial customers. I mean one of our major enterprise businesses is an environmental business and it's really there to solve customers' environmental problems, i.e. waste disposal problems. So we have a big focus on serving the customer and saying to the business customer 'we can deal with your other waste problems too.'

However, the reputational benefits the water companies hope to achieve may also adversely work in reverse, since they will also incur the reciprocal risk of suffering a serious accident or major disaster in waste management which would reflect negatively on their image as competent and environmentally sound water companies.

The companies have pursued different strategies towards the waste management business. Two companies have made major commitments to waste management. Severn Trent acquired Biffa Waste Services Ltd from BET in May 1990 for £212 million which now makes Severn Trent one of the biggest UK operators in waste management. This has been the biggest single acquisition of any of the Water plcs so far. As such it has attracted a lot of attention and has frequently prompted the criticism that Severn Trent paid too much for it. Having failed earlier in 1991 in its bid of £78 million to buy another waste management company, Caird, Severn Trent was determined to secure Biffa when BET, its previous owner, announced it was for sale.

---

7. Although there are examples of diversification into unrelated areas of activity these have been few and far between and have been on a small scale. Welsh Water, for example, through its recreation and leisure subsidiary Hamdden, purchased during 1990 and 1991 five country house hotels in Wales for some £8 million. However, the venture has not been successful and Welsh Water has now withdrawn from it.

Severn Trent justified the price of £212 million paid for it, both in terms of the future benefits expected to flow from it, and the intense competition that it had to beat to secure the deal. Not far behind is Wessex who entered into a joint venture with an American company, Waste Management International, which is the world's largest waste management company. The new company, Wessex Waste Management, acquired Wimpey Waste in 1991 for £105 million and Waste Management Ltd from NEC in 1992 for £113 million. On a regional basis South West Water, Yorkshire and Northumbria have initiated significant developments aimed at regional markets. South West acquired Haul-Waste, the largest waste management business in the South West, from English China Clay in early 1993 for £27 million, and expects synergies with its existing liquid waste disposal operations conducted through its subsidiary Peninsula Waste Technology Ltd. Yorkshire's principal focus is liquid waste, where it has in-house expertise but is fast developing its business in clinical waste incineration through its subsidiary White Rose Environmental. Southern began by confining its activities to the operations of the appointed business but has recently begun to expand on a regional basis its liquid waste collection and disposal activities through its subsidiary Ecoclear Ltd, landfill operations through Greenhill Enterprises, and has formed a joint venture, Clinical Waste, with Mediwaste of New Zealand to take advantage of the regional market for collecting and disposing of clinical waste. Welsh has so far focused on developing a niche market within their region in liquid waste collection and disposal, and is now looking through its subsidiary company Welsh Water Industrial Services to offer industrial clients design, project management, transportation and operation of treatment facilities, on or off the client's site. However, there have been some mistakes and false starts: for example, both Welsh and Southern have experienced withdrawals. They pulled out of joint ventures with the French company SAUR after the companies Cambrian Environmental (Welsh) and Stalward (Southern) failed to win sufficient municipal contracts to remain viable. Northumbrian, hoping to develop business in high-temperature incineration, had planning permission for two incinerators turned down, and consequently refocused their efforts on winning contracts for municipal and clinical waste disposal. Thames has a relatively low level of activity to date which is mainly related to the core utility business. Anglian is similarly placed, but as it showed interest in Biffa prior to its acquisition by Severn Trent, it may well increase its involvement. Even though Thames and Anglian have to date not established major presences in waste management they have not yet taken the position of North West which exceptionally has taken a definite decision not to enter this market.

The other main area of diversification has been into international work with an emphasis on securing operating contracts, and build, operate and transfer contracts which are becoming increasingly common. Both markets are expanding and the UK companies – particularly the big four, Thames, North West, Severn Trent and Anglian – have been keen to develop their overseas presences and compete more effectively with the leading French companies, Compagnie Générale des Eaux and Lyonnaise des Eaux. Again the Water plcs are hoping to achieve competitive advantage in international business by demonstrating a reputation for good performance in the home regulated business of providing water and sewerage services. One senior manager interviewed commented on these links as follows:

> We are seriously into the world market in terms of our international business, which relates straight back to our core in the sense that we cannot sell water technology in the world

if we can't demonstrate that the company is the league leader in the UK. So we can bring you to the UK from wherever you are elsewhere in the world and we show you the incredible achievements of the core business here as part of the process of selling you whatever we're trying to sell you for our international business.

Thames Water International, for example, now markets a wide range of technical and managerial services ranging from specialist tasks such as leakage control to long-term management of water utilities. Current projects include water operations and management in Indonesia, Malaysia, Thailand and Argentina, and consulting and training in India, Pakistan and Nigeria. During 1993 it has formed a joint venture with Binnie and Partners to develop its consultancy and training activities. Thames' major international activity, however, is in the design and building of water and waste water treatment plant for drinking water, sewage and industrial applications through its subsidiary PWT worldwide. This contributes £118 million turnover (48 per cent of turnover of the non-appointed businesses) and has recently been strengthened by the acquisitions of UTAG, a German company, in 1992, and in 1993 the waste water treatment activities of Simon Engineering. Its largest order in 1993 was for a £28 million water treatment plant for Karachi, Pakistan.

Severn Trent is also attempting to establish a leading world position in the water and waste water utility sectors through the activities of Severn Trent Water International. Through acquisitions it has operations in the USA, Mexico, Belgium, Italy and Germany, and has won contracts to manage and advise on developing water services in Puerto Rico, Mauritius, Malaysia, Swaziland, India, Chile, Hong Kong and Ethiopia.

North West Water has perhaps been the most successful so far of those seeking to win substantial business overseas both in consultancy, design and build, and management of water services. It has invested heavily in developing its engineering capability and its expertise in process technology to provide the basis for its focus on water and waste water operations and products. This is seen by the company as essential to its international business, conducted through North West International, since it believes that it must offer the same wide range of products and services as its main rivals, the big French companies, if it is to compete successfully with them. In 1993 it won a large contract (£11 million) to design, build and operate a water treatment plant for Melbourne and has followed that with a similar contract to do the same for Sydney (£50 million) as well as with successful bids for a ten-year operating contract (£285 million) to provide water and waste water services for Mexico City, and a 28-year contract worth £1.25 billion over the first 18 years to upgrade, extend and operate Malaysia's sewerage system. The company is also active in the USA; for example, US Water Inc., based in New Jersey, is providing contract operations and maintenance services to municipal and industrial water and waste water facilities.

Anglian Water is the fourth of the major players in the international market. Its acquisition in 1993 of the Swedish-based international water process engineering group of Nordic Water strengthened its process engineering activities which were reorganized in a new company, Anglian Water Process Engineering. It is intended that the business and process engineering skills provided by AWPE will assist in building the business of its international operating and consulting subsidiary, Anglian Water International, formed in 1992. Some of the other companies have some international business, usually consultancy, but it is on a limited scale.

REFERENCES   Office of Water Services (Ofwat) 1993. *Annual Report 1992*. Birmingham, Ofwat.
Ramamujan, V. and P. Varadarajan (1989) 'Research on corporate diversification: a synthesis',
Management Journal, Vol. 10, pp. 523–51.

SECTION 5

Consumer products

Case 12   The European food industry and Groupe BSN
           J.R. Anchor and C.M. Clarke-Hill, University of Huddersfield

Case 13   Glaxo Holdings Plc
           J. Fernie, University of Abertay Dundee

Case 14   Kwik-Fit Holdings
           J.G. Gallagher and R.S. Scott, Napier University

Case 15   Chrysalis Group
           J. Day, University of Huddersfield

The European food industry and Groupe BSN

J.R. Anchor and C.M. Clarke-Hill

FOOD INDUSTRY ANALYSIS

The technology of food production

The food processing industry is, as its name implies, the central link in a chain of production which involves the transformation of certain types of agricultural output into products which can be purchased by consumers in retail outlets. Of course, a major share of agricultural output, such as fruit and vegetables, finds its way into shops in an unprocessed form. Nevertheless, during the twentieth century an increasing proportion of the daily food intake in advanced industrial nations has been processed in one way or another.

The impact of technological change upon the food industry has taken a variety of forms. As has already been indicated, the interaction between product and process innovations has, in many cases, been complex. Food science and technology has been concerned not only with new or improved products but also with product quality and standardization, with cost reduction via decreasing labour and energy intensities and with attempts to obtain scientific understanding of the processes involved. Technological change has also had a considerable impact upon the food distribution sector, particularly with regard to the development of electronic point of sales systems, item price marking and stock control.

The food processing industry has a relatively low level of value added compared to manufacturing industry as a whole. However, capital investment assumes a greater proportion of net output in the food industry than in manufacturing as a whole. In both cases, the contribution of capital to net output has increased, with the rate of growth in the food sector being the greater.

The paragraph above refers to the situation in the food industry as a whole. In fact, the various food processing sectors differ significantly in their capital intensities and in their production methods. Nevertheless, in nearly every case, it would appear that major production scale economies do not exist. Empirical surveys have indicated, for instance, that the minimum efficient scale of production is only 0.5 per cent of sales in the case of plant bread and approximately 10 per cent for potato crisps. Therefore the food industry is unlike, in this respect, many other process industries which frequently exhibit both a high level of capital intensity and major production economies of scale.

Firm-level scale economies may, however, be of greater significance in the food processing industry. This may partially explain the large number of mergers which have occurred.

Industrial structure

In an overall sense, the structure of the food industry may be considered to be a relatively fragmented one. This is due to the highly varied nature of its output. Different companies tend to have different product specialisms. Indeed, firms engaged in food processing at the start of the twentieth century were typically relatively small compared to those in other manufacturing sectors. However, the lifting of wartime controls, the growth of supermarkets, the development of own brands and the abolition of resale price maintenance all served to increase competition within the industry during the postwar period.

As a result, there was a relatively large fall in the number of food processing firms during the 1960s. The horizontal and conglomerate mergers which brought about this resulted in a significant increase in industrial concentration. In several food markets, one or two firms obtained a major presence. Indeed the process of concentration increased to the extent that a number of food companies constituted some of the largest firms in manufacturing industry. Product market concentration appears to have stabilized during the 1970s compared with the rapid increase of the 1960s. However, the 'merger mania' which developed during 1985 threatened to increase the level of concentration further.

The proposed merger between the Australian company Elders and the British conglomerate Allied-Lyons illustrates the increase in the international orientation of the food industry which has taken place during the postwar period. The growth of international travel and improved communications have been major causes of this trend. Such developments have tended to erode culturally based differences in eating habits.

In the United Kingdom, this has taken the form of an increase in the demand for products such as rice, pasta and spaghetti as substitutes for potatoes and the growing use of peppers and more exotic flavourings in addition to salt and pepper. Indeed, in many households the traditional 'meat and two veg' meal is probably served only on a minority of occasions. Concomitant with this, the familiar and much loved English pudding has declined in usage in the face of competition from continental 'light sweets' such as yoghurt, caramels, fruit, and cheese and biscuits. However, a growing concern with the calorific content of food and increasing health consciousness have also stimulated the latter trend. The EU's common agricultural policy and food law harmonization programme have made a specific contribution towards the development of a European 'milieu' in which the food industry can exist.

Technological changes which have led to productive and infrastructural developments have also contributed to the internationalization of the food industry. For example, the development of new packaging materials and preservative techniques has facilitated the transportation of processed foodstuffs. Fresh food is also much more readily transported as a result of the development of container ships which are able to deploy techniques for the large-scale freezing and preservation of such goods.

As in many other mature sectors the European food industry is becoming increasingly concentrated. This trend is evidenced both within individual countries and also at the pan-European level. To a considerable extent, this trend mirrors a more general European-wide merger boom which occurred during the late 1980s/early 1990s as companies prepared for the advent of the European single market on 31 December 1992.

Statistics on the merger activity of Europe's largest 1,000 industrial companies show that by late 1989 cross-border mergers were almost as common as national mergers (Fig. 12.1). There seems to have been a significant shift away from the historically most common motive of restructuring towards strengthening of market position. Indeed, reinforcement of market position or expansion of commercial activities are reasons quoted in three out of four European mergers in 1988/89 (Fig. 12.2).

The changing shape of the European food industry has led to the emergence of three major conglomerates – Nestlé, Unilever and BSN – which enjoy representation in most geographical and product markets.

The French and UK industries are more than averagely concentrated with the largest fifty companies accounting for more than 50 per cent of total output. By comparison with other industries, however, this level of concentration is not particularly high. In some southern European countries, the level of fragmentation is even higher. In Italy, for example, there are estimated to be approximately 40,000 food and drink processors, with an average company size of approximately ten employees. At a European level, the three largest food processors – Unilever, Nestlé and BSN – account for less than 10 per cent of total European consumer expenditure.

The merger movement in the European food industry is likely to reduce this fragmentation somewhat. Germany heads the league table of mergers – an unsurprising situation, given the relatively low level of concentration of the German industry

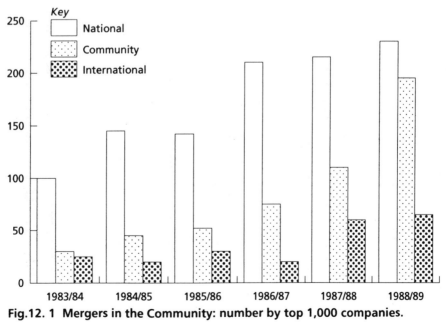

Fig.12. 1 Mergers in the Community: number by top 1,000 companies.
Source: EC Competition Policy Reports.

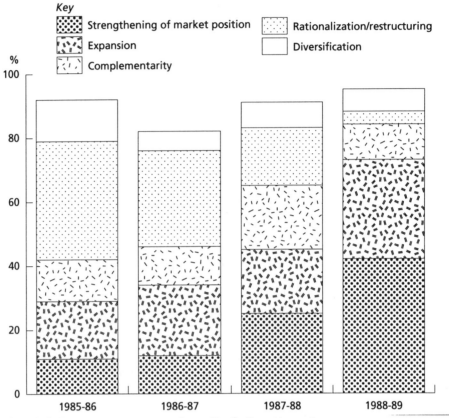

Fig. 12.2 European merger motives: % of all motives given.
Source: EC Competition Policy Reports.

compared with its northern European counterparts. The UK food industry comes second in the league table of merger activity. One survey has estimated, however, that between January 1988 and May 1989, one-third of mergers and acquisitions within the European food industry were cross-border deals, with UK companies the most active. The Netherlands has been the most attractive target market for cross-border acquirers. The physical location of Holland – with over 50 per cent of the EU's population living within 600 km (375 miles) of the centre of the country – may account for this fact.

US food companies have become increasingly active acquirers within the European food industry. Pepsico, for instance, acquired the Walkers and Smiths crisps and snacks business from BSN in 1989. This provided it with a major platform from which to develop its European food interests.

BSN is one of the most active European cross-border acquirers. In 1987, it made 11 acquisitions of which nine were outside France. In 1988/89, BSN acquired HP Foods in the UK for £199 million. In June 1989, BSN was involved in two of the largest ever cross-border acquisitions in the industry – the purchase of Nabisco's European food assets for $2.5 billion.

It is, perhaps, worth noting the impact which mergers and acquisitions can have on an individual company. At the end of 1988, United Biscuits was the largest biscuits producer in Europe and its KP subsidiary held a very strong position in the UK snacks, nuts and crisps market, facing essentially UK focused competitors – Smiths, Walkers and Golden Wonder. By the middle of 1989, however, it faced a very different environment. BSN's purchase of Nabisco's European biscuits interests gave it clear European leadership, with strong portions in each of the five major European markets. In addition, the acquisition of Nabisco's UK crisps and snacks business by Pepsico put KP up against a major US competitor.

The demand for food

Food is a non-durable consumer good. In most advanced industrialized nations, the overall demand for food (and hence its consumption) is relatively stable. This is due primarily to their low or even negative rates of population growth and an adequate level of nutrition for the most part, although at a lower level of aggregation there are many cases of 'over-eating' and an inadequate diet. Moreover, despite the fact that the overall demand for food is stable and relatively income and price inelastic, shifts in demand do take place at the individual product level, even over relatively short periods of time. In the case of less developed and newly industrializing countries, of course, the income and price elasticities of demand with respect to food will be much higher.

Of course, there are a number of food products which will be experiencing demand growth at any particular point in time. For instance, the demand for many categories of frozen foods increased substantially in the United Kingdom during the 1970s. The related product category of 'fast food' also experienced rapid growth during the 1970s and 1980s, especially in the United Kingdom and West Germany. This had a major impact not only on the food manufacturing industry but upon the structure of retail outlets too. Indeed snack foods of various categories, especially savoury snacks, grew in popularity during the early 1980s.

Health foods also experienced a growth in demand during the late 1970s and early 1980s. Pressure from bodies such as the UK government's Committee on Medical Aspects of Food Policy on Diet and Cardiovascular Disease (COMA) has been a major cause of this trend. In spite of these pressures, there is evidence that taste and value for money considerations still play a major role in consumers' choice of their food products. A further spreading of health consciousness, however, would have a significant impact upon the structure of the food industry.

The food industry in the advanced industrialized nations may be considered to be 'mature' in the sense that per capita food consumption is becoming less responsive to changes in income and is reaching a saturation level. Nevertheless, as has just been indicated, there have been a number of changes in the *pattern* of that demand. These have been caused by a combination of socio-economic factors.

An increase in the proportion of 'white-collar' employment has led to a reduction in the average level of physical exertion associated with work. This had led to a decline in the importance of the midday meal and a preference for snack products. A large midday meal is not conducive to the exercise of the brain, which is a key feature of most sedentary, white-collar jobs.

A second factor which has compounded the first is the increase in the proportion of married women who undertake paid employment. In the United Kingdom, this proportion had reached well over 50 per cent by the early 1980s. This trend has reduced and in most cases eliminated the possibility of a man coming home for a midday meal which has been cooked by his wife. It has also increased the demand for convenience-style foods for the evening meal since there is less time to cook that as well.

A large increase in the number of single-person households – mainly old people and young people – has been another cause of the growth in demand for convenience foods. For many people living on their own, there is little incentive to cook 'fully blown' meals, especially if they have to do all of the washing up as well. An increasing amount of leisure time for the majority of the population has also contributed to the growth of demand for snacks and 'fast foods'. On the face of it, this is the reverse of what might be expected since an increase in leisure time might be expected to provide more time for cooking. In practice, however, it seems that more free time simply encourages people to fill it with other activities which themselves serve to reduce the time available for meal preparation.

The growth in real disposable incomes which has taken place in the advanced industrialized nations during the postwar years, coupled with the relevant technological developments, served to stimulate the purchase of consumer durables such as refrigerators and freezers. These have provided the means for the preservation of frozen and other convenience foods.

Another major factor influencing the pattern of demand for food – one alluded to earlier – has been increasing consumer 'self-awareness'. This has taken the form of a growing concern about both the total amount of food eaten and its nutritional/health properties. It would probably be true to say, however, that this movement has been associated largely with higher income groups.

A study based on UK National Survey data has indicated that a number of household characteristics are important explanations of food consumption patterns. As well as income levels and household composition – factors which were highlighted above – the age of the housewife, freezer ownership, housing tenure and location were all found to be important determinants of demand at the household level.

The net effect of the above trends has been to reallocate consumers' expenditure on food. However, the absolute level of resource allocation has remained flat. Indeed, the share of consumers' expenditure on food has declined significantly during the postwar period. Between 1955 and 1980, it fell from 27.5 per cent to 17.2 per cent in the UK.

The five major European markets – UK, France, Germany, Italy and Spain – account for approximately 70 per cent of the total. There is, however, considerable variation in the rate of growth of both geographical and product markets. Northern European markets, such as the UK and Germany, are showing little real growth while some southern ones – Italy and Portugal, for instance – are enjoying rapid expansion. There are also wide variations in consumption levels for individual food categories across Europe. The French for instance, are estimated to be four times as interested in gourmet-style foods as the British. The converging consumer, demographic and lifestyle trends, already referred to, seem very likely to result in some homogenization of consumer taste.

In many product markets, only the brand leader and possibly the number two company make significant profits. Market leadership within a particular product category is therefore increasingly emphasized. In the more developed geographical outlets the top two branded manufacturers, within a particular product category, typically have a combined market share of over 40 per cent. Nestlé, for instance, is the leader in nine out of ten major European instant coffee markets, with a market share in each of the nine markets in excess of 40 per cent. Kelloggs has a similar position within the European ready-to-eat cereals market while Unilever dominates the European ice cream market. Such pan-European dominance is not common, however, and many product markets still remain largely in the hands of domestic operators with no dominant pan-European supplier.

Of growing significance to European food manufacturers, particularly those with pan-European corporate and brand portfolios, is the emergence of pan-European food retailers and buying groups. The French and German retailers have been the most active with Aldi, the major German discount retailer, now operating in seven European countries. A number of French supermarket chains have been particularly active in southern European markets. In addition, a number of pan-European buying and marketing groups have emerged.

Competition in the food industry

As was noted above, individual food markets tend to exhibit a relatively high level of firm concentration although the industry as a whole may be considered to be fragmented, in the sense that it is populated by a large number of firms. Moreover, mergers of both a conglomerate and a horizontal nature have exerted an upward pressure on levels of market concentration, although these have tended to occur at particular periods of time, such as during the 1960s and the mid 1980s. At other times – during the 1970s, for instance – concentration levels have been much more stable and may even have declined somewhat as a result of the implementation of post-merger 'sorting out' strategies. Nevertheless, competition within individual food markets is for the most part a case of 'competition among the few'. Indeed it has been stated that 'oligopolistic competition is the norm and not the exception.

The next section will highlight the fact that as far as many food manufacturers/ processors are concerned increasingly it is the pressure exerted by retailers in a vertical direction which has been their major source of competition. However, this section will concentrate on horizontal competition – *between* the food manufacturers themselves. As is often the case in oligopolistic markets, competition tends to emphasize non-price forms although it would be wrong to conclude that price is a totally unimportant variable in this context.

'Horizontal conflict' among food processors takes a number of forms. First of all, there is a significant level of competition for shelf space in retail outlets. The advent of large multiple retailers has tended to increase the level of this form of competition and has led to the 'delisting' of less popular brands – even those which are second or third in terms of overall sales – in favour of market leaders or retailers' own-label products. The key role played by leading brand names was thought to be one of the major driving forces behind the merger movement which affected the food and drink industries during the mid 1980s.

The food industry exhibits a relatively high level of new product development. During the 1970s and the 1980s, for instance, snack foods of various types have been developed in Britain, as have cheesecake and muesli. The latter two classes of product are examples of the utilization of ideas from abroad by the UK food industry.

Advertising is another important form of non-price competition within the food industry. A high level of advertising is thought to stimulate impulse purchases of products such as snack foods – crisps, chocolates and sweets, for example. However, advertising is also an important feature of other food sectors, since it is held to stimulate brand awareness. This is the case in the breakfast cereals industry, for instance, where advertising and new product development are closely linked.

Except where retailers' own-label products are in competition with manufacturers' brands, the breakfast cereals market is one in which companies compete through the appeal of different brand products and via a search for new varieties which will expand the market and their own sales. While appeal and quality of product are regarded as essential prerequisites for success, advertising and promotion have always been, and still are, regarded as necessary means of securing and retaining sufficient public acceptance of the brand products to ensure profitable and, if possible, growing volume of production.

As was noted earlier, economies of scale in food production are generally not of any great significance. However, the problem of winning shelf space in supermarkets and the need for a high level of marketing expenditure in support of new product development may well constitute major barriers to entry. Indeed the Monopolies Commission concluded in 1973 in the case of the British breakfast cereals industry that this factor was of considerable importance. The dominant position of Kellogg and its very wide product range simply served to accentuate this situation.

In summary, competition within many food markets is clearly of an oligopolistic nature. Image-based barriers to entry are relatively high and branding is of considerable importance. Although a certain amount of new entry competition has taken place in a number of markets, the existence of significant entry barriers has generally acted as a major disincentive. Where new product development has taken place, it has usually been by existing producers or has required the backing of a firm with large financial resources. A good example of the latter is Golden Wonder's introduction of flavoured crisps following its acquisition by the Imperial Group during the 1960s.

Vertical linkages and interfaces

The food manufacturing or processing industry is at the centre of a so-called 'food chain' which transforms agricultural output into products which can be bought in retail outlets.

Technological development has made a major contribution to the changes which have occurred in the relative importance of the different parts of the so-called 'food chain' during the postwar period. Since mass production technologies have made possible the continuous processing of homogeneous food products, firms have needed to secure standardized raw materials. Consequently, they have invested in agricultural production themselves or engaged in fixed contractual relations with farmers – a case of backwards vertical quasi-integration.

Chemical and pharmaceutical innovations have also contributed to this change in the relative importance of the various components of the food chain. An increasing number of crops are no longer viewed as finished or even semi-finished goods but are, rather, valued for what they contain; sugars, starches, fats and proteins, for example. By the use of advanced chemical engineering techniques, these constituents may be isolated and restructured to change their properties.

Primary processing firms can now produce purified and stabilized intermediate food products with well-defined technological and nutritional properties. Downstream firms, which are no longer directly dependent on agricultural supply, can then reconstitute these basic elements into finished products. The agricultural sector has now become essentially the link in the chain which provides the material for primary processing.

The extent of vertical linkages, in a backwards direction, between the food industry and the agricultural sector and, in a forwards direction, between the industry and the retail sector varies from country to country. Backward vertical linkages are especially important in Denmark and the United Kingdom but much less so in Italy, for instance. Forwards integration between food processors and distributors or retailers is more common in the United Kingdom than in any other European country. It is the latter type of linkage which will be the main focus of this section since it is this which has had a major impact upon food manufacturers' competitive strategies. However, the relationship between agriculture and the food industry is also of considerable importance.

Agriculture – food industry linkages

In the modern era, only a minor proportion of agricultural output reaches the consumer in the same form that it leaves the farm. Technological change has been largely responsible for this state of affairs (see above). As a consequence, close links have been formed between farmers and food companies in many countries and between farmers and distributors in some cases.

Up until the interwar period the flow of food distribution was from large numbers of farmers to large numbers of retailers via wholesale markets. Therefore, the food market can be said to have corresponded to the economic model of perfect competition. However, the emergence of specialist food processing companies, via mergers and natural growth, led to them obtaining a significant amount of market power over farmers. The subsequent growth of multiple retailers at the expense of independents has added to the pressure on the agricultural sector to improve the quality and packaging of its output. The major requirements of multiple retailers are continuity of supply, product standardization and packaging which is suitable for bulk handling. The major multiples do not buy through wholesale markets but rather use their existing distribution network for processed food to distribute fresh produce. They therefore seek to deal with suppliers who can offer large quantities of produce of a standardized nature and which is available over a considerable period of time. In the face of a relatively fragmented domestic agricultural sector, UK multiple retailers have often preferred to import fresh food.

The relationship between farmers, food processors and the distributive trades has varied from country to country. In a search for an improvement in the profitability of food and farming, there have been attempts at vertical integration between the two stages of production. The intensive livestock sector is the one in which vertical integration has been most highly developed due to the extent to which pig and poultry production can be organized on a 'factory' scale. In other sectors, however, quasi-integration via contract farming has been the most prevalent phenomenon.

Contract farming has been defined as a system 'for the production of and supply of agricultural and horticultural produce under forward contracts, the essence of such arrangements being a commitment to provide an agricultural commodity of a type, at a time and in the quantity required by a known buyer'. Such arrangements have existed for many years in a number of sectors. They have traditionally been based on an agreement that the price paid should bear some specific relationship to a standard 'indicator' price – the local wholesale market price, for example. However, the expansion of the food processing industry, the changes in the pattern of demand for food which were noted above and the changes in the distribution network which are discussed below led to a growth in the importance of contract farming.

There are various categories of contract, the relative importance of which has varied over a time and from product to product. A number of types of contract have been adopted. These include marketing contracts which specify only the conditions of sale for farm outputs; contracts in which the buyer also supplies the major inputs and specifies how the production process is to take place and usually retains ownership of the commodity; and contracts in which the buyer supplies some inputs and has a share in making the production decisions but does not acquire ownership of the product until it leaves the farm. In addition 'joint ventures' or 'market linked' contracts have been developed. Under the terms of these agreements, the processor and the farmer share the risks of producing, freezing and storing the product.

Manufacturer–distributor linkages

The relationship between food processors and their distributors – both wholesale and retail – has changed significantly during the postwar period as the structure of the latter has evolved. The growth of, first of all, self-service and, more recently, supermarket outlets, has taken place in most developed countries.

Concentration in food retailing tends to be particularly pronounced in the grocery sector. However, large firms are also significant in the sale of fresh milk and cream, fresh fish, poultry and game, and bakery products. In the dairy food retail market and to a lesser extent in some other food retail sectors, there is a significant level of vertical integration between producer/wholesalers and retailers. This is the case, for example, in the bakery and butchery trades where in the UK independents still account for three-quarters of the specialist outlet sales and plant-bakers and meat slaughterers/processors own significant numbers of retail outlets.

Within the grocery sector, concentration tends to be higher in the market for packaged products than for groceries as a whole since the grocery market now includes significant sales of fresh meat and fish, fresh fruit and vegetables. Indeed one of the most significant changes in the major grocery chains' merchandising policies during the 1970s was the move towards fresh foods. Meat and dairy produce departments were among the first to be introduced. During the 1980s, delicatessen sections, in-store bakeries and fresh fish departments have been introduced.

The growing concentration of the retail food market in general and the grocery market in particular has had a number of consequences – both for the retail sector itself and for the food manufacturing industry.

Within the grocery retail sector, companies have placed an increasing emphasis upon price in their market strategies. To a significant extent this was caused by the very high inflation rates of the 1970s which led to a growing price consciousness on the part of consumers. As a consequence, most of the major chains in the UK, apart from 'the Co-op', abolished trading stamps on their goods and concentrated on keeping their prices as low as possible.

Examples of price cutting operations in the UK include Tesco's 'Operation Checkout' which was launched in June 1977 and Sainsbury's 'Discount '78' which was instigated in the following year. Other companies also adopted increasingly price-conscious market strategies. However, there seems to be some doubt as to whether the response to 'Operation Checkout' by other firms was due to the free play of market forces or whether it was simply an example of oligopolistic behaviour – competition amongst the few. Not all companies adopted strategies in which price was the key variable. Marks and Spencer, for instance, relied upon their high quality image and upon new product development.

The 1970s also witnessed a sustained increase in retailer advertising with the most significant changes being observed during the period of 'Operation Checkout'. Between 1976 and 1977, advertising expenditure by the 'big three' (Asda, Sainsbury and Tesco) doubled. This was almost double the rate for retailers as a whole. Television advertising has been the major form of increased expenditure by the multiple retailers. This medium facilitates the building up of a store image or 'franchise'. For similar reasons, price cutting has tended to be of an increasingly 'across the board' nature, rather than concentrated on specific items.

In spite of this growth in the level of advertising by retailers, their total outlay remained considerably less than that of food manufacturers. In 1982, for example, the thirty largest food retailers in the United Kingdom spent a total of £54 million on advertising. During the same period, however, Unilever's four main subsidiaries alone spent over £56 million.

One rather important aspect of competition in grocery retailing has been the changing balance between brands, own-label and generic products.

The initial exploitation of self-service and the growth of multiple retailers were associated with food manufacturers' branded products. However, the price cutting of the mid 1970s served to put pressure, in the short term at least, on retailers' profit margins. This caused them to attempt to obtain compensation from the manufacturers. In addition, own-label products, which had been used successfully by a number of companies, notably Sainsbury, for many years, became increasingly attractive to the multiples since they were not in direct competition with one another.

A second factor which helps to explain the growth of own-label products at the expense of brands is the development of the 'store franchise' concept described above. This meant that retailers were increasingly keen to establish their own identities rather than those of their suppliers.

Thirdly, the growing concentration of the retail grocery market provided the firms concerned with greater leverage *vis-à-vis* their suppliers. This enabled them to obtain more favourable terms for both branded and own-label products supplied by the food manufacturers.

There is a growing tendency for the quality of own-label products to be upgraded towards the level of manufacturers' brands, although this may have been at the expense of a reduced price differential. More importantly, however, this trend has left a gap in the market for grocery products at the lower end of the price range. In some cases, this gap has been filled by the introduction of 'generic' products. These are products which have been stripped of any additional packaging or promotion costs. Their only guarantee or 'name effect' is the store franchise itself.

Generic products were first introduced by Carrefour in France in April 1976. Subsequently the idea caught on in other countries with consumer acceptance having been stimulated, in many cases, by the prior introduction of own-labels. In Britain,

Fine Fare and International led the way. Later on, however, other multiple retailers introduced generic lines. It would seem that most of the cost saving on generic products comes from the exploitation of the power of the major retailers over the food manufacturers – a power which was increased by the recessionary economic conditions of the 1970s and 1980s.

The introduction of own-label and generic products in grocery retailing has had a number of consequences for competition in both the food retailing and manufacturing sectors. Perhaps the most important of these relate to the allocation of shelf space within the retail outlets and the pressure on second and third brands.

There is a considerable amount of evidence that multiple retailers have devoted more time and effort to providing shelf space of own-labels and generics than for brands, due to the greater profitability of the former. The growing interest in fresh foodstuffs by the multiple retailers has also reduced the amount of space available for tinned and packaged goods.

The development of own-labels and generics has meant that retailers have been able to delist manufacturers' brands which do not sell quickly. Unless a brand is the leader in its field, its manufacturer may have considerable difficulty in obtaining access to shelf space. Many retailers prefer instead to stock the brand leader together with their own-label product and/or a generic. The retention of the brand leader serves a dual purpose. First of all, it stimulates interest in the product line concerned. Secondly, it allows price comparisons to be made between the brand leader and own-labels/generics.

Therefore it may be seen that many of the most important developments in food retailing have been brought about by and have themselves been the causes of the growing power of the retailers *vis-à-vis* the food manufacturers. As was noted earlier, this has been the experience of a number of countries, not just the United Kingdom. The reasons for this occurring vary, of course, from country to country.

In the United Kingdom the causes of the emergence of what has been termed a 'bilateral oligopoly' included the adoption of new production and packaging methods by the food manufacturers which led to a greater capital intensity of production, and favourable demand and supply conditions for the development of large supermarkets. However, it is the *implications* rather than the causes of growing retailer power *vis-à-vis* the food manufacturing industry which is of the greatest importance from the point of view of the implementation of the competitive strategies of the latter.

As has already been noted, the increased power of food retailers has enabled them to introduce own-label and generic products, many of which are supplied by the leading food manufacturers. In the United States, it seems that the largest retailers are supplied in many cases by small, 'fringe' food manufacturers. In the United Kingdom, however, many of the large food processors also supply the large retailers.

As well as using their market power to introduce own-label and generic products, the large food retailers have also been able to obtain substantial discounts on branded products. A Monopolies and Mergers Commission report in 1981 found that this practice was not harmful to the consumer interest. More importantly, however, from the point of view of this discussion, the Commission reported that manufacturers often granted discounts to large retailers which were greater than that which was justified by the cost savings involved. This was due in part to the fact that it is difficult to calculate costs on individual orders and that in any case suppliers generally have to take a broad view of customers' businesses. The Commission concluded, in effect, that discounts to retailers would not be made unless they could be commercially justified and that, therefore, the pressure exerted by retailers could not be excessive.

More recently, however, there have been instances of manufacturers claiming that they have been unfairly treated by multiple retailers. Certainly there does appear to be room for arguing that the multiple retailers have made full use of their increased bargaining power *vis-à-vis* the food manufacturers. On the other hand, the major multiple grocery retailers can offer savings in terms of delivery costs, especially for products such as bread, biscuits and fresh food. Moreover, their buying policies may be more skilful and they may offer more effective and coordinated sales and promotion opportunities to manufacturers.

Competitive strategy in the food industry

It is apparent from the preceding discussion that the competition experienced by food manufacturers emanates as much if not more so from the retail sector as from other manufacturers. Indeed many in the food industry are worried about the effects of discriminatory discounting on manufacturers' finances and the harmful effects the paring of manufacturers' profit margins has on their ability to invest and conduct research. It has been suggested, therefore, that it is essential for the main multiple retailers to work closely with food manufacturers in developing generic and own-brand products (as part of their strategy to 'brand' their own operation and differentiate themselves from their competitors) but in such a way as not to erode the long-term competitive and financial base of the manufacturers.

Many manufacturers, however, have not been content to trust their futures to the generosity of the multiple retailers. The response of many of the leading UK manufacturers has been directed towards improving the competitiveness of their leading brands. This has involved increased levels of advertising aimed at appealing direct to the consumers of their products over the heads of the major retailers. In addition, there has been a concerted effort by manufacturers to improve their cost efficiency and to increase the rate of their process and product innovation. The fact that the own-label and generic producers do not have to incur heavy marketing outlays has enabled them to concentrate on cost reduction. By doing so, they have been able to obtain an important competitive advantage over the major brand manufacturers.

This 'counter attack' by the major food manufacturers began in the early 1980s. It seems to have achieved a certain degree of success. One of its effects has been to strengthen the position of the brand leader *vis-à-vis* other branded products in a given market. This accentuates a trend which has already been apparent for some time, namely that of a move towards a situation in which food markets are dominated by the brand leader and own-label producers.

The competitive strategies employed by food manufacturers have included, at various points in time, both the cost leadership and product differentiation options as defined by Porter. Product differentiation is a strategy which lends itself to a consumer goods industry such as food. However, there is a danger, both from the point of view of the firm and of consumer welfare, that this strategy may get out of hand and may result in excessive levels of advertising and other marketing expenditure. This can lead to the cost differential between low-cost producers and those which are employing the differentiated strategy becoming too great for the latter to retain brand loyalty. Furthermore the development of generic products may reduce the perceived differentiation of brands on the part of consumers.

The cost leadership strategy has been successfully employed by the suppliers of own-label products to the major food retailers. As a consequence the major brand manufacturers have been forced, as was noted above, to pay greater attention to their own cost levels. In the major industrialized nations where food requirements are generally satisfied and fall within the 'basic necessities of life' category, price may be an important influence upon the demand for staple foodstuffs. For other, more luxurious, categories of food, this may not be the case. The response by UK brand manufacturers to the development of own-label products illustrates that 'image' is still an important factor in consumers' purchasing decisions in this area. It may be that if the brand manufacturers can reduce their costs significantly, own-brand manufacturers may begin to feel a 'backlash' from consumers who prefer 'a little style with their food'.

The focus strategy is one which is difficult to employ in a deliberate sense in the food industry since, by definition, each product market constitutes a separate niche. It is inevitable in such circumstances that food companies will tend to specialize in particular areas, although there are a number which are of a conglomerate nature. Nevertheless, the fact remains that cornflake producers are not in competition with processors of tinned peas.

The strategies which have been employed by food manufacturers mirror those which have been deployed by the retailers. This is to be expected given the nature of the interface between the two sectors.

Cross-border acquisition strategies in the European food industry

Any merger needs to take account of the fact that many major food markets and product categories are in a state of maturity. In addition the structure of many national industries may consist increasingly of a combination of 'Euroscale' competitors such as BSN, Unilever and Nestlé and entrenched local competitors.

Four different cross-border acquisition strategies have been identified in relation to the European food industry. These are consolidation, growth engineering, pan-European distribution and remarging.

The consolidator looks for markets and product categories which have fragmented competitive structures. The aim of the consolidator – via the acquisition of several small companies or a few large companies – is to gain market share by the exploitation of economies of scale which may be obtained from the putting together of formerly separate production capacities.

The Italian pasta market has seen the implementation of a consolidation strategy. The industry is relatively fragmented with most companies having individual market shares of less than one per cent. In the second half of the 1980s, for instance, BSN acquired, or took investment stakes in, six small companies and now holds the number two position in the market with a share of approximately 15 per cent behind Barilla which had gained market share via a similar strategy.

The consolidator may face difficulties in implementing its chosen strategy. Unless brand rationalization is possible, for instance, the need to manufacture and support several different brands may mean that both firm- and plant-level economies of scale may not be realized. It was, perhaps, for this sort of reason that BSN's more recent acquisitions in the European pasta market have involved buying a single major competitor as opposed to several small companies. In 1989, for instance, BSN acquired La Familia which at the time held a 9 per cent share of the Spanish pasta market. When this was combined with its existing share of 8 per cent, this gave BSN an overall market share of 19 per cent and the number two position in the industry. In the same year, BSN purchased Birkel, the largest German pasta manufacturer with a market share of approximately 20–25 per cent.

Markets which comprise numerous small local competitors with strong local or regional consumer brand franchises may represent significant obstacles to a company attempting to gain market share, as may the presence of large competitors which may be in a position to block attempts to gain market share.

The *growth engineer* looks for markets and product categories which are either growing strongly already, or which appear to have strong growth potential given the necessary marketing investment. The Spanish biscuits market is an example of such a growing market. During the second half of the 1980s, this market grew by 10 per cent per annum. The UK biscuit market, by contrast, grew by only 2 per cent per annum during the same period. During this period, BSN acquired a number of Spanish biscuit companies.

A growth engineering strategy needs to be implemented carefully in markets where there is a relatively fragmented retail structure – in Spain or Italy, for example. As such retail environments become increasingly concentrated, the growth engineer may experience lower rates of value growth (as opposed to volume growth) as private labels are developed and individual customers become more sophisticated and powerful.

The *remarginer* seekers to identify markets in which there is an opportunity to inject value growth, either by creating new brands which command a price premium or by developing a premium higher value segment. The French pasta market is one in which a remargining strategy has been implemented during the 1980s, via high levels of advertising behind a premium segment. The premium segment of the French pasta market accounted for 30 per cent of the total market, compared to 15 per cent at the beginning of the decade.

The *pan-European distributor* seeks to identify product categories which appear to increasingly have or could have broad pan-European consumer appeal. It then aims to 'export' these brands throughout its existing pan-European selling and distribution network. This strategy is available, therefore, only to companies which have a pan-European business infrastructure.

The return for the pan-European distributor will depend, in part, on the size of marketing investment required to build brands. In the UK, for example, significant marketing expenditure is required if multiple grocers are to list a product. As the retail environment becomes increasingly concentrated over time, the value of this particular strategy will probably diminish and only small salesforces will be required to service centrally controlled multiple grocers.

The pan-European distribution strategy aims to exploit or develop the homogenization of consumer taste which was discussed earlier. It is the opinion of some industry observers, however, that this feature is far less common than it might appear.

Italian food, however, does appear to be one category with widespread consumer appeal across Europe. A number of large-scale food producers have, as a consequence, acquired companies which possess portfolios of traditional Italian products. BSN, for instance, has acquired several small pasta companies, as well as Galbani, the leading Italian cheese and salted meats producer, and Star, one of Italy's largest Italian packaged goods suppliers. It has also acquired Peroni beer. Its purchase of Galbani has provided BSN not only with some attractive brands for 'export' throughout Europe, but also with a significant selling network through which it can be expected to push some of its existing non-Italian products.

The four strategies are not mutually exclusive. It is quite likely, however, that the 1990s will witness a change in the prevalence of each of them. During the early 1990s a number of industry experts expected to see a steady reduction in the number of opportunities for consolidators and growth engineers, as fragmented markets became concentrated and relatively high growth markets began to mature. Remargining, however, will represent an increasingly important source of value added for cross-border acquirers as growth within markets or product categories slows down. Similarly, a pan-European distribution strategy can be expected to become more common as increasing numbers of companies build extensive European business infrastructures.

The 1990s are also likely to see cross-border 'unbundlers' at work as some acquisitions made in the 'heat of the moment' fail to meet the expectations of their acquirers. Even BSN, Unilever and Nestlé, the three Euro-scale players, may be ripe for unbundling.

GROUPE BSN

Introduction

Groupe BSN was formed as a result of a merger between two glass manufacturing companies – Souchon Neuvessel, a glass packaging company, and Boussion, an industrial glass manufacturer. Since the merger, BSN rapidly orientated its business towards becoming a major player in the French and later the European food industry. It achieved this by a mixed strategy of merger and acquisition, and divestment. By 1982, Groupe BSN had completely divested its industrial glass interests and had strengthened its food packaging businesses so as to become a partial-integrated food processing and marketing company. By 1989, Groupe BSN was the premier food group in France and the third largest food company in Europe, after Unilever and Nestlé.

Its geographic spread had grown from being primarily focused on the French market, to that of a global player. By 1990, BSN was active in the following sectors of the food industry: biscuits, fresh products, grocery products, beer, champagne and mineral waters, and packaging.

One of BSN's first acquisitions was the takeover of Kronenbourg Breweries along with another European brewery company giving BSN control of breweries and the Kronenbourg label, which it subsequently developed as a pan-European brand. Along with its entry into the beer sector, BSN also acquired the mineral waters company that marketed a series of mineral waters, the most famous being Evian. In 1973 BSN moved into the dairy foods and grocery sectors, by the acquisition of the Compagnie Gervais Danone (yoghurts and other dairy products) and its affiliates Panzani and Gallia (dried pasta and other grocery products). Further brewery and beer interests were added to the company's portfolio in 1979 by the acquisition of controlling interests in a brewery company in Belgium. 1980/81 saw BSN develop its dairy interests further by a series of small-scale acquisitions and it took its Dannone brand of dairy products into the Japanese and US markets.

BSN strengthened its grocery division by further acquisitions in France, Belgium and Italy. In 1984, it added to its drinks portfolio by taking over the champagne firm of Pommery and Lanson (later to be divested in 1990). It was in 1986 that BSN entered the biscuit market as a significant player. The acquisition of General Biscuits and its affiliates Sonnen-Bassermann in Germany gave BSN command of a number of important European and US brands and further strengthened its grocery interests in Germany. As the 1980s continued, further acquisitions were made by BSN which strengthened its market presence in Europe and gradually turned the company into a significant multinational food group.

Perhaps the most important deal the company made was the purchase of the biscuit interests of Nabisco in Europe in 1989. Nabisco was part of the giant R.J.R. Nabisco Inc. of the USA that was the subject of a successful leveraged buy-out and subsequent break-up by Kravis Kohlberg and Roberts. In one deal BSN gained control of a number of premium biscuit brands across Europe. By 1990, BSN was the market leader in the biscuit sector in a number of national EC markets and the largest biscuit manufacturer in Europe.

Further full-scale acquisitions, minority stake building and joint ventures followed in 1990 as BSN picked up further biscuit interests of Nabisco in overseas markets, notably in India, the Far East and Australasia. Table 12.1 gives details of acquisitions made in 1989/90. 1990 also saw BSN initiate a development programme orientated towards Eastern Europe by signing joint venture agreements in the dairy product sector with companies in East Germany and Hungary.

In generic terms BSN could be described as a multi-domestic company which operates in multiple related consumer goods businesses across the world, with strong perceived product differentiation arising from strong branding. BSN has always been multi-domestic in character (as opposed to global or transnational).

Table 12.1 Strategic developments in 1989/90 – external growth

Company	Country	Type of business
Star[1]	Italy	Grocery products
Starlux[1]	Spain	Grocery products
Scharffenberger Cellars	USA	Sparkling wine
La Familia	Spain	Pasta
Belin	France	Biscuits
Saiwa	Italy	Biscuits
Jacob's	UK	Biscuits
Henniger Hellas	Greece	Beer
Galbani[1]	Italy	Dairy products
Birkel[1]	Germany	Pasta
Britannia[1]	India	Biscuits
Griffen and Sons[2]	New Zealand	Biscuits/Grocery products
Nabisco Brands Malaysia[2]	Malaysia	Biscuits/Grocery products
Nabisco Brands Ltd[2]	Hong Kong	Biscuits/Grocery products
Peerless Foods	Hong Kong	Biscuits/Grocery products

1. Minority interests taken in these companies by BSN.
2. Joint ventures with the Pallai Group.

Financial highlights and group strategy

Financial
highlights

BSN had grown in scale and scope over the latter part of the 1980s to become the third largest food group in Europe challenging the market position of Nestlé and Unilever. By early 1990, BSN was the sixth largest quoted company on the Paris Bourse by market capitalization. Sales and net income continued to grow up to 1990. Its acquisition policy, funded by a mixture of new shares, long-term borrowing and asset disposals helped fuel this growth and turn BSN into a company with world-wide interests. The key acquisition of the Nabisco interests worldwide made BSN the world's largest biscuit-maker.

Due to BSN's heavy acquisition programme, the company, as was the prevailing fashion, included in its balance sheets the valuation of brands and goodwill that arose as a surplus over the asset value of acquired companies. To quote from the 1989/90 annual report:

> The separate identification of brands in the fair value assigned to net assets acquired relates primarily to the recent acquisitions of the biscuit companies of Nabisco (1989) and the sauce companies HP Foods and Lea and Perrins (1988). For consistency purposes the brands of the General Biscuit Group, included in the goodwill at the date of acquisition in 1986 and 1987, have also been separately identified and subsequently allocated to the fair value assigned to net assets acquired.

> The brands which have been separately identified are only premium brands, with a value that is substantial and considered to be of a long-term nature, sustained by advertising expenses.

> The valuation, conducted in conjunction with a specialist international branding consultancy, takes into account various factors including, particularly, the reputation and earnings of the brands. These brands, which are legally registered and protected, have no predeterminate finite life, and accordingly are not amortized. In the event that the recorded value of the brands become permanently impaired, a provision would be charged to the income.

Table 12.2 Financial highlights 1986–89

	1986	1987	1988	1989
Employees	42,780	41,285	42,234	49,693
Earnings per share (FF)	n.a.	34.0	41.7	49.7
Dividends per share (FF)	n.a.	8.5	10.0	11.5
	FF m	FF m	FF m	FF m
Sales	33,623	37,156	42,177	48,669
Operating profit	2,724	3,296	4,527	5,022
Net income	1,081	1,550	2,189	2,698
Shareholders' equity	9,612	14,344	16,415	19,782
Long-term debt	4,664	4,148	5,288	14,436
Capital employed (gross)[1]	17,934	23,094	26,617	39,634
Capital investment	n.a.	2,371	2,403	2,933
Market capitalization (31 December)	17,253	22,584	33,309	42,348

1. Includes goodwill and other intangible assets such as brand values.

Source: Company accounts.

Purchased goodwill, licences, patents and tenancy rights are recorded at cost. Purchased goodwill is amortized on a straight-line basis over a maximum period of 40 years. Other intangible assets are amortized on a straight-line basis over their estimated useful lives.

(*Source*: BSN Annual Report, Note 1D, p. 43)

Tables 12.2 to 12.5 provide an overview of BSN's financial performance between 1986 and 1989/90.

Table 12.3 Sales and operating income 1987–89

	Sales (FF m)			Operating income (FF m)		
	1987	1988	1989	1987	1988	1989
Dairy products	9,796	11,065	12,627	534	841	964
Grocery products	7,948	9,177	9,936	816	939	952
Biscuits	7,230	8,275	11,119	732	796	1,030
Beer	5,577	6,260	6,188	526	628	806
Champagne/mineral water	2,975	3,476	4,320	470	528	642
Containers	4,626	4,997	5,557	410	565	620
Internal transactions	(996)	(1,073)	(1,078)	—	—	—
Unallocated income	—	—	—	(192)	230	8
Total	37,156	42,177	48,669	3,296	4,527	5,022

Source: Company accounts.

Table 12.4 Geographic breakdown of sales and operating income

	Sales (FF m)			Operating income (FF m)		
	1987	1988	1989	1987	1988	1989
France	25,268	27,959	30,712	2,679	3,248	3,729
Rest of Europe	8,320	10,141	13,100	656	774	1,039
Outside Europe	3,568	4,077	4,857	153	275	246
Total	37,156	42,177	48,669	3,488	4,297	5,014

Source: Company accounts.

Table 12.5 Capital investment and operating cash flow

	Capital investment (FF m)			Net operating cash flow (FF m)		
	1987	1988	1989	1987	1988	1989
Dairy products	385	418	423	585	777	891
Grocery products	318	351	428	581	663	664
Biscuits	466	292	620	543	608	537
Beer	539	546	540	730	960	872
Champagne/mineral water	211	275	392	300	358	512
Containers	443	483	517	510	683	673
Total	2,362	2,365	2,920	3,378	4,249	4,330

Source: Company accounts.

Group strategy   In 1988, the chairman of BSN, Antoine Riboud, articulated five key objectives that would be the guiding principles of the company's strategy for the late 1980s and early 1990s.

1 BSN would develop and conserve a high degree of flexibility in the company's management and resist the encroachments of bureaucracy in its organization.

2 BSN would continue to improve the working conditions and situation of its employees, and intensify training so that employees can better understand the constraints under which BSN operates.

3 BSN would pursue an active strategy of acquisitions and alliances in Europe in order that all its operations may be present in sufficient strength in the unified European market of 1992, which, with a population of 320 million, will be the world's largest.

4 BSN would continue to develop research and innovation in order to place on the market new products and new packaging approaches.

5 BSN would continue its efforts in rationalization and improving productivity in manufacturing and logistics, in order to be able to face the competitive challenges and to keep pace with the changing trends in distribution that an expanding and restructured Europe will present, thereby maintaining and improving net margins.

BSN had always courted the investor, believing that good investor relations with the company had strategic advantages. In 1988, taking account of favourable stock market conditions, the company split its shares on a 10 for 1 basis, thereby leaving the sector of the high priced share and joined the ranks of the more moderately priced ones. Furthermore, BSN had always been committed to providing its shareholders with full information. Advertising campaigns were scheduled throughout the year designed to show and explain BSN's range of products and what the company stood for.

Group activities

Dairy products   BSN's sales of dairy products by product class for 1987–89 are detailed in Table 12.6. In a growing market for dairy products in Europe, BSN's premier brands all showed market share gains after a difficult trading year in 1987. This was achieved by a mixed strategy of new product introductions, efficiency improvements in production and rationalization of product lines and manufacturing location.

Market growth in the French market reduced from 11 per cent in 1988 to about 4 per cent in 1989, but growth rates in the German market stabilized at around 2–3 per cent over the period 1988–89. This allowed the key brands controlled by the company to hold and indeed increase market share. The fastest growing market in the EC was Italy, where the dairy sector recorded an increase of 19 per cent in 1988 that continued to be sustained in 1989. BSN's success in the Italian market was through its Galbani subsidiary, marketing fresh cheeses, pasta, desserts and yoghurts to the Italian public. In mid 1990, BSN increased its equity holding in its Italian affiliate to 50 per cent. Spain was also a key growing market for the dairy

Table 12.6 Sales of dairy products by product class

	1987 FF m	1988 FF m	1989 FF m
Sales	9,796	11,065	12,627
Operating income	534	841	964
	%	%	%
Desserts	16.5	15.8	15.4
Natural cheeses	32.9	33.2	32.7
Yoghurts	42.6	45.2	45.6
Miscellaneous	8.0	5.8	6.3

products division, which occupied a dominant market position and confirmed its leadership role in that market by the successful introduction of new product lines transferred from the French market.

BSN also operated in markets outside Europe, notably in North America and increasingly in South America, where in both Mexico and Brazil, the Danone brand of products were all displaying market share growth. The US subsidiary was also involved in a number of new product introductions that met local market needs and continued to keep the company competitive. Developments in the Far Eastern and Chinese markets were reported to be on track and in some cases to have exceeded their targets, particularly in China.

Capital investment in production efficiency and new product development continued at a consistent level to sustain the division's competitive advantage in an increasingly competitive market sector. Changes in consumer tastes and an increasing demand for low calorie and natural products had to be catered for. BSN responded by marketing a number of products to meet this demand; a notable success in Europe had been the Bio brand. Bio was a type of yoghurt that was manufactured using the bifidus fermentation method and flavouring the yoghurt culture with natural fruits. This brand was marketed by Danone in most European countries and complemented the company's other important dairy product brands and cheeses on the supermarket shelves in Europe.

Grocery products BSN's sales of grocery products by product class for 1987–89 are detailed in Table 12.7. As a result of a number of key acquisitions in the pasta and sauces market,

Table 12.7 Sales of grocery products by product class

	1987 FF m	1988 FF m	1989 FF m
Sales	7,948	9,177	9,936
Operating income	816	939	952
	%	%	%
Soups, jams and others	21.6	21.8	18.9
Health and baby foods	19.2	18.1	17.9
Prepared dishes	14.8	15.9	17.0
Sauces and condiments	19.4	20.9	24.0
Pasta	25.0	23.3	22.2

BSN gained major market positions in a number of EC countries. In Germany and France, BSN occupies the premier position in the market. In Italy, Belgium and Spain, BSN is number two in the market. Because complementarity existed between pasta, sauces and prepared dishes, this allowed BSN to make these three product sectors the basic supports for its expansion strategy in the European grocery products area.

The main product sectors that BSN operated in exhibited a number of differing characteristics that impacted on growth and rates of profitability. Each product sector may be examined in turn.

Pasta and prepared dishes

The total market for pasta fell slightly in 1989 in France. Much of this was put down to the mildness of the weather. However, aggressive marketing and promotion of own-labels and retailer's private labels did create a more aggressive marketing environment. BSN brands did well to hold their share under such unfavourable conditions. Pasta sales in other European markets also showed mixed trends. In Italy, market growth was less than 1 per cent for dried pasta, but considerably higher at 5 per cent for the premium fresh egg pasta segment. The Italians were particularly partial to pre-cooked rice and the segment grew by 7 per cent. BSN were particularly pleased with their exports of pasta and pasta products to Japan and the US which recorded very significant volume and value increases. The German market showed signs of increasing competition, and BSN brands in the pre-cooked microwave meals segment did particularly well, but in dried pasta, jam and dry bread products, sales levels were flat. The rapidly expanding market for these product classes in Spain meant that BSN brands continued to make good progress and reinforce their brand positions.

Sauces and condiments

The market for sauces and condiments includes three types of products: red sauces (tomato and prepared tomato-based sauces and ketchups), yellow sauces (mustard, mayonnaise, vinaigrette) and brown sauces (Worcestershire sauce etc.). BSN had a strong presence in all these segments.

In France, the very dynamic market for sauces, mustards and condiments was characterized by growing segmentation and an increased demand by consumers for better quality and greater convenience in using the products. BSN's sauces were well placed to benefit from these trends. BSN brands were also increasing their penetration in institutional markets as well as consumer ones. A number of their leading brands occupied premium positions in these segments. In other European countries, BSN brands were equally well placed although growth rates in these markets varied as did marketing conditions.

Baby foods, health foods and jams

In spite of the levelling off of the birth rate in France, some segments of the baby foods market displayed significant growth, i.e. soups, junior portions of prepared dishes, mashed foods and infant formulas. BSN brands in these segments continued to be strong. A number of pre-prepared baby products and infant formulas, sold by BSN through pharmacies, began to be sold through the supermarkets and general retail trade. This gave BSN's brands in this sector a wider customer coverage. Adult health foods in France as in other EC markets also displayed growth potential and BSN, through new product development and marketing, continued to maintain and increase market share. Consumption of jams in France rose by 3 per cent in 1989; much of this increase came from the low calorie segments.

Biscuits

Sales of biscuits by geographic area for BSN in 1987–89 are detailed in Table 12.8. In 1985, BSN was not represented in the biscuit market, but by 1990, through a series of key acquisitions and equity participation, it had become the largest European biscuit-maker and the second biggest in the world.

Table 12.8 Sales of biscuits by geographic area

	1987 FF m	1988 FF m	1989 FF m
Sales	7,230	8,275	11,119
Operating income	732	796	1,030
	%	%	%
France	58.0	56.4	53.2
Europe outside France	24.6	25.9	36.3
Outside Europe	17.4	17.7	10.5

The biscuit division in Europe had reached genuine European size, with some FF 4.7 billion sales coming from the Nabisco interests alone in a full year. Coverage in Europe included, in addition to France, all the main food markets, the UK, Germany, Italy and Spain.

The biscuit market in Europe registered only moderate growth in volume terms, due primarily to unusually warm weather in the spring and summer, which did not favour consumption of this product. Competition in this food sector was strong with many local companies holding significant brand share positions. The established policies of innovation in products, packaging and campaigns designed to reduce costs, were pursued by the company. This meant that a number of production units were closed and others upgraded. Higher productivity and production efficiency was the prevailing strategy among the many companies that comprised this division. Brand strength across Europe was maintained and improved as a result of the brand-buy strategy that BSN had followed for this division. Growth in market share in this food sector was as difficult as it was expensive and the many sub-sectors that BSN was represented in meant that the company had an overall balanced profile.

At the time of writing, the many new overseas ventures that BSN had entered into in 1990 had yet to report trends and operational details. However, the US operation had mixed success. Growth in demand for BSN's brands on the West Coast of the US displayed gains. On the Eastern side, however, sales were less favourable. In May 1990, BSN put its US biscuit division up for sale and the company was to use the money raised from the sale to fund its expansion plans in the Far East and Eastern Europe.

Through equity participation and joint venturing schemes, BSN extended its biscuit interests in Asia. BSN forged a link with Britannia Biscuits in India by taking a substantial equity stake in that company. BSN had plans to transfer technology and brands to the Indian company to enable Britannia to increase its dominance in the growing biscuit market in India and other parts of Asia. Consumer habits in Asia were changing, and many Western type products were becoming increasingly popular and being incorporated into the eating habits of consumers. Furthermore, a shift away from a savings to a consumer mentality was becoming a noticeable trend in many Asian markets.

Beer

Sales of beer by geographic area for BSN in 1987–89 are detailed in Table 12.9. In 1988–89, Kronenbourg and Kanterbräu, two of BSN's premium brands of beer, showed gains of around 3 per cent in volume terms enabling BSN to account for 47 per cent of French beer consumption and 53 per cent of beer production. 1989 was a good year for the brewers; exceptionally warm weather and a long summer helped boost beer sales. Packaging and other changes also meant that BSN brands sold through the retail trade held or increased market share. Trends in the French market, as elsewhere in Europe, towards low alcoholic and non-alcoholic beverages meant that significant segments were being created. BSN beer brands were to be found in these segments. The acquisition policy of the company ensured that by 1990, BSN was Europe's second largest brewer. Divisional strategy took the form of a number of policies. Firstly, a programme of restructuring and workforce reductions at a number of production sites was implemented, along with capital investment in new technology designed to bring production costs down. Secondly, the ten-year international strategy built around the promotion of the brand Kronenbourg across Europe was strengthened by an acquisition programme and by licensing and franchising agreements that brought the brand into new geographic markets, like the UK, Belgium, Spain and Greece. BSN's exports of its key beer brands in both the premium and non-premium sectors continued to grow and accounted for some 80 per cent of all French beer exports in 1989.

Table 12.9 Sales of beer by geographic area

	1987 FF m	1988 FF m	1989 FF m
Sales	5,577	6,260	6,188
Operating income	526	628	806
	%	%	%
France	83.3	78.3	82.5
Outside France	16.7	21.7	17.5

Champagne and mineral water

Sales of champagne and mineral water by product class for BSN in 1987–89 are detailed in Table 12.10. In France, the market for carbonated and non-carbonated mineral water, which had been dynamic for a number of years, showed a dramatic

Table 12.10 Sales of champagne and mineral water by product class

	1987 FF m	1988 FF m	1989 FF m
Sales	2,975	3,476	4,320
Operating income	470	528	642
	%	%	%
Mineral water	65.8	67.0	72.3
Champagne	27.8	27.6	23.3
Soft drinks	6.4	5.4	4.4

acceleration in demand in 1989–90 as a result of the weather conditions. In this context BSN's brands, Badoit and Evian, strengthened their market position. Perrier had withdrawn its mineral waters from the market for about a ten-week period over a purity issue. As a consequence BSN had difficultly in meeting demand. Other variants of the Badoit brand in the carbonated segment, flavoured with menthol and lemon, continued to be successful. BSN's mineral water brands in Italy performed particularly well, holding and increasing market share in a number of sectors. The market for mineral water in Spain continued to show some growth, with BSN brands holding market share in both the carbonated and the non-carbonated sectors. Mineral water exports to countries like the UK continued to be profitable, especially as mineral water was becoming increasingly popular in the British market.

Champagne was also a growth area for BSN and recorded a sales increase of some 3 per cent in the year to 1989. However, the luxury drinks business was undergoing dramatic change, and BSN came to the conclusion that it was at a strategic disadvantage in the champagne business. The way to protect brand image was to keep a number of brands with the same identity in the same network, ideally under the same control. BSN recognized that its champagne businesses were at a strategic disadvantage against the large drinks companies which had a wider range of brands in their portfolios. BSN decided to dispose of its champagne businesses. The two premium brands of Pomery and Lanson were sold to the French drinks and luxury products group LVMH (Louis Vitton Moet Hennessey). BSN sold the champagne brands and associated stocks, production processes and vineyards for FF 3.1bn.

Containers

Sales of containers by product class for BSN in 1987–89 are detailed in Table 12.11. This division represented the historical roots of the modern company with the containers division key operating company being Verreries Souchon Neuvessel. The late 1980s saw BSN increase its investment in this division in order to keep pace with market growth, particularly in the area of beer and soft drinks bottles and plastic containers. This investment was designed to increase productivity and reduce costs. In the Spanish market, BSN had two operating subsidiaries that began to operate much more closely together in order to exploit potential synergies and to continue to consolidate their market presence. New investment in this geographic area was seen to be crucially important.

The BSN bottling plant in France commissioned two new glass-making furnaces and retired five older machines. Output in 1989 of the beer bottling lines amounted to some 4 billion units. Other areas of the containers business included wine bottles of various types, plastic bottles for the soft drinks and mineral water markets, jars

Table 12.11 Sales of containers by product class

	1987 FF m	1988 FF m	1989 FF m
Sales	4,626	4,997	5,557
Operating income	410	565	620
	%	%	%
Bottles	77.7	75.7	75.1
Flasks	9.0	9.4	8.8
Plastic containers	8.6	9.3	9.5
Miscellaneous	4.6	5.6	6.6

and bottles for jams and foods, glasses and associated tableware.

BSN had recognized the increased pressures placed on manufacturers by the environmental lobby to produce environmentally friendly packaging. It responded by changing the brief of its new products section (the Packaging and Environmental Department), and charged it with developing new packaging and containers that took into account the environmental pressures on the packaging industry. Greater cooperation between packaging manufacturing plants and customers resulted, and there was a move towards a more active policy in the collection and recycling of packaging materials.

Human resources

In 1989, BSN employed some 50,000 people worldwide; 54.3 per cent in France, 34.7 per cent in the rest of Europe and 11 per cent overseas. BSN recognized that the late 1980s and early 1990s would be the 'age of consolidation', when growth had to be planned and new businesses that had been acquired had to be integrated and developed within the BSN framework.

Changes that had been recognized by the company had been of three principal types: changes in occupational specialities, the combination of renewed growth and the rigour of competition, and the fragmentation of markets. This meant that the organization had to be flexible in its operations.

BSN believed that strategic decisions would increasingly take on a European dimension and that the national framework had become too narrow. As brands become more international and production of those brands also took on international aspects, there is a need for departments and operating companies to increase cooperation between each other. The single market in 1992 would increase pressure on companies like BSN to think of Europe as one home market and not as a series of discrete national ones. The human resource policy had recognized this and had attempted to respond.

BSN's human resource directorate had begun to develop an extensive programme of retraining, job review and job mobility within the group in order to reduce the dislocation felt by those who found that their jobs had to go. Links with the French Ministry of Education promoted in-house training schemes to improve worker qualifications, and links with higher education providers to establish tailored programmes for managers and scientists were developed. The model preferred was that of the German apprentice training scheme. Other programmes developed by BSN aimed to increase the sensitization of employees to EC 1992 and to promote good industrial relations and training across the group. Regular seminars were held for the industrial relations and training directors of subsidiary firms to exchange and develop good industrial practice and training across the group and its many geographic borders.

Appendices 12.1 and 12.2 give details of BSN's accounts for the years 1987–89 and tables 12.12 and 12.13 show BSN's key financial ratios and those for the French food manufacturing sector for the years 1985–89.

APPENDIX 12.1
CONSOLIDATED STATEMENTS OF INCOME
(FOR THE YEARS ENDED 31 DECEMBER)

	1989 FF m	1988 FF m	1987 FF m
Net sales	48,669	42,177	37,156
Cost of goods sold	(26,448)	(23,027)	(21,192)
Selling expenses	(11,524)	(9,664)	(7,807)
General and administrative expenses	(2,537)	(2,340)	(2,228)
Research and development expenses	(297)	(269)	(244)
Other incomes and expenses	(588)	(328)	(601)
Depreciation	(2,253)	(2,022)	(1,788)
Operating income	5,022	4,527	3,296
Interest income	660	209	186
Interest expense	(1,731)	(818)	(681)
Income before provision for income taxes and minority interests	3,951	3,918	2,801
Provisions for income taxes	(1,397)	(1,627)	(1,274)
Income before minority interests	2,554	2,291	1,527
Minority interests	(119)	(75)	(70)
Income from affiliated companies	263	(27)	93
Net income for the year	2,698	2,189	1,550

APPENDIX 12.2
CONSOLIDATED BALANCE SHEETS (AS AT 31 DECEMBER)

Assets	1989 FF m	1988 FF m	1987 FF m
Current assets			
Cash and time deposits	1,154	1,265	1,209
Marketable securities	359	464	347
Accounts receivable	8,715	7,536	6,273
Short-term loans receivable	400	329	143
Inventories	6,096	5,289	4,891
Other accounts receivable and prepaid expenses	2,760	1,579	2,227
	19,484	16,462	15,090
Capital assets			
Property, plant and equipment	28,660	23,782	21,168
Less depreciation	13,360	11,355	9,702
	15,300	12,427	11,466
Intangible assets			
Goodwill	8,214	4,698	3,144
Brand names	4,820	—	—
Other intangible assets	1,638	1,714	1,627
Less amortization	862	795	718
	13,810	5,617	4,053
Other assets			
Long-term loans	537	439	508
Long-term investments	1,261	1,686	1,395
Equity in affiliated companies	5,398	1,893	1,558
Other	519	315	277
	7,715	4,333	3,738
Total assets	56,309	38,839	34,349

Liabilities and shareholders' equity	1989 FF m	1988 FF m	1987 FF m
Current liabilities			
Short-term debt and overdrafts	4,490	1,856	1,855
Trade accounts payable	7,045	5,933	4,903
Other accounts payable and accrued expenses	5,140	4,433	4,497
	16,675	12,222	11,253
Deferred taxes	1,570	1,526	1,439
Provisions for retirement indemnities and pensions	1,110	1,113	1,224
Provisions for other risks and charges	1,992	1,601	1,345
Long-term debt	14,436	5,288	4,148
Consigned containers	744	674	594
Minority interests	874	715	494
	20,726	10,917	9,244
Shareholders' equity			
Capital stock	547	521	520
Capital reserves	9,681	8,173	8,160
Retained earnings	9,165	7,072	5,230
	19,393	15,766	13,910
Treasury stock	485	66	60
Total shareholders' equity	18,908	15,700	13,850
Total liabilities and shareholders' equity	56,309	38,839	34,349

Table 12.12 Groupe BSN – key ratios

Key item description	1985	1986	1987	1988	1989
Return on shareholders' equity (%)	10.22	15.89	15.64	10.23	39.54
Return on capital employed (%)	16.87	20.10	18.79	15.38	19.15
Operating profit margin (%)	6.45	8.49	9.49	7.70	9.97
Pre-tax profit margin (%)	5.23	7.07	8.13	6.30	7.77
Net profit margin (%)	2.77	3.81	4.55	2.88	5.54
Income gearing (%)	28.98	22.87	18.62	23.09	31.39
Borrowing ratio	0.54	0.89	0.56	0.64	2.90
Stock ratio (days)	48.53	49.72	48.05	45.77	45.72
Debtors ratio (days)	67.95	84.92	89.06	76.88	86.06
Creditors ratio (days)	104.56	114.91	121.04	102.56	107.01
Working capital ratio	1.29	1.25	1.22	1.29	1.13

Source: Datastream Program 190D. Reproduced with permission of Datastream International.

Table 12.13 French food manufacturing sector – key ratios

Key item description	1985	1986	1987	1988	1989
Return on shareholders' equity (%)	10.89	12.48	15.34	14.45	21.55
Return on capital employed (%)	15.38	15.57	15.83	15.47	16.60
Operating profit margin (%)	5.78	6.81	7.57	6.84	7.73
Pre-tax profit margin (%)	3.66	4.55	5.68	4.93	5.60
Net profit margin (%)	2.11	2.47	3.46	2.77	3.69
Income gearing (%)	44.97	38.80	32.25	35.33	36.27
Borrowing ratio	1.25	1.42	1.21	1.50	2.02
Stock ratio (days)	71.24	71.75	66.97	62.95	57.04
Debtors ratio (days)	72.63	80.83	84.23	74.22	76.42
Creditors ratio (days)	104.25	114.89	112.44	104.37	97.92
Working capital ratio	1.59	1.29	1.32	1.14	1.14

Source: Datastream Program 190D. Reproduced with permission of Datastream International.

Glaxo Holdings Plc

J. Fernie

The year 1993 was a difficult one for Glaxo. After more than a decade of exceptional success Glaxo, like its pharmaceutical counterparts, was out of favour with the stock market. In 1991 Glaxo was the largest company in Britain in terms of market capitalization, but more than £10 billion has been wiped off its market value since mid 1991. This reversal in fortunes can be attributed to a combination of the following factors:

- the pressure on health care budgets leading governments to review drug prices;
- the escalation of R&D costs from £77 million in 1984 to £739 million in 1993;
- industry estimates that it now costs around £200 million to develop a new drug;
- patent challenges to two of its drugs, Zofran and its best seller, Zantac;
- the boardroom tussle between the chairman, Sir Paul Girolami, and his supposed heir apparent, Dr Ernest Mario, the Chief Executive, which resulted in Mario abruptly leaving the board in March;
- speculation that the company would change its strategic direction.

BACKGROUND

Until the 1960s Glaxo was mainly known for its infant milk business which had been established in the UK at the turn of the century. Its origins go back to 1873 when the founding business, Joseph Nathan and Co., was established in New Zealand.

Nutritional advances and the development of Ostelin (vitamin D) led Glaxo into pharmaceuticals; in the 1930s it founded Glaxo Laboratories (1935) and began pharmaceutical manufacturing overseas. By the 1940s and 1950s the company had become a major supplier of antibiotics, vaccines and corticosteroids. In the wake of Glaxo becoming a public company in 1947, it began to diversify in the ensuing 20 years, primarily in the fields of surgical instruments and drug wholesaling. It also consolidated its position in the baby food market with its purchase of Farley's Infant Food.

Until the early 1960s, Glaxo's main strengths were in the development and marketing of products rather than in the discovery of new drugs. This began to change with the introduction of basic research and the deliberate and planned search for new entities. The principal Glaxo discoveries from 1964 are shown in Table 13.1.

One of the biggest challenges that faced the pharmaceutical industry in the 1970s and early 1980s was a reduction in the rate of new product introductions and an increase in the time taken to develop a new drug (see Fig. 13.1). The reasons for this were attributed to regulatory requirements and a slowdown in drug innovation. The response by the industry to these pressures is illustrated in Fig. 13.2. Companies moved into international markets, developed copies of original products or diversified away from pharmaceuticals into medical and related technologies.

Table 13.1 Principal discoveries and launch dates

Brand name	Generic name	Type	First launch
Betnovate	Betamethasone Valerate	Dermatitis	1964
Ceporin	Cephaloridine	Injectable antibiotic	1964
Ventolin	Salbutamol	Anti-asthmatic	1969
Becotide	Beclomethasone	Anti-asthmatic	1972
Dermovate	Clobetasol propionate	Dermatitis	1973
Beconase	Beclomethasone	Anti-rhinitic	1975
Trandate	Lebetalol	Anti-hypertensive	1977
Zinacef	Cefuroxime	Injectable antibiotic	1978
Zantac	Ranitidine	Anti-ulcerant	1981
Fortum	Ceftazidime	Injectable antibiotic	1983
Volmax	Salbutamol	Anti-asthmatic	1987
Zinnat	Cefuroxime axetil	Oral antibiotic	1987
Flixonase	Fluticasone propionate	Anti-rhinitic	1990
Serevent	Salmeterol	Anti-asthmatic	1990
Zofran	Ondansetron	Anti-emetic	1990
Cutivate	Fluticasone propionate	Dermatitis	1990
Lacipil	Lacidipine	Anti-hypertensive	1991
Imigran	Sumatriptan	Anti-migraine	1991
Flixotide	Fluticasone propionate	Anti-asthmatic	1993

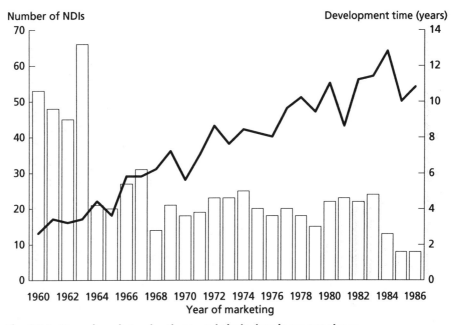

Fig. 13.1 New drug introductions and their development times.

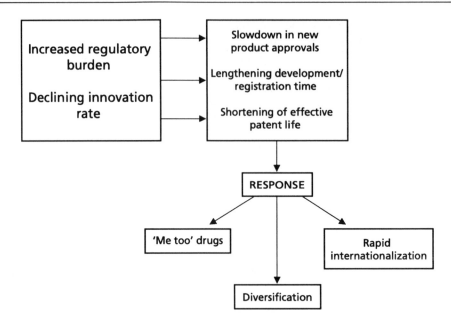

Fig. 13.2 Industry pressures and responses 1970s–80s.

Although Glaxo had discovered several new drugs by the mid to late 1970s, profits remained stagnant from 1976 to 1980 as the company incurred increasing R&D costs (see Table 13.2). Then in 1979 its research department discovered Zantac which was to lever Glaxo into a major multinational company in the 1980s.

THE 1980s: THE DECADE OF GROWTH

The rapid growth strategy pursued by Glaxo coincided with the launch of Zantac and the appointment of Paul Giralomi as chief executive officer in 1981. Initially growth was focused on selling Zantac into as many markets as possible but by the time Girolami became chairman in 1986 this growth strategy was firmly based on the following policies:

- the concentration of resources on prescription medicines;
- the worldwide extension of Glaxo's activities and markets;
- the expansion and improvement of research, development and technological resources;
- to grow from internal resources, by organic growth rather than acquisition;
- the creation of a flexible international organization capable of meeting the needs of Glaxo's worldwide business.

Unlike many of their competitors Glaxo reversed the trend towards diversification. In the 1980s Girolami concentrated upon ethical pharmaceuticals thereby selling a range of diverse activities from UK wholesaling to the retail chemist (Vestric), surgical products (Eschmann), furniture manufacturing (W.H. Deane) and baby foods (Farley). Thus, in 1988 Girolami could state in the annual report and accounts that the company was now:

... by deliberate policy, wholly devoted to the discovery, development, manufacture and sale of prescription medicines ... with the intention of continuing Glaxo's success as a world leader in the pharmaceutical industry   (p. 5)

At the same time as Glaxo was focusing its resources on ethical pharmaceuticals, it was internationalizing the business. The main thrust of this strategy in the late 1970s/early 1980s was to launch Zantac into as many lucrative markets as possible. The US, the largest market, was the first to be targeted. Glaxo bought a small company in the US in the late 1970s to provide the basis of a marketing team to build up a medical and registration department to carry out clinical tests and obtain registration of its drugs from the US Federal Registration Agency, the FDA. To achieve greater market penetration, Zantac was co-promoted with Hoffman-la-Roche. This approach was also adopted in other countries; for example, in Germany a joint venture was established with E. Merck, and in Japan with Sankyo.

It was important to Girolami that international markets should be tackled in different ways and genuine delegation was left to local management on how to market drugs for different cultures and variations of diseases from country to country. In the 1980s, therefore, Glaxo expanded its overseas subsidiary operations and developed joint ventures in addition to building up one of the largest marketing salesforces in the pharmaceutical industry. The effectiveness of this policy at penetrating world markets is shown in the geographical distribution of group sales detailed in Table 13.2.

Coupled with this international growth has been the increased commitment by Glaxo to R&D expenditure and a globalization of its R&D facilities (see Table 13.2 for R&D expenditure). Glaxo realizes that profits from Zantac need to be reinvested to discover new drugs to be commercialized in world markets. As a truly global company this has meant the expansion and new construction of R&D facilities in its major markets: the triad of Europe, North America and the Far East.

With the cost of R&D being so high and the maintenance of a worldwide distribution network requiring vast resources, City analysts have predicted that integration and rationalization of the world's pharmaceutical industry would take place. However, Girolami did not waver from his commitment to grow through organic means rather than acquisition. Indeed, he wrote in the 1989 Annual Report:

> We are already witnessing the start of the integration process in other companies, but it is not one in which I believe it is necessary for Glaxo to take part. Our growth in the world market has been achieved through discovering and selling our own products, not by buying market share through acquisition.   (p. 7)

As Glaxo developed its international business, it became a more flexible organization with a more relaxed open style of management than in the past. With such a vast array of geographically dispersed activities, Glaxo's approach was to combine strong central leadership with the delegation of full operating responsibility to subsidiary and associated companies. Thus general managers of Glaxo's operating companies are encouraged to act as entrepreneurs in the markets for which they have responsibility.

The role of the headquarters function is to provide leadership and command in order that operating companies can thrive on the freedom granted to them. Glaxo's main board of directors has the task of establishing a common strategy and monitoring policies to ensure that the strategy is realized. The coordination role

Table 13.2 Glaxo Holdings Plc 1974–93

	1993 £m	1992 £m	1991 £m	1990 £m	1989 £m	1988 £m	1987 £m	1986 £m	1985 £m	1984 £m	1983 £m	1982 £m	1981 £m	1980 £m	1979 £m	1978 £m	1977 £m	1976 £m	1975 £m	1974 £m
Group turnover[1]																				
Pharmaceuticals and foods	4,930	4,096	3,397	3,179	2,570	2,059	1,741	1,429	1,161	892	757	639	515	415	379	388	352	299	228	188
Surgical and other products	—	—	—	—	—	—	—	—	25	23	22	24	22	19	18	22	23	20	18	15
Wholesaling	—	—	—	—	—	—	—	—	226	285	248	203	173	184	142	133	113	92	72	56
	4,930	4,096	3,397	3,179	2,570	2,059	1,741	1,429	1,412	1,200	1,027	866	710	618	539	543	488	411	318	259
Geographical analysis of group turnover (excluding wholesaling)[1]																				
Europe	1,968	1,724	1,481	1,338	1,081	937	830	735	611	514	447	361	298	252	230	219	203	171	140	113
North America	2,132	1,715	1,359	1,316	1,163	831	662	469	333	193	66	45	28	22	23	24	24	18	9	9
Rest of world	830	657	557	525	326	291	249	225	242	208	266	257	211	160	144	167	148	130	97	81
	4,930	4,096	3,397	3,179	2,570	2,059	1,741	1,429	1,186	915	779	663	537	434	397	410	375	319	246	203
Group profits and dividends[1]																				
Trading profit	1,525	1,287	1,088	1,040	876	777	709	517	363	249	182	133	91	69	74	83	86	76	46	46
Net investment income	150	140	179	142	130	68	51	95	27	7	4	1	(4)	(3)	(2)	3	1	(2)	(5)	(3)
Profit before taxation	1,675	1,427	1,267	1,182	1,006	845	760	612	390	256	186	134	87	66	72	86	87	74	41	43
Profit for appropriation	1,207	1,033	881	807	688	581	510	400	264	169	109	80	61	42	47	42	42	35	20	25
Dividends	667	512	420	329	260	185	141	104	74	48	33	24	19	16	13	10	9	8	6	5
Retained profit	540	521	461	478	428	396	369	296	190	121	76	56	42	26	34	32	33	27	14	20
Research and development expenditure[1]	739	595	475	420	323	230	149	113	93	77	60	50	40	32	25	20	17	14	12	8
Share statistics[1]																				
Earnings per ordinary share	39.9p	34.3p	29.4p	27.0p	23.1p	19.6p	17.2p	13.5p	8.9p	5.7p	3.7p	2.9p	2.2p	1.5p	1.7p	1.5p	1.5p	1.3p	0.8p	0.9p
Dividends per ordinary share	22.0p	17.0p	14.0p	11.0p	8.7p	6.2p	4.7p	3.5p	2.5p	1.6p	1.1p	0.8p	0.7p	0.6p	0.5p	0.3p	0.3p	0.3p	0.2p	0.2p
Net assets[2]																				
Fixed assets	3,020	2,373	2,109	1,628	1,187	882	701	582	456	388	316	274	235	197	172	152	129	109	95	83
Net liquid funds	1,815	1,332	1,212	1,127	1,124	912	729	479	293	86	47	10	16	14	19	25	61	55	16	20
Other assets and liabilities	(178)	(66)	(39)	50	2	9	34	39	87	209	183	150	136	131	128	37	9	—	(8)	(13)
	4,657	3,639	3,282	2,805	2,313	1,803	1,464	1,100	836	683	546	434	387	342	319	214	199	164	103	90

Table 13.2 Cont.

	1993 £m	1992 £m	1991 £m	1990 £m	1989 £m	1988 £m	1987 £m	1986 £m	1985 £m	1984 £m	1983 £m	1982 £m	1981 £m	1980 £m	1979 £m	1978 £m	1977 £m	1976 £m	1975 £m	1974 £m
Capital employed[2]																				
Share capital and reserves	4,546	3,572	3,208	2,732	2,291	1,784	1,450	1,090	827	675	542	428	382	338	315	208	193	159	99	87
Minority interests	111	67	74	73	22	19	14	10	9	8	4	6	5	4	4	6	6	5	4	3
	4,657	3,639	3,282	2,805	2,313	1,803	1,464	1,100	836	683	546	434	387	342	319	214	199	164	103	90
Profit before taxation[2]	1,675	1,427	1,267	1,182	1,006	845	760	612	390	256	186	134	87	66	72	86	87	74	41	43
Return on capital employed[2]	36.0%	39.2%	38.6%	42.1%	43.5%	46.9%	51.9%	55.6%	46.7%	37.5%	34.1%	30.9%	22.5%	19.3%	22.6%	40.2%	43.7%	45.1%	39.8%	47.8%
Capital expenditure[2]																				
United Kingdom	311	281	270	340	146	155	126	153	79	46	43	25	29	31	29	27	21	13	10	9
Overseas	339	285	351	297	227	120	67	48	47	52	27	40	26	16	12	11	8	6	8	5
	650	566	621	637	373	275	193	201	126	98	70	65	55	47	41	38	29	19	18	14
Average number of group employees[2]																				
United Kingdom	12,149	11,968	12,422	12,291	11,444	11,035	10,867	11,815	13,463	13,685	13,605	13,188	13,725	14,816	15,602	15,881	15,944	16,132	17,084	16,344
Overseas	27,875	25,115	23,218	20,934	17,266	15,388	14,087	12,913	12,171	11,368	14,163	14,918	14,493	14,371	14,179	15,020	14,596	14,551	14,436	13,735
	40,024	37,083	35,640	33,225	28,710	26,423	24,954	24,728	25,634	25,053	27,768	28,106	28,218	29,187	29,781	30,901	30,540	30,683	31,520	30,079

1. These figures comprise those originally published except that: (i) the figures for 1990 have been restated to consolidate Nippon Glaxo Ltd, Glaxo-Sankyo Co., Ltd and Cascan GmbH & Co. KG as subsidiary undertakings, (ii) the figures for 1990, 1985, 1983 and 1979 have each been adjusted for the changes in accounting policy which occurred in the following year, (iii) dividends and earnings per share have been adjusted for any scrip issues, and for the subdivision of share capital in 1991, (iv) trading profit, profit before taxation and earnings per share for 1991, 1988, 1987 and 1985 have been adjusted to reflect the reclassification of extraordinary items as exceptional in accordance with FRS3.

2. These figures comprise those originally published except that: (i) the figures for 1990 have been restated to consolidate Nippon Glaxo Ltd, Glaxo-Sankyo Co., Ltd and Cascan GmbH & Co. KG as subsidiary undertakings, (ii) the figures for 1990, 1985, 1983 and 1979 have each been adjusted for the changes in accounting policy which occurred in the following year, (iii) profit before taxation and return on capital employed for 1991, 1988, 1987 and 1985 have been adjusted to reflect the reclassification of extraordinary items as exceptional in accordance with FRS3.

of integrating day-to-day activities of the global business to efficiently manage the discovery, development and marketing of Glaxo's drugs was performed by the board but in 1989 this responsibility was given to Glaxo Group Limited, under the direction of the chief executive of the holding company, Dr Ernest Mario, who had been mooted as the heir apparent to Sir Paul Girolami.

THE 1990s: A DECADE OF UNCERTAINTY

All pharmaceutical companies are facing a much tougher environment in the 1990s than in the previous decade. The major environmental pressures on the industry are outlined in Fig. 13.3. Glaxo is well placed to respond positively to these changes. It has invested heavily in biologically orientated research technologies and ensured speedy development of its drug discoveries through a commitment of resources to the preparation of international registration documents and the marketing of approved drugs. Its success with the 'blockbuster' Zantac illustrates this in that Zantac was sold in all of the world's major markets within three years of its launch in 1981. Its new products are developed in one unified programme, not a piecemeal, country-by-country approach. This compresses the time taken up by the costly development phase allowing a longer period to maximize revenues before patent expiry. Glaxo has the ability to submit a registration dossier for a new drug in every major market within a year, while some of its smaller competitors can take several years to reach this stage. Also, compared with the average time taken by pharmaceutical companies to commercialize a drug from test-tube to market place (8 to 12 years), Glaxo has shortened this period to five years in the case of its drug, Zofran, which is used to treat nausea and vomiting in cancer therapy.

Clearly pressures on health care budgets have forced governments to instruct state health services to prescribe generic drugs where branded products do not offer novelty or clear benefits. The generic threat poses fewer problems to Glaxo because it has segmented the drugs market into a number of distinct areas and offered 'unique'

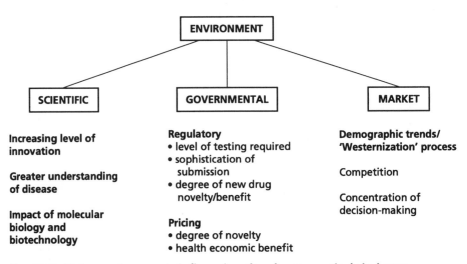

Fig. 13.3 Major environments influencing the pharmaceuticals industry.

benefits to the user. This has ensured a premium pricing strategy. Furthermore, in such a competitive marketing environment the creation of a large salesforce is a prerequisite to the marketing of branded prescription medicines. The average size of a top 40 pharmaceutical company's detailing force is 2,500 representatives worldwide. In the early 1990s Glaxo's worldwide detailing force was around 6,000 representatives.

Although Glaxo is well positioned to compete in this tougher environment, it has made a series of tactical errors which has jeopardized its position as a leading player in the pharmaceuticals market. As Ernest Mario was alleged to be mainly responsible for these mistakes, it is not surprising that he was forced to resign by Girolami in March 1993. Girolami had built up the business through smooth relations with regulators in order to maximize profits from compounds before their patents ran out. Mario succeeded in alienating regulators with extravagant claims of future sales for newly launched drugs and an over-aggressive approach with its established products. As one of the regulators is the FDA, which openly accused Glaxo of violating US drug laws by promoting Zantac illegally in January 1993, Glaxo was alienating the regulator of the largest pharmaceutical market in the world (see Table 13.3). Coupled with the Clinton administration's commitment to fairer prices for drugs, this is putting a squeeze on profit margins, especially on new drugs such as Imigran which undoubtedly would have been launched in the US at a higher price if the political environment was more favourable. In view of the importance of the US market to Glaxo (sales of £1,985 million in 1993, profits of £575 million[1] out of sales of £2,132 in North America in 1993), such tactics are questionable for a company which is committed to developing new prescription drugs as its main strategic objective.

Another source of friction between Girolami and Mario concerned the nature of Glaxo's involvement in the over-the-counter (OTC) medicine market. Girolami had always been consistent in his view that Glaxo would focus on prescription medicines and growth would be achieved through organic growth or joint ventures. Nevertheless, the changing health care market with governments keen to see the consumer pay more of their own health care has led analysts to predict that the OTC market

Table 13.3 Leading pharmaceutical markets in 1993

Country	Market size (£ million)	% of world market	% growth
USA	32,600	29	6
Japan	19,900	18	3
Germany	9,500	9	5
France	8,200	7	8
Italy	6,800	6	5
UK	3,600	3	13
Spain	3,000	3	11
Canada	2,400	2	9
Brazil	1,900	2	19
Korea	1,800	2	15
Others	20,900	19	15
Total	110,600	100	8

1. US figure is not disaggregated.

will be the fastest growing drug market into the early years of the next century. The major pharmaceutical companies have been consolidating their position in the OTC sector through joint ventures (Merck/Johnson & Johnson, SmithKline Beecham/Marion Merrell Dow) or acquisitions (Roche/Nichol Labs and Fisons' OTC business). While Girolami acknowledged that Glaxo products might have OTC potential, it appears that Mario was keen to take over Warner-Lambert, the world's largest OTC company. This would be counter to the approach sought by Girolami and was an added factor in Mario's premature exit from Glaxo. In the end Wellcome, which already had a £400 million OTC business, agreed to merge their non-prescription business with Warner-Lambert to form Warner-Wellcome Consumer Health Products and, at the same time (July 1993), the new company agreed to a joint venture with Glaxo to develop and market any non-prescription drugs from the Glaxo portfolio, in particular an OTC version of Zantac.

GLAXO'S PRODUCT PORTFOLIO

Glaxo's current portfolio of products are sold in seven therapeutic areas: anti-emesis, anti-ulcerants, respiratory, systemic antibiotics, anti-migraine, cardiovascular and dermatologicals (see Table 13.4). Table 13.4 shows the importance of anti-ulcerants, primarily Zantac, in Glaxo's product portfolio. Nevertheless Glaxo's strategy has been to extend the product lifecycle of Zantac and other best-selling drugs, such as Ventolin, to provide revenue for the cash cows of tomorrow such as Zofran and Serevent. Table 13.5 lists the sales of Glaxo's major products.

In order to maximize cash flows from Zantac, Glaxo has marketed the drug to increase frequency of purchase, encourage new product uses, and obtain price increases. More specifically, these include:

- increasing the use of Zantac in hospitals to prevent stress ulcers and to reduce acidity pre-operatively;
- switching from acute to episodic therapy to maintenance therapy. Around 30 per cent of Zantac prescriptions are written for maintenance therapy. The volume of drugs consumed on maintenance therapy is double that seen in acute therapy;

Table 13.4 Therapeutic analysis of group pharmaceuticals and foods turnover

	1993 £m	1992 £m	1991 £m	1990 £m	1989 £m	1988 £m	1987 £m	1986 £m	1985 £m	1984 £m
Anti-ulcerants	2,172	1,807	1,606	1,551	1,291	989	829	606	432	248
Respiratory	1,087	964	775	723	585	457	362	287	255	217
Systemic antibiotics	827	681	608	560	896	299	226	181	112	95
Anti-emesis	365	259	78	2	—	—	—	—	—	—
Dermatologicals	168	145	128	126	101	96	86	77	74	70
Anti-migraine	116	43	2	—	—	—	—	—	—	—
Cardiovascular	67	63	43	50	46	48	46	36	33	19
Other pharmaceuticals	115	124	147	155	138	138	149	174	154	130
Foods and animal health	13	10	10	12	13	32	43	68	101	113
	4,930	4,096	3,397	3,179	2,570	2,059	1,741	1,429	1,161	892

Table 13.5 Sales and market share of Glaxo's major products, 1993

Product	Type	Sales[1] £ million		Market share[1] %	Market share 1990
Zantac	Anti-ulcerant	2,172	(1,606)	37.9	(40.0)
Ventolin	Anti-asthmatic	484	(384)	13.5	(15.5)
Zofran	Anti-emetic	365	(78)	38.7	(1.0)
Zinnat	Oral antibiotic	348	(206)	4.5	(3.3)
Becotide	Anti-asthmatic	345	(237)	9.2	(9.2)
Fortum	Injectable antibiotic	293	(248)	5.5	(5.0)
Beconase	Anti-rhinitic	143	(100)	19.8	(18.9)
Imigran	Anti-migraine	116	—	N/A	—
Serevent	Anti-asthmatic	73	—	N/A	—

1. 1990 figures in brackets.

- increasing use of Zantac in non-ulcer conditions such as reflux oesophagitis;
- using Zantac for patients receiving NSAIDS, where the corrosive effects of the NSAID are mitigated by concurrent administration of Zantac;
- increasing prices where appropriate;
- developing an OTC version.

Whilst Zantac has hogged the limelight with regard to Glaxo's product performance, the company dominates the anti-asthma market and its sales of antibiotics have exceeded growth rates in the world market (see Tables 13.1 and 13.4 for brand names and sales of therapeutic classes).

The growth in the anti-asthmatic market was fuelled by Ventolin, the leading bronchodilator, which was launched in 1969 and followed in 1972 by Becotide, which treats the inflammatory condition rather than the symptoms as with bronchodilators. Ventolin's patent expired in 1987 but it is still the market leader and is one of the best selling prescribed pharmaceutical products in the world. Becotide has emulated Ventolin's success and during 1987 it became the world's second largest selling inhaled anti-asthma product, a position that it has consolidated in the late 1980s/early 1990s. In this market, Glaxo has developed the diskhaler which has aided the way in which its anti-asthma drugs can be inhaled. Moreover, the company has added 13 line extensions to its Ventolin range, including Becloforte, a higher strength form of Becotide, and Volmax, a new controlled release delivery system for Salbutamol.

The other main market in which Glaxo is a major player is its original drug market, that of antibiotics. Its four main products in this area, Ceporex (launched in 1964), Zinacef (1978), Fortum (1983) and Zinnat (1987), are used to treat a variety of bacterial infections. Fortum has established itself as the third largest selling product in the injectable cephalosporin sector worldwide and Zinnat, the oral antibiotic cefuroxime axetril, has quickly become number six in world sales for this type of oral antibiotic product. The market for oral cephalosporins is approximately half of that of the injectable market (Fortum) but is growing at a faster rate. Glaxo hopes to be able to market Zinnat successfully to challenge the top three antibiotics in its class.

Since 1990, the portfolio of products launched has achieved sales of £592 million in 1993, accounting for 12 per cent of group sales. With the exception of respiratory medicines (notably Serevent), most sales have been generated from new therapeutic classes, anti-emesis (Zofran) and anti-migraine (Imigran).

In 1993 Glaxo had ten compounds in full development with 16 at the exploratory stage. Several of these new drugs are being developed in conjunction with biotechnology companies to share R&D expertise and are in new therapeutic classes for Glaxo, for example AIDS, hepatitis and diabetes. Nevertheless, two compounds which moved from the exploratory to full development phase were in the new categories, anti-emesis and anti-migraine. In addition, programmes are also in progress to extend the value of existing compounds to new areas or to produce formulations for different uses.

While Glaxo has successfully repelled a challenge to the Zantac patent in 1993, the company has only until 2002, the patent expiry date, to develop another 'blockbuster' or a series of highly profitable drugs from its current research portfolio.

CASE 14

Kwik-Fit Holdings[1]

J.G. Gallager and R.S. Scott

Few men can claim to have changed the face of their industry and even fewer are given the credit for it. One man who can justifiably make this claim and take the plaudits is Tom Farmer the 47-year-old chairman and chief executive of Kwik-Fit Holdings plc.

Kwik-Fit's turnover for 1988 exceeded £125 million. With a market share of 12 per cent in the replacement tyre market, 23 per cent in the exhaust systems market and 20 per cent of the free market for shock absorbers Kwik-Fit is Europe's largest independent tyre and exhaust retailer.

The UK car aftercare market is the last fragmented market of its size still dominated by very small-scale operators – car dealers and back-street workshops, whose reputation is one of high prices, low levels of service and often sharp practices. It is from this environment that Farmer has hoisted his 'Kwik-Fit' business to become the market leader providing a product and service that few others come anywhere near matching.

ORIGINS AND GROWTH

In 1954 at the age of fourteen Tom Farmer left school and went to work as a stores boy in the tyre business. Later, after working for two years in one of Good Year's subsidiaries as a sales representative, Farmer opened his own business in 1964. This consisted of a corner shop in Buccleuch Street, Edinburgh at a rent of £5 per week and with a stock of 100 tyres on a sale or return basis.

The long-awaited abolition of Resale Price Maintenance in 1964 provided the fillip to growth which Farmer sought. This combined with an article in a Sunday paper highlighting his problems with his suppliers, proved an excellent vehicle for advertising his discount tyres. Growth quickly followed.

Farmer's success did not go unnoticed. Albany Tyre, a London-based company, founded in the early 1960s by Alex Stenson and Andrew Knight in 1968, paid £400,000 for Farmer's business in addition to making him a director of Albany with responsibility for all business north of Birmingham.

The tale is often told at Kwik-Fit's headquarters in Corstorphine that when showing Alex Stenson around a depot Stenson asked Farmer how often he 'turned over' his tyres. Farmer replied that he never turned them over he just left them as they were! When then asked how often he sold his tyres he responded that 'he didn't know how often they sold them in England but in Scotland we only sell them once!' From this early meeting developed a strong working relationship between Farmer and Stenson.

---

1. This case was made possible by the cooperation of Kwik-Fit Holdings, Tom Farmer and Duncan Whyte.

Two and a half years later when Albany merged with Brown Brothers, a motor components business, Farmer left to retire and settle near San Francisco in the United States. He was then only twenty-nine years old.

Within six months Farmer and his family were back in Scotland. He had seen in the United States local 'muffler shops' specializing in fitting exhausts. In 1971 he set up, from scratch, an exhaust fitting business, Kwik-Fit. The tale is often told how it was whilst in bed with flu that one of his company's greatest assets, its name, suddenly came to him.

Kwik-Fit came into existence in 1971 and in 1974 Tom Farmer invited Alex Stenson who had retired from business to become non-executive chairman of Kwik-Fit, with the view to making the company the UK's biggest and best tyre and exhaust retailer. Stenson provided the company with not only his financial expertise, but also a figure-head known to the City.

Initially, tyres were to be a sideline. But, it was not long before Farmer was back into selling tyres as his primary product, accounting for 80 per cent of Kwik-Fit's sales with exhausts accounting for the rest.

For Farmer and Stenson this was not just a case of treading a familiar path. Farmer's philosophy underpinned their business strategy, the crux of which as stated by Farmer in his 1972 Annual Report was that the customer was the most important element in the business and therefore had to be wooed. This was pursued through a policy which combined keen prices, well equipped service bays, a clean reception area and the promise of 100 per cent customer satisfaction. To achieve and maintain this all staff are trained to adhere to the Kwik-Fit Code of Practice which ensures that every customer's vehicle receives the highest standard of service (see Fig. 14.1).

This is further enhanced by the policy whereby:

Kwik-Fit customers are given a binding quotation before any work commences and on completion they are invited to inspect the work. Along with their invoices, our customers receive details of our guarantees and a satisfaction card. Through this questionnaire and our retail advertising, customers are asked to contact the Centre Manager or our Chairman

---

OUR CODE OF PRACTICE MEANS THAT THE STAFF OF THIS DEPOT WILL:

■ Treat your vehicle with care and fit protective seat covers.

■ Examine your vehicle with you and give an honest appraisal of work required.

■ Give, on request, a binding quotation before work commences.

■ Ensure that all work is carried out in accordance with the Company's laid down procedures.

■ Inform you immediately of any complications or delays.

■ Examine all finished work with you before your vehicle leaves the premises.

■ Make available to you, on request, all parts removed from your vehicle.

WE NEVER WANT OUR CUSTOMERS TO HAVE ANY DOUBTS ABOUT OUR RECOMMENDATIONS.

IF YOU HAVE A QUERY, SPEAK TO THE MANAGER WHO IS HERE TO HELP YOU.

Fig. 14.1 Kwik-Fit Code of Practice.

if there is any cause for dissatisfaction with either our service or our products, so that improvements can be made.

Three years after starting Kwik-Fit, in 1971, Farmer sold the business to a quoted mini-conglomerate – G.A. Robinson – for £700,000 plus a seat on their board. Some six months later, amid boardroom squabbles, G.A. Robinson ran into difficulties during the three-day week of 1974. Farmer seized this opportunity to buy out his co-directors and sell off everything other than the fast-fit operation. He then renamed the Robinson Company Kwik-Fit, thereby creating for himself a quoted company at very little cost.

It was in order to strengthen the image of this 'newly' quoted company that Farmer invited Stenson to join the company.

Progress between 1974 and 1979 was steady and predictable. By the end of the 1970s Kwik-Fit was operating 52 outlets. But 1980 was to prove a remarkable year on two counts. In January 1980 the London based Euro Exhaust Centre Holdings were acquired for £10 million, thereby doubling the number of depots Kwik-Fit held. Additionally, this acquisition opened up new market segments to Kwik-Fit; the south of England and the Midlands, and a toehold in continental Europe.

The second major event was the purchase in September 1980 of 180 retail depots from Firestone Tire and Rubber for £3.2 million. A month later Farmer resold 80 of these depots to Dunlop for £3.2 million. Kwik-Fit, had, therefore, nearly doubled its size at no cost. Of this deal Farmer said: 'Opportunities come along, and unless you chase them they go past you.'

In essence Farmer and Stenson had deduced from Firestone's closure of its Brentford manufacturing plant and from trade rumours that the US group would soon want to pull out of UK retailing. When they approached Firestone they found that Firestone wished to cut its British losses as quickly as possible and consequently were only asking the book value of their depots.

Unfortunately, the near quadrupling of depots from 50 to almost 200 (some were closed down) did little for Kwik-Fit's performance. The nearly 200-strong chain was making heavy trading losses partially due to recurring management problems and the poor siting of depots (some of the former Firestone depots proved not such a bargain after all since they did practically no business).

In the year to February 1981 the company reported £4 million pre-tax profits on sales of £34.4 million. The following year profits slumped to £1.4 million whilst turnover rose by only a quarter, to £43.4 million. Additionally, Farmer ran into trouble at year end 1983 with his shareholders when he tried to merge his property company, Crest International, with Kwik-Fit. With the addition of 'dumping' by parts manufacturers which reduced margins dramatically, Kwik-Fit's growth image in the early half of the 1980s was under severe pressure. It was not until after 1984 that real recovery was achieved.

COMPUTERIZATION

The problems of welding Firestone, Euro Exhaust and Kwik-Fit into a single, cohesive organization were proving more problematic than Farmer had foreseen. Farmer comments that:

We had an administrative operation that was good for 50 outlets but not for 180 ... The whole structure began to creak.

Two areas were identified for attention, administration and motivation. The first was resolved by integrating the new acquisitions, and by harmonizing trading practices and reporting systems through computerization.

First attempts at this proved fruitless. The UK computer manufacturers could only offer part solutions to Kwik-Fit's problem. They failed to reflect an understanding of Kwik-Fit's underlying needs. Furthermore no one inside the company had any knowledge of computers. It was one of the non-executive directors John Padget who had convinced Farmer that the only way to maintain control of the business was to install a computer terminal in every depot.

It was Padget, an American who had once run the European operation of the US conglomerate Tenneco, who fortuitously came across an article in the *Wall Street Journal* which helped to solve Kwik-Fit's computer problem. The article described the system developed by the US fast food chain, Church's Fried Chicken.

Farmer phoned Church's and discovered that they had just set up a joint venture to market their system. One of their executives, who flew over to Scotland, understood retailing, and he managed one of Kwik-Fit's depots for a week in order to understand properly Kwik-Fit's operation.

By 1 March 1982 some 200 terminals were installed. These machines were known as MATs (management action terminals) for it was felt that the word 'computer' could have a detrimental effect on staff. The machines themselves are robust with fat keys designed for stubby fingers. They perform all essential functions of a centre's administration including quotation and invoice production, the recording of customer and banking transactions, confirmation of stock levels and the recording of staff working hours for payroll. Depot managers, but not, programmers, help draw up the specification for the computer system. The system has so far suffered no serious hiccups, though it has been modified. The effect of computerization may be measured by Farmer's reaction:

Computerization was the biggest thing that's happened to our business ... we can see the effects of pricing decisions in 24 hours.

During the day 'MAT' operates as a free-standing computer in the centres. Overnight it becomes a slave terminal to the mainframe computers in the central office in Edinburgh.

At the close of trading each evening, the day's transactions are polled and collated by the mainframe computers and any information for the centre manager's attention is transmitted. By 7 a.m. the next morning, management have detailed trading analyses and other vital information required to operate effectively.

EPOS equipment has conferred further benefits so that the organization does not choke on paper. It allows sales to be converted into orders which are automatically transmitted to four of the biggest suppliers overnight which as Duncan Whyte, the Finance Director and formerly Arthur Andersen's managing partner, points out: 'gives us a 48 hour cycle of delivery'.

In 1985 a further step was taken to maximize the potential benefits accruing from computerization. Both Access and Visa were linked into the system thereby allowing instant payment on credit card transactions which represented around 35 per cent of total sales.

Kwik-Fit has spent more than £3 million in hardware and programming. The result according to Whyte is that the existing system could now cope with up to 1,000 outlets.

THE ENVIRONMENT

The size of the market is growing. The recession and slump (1979–80) in new car sales led to more old cars being on the roads and a greater need for replacements of fast wearing parts. Additionally, the tightening up of Department of Transport regulations has also helped. Shock absorbers were added to the list of components that had to be tested. So since 1980 Kwik-Fit has been replacing them, too.

Kwik-Fit's success has done much to galvanize the rest of the after-market; competition is rapidly becoming more powerful and professional. It is probable that competition will come not from the complacent garage-owners but rather from the chains belonging to the tyre manufacturers and large retailers, some of whom exceed Kwik-Fit in numbers of outlets. These chains have smartened themselves up whilst adding new equipment to their outlets. Furthermore, new entrants into the market-place, often closely modelling themselves on Kwik-Fit, have added their pressure to the competitiveness of this market.

Perhaps the most significant emerging factor is the move by several large retailers such as Woolworth's B&Q subsidiary and Ward White's Halfords penetration into Kwik-Fit's market. By the end of 1987 B&Q had six 'autocentres' on stream, each one of which will be six times the size of the typical Kwik-Fit depot. Furthermore, each will have a large auto-parts shop and valeting department in addition to its fast-fit bays.

At present Kwik-Fit's product base is balanced between tyres and exhausts:

- 45 per cent tyres plus add-ons – wheel balancing, alignment;
- 45 per cent exhausts;
- 10 per cent shock absorbers, batteries and radiators;

but it is broadening. The year 1982 saw the launch of specialist Stop 'n' Steer centres which offered brake and steering adjustment. 1985 saw the introduction of the Kwik-Lube oil change facility and latterly fixed-price servicing.

Underlying this strategic development of Kwik-Fit was the desire by Farmer to dominate the autocare industry. He was well aware that this industry was not going to get any less competitive. In response he intended to turn his company into the 'Marks & Spencer' of the industry. Each centre carries a comprehensive range of tyres, shock absorbers, batteries and radiators. Other services offered include while-you-wait Kwik-Lube engine oil and filter change, introduced into all centres in July 1986. This was quickly followed by Kwik-Lube Plus which includes the checking and replenishing of all lubricant and coolant levels. The introduction of these lubrication services formed the basis of menu priced car servicing, whereby the customer can see what he is paying for. This was introduced into 42 centres in 1986 in Scotland and introduced into selected centres throughout Britain during 1987. Computerized wheel balancing and alignment, and puncture repair were also offered. Moreover, since 1984 own-label produced have been introduced (see Table 14.1).

All of these products are, in Kwik-Fit's opinion, of premium quality and priced

Table 14.1 Kwik-Fit own-label products

- **Centaur supreme** steel radial tyres, introduced last year and already proving very successful, offer the exclusive after-sales benefits of free wheel balancing and free puncture repair for the legal life of the tyre.
- **Centaur supreme** batteries are guaranteed for three years' unlimited mileage.
- **Centaur** steel-braced remould tyres are 'S' rated (the same rating applied to new radial tyres).
- **Centurion supreme** exhausts are manufactured exclusively for Kwik-Fit to our own specifications. These high-quality systems are constructed from stainless and aluminized steel and covered by a three-year warranty.
- **Centurion** heavy-duty shock absorbers are covered by a three-year guarantee, and
- **Centurion supreme** gas-filled shock absorbers are guaranteed or as long as the customer owns the car.
- **Centurion** radiators are available for a wide range of vehicles – meeting motorists' requirements for a fast-fit replacement service.

competitively. In addition, along with the introduction of Autocharge, Kwik-Fit's own credit card, a deal was struck with General Accident, Britain's largest motor insurance company, to offer motor insurance through any Kwik-Fit centre.

In 1987 the Department of Transport granted MOT test station licences to fifteen Kwik-Fit and Stop 'n' Steer outlets and a further thirty licences have been applied for.

Stop 'n' Steer Centres specialize in the replacement of brakes, clutches and steering and suspension parts. All Stop 'n' Steer Centres offer fixed-price menu servicing and wherever possible are located next to Kwik-Fit Centres in order to provide a convenient 'one stop' facility. The Stop 'n' Steer services are also being incorporated into selected Kwik-Fit Centres to create the new 'Autocare' Services Centres.

The year 1986 saw the opening of the first Kwik-Fit Autocare Service Centre in Rochdale. Others quickly followed in Sutton Coldfield, Paisley, Worksop, Clacton, Leeds and Newcastle upon Tyne.

It is planned to extend the Stop 'n' Steer chain to a network of over 150 specialist centres in conjunction with the development of the Kwik-Fit 'Autocare' Service Centres.

The development of these new and larger outlets provided an ideal opportunity for Kwik-Fit to introduce a more modern retail identity. Brighter, more comfortable waiting areas with drinks dispensers and reception counters, new lighting, flooring and racking with well-displayed point-of-sale material – all these help to create an atmosphere of a well managed and efficient outlet and which gives the customers confidence. Every relevant outlet will be upgraded in line with this new scheme over the next three years.

MOTIVATION – STRUCTURE – MANAGEMENT

In 1972 Farmer commented that:

> At Kwik-Fit the most important person is the customer and it must be the aim of us all to give 100 per cent customer satisfaction 100 per cent of the time.

With this philosophy in mind it was a simple step to recognize two critical factors.

First,

> Our continued success depends on the loyalty of our customers. We are committed to a policy of offering them the best value for money with a fast, courteous and professional service. We offer the highest quality products and guarantees.

Second:

> We at Kwik-Fit recognize that our employees are our most valuable asset. The managers and staff at our centres are the all-important contact with the customers and they are the key to the success of the Kwik-Fit Group.

Kwik-Fit has thus always been committed to training but now even greater emphasis has been placed on staff development. Continuous 'on-the-job' training is still a major feature whilst the training centres at Edinburgh and Newcastle-under-Lyme provide training courses for both new and existing members of staff covering business aspects such as technical and product knowledge, depot management, sales methods and communications skills.

To aid training and assessment a new series of modular training programmes was introduced. Each programme is related to one of the four areas of the Group's activities – Sales, Technical, Administration and Management.

Kwik-Fit is also a strong supporter of the government's Youth Training Scheme. Each year Kwik-Fit sends about 220 YTS trainees on 12-week residential courses held in conjunction with the Road Transport Training Board at MOTEC in Livingston, Scotland. These courses include a week spent at Loch Eil Outward Bound Centre in the Scottish Highlands. Once their training period is over, almost all these youngsters have been offered permanent employment.

Kwik-Fit's policy has always been to recruit its management staff from within the company. Many of the Group's partners and master managers started in the company as fitters or YTS trainees.

In the days when Kwik-Fit had only 50 depots, 'Managing staff', states Farmer, 'was easy – a matter of personality and example'. He tells of arriving recently at a busy depot where things were getting out of hand, stripping off his coat and changing tyres with the best. But, in a company employing over 2,000 people it may be thought that such methods are less effective.

Since 1 March 1981 all new recruits, whether management, clerical, accounting or advertising, have had to serve an initial induction period working in the depots so that they understand the (depot) manager's problems. Computerization was designed, partly, to take troublesome chores from managers' shoulders allowing them to spend less time on administration and more on managing. Farmer firmly believes that: 'The good Kwik-Fit manager is not an administrator, he's a doer'.

The rationale which underpinned the changes in Kwik-Fit since 1981 was that Farmer believed that the majority of Kwik-Fit depots were trading at well below their potential profitability and that more able and experienced managers could change this situation. The most profitable depots were those that were the longest established:

> ... the reason for this is that the guys who run them are much more experienced. They know how to handle customers and to get them to wait, even when the depot is very busy and they feel like turning around and going away. They know the secret. Service to the customer.

In the early 1980s Farmer thought that his business was one with high margins which meant that:

Once a depot reaches a certain sales figure and covers its fixed costs, then almost all the gross takings go right down to the bottom line.

Financial motivation plays a vital role throughout the company. For the past three years depot managers have been paid a minimum salary (currently £7,500) with the rest of their remuneration depending entirely on profits. This profit-sharing scheme replaced the conventional bonus scheme calculated on depot performance. Now, the proceeds of each month's sales are notionally divided between the company and the depot. Out of its 50 per cent the depot pays the controllable costs and of what's left the depot manager gets 5 per cent. Regular bonuses can take master manager's salaries up to £40,000. The average master manager's salary is around £20,000 which is nearly double the industry norm.

For the sake of control and career structure, and to encourage the impression that Kwik-Fit consists of local businesses whose bosses have a stake in the enterprise, depots are grouped in threes. The senior manager of the trio, called a 'partner', supervises the other two depots and collects a further 2.5 per cent from the kitty of each satellite.

Since September 1986 fitters have been included in the scheme – 50 per cent of the manager's profit share is pooled and paid out to fitters according to grade. This may be worth up to £22 in the weekly pay-packets.

According to Farmer the impact on costs of the 50-50 formula has been dramatic. In the first winter after its introduction the company's electricity bill fell by £200,000. Essentially, it forces the manager to focus on costs as well as revenues.

Surprisingly, Farmer argues that money is only the starting point of motivation. A constant effort is made to foster the idea that everyone in Kwik-Fit is a partner. To this end a share allocation scheme under which all employees of over three years standing are allocated an equal bundle of shares depending on the year's profit was introduced.

MANAGEMENT-STRUCTURE

Kwik-Fit comprises nine business units – five geographically located divisions, the relatively new Fleet Division, the Stop 'n' Steer division, and two overseas divisions. Each division is responsible for all retail operations. Each business unit is controlled by a director who is responsible for its profitability. He is assisted by a tight-knit management team with individual responsibilities for retail sales, staff welfare and training, property maintenance and development, and centre administration. The offices and warehouses of each of these business units are strategically located close to the major communications links at Broxburn near Edinburgh, Warrington, Derby, Harlow and Reading. This operating structure keeps management in close touch with local market conditions (see Fig. 14.2).

Two further business units operate on the continent. These are the USN wholesale and distribution subsidiary and the Kwik-Fit retail chain of 41 tyre and exhaust replacement centres in the Netherlands and Belgium, seven centres of which were opened in 1985/86.

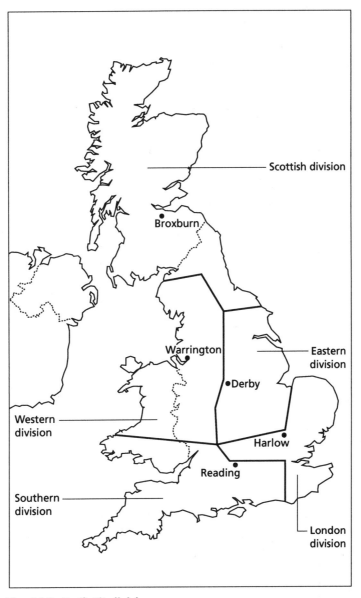

Fig. 14.2 Kwik-Fit divisions.

The Dutch wholesaling subsidiary, Uitlantservice Nederland BV, supplies tyres, exhausts, batteries and shock absorbers not only to Kwik-Fit outlets but also to wholesalers, garages and other fitting centres in Holland, Belgium and West Germany. USN, with a stockholding of over 150,000 items, is now the largest independent importer and distributor of such parts in the Dutch market.

One advantage of Kwik-Fit national coverage is that it can now push its services nationwide to fleet operators. To this end it has created a separate division to deal with fleet sales.

It is estimated that 25 per cent of the cars now on Britain's roads are owned by companies and that last year approximately 70 per cent of new cars were registered

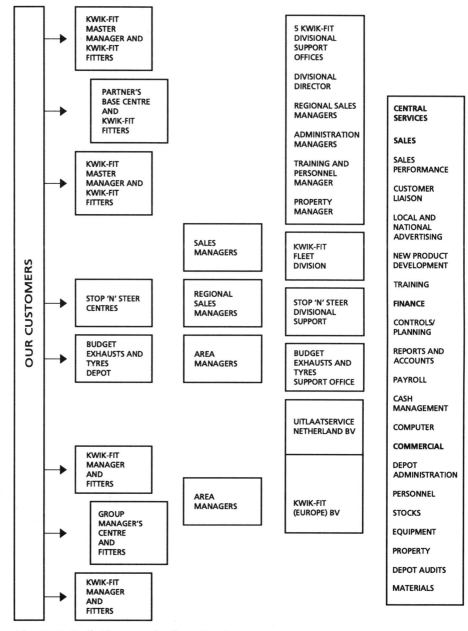

Fig. 14.3 Kwik-Fit: organization structure.

under company names. This makes the UK company car market one of the most concentrated in the world.

Each year this sector of the car after-market spends over £150 million on tyres and exhausts and of this Falmer estimates that fleet contracts could add £10 million to his sales. By 1987 end sales are expected to be in excess of this estimated £10 million and double that in 1988.

Kwik-Fit Fleet's customers already include the Ministry of Defence, Thames Water

Authority, the Scottish Office and such well known companies as Hertz, Avis, Hotpoint, Thorn EMI, GEC and Rowntree Mackintosh, and major car-leasing companies such as Gelco, PHH, Lax, Motorent and Swan National.

In terms of company structure Farmer is a believer in maximum decentralization. Before computerization the company employed over 100 clerical staff. Now, with over 300 depots, it has 30.

Central Services in Edinburgh provides centres and field management with support in key areas of sales, commerce and finance, with senior executives having specific responsibility for sales analysis, finance, training, marketing and advertising, customer services, stock control, purchasing and property.

Day-to-day running of the company is therefore in the hands of a management board interposed between the main board and the regional managers.

The structure which Kwik-Fit has developed is seen as a pyramid lying on its side (see Fig. 14.3). The result of this is that the depots are the front-line rather than the base and the management organization – regional managers, management board and the main board – come behind them as a backup team, rather than above them.

Farmer claims that:

We're not a big 'organization', we're a collection of small businesses ... In our company culture, head office is seen as just a support operation.

To reinforce this attitude that the basic unit is the 'partnership' of three depots, Farmer insists that all administrative staff spend a week every year working at one of the depots. At the same time, he makes sure that all his senior managers travel regularly around the country – and muck in.

The business strategy during 1986–87 was to reinforce the Group's positive, customer orientated image. Satisfied customers are fundamental to Kwik-Fit's success. To this end 1986 was designated 'The Year of the Customer' where every member of staff was constantly reminded of the need to achieve 100 per cent customer satisfaction at all times.

As a result of the press and television advertising campaign 'You Can't Get Better Than a Kwik-Fit Fitter', Kwik-Fit is now the best known tyre and exhaust company in Britain and claims to receive fewer than two complaints per 10,000 customers all of which are answered by Farmer himself.

The Granada TV survey of Kwik-Fit awareness for the UK showed:

Spontaneous	56%
Prompted	92%

Advertising in 1987 is likely to be in excess of £8 million. Some of this is accounted for by the regular market research carried out to keep management fully informed about trends, the effectiveness of advertising and to provide other information necessary to enable the Group to maintain its leading position in the market.

In reality Kwik-Fit is Tom Farmer. Farmer takes the trouble to state that:

We are not a one-man company. Our management structure has been carefully developed and depots run as a small independent businesses.

He has gained a reputation as a shrewd, aggressive entrepreneur, a man who demands a high level of commitment to the company and one who is sometimes difficult to work for. Farmer often works late or at weekends in his headquarters. He visits at least once a year every one of his UK depots and is usually on first name terms with most of his employees.

Although the business is a major part of his life, his family is as important, if not more so, and he takes great care to keep family and business affairs separate.

Duncan Whyte and Peter Homes are the only other executives with seats in the boardroom. There are several more 'directors' but they are more in the nature of staff officers.

In response to being asked how he saw Kwik-Fit's long-term planning or strategy developing Whyte said:

> My role as I see it is to feed things to Tom and Tom would probably say that he didn't use such highfalutin words as strategy. For him, long-term planning is what we're going to do tomorrow.

FINANCE

The substantial reserve of cash raised to pay for the Firestone purchase and from the £1.8 million sale of Kwik-Fit's Dutch subsidiary in November 1980 was used for consolidation, not further acquisition.

Around £1 million was spent on the computerization programme whilst £350,000 was used to facelift some of the properties. In 1980 a new training scheme was introduced. In its first year it cost £150,000. Kwik-Fit now have two training centres, in Edinburgh and in the Potteries.

For Farmer these changes in 1980 were necessary because:

> Our plan for the next period is to make the improvements to the company that we have always been aware needed to be made, but got shelved because we were too busy with expansion.

Kwik-Fit's rapid expansion has been financed largely by frequent and substantial issues of new equity. Since 1982, earnings per share have increased by an annual average of more than 20 per cent, while profits growth at pre-tax level, compound, has been above 45 per cent to reach £6.6 million in the year to end February 1986.

The strong advance that has taken place in Kwik-Fit's earnings since 1982 was not reflected in its share price until 1986 (see Fig. 14.4). In 1983 the market was unsettled by the offer for Crest International by Farmer and two other directors at a price which some of the institutional shareholders thought to be too high. Ultimately, Kwik-Fit bought Crest, after an adjustment in terms, for £4 million.

According to analysts, and Farmer, Kwik-Fit is now in a position to expand its depot network by 10–12 per cent a year, funded from cash flow. Ultimately, the aim is a UK chain of around 1,000 outlets (of which some 150 would be large Autocare centres) with virtually every aspect of autocare catered for somewhere in the group.

During the past three years the resurgence of Kwik-Fit's shares opened up the possibility of reaching that goal much more quickly through a capital raising. Although that option is available there are constraints such as finding suitable management and staff. A more cautious Farmer commented:

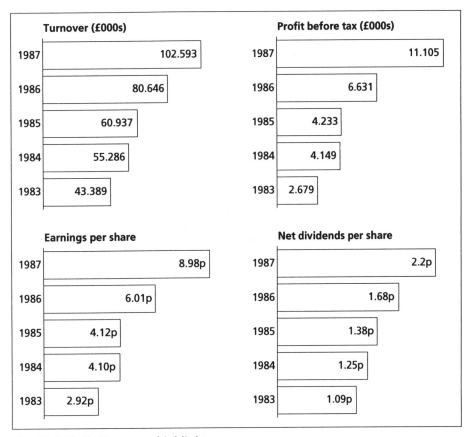

Fig. 14.4 Kwik-Fit: group highlights.

I wouldn't like to give the impression that we're overreaching ourselves ... But, after all its not as if Kwik-Fit has to worry unduly about competitors breathing down its neck. Apart from fast-fit chains tied to specific manufacturers (like Michelin, Goodyear and BTR's National Tyre), and retail multiples aimed at the DIY trade (like Halfords) there is little serious competition in the market place.

The interim profit (half year 31/8/87) was almost 50 per cent up on the corresponding period of the previous year whilst the interim dividend had risen by 25 per cent to 1.25p.

The improvement indicated by the interim report reflected not only increased market share in its traditional tyres, exhausts and batteries business, but shock absorbers also received a boost from new MOT requirements introduced in 1986. There was also continued movement into higher-margin business such as brake replacement and a further tightening of financial controls.

The investment community has shown some concern that Kwik-Fit is in danger of slipping out of its specialist niche. Farmer's solution is to draw a broad line between straightforward replacement operations which would fit into the existing depots' traditional business and others which are more complicated. The latter would become parallel businesses run as joint ventures with other companies.

Farmer is also unwavering in his strategy for expanding the number of Kwik-Fit depots. In the first half of 1987 another 20 were opened, bringing the total to 359, with another 25 under development. The target was to open 60–70 depots during the financial year following. By 15 January 1988 the total stood at 390. Ultimately a near doubling of ordinary depots to some 750 and the establishment of 150 new depots for both the Stop 'n' Steer and Autocare chains was envisaged by 1991. In addition, Farmer is particularly keen to expand within the M25 'ring'. Kwik-Fit already has some 70 depots in the area but Farmer believes it could support another 100.

The outcome of such an expansion programme is the increase of market share in tyres to 20 per cent and exhausts to 30 per cent.

OVERSEAS

The company already operates a sizeable chain in Holland and Belgium which continues to expand alongside its UK operations. Elsewhere, though, Farmer is wary of direct involvement:

> We think we're a bit like McDonald's in that we now have a first-class system to sell to potential partners internationally. Our input would be at boardroom level – we're definitely not interested in day-to-day management.

Of acquisitions Farmer takes the view that these hold little attraction: 'Why pay for goodwill when we can just open up nearby and take the business away from them?' Nevertheless, in April 1988 Kwik-Fit expanded into France through an 80 per cent acquisition of Tours Pneus which ran seventeen outlets.

Joint ventures may, however, be a different proposition. In July 1987 Kwik-Fit announced its first venture into Northern Ireland through a joint venture with Hampden Homecare, an Irish company which is Ireland's largest homecare and DIY retailer, having the franchise for seven Texas Homecare stores.

This venture allowed Kwik-Fit initially to set up six tyre and exhaust centres before building the business up to a total of about 25 centres. The initial approach was made by Hampden and under the joint venture Kwik-Fit provided the marketing, training, computerization, central management services and site layout plans, while Hampden provided local management. According to Farmer:

> Northern Ireland was not an area we had on our priority list, but the opportunity came along to start up this joint venture and it made a lot of sense.

APPENDIX 14.1
FINANCIAL STATISTICS

Tables 14.2 to 14.7 and Figs 14.5 to 14.13 provide a range of financial and other information regarding Kwik-Fit Holdings plc for the period to 1988.

Table 14.2 Chairman's statement (22 September 1987)

Our Aim is 100% Customer Satisfaction

In the fist six months of the current financial year Group profits before tax have increased by 50% to £8.031 million compared with £5.352 million last year. Turnover has risen by 22% to £62.924 million from £51,661 million last year.

We have continued to improve our market share both in the UK and in Holland with increased sales of our main products – tyres, exhausts, batteries and shock absorbers. New products and services which complement our existing activities are being researched and introduced into selected centres. Kwik-Fit Fleet, our new operating Division established January this year, has already succeeded in capturing a significant share of the tyre and exhaust replacement business within the fleet sector. This is an important market with 25% of cars in the UK being company owned.

During the last six months, we opened 20 new centres and at 31st August the Group was trading from 359 specialist automotive repair outlets. A further 25 new specialist automotive repair outlets. A further 25 new sites are currently under development, whilst we are continuing with our refurbishment programme to upgrade the facilities offered through existing centres.

In order to maintain the highest possible standards of service – in line with our position as market leader – the scope and content of our training programmes have been further extended to ensure that our staff always have the technical skills and expertise necessary to meet the expectations of today's motorists. These training programmes together with ongoing reviews of our centres' operating procedures will ensure that Kwik-Fit continues to win and retain the motorist's confidence.

Our management operating structures and our past investment in computerization together with our dedication to 100% customer satisfaction, has not only enabled us to achieve record sales and profits for this six month period but has reinforced Kwik-Fit's position as the dominant force in the car repair and servicing business.

We go into the next six months of our financial year with confidence.

The interim dividend is being increased to 1.25p per share compared with 1.0p per share – an increase of 25% – and will be paid on the 30th November 1987 to shareholders on the register at 31st October 1987.

TOM FARMER

Table 14.3 Unaudited results for the half-year ended 31 August 1987

	Half year 31.8.87 £000s	Half year 31.8.86 £000s	% increase	Year to 28.2.87 -£000s
Turnover –				
continuing operations	62,294	51,661	+21.8	102,593
Operating profit	8,286	5,653	+46.6	11,792
Investment income	216	545		769
Interest payable and similar				
charges	(471)	(846)		(1,456)
Profit on ordinary activities	8,031	5,352	+50.1	11,105
Tax on profit on ordinary				
activities	2,889	1,544	+87.1	(3,496)
Profit on ordinary activities				
after tax	5,142	3,808	+35.0	7,609
Extraordinary items	—	(321)		(332)
Profit for the financial period	5,142	3,487	+47.5	7,277
Dividend per share	1.25p	1.0p	+25.0	2.2p
Cost of dividend	£1,062,089	£848,138	+25.2	£1,868,099
Earnings per share based on:				
Profit on ordinary activities				
before tax	9.46p	6.32p	+49.7	13.11p
Profit on ordinary activities				
after tax	6.06p	4.50p	+34.7	8.98p
Earnings per share based on				
the weighted average				
number of shares of	84,864,647	84,637,640		84,725,013

Table 14.4 Consolidated profit and loss accounts (for the years ended 29 February 1988 and 28 February 1987)

	1988 £	1987 £
Turnover	125,495,790	102,592,962
Cost of sales, inclusive of marketing costs	(104,906,656)	(87,251,221)
Gross profit	20,589,134	15,341,741
Administrative expenses	(5,150,687)	(3,999,715)
Profit on sale of tangible fixed assets	419,683	449,823
Operating profit	15,858,130	11,791,849
Investment income	1,323,597	769,161
Profit before interest and taxation	17,181,727	12,561,010
Interest payable and similar charges	(1,172,908)	(1,456,393)
Profit on ordinary activities before taxation	16,008,819	11,104,617
Tax on profit on ordinary activities	(5,711,031)	(3,495,946)
Profit on ordinary activities after taxation	10,297,788	7,608,671
Extraordinary items	—	(331,943)
Profit for the financial year	10,297,788	7,276,728
Dividends paid and proposed	(2,434,652)	(1,868,099)
Retained profit for the year	7,863,136	5,408,629
Earnings per share based on:		
Profit on ordinary activities before taxation	18.80p	13.11p
Profit on ordinary activities after taxation	12.10p	8.98p

Table 14.5 Consolidated balance sheets (at 29 February 1988 and 28 February 1987)

	1988 £	1987 £
Fixed assets		
Tangible assets	55,435,279	45,413,112
Investments	802,885	1,009,331
	56,238,164	46,422,443
Current assets		
Stocks	18,344,380	14,063,404
Debtors	6,477,625	5,523,491
Cash at bank and in hand	3,300,525	5,155,588
	28,122,530	24,742,483
Creditors: amounts falling due within one year	(32,735,245)	(26,484,146)
Net current liabilities	(4,612,715)	(1,741,663)
Total assets less current liabilities	51,625,449	44,680,780
Creditors: amounts falling due after more than *on year*	(10,667,665)	(11,137,054)
Provisions for liabilities and charges	(1,803,350)	(1,242,306)
	(12,471,015)	(12,379,360)
Net assets	39,154,434	32,301,420
Capital and reserves		
Called-up share capital	8,567,024	8,481,383
Share premium account	6,447,682	6,128,012
Profit and loss account	24,139,728	17,692,025
Total capital employed	39,154,434	32,301,420

Table 14.6 Company balance sheets (at 29 February 1988 and 28 February 1987)

	1988 £	1987 £
Fixed assets		
Investments	31,213,368	28,074,801
Current assets		
Debtors	29,633,238	20,341,885
Cash at bank and in hand	—	277,988
	29,633,238	20,619,873
Creditors: amounts falling due within one year	(15,222,672)	(9,073,754)
Net current assets	14,410,566	11,546,119
Total assets less current liabilities	45,623,934	39,620,920
Creditors: amounts falling due after more than one year	(6,469,500)	(7,319,500)
Net assets	39,154,434	32,301,420
Capital and reserves		
Called-up share capital	8,567,024	8,481,383
Share premium account	6,447,682	6,128,012
Revaluation reserve	16,934,472	13,589,459
Profit and loss account	7,205,256	4,102,566
Total capital employed	39,154,434	32,301,420

Table 14.7 Consolidated statements of source and application of funds (for the years ended 29 February 1988 and 28 February 1987)

	1988 £	1987 £
Source of funds		
Profit before extraordinary items	10,297,788	7,608,671
Items not involving the movement of funds:		
Employee share scheme	238,810	189,524
Depreciation	2,847,951	2,312,073
Increase in net assets of related company	(261,069)	(85,944)
Increase (decrease) in deferred taxation	561,044	(663,843)
Translation (loss) gain	(96,125)	145,996
Total generated from operations	13,588,399	9,506,477
Net book value of tangible fixed assets sold	1,721,035	8,358,927
(Decrease) increase in creditors falling due after more than one year	(469,389)	948,893
Shares issued during the year	166,501	—
Net book value of fixed asset investment sold	519,820	—
	15,526,366	18,814,297
Application of funds:		
Purchase of tangible fixed assets	14,591,153	9,868,305
Acquisition of fixed asset investments	52,305	750,000
Dividends	2,434,652	1,868,099
Extraordinary items less taxation	—	210,130
Purchase of goodwill at cost	1,319,308	—
(Increase) decrease in net current liabilities as shown below	(2,871,052)	6,117,763
	15,526,366	18,814,297
Decrease (increase) in net current liabilities:		
Stocks	4,280,976	1,818,863
Debtors	954,134	986,728
Creditors falling due within one year	(3,284,086)	(5,494,604)
	1,951,024	(2,689,013)
Movement in net liquid funds:		
(Decrease) increase in cash	(1,855,063)	4,981,717
(Increase) decrease in bank overdrafts	(2,967,013)	3,825,059
	(4,822,076)	8,806,776
(Increase) decrease in net current liabilities	(2,871,052)	6,117,763

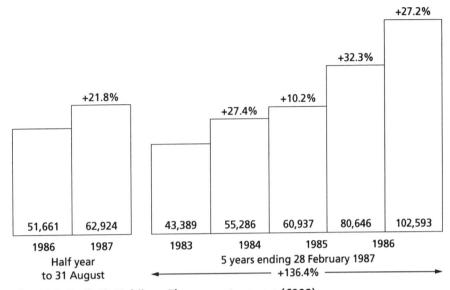

Fig. 14.5 Kwik-Fit Holdings Plc: group turnover (£000).

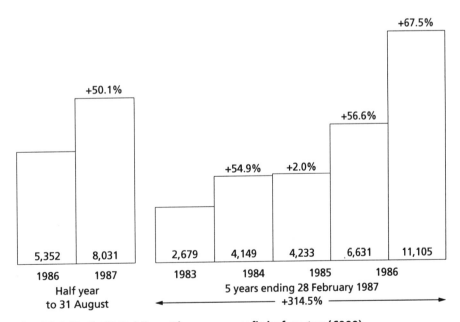

Fig. 14.6 Kwik-Fit Holdings Plc: group profit before tax (£000).

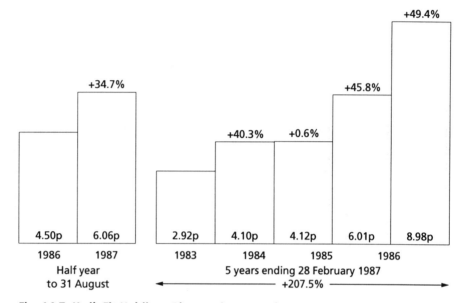

Fig. 14.7 Kwik-Fit Holdings Plc: earnings per share.

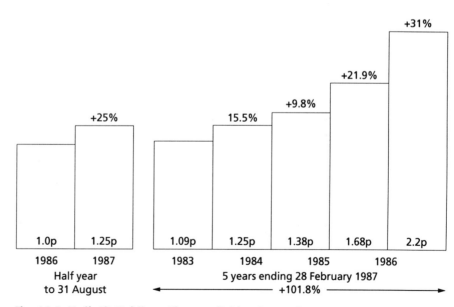

Fig. 14.8 Kwik-Fit Holdings Plc: net dividends per share.

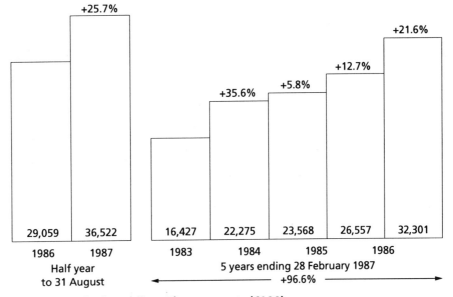

+25.7%

+21.6%

+12.7%

+35.6%

+5.8%

| 29,059 | 36,522 | 16,427 | 22,275 | 23,568 | 26,557 | 32,301 |

| 1986 | 1987 | 1983 | 1984 | 1985 | 1986 | |

Half year
to 31 August

5 years ending 28 February 1987

+96.6%

Fig. 14.9 Kwik-Fit Holdings Plc: net assets (£000).

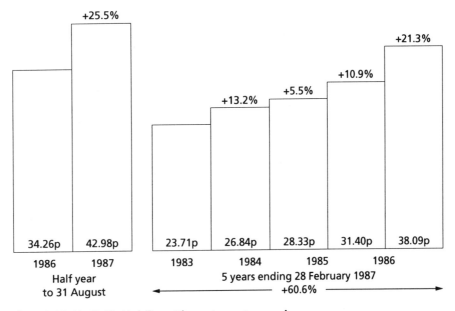

+25.5%

+21.3%

+10.9%

+13.2%

+5.5%

| 34.26p | 42.98p | 23.71p | 26.84p | 28.33p | 31.40p | 38.09p |

| 1986 | 1987 | 1983 | 1984 | 1985 | 1986 | |

Half year
to 31 August

5 years ending 28 February 1987

+60.6%

Fig. 14.10 Kwik-Fit Holdings Plc: net assets per share.

	Half year 1986	1987	1983	1984	1985	1986	1987
Profit before taxation as a % of turnover	9.9%	12.8%	6.2%	7.5%	6.9%	7.9%	10.8%
Return on capital employed	16.0%	19.7%	13.9%	14.5%	15.1%	19.4%	30.7%
Dividend cover (times)	4.1	4.8	2.67	3.15	2.55	3.23	3.9
Gearing ratios	23%	14%	45%	69%	64%	57%	20%

Fig. 14.11 Kwik-Fit Holdings Plc: summary of financial ratios.

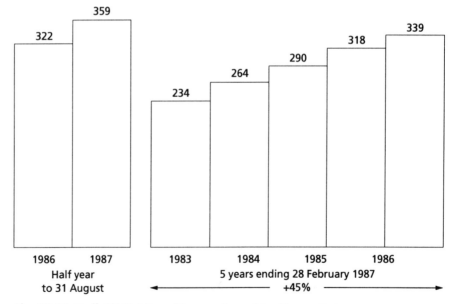

Fig. 14.12 Kwik-Fit Holdings Plc: number of trading outlets.

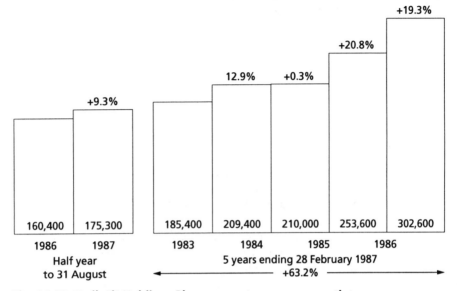

| 160,400 | 175,300 | | 185,400 | 209,400 | 210,000 | 253,600 | 302,600 |

Fig. 14.13 Kwik-Fit Holdings Plc: average turnover per outlet.

Chrysalis Group Plc

J. Day

INTRODUCTION

This case is about Chrysalis Group Plc which was formed by the reverse takeover of MAM Plc by Chrysalis Group Ltd. By the time of the merger in 1985 Chrysalis Group Ltd had grown to be one of the most successful 'mini-major' recording companies in the UK. MAM Plc was also in the music business but had used the funds generated to diversify into more general leisure activities. In addition to the interests that Chrysalis Group acquired MAM had been active in corporate aviation, a marina and fast food franchising.

In the years immediately following the merger the company developed a more diverse leisure portfolio resulting on the whole in increasing profits. However, from 1988 onwards the company has had to address both internal and external problems and to search out a viable strategic focus within the leisure industry. In 1993 they announced the setting up of a new record label. In 1989 and 1991 they had sold their existing record company in two tranches to Thorn-EMI and accepted a non-compete clause expiring in 1993.

They have not turned a full circle but if the record label is successful then once again they will have broadly similar interests to those of the 1980s. However, the real difference as recognized by Chrysalis Group Plc itself is the changed nature of both the record and leisure industries. This will require that their strategy, approach and range of products and services continue to be adjusted accordingly.

Whilst many businesses cannot flourish without paying regard to creativity and trying to manage risk, the recording industry is a peculiar mix of artistry, creativity and hard-headed business sense. This case study deliberately avoids a narrow financial analysis of Chrysalis Group Plc. Readers keen to pursue such will find plenty of financial data on the usual databases.

CHRYSALIS GROUP LTD: THE BEGINNING THROUGH TO 1985

Chris Wright became involved in the music business during the 1960s when, as the social secretary of his student union, he booked and arranged pop groups at his university. On graduation he managed the band Ten Years After. Early on he combined with Terry Ellis and they formed the Ellis Wright Agency which became a successful agency and management concern that guided the fortunes of not only Ten Years After but also Procul Harem and Jethro Tull (Ian Anderson). By 1968 they had launched the Chrysalis Record Label and an associated music publishing company, the name chosen as a close acronym of Chris and Ellis. The original record company was under licence to Island Records but as Chrysalis matured this arrangement was changed to one for pressing and distribution only. In subsequent years they have used Polygram, CBS and EMI. For a time in the USA they did arrange their own distribution through independent distributors. As their other interests grew they moved out of the direct management of rock bands. Notable Chrysalis artists in this period were, to name a handful, Blondie, Billy Idol, Pat Benetar, Huey Lewis and the News, Spandau Ballet, Ultravox, Go West and the Housemartins. As well as administering the song catalogues of their own artists they had signed catalogues from other artists and counted Leo Sayer, Chris de Burgh and David Bowie amongst them.

The precedent for diversifying into related businesses was set as early as 1973 when Wessex Sound was purchased which brought to the company recording studio facilities. Later the AIR Group which owned recording studios was acquired; it had, and still has, the services of George Martin, the record producer and composer. As head of Parlophone he had signed The Beatles and went on to produce all of their subsequent records. The company had interests in visual programming although by 1985 with one or two notable exceptions these had been abandoned. Their artist roster was strong and indeed they were the only UK independent record company to have full-scale trading operations on both sides of the Atlantic. In respect of responsibilities Chris Wright was proactive in building up the UK operation and Terry Ellis the one in the States, each operation having reciprocal licensing and sub-publishing agreements with the other. Over the period 1977 to 1985 they held no lower than a minimum of 2 per cent and maximum 5.7 per cent of the overall UK market, their median value being 3.6 per cent. Comparative figures for Island and Virgin being 1.4 per cent, 8.0 per cent, 2.8 per cent and 1.5 per cent, 9.9 per cent, 4.3 respectively. Over the period 1974 to 1988 they had achieved two 'Platinum', twelve 'Gold' and 32 'Silver' British Phonographic Certified Sales Awards for single releases. Album artists had been awarded three 'Double Platinum', 20 'Platinum', 30 'Gold' and 31 'Silver' Certified Sales Awards.

So by 1985 Chrysalis Group Ltd had record companies in the US and the UK along with associated music publishing companies and both represented and managed artists and record producers. In terms of facilities they operated Air and Wessex recording studios and had some interests in visual programming. Lastly they ran a profitable property company designed to both utilize group cash and provide surplus cash to invest in the core business.

CHRYSALIS GROUP PLC: 1985 TO THE EMI JOINT VENTURE IN 1989

In 1985 three major events took place. First Terry Ellis left after selling back his interest to Chris Wright for £17.5m in what *Music Week*, the key trade paper, described as 'one of the biggest business transactions in the history of the record industry'. Secondly Chrysalis Group Ltd engineered a reverse takeover into a public limited company MAM. Thirdly, the renamed company – Chrysalis Group plc – raised £5.35m through an offer for sale of 4.3m shares.

The departure of Terry Ellis as one would expect impacted on the company but leaving aside naive judgements it is unclear how and to what extent. In the offer for sale document Chris Wright acknowledges that Ellis was instrumental in the establishment of the record operations in the USA (moving to Los Angeles in 1974 to build up the US arm) and for its management in the formative years. However, in the latter years it was managed by a locally appointed president whilst Ellis himself became progressively less involved with the record business and more involved with visual programming. Except for promotional music videos and the exploitation of Max Headroom (a computer generated fictional hero) Wright discontinued visual programming. In the offer for sale document he argued that the departure of Ellis had not and would not adversely affect the company.

Given the nature of this industry and the durability of the partnership there was obvious interest in the change but both partners confided little in the media. *Music Week* attributed the split to Ellis's wish to extend the company into films and video production and the company cutting back the US operation, closing the Los Angeles office and relocating to New York. In a rare interview in *Music Week* (27/7/85), Chris Wright conveys the impression of two partners whose interests were pulling in separate directions but whose personalities, abilities and interests were such that they could not be disentangled from each other or the company itself. What was clear to them, however, was that the company had lost momentum and that the only viable solution would be for one of the partners to buy the other out. Terry Ellis in 1990, five years after the buy-out, moved to New York and started a new record company, Imago, as a co-venture with BMG. In the interim he dealt in property. He has also been chairman of both the UK (British Phonographic Industry) and USA (Record Industry Association of America) trade bodies, and in 1989 was elected to the board of IFPI (International Federation of Phonographic Industries). Chris Wright has also been chairman of the BPI and on the board of the IFPI.

Chrysalis Group Ltd had begun to build up a small shareholding in MAM and Chris Wright suggests that this was part proactive and part defensive. Their finance director at that time, Nigel Butterfield, had been with MAM from 1972 to when he joined Chrysalis in 1976. Again quoting from *Music Week*, Chris Wright commented:

> We may have been interested in going public, or even buying MAM, and we decided to build up a small shareholding in the company to establish a stake and pre-empt anyone else doing anything without talking to us.

Their shareholding then exceeded the 5 per cent disclosure level and 'MAM popped over and said "How would you like to do something?"' (*Music Week*, 27/7/85).

MAM was formed originally in 1969 to acquire the services of, and to manage, artists. In 1969 it acquired for shares the major part of the entertainment earnings of Tom Jones, Englebert Humperdinck and their manager Gordon Mills who became chairman of the company. The value of this income flow diminished as the contracts became less restrictive and less remunerative; however, the substantial earnings produced had allowed MAM to diversify into other activities within the leisure industry. At the point of the merger MAM had enlarged its promotion and management activities and diversified into hotel ownership and operation; the supply of post production facilities and services to the television, film and video industry; the operation of juke boxes and amusement machines in public houses and clubs; the supply of background music equipment; the sale of electronic organs and pianos; and the production of an animated cartoon series about the Loch Ness Monster created by the cartoonist, Peter Maddocks. MAM had also had interests in fast food franchising, corporate aviation services and a marina, but these had been sold by 1985.

The offer for sale document cited the general advantages of the merger as:

> The Directors believe that the combined Group will gain substantially from the merger of the CGL Group, with its active management and prominent position in the record and music business, and the MAM Group, with its strong balance sheet and spread of established businesses.

Specific benefits were claimed to be:

- Music Publishing is an excellent long-term investment but to achieve maximum profitability songs must be actively promoted and marketed. CGL has such expertise and the MAM Group catalogue contains many valuable 'standards'.
- MAM will shortly regain the right to administer its own catalogue in many overseas territories (currently in the hands of independent agents) and the two catalogues will be merged, resulting in administrative cost savings, maximization of income and strength from the combined portfolio.
- The MAM back catalogue is still capable of further exploitation through, say, budget and mid-price lines.

Since CGL used video production facilities, an in-house facility through the 75 per cent ownership of Research Recordings Ltd (later renamed Air tv) was seen to be of great potential advantage. Additionally it was anticipated that there would be synergy between Research Recordings, Air Group and Wessex Studios. With regard to agency and promotion, World Service Agency owned by CGL concentrated on rock and pop stars whilst MAM's agency was biased towards international entertainment artists. Finally there seemed to be potential for the combined group to reduce central overheads and in particular CGL had sufficient spare office space to accommodate MAM.

The combined group (Chrysalis Group Plc) stated that it was 'principally a record and music company with additional interests in the leisure sector'.

The offer for sale of 4,300,000 shares at 200p per share was to yield after floatation expenses about £5.35m and to be used to expand the scale of the new combined group. The directors believed that:

> There are excellent opportunities for expansion and development of the new Chrysalis Group's activities in the UK, USA and elsewhere. To date the growth of the record and music publishing business of the CGL Group has been achieved on a low capital base in relation to the scale of the business undertaken. The increased capital base achieved through the shares now being issued will strengthen the combined group and its future expansion.

The offer for scale document formally stated the prospects for the future:

> The merger and offer for sale would allow for a more diverse range of activity to be undertaken whilst retaining the record division as the core business. This would allow continued use of the management's proven skills in finding, developing, promoting and exploiting new acts and continuing the process as artists become established.

Particular note was made of the concerted efforts to sign and develop new bands during 1984 and that results were already in hand with three new acts charting in the top 5 in the UK, two of these artists achieving a considerable degree of international success. The record release schedule for the next year was very full and hence there was the anticipation of financial success.

The directors then highlighted four key areas: the potential for cost savings;

synergistic and commercial benefits in the common areas of music publishing, agency and promotion and facilities management; and:

> ... that the hotels, which currently have high occupancy rates, will continue to trade at a high level of profitability, and that there are indications that the juke box and fruit machine operations, which have in recent years suffered reductions in profit margins, will be able to improve their terms of trade.

> The Directors are confident that the combined Group's strong management, marketing skills, tight financial control, strong cash flow and ability to identify and develop new acts, will ensure that Chrysalis plc is able to exploit its medium and long-term growth opportunities.

Chrysalis Group Plc was to operate with five divisions (see Table 15.1). Chris Wright was to be executive chairman supported by four other CGL directors and five MAM directors. The senior management team consisted of 28 managers, the youngest being 31 and the oldest 61, between them having about 238 years of service to their respective companies. Nigel Butterfield at 37 was the youngest director and Kenneth Chappellow at 62 the eldest. Chris Wright was 40 and his MD, Terry Connolly, 41. Sadly, Gordon Mills died in 1986.

In the *Music Week* interview cited previously Chris Wright talked about the merger and offer for sale in a more informal way. He saw MAM as having useful and complementary interests that would interface with Chrysalis Group Limited (with the exception of the hotels) and that 'juke boxes and amusement machines are not terribly fashionable but they are a good business to be in and MAM has a good business in those areas.' He felt that despite Gordon Mills' undoubted talent, his lack of recent involvement with MAM's musical activities had meant that the company had been unable to maintain its ability as a music company. Thus the merger would bring the company back to being a 'creative music-orientated operation'.

Wright saw the opportunity realized by the new capital to be the ability to set up new companies in overseas territories rather than in the buying in of new acts. Equally he did not see Chrysalis becoming a more broadly based leisure company but one whose core would remain the music business. He stated: 'I see the future for record companies in selling items of "home entertainment software" for the combined CD/laser video disc player'.

At the time of the merger the company had grown to become one of the

Table 15.1 Chrysalis Group Plc operating divisions

Division	% turnover[1] (1984)	% profit before taxation[1](1984)	Employees[2] (actual)	UK/USA split[3]
Records & Publishing	64	62	109	(64/45)
Facilities Management	4	11	83	
Hotels & Machines	23	18	1,208	
Agency & Promotion	3	4	17	
Other	6	5	39	
Finance & Administration			71	(56/15)
Total			1,527	

1. Percentage profit and turnover are a pro forma estimate as if the combined group had traded in 1984.
2. Employee totals are as 1985.
3. Figures in parenthesis are the split between UK and USA respectively.

'mini-majors', and one which enjoyed and benefited from a good artist roster. It had astutely reverse merged into MAM, handled the loss of a long-time partner and raised £5.35m of new capital to enhance its strategic goals. The information provided in the tables in Appendix 15.1 details the company's aspirations and performance as evidenced in their Annual Reports over the period 1986 to 1992.

Tables 15.4 and 15.5 give details of the percentage contribution to turnover and profit by the various operating divisions of the company. Chrysalis Group Plc operated over this period, and still does, through a series of associated and subsidiary companies which numbered 84 in total and were a changing mix due to acquisition and disposal. They were also shuffled around in changing corporate structures, and to understand the company an overview of these associated and subsidiary companies is useful – Tables 15.6 and 15.7 seek to provide just this. Table 15.8 illustrates some key financial data but some care needs to be exercised over the 1985 figures since, due to the timings and complexities of the merger, unless adjusted the accounts include only about half a year of the Chrysalis Group figures and eleven months of MAM. Also the half year of figures for Chrysalis does not include Christmas, traditionally a period of high sales. Tables 15.9 and 15.10 track key changes and issues addressed by the company and its hopes and aspirations as revealed in their Annual Reports. Finally, Table 15.11 highlights the key acquisitions and disposals made by the company. These tables should be read in conjunction with commentary below on the company and its markets.

THE POST-MERGER YEARS 1985 TO 1988

An interesting and volatile period for the pop business and hence the company. Although producing acceptable profits right up until the poor £1.8m result in 1988, the company had several times disappointed the market by not meeting its forecasts essentially because of the late delivery or non-appearance of high charting material by its established artists. To be fair part of this disappointment is due to the City's inability to understand fully the risky and unpredictable fortunes suffered by companies in this line of business. In general the 1986 figures received a good press, artist potential looked good and the loss-making parts of the facilities business were being re-equipped. The contribution by the music division to profits was planned to fall as other divisions developed. Early in 1987 attitudes were also positive. The hotels had been sold and this was regarded as a good move as it had reduced substantially their borrowing needs, and at little loss to the Group's overall profitability. Additionally the hotels had been sold for almost twice their valuation at the time of the merger. Difficulties were noted with the late delivery of material by US artists but earnings from newer groups such as The Housemartins were encouraging. Final pre-tax profits came in at £6.2m plus an exceptional £1.06m (gained on the disposal of surplus MAM office space). Whilst this was a 15 per cent increase on the previous year the City was disappointed since it had been anticipating around £8m and the figures did mask a downturn in the second half. The volatility of this business was well illustrated by the *Financial Times* article heading 'Chrysalis disappoints with rise to £7.26m', and its comment:

> If you have two big name artists which don't come up to expectations, you will suffer, and Chrysalis has. In addition to the problems over Billy Idol's Whiplash Smile Album,

Huey Lewis's latest has not sold as well as hoped. In fact if it had not been for the £1m contribution from the computerized video star Max Headroom and the strong performance of Lasgo, the record wholesale export business, record earnings would have been lower than last year.

(Financial Times, 21/11/87)

Yet six months earlier In respect of the first half figures, *Music Week* and *The Financial Times* were saying:

Chrysalis Group has delighted the City with interim profits more than doubled to £5m, yet remains hungry for further acquisitions in the leisure field. Any acquisitions are unlikely to include other record companies because, explains chairman Chris Wright simply, 'there are no other record companies for sale'. So resigned to growing Chrysalis Records 'organically' he is looking for another string to our bow, another 'profit earner'.

(Music Week, 2/5/87)

'Chrysalis has taken a firm grasp of the volatile record industry. Its impressive profits growth reflects a broadening of its stable of pop stars, good management and a policy of developing related business. This has given it a firm base for further expansion.

(Financial Times, 24/4/87)

By early 1988 first half earnings were down by 60 per cent and the US operation was generating losses. Property trading had almost ceased as there was no property in stock and the machines division suffered lower operating profits due to internal reorganization and reduced rentals. The facilities division showed an improvement but audio studios were affected by unfavourable movements in the sterling/dollar exchange rate, which discouraged US artists recording in the UK. In July there was a second warning about profits and the press became less enthusiastic about the company's prospects. As well as noting the problems caused by late delivery of product the quality of the more established artists was questioned. When the results for the year ended August 1988 (the year end having been changed from June) were announced they were received without enthusiasm given that profits amounted to only £1.8m on an increased turnover of £117m. The greatest loss was £3.8m from the US division; however, most other parts of the company had performed well and the non-US operations were ahead of budget. However, this time the comment from the *Financial Times* was rather less generous:

Those investors who shunned Chrysalis' floatation three years ago have proved pretty perceptive. The shares, after yesterday's 4p fall to 103p, are little more than half their offer price. Artists are temperamental and the record buying public is fickle; it is accordingly hard for a small company like Chrysalis to avoid the occasional lean year. However, whilst one can have sympathy for Chrysalis, it is harder to be enthusiastic about its prospects. Short of slashing costs drastically (which would mean effectively withdrawing from the market) or hiring Bruce Springsteen, it is difficult to see how a turnaround in the US can be achieved in the short term. So, for a swift upturn in profits, shareholders will have to rely on the TV operations (another extremely competitive business) or a surprise hit from the group's roster of middle ranking artists. The shares are only for the brave, or for fans of Pat Benetar.

(Financial Times 9/12/89)

For the financial year ending 31 August 1989, Chrysalis was reporting pre-tax losses of £11.5m but due to the partnership with Thorn-EMI was able to report a twelve to thirteen-fold increase in shareholders' funds. In March 1989, *Music Week* was reporting that Chrysalis was in the final throws of negotiations to find a world-wide trading partner, and the speculation was that BMG was the likely prospect. By the end of the month the confirmed partner was EMI. They had sold EMI a half share in the record company giving EMI access to current artists including Sinead O'Connor and The Proclaimers and back catalogue including Jethro Tull, Blondie and Ultravox. This deal followed on less than two months after EMI had paid £187m for the SBK song catalogue. EMI had the option to purchase the other half of the company between seven to ten years in the future for a consideration based on profit performance. Chrysalis would run the record companies independently of EMI but they would be jointly responsible for their funding. Chrysalis would still have the music publishing, recording studios, broadcasting, wholesaling and machines divisions. This performance related deal was worth around £46m initially and potentially up to another £15m over the subsequent four years. Reaction to this deal is best covered by reference to some germane press quotes:

> The EMI deal appears to vindicate the Virgin argument (that UK investors undervalued and misunderstood the music business). One city analyst said yesterday: It shows what twits investors really are if all of a sudden Thorn can spend this much money for a piece of Chrysalis. Thorn-EMI clearly knows its business and is intending to be in the music market as a long term player.
>
> (*The Independent*, 23/3/89)

> Mr Chris Wright, the co-founder of Chrysalis, conceded that the deal was a symptom of the enormous competition for rights and artists in the international music business and the increasing difficulties faced by the independents. Following well publicized losses in the US, it had been essential for Chrysalis to see that 'the company had a clear cut future'.
>
> (*Financial Times*, 23/3/89)

> The deal with Thorn will eliminate gearing and leave the group with £20m to £30m to expand other parts of the business. But Mr Wright is in no hurry to spend the money... 'There are other aspects of restructuring we want to get out of the way first, including changes in central management.'
>
> (*The Independent*, 17/6/89)

By August 1989, Chrysalis had earned a profit of just £5,000, its operating profits of £1.78m written down by foreign exchange losses. The good news was that the non-US record business was doing well; however, the US records loss was around £1.6m. Asked when the American division would make a profit, Chris Wright answered 'not this year, possibly next year, certainly the year after'. (*The Times*, 8/12/90). Any reader not yet convinced about the vagaries of this industry and its performers should consult this reference in full! Two important events were the joint venture with Pioneer for the new Air Studio and the stake taken in Metro Radio.

The year 1991 was particularly difficult for the company and it made a loss before tax of £9.33m. The joint venture was fully sold to EMI. Ambitions to consolidate and develop the media side of the company led to the participation in two television franchise bids. By the 1992 year-end they had achieved a before-tax profit of £5.63m. The company appointed Steve Lewis to become Chief Executive of their proposed new record business to be started once the non-compete agreement with EMI terminated in early 1993. Taking out the impact of the EMI payment there was an operating loss of about £4.8m of which £1.8m was due to worsening conditions in the fruit machines business. The media business contribution was encouraging. Finally, they announced that they would be appointing three non-executive directors, the first of whom was Charles Levinson a lawyer and previous managing director of WEA Records/Warner Home Video (UK) and of Virgin Broadcasting.

Commentators saw the company as being pro-active in respect of its long-term future but suffering from short-term problems. Their harshest critic was an article in *BusinessAge* in July 1992 which described them as 'a business without strategy, stumbling from loss to loss'. By November 1992, however, in an article about the impact of Nick Watkins (recruited to head up the Communications Division in 1989) *BusinessAge* was distinctly bullish about the company, its proprietor and the future.

Interim results announced in June 1993 were mixed. The amusement machines division had replaced the US records operation as the cash and profit hemorrhage with predicted losses of at least £5m. A new management team was briefed to restructure the machines side and to seek out more profitable locations. Once again Lasgo performed well as did music publishing. The company has bid for two commercial radio franchises in London and failed to win one in the north of England. The television interests were making good progress and they were the fifth biggest independent supplier of programmes. The new record label was on target for the end of the year. Profits of £104,000 for the half year to February were due to interest received on the funds from the EMI sale; however, operating losses were marginally improved on the previous comparative half year. Turnover was up from £38m to £39.2m and operating losses down to £853,000 against £913,000.

In August 1993 they decided to close MAM Leisure (excluding MAM Communications Systems); the estimated loss was reported to be £6.1m in addition to £3.1m in 1991–92. Winding down the division, which by then was operating and supplying about 10,500 machines throughout the UK, would be at a cost of about £10m. About 400 jobs would be lost. Never an easy business to be in, the contemporary problems which had faced the division were increasing overheads due, for instance, to CD juke boxes costing £1,000 to stock rather than £50 for vinyl singles, the recession, fewer 18–25 year olds and competitive pressures from other operators and home amusement machines. The change in the structure of the public house market had added to operational problems.

In August Chrysalis and Unique Television joined forces to supply advertiser supplied programming, this being a logical development from Chrysalis's IndyCar '93 series funded in full by Texaco. Carlsberg Export lager were going to sponsor the Italian football coverage. Michael Pilsworth, the Managing Director of SelecTV moved to Chrysalis to be MD and Chief Executive of a newly created visual entertainment division which grouped together the TV production company, the home video operation and Red Rooster Film. Quoting Michael Pilsworth:

> For me Chrysalis is a fantastic global brand name in the record business; it provides a great opportunity to capitalize on that goodwill for the visual entertainment side.
>
> (*Financial Times*, 25/8/93)

In September Chrysalis had signed a deal with the Japanese record company Pony Cannon which gave them a 25 per cent stake in the Echo record label. This valued the label at around £42m, greater than the valuation placed on the mature label when sold to EMI. Chrysalis shares rose from 77p to 116p. Steve Lewis had a 19–25 per cent stake in the label Echo and:

Mr Wright said yesterday that, while there was no guarantee of success, the label should prosper because 'I've done it once and Steve Lewis has done it before at Virgin'... 'The main thrust is going to be on ground-floor A&R (discovering and promoting new talent) but there may well be established artists who want to talk to us,' he added. He said the first signing 'is imminent'. The Japanese will get the rights to Asian distribution of Echo's artists.

(*Daily Telegraph*, 3/9/93)

'It's a brilliant deal from our standpoint,' Mr Wright said, adding that it gave Pony a foothold in a market increasingly dominated by a few conglomerates.

(*The Independent*, 3/9/93)

For the 1993 financial year the group declared a pre-tax loss of £14.6m compared to a pre-tax profit of £5.6m in 1992 but paid the first dividend since April 1991. This was a 'one-off' payment funded by the proceeds of the Thorn-EMI sale and the Pony Cannon injection of funds. The company was to operate with three divisions – music, visual entertainment and radio – and Chris Wright seemed to want to replicate his successful music industry strategy – the building up of a few distinctive record labels – in television production. That would endow the company with a stock of material to be offered to the growing number of cable, terrestrial and satellite broadcasters. Chrysalis acquired the outstanding half of Red Rooster and bought a 50 per cent stake in Stand and Deliver Productions. *The Financial Times*, December 1993, estimated that of the 300 or so independent TV production companies only about a dozen will make steady profits and that in the long term the sector will shake down to around ten major independent production groups. Chrysalis clearly intends to be one of them.

Half year results to February 1994 showed reduced pre-tax profits but a substantial boost to retained profits having taken into account minority interests. The group had invested heavily in new artists and both songwriter and artist advances. The Echo Special projects label had been set up as well as a new publishing company for contemporary composers AE Copyrights (with Air-Edel).

David Puttnam became the second non-executive director in September, and in October Nick Watkins resigned as a director to head a management buy-out of its multimedia and in-flight television interests. (Chrysalis kept 15 per cent.) Watkins had joined the company in 1989 to help refocus its business and felt that he had succeeded to the point where he did not feel that Chrysalis had a place for him any longer.

Its focus is now on the music business – which it re-entered last year – and on television broadcasting activities. Watkins believes both sides of the business require managers with a creative background, 'I'm more of a corporate suit', he says.

(*Financial Times*, 8/10/93)

In October the company was awarded a regional FM licence for the West Midlands for an adult orientated service to be called Heart FM. Richard Huntingford, Chrysalis' Development Director, stated that 'along with Chrysalis' 18.7% stake in Metro Radio, the new station will form the basis for a new core division at the group. "We want to build ourselves into a major player in UK commercial radio"' (*Daily Telegraph*, 12/10/93).

In one sense Chrysalis has come almost full circle given their desire to again run a record company but they are well aware of and very keen to take advantage of multimedia operations and complementary broadcasting opportunities. Can Chris Wright and his team 25 years on create and sustain a viable record company in an industry so unlike that of the 1960s? That will, of course, depend upon his character and skills, his ability to find a strategic niche and the lessons learnt from the past. This section concludes with quotations from three recent articles which attempt to get close to his character, or at least as close as anyone will get in public!

On Chris Wright himself:

But Wright likes his independence. Despite what he might say he likes his stock market quote and he enjoys business. Without that buzz life would have little meaning. In some ways he has no choice. The stock market constantly refuses to value Chrysalis at anywhere near its break-up value. But it has always been that way because Chrysalis's biggest and worst asset is its chairman. On the one hand, he is a whiz at the music business and has a deep understanding and knowledge of copyrights, which means that Chrysalis's intellectual value (far more valuable than property and other tangible assets these days) keeps growing and growing. He provides the perfect entrepreneurial drive at the top of the company. But Wright himself will admit that he is no administrator and probably hates management. He is also a softie deep down and often lacks the final cut and thrust a businessman at the top of any company requires in the 1990s. But Chris Wright puts his money where his mouth is. He is not the sort to walk away – all his wealth is tied up in the company.

(*BusinessAge*, 1/10/92)

Wright's decisiveness secured the Italian Football deal. Neil Duncanson, Head of Chrysalis Sport, then ran straight into Wright's office 'We can have the Italian footy, but it will cost us £750,000 and they need to know by 5pm today'. Wright looked at his watch. It was 3.55pm in London – 4.55pm in Rome. 'I thought for, oh, all of ten seconds, and said, "Go for it",' he recounts. After he left I started working out who we would sell it to.

(*Independent on Sunday*, 7/2/93)

... Wright, a tall, balding and imposing figure, with a reputation both for indecisiveness and not suffering fools gladly, and an enthusiasm for music more than matched by one for sports ... The entrepreneurial, independent minded Wright, a football and tennis fanatic whose myriad of interests outside of the music business stretch as far as a string of racehorses bred by himself ...

(*Music Business International*, Vol. 3, No. 4, 1993)

From fellow director George Martin:

He puts his money where his mouth is and I applaud him for that. He is that rare combination of sound business manager and gambler. He thinks about things carefully and takes calculated risks. And if more people were prepared to take risks the business would be in a healthier state than it is now. It beats sitting safely behind a desk counting numbers and making predictions. If justice is done then fortune will favour the brave.

(*Music Business International*, Vol. 3, No. 4, 1993)

On the new record company:

There is ample room for a creatively led record company in a market that is becoming increasingly polarised towards the multimedia multinational companies. A clear window of opportunity exists for an independent record company. We are a creatively led music, media and communications group and now the solid foundations have been laid we shall be uniquely placed when the recession does end to take advantage of the opportunities.

> The second coming of Chrysalis, a quarter of a century on, will be inexorably linked to the multimedia world the music business is now part and parcel of.
>
> The record company will start small and grow organically. That is why Steve Lewis is here. We want a marriage of the old Chrysalis and Virgin philosophies linked into the economic realism of the multimedia 90s.
>
> *(Music Business International*, Vol. 3, No. 4, 1993)

On lessons learnt:

> We have no intention of repeating the mistakes of last time. We are not going for the same kind of US operation with massive infrastructure and overheads. We shall not be looking at having manufacturing and distribution facilities in territories like Australia and Brazil ... In the old Chrysalis we felt like we needed to be in the US, with offices in New York and LA. But you do not need to have a presence in these places, where you need to be is in the charts. Chart success is the exposure you need.
>
> *(Music Business International*, Vol. 3, No. 4, 1993)

> We sold the first half [of Chrysalis Records] to EMI for what we thought was a lot of money. Circumstances later proved that it was not a lot of money ... We'd have been better off selling our fruit machines.
>
> *(Independent on Sunday*, 7/2/93)

BRIEF INDUSTRY BACKGROUND

The core business of a record company is simply the exploitation of musical copyright either as an item in itself or converted into a mechanical, that is a playable, form. In the latter case revenue is earned both by selling the playable format and by receiving payment when it is played in public. Organizations exist to monitor and recoup royalties in respect of public performances. Companies are concerned with the exploitation of 'rights', be they musical rights, visual rights or printed rights, and their strategy should be one of maximizing the returns from such intellectual property. There are several operational strategies to achieve this, a company might want to become vertically integrated from production to distribution, or to set up joint ventures or to be involved in only one part of the process. To use a computer analogy, hardware producers may decide to become the owners of software or vice versa. Clearly Sony has decided to do just this whilst Thorn-EMI has always declined to be involved in the hardware side. Since everything apart from innate talent can be subcontracted there is no need to have recording, manufacturing or distribution facilities.

The nature of the product is such that a world rather than national market is crucial. Hence the importance of the United States which is the largest market, followed by Japan, Germany, the UK and France in order of importance. Such international trade rarely consists of the physical shipment of product but rather the selling of the right to exploit an artist or music in a given territory. In order to ensure a stable supply of exploitable rights record companies will endeavour to contract artists for a given period of time such that they have the opportunity to recoup their investment in the artist. There is no such thing as a standard contract but most companies will try to contract for around six albums. The George Michael case in 1993 has given us a great deal of insight into the nature of the relationship. Finally the successful record company will seek to contract a mix of established, middle ranking and new artists so that it can cross subsidize new acts and ensure continuance of revenues.

The role of technology can easily be overstated – information super highways, multimedia, virtual reality, digitization and so on are on their own irrelevant. Whether music is reproduced mechanically on a wax disc or vinyl seven-inch record is of no consequence unless the new format delivers new customers due to better quality or cheaper and more convenient access. The industry has been and still is littered with technically excellent but unloved and unadopted formats. Whilst ever hardware and software companies are separate and striving for competitive advantage this is inevitable; however, there have been decisive technological advances. Key advances for this business are:

- increasingly more convenient methods of recording and playing back music, from easily broken 78 rpm records post Second World War to the smaller, convenient and virtually indestructible compact disc and minidisc;
- the ability to produce audio and visual tape recordings of a quality, convenience and cost that is attractive to the domestic consumer;
- the development of cheap and powerful personal computers, particularly for multimedia applications;
- the use of digital rather than analogue techniques to record and reproduce visual or audio signals, both for consumers and the originators of the material;
- the development of transmission systems from traditional terrestrial based systems to satellite and cable transmission, and equally the impact of digital techniques such as digital broadcasting and digital compression which enables the signal carrier to be used far more intensively and hence yield gains in cost and choice;
- the potential for the consumer to be able to make digital recordings.

Thus profit is available either from the provision of the hardware or the software. Hardware companies need not be software providers and vice versa, but hardware success and software availability is linked. Thorn-EMI has become a major owner and controller of music software but feels no desire to manufacture the hardware. Sony, on the other hand, who are primarily hardware manufacturers desire to control audio and video software as well. One might speculate that this is due to their unhappy experience with the technically superior Betamax video tape system which lost market share to the reputedly technically inferior VHS system. As Philips can well testify, this business is not about the best system – whilst they revolutionized the industry with the development of compact audio cassettes they have failed to do so with some other equally innovative technologies.

Along with these technical changes the industry is being driven by economic and commercial forces such as changing demographics and consumer expectations, the emergence of new markets, and the liberalization of broadcasting regulations and access rules. Key players in this business are becoming increasingly multifunctional and global. Local markets and tastes and the need to be proactive not reactive in spotting niches will ensure that there is a need for the smaller, creative and independent producer of repertoire.

This section concludes with a brief overview of the recorded music market in the UK and some comments on amusement machines since both these represent key areas for the understanding of Chrysalis Group Plc. Record sales in 1993 in the UK of £785.7m were about 13 per cent up on 1992 figures. The industry is cyclical – in real value terms industry sales have fallen since 1989 and have still to return to that level. The data in Table 15.2 show constant value (deflated by the Retail Price Index) of trade deliveries.

Table 15.2 UK sales of all recorded music formats, trade deliveries, 1972–93 (deflated by RPI)

1972	1972 = 100	69.4	
1973		95.6	
1974		109.6	
1975		101.5	
1976		93.8	
1977		91.5	
1978		108.5	
1979		101.7	
1980		81.6	
1981		75.1	
1982		72.5	
1983		73.6	
1984		80.0	1984 = 100
1985		85.3	107.5
1986		94.3	117.9
1987			140.5
1988			155.4
1989			160.2
1990			145.8
1991			144.1
1992			135.6
1993			151.5

Source: Monopolies Commission, Cm 2599, 1994, BPI.

Compact discs are now the best selling format in history and the CD single market is worth about half that of the traditional singles format. In 1992 singles accounted for 11 per cent of total sales, vinyl albums 3.5 per cent, cassette albums 29 per cent, CD albums 56.5 per cent. Compilation albums comprising mainly of back catalogue which traditionally enjoy lower royalty payments account for almost 20 per cent of album sales. Sales have a seasonal element with 30–40 per cent of the product sold in the fourth quarter leading up to Christmas. Pop music remains the most popular musical category (45 per cent of sales) followed by Rock (15 per cent), Classical (12 per cent) and MOR (10 per cent). Tastes and purchase behaviour vary with age and demographic characteristics. A survey commissioned from Gallup by the BPI indicates that young people buy more records than other groups. Sixteen to twenty-four-year-olds comprise only 16 per cent of the population (aged 16 and over) but buy 27 per cent of albums and 39 per cent of singles. So not surprisingly 35 per cent of album sales can be categorized as Pop, 24 per cent as Rock, with Classical and MOR each taking 9 per cent of sales. However, these sub-markets are commercially important, for example, whilst the 45 plus age group is under-represented in terms of purchasing records, since they comprise 47 per cent of the population aged 16 and over but only account for 27 per cent of album purchases and 21 per cent of singles purchases, they are still an important source of revenue.

Work by Manchester Business School, Belifante and Davis in America and the Monopolies Commission in the UK indicates that the important variables are:

- advertising
- age
- artist loyalty
- artist status (evidenced by chart success of last recording)
- audio equipment type and ownership
- current chart position
- disposable income
- fashion
- formats
- gross domestic product
- music press
- price and discounts
- quality
- radio airplay
- seasonality
- sub-market appeal reflected by specialist charts
- substitutes
- television exposure of artist
- word of mouth

Whilst there are around 600–700 small to very small independent record companies, about 500 music publishing ventures and around 4,250 retail outlets selling records in the UK, the industry is dominated by major suppliers in publishing, production and distribution. However, competition generated between the existing companies, the relative ease of entry and the absence of heavy sunk costs due to subcontracting arrangements ensures that excessive profits are not earned. Indeed, given that this is a high-risk industry, the average rates of return are relatively modest. Using PBIT as a percentage of revenue to measure the average for the five major record companies has fallen from 7.1 per cent in 1989 to 2.8 per cent in 1992 but (at the time of the calculations) was expected to almost double in 1993.

By definition most record releases fail. In 1991, a fairly typical year, only 300 out of 10,800 new album releases made it into the Top 40. Most singles make a loss for the company but are still seen as a way to market artists and to secure sales of profitable album formats (including cassettes and CDs). Singles can cost between £50,000 to £100,000 to market. In 1986 the average chart life of a Top 75 single was 6.5 weeks; by 1992 this had dropped to 4.2 weeks. In 1992 the average album, if such a thing exists, sold fewer than 5,000 copies across all formats and the average sales per single was just under 11,000 copies. This average masks the wide difference between success and failure – a single such as Whitney Houston's 'I Will Always Love You' selling in the order of one million copies, and George Michael's first solo album, *Faith*, which has sold close on 14 million copies. An album charting at Number One for a week will sell around 67,000 units, while an album at Number One Hundred will sell just under 2,000 copies.

Whilst the next logical step would be to compare volume, price and cost data, the latter is exceptionally unreliable as the recent debate in the UK on CD prices has shown. A crude indication of costs involved in this business can be drawn from the 1993 Monopolies and Mergers Commission Report: for a full price CD selling at £12.99, VAT represents 17.5 per cent; retailer gross margin 30 per cent; manufacturing costs 10 per cent; mechanical royalties, artists royalties and licence fees 15 per cent; leaving 30 per cent to cover distribution, marketing administrative costs and supporting A&R activities. Given that there are full-price, mid-price and budget segments, and that artists' royalties vary substantially depending upon the relative bargaining power of the artist, one needs to be particularly cautious about such data.

The income generating potential from music publishing rights should never be under-estimated – witness the multiples of earnings, assets and sales that sellers of music catalogues can obtain. To illustrate this, Polygram's acquisition of Motown has given it 30,000 back catalogue recordings. Thorn-EMI in 1993 agreed a $70 million deal to exploit Michael Jackson's ATV catalogue which is notable for holding the publishing rights of most of The Beatles songs.

A more detailed breakdown of the industry structure is given in Table 15.3.

Table 15.3 Industry structure: UK majors

The top five majors 1993	%	The top music publishers 1992/93[1]	%	The top five retailers 1992	%
EMI Records Ltd And Virgin Records Ltd	23.8	Warner Chappell Music Ltd	20	W.H. Smith Group Plc (W.H. Smith)	8.1
Polygram UK Holdings Plc (Polygram)	21.3	EMI Music Publishing Ltd	20	Our Price Limited (Our Price) (subsidiary of W.H. Smith)	18.5
Warner Music UK Ltd (Warner)	10.3	Polygram Music Ltd	11	Woolworth's Plc (Woolworth's)	15.0
Sony Music Entertainment (UK) Ltd (Sony)	9.6	MCA Music Ltd	9	HMV UK Limited	13.5
BMG Records (UK) Ltd (BMG)	7.0	Carlin Music Corporation; Sony Music Publishing; BMG Music; Zomba Music Publishing; Chrysalis Music Ltd;	20	Virgin Retail Ltd (Virgin Retail) (at that time by 50% owned W.H. Smith Ltd)	4.2
		All Boys Music Ltd	20		
		Others	20		

Source: Monopolies Commission, Cm 2599, 1993.

1. Gallup survey, published in *Music Week*, 7/8/93, to determine source of top 100 singles and top 50 albums in previous 12 months

The fruit machine, or more formally the amusement with prizes (AWP), business has always been a difficult market in which to succeed and has become more so from 1990 onwards. It is heavily regulated both in respect of maximum charge per play and the prize level; these aspects are regulated by the Home Office who carry out three-yearly reviews. Machines have a very short life – at best no more than four years, at worst only two. Additionally, machines usually spend no more than 3–6 months in their first prime site; subsequently they are rented out to increasingly less salubrious and profitable locations. At present payout is set at 70 pence in the pound leaving the operator with 30 pence. Set against this margin are not only the factors above but also that the most popular and lucrative sites – public houses – are themselves declining and under financial pressure due to structural changes in their industry. Most players are not gamblers in the true sense but spend some money on an AWP machine as part of a night out at the pub. So even factors such as a good summer which induces drinkers into the beer garden can cause a marked reduction in profits. By 1992 Chrysalis-MAM was one of the six key suppliers in the industry with a 5 per cent market share. The others were Kunick, 16 per cent; Rank 14 per cent; Bass 11 per cent; Stretton 4 per cent; and Brent Walker 3 per cent. Yet, as can be seen from Appendix 15.1, managed successfully it can be a profitable business.

APPENDIX 15.1
CHRYSALIS GROUP PLC: FINANCIAL AND RELATED DATA

Table 15.4 Chrysalis Group Plc: Percentage[1] contribution to turnover and profit/(loss) before taxation, 1984–88

Activity	1984[2]		1985		1986		1987		1988	
	Turnover	Profit	Turnover	Profit	Turnover	Profit	Turnover	Profit	Turnover	Profit
Records & Music Publishing	64	62	34	3	51	44.5				
Facilities Management	4	11	8	26	5	(1.85)	4.5	2.6		
Hotels			14	25	9	8.4	3	2.5		
Juke Boxes & Amusement Machines	} 23	18	31	74	21	20	18.4	31	23.3	60
Agency and Promotion	3	4	4	3	3	1				
Other	} 6	5	7	(36)	2	3.7				
Property Development			1.5	5	10	24	11	19	0.21	(0.02)
Records, Music Publishing & Entertainment							63	45		
Records: USA									20	(63)
Records: UK and non-USA									24	31
Other Musical & Entertainment Activities									21	46
Audio Facilities									4.5	16
Wholesale Export[3]										
Television/ Communications (post 1989 Communications and Media)									7	10
Corporate[3]										

1. Percentage is percentage of overall turnover or percentage of overall profit or loss. Errors in summing are due to rounding.
2. 1984 is a pro forma estimate in the offer for sale document, i.e. if the merged company had existed in that year.
3. See Table 15.5.

Source: Annual Reports.

Table 15.5 Chrysalis Group Plc: Percentage[1] contribution to turnover and profit/(loss) before taxation, 1989–92

Activity	1989		1990		1991		1992	
	Turnover	Profit	Turnover	Profit	Turnover	Profit	Turnover	Profit
Records & Music Publishing[2]								
Facilities Management[2]								
Hotels[2]								
Juke Boxes & Amusement Machines	26.3	17	22	26	23	(14.5)	26	(33)
Agency and Promotion[2]								
Other[2]								
Property Development	6.6	(14)	2.79	(20)	2	(13)	8.3	(6)
Records, Music Publishing & Entertainment[2]								
Records: USA	5	(129)	12	(43)	} 27.5	} (41)	} 10	} (3)
Records: UK and non-USA	23.5	7.1	21	89				
Other Musical & Entertainment Activities	20	15	22.4	30	11	13	13	3.6
Audio Facilities	3.1	4	2.75	5	1.6	(9)	1.6	(7)
Wholesale Export[2]					19	9.5	23	7
Television/ Communications (post 1989 Communications and Media)	15.6	0.46	16	12	15	(29)	17	(36)
Corporate				0.75	1.2	(16)		

1. Percentage is percentage of overall turnover or percentage of overall profit or loss. Errors in summing are due to rounding.
2. See Table 15.4.

Source: Annual Reports.

Table 15.6 Chrysalis Group Plc: Divisional structures, 1986–92

Division	Year	Principal subsidiaries and associated companies of Chrysalis Group Plc[1]
Agency and Promotion	1986	23 25 84
Facilities Management	1986	19 20 37 38 82
Hotels	1986	22
Juke Boxes and Amusement Machines	1986	21 26 37
Other	1986	31 47 63 12 28 29 30
Property Development	1986	54
Records and Music Publishing	1986	2 5 6 11 13 14 15 17 18 24 33 35 36 42 47 52 56 66 67
Facilities	1987	19 20 30 31 37 38 73 82
Juke Boxes and Amusement Machines	1987	21 26 27
Properties	1987	54
Records, Music Publishing and Entertainment	1987	2 5 6 7 11 13 14 18 24 25 29 33 35 36 42 47 52 56 63 65 66 67 77 84
MAM Leisure Group	1988	21 26 68 69 70
Properties	1988	48 49 50 54
Records, Music Publishing and Entertainment	1988	2 4 5 6 7 11 13 14 18 24 29 33 35 36 42 47 52 56 63 64 65 66 67 77 84
Television and Facilities	1988	9 16 19 20 30 31 37 38 40 53 73 76 82 83
Audio Facilities	1989	9 16 20 37 38 82
Joint Venture Record Companies	1989	4 18 56 64 65
Machines	1989	21 26 68 69 70 71
Music and Other Entertainment Activities	1989	2 5 6 7 11 13 14 24 30 31 33 34 35 36 42 43 47 52 66 67 84
Properties	1989	48 49 50 54
Television/Communications	1989	19 40 53 59 60 61 63 76 80
Audio Facilities	1990	9 16 37 38 82
Communications and Media	1990	19 44 46 59 60 61 62 63 76
Joint Venture Record Companies	1990	4 18 55 56 64 65
Machines	1990	21 26 68 70 71
Music and Entertainment	1990	2 5 6 7 11 13 14 24 30 31 32 33 34 35 36 42 43 47 52 66 67 84
Properties and Other	1990	49 50 54 69
Audio Facilities	1991	37 38 39 82
Communications and Media	1991	19 41 44 46 59 61 62 63 72 74 76
Joint Venture Record Companies	1991	4 18 55 56 64 65
Machines	1991	26 68 70 71
Music Publishing and Other Music and Entertainment	1991	2 5 6 7 8 10 13 14 24 31 32 34 35 36 42 43 47 52 66 81
Properties and Other	1991	49 50 54 69
Wholesale Export	1991	33 67
Audio Facilities	1992	37 38 39 82
Communications and Media	1992	41 44 45 51 58 59 61 62 63 72 74
Corporate	1992	43 47
Machines	1992	26 70 71
Music Publishing and Other Music and Entertainment	1992	1 3 6 7 8 10 13 14 31 32 34 35 36 42 52 57 66 75 78 79 81
Properties and Other	1992	49 50 54 69
Wholesale Export	1992	33 67

1. Numbers refer to Table 15.7

Source: Annual Reports.

Table 15.7 Chrysalis Group Plc: Associated and subsidiary companies[1] and divisional structure, 1986–92

Company	1986	1987	1988	1989	1990	1991	1992
Operations registered abroad							
Australia							
1 Chrysalis Music Publishing (Australia) Pty							•
2 MAM Music Publishing Pty Ltd	•	•	•	•	•	•	
Germany							
3 Chrysalis Music Publishing GmbH							•
4 Chrysalis Records GmbH			•	•	•	•	
5 MAM Music Publishing GmbH	•	•	•	•	•	•	
Sweden							
6 A.I.R. Music Scandinavia AB	•	•	•	•	•	•	•
USA							
7 Chrysalis Music Group Inc.	•	•	•	•		•	•
8 Chrysalis Music Holdings Inc. (Delaware)						•	•
9 Chrysalis Recording Studios Inc.			•	•	•		
10 Chrysalis Records Inc. (Delaware)						•	•
11 Chrysalis Records Inc.	•	•	•	•	•		
12 Chrysalis-Yellen Productions Inc.	•	•					
13 MAM (Music Publishing) Corp.	•	•	•	•	•	•	•
14 Management Agency & Music Publishing Inc.	•	•	•	•	•	•	•
15 Rare Blue Music Inc.	•						
16 Record Plant Inc.			•	•	•		
17 Red Admiral Music Inc.	•						
18 Terwright Records Inc.	•	•	•	•	•	•	
Domestic operations gained through reverse takeover of MAM							
19 AIR tv Facilities Ltd		•	•	•	•	•	•
20 Audio International Recording Studios Ltd	•	•	•				
21 Kenmar Leisure Ltd		•	•				
22 Kingsmead Hotels Ltd	•						
23 MAM (Agency) Ltd	•						
24 MAM (Music Publishing) Ltd	•	•	•	•		•	
25 MAM (Promotions) Ltd	•	•					
26 MAM Communication Systems Ltd	•	•	•	•		•	•
27 MAM Inn Play	•	•					
28 Minns and Crane Music Ltd	•						
29 The Ness Company Ltd	•	•	•				
30 Tughan-Crane (Music) Ltd	•	•	•	•	•		
Domestic operations registered in UK							
31 A.I.R. Edel-Associates Ltd	•	•	•	•	•	•	•
32 A.I.R.-Edel Recording Studios (formerly 20)					•	•	•
33 ACD Trading Ltd	•	•	•	•	•	•	•
34 Air Management Services Ltd					•	•	•
35 Air Music (London) Ltd	•	•	•	•	•	•	•
36 Air Music Publishing Ltd	•	•	•	•	•	•	•
37 Air Records Ltd	•	•	•	•	•	•	•
38 Air Studios Ltd	•	•	•	•	•	•	•
39 Air Studios (Lyndhurst) Ltd						•	•
40 Blackrod Interactive Services Ltd			•	•	•		
41 Blackrod						•	•
42 Chrys-A-Lee Music Ltd	•	•	•	•	•	•	
43 Chrysalis Holdings Ltd				•	•	•	•
44 Chrysalis Home Video Ltd					•	•	•
45 Chrysalis Inflight Entertainment Ltd							•
46 Chrysalis Interactive Services Ltd (formerly 80)					•	•	
47 Chrysalis Investments Ltd	•	•	•	•	•	•	
48 Chrysalis Knightsbridge Estates Ltd			•	•	•	•	
49 Chrysalis Land (Mayfair)			•	•	•	•	
50 Chrysalis Land Ltd			•	•	•	•	•
51 Chrysalis Multi Media Ltd							•
52 Chrysalis Music Ltd	•		•	•	•	•	•
53 Chrysalis News and Sports Ltd			•	•			
54 Chrysalis Properties Ltd	•	•	•	•	•	•	•
55 Chrysalis Records International Ltd					•	•	
56 Chrysalis Records Ltd	•	•	•	•		•	
57 Chrysalis Songs Ltd							•
58 Chrysalis Television Facilities Ltd							•

Table 15.7 *Continued*

Company	1986	1987	1988	1989	1990	1991	1992
59 Chrysalis Television Group Ltd				•	•	•	•
60 Chrysalis Television Ltd (formerly 83)				•	•		
61 Chrysalis Television Mobiles Ltd (formerly 73)				•	•	•	•
62 Chrysalis Television Productions Ltd (formerly 53)					•	•	•
63 Chrysalis Visual Programming Ltd	•	•	•	•	•	•	•
64 Dover Records			•	•	•	•	
65 Ensign Records Ltd		•	•	•	•	•	
66 Ian Anderson Music Ltd	•	•	•	•	•	•	•
67 Lasgo Exports Ltd	•	•	•	•	•	•	•
68 MAM Amusement Sales Ltd			•	•	•	•	•
69 MAM Inns and Restaurants Ltd			•	•	•	•	•
70 MAM Leisure Ltd			•	•	•	•	•
71 MAM Leisure (Holdings) Ltd				•	•	•	•
72 Metro Radio Group Plc						•	•
73 Recording & Production Services Ltd		•	•				
74 Red Rooster Film and Entertainment Ltd						•	•
75 Redemption Songs Ltd							•
76 REW Video Hire			•	•	•	•	
77 Showplay		•	•				
78 Speaking Books Ltd							•
79 The Hit Label Ltd							•
80 The Video Disk Company				•			
81 Tughan-Crane Music Ltd (Northern Ireland)						•	•
82 Wessex Sound Ltd	•	•	•	•	•	•	•
83 Workhouse Productions Ltd			•				
84 World Service Agency Ltd	•	•	•	•	•		

1. Principal subsidiaries as detailed in Annual Reports. Percentage owned varies between 100 per cent and 18.7 per cent.

Source: Company Annual Reports, except 1988 Extel Annual card.

Table 15.8 Chrysalis Group Plc: Some key financial data, 1985–92

Units		1985[2]	1986	1987	1988[3]	1989	1990	1991	1992
Group turnover	£000	46,253	82,872	105,769	117,025	95,590	107,380	93,396	74,400
attributable fully to the company	£000						73,495	68,345	65,968
associated companies & joint ventures	£000						34,300	25,042	8,432
Turnover attributable to USA[1]	%	13	16	21	23	8	15	11	6
Turnover attributable to UK[1]	%	87	84	79	77	92	81	84	90
Turnover attributable to Europe[1]	%						4	5	4
Gross profit (turnover less sales cost)	£000	13,002	27,084	29,313	34,999	20,113	18,802	13,840	11,913
Profit (loss) before tax	£000	[5,598] 516	5,309	7,258	1,805	11,519	5	(9,330)	5,628
Profit (loss) before tax and interest	£000							(8,118)	5,045
continuing operations	£000							(1,084)	(4,606)
on discontinued operations	£000							(7,034)	9,651
Profit (loss) after tax	£000	[3,368] 656	3,213	4,864	547	(11,502)	(395)	(8,685)	7,078
Dividends	p/share	6.95	5.6	7.0	4.0	4.0	4.0	none	none
Profit (loss) retained for financial year	£000		1,582	9,770	300	39,231	(1,935)	(8,292)	7,016
Earnings (loss) per share	p/share	3.99	12.10	17.08	1.5	(40.2)	1.6	(30.06)	26.02
Shareholders' funds	£m (a)	(a) 3	(a) 7.4	(a) 8.3	4.8	53	50	48.4	54.4
Employees (including directors)	Actual	1,495	1,529	1,251	1,226	1,104	1,078	942	844

1. Turnover attributed to regions is on all business activity.
2. 1985 figures include only six months of Chrysalis Group Ltd because of merger date and year end differences.
Figures in parenthesis adjust as if combined group has traded that year and are a better comparison.
3. 1988 is 14 months.
(a) Signifies net assets as shown on Balance Sheet, thereafter shareholders' funds.

Source: Company Annual Reports.

Table 15.9(a) Key activities as detailed in Annual Reports, 1985–87

Activity	Report for year to June 1985	Report for year to June 1986	Report for year to June 1987
Hotels	Profit growth over the previous year.	Sold to Mount Charlotte Investment Plc, another hotel chain. The capital intensive nature of hotels was not felt appropriate for the company at this stage.	
Other	Max Headroom makes a significant breakthrough.	See Records and music publishing & entertainment.	
Musical Instruments (retail supply of)	Minns and Crane Music subsidiary made losses and hence decided to discontinue this activity. Tughan Crane Music in Northern Ireland produces satisfactory profits.	Completed closure of Minns and Crane resulting in further extraordinary losses. Tughan-Crane Music continues to trade successfully.	See Facilities. See Music & Other entertainment activities.
Music Promotion and Advertising Jingles	Air-Edel Associates is the leading European producer of music for films, TV and commercials.	Air-Edel still leading European producers.	See Facilities. See Music & Other entertainment activities.
Juke Boxes and Amusement Machines	Trading successfully, high degree of acceptance of new video juke box. Re-equipment, conversion and maintenance costs have lessened the impact on profit margins from accepted and growing use of the £1 coin.	Division achieved good profit growth – main customer base is with tied brewery houses. Background music operation has been hived off as a stand–alone company and expects considerable growth. Clients include an increasing number of high street multiples. Division as a whole contributed £1.4m profits.	Integration of the management of Kenmar Leisure Ltd and MAM Inn Play bring cost and management gains. Disposal of MAM Inn Play HQ buildings. MAM Amusement Sales is set up to sell and distribute machines. MAM Communication Systems is a leading operator in background music systems.
Property Development	Active in development and dealing resulting in highly satisfactory profits	Active in Docklands – good profit of £1.68m. Other residential projects in hand.	Marginally lower profits and some concern that the market is getting overheated.
Agency and Promotion	Successful.	MAM Agency and Promotion closed and small net losses. World Service Agency Ltd which acts as a booking agent for many well known rock and pop artists continues to trade successfully. In October 1986 acquired 50 per cent of Showplay Ltd, a company new formed to arrange promotion of product launches, conferences and similar events.	See Records and music publishing & entertainment. See Music and Other entertainment.
Records and Music Publishing. See Table 15.6 for detailed changes to divisional title.	Profits of Chrysalis Group comfortably exceeding its own expectations and made up for MAM shortfall. MAM and Chrysalis music catalogues merged. Air Music Scandinavia AB in which they have a 50 per cent share increases profit.	Despite delay of major product still managed pre-tax profits of £3m. Over last two years have invested heavily in new talent and this is showing in profits and sales. Lasgo Exports pre-tax profits growth. Good contribution from compact discs, particularly in markets where no indigenous manufacturing.	Continued investment in new artists. Good results from Ensign, Cooltempo, China label (licensed). Moves distribution from Polygram to CBS. Opens record operations in Holland and Germany to complement Sweden (opened last year). Problems with American operation and senior staff changes. Lasgo has another good year. Good performance from own and the purchased MAM catalogue. World Service Agency has a quiet year. Chrysalis Visual Programming Ltd gains from the Max Headroom character but his future will be in merchandising (including Coca-Cola) not programming.
Facilities 1988 TV and Facilities 1989 on Audio Facilities	New division bringing together Air, Wessex, MAM Research Recordings and Audio International Recording Studios (50 per cent interest in partnership with Radio Luxembourg) enjoyed a successful year except for MAM Research Recordings and other TV facilities (video production facilities). Now under new management.	Problem with TV facilities showing a loss for the year. Lost an important transmission contract – relaunched as Air tv, May 1986, and now improving client base. Audio studios continue to show a profit.	Now comprises: Air and Wessex Recording Studios, Air tv and Tughan – Crane and 50 per cent interests in A.I.R.S and Air-Edel. Air tv has received significant satellite transmission contracts with MTV Europe and Scansat. Recording studios another good year despite strong competition. Investment has kept the studios in demand. RPS and REW video hire purchased. Controlling interest in Los Angeles based Record Plant Recording Studio taken. Tughan-Crane has best year yet.

Source: Company Annual Reports.

Table 15.9(b) Key activities as detailed in Annual Reports, 1988–90

Activity	Report for year to June 1988	Report for year to June 1989	Report for year to June 1990
Juke Boxes and Amusement Machines 1988 MAM Leisure Group.	Relaunched as MAM Leisure Group will move into development of small business hotels under the name MAM Inns and Restaurants.	Amusement machines a difficult market, pressure on margins on sales/distribution but sole UK/Europe distributor for Rowe Jukeboxes. MAM Communication Systems makes excellent progress. MAM Inns and Restaurants concentrated on the redevelopment of one pub in Theale.	Difficulties apparent because of recession, changing technology (CD juke boxes), competition and so on. MAM Communications Systems audiovisual operation prospers and will form a larger part of the business.
Property Development	Breaks even only.	Winding down of portfolio and no new projects anticipated.	Continued wind down of portfolio. Pub/restaurant in Theale had a disappointing year.
Records and Music Publishing	US records division suffering lower than anticipated sales and high costs. Reported loss of $7m. Max Headroom makes zero contribution. UK and European record operations ahead of budget. Cooltempo, Ensign, Dover labels successful. Opens operation in France. Chrysalis Visual Programming gained recent European contract and potential for future income albeit reduced over previous levels.	Severe losses on USA operation due to low sales activity aggravated by a combination of exceptional and adverse factors. UK division suffering slippage from some of the US artists but some pleasing UK performances. For the first time disappointing German results, management changes and new head of division. Lasgo continues good performance and addresses new markets in Asia/Middle East. All-time profit record for the publishing group. Tughan-Crane disappointing but profitable year. Air-Edel maintains its position as the market leader with 'blue chip' contracts and takes over A.I.R.S. World Service Agency faced difficult year and restructured. Sells 50 per cent of record company to Thorn-EMI.	First full year as joint venture with Thorn-EMI Plc. Considerable success and gain in international market share and resurgence of Chrysalis Record label throughout the world. Manufacturing and distribution contracted to EMI. Considerable progress in reducing the trading losses in the USA due to attention paid to cost base and all-time sales level. Lasgo continues to do well, now operating in Eastern European markets. Music publishing turnover up, profit down slightly (investment in new writers and copyrights). Increases share in Air Music Scandinavia to 75 per cent. Tughan-Crane increased profits, Air-Edel largest UK jingle producer. World Service Agency closed after disappointing year.
Facilities 1988 TV and Facilities 1989 Audio Facilities	Recording and production services living up to profit expectations and was a key component in successful bid for Football League contract. Purchased Workhouse and Blackrod which will now form the backbone of TV programmes and corporate video business. New Chrysalis TV News & Sports operation to handle the football contract and set up as springboard into sports and current affairs. Bidding to televise House of Commons through Portcullis productions. REW Video Hire relaunched and set to become market leader in broadcast and industrial equipment hire. Contract from HBO to broadcast Wimbledon. Air tv launched and has satellite transmission contracts but post production facilities in very difficult market. Air Studios had a good period whilst Wessex and A.I.R.S fought hard for business. Record Plant affected by Guild of Screen Writers strike. Air-Edel credible results again. Tughan-Crane has a successful year.	Air Studios twenty-first successful year. imminent move to new complex. Wessex studios concentrating on young, emerging rock bands. Record Plant difficult year, restructuring management team.	Building of new Air Studios commenced. Joint venture with Pioneer Electronic Corporation. Air Studios and Wessex Studios satisfactory albeit reduced contribution to divisional profits. Record Plant had a difficult year with continuing losses and its long term future is under review.
Chrysalis Communications Division (1988 onwards) Chrysalis TV Division (prior name). 1990 onwards Communications and Media.		Disappointing results but foundation for future growth. Chrysalis News & Sports continued successful relationship with Football league and LWT News contracts. New opportunities await and robust future. Chrysalis Television Mobiles synergistic benefits with Football League contract. Also significant client roster. Blackrod and Chrysalis Television maintained reputation for quality corporate programmes. Blackrod Interactive Services winning several major contracts. Chrysalis Television projects coming to fruition. Chrysalis Visual Programming (Max Headroom) revenues falling away and write-offs leading to loss. Air tv facilities uncertain year but clear future, two satellite transmission contracts will secure future. REW Video Hire – competition and limited demand led to difficult year, hopes for a more active market next year.	Restructuring, rationalization completed. Clearly defined strategy, well focused management team. Split into factual and non-factual programming. Chrysalis TV Productions an amalgamation of the Chrysalis Television News and News & Sport operations will concentrate solely on factual programmes. Joint venture with Red Rooster production company. Acquired 9.99 per cent interest in Metro Radio Plc and increased when Metro takes over Yorkshire Radio Network Plc.

Source: Company Annual Reports.

Table 15.9(c) Key activities as detailed in Annual Reports, 1991–92

Activity	Report for year to June 1991	Report for year to June 1992
Juke Box and Amusement Machines 1988 on MAM Leisure Group. 1989 on Machines.	Faced worst trade conditions for many years, despite strict overhead and capital expenditure control – losses incurred for the year. But has gained new customers. MAM Communications Systems continued to trade profitably.	Along with major competitors suffered badly in the recession. Fundamental changes to strategy and management. Concentrated sales effort into non-traditional outlets. MAM Communications Systems a substantial improvement in profits despite recession.
Property Development	Some disposals made.	Only two left and some lettings.
Records and Music Publishing From 1987 Records, Music Publishing and Entertainment; from 1989 Music and Other Entertainment Activities; from 1990 see Table 15.6.	Exceptionally quiet Christmas 1990 and despite some success in US and UK charts, overall turnover very disappointing and significant losses. Chrysalis 50 per cent share of these equal to £4.7m. After extensive discussions agreed to terminate joint venture prematurely and for EMI to acquire remaining 50 per cent earlier than anticipated. Once again increased turnover and profit for Lasgo now the core of the Wholesale Export division. In the Music Publishing and Other Music and Entertainment division, Chrysalis Music Publishing has a successful year with improved turnover and profits. Chrysalis Music Inc. performs well. Tughan-Crane and Air-Edel unspectacular but a satisfactory contribution given the adverse trading environment.	Restrictions placed post EMI sale on participation in record business other than in compilations and spoken word, so launched the Hit Label and the Speaking Book Company as a joint venture. Secured services of Steve Lewis to become head of new Music Division when non-compete restrictions terminate in 1993. UK turnover and gross margins maintained but profitability down due to higher costs. Expanded the book and magazine side of Lasgo since they enjoy a higher profit margin compared to audio and video. Good first quarter 92/93 performance. Music publishing income held up but investment on new signings reduced products. Air-Edel significantly improved contribution. Tughan-Crane made a loss.
Facilities	New Air Studio complex scheduled to open September 1992. Profits and turnover down slightly but this quality sector of the sound recording market remains relatively healthy. Wessex, however, made small loss due to its particular customer profile. Record Plant sold in February 1991.	Lyndhurst Hall audio complex opened December 1992. Air Studio level of activity as would be expected ran down prior to change over. Wessex made a small loss.
Chrysalis Communications Division Chrysalis TV Division. 1989 Communication and Media.	Paralysis gripped the Independent Television Sector up to the Channel 3 franchise awards and economic conditions made the trading environment difficult. Participated in two TV franchise applications and were unsuccessful but a nominated programme supplier for others. Air tv used quiet trading period to upgrade facilities. Chrysalis Mobiles affected by demise of BSB but regained Football League contract and five-year SIS (race course broadcasting) contract. REW hit by recession and sold. Blackrod remains at forefront of corporate communications. Chrysalis Interactive Services continue to develop software for CD-I market. Chrysalis Multi-Media formed from Blackrod/Chrysalis Interactive Services merger. Increased stake in Metro Radio to 19.55 per cent.	Year of development and substantial investment which materially contributed to the reported loss but will allow the Division to emerge as a profitable core business for the future. Chrysalis Television Facilities and Chrysalis Television Mobiles gained long-term contracts from Kanal 6 & SIS – which will go a long way to underwrite fixed costs. Post production facilities reduced due to poorer trading environment. Chrysalis Television Productions Italian Football for C4 success, light entertainment contracts gained. Red Rooster Film and TV Entertainment notable success. Chrysalis Mobiles at the leading edge but market affected by recession and recent restructuring to meet challenges. Chrysalis Home Video label continues to act as conduit and obtainer of material in own right. Chrysalis Inflight Entertainment established in 1992 to service total in-flight media has won first major contract. All costs of setting up that business were expensed during the year.

Source: Company Annual Reports.

Table 15.10 Headline statements and prospects for the coming year as stated in their Annual Reports 1986–92

1986

I am convinced that the current year's results will show a substantial advance on last year.

I have already referred to our extensive artist investment programme as a result of which I feel more confident than ever before about the depth of talent in our artist roster. With all the divisions in the Group trading ahead of budget, I am convinced that the current year's results will show a substantial advance on last year. Your Board intends to use the proceeds of the recent Kingsmead Hotels disposal as the basis for expansion and to that end we have identified and are pursuing a number of potential leisure based acquisitions. Finally, shareholders will be aware that our continuing success is entirely due to the enthusiasm and commitment of our artists, directors and staff and on your behalf I would like to thank them all.

1987

The past year has again been a very successful one, both in terms of the results and the work that has been done in laying a base for future growth.

For reasons already indicated, the first half of the current year will not, in profit terms, be as buoyant as the first half of last year. Whilst I still anticipate continued growth in our overall annual profits, these will clearly be weighted towards the second half. I have already listed important record product coming later in the year and I believe that we have the right people, structure and strategies to get the best in sales and profit terms from these records.

Elsewhere in the Group the current year is one for steady growth on levels of success already achieved, together with a programme of strategic acquisitions.

Finally, two Group Board Directors retired during the year, Bill Smith, former MD and co-founder of MAM, and Ken Chappellow, founder and former MD of Kenmar Leisure. To them and our artists, directors and staff, I would like, on your behalf, to say thank you.

1988

The poor profit performance in the period under review, primarily in America, will undoubtedly affect the first half of the current year. The Board are reviewing the basis of our US operation and it is to be hoped that this will lead to an upturn in profitability in the second half. The television division looks set to become a key element in the Group's growth.

1989

The losses in America have been the dominant factor in the Group's trading problems for several years. It became clear during the financial year that proactive and strategic measures were demanded to rectify the situation and to bring about a state of change.

The sale of 50% of Chrysalis Records has increased our net worth and eliminated our net gearing providing us with the security of a sheltered state from which we now feel confident that we are ready to emerge and develop our core activities.

The financial benefits of the THORN-EMI Plc transaction and our healthy balance sheet, coupled with the recent management changes, will I believe provide an excellent foundation for the successful development and expansion of the Chrysalis Group into the 1990s. In this regard, your Board are currently investigating a number of potential acquisitions and projects both in existing and new areas of activity. However, with interest rates at their current high levels and doubts about the economy as a whole, we will take a cautious and prudent approach to investment opportunities.

The severe problems of the US Record Company and the long-term nature of our efforts to rebuild a successful operation mean that its profitability is unlikely to be restored for some while and certainly not within the current financial year. I am confident, however, that good progress has already been made in remedying the position and that its level of trading losses for the year will be significantly reduced. Our joint venture arrangements with THORN-EMI Plc will in addition reduce the Group's exposure to these losses.

The first quarter's trading from the UK Record Company has been extremely encouraging and well above expectations with some considerable chart success. With other companies in the Group presently performing close to expectations, and with the very positive impetus provided by new management, I am optimistic for the group's trading prospects for 1990.

The Spring of 1990 will also see Chrysalis moving to a new corporate headquarters. We have recently purchased the freehold of a 32,000 square foot office building in Holland Park, London W10 which will enable us to bring together our Records, Publishing and Communications activities under one roof. The building will provide an ideal environment for the Group to become one of the leading media and communications businesses of the 1990s at the cutting edge of creativity. I look forward to the opportunity of welcoming shareholders in the future to our new home.

1990

The financial year to 31st August 1990 has seen the Chrysalis Group Plc return to profitability after the heavy losses suffered in the previous year. The partnership with THORN-EMI Plc and the management changes effected towards the latter part of last year have played a major role in this turnaround and I am confident that we now have a solid base upon which to build for the future.

The past year has been one of major reorganization and restructuring throughout the Group, resulting in a number of substantial one-off costs which have been expensed in the period. Whilst during the year good progress has been made by laying firm foundations for the long-term future, the current economic recession in our major markets makes it difficult to be optimistic about short-term trading prospects.

Initial trading results for the early part of the current year have been satisfactory. However, it is clear that the full year's results will be influenced by economic factors beyond our control and will depend on our continued ability to develop and successfully establish new products and services.

The Group has recently moved its corporate headquarters, bringing UK Records, Publishing and Communications activities under one roof at Bramley Road, London W10. We are already reaping the benefits of this and I am confident that we have in place a winning team of management and staff to see the Group successfully through the current uncertain economic climate into the 1990s.

1991

In the light of the Record company disposal, the Board has undertaken a long-term review of the Group's strategic direction and investment plans. This includes a major expansion of our television production and music publishing interests and in due course, once non-compete restriction periods have expired, a return to the record business.

This strategy, which will require substantial investment over the next few years, will be heavily geared towards the longer term and focused on areas which are generally thought to involve high levels of operational risk and earnings volatility.

As you will recall it was announced on 12th November 1991, that subject to the completion of the Record Company disposal, I was considering making an offer for those shares in the Company that I do not already own. Accordingly, together with my colleagues on

Table 15.10 *Continued*

the Board, I have been discussing the feasibility of making such an offer with my advisers in order to provide shareholders with an opportunity to realize their investment before the implementation of our plans for the long-term development of the Group. I hope to be able to inform you shortly of the outcome of these discussions.

The current financial year has started slowly with trading conditions remaining difficult. The disposal or closure of a number of the loss-making businesses will undoubtedly benefit overall future results; however, it is difficult at present to foresee any significant upturn in trading for the remaining companies ahead of the economic recovery in our major markets.

1992

Our strategy is to create an integrated music, media and communications group, where a blend of creative flair, technical excellence and innovation provides the firm foundation for growth in profits, earnings and long-term capital value.

The current year has started slowly, although we are now beginning to see clear signs of improved trading from some of our Group companies. The first quarter's results, in particular those from Lasgo and from our Television Productions and Facilities companies, are encouraging. However, the conservative accounting treatment we apply to the continuing long-term investments in our Television, Music Publishing and new record label interests will inevitably impact on the Group's short-term profits. Furthermore the state of the amusement machine industry continues to be of considerable concern and it is therefore difficult at this stage, despite the early encouraging signs, to predict with any certainty an optimistic outcome for the year as a whole.

Source: Company Annual Reports except 1988 which is Extel Annual Card.

Table 15.11 Key acquisitions, disposals and joint ventures 1985–94

Date	Acquisition	Reason	Terms & financed by	Disposal/Joint venture	Reason
December 1985	Lasgo Exports Ltd	Wholesaler of pre-recorded music and video	75%, cash & shares & profit-related final sum depending up profit contribution. Fully owned May 1989		
May 1986				MAM Agency and MAM Promotions	Following departure of director
June 1986				Minns and Crane	Continues to make losses
September 1986	Showplay Ltd	Provision of video and audio services for events and conferences	50%, shares		
October 1986	Ensign Records Ltd	Good stable of artists and above average hit rate	100%, cash		
December 1986				Kingsmead Hotels Ltd	Nature of the business
March 1987	AIR tv Facilities	Acquisition of remaining 25%	Cash		
April 1987	Recording and Production Services Ltd	Nottingham based TV facilities and outside broadcast company	100%, cash and shares & profit-related final sum		
October 1987	REW Video Hire	Industrial and commercial video company	55%, cash		
December 1987	Record Plant Inc.	Los Angeles based recording studio, good reputation to build on for growth	Controlling interest (51%), option to acquire balance, cash		
March 1988	Workhouse Productions Ltd, Blackrod Ltd	Income flow and in preparation for future role in commercial broadcasting	Cash and loan stock		
May 1989	Remaining 12.5% of Lasgo Exports Ltd		Cash and loan stock		
August 1989	Remaining 49% of Record Plant Inc. acquired		Cash	Chrysalis Record companies, 50% interest sold to EMI for mainly cash but some Thorn-EMI loan stock. Adjustment to price depending upon profit outcome.	Proactive response to trading problems in North America whilst maintaining an active presence in North America
July 1990	9.99% interest in ordinary share capital of Metro Radio Group. With Metro's takeover of Yorkshire Radio Network in November 1990 subscribed to further shares and holding increased to 19.55%	To broaden the base of its activities and to be ready to capitalize on future opportunities	Cash		
September 1990				Sold interest in TV premises, certain plant & equipment to M Blakstad.	Mr Blakstad decided to return to independent production in the provinces.
				World Service Agency Ltd ceases trading	Steady decline in the level of business
October 1990	Further 25% of Air Music Scandinavia AB acquired and option for remaining 25% at end of 1993				
December 1990				With Red Rooster Films for joint venture television production company to be known as Red Rooster Film and Television Entertainment Ltd. Cash for 50% share and loan facility made available up to £1m	To develop drama, light entertainment and children's programming

Table 15.11 *Continued*

Date	Acquisition	Reason	Terms & financed by	Disposal/Joint venture	Reason
December 1990				With Pioneer Electronic Corporation and Air Studios Ltd to develop Lyndhurst Hall London as replacement for Air Studios in Oxford Street	End of lease at original Air Studios at Oxford Street and desire to continue to have a state-of-the-art facility with the additional multimedia theatre
February 1991				Record Plant Inc. ceased activities and premises and plant sold for $3.5m	
May 1991	50% of Giltbrook Studios acquired for circa £250,000				
September 1991				Giltbrook ceases trading	
October 1991				REW Video Hire Ltd	
November 1991				Other 50% of record company to EMI	Exceptional losses from the venture. Opportunity to use funds for long term investment
May 1992				Joint venture music publishing company – Redemption Songs	With former Rough Trade executives Geoff Travis and Richard Thomas
July 1992				The Hit Label and The Speaking Book Company	EMI non-compete agreement allowed them to operate in compilations and spoken word. Set up with John & Phil Cokell who had developed the highly successful Dover Records Division

Date	Event and commentary
April 1993	Echo Record Label set up with Steve Lewis
May 1993	The Hit Label issues a tie in Album 'The Legendary Joe Bloggs Dance Album' for Joe Bloggs goods
July 1993	Chrysalis and Cadbury Schweppes co-fund sponsorship for Chris Bailey, the English tennis player
August 1993	Announces the closure of MAM Leisure, with the exception of MAM Communications Systems
August 1993	Carlsberg Lager is to sponsor C4s Italian Football coverage produced by Chrysalis (Gazetta Italia and Football Italia)
August 1993	Joint venture with Unique Television to develop advertiser supplied entertainment programming for TV stations
August 1993	Michael Pilsworth joins as Managing Director and Chief Executive of newly created visual entertainment division which will group together the TV production company, the home video operation and Red Rooster Film
September 1993	Appoints sponsorship consultancy Wood Lynds to handle on-air sponsorship, off-air merchandising and licensing activities for their sports programming. Chrysalis have produced about 360 hours of such in the last year
September 1993	Pony Cannon, the music division of Fujisankei, the Japanese communications group, buys a 25% stake in Echo Records for £11.7m
October 1993	Chrysalis is awarded a regional FM licence for the West Midlands and will run an adult orientated service – Heart FM. Catchment, area is around 2.5m adults. '... the new station will form the basis for a new core division at the group ... we want to build ourselves into a major player in UK commercial radio' Richard Huntingford, *Daily Telegraph*, 12/10/93. Their business plan records a £1.25m investment and operational breakeven after two years
October 1993	Nick Watkins resigns as a director to head a management buyout of its multimedia and in-flight interests. Chrysalis will retain a 15% interest
May 1994	*Sunday Telegraph* 8/5/94 believes Chrysalis to have acquired a 25% stake in Transworld, the publishing and ILR company
May 1994	Ryan Giggs, Manchester United, Bobby Charlton and Chrysalis Sport to make six half-hour TV programmes on soccer skills. Video and book as well
May 1994	Wire TV, a cable company, gain secondary rights to Wimbledon tennis and Chrysalis Sport produce programming for them

Source: Company Annual Reports, McCarthy.

SECTION 6

Industrial products

Case 16   Volkswagen Group
           I.D. Turner, Henley Management College

Case 17   Fisons Plc
           J.R. Anchor, University of Huddersfield

Case 18   Redland Plc
           B. Kenny and E.C. Lea, University of Huddersfield

Case 19   ICI and Hanson – a contrast in styles
           J.R. Anchor, University of Huddersfield

Volkswagen Group

Ian D. Turner

HISTORICAL BACKGROUND

Volkswagen has long enjoyed a reputation as a manufacturer of high quality cars, particularly in the volume car market. Historically the company owes its origins to Hitler's obsession with producing a 'People's Car' or 'Volkswagen'. A factory was purpose built in Germany in 1938 to manufacture cars to a design by Ferdinand Porsche. Following the war, and postwar reconstruction under British direction, ownership of the plant was vested jointly in the Federal Government of Germany and the provincial government of Lower Saxony. In 1961 60 per cent of the shares in VW were sold to the general public. The remaining 40 per cent were divided equally between the federal and provincial governments. In 1988 the federal government disposed of most of its shares leaving only 17.6 per cent in public ownership. Nevertheless, the pattern of share ownership and Germany's co-determination laws ensure that VW's supervisory board contains representatives from the regional government, the banks and the trade unions.

In a postwar world which required vast numbers of robust, practical, utility vehicles to replace wartime losses and satisfy the demands of a rapidly expanding international economy, VW was ideally placed. Under the leadership of the legendary Heinrich Nordhoff the company took full advantage of this opportunity. Nordhoff's strategy was three-pronged. At home he achieved market dominance in the mass car segment. This was complemented by aggressive exporting, initially to other European countries, but by the mid 1950s to the USA as well. Finally, Volkswagen became a true multinational company with the location of plants overseas, initially in South America. All this was achieved with one main product: the Volkswagen Beetle.

Favourable world conditions and a product which rapidly caught people's imaginations ensured that Nordhoff's strategy was phenomenally successful in the 1950s and 1960s. The Beetle became the most successful car of all time. By the end of that decade, however, it had become clear that the world was changing. The public was demanding better standards of comfort, safety, economy and environmental consciousness. The transition period at VW was painful and protracted. Nordhoff was unable to make the necessary changes and his successors had to try to adjust the company's strategy to new circumstances. In 1974 the weaknesses of the company's product strategy were cruelly exposed by the energy crisis and the economic recession. VW weathered the storm but not after some hard decisions had been taken and a sizeable portion of the workforce had been laid off. In the mid 1970s a new range of products came on stream and VW's fortunes looked up again. The Polo and the Passat were adapted from existing models designed by VW's Audi subsidiary,

Table 16.1 The Volkswagen Group in figures

	1983	1984	1985	1986	1987	1988	1989	1990	1991	1992[4]
Sales (DM million)	40,089	45,671	52,202	52,794	54,635	59,221	65,352	68,061	76,315	85,403
Change on previous year in %	7	14	15	1	3	8	10	4	12	12
Domestic	14,453	14,638	16,171	18,839	22,555	22,653	23,682	26,929	36,360	39,508
Abroad	25,636	31,033	36,331	33,955	32,080	36,568	41,670	41,132	39,955	45,895
Export of domestic Group companies	15,460	20,108	24,025	23,414	22,898	24,395	27,601	28,323	28,093	33,884
Net contribution of foreign Group companies	11,812	12,864	14,698	14,127	13,080	15,961	18,256	18,242	18,809	15,412
Vehicle sales (thousand units)	2,127	2,145	2,398	2,758	2,774	2,854	2,941	3,030	3,237	3,433
Change on previous year in %	0	1	12	15	1	3	3	3	7	6
Domestic	750	708	722	838	921	848	849	945	1,264	1,211
Abroad	1,377	1,437	1,676	1,920	1,853	2,006	2,092	2,085	1,973	2,222
Production (thousand units)	2,116	2,148	2,398	2,777	2,771	2,848	2,948	3,058	3,238	3,500
Change on previous year in %	−1	2	12	16	0	3	4	4	6	8
Domestic	1,413	1,474	1,635	1,654	1,666	1,694	1,783	1,816	1,814	1,929
Abroad	703	674	763	1,123	1,105	1,154	1,165	1,242	1,424	1,571
Workforce (thousand employees)[1]	232	238	259	276	260	252	251	261	277	273
Change on previous year in %	−3	3	9	7	−6	−3	−1	4	6	−1
Domestic	156	160	170	169	170	165	161	166	167	164
Abroad	76	78	89	107	90	87	90	95	110	109
Capital investments (DM million)[2]	4,858	2,782	3,388	6,371	4,592	4,251	5,606	5,372	9,910	9,254
Change on previous year in %	−1	x	22	88	−28	−7	32	−4	84	−7
Domestic	3,476	1,889	2,508	3,849	4,000	3,546	4,477	3,016	6,311	4,853
Abroad	1,382	893	880	2,522	592	705	1,129	2,356	3,599	4,401
Additions to Leasing and rental assets (DM million)		2,021	3,217	2,738	3,318	3,447	4,069	4,419	4,961	6,139
Change on previous year in %			59	−15	21	4	18	9	12	24
Cash flow (DM million)[3]	5,207	4,081	4,558	4,285	4,874	5,018	5,412	5,701	7,133	7,004
Change on previous year in %	51	x	12	−6	14	3	8	5	25	−2
Net earnings/loss (DM million)	−215	228	596	580	598	780	1,038	1,086	1,114	147
Dividend of Volkswagen AG (DM million)	—	120	240	306	306	306	336	369	369	66
Ordinary shares (DM million)	—	120	240	240	240	240	264	297	297	54
Preferred shares (DM million)				66	66	66	72	72	72	12

1. Workforce at year end; as of 1986 average over year.
2. Up to 1983 including additions to leasing and rental assets.
3. Up to 1983 including depreciation on and disposal of leasing and rental assets.
4. SKODA, automobilová a.s. was included in the consolidated figures for the first time in 1992, for 1991 the quantitative data in respect of the abbreviated fiscal year (16 April to 31 December, 1991) have been taken into account, whereas the financial data have not been adjusted.

Source: 1992 Volkswagen Annual Report.

Table 16.2 The major companies within the Volkswagen Group

VOLKSWAGEN	SEAT	SKODA	AUDI	OVERSEAS OPERATIONS	FINANCIAL SERVICES	FINANCING COMPANIES
VOLKSWAGEN AG Wolfsburg Subscribed capital: DM 1,664,425,000	**SEAT, S.A.** Barcelona, Spain ESP 84,000,000,000 99.99%	**SKODA, automobilová a.s.** Mladá Boleslav, Czech Republic CSK 9,642,000,000 31%	**AUDI AG** Ingolstadt DM 215,000,000 98.99%	**Volkswagen of America, Inc.** Auburn Hills, Mi., USA USD 242,422,222.92 100%	**V.A.G. Bank GmbH** Brunswick DM 600,000,000 100% Volkswagen Finanz GmbH	**Coordination Center Volkswagen S.A.** Brussels, Belgium BEC 14,000,000,000 60% Volkswagen AG 40% Volkswagen Bruxelles S.A.
Plant locations: Wolfsburg Hanover Kassel Emden Salzgitter Brunswick	**Seat Deutschland GmbH** Mörfelden-Walldorf DM 10,000,000 100% SEAT, S.A.	**SKODA France Automobiles S.A.** Paris, France FRF 15,000,000 99.95% V.A.G. France S.A.		**Volkswagen Canada Inc.** Toronto, Ontario, Canada CAD 500,000 100%	**V.A.G. Leasing GmbH** Brunswick DM 100,000,000 100% Volkswagen Finanz GmbH	**Volkswagen International Finance N.V.** Amsterdam, Netherlands NLG 226,000,000 100%
Volkswagen Sachsen GmbH Mosel DM 10,000,000 100%	**SEAT, S.A.** Seat France, S.A. St. Quen l'Aumone, France FRF 50,000,000 100% SEAT, S.A.	**SKODA Automobili Italia S.r.l.** Verona, Italy ITL 1,000,000,000 100% AUTOGERMA S.p.A.		**Autolatina Comércio, Negócios e Participações Ltda.** São Paulo, SP, Brazil BRE 364,050,926,000 51%*	**V.A.G. Financement S.A.** Paris, France FRF 95,000,000 99.68% V.A.G. France S.A. 0.32% Volkswagen AG	**Volkswagen Investments Ltd.** Dublin, Ireland DM 600,000,000 100%
Volkswagen Bruxelles S.A. Brussels, Belgium BEC 1,925,000,000 100%	**Seat Italia, S.p.A.** Milan, Italy ITL 20,000,000,000 100% SEAT S.A.			**Autolatina Brasil S.A.** São Paulo, SP, Brazil BRE 849,414,336,936 42.58%*	**Financiera Seat, S.A.** Madrid, Spain ESP 8,207,390,000 100% SEAT, S.A.	**VW-GEDAS & Co. Projekt-management OHG** Berlin DM 300,000,000 99.97%
V.A.G. France S.A. Paris, France FRF 50,000,000 100%	**Seat UK Ltd.** Crawley, West Sussex Great Britain £4,000,000 100% SEAT, S.A.			**Autolatina Argentina S.A.** Buenos Aires, Argentina ARS 99,651,856 51%*	**VW Credit, Inc.** Auburn Hills, Mi., USA USD 100,000 100% Volkswagen of America, Inc.	
AUTOGERMA S.p.A. Verona, Italy ITL 90,000,000,000 100%	**Gearbox del Prat, S.A.** El Prat de Llobregat, Spain ESP 9,800,000,000 100% SEAT, S.A.			**Volkswagen de Mexico, S.A. de C.V.** Puebla/Pue., Mexico MXP 304,343,224,000 100%	**FINGERMA S.p.A.** Verona, Italy ITL 10,000,000,000 100% AUTOGERMA S.p.A.	
AutoEuropa Automóveis Lda. Palmela, Portugal ESC 4,000,000,000 50%				**Volkswagen of South Africa (Pty.) Ltd.** Uitenhage, C.P., South Africa ZAR 9,362,650 100%	**SkoFIN s.r.o.** Prague, Czech Republic CSK 30,000,000 100% Volkswagen Finanz GmbH	
V.A.G. Sverige AB Södertälje, Sweden SEK 84,000,000 33.33%				**Volkswagen of Nigeria Ltd.** Lagos, Nigeria NGN 38,000,000 40%		
Volkswagen Bratislava, spol. s.r.o. Bratislava, Slovak Republic CSK 1,054,800,000 80%				**Shanghai-Volkswagen Automotive Company Ltd.**** Shanghai, China CNY 958,000,000 50%		
V.A.G. Transport GmbH & Co. OHG Wolfsburg DM 1,000,000 81% Volkswagen AG 19% AUDI AG				**FAW-Volkswagen Automotive Co. Ltd.**** Changchun, China CNY 1,440,000,000 40%		
VOTEX GmbH Dreieich DM 1,000,000 100%				**Volkswagen Audi Nippon K.K.**** Toyohashi, Japan JPY 15,360,000,000 100%		
Europcar International S.A. Boulogne-Billancourt FRF 553,500,000 50%						

* Volkswagen AG's direct and indirect holding.
** Assigned to the 'Asia Pacific' division since 13 January, 1993.
Source: 1992 Volkswagen Annual Report.

acquired in 1965. But above all it was the Golf, designed in-house and creating a class of its own in the mass car market, which revived VW's fortunes. Table 16.1 (page 336) gives a statistical overview of the company's performance from 1983–92.

CURRENT SITUATION

The Volkswagen Group – comprising the four main marques Volkswagen AG (54 per cent of sales in 1992), Audi AG (16 per cent), SEAT-SA (13 per cent) and Skoda automobilová a.s. (2 per cent) – is the world's fourth largest car manufacturer. (The Group structure is depicted in Table 16.2 on page 337.) In 1992 the group sales exceeded 3.4 million vehicles worldwide. Some 52 per cent of the group's turnover is outside Germany. VW also has production facilities in many countries. Table 16.3 describes the company's worldwide locations with a breakdown of production at each foreign operation. The lion's share of production, however – some 54 per cent in 1992 – is still in Germany.

At Volkswagen AG, sales rose over 11 per cent by value in 1992 and over 7 per cent by unit, helped by sales of the newly launched Golf III. At Audi, VW's upmarket subsidiary, sales rose 13 per cent from DM 14.8 billion in 1991 to DM 16.7 billion in 1992. Despite a difficult year in Germany, Audi increased its sales slightly in its

Table 16.3 Foreign production facilities in VW Group 1992

Location	Firm/holding	Plants/workforce	Product range	Production	Sales DM million
Spain	SEAT/99%	Barcelona, Pamplona Martorell, Prat 27,738	Polo, Ibiza Marbella, Toledo, Malaga, Terra	578,432	10,350
Belgium	VW/100%	Brussels 7,144	Passat, Golf	215,994	4,050
Slovakia	VM Bratislava/80%	Bratislava 434	Passat	2,230	54.7
Czech Republic	Skoda/31%	Mlada Boleslav 17,105	Favorit	200,057	1,677
Mexico	VW/100%	Puebla 16,659	Golf, Jetta, Beetle	188,449	3,178
Brazil/ Argentina	Autolatina/51%	Buenos Aires São Bernado 26,159	Golf, Passat, Transporter, Trucks	341,179	4,034
South Africa	VW/100%	Uitenhage 8,231	Golf, Jetta Caddy, Passat, Transporter, Audi 100	44,480	1,289
China	Shanghai- Volkswagen/50%	Shanghai 5,883	Santana, Engines	65,000	1,967
China	FAW- Volkswagen/40%	Chang Chun	Audi 100, Jetta	N/A	N/A

home market helped by sales of the Audi 80. Audi recovered some ground in the USA, boosting sales by 20 per cent. This followed a disastrous 40 per cent drop in sales in 1991 due to tough economic conditions and the introduction of a luxury car tax. Despite successful new models Audi has yet to recover fully from its image problems of the late 1980s – when it was alleged some Audi automatics accelerated of their own accord – and this has made it difficult to respond to the Japanese upmarket offensive. Sales in other export markets rose by over 7 per cent and, in China, where the Audi 100 is built in cooperation with FAW (see below), 15,000 vehicles were sold.

SEAT closed with a loss of DM180 million in 1992. The first half of the year saw an unexpected surge in the demand for new cars in Spain. SEAT increased its sales in Spain – but only by 3 per cent retaining just under 18 per cent of the market. The rapid growth in sales in Germany in 1991 – mainly of VW's Polo which is now produced exclusively in SEAT's Pamplona plant – was followed by a 3 per cent drop in 1992. Italy proved a more promising market and SEAT increased its sales there by 3.7 per cent to 62,000. The first half of 1993 saw SEAT falling into unexpectedly deep losses.

Things looked brighter during 1992 at the Group's latest acquisition, the Czech company Skoda. VW assumed management responsibility at Skoda in April 1991. Sales rose to nearly 200,000 units in 1992. Of these almost half were sold domestically, virtually doubling sales there. Skoda was also able to offset the fall off in demand in its Central European markets by increasing penetration in Western Europe. Overall, Skoda made a profit of $43 million on sales of $1.1 billion in 1992.

WESTERN EUROPE: THE COMPANY'S MAIN MARKETS

VW is an international company with its strength in Europe. Over 70 per cent of Group turnover is in Europe. Even within Europe the company's market share varies considerably from country to country as can be seen from Table 16.4. The VW group has for some years had the largest share of its home market: at nearly 30 per cent almost double its nearest rival Opel and twice as much as all Japanese firms put together. In 1992 the VW Group was still the market leader in its home market – its units sales grew by 2.8 per cent – against a declining market.

Sales continued to grow during 1992 in Europe as a whole (up 6.3 per cent). In Western Europe, VW has consolidated its position as market leader (17.5 per cent in 1992) through acquisition and strong organic growth. The Fiat challenge – strong in the mid 1980s – now seems to have receded.

In 1992, therefore, Volkswagen Group was able to maintain its sales growth – but at wafer thin margins. The results for the first half of 1993, however, give cause for alarm as sales collapsed by 12 per cent against an overall market decline in Western Europe of 17 per cent.

Table 16.4 Volkswagen Group market shares of key West European markets

	Germany	France	Italy	United Kingdom	Spain
1991	30%	10.0%	12.4%	6.5%	17.6%
1992	28%	9.6%	14.6%	6.5%	18.0%

PRODUCT RANGE

The VW Group has an extensive product range which covers much of the car market, although not without some overlap between subsidiaries (see Table 16.5). Volkswagen Group product policy is to focus the SEAT range on the DM 10–20,000 bracket, the core VW models (Golf and Passat) on the DM 15–50,000 segment and the Audi marque on the DM 30–100,000 category. Skoda's Favorit is positioned as a low priced alternative to the Golf.

Table 16.5 Vehicles delivered to customers

	1992	1991	Change %
Western Europe	2,556,929	2,404,838	+6.3
Germany	1,248,833	1,214,962	+2.8
Italy	363,916	311,513	+16.8
France	217,226	190,454	+14.1
Spain	184,190	178,977	+2.9
Great Britain	106,793	111,018	–3.8
Belgium	87,906	84,322	+4.3

The VW range starts with the small car Polo, currently available in three forms, of which the hatchback is the most common. It received a facelift in 1990 and will be replaced in the mid 1990s, complemented by a new smaller 'city-car', the 'Chico'. The VW Golf – now in its third form – effectively created its own segment as a medium-sized hatchback in the mid 1970s and the GTI variant created a lucrative niche within that. The Vento is the booted version of the Golf and the Passat is a family saloon/estate, last renewed in 1988. The Corrada is an upmarket sports coupé based on the floorpan of the Golf. It was introduced in 1988 and is coming to the end of its product lifecycle.

A gap in the emerging 'people carrier' segment – competing against cars like the Renault Espace – is to be filled by a new model designed and produced jointly with Ford from 1994 onwards at a plant in Portugal. Total costs of the project, known as 'Auto Europa', are estimated to be DM 4 billion. The total capacity of the new Portuguese plant will be 180,000 cars per year aimed at a segment VW estimates should grow to 500,000 units per year by the end of the decade.

Through its acquisition of the Spanish SEAT company in 1986 (the Group owns 99 per cent of SEAT) VW has a presence in the utility small car segment. SEAT's Marbella is a variant of the Fiat Panda. A replacement is due in the mid 1990s. SEAT's first completely new model – the mid-range saloon Toledo – was launched in 1991 and has been well received. Although distinctive in design the Toledo shares many common components with other VW Group models. SEAT's mainstay – the hatch-backed Ibiza – has been redesigned and relaunched to critical acclaim in 1993.

VW moved into the higher priced car bracket in the 1960s through its acquisition of Audi. Audi specializes in medium to large refined saloon cars. Since 1991 the Audi range has been extensively revised and updated. The Audi 80 series of medium saloon cars was launched in its fourth generation form in September 1991, and the range includes an elegant convertible. The new Audi 100 range of large saloons was first introduced at the start of 1991 and was complemented by the launch of an estate – the Avant – in the same year. Audi cars are prized for their design and innovation. A particular feature has been the emphasis on safety, including the development of the 'procon-ten' system for improving the survivability of front-seat passengers in a crash. In common with other German manufacturers of luxury cars, Audi is also actively considering production of a smaller mid-range vehicle.

Skoda currently produces only one model, the Favorit, available as hatchback or estate. Designed with Western assistance, the Favorit was widely regarded as a breakthrough in the standards of Eastern European car production at its launch in 1989. Since the arrival of VW quality standards at Skoda have improved, but the image of the marque still leaves something to be desired. VW has plans for an additional model series in the future. Table 16.5, in addition to giving a breakdown of production for the Group's models, also shows the centrality of passenger car production to its operations.

Despite the breadth of the product range, the continued success of the Golf – consistently Europe's best selling car – is clearly critical to VW's position in Europe. The Golf accounts for around 40 per cent of VWs European sales. The latest model – only the third to be launched since 1974 – came on to the market in 1991/92 and has successfully maintained VW's lead in this all-important market segment. But competition is fierce and consumers are becoming more demanding.

PROFITABILITY AND PRODUCTIVITY

Despite the manifest achievements of Volkswagen there are weaknesses in its performance. Tables 16.1 and 16.6 summarize the company's financial performance since 1983. Profit margins at VW have been chronically low and they dropped precipitately in 1992. Arguably, however, profitability ratios are not the best measures of success when considering VW's performance. In common with other German companies, VW's accounting policies are extremely conservative. High depreciation charges depress profitability but also reduce tax liabilities. Thus in 1992 VW Group's net income declined by nearly 90 per cent. Cash flow, widely held to be a better measure of performance, fell in the same period by only 2 per cent. As a result the Group is able to fund more than two-thirds of its investment needs internally from cash flow. Nevertheless, it remains cause for serious concern that VW AG made operating losses of over DM 600 million in both 1990 and 1991 during periods of extraordinary growth in domestic demand when plant was operating at full capacity. Audi is widely believed to be the only profitable part of the Group's car operations. With sales falling drastically in early 1993, VW is widely predicted to show an overall loss for the year as a whole. Publicly, VW predict that the Group will return to profit in 1994. In reality Volkswagen is in the midst of a deep crisis. Its breakeven point is thought to be over 100 per cent of its capacity utilization and Piëch knows he must reduce the breakeven point to 80 per cent or less.

VW was counting on future cash flows – mainly from the car business – to finance its colossal investment programme. DM 82 billion was earmarked for investment worldwide – DM 51 billion in the car operations and the remainder in its financial services (leasing and credit). The investment programme includes current commitments – like Skoda and Eastern Germany – but also makes provision for further acquisitions. However, the ambitious investment plans depended critically on a projected continued volume growth worldwide – 33 per cent between 1992 and 1996 – in

Table 16.6 The Volkswagen Group in figures

Balance-sheet Structure (DM million)

31 December	1983	1984	1985	1986	1987	1988
Assets				2	29	76
Tangible assets	11,801	9,082	8,740	12,111	13,406	13,836
Financial assets	464	544	574	1,099	1,125	1,304
Leasing and rental assets		2,433	3,717	4,106	4,919	5,427
Fixed assets	12,265	12,059	13,031	17,318	19,479	20,643
Inventories and advance				6,802	6,618	6,506
Payments to suppliers	5,878	6,654	6,348			
Receivables and the like	6,269	7,388	7,157	8,675	9,403	11,848
Liquid funds, trade accept.	1,815	5,253	4,326	364	426	488
Securities, treasury stock	2,528	1,588	3,960	8,553	8,135	10,809
Current Assets	16,490	20,883	21,791	24,394	24,582	29,651
Total Assets	28,755	32,942	34,822	41,712	44,061	50,294
Stockholders' Equity a.Liab.						
Capital stock	1,200	1,200	1,200	1,500	1,500	1,500
Reserves of the Group	5,227	5,165	5,929	7,891	8,496	9,040
Minority inter. i. consol. subs.	281	320	266	408	405	405
Stockholders' Equity	6,708	6,685	7,395	307	308	308
Undetermined liabilities						
in respect of old-age pensions	4,235	4,739	5,029	3	17	42
Other undetermined liabilities	5,597	7,417	9,343	1,828	2,203	2,452
				10	9	9
Undetermined Liabilities	9,832	12,156	14,372	11,947	12,933	13,750
Liabilities payable within				5,294	5,889	6,314
more than				992	925	1,358
4 years	1,283	992	947	8,228	8,050	9,418
1 to 4 years	1,004	1,411	1,291	14,514	14,864	17,090
up to 1 year	9,925	11,570	10,569			
Liabilities	12,212	13,973	12,807			
Net earnings available for				1,344	1,217	1,929
distribution (Volkswagen AG)	—	124	244	1,456	1,999	2,121
Minority interest in earnings				12,451	13,043	15,398
to be distributed	3	4	4	15,251	16,259	19,448
Outside Capital	22,047	26,257	27,427	29,765	31,123	36,538
Total Capital	28,755	32,942	34,822	41,712	44,061	50,294
Statement of Earnings (Condensed) (DM million) January–December						
Gross performance	40,680	46,772	52,709	52,794	54,635	59,221
Cost of materials	20,852	23,824	26,623	46,746	48,526	51,315
Labour cost	12,371	13,227	13,913			
Depreciation and write-down	3,689	2,961	3,411	5,380	5,498	6,321
Depreciation on leasing and						
rental assets		1,060	1,259	632	931	38
Taxes	580	1,368	2,124	295	68	513
on income,						
earnings and				1,595	1,610	2,136
property	494	1,266	1,993	−473	−443	—
Sundry expenses less sundry income	3,403	4,104	4,783	542	569	1,356
Net earnings/Loss	−215	228	596	560	598	780

As of 1986 presentation in accordance with the new Accounting and Reporting Law.

1989	1990	1991	1992	Change 1992/91 in %	Balance-sheet Structure (DM million) 31 December
					Assets
134	261	372	631	69.8	Intangible assets
15,493	16,826	21,126	24,050	13.8	Tangible assets
1,621	1,418	2,655	2,747	3.5	Financial assets
5,561	5,834	6,293	7,393	17.5	Leasing and rental assets
22,809	24,339	30,446	34,821	14.4	*Fixed assets*
7,301	8,703	9,049	9,736	7.6	Inventories
					Receivables and other
14,472	15,065	19,011	21,394	12.5	assets
2,360	2,764	2,329	1,497	−35.7	Securities
9,929	11,842	9,255	7,836	−15.3	Liquid funds
34,062	38,374	39,644	40,463	2.1	*Current Assets*
56,871	62,713	70,090	75,284	7.4	*Total Assets*
					Stockholders' Equity and Liabilities.
1,500	1,650	1,656	1,664	0.5	Subscribed capital
9,667	11,491	12,098	11,800	−2.5	Reserves of the Group
439	145	164	859	x	Minority interest in consolidated subsidy
339	374	373	71	−80.9	Net earnings available for distribution
					Minority interest in net earnings to
54	33	12	68	x	be distributed
2,925	2,882	3,823	3,659	−4.3	Special items with an equity portion
12	13	19	18	−5.3	Special item for investment subsidies
14,936	16,588	18,145	18,139	0	*Shareholders' equity*
6,652	7,283	8,089	9,113	12.7	Undetermined liabilities (pensions)
2,001	1,828	2,032	1,773	−12.8	Undetermined liabilities (taxes)
10,454	10,680	10,161	11,323	11.4	Other undetermined liabilities
19,107	19,791	20,282	22,209	9.5	*Undetermined liabilities*
					Liabilities payable within
1,934	1,840	3,813	4,557	19.5	more than 5 years
3,289	3,339	3,900	6,222	59.6	1 to 5 years
17,605	21,155	23,950	24,157	0.9	up to 1 year
22,828	26,334	31,663	34,936	10.3	*Liabilities*
41,935	46,125	51,945	57,145	10.0	*Outside Capital*
56,871	62,713	70,090	75,284	7.4	*Total Capital*
					Statement of Earnings (Condensed) (DM million) January–December
65,352	68,061	76,315	85,403	11.9	Sales
56,196	61,890	69,472	79,155	13.9	Cost of sales
7,151	7,308	7,599	7,977	5.0	Selling and administration expenses
					Other operating income less
209	2,615	1,302	1,612	23.8	other operating expenses
773	914	1,239	719	−42.1	Financial results
					Results
2,987	2,392	1,785	602	−66.3	from ordinary business activities
—	—	—	—	—	Extraordinary results
					Taxes on
1,949	1,306	671	455	−32.2	income
1,038	1,086	1,114	147	−86.8	Net earnings

an era of increased turbulence and competition. The plans have since been scaled back somewhat. Overall investment in 1993 has been halved. Investment in SEAT in 1993/94 has been reduced by a third. All comparable cuts have been made at Audi. At Skoda, VW was looking for long-term finance from the EBRO, IFC and EIB, but this was placed on hold in 1993. Cherished projects like the joint venture with SWATCH to develop an electric car and a collaborative effort between Suzuki and SEAT to develop a successor to the Marbella have been shelved and capital programmes extended into the future.

Notwithstanding massive investment in technology VWs workforce actually grew in the mid 1980s and productivity has made only modest advances since then. The trend from 1983–92 is shown in Table 16.1. In 1985 German workers won the right to a shorter working week and with the concentration of VW's facilities in the Federal Republic this inevitably had a negative effect. As a result of efforts to rationalize, however, the size of the Group's workforce fell again in 1989 to 250,000 employees worldwide, down from 276,000 in 1986. The surge in demand in Germany in 1991 put paid to attempts to reduce the workforce.

High wage costs, overtime payments, fringe benefits and other concessions continue to gnaw at the company's profit margins. In 1988 VW management estimated that hourly labour costs in VW's West German plants were averaging $31 per man. Fiat and Peugeot meanwhile had to find only $17.50 and $20 respectively. Fiat and Peugeot's labour cost/sales ratio stood at around 20 per cent in 1988; VW's stood at 28 per cent overall. As part of a five-year cost reduction programme to 1992, DM 2.5 billion was spent on labour cost reductions, but VW is shooting at a moving target. Its labour costs/sales ratio fell to 25 per cent in 1992 but Renault and Peugeot managed 17–19 per cent. As part of a restructuring programme 36,000 jobs are to go by 1997, 20,000 of them to be shed in 1993, mostly in Germany. The Group's cost position remains perilous and plans have been announced to reduce the German workforce by 12,500 people between 1992 and 1996. The question for VW becomes whether the labour representatives on the company's supervisory board will accept the radical changes in working practices necessary, particularly in Germany, to approach Japanese productivity levels.

INVESTMENT IN NEW TECHNOLOGY

VW is a leader in the application of modern technology to both products and processes. In 'Halle 54' of its Wolfsburg plant the company installed one of the world's most advanced automated production lines and in its Emden plant for the Passat and the new East German plant at Mosel, JIT methods have been incorporated. An indication of the investment that the company has undertaken over recent years can be obtained from Table 16.1. Although the bulk of investment in the 1980s went to the Federal Republic, the massive capital investment programme for the 1990s is aimed at turning VW into Europe's only truly global car-maker. Of the DM 51 billion originally to be invested in car production, DM 9 billion was to go to Skoda and a further DM 880 million was to be invested in a joint venture in Slovakia. DM 5 billion was to go to the new VW plant in Mosel. Further large sums were likely to be invested in the new Martorell facility in Spain and in VW's Mexican subsidiary. Smaller sums were earmarked for investment in China and the Far East.

As already mentioned these investment sums have been scaled down – from DM 51 billion in 1992–96, to DM 45 billion, 1993–97.

A large part of the investment funds will be spent in the development of new vehicles. Product R&D expenditure stood at DM 3.0 billion in 1992. As far as new products are concerned VW has been at the forefront of applying catalytic converter technology to reduce engine emissions and was amongst the first to introduce permanent all-wheel drive on saloon vehicles. The company has also majored in the field of diesel and turbo-diesel engines. Recent innovations include the use of 16-valve engines and the adoption of fully galvanized bodywork on Audi models. Advanced passive safety features and recyclable components have both featured prominently on the new Golf, whilst the company continues to experiment with electric and hybrid vehicles. In the longer term VW is also working on traffic guidance and parking systems. The first product of this development was presented in 1989 in the shape of the revolutionary Futura passenger car.

DISTRIBUTION AND RENTAL

VW is seeking to apply IT to the distribution of vehicles. Starting in Germany in 1989, the company abolished the twelve regional wholesalers and substituted a direct dealer system. The 1,700 VW dealers in Germany are now linked directly to the sales department at Wolfsburg. VW's intentions are clear:

> With this introduction of direct sales we aim to speed up effectively the ordering and delivery process for the customer, cover the automobile market on a more comprehensive scale and ensure still greater delivery readiness and clarity.

VW, in common with other car manufacturers, has also moved into the important car rental sector by taking a 50 per cent stake in 1989 in Europcar, an EC based car rental company. The company has also reorganized its leasing, credit and banking subsidiaries which are targeted to grow rapidly in the 1980s. At the same time VW has also moved to take control of its wholesale distribution systems in the major markets of Western Europe.

SUPPLY

The moves in the distribution system parallel moves on the supply, where increasing reliance is being put on high-tech component suppliers – throughout the world – to provide ready made sub-systems. In contrast to Japanese manufacturers VW eschews equity stakes in its suppliers. Already in early 1993 VW had announced price cuts of 5–10 per cent for bought in components, as a way of reducing the group's DM 50 billion annual purchasing bill. A further acceleration of changes in supply was prompted by the arrival at VW of GM's former logistics expert José Ignacia Lopez (see below). A new global purchasing strategy is being implemented. Seven regional offices around the world are to coordinate the group's strategy to take fullest advantage of low cost production locations. This means, for example, that VW is to reduce its reliance on its traditional former supply base in favour of French and British component suppliers. Lopez has also moved rapidly to reduce the range and complexity of VW's componentry, focusing in-house production on core technologies and reducing the number of primary level suppliers. Lopez came with a formidable reputation for cutting costs at GM's European supply base. This was achieved by rigorous analysis of suppliers' processes by GM's feared PICOS team (Purchased Input Concept Optimization). The results, Lopez claimed, produced efficiencies which surpass even the Japanese lean production methods. Some of the components companies subjected to the relentless scrutiny of Lopez's PICOS team, however, complained that much of the savings were achieved by heavy-handed negotiating tactics which ultimately may backfire.

INVESTMENT IN SPAIN

As noted above, the bulk of VW's production is located in Germany, though operations elsewhere have increased significantly in recent years.

Since acquiring SEAT in 1986, VW has undertaken extensive restructuring and investment. VW is determined to integrate SEAT fully into its global automotive operations and future models, though distinct, will share common VW components. Some DM 10 billion are being spent over five years both to build a revolutionary new assembly plant at Martorell and to modernize existing production facilities. By 1994 330,000 cars a year will be produced in Martorell and SEAT will be able to launch a major assault on the small car market with its newly designed Ibiza.

STRATEGIC ALLIANCES WITH JAPANESE MANUFACTURERS

The company also has a number of collaborative agreements with Japanese car makers. VW has worked for many years with Toyota in Germany on the production of transporters. A joint venture with Nissan, under which VW Santanas and Passats were assembled at Nissan plants in Japan, was set up in the early 1980s but wound up subsequently when no sales breakthrough was achieved.

In 1989 the Group established a new wholly owned distributor in Japan, VW-Audi Nippon KK. Encouraged by the good showing of German producers in Japan, VW plan to double sales to 100,000 cars a year by 1995. The sales strategy is to be achieved in part through a cooperation deal with Toyota's Japanese dealer network and partly through VW/Audi's own network of dealers. So far, however, sales have suffered due to the fall in the Japanese market and the group sold only 41,265 vehicles in 1992.

GERMAN UNIFICATION

VW has long been active in what used to be East Germany. In the late 1980s it supplied a production line for Golf engines to the IFA works which produced Trabant cars. In return, IFA supplied small quantities of engines to VW. This cooperation was intensified following unification in 1990 with the establishment of a company at Mosel, near Zwickau, to manufacture cars in Eastern Germany. The company – VW Sachsen GmbH – is now wholly owned by VW. VW is to invest DM 3.5 billion in a new plant to produce Golfs, as well as the necessary supply and distribution infrastructure. Production was originally intended to reach 250,000 units a year by 1994 although the execution time has now been extended to spread the cost. An additional DM 700 million is being invested in an engine plant in Chemnitz which eventually should be capable of producing 460,000 engines a year. Production of Golf bodyshells at Mosel reached 34,000 in 1992 and the Chemnitz plant produced a total of 184,000 engines.

EASTERN EUROPE

Since the events in 1989 VW has had its eyes firmly on Eastern Europe. The company estimates that the market there should grow to some 3 million units a year by the end of the century. The market potential and the attractions of a low cost production location brought VW in 1990 to Skoda. As the most advanced East European motor manufacturer, Skoda was a much sought after prize and VW had to beat off rival bids from competitors, notably France's Renault, before securing control of Skoda.

Under the terms of the agreement, VW acquired a 31 per cent stake of Skoda to be increased to 70 per cent by 1995. Skoda is to be kept as a separate marque within the Group, alongside Audi and SEAT. DM 9.5 billion is to be invested in Skoda including the construction of a new assembly plant, transmission and engine works. The development of the 'new' enterprise has benefited from a two-year tax holiday and generous depreciation allowances. The imposition by the Czech government of stiff import tariffs on foreign cars – new and used – has helped Skoda consolidate its position in its home market. VW is currently in dispute with the Czech government which is unhappy about the rising prices of Skoda cars, which enjoy a virtual monopoly of the Czech market, and the level of local content. Vague threats have come from the government about reducing import levies on new and used cars in retaliation.

VW also has an 80 per cent stake in an assembly plant in Bratislava, capital of the newly created Slovak Republic. The first vehicles – Passat saloons – were produced in 1991 and the plant is still in its start-up phase.

VW also owns 49 per cent of TAS, a Slovenian car factory which produces a small number of Golf saloons and the Caddy – a pick-up based on the Golf platform. Production fell in 1992 and only modest investments are planned for the future.

ASIA

In the mid 1980s VW established a joint venture assembly plant in Shanghai, China. There were ambitious plans to produce 60,000 VW Santana saloons by 1990 and eventually as many as 300,000 cars a year. Development of Shanghai-Volkswagen Automotive Company slowed after Tiannenmen Square. Production reached 65,000 units a year in 1992, however. A paint shop was opened in 1989 and a new engine plant with a capacity of 100,000 engines a year was opened in 1990. This supplies Europe as well as local markets. A neighbouring car plant was taken over in 1992. In the course of 1993 VW is to raise production to 100,000 vehicles. By 1995 150,000 cars a year and a new model variant are to be produced. Local content of the cars had reached 75 per cent by 1992. VW was able to take advantage of the phenomenal economic growth in Southern China doubling its sales in 1992. The VW Santana taxi is now ubiquitous in Southern China. VW predicts that China will be its third largest market worldwide by 1996. By the year 2000 VW intend that the Chinese operation should not only serve an important home market but also compete with producers from the other markets in the growing Pacific/Asiatic areas.

China itself has not been an easy market. Most cars in China were sold to economic or political organizations. Distribution of cars in China has always been problematic: excessive bureaucracy, nepotism and corruption are endemic. After a period of uncertainty, when it seemed that the commitment of the Chinese government to the motor industry was in doubt, cooperation between VW and the Chinese government is now proceeding apace. A new joint venture was formed in November 1990 with China's largest car plant, the 'First Automotive Works' in Changshun, South China. VW is to provide 60 per cent of the DM 1.5 billion to be invested in the venture, including a new vehicle assembly plant to come on stream in 1994. FAW has built Audi 100s – 30,000 to 1992 – under licence from VW since 1988. The operation is to be provided with plant from the United States where VW of America's old works in Westmoreland has been purchased in its entirety. Assembly of Jetta cars from kits began at the end of 1991 and is set to rise to 150,000 a year when the new plant is in full operation in 1996. Local content should by that point have reached 90 per cent and some 15 per cent of production is to be exported to SE Asia.

In 1991 VW also concluded a joint venture in Taiwan to produce 30,000 transporter vans a year. VW holds 33 per cent of the shares in the Ching Chung Motor Company.

In the course of 1992 the VW Group consolidated its activities in China, Taiwan and Japan into an 'Asian–Pacific Division' under a main board director.

LATIN AMERICAN OPERATIONS

A major problem for the group in the 1980s was its South American companies. Profitable in the 1960s and 1970s, the Brazilian and Argentinean operations suffered in the 1980s from a collapsing car market and hostile government actions. At the same time VW's share of the principal market, Brazil, fell from a commanding 57 per cent in the late 1970s to only 37 per cent by 1987 and the South American operation made losses or marginal profits between 1980 and 1988.

In November 1986 VW merged its activities in these countries with Ford to create Autolatina, a holding company with a joint German-American management structure. Autolatina distributes Ford and VW vehicles jointly and exports cars to other countries in South and North America.

Despite a promising start, by mid 1987 Autolatina was staring a loss of $400 million in the face: wage costs in Brazil had risen but government policy forbad any increase in car prices. Autolatina's management decided to raise prices despite the government invocation and the losses were reduced to some DM 170 million. Relations with the government had been strained but the restrictive price policy was finally ended in September 1991. Autolatina was able to benefit from the results of market liberalization in South America in 1992, boosting sales by nearly 10 per cent. VW's share of production rose by over 15 per cent. In Brazil, VW increased its market share to nearly 40 per cent and in Argentina VW more than doubled its sales in 1992, admittedly from a low base. Of the 507,488 vehicles produced in 1992, 342,948 were VWs. VW, it should be noted, is also a significant manufacturer of commercial vehicles in Brazil. The Brazilian market remains distorted by government intervention, however – despite recent cuts car taxes are still high, inflation is still rampant and materials costs are exorbitant. VW made a 'profit' on its sales in Brazil and Argentina in 1992 for the first time in many years.

VW's attempts to use its South American plants as platforms for exporting to other parts of the world have, however, been disappointing. In 1988 over 40 per cent of VW's Brazilian output was exported, principally to the USA and Canada, but also to Iraq where payment was in crude oil. With the closure of VW's US assembly plants (see below), VW planned to export from Brazil to the USA 100,000 Fox model saloons rising eventually to 150–180,000 units a year. Exports of the Fox to the USA peaked, however, in 1987 at 74,000. Sales fell by 1990 to only 15,000 units before the model was withdrawn. Here the over-valuation since 1987 of the Brazilian cruzado against the dollar was partly to blame, raising the selling price in the United States from $6,000 to $10,000. The uncertain economic situation in Brazil also put paid to future business in Iraq: a contract for the supply of 100,000 cars was reluctantly rejected by VW in 1989 as too risky. In 1992, Volkswagen exported 41,275 vehicles from Brazil compared with 14,795 vehicles in 1991.

MEXICO

VW has long had a major presence in Mexico. For many years the Mexican market was a steady source of income, but for much of the 1980s VW's involvement in Mexico was a serious cause for concern. Starting in 1982 the Mexican car market collapsed from a high of 600,000 to 200,000 in 1988. VW's vehicle sales declined to around 60,000 by the latter date. By 1987 the Mexican operation was making a loss of DM 48 million. Clearly, the massive indebtedness of the Mexican government had an impact on the car market, not least through punitive taxation on cars. But VW was faced with increased competition from other manufacturers, notably Nissan, and the company was plagued by strikes and poor labour relations.

In retrospect 1988 was a turning point. VW's market share still declined from 33 per cent to 26 per cent, but production was up, boosted by a revival in sales, and losses were manageable. In 1989 the Mexican operations made a profit again and in 1990 VW boosted its sales by 40 per cent to gain a commanding 38 per cent market share. VW's share fell slightly in 1991 as production failed to keep pace with growing domestic demand and again in 1992 due to a four-week labour dispute.

The strong recovery was mainly due to the success of the venerable Beetle – now complete with catalytic converter. The Beetle sells for $5,250 in Mexico making it one of the cheapest cars in the world. VW has a DM 1.5 million investment programme in Mexico with plans to expand production to 390,000 units a year by 1994. Apart from satisfying the demand from a booming domestic economy, VW's main aspirations for its Mexican operation in the short and medium term is as a supplier of engines to Europe and as a low cost location for making cars for export to North

America. Of the 188,500 cars built by VW di Mexico in 1992, 27,985 were exported to North America, down substantially on 1991. From 1993 all Golf and Jetta cars sold in the USA will be produced in Mexico. Labour costs in Mexico can be as little as 5 per cent of those in the USA, and with the creation of the North American Free Trade Area this will prove a promising strategic location.

THE US WITHDRAWAL

VW suffered a major setback in the USA in the late 1980s. Once a major export market for VW, the USA became a problem child. In response to adverse exchange rate trends, VW took the decision to establish production facilities in the USA in the late 1970s. However, a misguided marketing campaign and competition from Japanese small car manufacturers meant that initial plans had to be revised. One plant was sold off and a new marketing strategy adopted.

The Westmoreland plant, where VW production was concentrated, suffered from high wage costs and inflexible working practices – the UAW trade union ensured that labour relations were more akin to the pattern prevailing in US car plants in Detroit than in the Japanese 'transplants'. Sales of the Golf equivalent were also badly hit, not only by Japanese competition but also by low-priced cars from South Korea and Yugoslavia.

US sales of *imported* VWs were also affected by the appreciation of the DM against the $ – some 35 per cent in 1986 alone, so that the company's then chief executive, Carl Hahn, could argue that the US facilities were VW's insurance policy against an appreciating DM. Evidently, the premium became too expensive. By 1987 VW of America was losing DM 572 million a year and in November 1987 VW took the decision to close down its plant in Westmoreland. This occurred in 1988. Subsequently, VWs sold in the USA have been supplied either directly from Germany or, increasingly, from the company's subsidiaries in Mexico and Brazil.

VW's sales in the USA have slumped since 1989 from 133,000 units to 75,873 in 1992. VW thus has currently less than 1 per cent of the US market, a far cry from the heady days of the 1950s and 1960s when it was America's best selling importer of cars.

TOUGH AT THE TOP

Like all public companies in Germany the VW group has a dual top management structure. A supervisory board is responsible for overall strategy and policy decisions. Out of 20 members, six are representatives of the works council and three represent the powerful IG Metall union. The Lower Saxony government – currently Social Democratic – is represented by the Minister President and a ministerial colleague.

Beneath the supervisory board is an eight-man management board headed by the chairman or chief executive. This is currently Ferdinand Piëch (55) who replaced Carl Hahn in January 1993. Hahn had led the company since 1982. Piëch came to the post after a successful period as chief executive of Audi. Piëch, a grandson of Beetle designer Ferdinand Porsche, developed a reputation as a hard-headed and abrasive engineer who is not afraid to grasp unpleasant matters. Piëch's main contender for the crown was Daniel Goeudevert, a former head of Ford Germany, who has now been made chairman of the VW 'marque' management body.

A recent and controversial new member of VW's main board is José Ignacio Lopez de Arriortúa. After much highly visible toing and froing, Lopez joined VW in March 1993 as head of 'Production Optimization and Procurement'. This followed similar positions at GM in Europe and the USA. Lopez's arrival at VW sparked a heated public and legal battle with GM over allegations of industrial espionage. The allegations implicate Lopez's associates, recruited at the same time from GM, in the possession of documents including internal GM plans for a new low cost plant – the so-called 'Plateau Six' – which Lopez had originally hoped to build in his native Basqueland.

At the time of writing the outcome of the Lopez case and the future of Lopez and his patron Piëch are still uncertain. It is almost certain to end in tears, however.

This case has summarized the current situation at VW. The 'World Motor Industry' (*The Economist*, 17 October 1992) brief also draws your attention to other relevant trends in terms of market developments, capacity and competition.

Fisons Plc

J.R. Anchor

The financial performance of Fisons was extremely poor during the late 1970s, with its Fertilizer and Agrochemical Division being particular centres of under-achievement. Lack of competitiveness on a global scale was the main reason for this performance. A combination of a high level of gearing and rising interest rates also meant that Fisons' operating profits were being eaten up by the costs of debt financing.

This corporate crisis led to a change of top management and to the appointment in 1980 of a new chief executive, John Kerridge. Company headquarters were moved from London to Ipswich – the home of its Fertilizer Division. Fisons' Agrochemical Division was merged with a similar business owned by Boots Plc. The combined operation was named FBC Ltd.

Fisons then set about devising a strategy to restructure its portfolio of businesses. This strategy was based on two key principles. First of all it would retain a presence only in industries which demonstrated significant growth and profit potential and in markets in which the company's management skills and financial resources could make it an effective competitor.

The most significant event in this reorientation of the company occurred in 1982 with the sale of Fisons' Fertilizer Division to Norsk Hydro for £59 million (see Appendix 17.1). This move disconnected the company from the line of business on which it was founded. Fisons' exit from agricultural products was completed by its disposal of its half share in FBC to Schering AG, the West German chemical company, for £60 million.

The cash which was realized from these disposals was used to eliminate the company's debt and to reinvest in its three remaining 'growth' businesses: pharmaceuticals, scientific equipment and horticulture. Growth in the future would be mainly via organic means, with acquisitions used as an augmenting mechanism. As a consequence of this activity, a record pre-tax profit of £31.2 million was recorded by Fisons in 1983.

Sales of Fisons' ethical pharmaceutical products, led by the asthma treatment Intal, continued to grow worldwide with particular success being achieved in the US market. Capital investment expanded further the company's manufacturing capacity. Curtin Matheson Scientific became Fisons' largest single subsidiary when it was acquired in 1984. CMS was a major distributor of clinical and industrial laboratory products in the important US market. The acquisition of Italian-based Carlo Erba Strumentazione (CEST) increased Fisons' presence in another important growth business – the manufacture of market-leading, high technology analytical instruments. By 1985 more than 80 per cent of the company's business was done outside the UK.

In addition, its market capitalization, which had stood as low as £41 million in 1981, had passed the £1 billion mark.

In 1984, John Kerridge was appointed to succeed Sir George Burton – a member of one of the company's founding families – as chairman. This change re-emphasized Fisons' reorientation away from its historic roots.

Sales of established pharmaceutical products continued to grow during the mid 1980s, and a number of significant product innovations were also launched. In addition, a major investment programme expanded Fisons' pharmaceutical research and production facilities. The acquisition of Applied Research Laboratories – a leading manufacturer of spectrometers in the USA and Europe – expanded the company's worldwide interests in scientific equipment.

By 1987 Fisons was able to boast of profits of £100 million and that its declared strategy of augmenting strong organic growth with selective acquisitions had been boosted by the speed and effectiveness with which new companies had been absorbed into the group's operations.

This pattern of growth was continued at the end of the decade. In 1988 Fisons acquired the Pharmaceutical Division of the US-based Pennwalt Corporation for $441 million – its largest acquisition to date, and one which provided an established range of prescription and over-the-counter products, a larger sales force, and enhanced R&D capability and substantial manufacturing facilities. In 1989, Fisons expanded its Scientific Equipment Division through the £270 million acquisition of VG Instruments, a leading world supplier of state-of-the-art analytical instruments. This acquisition led to Fisons becoming the fourth largest manufacturer of scientific instruments in the world.

As it entered the 1990s, Fisons had been transformed from the organization which had existed a decade earlier. Its 1991 report stated:

> The Fisons of the 1990s has grown and developed from the Fisons of the 1980s. Over the 10 years, Fisons has been transformed into a group whose resources are channelled firmly into international growth industries with good profit potential. Three strong Divisions operate with high levels of autonomy in attractive markets where Fisons competes effectively. Operating on every continent and in over 100 countries worldwide Fisons' businesses span pharmaceuticals and consumer healthcare, scientific instruments and equipment distribution and horticultural products for the consumer and professional grower. Over many countries its products are market leaders.

Although the above statement may be infected by a certain degree of hyperbole, it does provide a clear indication of the evolution of the company during the previous decade. In spite of these developments, however, Fisons' fortunes took a turn for the worse during the early 1990s.

In spite of the optimism of the above statement, Fisons was forced to admit that it suffered from an identity problem. Although it had been eight years since its exit from fertilizers, many of the general public still associated it with those and other divested products. Indeed the group's involvement in horticultural products – which supplied the amateur gardener – was felt to contribute to the continued popular association of Fisons with fertilizers and agrochemicals. Nevertheless, a programme of public education/awareness raising was very low down on Fisons' list of priorities during the 1980s. The emphasis then was very much on turning round the company, rather than on external relations. This preoccupation with internal affairs, to the exclusion of other matters, was a theme which was to return to haunt Fisons during the early 1990s.

In April 1990, Kerridge defined Fisons' strategy as being one of 'developing a portfolio of businesses in attractive growth markets where Fisons can be an effective competitor'. The key terms here are 'portfolio', 'attractive growth markets' and 'effective competitor'. The latter two criteria had not been met by Fisons' fertilizer and agrochemical businesses ten years previously, according to Kerridge. The company's portfolio approach was justified on the basis that it was thereby enabled to grow at different speeds, to incur setbacks and to make investments.

In spite of this emphasis upon its portfolio of products, Fisons did not try to pretend that strategic or defensive synergies existed between its pharmaceuticals, scientific equipment and horticultural products divisions. As a consequence, transferable skills between the divisions were limited. The reason for Fisons having a presence in them was simply that they were perceived to be growth industries which offered a reasonable financial return and in which the company could be an effective competitor either globally or locally.

On the face of it, Fisons' strategy had enjoyed a considerable degree of success with profits growing from £3.2m in 1980 to £169m by 1989. In spite of this improvement in the company's fortunes, a number of City observers remained unimpressed. It was suggested, for instance, that Fisons' development of its scientific equipment business was simply an attempt to reduce its dependence on pharmaceuticals. Moreover, the company was felt to be over-reliant upon acquisitions at the expense of organic growth. This latter suggestion was refuted by Kerridge who stated:

> We may be an acquisitive company, but it would be wrong to say we are acquisition driven ... Our priority is for organic growth and I can't think of a year in the past ten where our organic growth has not been much greater than that from acquisitions ... Our bigger acquisitions have never diluted; they have always added to earnings within the first year.

Although there was clearly a difference of opinion about the appropriateness (or otherwise) of Fisons' corporate and business strategies, there was a consensus that its financial management skills were strong. Financial control, like strategy formulation, was exercised from the centre. Active tax management was a feature of Fisons' financial control. Kerridge would have preferred that Fisons' performance be judged purely on its financial results. Attention continued to be focused, however, on its individual businesses.

The pharmaceuticals division was the one which attracted the most attention in the City. The major issue was whether or not its research and development activities were sufficient to ensure long-term growth. There was concern, in particular, that Fisons might be over-dependent on Intal. Since the product had been around for more than 15 years, some observers were concerned that the pharmaceutical division's performance would decline as patents on Intal's chemical constituent, nedocromil, expired. However, other formulation patents existed which could help to ameliorate this development. In addition, an offshoot drug with wider application, Tilade, had been launched successfully in Europe and its approval in the United States was expected to take place in late 1990.

To a certain extent, Fisons' pharmaceuticals division mirrored the group's portfolio. Approximately one third of the division's sales were in respiratory drugs, such as Intal, while the rest came from a variety of products such as vitamins and veterinary medicines. In early 1990, it was expected that there would be further spin-offs in the respiratory products area, including ophthalmic and nasal versions of Intal. In addition, developments were expected in the cardiovascular, gastro-intestinal and dermatological fields. To a considerable extent, these product lines demonstrated a significant degree of synergy since they all revolved around the concept of allergic reactions, variations of which can be blamed for a diverse range of conditions. It was hoped that the same kind of synergy would exist in the case of compounds which were currently at the R&D stage, as well as those obtained in acquisitions such as the 1988 purchase of Pennwalt.

As in other areas of activity, Fisons adopted a tough attitude towards the financial control of its R&D. Kerridge's words exemplify this approach:

> Research is cheap, it's the development of a product and bringing it to market that will cost you millions ... Companies go through periods of being very barren and then they strike a rich vein. We don't look at R&D in terms of a percentage of turnover; we look at it as a cost towards achieving a certain profit. If the number gets too high, then we have to have the management discipline to stop a programme.

Fisons' bullishness continued into 1991. Its 1990 pre-tax profits rose by 36 per cent to £230.2m. Twenty per cent of this profit growth was said to be accounted for by growth in existing businesses with the acquisition of VG Instruments being responsible for the remaining 16 per cent. Kerridge stated that above-average growth could be expected throughout the 1990s, boosted by 'its promising new drugs in the development pipeline'. All three divisions saw their sales and profit rise.

Tilade was said to be selling better in continental Europe than in the UK. Its approval by the US Food and Drug Administration was 'just around the corner'. By September 1991, when the first half results were announced for that year, Tilade had achieved a market share of more than 5 per cent in several European countries. Indeed, by that time respiratory and allergy products accounted for just over 50 per cent of pharmaceutical sales. Just three months later, however, Fisons felt obliged to issue a profits warning.

On 11 December 1991 Fisons announced that two of its pharmaceutical products had been banned from being imported into the United States by that country's Food and Drug Administration – a regulatory watchdog. The FDA had become concerned about the production quality of both Opticrom, a hayfever medication, and Imferon, a blood product. Fisons also announced that disruption to other markets for Opticrom in spring 1992, the peak season for hayfever sufferers, would also hit profits.

Fisons' difficulties actually started in October 1989 when the FDA asked for Opticrom to be withdrawn following problems with testing specifications. In January 1990, Imferon was also withdrawn after the FDA discovered that Fisons' manufacturing processes did not meet its specifications. Fisons' announcement shocked analysts who had been promised only three months earlier that both Opticrom and Imferon had been cleared for sale by the FDA.

Fisons claimed that it had been caught out by increasingly rigorous standards set by the FDA following a number of scandals in the generic (or non-patented) US drugs market. The company also pointed out that other pharmaceutical groups had been similarly hit, but that it was particularly vulnerable because it did not have dual sourcing, i.e. production from more than one source.

Financial analysts were not impressed by this line of argument, however. They were particularly critical of Fisons' lack of dual sourcing arrangements. The company's failure to communicate effectively with investors led to questions being asked about Kerridge's position. It was suggested that although his autocratic style had been appropriate during Fisons' 1980s transformation, he might not be the right man for its future development. Kerridge's wish that Fisons should 'go it alone' in pharmaceuticals was a particular cause of concern, given the increasingly high costs of marketing and R&D in the pharmaceuticals industry. More specifically, it was felt that there was a gap in the company's product pipeline to replace Intal as it came off patent during the early 1990s.

Fisons' credibility was further undermined two weeks later when it became known that the FDA had discovered 'significant deviations' from good manufacturing practice at one of Fisons' Cheshire plants which manufactured Intal. Indeed, it was stated that Intal was only allowed to remain on sale because of its popularity with patients. Other allegations related to Imferon and Opticrom.

In spite of an attempt by Fisons to reassure the markets, City confidence remained low. Less than frank and, in some cases, misleading statements combined with a reputation as the world's most secretive drug company had taken their toll on investor relations. This was reflected in a 6 per cent rise in Fisons' shares when John Kerridge abruptly resigned as chairman and chief executive on 14 January 1992 'on grounds of ill-health'.

Kerridge was described by those who had worked with him as 'a highly complex personality; a brilliant strategic thinker, but obsessive over detail; self-confident and at times apparently arrogant, but abnormally thin-skinned'. This sensitivity undoubtedly played a major role in souring Fisons' relations with the investment community and the press. The company did have a history, however, of over-optimistic forecasts and, to some extent, could be regarded as 'accident prone'. In the 1960s, for instance, the company botched the launch of Intal in the United States. Kerridge's appointment in January 1981 had coincided with the announcement that Proxicromil, supposedly a major pharmaceutical breakthrough, was being scrapped at the last moment because of side-effects. The City complained at the time that the company had been reassuring right up to the moment of disaster. Again, Fisons raised hopes too high during the mid 1980s about the prospects for Tilade.

Fisons immediately replaced Kerridge as chairman with one of its non-executive directors, Patrick Egan, a long-time Unilever employee. Egan, while defending Kerridge's record, announced that he would have a more open style and that Fisons' tradition of secrecy would change. Just over one week after his appointment, the company gave its first R&D presentation in four years. The event was not a total success, however. Although analysts were impressed by Egan's commitment, they felt that the company was still guilty of some wishful thinking, particularly in relation to the likely timescale for the introduction of the company's new drugs.

Fisons continued to be dogged by bad news after Kerridge's resignation. Two days later the US Food and Drug Administration released documents which indicated that Tilade had been breaking US regulations in relation to both manufacturing processes and testing. It also indicated that there had been further inadequacies in quality control relating to Intal, Opticrom and Imferon.

The pressure on Fisons was increased further by an announcement from a US pharmaceutical group that its UK subsidiary had received a licence from the UK authorities to license and market a generic version of Intal, following its overcoming of certain inhaling technology problems. Although Intal had been off patent for some years, generic producers had had problems designing an aerosol inhaler which would deliver the product efficiently to asthma sufferers' lungs.

On 2 April 1992, Fisons announced the resignation of Peter Fothergill, chairman of its pharmaceutical division. More significantly it announced the appointment of Cedric Scroggs, chairman of the group's scientific division, as chief executive of the company and chairman of its pharmaceutical division. It was stated that Scroggs' appointment would end alleged deficiencies in communication between the pharmaceuticals management committee and the main board. As a consequence, the company's divisions would no longer operate as independent entities. Egan, the company's chairman, stated that a merger with another company was not being contemplated, but that co-development and co-marketing projects, particularly in the cardiovascular field, were being actively examined. He also stated that there was no intention to sell the horticultural business.

Four weeks later, Fisons announced that it was offering for sale its horticultural and consumer health businesses, as part of a fundamental restructuring of the group. The decision to sell the horticultural business represented a final break with Fisons' roots. Scroggs stated that the decision to concentrate on pharmaceuticals and scientific instruments was not made because the horticultural or consumer health products were poorly managed or unprofitable. Rather it was because Fisons wanted to have global businesses and this goal was not achievable in either area without significant investment, not least in advertising. Within the pharmaceuticals division, Fisons would concentrate on anti-inflammatory products and drugs for the central nervous system. The company's generic non-patented products would eventually be divested.

These changes were generally welcomed by analysts. Nevertheless, some questioned whether Scroggs, with no background in pharmaceuticals, was the right man to take the new-look company forwards.

On 12 June 1992, Fisons surprised City analysts by issuing yet another profits warning, citing continuing difficulties in both its pharmaceuticals and scientific instruments division. In the case of pharmaceuticals, it was stated that there had been additional costs associated with upgrading Opticrom's manufacturing facilities. In addition, 'the attention paid to Opticrom and a desire not to market drugs with quality deficiencies had meant that sale of other products had suffered.' In other words, Fisons' profits had been hit by a double squeeze – an increase in costs combined with a reduction in sales. The unexpected nature of the profits warning lead to a sharp fall in Fisons' share price and, in the view of at least one observer, to the credibility of the company's management being in tatters. The fact that none of the company's board had any experience in pharmaceuticals raised further doubts about the credibility of its strategy.

The company's difficulties were exacerbated by its management's expressed wish not to enter into an agreed merger. Hostile takeovers are virtually unheard of in the pharmaceuticals industry, in view of the need to avoid upsetting the employees with whom the future of the company is so intimately bound up. Fisons also stated that it would not be pushed into selling its horticulture, consumer health care and generic pharmaceuticals businesses.

Fisons' share price dropped further in September 1992 following the announcement of poor first half figures, mainly as a result of poor drug sales, particularly in the United States. The failure of Fisons to obtain the speedy reintroduction to the

US market of its withdrawn products led to the resignation of the head of its US operations in October 1992. The full year results for 1992 reflected the half year figures and saw pre-tax profits fall from £162.6m in 1991 to £123.6m in 1992.

In January 1993 Tilade eventually obtained the approval of the Food and Drug Administration. Nevertheless, Fisons waited for the results of a further clinical trial to show that the medicine was more effective than Intal, its other asthma treatment. As a result, it did not begin marketing Tilade until June of that year. The significance of this event for the company can be judged by the comment of one drugs analyst who said that it was 'Fisons' last throw of the dice to remain a viable pharmaceutical entity'.

Fisons' half year results for 1993 revealed a significant improvement in the performance of its pharmaceuticals division, but a loss in the scientific instruments operation. This was doubly ironic in the sense that most of its recent difficulties had been in the pharmaceuticals area. In addition, the company's new chief executive, Cedric Scroggs, had previously been in charge of the scientific instruments' business.

In November 1993, Fisons' fortunes took another turn for the worse when it was discovered that some of its pharmaceuticals sales staff in the West Midlands had been involved in illegal marketing practices. These included inducements to doctors to prescribe the company's products. Such inducements are against the pharmaceutical industry's code of practice and could have led to expulsion from the Association of the British Pharmaceutical Industry and prosecution by the UK government's Medicines Control Agency. Following an internal company investigation, one employee was dismissed and another was disciplined. It was suggested that Fisons' complicated organizational structure may have contributed to the ability of certain employees to practise illegal marketing techniques; there were up to six layers of management between the chief executive and individual members of the salesforce. A cost-cutting exercise in the pharmaceuticals division, entitled 'Funding Fisons' Future' (FFF) was also considered to have damaged employee morale.

On 11 December 1993, Fisons' finance director, Roy Thomas, resigned following the discovery of dubious, although not illegal, accounting practices within the pharmaceuticals division. It was apparently boosting sales and profits by offering heavy discounts to wholesalers towards the year-end. This policy, which started in 1984, was estimated to have led to additional sales of £78m out of a divisional turnover of £427m by 1991. The collapse in profits from the scientific instruments' division made this policy unsustainable. A board meeting on Sunday 13 December led to the sacking of the company's chief executive, Cedric Scroggs. In the words of one observer this left the company 'in disarray without a chief executive, without a finance director and without an apparent strategy'. It also left the company more vulnerable than ever to a takeover.

Given the difficulties which Fisons had experienced in filling the chief executive's post at the time of Scroggs' appointment – it was unable to find a suitable external candidate – it was felt that chairman Patrick Egan would be running the company for some time to come.

Egan was the son of an Indian civil servant, conversant in Urdu and Punjabi, and was a hunting, beagling and polo-playing enthusiast. After national service and without a university degree, Egan had joined Unilever in 1951. In 1978 he became a director of that company and in 1982 chairman of its UK operations. In 1987 he was appointed regional director for Latin America, Central Asia and South Africa. In 1985 he joined the Fisons' board and in January 1992 took over as executive chairman following the resignation of John Kerridge. His forty-year career in Unilever's consumer products businesses was a very different role from the one which he would now be required to play for Fisons.

The prospects for the company at the end of 1993 were not good. At the time of Kerridge's departure Egan had claimed that the scientific equipment business was a healthy one. Yet its profits subsequently declined from about £40m in 1991 into a £16m loss in 1993. Egan had also been over-optimistic about the pharmaceuticals division, particularly in relation to the state of its pipeline of new products. The strategic review which he had initiated in January 1992 concluded with a decision to sell the consumer health and horticulture operations. With hindsight, the company should have kept the consumer businesses, which provided steady revenue streams, and sold the more cyclical scientific equipment operations, said analysts.

APPENDIX 17.1
GROWTH AND MATURITY IN THE UK FERTILIZER INDUSTRY, 1953–82: A STUDY OF ENTRY AND EXIT

Introduction

The major classes of fertilizers are known as 'straights' and 'compounds', with nitrogen-based products being the most important subset of the former category.

During the early and mid 1950s, ICI had a virtual monopoly in the production of straight nitrogen fertilizers. Fisons was the leader in the compounds sector at this time, with a 40–45 per cent market share. ICI had a 20 per cent share. In addition, a large number of small firms bought intermediates from 'the big two' and mixed them to produce their own compound fertilizers.

Entry competition, 1953–73

Entry into the fertilizer industry took the form of new entry (that is, by companies without a previous presence in the industry) and cross entry (that is, a reorientation by existing fertilizer producers). Shell Chemicals is the major example of the former category. It entered the straight nitrogen sector in 1956 and the compounds sector in 1960. In both cases, the means of entry was via imports from abroad – domestic production began several years later. In the case of the straight nitrogen sector, Shell pursued a market share building strategy by the use of delivery rebates which reflected transport cost savings.

Cross entry occurred when ICI, which had not hitherto maintained a major presence in this area, widened its product range in the compounds sector during the early 1960s. At this time, the compounds market was growing more rapidly than the straight nitrogen one. The second major example of cross-entry was the introduction by Fisons, in 1963, of a straight nitrogen fertilizer, a sector from which they had previously been excluded. ICI's hold on the straight nitrogen sector was weakened in that year by government policy. The Restrictive Practices Court made a ruling that ended its position as sole selling agent for the British Sulphate of Ammonia Federation – a decision which reduced a major barrier to entry into this sector.

Other (and possibly less important) new entrants included the heavy inorganic chemicals producer, Albright and Wilson, which gained a presence in both the major fertilizer markets, and several firms – both large and small – which began to supply liquid or gaseous (rather than solid) products. Albright and Wilson's entry strategy was one of acquisition, while the liquid and gaseous fertilizer markets were relatively new ones.

Barriers to entry

In addition to ICI's exclusive supply position with regard to ammonium sulphate – even Fisons was dependent upon its main rival – the fertilizer industry featured a number of other barriers to entry. These included the existence of significant economies of scale in fertilizer intermediates production, particularly in the straight nitrogen sector. This fact was largely responsible for the eventual emergence of a fertilizer industry structure which consisted of a three-member oligopoly and a competitive fringe.

The existence of import duties on both nitrogen and compound fertilizers constituted a barrier to overseas competition during the 1950s and 1960s. However, the duty on imports from the EEC was progressively reduced during the 1970s.

The fact that product differentiation did not constitute an effective barrier to entry was largely due to government policy. Although branding was supported by intensive advertising there was a legal requirement that firms display the plant food content of fertilizers on their bags.

The response to entry

The major feature of firms' competitive response to the entry which took place during the late 1950s and early 1960s was its accommodating nature. Price parallelism – in which the major firms' list prices consistently moved together upwards and downwards – was especially noticeable. Nevertheless, conduct was not uniform throughout.

During the early 1970s, the price war was brought to an end by a series of intra-industry agreements and there was a resumption in the upward trend of parallel pricing. The major producers accepted that attempts to significantly increase their own market shares by price cutting would simply result in reduced profits or losses, as rivals retaliated.

The initiative in halting the price war was apparently taken by ICI which refused to sell compounds and straight nitrogen fertilizers below certain levels. This occurred in conjunction with informal talks between ICI, Fisons, Shell and, later, Albright and Wilson on industry problems. In addition, Shell had apparently abandoned its ambition to obtain a 25 per cent share of the UK market.

The effect of entry on product competition and technical change

Technical change occurred in conjunction with and was, to an appreciable extent, stimulated by new entry competition. In particular, there was a move towards fertilizers with a higher plant food content, particularly nitrogen. These offered savings to the farmer in time, transport costs and storage costs. Manufacturers also benefited from reduced transport and storage costs. In addition, they gained from reduced production costs; a given plant food tonnage requires a lower total tonnage to be processed as plant food concentration increases. These trends were especially marked in the straight nitrogen sector. In the compounds sector, plant food concentration had been increasing prior to the new entry competition taking place. Nevertheless, the latter did have a significant impact.

In addition to product innovations, there were a number of significant process innovations which resulted in cost reduction and increasing production economies of scale. Moreover, some product innovations had a major impact upon the manufacturing and distributive process. These included the production of fertilizers less susceptible to caking in the bags or clogging the fertilizer spreading equipment. Nevertheless, many of the innovations within the industry were developed by the smaller firms, some of which were new to fertilizer production. The introduction of liquid fertilizers is one example of this. The major firms did, however, 'keep an eye on the situation' by pursuing a strategy of investment in small firms which were active in developing the liquid fertilizer market, in case the latter became of major importance.

During the pre-entry period (1953–58/59), price competition was more severe in the compounds sector than in the straight nitrogen market, although conditions in both tended to favour producers rather than consumers. During the early part of the post-entry period (1959/60–69/70) there was increased price competition, particularly in the compounds sector, although the list prices of the three major companies tended to move in parallel. This culminated in a price war during 1969.

ICI was partly responsible for initiating the increased price competition. In 1965, it introduced a nitrogen fertilizer which was sold at a lower price per unit of nitrogen than the less concentrated nitrogen fertilizers. There were a number of reasons for the adoption of this strategy. First of all, there were cost considerations – the new product was manufactured in a plant which took advantage of both economies of scale and new technology. Secondly, its higher concentration than competitive products probably allowed some saving in manufacturing and transport costs per unit of nitrogen. This factor may also have made a comparable price per unit of nitrogen seem too large a gap when considered on a price per tonne basis. Thirdly, ICI was facing competition from both Shell and Fisons by 1965. Therefore, it may well have decided to adopt a relatively aggressive pricing policy in order to build up sales quickly, to utilize its new capacity and to defend its dominant position in the nitrogen sector of the fertilizer market.

External factors – such as the weather and changes in government policy – were also responsible for the increasing competition during this period. The build up of Shell's imports and its publicly announced intention to capture 25 per cent of the UK fertilizer market were other significant factors. In anticipation of the planned opening of a new plant in 1968, Shell significantly increased its imports in an attempt to build up market share so that competitive pressure preceded the actual commissioning of the plant.

The evolution of the fertilizers industry

Although new product innovation continued during the 1970s, it did so at a reduced rate. More specifically, competition via increasing plant food concentration had virtually played itself out by the end of the 1960s, mainly because of natural resource limitations. This fact may have been at least partly responsible for the price war of 1969. At any rate, there was an increasing emphasis on price competition via cost reduction from this date. The stronger competition in the compound fertilizer sector at this time was largely due to the fact that consumption was only slightly greater that it had been ten years previously. The continuing growth of consumption in the straight nitrogen sector enabled new entry competition to take place with much less disruption.

The rates of growth of demand for straight nitrogen and compound fertilizers have differed substantially at various points in time. Until 1965/66, there was a move towards the increased use of compounds and away from straights. After this date, however, the trend was reversed. In addition, there was a continuing move towards increasing the nitrogen concentration of compound fertilizers, but no corresponding change in the concentration of phosphoric acid or potash.

Evidence of the industry's increasing maturity during the 1970s is provided by the considerable decline in the price elasticity of demand for fertilizers between the late 1940s and the mid 1970s. By the latter period, it was considered to be highly inelastic, although there was apparently some concern that the oil induced price increases which took place during the 1970s might increase buyer resistance.

Structural change and Fisons' divestment of its core business

In 1973, Shell's fertilizer interests, which had for a time been known as Shellstar Ltd, were sold to UKF, a Dutch producer. It seems likely that the increasing maturity of the fertilizer industry was the main reason for Shell's exit.

The 1973/74 oil crisis turned the fertilizer industry from a 'cash cow' into a 'commercial cripple'. However, Fisons' did not realize this for some time. ICI was able to weather the commercial storm which took place, both after this event and the second oil crisis of 1978/79. One major factor in its relative success was a long-term (and cheap) supply contract for methane – used in the production of ammonia – which it had negotiated with British Gas.

Fisons, however, possessed no similar advantage and incurred heavy losses. Indeed, it was dependent upon ICI for half its supply of ammonia; the other half of its requirements was imported. During the early 1960s, Fisons had chosen to diversify into pharmaceuticals rather than integrate backwards into ammonia production. Its strategy had been to use the cash generated by its (more mature) fertilizer and scientific equipment divisions to finance pharmaceutical and agrochemical research.

Although Fisons had been a very 'visible' company for a number of years, its performance had suffered due to a lack of financial resources to match. Indeed, the fertilizer industry was increasingly dominated by the major chemical companies and by government owned enterprises – such as the Norwegian, Norsk Hydro, and the Dutch, DSM – during the 1970s, as its business became more cyclical in nature and its products developed 'commodity' type characteristics.

During the 1970s, the fertilizer industry was hit by a reduction in farmers' demand and in stockpiling. More specifically, Fisons was dwarfed by ICI in the growing market for straight nitrogen fertilizers – they had approximately 15 per cent and 60 per cent shares respectively. In addition, it had lost its lead in the now declining compound fertilizer market – 35 per cent to 25 per cent. These trends were at least partly due to its policy of offering a wide product range to its customers. Indeed, it produced a fertilizer to satisfy virtually every need.

By contrast, ICI and UKF/Shellstar pursued a fundamentally different strategy. They sought to achieve economies of scale by restricting the range of their products to the minimum necessary to cover all the major segments of market demand. Together with the decline in customer loyalty to any particular producer, which took place during a period of intense price competition in the late 1960s, these facts led to ICI displacing Fisons as the largest UK fertilizer producer.

This trend led to Fisons pursuing a policy of gradual withdrawal from fertilizers from about the early 1970s. However, the existence of a major barrier to exit – a buyer would have needed to have access to cheap methane feedstocks – led it to begin a process of rationalization. Consequently, it withdrew from deep sea exporting and then closed down an independent R&D unit. Although Fisons' overall financial results improved in 1981 and the slimmed down fertilizer division moved back 'into the black', its performance was still unsatisfactory and the company continued to look for a possible buyer.

The competition policy authorities were prepared to accept ICI's acquisition of Fisons' 25 per cent share of the total UK market, provided that it loosened its stranglehold on the supply of methane. This would have required a renegotiation of its contract – on less favourable terms – with British Gas. ICI was not prepared to do this. Indeed it renewed, on still favourable terms, its contract with its monopolistic supplier. Therefore, Fisons sold its fertilizer business for £50m to Norsk Hydro, the Norwegian energy group, on 1 February 1982. Norsk Hydro had its own secure supplies of cheap methane from the North Sea.

APPENDIX 17.2
ACCOUNTING POLICIES

Basis of preparation	The accounts of the Group (see Tables 17.1 to 17.3 which follow below) are prepared in accordance with applicable accounting standards under the historical cost convention with certain assets included at revalued amounts, and deal with the results of Fisons plc, all its subsidiaries and its associated companies for the year ended 31 December. In the case of acquisitions and disposals during the year only the results relating to the period of ownership are dealt with in the Group accounts.
	The Group has opted to prepare its accounts in accordance with Financial Reporting Standard No. 3, Reporting Financial Performance. Comparative figures have been restated where necessary.
Foreign currencies	Assets and liabilities in foreign currencies are expressed in sterling at the rates of exchange ruling at 31 December. The differences arising in translation are taken directly to reserves. The results for the year of overseas companies are expressed in sterling at the average rates of exchange prevailing during the year. Currency gains and losses on trading items are taken to profit and loss account.
Turnover	Turnover represents sales by Group companies to external customers.
Pensions	The cost of providing pensions is, together with surpluses and deficits arising on revaluation of pension scheme assets and liabilities, charged against trading profits on a rational and systematic basis over the average remaining service lives of current benefit scheme employees.
Fixed assets and depreciation	Fixed assets are stated at cost or valuation less depreciation, except in the case of freehold land which is not depreciated. The values of land and buildings are professionally reviewed on a regular basis. Depreciation is provided on a straight line basis at an annual rate over

the expected economic lives of the assets. Within the following asset classifications the expected economic lives are approximately:

(a) Freehold buildings (other than in (c))   – 50 years
(b) Leasehold land and buildings:
                                        long   – 50 years
                                      short   – Life of lease
(c) Plant and equipment (including industrial buildings, housing
     or linked to plant)   – 10 years
(d) Motor vehicles   – 4 years

Leases

Assets held under finance leases are treated as if they had been purchased outright at the present value of the outstanding rentals payable, less finance charges, over the primary period of the leases. The corresponding obligations under these leases are shown as creditors. The finance charge element of rentals payable is charged to profit and loss account. Rental payments under operating leases are charged to profit and loss account.

Research and development expenditure

Research and development expenditure is charged against trading profits as incurred.

Intangible assets

Individual elements of purchased goodwill are either written off directly against reserves or are amortized through the profit and loss account. Other tangible assets are amortized through the profit and loss account.

Stocks

Stocks are stated at the lower of cost and net realizable value on a basis consistent with previous years. Cost includes appropriate overhead expenses.

Deferred taxation

Provision is made for deferred taxation where it is probable that a tax liability will become payable within the foreseeable future.

Table 17.1 Consolidated profit and loss accounts (year ended 31 December 1992)

	1992 £m	1991 £m
Turnover		
Continuing operations	1,211.0	1,151.8
Discontinued operations	73.2	88.1
	1,284.2	1,239.9
Trading profit		
Continuing operations	117.3	193.5
Discontinued operations	0.1	3.9
	117.4	197.4
Profit/(loss) on disposal and termination of businesses, after charging goodwill of £66.0m (1991 – £2.6m) written off against reserves in prior years	23.3	(24.6)
	140.7	172.8
Finance charge	(17.1)	(10.2)
Profit before taxation	123.6	162.6
Taxation	(26.9)	(41.4)
Minority interest	(1.0)	(1.4)
Profit attributable to shareholders	95.7	119.8
Dividends	(60.2)	(60.2)
Retained profit	35.5	59.6
Earnings per 25p ordinary share	13.9p	17.4p

Table 17.2 Consolidated and Fisons Plc balance sheets (31 December 1992)

	Group		Fisons plc	
	1992	1991	1992	1991
	£m	£m	£m	£m
Fixed assets				
Tangible assets	433.1	380.2	197.5	191.5
Investments	—	—	526.2	560.9
	433.1	380.2	723.7	752.4
Current assets				
Stocks	266.4	243.7	96.9	102.4
Debtors	630.7	422.9	590.8	413.2
Investments	169.0	201.0	—	—
Cash at bank and in hand	65.0	84.6	23.4	40.3
	1,131.1	953.0	711.1	555.9
Current liabilities				
Creditors – amounts falling due within one year	962.1	826.2	559.8	466.7
Net current assets	169.0	126.8	151.3	89.2
Total assets less current liabilities	602.1	507.0	875.0	841.6
Creditors – amounts falling due after one year	68.0	51.1	104.8	96.2
Provision for liabilities	6.1	6.1	—	—
	528.0	449.8	770.2	745.4
Capital and reserves				
Called-up share capital	172.8	172.6	172.8	172.6
Share premium account	32.3	30.8	32.3	30.8
Special reserves	—	—	467.6	467.6
Revaluation reserve	14.8	33.0	5.7	21.0
Profit and loss account	302.4	209.5	91.8	53.4
	522.3	445.9	770.2	745.4
Minority interests	5.7	3.9	—	—
	528.0	449.8	770.2	745.4

Table 17.3 Five-year record

	1988 £m	1989 £m	1990 £m	1991 £m	1992 £m
Turnover					
Continuing operations	732.2	900.5	1,099.2	1,151.8	1,211.0
Discontinued operations	50.7	88.7	96.4	88.1	73.2
	782.9	989.2	1,195.6	1,239.9	1,284.2
Profits					
Continuing operations	121.9	160.5	218.4	193.5	117.3
Discontinued operations	0.2	0.6	7.4	3.9	0.1
Trading profit	122.1	161.1	225.8	197.4	117.4
Exceptional items	(22.3)	(15.8)	(34.8)	(24.6)	23.3
Finance income/(charge)	8.4	2.0	0.9	(10.2)	(17.1)
Profit before taxation	108.2	147.3	191.9	162.6	123.6
Taxation	(29.5)	(32.1)	(44.6)	(41.4)	(26.9)
Minority interests	—	(0.2)	(0.7)	(1.4)	(1.0)
Net profit attributable to shareholders	79.7	115.0	146.6	119.8	95.7
Dividends	(29.4)	(40.1)	(51.5)	(60.2)	(60.2)
Transfer to reserves	50.3	74.9	95.1	59.6	35.5
Assets employed					
Long-term assets	266.6	325.6	344.7	380.2	433.1
Net current assets	109.5	183.3	149.4	126.8	169.0
	376.1	508.9	494.1	507.0	602.1
Financed by					
Ordinary shares	147.7	148.8	171.8	172.6	172.8
Reserves	181.0	221.8	242.9	273.3	349.5
Shareholders' interests	328.7	370.6	414.7	445.9	522.3
Minority interests	0.9	1.6	3.4	3.9	5.7
Loans	44.6	131.0	70.0	51.1	68.0
Taxation accounts	1.9	5.7	6.0	6.1	6.1
	376.1	508.9	494.1	507.0	602.1
Statistics					
Ratio of activity profit to average operating assets employed	30.3%	31.8%	36.7%	28.8%	15.2%
Earnings per share (FRS 3 basis)[1]	14.8p	19.1p	21.5p	17.4p	13.9p
Dividend per share (gross including tax credit)	6.67p	8.27p	10.00p	11.6p	11.6p
Dividend earnings (time covered)	2.7	2.9	2.8	2.0	1.6
Number of shareholders	33,000	30,500	34,000	44,000	50,000

1. Earnings per share figures have been adjusted for the bonus element of the rights issues of 1 for 6 in 1988 and 1 for 8 in 1990.

Redland Plc

B. Kenny and E.C. Lea

In March 1991 Redland, one of the world's largest producers of building materials for the construction industry, announced the formation of a joint venture with Stresnik Industria Gradbenega Materials of Yugoslavia. Through its German partner Braas Co GmbH, Redland acquired a 50.69 per cent stake in the venture while Stresnik took 39.62 per cent and SGP Kograd Dravograd Prodjetje, another Yugoslavian company, acquired a 9.69 per cent holding. This venture followed closely on the heels of Braas' acquisition of West Germany's leading prefabricated chimney manufacturer, Schiedel, for £30m.

This typified the strategy of Redland which from 1949 had grown largely through the formation of alliances in no less than thirty different countries spanning Australia, the United States, Europe and the Middle East. On the question of this approach to international expansion Redland's chairman, Sir Colin Corness, commented:

> I think life at Redland would be impossible if we were trying to manage all our joint ventures from the UK – there would not be time to sleep ... it is not always easy finding a suitable partner. And once you have found one, you then have to learn to work with people from different countries, where there are different norms of behaviour and different business practices ... If a company goes through a process of consultation and joint decision-making it is far more likely to produce a soundly based strategy than if the management simply arrive in a country, make a quick market survey then jump to a conclusion about what it should do.
>
> (*Acquisitions Monthly*, December 1990, p. 56)

Table 18.1 shows Redland's major joint ventures.

The nature of the products of the construction and building material industry meant that exporting was not a viable option due to the weight/value ratio of the products and also because of the local and regional traditions in using certain kinds of materials. In this sense the industry was not a global industry as was often the case with multinational companies. Redland was involved in four major areas of the industry:

- *Roofing*. Redland was the world's leading producer with over 130 plants in 22 countries.
- *Aggregates*. Redland was the fourth largest supplier of construction aggregates in the UK, one of the largest in the USA and also had operations in France and the Middle East.
- *Bricks*. The company was the fourth largest producer of clay facing bricks in the UK, a leading supplier in Holland and Australia and had brickworks in Belgium and Germany.
- *Plasterboard*. Although the company had only recently entered the UK market with the opening of a plant in 1990 Redland had achieved a market share of

Table 18.1 Redland Plc: Major joint ventures

Company	Partner	Product(s)	Stake	Year
Vereeniging Tiles (South Africa)	Vereeniging Brick & Tile	Roof tiles and bricks	Initially 49%	1949 Sold in 1989
Braas (Germany)[1]	Various	Roofing products	Initially 12% now 50.8%	1954
Redland-Braas-Bredero (Netherlands)	Bredero (until 1986)	Roof tiles	Initially 55% now 100%	1963
Société Française Redland (France)	St Gobain	Roof tiles	42.7%	1966
Redland Iberica (Spain and Portugal)	Uralita	Roof tiles	47%	1972
Zanda (Sweden and Norway)		Roof tiles	49%	1974
Several in Middle East	Various	Ready-mixed concrete	40/49%	1976/80
Western-Mobile (USA)	Koppers (until 1988)	Aggregates	Initially 50% now 100%	1986
Redland Plasterboard (Europe)	CSR Since 1990 Lafarge Coppee	Plasterboard	Initially 51% now 20%	1987
Monier PGH (Australia)	CSR	Roof tiles, bricks and pavers	49%	1988

1. Since 1954 Redland had obtained through Braas a presence in Austria, Italy, Denmark, Hungary and Eastern Germany.

Source: Redland 1991.

25 per cent in the UK. Redland had other plasterboard operations in Europe. (Redland's developments in the plasterboard industry are discussed further below.)

The senior management at Redland paid very close attention to the detail of their various activities around the world and concentrated their effort upon the identification of growth markets both geographical and product. They considered that the two main driving forces of interest to their businesses were economic welfare expressed through growth of gross domestic product and people expressed through demographic change. In terms of objectives the company was concerned to maintain real growth in earnings per share and continually compared their performance against competitors in the construction and buildings materials industry. They understood the value of and the role of the financial institutions and maintained a very close contact with them.

In March 1991 Redland made a £280 million 1-for-5 rights issue. It was speculated that the company was preparing to expand its Eastern European activities while other speculation suggested that some of its smaller rivals, suffering from the effects of the building recession in the UK at that time, might well be potential takeover targets. Redland stated in its documentation that the reason for the rights issue was '...to continue the significant capital investment and acquisition programme of recent years ... permitting gearing and interest cover to be maintained at conservative levels'.

GROWTH AND DEVELOPMENT

During the 1930s Redland had pioneered a process of extruding concrete roof tiles through a continuously moving machine which replaced the previous system whereby the cement and sand mixture was simply pressed into shape using wooden moulds. Following the end of the Second World War, when the demand for building materials was very heavy, the company embarked upon an expansion strategy which involved joint overtures in the Far East and South Africa and,in the early 1950s, West Germany. Redland technology, based on the original extrusion process, was central to these and subsequently similar joint ventures, even into the 1990s. Appendix 18.1 provides some information on the process.

Between 1960 and 1965 the expansion and diversification programme had proved very successful. Pre-tax profits increased more than fourfold and return on capital employed never fell below 18 per cent. Between 1966 and 1970, however, performance deteriorated, exacerbated by the effects of recession in the late 1960s (see Table 18.2). Appendix 18.2 provides further financial information on Redland.

In 1971 Lord Beeching, formerly head of British Railways, the UK's state-owned railway system, became chairman of Redland for just one year. He took over from Alex Young who had headed the company for 40 years and who then became a non-executive director. In the previous three years the two other main architects of Redland, Tony White and Harold Carter, had stepped down. In his first statement to shareholders Lord Beeching summed up his new philosophy:

> Although our United Kingdom business is sound and healthy it has no obvious features which make it likely to do more than grow and prosper in general conformity with the construction industry and the national economy. By contrast our overseas operations offer plenty of scope for expansion of our existing activities, but the necessity to finance their growth by loans and retained profits prevents them from making the same cash contribution as successful development at home. We shall therefore, seek for new products with better growth potential in the home market than our existing ones.
>
> (*Times Business News*, 24 May 1971)

At the end of 1971 Redland's pre-tax profit had risen to over £7 million on turnover over £65 million and a return on assets over 19 per cent. During this year turnover and profits from the group's overseas subsidiaries were £23.5 million and £3.6 million

Table 18.2 Redland performance 1961–70 (rounded figures)

Year	Turnover (£m)	Pre-tax profit (£m)	ROCE (%)
1961	11.5	2.5	25
1962	15.0	2.8	32
1963	25.0	3.0	18
1964	32.0	4.8	26
1965	38.0	5.1	27
1966	44.0	5.0	20
1967	45.1	5.1	15
1968	45.6	6.5	19
1969	42.8	6.0	14
1970	51.3	5.2	12

respectively. Return on assets had increased from 15.2 per cent in 1970 to 19.6 per cent.

Although Redland's profits continued to rise in 1973 the group's waste treatment and disposal offshoot Redland-Purle (acquired at the end of 1971 for £16.8 million), made no contribution following extensive write-offs, and at 100p on a price/earnings ratio of 9.25, the market appeared to take little account of Redland's strength in overseas earnings. For example, the profits from Germany were up by two-thirds over 1972 and dwelling completions for 1973 in that country were forecast to rise from 660,000 in 1972 to 725,000.

By 1980 Redland was firmly established as a major company in the international building materials market. Indeed, in 1980 the UK contribution to pre-tax profits (26 per cent) was considered the weakest area from its broadly based geographical spread of markets. Total pre-tax profits amounted to £57.3 million on a turnover of £397 million and net debt to shareholders' funds stood at 20.5 per cent. During the 1979/1980 recession drastic cuts in UK public expenditure coupled with sustained high interest rates depressed capital investment in buildings of all types. Chairman Colin Corness commented:

> We have drastic cuts in public expenditure at both central and local levels coinciding with exceptional and sustained high interest rates ... we witness the prospect of a government preferring to sacrifice long-term investment in the infrastructure of the country rather than facing up courageously to pruning public sector current expenditure.
>
> (*Financial Weekly*, 22 August 1980)

At the end of 1980 Redland disposed of its waste disposal business, Redland-Purle, which was at that time the largest private sector waste operator in the United Kingdom. The contribution from Purle during 1980 was estimated to be £3.25 million in pre-tax profit on a turnover of £28 million with a net book value of £15 million. Following the £20 million cash sale Colin Corness commented that he had never been completely comfortable with a business which was prone to throwing unpleasant surprises.

By 1981 continental Europe accounted for 51 per cent of Redland's profits on 39 per cent of sales, the North American profit contribution had fallen from 6 to 2 per cent and Monier (Australia) provided 13 per cent. Overall, pre-tax profit had declined to £45.6 million from £57.3 million in 1980 and the UK market had continued its decline. However, in spite of the UK's poor prospects, Colin Corness pointed to the need to see further acquisitions in Britain.

> ... we have a tax system which discriminates against overseas earnings by not allowing tax paid to be set against Advanced Corporation Tax liability. That means that there is a strong case for supplementing our flat UK earnings with acquired profits, attracting mainstream UK Corporation Tax as an offset to ACT.
>
> (*Yorkshire Post*, 28 August 1981)

In 1982 Redland made an offer for Cawoods (quarry owner, fuel distributor and with interests in off-shore oil) of £138 million with the agreement that the oil interests would be offered back to the Cawood shareholders for £21 million. This took Redland into the unfamiliar area of fuel (coal) distribution although the concrete and aggregates operations made a geographic fit. The combined market shares did not exceed the monopoly barriers in either industry and thus there were no obvious monopolies and merger competition problems.

At the end of 1986 Cawoods was merged with the British Fuel Company (which was jointly owned by British Coal and AAH Holdings). The resulting venture, named British Fuels, was managed by Redland with a 55 per cent share, AAH with 25 per cent and British Coal 20 per cent. Redland's financial director commented:

> The new group will enjoy a broader geographical spread and better product mix. There will be synergy and it will benefit from being a larger force in the market.
>
> (*The Times*, 18 December 1986)

Just 18 months later Redland sold its holding in British Fuels to a management buy-out in which British Coal retained a significant stake. An exceptionally mild winter in the UK during 1987 caused British Fuel profits to fall by some 9 per cent.

By 1989 Redland's exposure to the UK housing construction market represented only 10 per cent of group profits. The company had grown to be the world's biggest manufacturer of roof tiles and the fourth biggest brick-maker; it had also become number two in the manufacture of plasterboard. In tiles it had captured 60 per cent of the UK market while Braas, its West German associate, had a 56 per cent market share in West Germany. The company was also the biggest producer of roof tiles in the United States where it had 11 plants.

REDLAND AND BRAAS (GERMANY)

Redland's 51 per cent stake in Braas accounted for more than a quarter of the group's profit (before minority interests) in the first quarter of 1990 rising from £44 million in 1989 to £62.5 million.

Redland's entry into the German market had begun in 1954 when a joint venture was established with entrepreneur Rudolph Braas. The latter had built up a substantial business repairing and rebuilding war-damaged homes and Redland had provided the machinery and the technical expertise during the early days of Braas' operations.

As far back as 1971 the European contribution to Redland's profits, under Braas, amounted to some 40 per cent of the total. Despite the usual cyclical fluctuations suffered by the construction sector, Braas continued to be a major success story for Redland and the importance of this early entry into Western Europe proved to be instrumental in the group's expansion into Eastern Europe. This growth was helped by acquisitions and joint ventures managed through Braas and involved some level of diversification away from Redland's core business of roof tiles. For example, in 1971 Braas acquired a German company which produced plastic sheet and film for the cladding of flat and low pitch roofs. The rationale behind this was the tendency for high-rise accommodation developments in Germany and Eastern Europe, which precluded the need for roof tiles.

The chairman of Braas, Erich Gerlach, helped lead the Yugoslavian deal among other notable ventures. In 1990 he was instrumental in the acquisition of four out of five former state-owned East German tile plants for a price of DM25 million. Braas planned to produce up to 100 million tiles a year with just 320 workers working 39 hours a week in two shifts a day. Previously, the plants had employed a total of 690 workers working 42 hours a week, three shifts a day, producing 60 million tiles a year.

In a comment on the original workforce Erich Gerlach explained:

...about 150 workers were bureaucrats, they were not managers in the sense that Western companies would understand.. These were no salesmen. Cash flow and other financial controls were virtually nonexistent. Output was determined by how many houses the state had decided to build or repair and upon the ability of raw material producers to keep the company supplied and the availability of transport to deliver the finished product.

(*Financial Times*, 16 January 1991)

Braas was also quick to change the way these plants were run. Outdated British and German equipment, some of it more than 20 years old, was replaced. Bonus schemes were introduced linked to achievement of targets and computers were installed at the East German headquarters in a move to improve efficiency in order processing and accounting.

A major problem in Eastern Germany was the recruitment of salesmen. Because plants had never had to sell their produce, there was no concept of marketing or, indeed, the need to market. Other West German companies were already exporting roofing materials to Eastern Germany and over half of all roofing sales in 1990 were supplied by these companies. Sales from East German plants were some 20 per cent only of their 1980 figure.

It was considered by Redland that Eastern Germany could eventually contribute about 30 per cent of Braas' sales and profits.

REDLAND AND AUSTRALIA

In April 1987 Redland bid for the balance of the shares it did not already hold in the Australian based roof, tile and building materials group, Monier Ltd. At the time Redland held 49.9 per cent of the shares in Monier and the bid for the remaining 50.1 per cent was initially estimated to cost in the region of Aus$250.5 million (£112.3 million), at a price of Aus$3.14 per share.

CSR, the Australian building products, resources and sugar group, then offered Aus$3.50 per share for the balance of 50.1 per cent of Monier and at the end of April 1987, Monier agreed to accept an increased offer from CSR of Aus$3.80 per share. The increased offer had largely resulted from Redland's rejection as a major Monier shareholder of CSR's original offer. It was subsequently agreed between the two companies to run Monier as a joint venture.

Redland's finance director at that time indicated that the agreement was based on genuine compatibility of the two companies' aims in the building materials industry but that it was the intention to keep Monier as an independent jointly owned company. The decision to retain an interest in Monier was an indication that Redland believed that Australia was an attractive market and that with Monier's 100 per cent owner-ship of activities in the US this would give scope for further expansion in the latter.

During this period of bid, counter-bid and negotiation, Equiticorp Tasman, an acquisitive, diversified New Zealand group, had taken a 4 per cent stake in CSR and had indicated its intention of bidding for Monier. Subsequently, Redland increased its stake in Monier to 50.1 per cent, making Monier a subsidiary of Redland. However, Equiticorp Tasman succeeded in securing an initial 33.8 per cent shareholding in Monier and by the end of 1987, this had reached 48 per cent. Following negotiations Redland and Equiticorp, agreed to split Monier such that Equiticorp bought Redland's stake for Aus$320 million and Redland paid Aus$298 million to buy back the tile business. At the end of June 1987 Monier had a turnover of Aus$727 million and pre-tax profit of Aus$45 million. Roofing tiles contributed Aus$295 million of sales and Aus$45 million of pre-tax profit.

At the end of 1988 CSR, who had been overtaken by Equiticorp in its bid for Monier, entered into a joint venture with Redland. CSR bought the bricks and pipe businesses of BTR Nylex and this was merged with Monier Redland roofing operations. Commenting on the merger, Redland's finance director said:

> It makes a lot of sense to merge the largest roof and tile companies. Benefits include common administration and accounting systems, pooled management and the ability to push two important products through one distribution channel.
>
> (*Daily Telegraph*, 24 November 1988)

In addition, CSR took over management of the brick and tile business and had access to technologies developed by Redland for fixing up old brick kilns by increasing their output or enhancing them to make premium (or higher value added) bricks.

CSR's managing director, commenting after the merger, suggested that the companies would have to look abroad for expansion as there was not much else to buy in Australia.

Redland (51 per cent) with CSR (49 per cent) had, in 1987, set up a joint venture in the UK to manufacture plasterboard and a new plant, producing some 35 million square metres of plasterboard a year, had been built in Bristol. Redland had moved into plasterboard because of the long-term growth pattern in the market. Plasterboard is a dry, easily handled material generally used for internal house walls but increasingly being adapted to commercial property. In only a year of operation Redland/CSR gained some 15 per cent of the UK market which was previously dominated by BPB and to a lesser extent by West Germany's Knauf Group.

In spite of growth predictions the plasterboard market was not an easy market. As the lowest cost producer, BPB responded to the new entrants by price cutting causing losses for Redland/CSR.

REDLAND AND LAFARGE COPPEE

Lafarge Coppée, France's largest cement producer and second largest in the world), and one of the world's leading producers of construction materials, first approached Redland in the middle of 1990. The French group was keen to expand its plasterboard activities and to challenge British Gypsum (part of BPB Industries), one of only three plasterboard manufacturers active in the UK.

Redland/CSR's experience in the plasterboard industry made them more responsive to Lafarge and CSR withdrew on payment of £16 million by Redland leaving Lafarge (80 per cent) and Redland (20 per cent) to form a new venture. This joint venture between Lafarge and Redland significantly changed the balance of power in one of Europe's building materials market segments. Lafarge which held 80 per cent of the merged business, became Europe's second largest producer of plasterboard, reducing the gap between itself and BPB (see Fig. 18.1).

Redland had forecast annual plasterboard production capacity to rise to about 900 million square metres by the end of 1991 compared with an annual demand of just 600 million square metres. According to BPB at the time, prices of

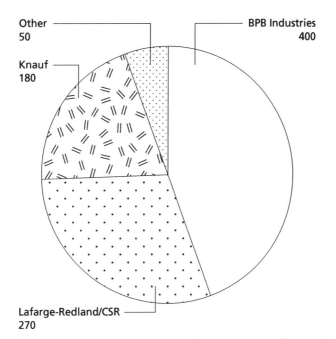

Other
50

Knauf
180

BPB Industries
400

Lafarge-Redland/CSR
270

Fig. 18.1 Plasterboard production capacity (millions of square metres).

plasterboard had fallen by 20 per cent between January and August 1989. Prices in France, where BPB was the largest supplier, had fallen between 10 and 20 per cent whereas in West Germany, where BPB was the second largest supplier behind Knauf, prices had fallen by up to 30 per cent from 1987.

Lafarge had four plasterboard plants in France and had operations in Spain in partnership with Uralit. BPB also had interests in Spain with a 65 per cent interest in Inveryeso, the country's biggest plaster company. The two companies were also competing fiercely in Italy, where Lafarge had a 20 million square metre plant near Pescara and where BPB was also building a new plant. Redland was considered a good geographical fit by Lafarge. The former had a 45 per cent shareholding in Norgrips covering Scandinavia and had plants in the Netherlands.

The joint managing director of Lafarge indicated that he expected the European plasterboard market to grow by an average of 5 per cent a year over the period 1990–95. Scandinavia, like the US, had by 1990 already switched from traditional plastering techniques and in the major markets of France, West Germany and the UK, plasterboard had displaced traditional plaster. In southern Europe, however, the substitution had hardly begun.

The subsequent withdrawal of Redland/CSR and the restructuring of the industry was commented on by Kevin Cammack, an analyst with Smith New Court:

> I would call it as dignified a withdrawal from the plasterboard market as was possible to make. There are now three clear players on a pan-European basis, and one could argue that the business will be a good deal more structured than with four groups in the market ... But I cannot see this deal lifting any of the gloom for at least two years. It will make the battle for market share even harder.

> (*The Sunday Times*, 5 August 1990)

In the newly negotiated joint venture with Lafarge, the latter held an 80 per cent interest and Redland 20 per cent. For its 80 per cent holding, Lafarge paid £39 million and with Redland's £16 million payment, the £55 million total accounted for CSR's original 49 per cent holding in the plasterboard operation.

With UK demand at little more than half the total production capacity of 315 million square metres, it was expected that 1991 would be a difficult year. However, the group was planning to make its presence known by reducing costs and improving service to customers served by the Redland plant at Bristol.

While Lafarge and BPB prepared for battle, Knauf believed its efforts to rapidly expand in the UK would erode further BPB's 70 per cent UK market share. Its Sittingbourne and Immingham plants would have a combined capacity of 65 million square metres a year using 'artificial' gypsum imported from Germany.

REDLAND AND THE UNITED STATES

Redland interests in the United States were added to indirectly, through its venture with Monier of Australia in the early 1970s. Monier had already invested in the US market by the time of the joint venture, on the basis that concrete roof tiles had yet to achieve wide-scale adoption in that market. In 1968 Redland acquired US Prismo Universal Corporation's highway-making business and successive losses from that company were turned into a £130,000 profit in 1973.

During the period 1980 to 1981 recession had hit the US construction industry and profit contribution from this area dropped from 6 per cent to 2 per cent, while the strength of sterling and the impact of high interest rates further diminished performance.

Redland increased its US interests at the end of 1982 through the acquisition of 80 per cent of the Texas quarry group Boston Industries for $70.4 million (nearly £44 million). Boston operated two limestone deposits, one with 100 million tons of reserves similar to Redland's Leicester-based quarry in the UK, and the other with 500 million tons. Total annual sales of the quarries amounted to $40 million and output was estimated to double by the late 1980s. Besides limestone aggregate for use with cement, the Boston operation also produced and marketed lime, ready-mixed concrete and other products.

Redland at this time also controlled seven other American companies involved in road-making, traffic control and roofing products. However, it was considered that no integration with Boston was planned as none of the three companies was Texas-based and many had suffered severely from the effects of recession.

In January 1985, faced with construction cuts and sluggish demand for its sand, gravel and stone at home, Redland again turned to the US for further growth through acquisition. David Taylor, Redland's director of the company's aggregate activities, commented:

> We have had to face a 30 per cent decline in the demand for aggregates in the past decade after being in growth for 25 years. After reaching a record 300m tonnes a year in 1973 UK demand has settled down to around 200m tonnes a year. Since we've got hooked on to growth, we've had to look for other markets and the US is the honeypot as nowhere else in the world has a higher per capita consumption of aggregates. During the next four

years we see a growth in the US of 10–15 per cent a year compared with a flat market in the UK.

(*Financial Times*, 22 January 1985)

During this period other UK companies were actively involved in developing US interests. Tarmac had purchased the Florida quarries of US cement company Lone Star for $79.3 million and both RMC and ARC cement companies were actively seeking aggregate companies.

A year after David Taylor's signalled intentions, Redland entered into a partnership with US insurance company USSA, to develop 800 acres of land in San Antonio, Texas. The residential and commercial project was estimated to take several years on land which was originally earmarked for quarrying stone. Ownership was split 49.3 per cent by Redland, 34.5 per cent by USSA and the remainder to a third party.

In September 1986 Redland formed a joint venture with Pittsburgh based construction materials company, Koppers. The company paid £24 million for a 50 per cent holding in the new jointly owned company Western-Mobile, and this resulted in the acquisition of aggregate company MPM operating in Colorado and New Mexico, and Western Paving, which shipped construction aggregates in Colorado, Kansas and Wyoming and was also a road-surfacer. Redland's financial director stated that:

> ... the acquisition will give quarries, gravel pits and readymix plants a complete backed-up road surfacing operation ... Kopper's management of Western Paving is now going to be the management of the Western-Mobile joint venture so we are confident there is scope for improving the performance of MPM where we will be able to cut back the loss-making operation.

(*Financial Times*, 25 September 1986)

Within a week of sealing the Kopper's venture, Redland had acquired Maryland based quarrying company Genstar Stone for $317.5 million (£220 million), from the Imasco Corporation of Canada. Genstar was described by Redland as a 'high quality aggregates business with all the characteristics we now know to look for of a large proven reserve economically located to serve a buoyant market'. Genstar's operating profits had grown from $11 million in 1981 to $30 million in 1985 and in the seven months to July 1986, it was $1 million ahead of the comparative period.

The acquisition gave Redland nine aggregates production sites with total estimated reserves of more than 1.5 billion tons – enough for more than 40 years' production. (The main market for aggregates in the US was in road construction valued at $3.96 billion a year, and spending on roads in Maryland alone was running at $500 million a year.)

STRATEGY, ORGANIZATION AND MANAGEMENT

Since the mid 1970s Redland's joint venture strategy had been based on a perceived need to reduce the risks associated with going into a foreign country, untried and uninformed. When setting up a venture Redland would agree with its partner to make particular key decisions jointly and such decisions would generally include:

- the investment of capital above a predefined limit;
- entry into new product areas or territories;
- approval of the annual accounts;

- agreement on the distribution of dividends; and
- the appointment of senior management.

These were considered in essence, to be the basis of an 'equal' partnership, irrespective of Redland's majority shareholding. The arrangements on dividend payments were normally that, unless otherwise agreed, 50 per cent of the annual net-of-tax profits would be distributed to the partners, pro rata their share in the company. This 'investor orientation' is also reflected in the group's obligation to protect shareholders' income against the effects of inflation by increasing the payments accordingly. This orientation was also predominant in the process of seeking out new ventures, as chairman Colin Corness pointed out when asked about bid speculation in the early 1980s:

> We are looking for a company where we can apply executive skills which will exploit our high liquidity and low gearing. The use of equity is not barred, but it will not be used if it disturbs our long view to maintain dividend increases to our shareholders.
>
> (*Financial Weekly*, 3 July 1981)

Subsequently the chairman responded to certain observers who had come to describe Redland as a 'nice' company with regard to its preference for joint ventures rather than aggressive takeovers.

> Sir Colin Corness says Redland's 'niceness' doesn't stem from an antipathy in principle towards hostile takeovers but rather from the force of circumstance ... we don't depend on growth through acquisition ... because we would be liable to regulatory constraints ... we are looking for a large number of small acquisitions (worldwide).
>
> (*Financial Weekly*, 10 August 1989)

Prior to Lord Beeching taking over as chairman of Redland in 1970 the management organization had evolved as a kind of pear-shaped structure. At the top (thin) end were three influential directors, Tony White, Alex Young and Harold Curter, whose style of management was both autocratic and entrepreneurial. Each of seven UK operating divisions had its own board of directors and these were visited every so often by the 'powerful triumvirate'. In essence, Redland was little more than a federation of companies which had been acquired over a decade or more. Typically, the managers of these companies had built up their businesses to the size which suited their managerial talents.

By the middle of 1971 there were two boards at the UK head office in Reigate, Surrey: the main board which dealt with the statutory formalities such as dividend policy and the appointment of directors, and the management board or group management committee. The management board had two tiers, the top level comprising the chairman Lord Beeching, managing director Colin Corness and finance director, Terry Dawson. The rest of the management board comprised the heads of the operating divisions, which replaced the previous subsidiary board structures. However, it was considered by the management that further structural changes would be necessary in a move towards establishing a board with a greater concentration of people whose interests were company-wide.

In June 1990 Redland appointed chairmen to head its three core businesses: Kevin Abbott aged 36 at 'Roof Tiles'; George Phillipson, 51, at 'Aggregates'; and Peter Johnson, 42, at 'Bricks'. All three had been board directors since April 1988. George Phillipson and Peter Johnson were previously managing directors of their businesses and Kevin Abbott was chief executive of roof tiles. These three were not young by Redland standards:

> Chairman, Sir Colin Corness, had taken over as managing director of Redland in 1967 at the age of 35 and had masterminded the group's overseas growth strategy.
>
> His attention for detail was well known and it was said he would put as much effort into correct phrasing of a paragraph in the annual report as to a multi-million pound deal. Holding a position on the Court of the Bank of England and non-executive directorships with textiles giant Courtaulds and merchant bankers Warburg, he was considered a part of the 'establishment' on doing things in their proper manner. This included ensuring that fellow directors were smartly turned out at company occasions, including board meetings. Nonetheless, he commanded respect and although considered too pernickity and occasionally peevish by some, he was respected by most who knew him and just as important, liked by them also. As one of his advisers said 'he is the model of what a British industrialist should be'.
>
> *(The Independent, 6 August 1990)*

CORPORATE PLANNING

Planning had always been an important function at Redland and this was handled by a small group in the planning team of up to five people out of the headquarters staff of 48.

The planning process involved all of the Redland companies worldwide. The chief executives of these companies following agreement of the plan with the local board, presented their annual plans to the group management committee.

Following agreement with the group management committee the plans were approved by the board of Redland in order that the budget preparations for the next financial year could take place.

The planners were responsible for preparing scenarios which would help the company take a view of how and why developments might take place which would affect the company. Part of this process included use of sophisticated forecasting methods which drew upon available national models and Redland's own in-house expertise.

In addition the planning team were responsible for a monthly economic progress report which could cover as many as thirty countries.

THE EAST EUROPEAN CONSTRUCTION INDUSTRY[1]

Inflation and monetary supply were considered to be the fundamental economic factors that would determine the short-to-medium term success of the major East European countries' transition to a free market economy.

To understand the problems that the new governments faced it was necessary to understand the political crises prior to *perestoika* and the collapsing rigid economic and political structures therein. Former Professor of Russian and Social and Economic Studies at the London School of Economics, Peter Wiles, pointed to the 'exaggerated levels of growth and the accompanying breakdown of the productive and

---

1. Data extracted from *Building*, 29 June and 6 July 1990, and reproduced in this section by kind permission of the publishers.

distributive processes' that threatened the economies of Eastern European countries, including the USSR (*Building*, 29 June 1990).

Poland's hyperinflation, Germany's reunification, Bulgaria's seeming indifference to change, Romania's hard-line attitude, Czechoslovakia's and Yugoslavia's willing attempts at enterprise, reflected the disparities and unrest so untypical of a once unified socialist system.

Against this background, the opportunities for construction business presented a challenge for Western European companies. To some extent both French and UK companies had established interests in Eastern Europe, while the absorption of East Germany into West Germany had virtually guaranteed the latter a stronghold in a major European market.

While comparative outputs in construction showed Western Europe to be well in the lead (see Fig. 18.2), the smaller output from the Eastern European countries belied the potential opportunities for growth and cooperative ventures arising from *perestroika*. Nonetheless the potential benefits of doing business through such opportunities had to be weighed against the possible financial risks signalled by recent economic indicators (see Table 18.3) and, of course, the uncertainties accompanying the need for radical internal changes.

The willingness of certain Eastern bloc countries to welcome overtures from the UK construction industry had already been established. Following a visit to Eastern Europe, Michael Spicer, UK Minister of Construction commented:

> I was impressed by the warmth of the welcome we received in all three countries, and by the genuinely expressed desire of the Hungarians, the Poles and the Czechs to do business with the UK. These countries recognize that our industry has much to offer and they welcome our participation in joint ventures ... Tourism, leisure and infrastructure are the main sectors where improvements and expansion are taking place, and the best way to exploit these opportunities is through a joint venture with a local concern.
>
> (*Euronews Construction*, Department of the Environment, No. 12, November 1990)

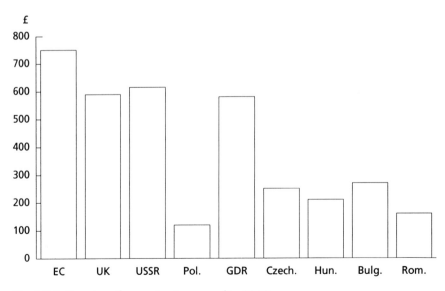

Fig. 18.2 Construction output per capita 1989.

Table 18.3 Economic indicators

	USSR	Poland	GDR	Czech.	Hungary	Bulg.	Rom.
Population (millions)	283	38	16	15	10	9	2
Area (000km)	22,400	312	108	128	93	111	23
GDP (£bn)	774	48	110	48	17	24	n/a
Growth (%) (1989)	2.5	0	2	2	6	−0.4	n/a
Inflation (%) (1989)	2	1000	10	1.4	20	11	n/a
Gross external debt (1989) (£bn)	30.8	23.8	12.4	4.8	12.0	6.25	3
Construction output (1989) (£bn)	17.4	4.2	54	3.8	2.26	2.9	4.0
Construction as % of GDP	21	10.2	7.6	5.4	13.6	10.9	9.2
Housing completions (000s) (1989)	2,100	150	220	90	50	63	n/a

Source: Adaped from *Building*, 29 June 1990, p. 36.

East Germany

East Germany's need for construction services was considered as great as any other East European country, but existing West German ventures and the reunification had taken up many of the opportunities, making it difficult for other Western nations to penetrate the market.

For Western companies to succeed in this market they would need to be very large, have subsidiaries in West Germany or provide highly specialized goods and services. Around 800,000 families out of a population of 16.5 million were inadequately housed, 20 per cent of roads and 60 per cent of urban highways were in urgent need of repair and the cost of reconstruction was estimated to be between DM 60 billion and DM 50 billion. Figure 18.3 shows construction output in East Germany.

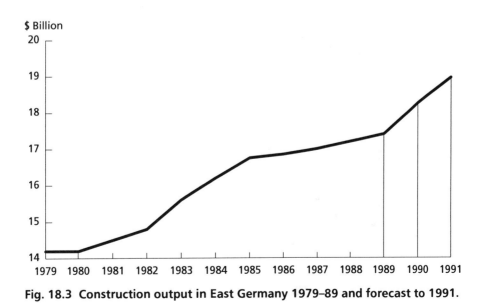

Fig. 18.3 Construction output in East Germany 1979–89 and forecast to 1991.

Poland

Of all the countries in Eastern Europe Poland had the lowest building work output per head of population, amounting to £120 in 1990. The need for building work spanned the range of domestic, commercial and industrial requirements, including factories, homes, offices and hotels. Approximately 30 per cent of pre-1945 homes needed modernizing and repair and some 1.5 million low-cost homes were required to alleviate a 20-year waiting list.

Poland's economic recovery programme was aimed at transforming the country from centralized socialist control to a completely free market. To support this transition the International Monetary Fund granted Poland a credit package of $723 million and the World Bank was to provide a further $1.5 billion. The main aims of the recovery programme were directed at: reducing inflation while maintaining a differential between this and higher interest rates; imposing severe wage restrictions and keeping increases below the level of inflation; removing price controls.

The injection of Western capital was considered vital for the regeneration of the construction industry and, in particular, to aid the privatization of companies within this sector. State construction fell some 8.9 per cent in 1989 while the total output had fallen dramatically since 1985 (see Fig. 18.4).

Slow construction progress typified performance across all sectors of industry (see Figure 18.5) which together accounted for more than 10 per cent of Poland's gross domestic product in 1989. There were approximately 2,000 construction companies split between private firms and collectives.

The poor state of the economy appeared to account for the relatively few foreign ventures in existence, although it was considered that the strength of the country's reforms would, if maintained, lead to stable long-term economic growth.

Czechoslovakia

In 1990 economists were predicting the deepening of Czechoslovakia's hard currency debt as imports of modern equipment increased. The government's inability to make

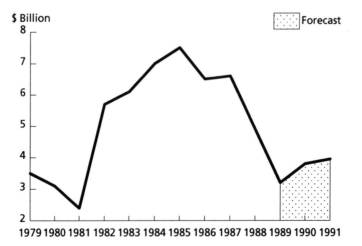

Fig. 18.4 Construction output in Poland 1979–89 and forecast to 1991.

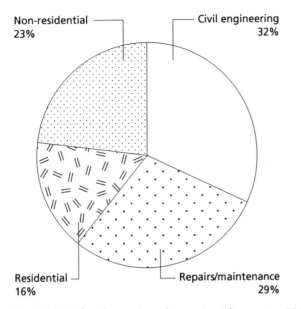

Fig. 18.5 Poland: construction output by sector 1990.

quick decisions had caused delays in the introduction of the legal framework for a market economy, including property valuation and foreign participation in business. Nonetheless, enthusiasm for joint ventures, less stringent currency laws and a massive need for housing refurbishment and improved infrastructure made the country the most attractive opportunity, for Western business, in the Eastern bloc.

Structural changes in the construction industry included the splitting up of 80 state-controlled large companies into at least 400 smaller firms, and these were to be sold to Czechoslovakian enterprises or individuals. The plan would allow for medium-sized firms to be changed to stock companies, letting foreign capital into the country, while the larger enterprises would be encouraged to establish joint ventures with Western companies.

Czechoslovakia had built some 3 million flats since the end of the Second World War in 1945. Typically, these were 14 storey prefabricated blocks containing apartments of only 62 square metres and with limited facilities. The government was planning to introduce a number of different types of prefabricated systems and to use them only for social housing which would account for some 30–50 per cent of the new-build market. More resources would also be put to the restoration of the country's dilapidated old housing stock which had been neglected since the end of the Second World War. Construction output by sector is shown in Fig. 18.6.

While the government hoped that their cheap concrete and steel would be competitive, supplies of high quality materials such as cladding, doors, windows and bricks had to be imported. To this end foreign investment for brick production was being considered.

As a result of the poor state of Czechoslovakia's infrastructure, civil engineering construction output was set to grow by 5 per cent per annum – the fastest growing sector over the two years to 1992, and the largest of the sectors by turnover (see Fig. 18.7).

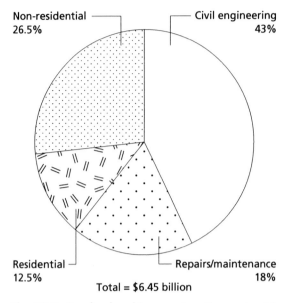

Fig. 18.6 Czechoslovakia: construction output by sector 1990.

The road and railway concern, Stavby Silinic A Zeleznic, had already signed contracts with Italian and French firms to start infrastructure repairs. The company head said:

> We are more than pleased to join with the firms from the West, but the question is how we can take part in the financing of developments. For example, we have built 30 km of road from Prague to Nuremberg – with 120 km still to go. We need banks to take part. They give us materials and the technology and we build. And then maybe we go to their countries. It has to be said that our advantage is very cheap labour.

> (*Building*, 29 June 1990)

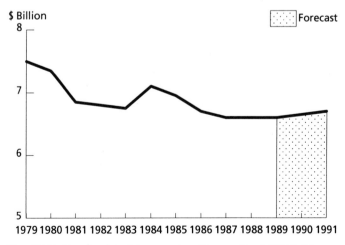

Fig. 18.7 Czechoslovakia: construction output 1979–91.

Hungary

In 1990 Hungary had the largest number of joint ventures with the West of all of the Eastern bloc countries. The country had been chosen by Redland and Ready Mixed Concrete (RMC) in their respective first ventures into Eastern Europe. In 1990 some 700 joint ventures had been established with Western construction firms. Foreign firms could export to Hungary, operate as independent contractors or, more recently, buy controlling interests in the host nation's companies through the new Budapest Stock Exchange.

The state was rapidly releasing its central control over the economy, but in 1990 it still had some way to go. Earlier in that year the country's new president announced a reduction from 90 per cent to 30 per cent of the public sector share of the economy, including a substantial privatization programme and plans to join the European Community.

Although traditionally known for its relatively healthy economy, Hungary's foreign debt at £12 billion and 30 per cent inflation rate in 1990 were causes for concern. Added to this unemployment was set to rise by a factor of 6 from a 1989 figure of 30,000.

Construction output had remained relatively stable over the decade to 1989 (see Fig. 18.8). The main derived demand factor was the tourist trade which brought in more than 20 million foreign visitors in 1990. Most major Western hotel chains, such as Trusthouse Forte and Novotel, were involved in building programmes, and an additional 40,000 rooms were planned for the period to 1995.

Although the situation regarding property had still to be clarified by the government, many owners including the public sector were speculating and prices were soaring due to demand exceeding supply. Demand for property in the capital, Budapest, and other populated areas reflected the opportunity for growth in shopping centres, company offices and the like. The housing sector was experiencing only marginal growth as a result of the phasing out of public sector involvement – 30,000 new units per year in 1990, compared with 100,000 units in 1979 – and most existing homes were in a poor state of repair.

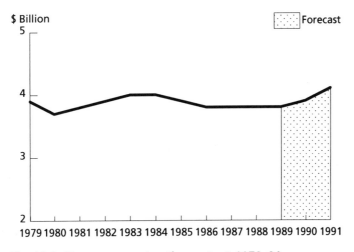

Fig. 18.8 Hungary: construction output 1979–91.

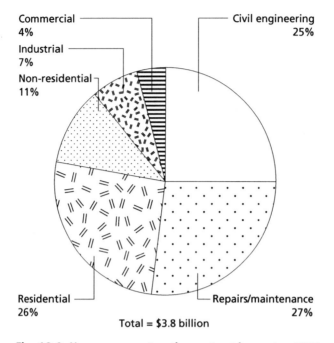

Fig. 18.9 Hungary: construction output by sector 1990.

The infrastructure was also in a bad state of repair and, as one industry observer pointed out, modernization could only take place if Western countries helped to finance the improvements.

Construction output by sector in shown in Fig. 18.9.

Bulgaria

The rapid industralization of Bulgaria since the end of the Second World War had transformed the country from what was predominantly a rural economy. The demand for housing, created by the population explosion in the capital, Sofia, and other major towns, coupled with a rundown in construction output over the period from 1985 (see Fig. 18.10), led to one of the country's biggest problems. The situation was further exacerbated by the generally poor state of housing in existence.

Private initiatives, together with construction cooperatives, were encouraged but, in the main, housing was not considered to be a promising sector for Western companies. However, the country was in desperate need for Western help in the carrying out of major infrastucture projects. A crumbling road system, a delayed underground system construction in Sofia and intended improvements to the main airport (in line with plans for tourism development) represented more hopeful opportunities. Construction output by sector is shown in Fig. 18.11.

Recent reforms in the banking system and new tax laws had allowed Bulgaria to take its initial steps towards a free economy.

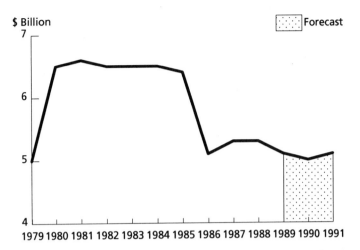

Fig. 18.10 Bulgaria: construction output 1979–89 and forecast to 1991.

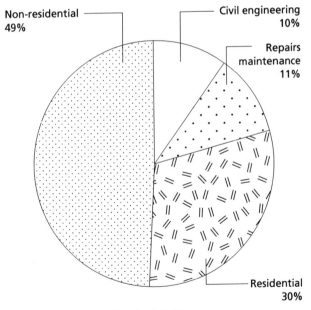

Total = $5 billion

Fig. 18.11 Bulgaria: construction output by sector 1990.

Romania

The need for new housing was perhaps more urgent in Romania than any of the other Eastern bloc countries. With the exception of monuments and private villas, virtually nothing was built in the country during the final years of Ceausescu's reign.

In response to the country's 100,000 homeless families, Romania was relying on cooperation from France for its reconstruction programme. French being a second language in Romania, it was considered that France would have a natural advantage in securing contracts and joint venture agreements. Projects already underway with French companies in 1990 included hotel chains, a world trade centre and railway construction. It was hoped that such cooperation would lead to benefits of technology transfer, for example in the fields of earthquake-proof building construction and drainage and water supply technology.

In transport, a medium-term plan had been developed to improve road links with other East European countries, to facilitate access to the tourist centres near the Black Sea.

Although Romania had reported growth in construction output over the ten years to 1989 (see Fig. 18.12), it emerged that many official statistics had been fabricated. The bureaucracy was evident at every level of contact with Romanian business and this, along with the aforementioned uncertainties, would have to be borne by potential Western investors.

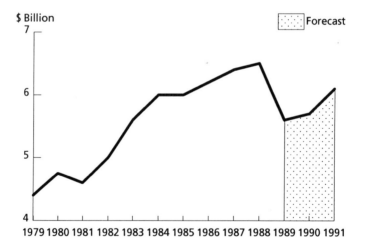

Fig. 18.12 Romania: construction output 1979–89 and forecast to 1991.

The Soviet Union

Over the period 1990 to 2000 the Soviet Union expected to embrace a Western-style mixed economy. The barriers to Western construction contractors and building material suppliers would be eroded following corporate restructuring and the introduction of property laws in 1990.

The Soviet construction industry employed more than 12 million people in 1989 within three major sectors (see Fig. 18.13). In Moscow five major construction

Fig. 18.13 The Soviet Union: construction output by 1979–89 and forecast to 1991.

companies employed more than 280,000 people in total, covering the construction activities of flats and factories, offices, heating, lighting and ventilation, roads, bridges and docks, and building materials.

Some Western companies, including Redland (tile manufacturing in Kiev) had established ventures with the Soviet Union.

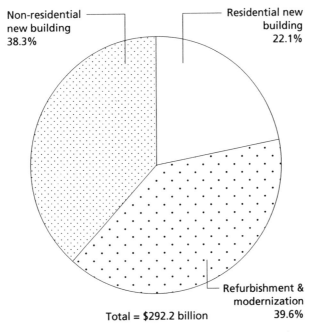

Fig. 18.14 The Soviet Union: construction output by sector 1990.

Commercial construction offered the most attractive opportunity for Western developers and contractors and more than 200 foreign companies were estimated to be waiting for offices in Moscow.

European construction Research (Copenhagen) had predicted a potential demand for 10 million square feet of hotel accommodation in Moscow over the period 1990–95.

Repair and maintenance was considered a further significant growth area along With industrial construction. In 1989, 865,000 houses were renovated and, according to some estimates 80 per cent of this work was done through the 'black economy'. Additionally infrastructure improvement represented an opportunity for growth. The USSR had limited major highways and water transport was hindered by the long winter freeze. Over the period 1985/90 freight had grown sixfold, but the rail network had only tripled in capacity, and a similar under-capacity existed in Soviet airports.

Construction output by sector is shown in Fig. 18.14.

APPENDIX 18.1
GROWTH OF TILE MANUFACTURE BASED ON EXTRUSION PROCESS

- Although concrete tiles of a sort had existed since the 1840s (Germany) the process was really pioneered by Redland after the First World War. Marley started production at about the same time and also very close, geographically, to Redland.
- Concrete tiles were initially made by hand, in plain tile form, and there was no patent cover available to either company at this stage. Even so, the hand-made product was very competitive against slate and clay.
- From the outset, hand-made concrete tiles possessed characteristic benefits over slate and clay:
  - dimensional accuracy;
  - wider colour range;
  - price advantage;
  - better technical performance through higher strength, lower weight and much better frost resistance;
  - geographic scope, due to more widely available raw materials, to make concrete tiles anywhere justified by the market.
- Concrete tile-making started in south-east England where the clays are technically inferior to the Staffordshire (Etruria) clays. To this advantage was added the extrusion process, developed for plain tile-making prior to the Second World War. There was still no patent cover at this stage.
- With its considerable production cost advantage, concrete started to gain share strongly against slate and clay, both of which remained manual processes before the Second World War. The moulding of clay tile was notably less efficient than the extrusion process used for concrete.
- After the Second World War came the first development of an interlocking concrete tile in the form of Redland's '49' tile (in 1949). This was a major step although the concept of an interlocking design was already established in the clay tile market. Moreover, the concrete tile enjoyed the protection afforded by registration of the design. Marley followed with its own interlocking ranges, modified in shape and detail to avoid infringement of Redland's rights.
- By this stage, the interlocking concrete tile had become a very efficient way of covering a roof through the use of a single layer of accurate and low-cost tiles.

International growth

- The concrete tile market expanded rapidly from this point. In 1950, Redland introduced Double Roman, still the most popular model in the UK and elsewhere. This was followed in the early 1950s by Renown, Regent and other models.
- The expansion was based on offering wide choice of colour, shape and profile. It therefore provided a new concept of roof design to architects.
- Throughout, Redland combined a strong business strategy with the developing technology. The success of the early 1950s therefore led to new UK plants and to overseas licensing of the process. This was highly opportune timing given the need to rebuild postwar Europe.
- The alliance with Braas (1954) was a key building block in Redland's international growth and a precursor to others in France (Saint Gobain) and elsewhere.

Technology, competitive advantage and ease of copying

- Technical process details are only available to joint venture licensees. These benefit from technology in which:

- product design is optimized both for processing and end performance;
- extrusion provides speed and accuracy of tile forming – effectively a continuous process. It is the tile forming which is the 'clever' aspect;
- highly developed expertise in formulation again balances processing characteristics and end performance.

- It is true to say that the process is relatively easy to copy. It is fairly straightforward and is patented only as to specific areas of the plant. However, design protection always exists and it is difficult for competitors to achieve Redland's high levels of efficiency.
- Redland has always managed to maintain its innovative and marketing edge. It has also stayed more closely focused on concrete tile as opposed to derivative businesses.

APPENDIX 18.2
REDLAND PLC: FINANCIAL INFORMATION

Consolidated profit and loss

	Year ended 31 December 1990 (£m)	Year ended 31 December 1989 (£m)
Turnover		
United Kingdom subsidiaries	409.2	470.1
Overseas subsidiaries	1,002.3	839.7
Group share of associates	228.4	237.7
	1,639.9	1,547.5
Operating profit (see below)		
United Kingdom subsidiaries	72.4	107.4
Overseas subsidiaries	155.9	119.8
Group share of associates	28.7	32.7
(principally overseas)		
	257.0	259.9
Interest payable, net	(12.0)	(9.7)
Profit on ordinary activities before taxation	245.0	250.2
Tax on profit on ordinary activities	(63.8)	(65.1)
Profit on ordinary activities after taxation	181.2	185.1
Minority interests	(27.5)	(17.1)
Preference stock dividends	(9.9)	—
Profit attributable to Redland Plc before extraordinary items	143.8	168.0
Extraordinary items after taxation	(9.9)	—
Profit after extraordinary items	133.9	168.0
Dividends	(69.8)	(64.3)
Retained profit	64.1	103.7
Earnings per share	52.3p	61.2p
Dividends per share	25.0p	23.35p

Analysis of operating profit

	Year ended 31 December 1990 (£m)	Year ended 31 December 1989 (£m)
By product:		
Roofing	139.1	107.5
Aggregates	75.0	100.0
Bricks and other	42.9	52.0
Total operating profit	257.0	259.9

	Year ended 31 December 1990 (£m)	Year ended 31 December 1989 (£m)
By geographical region:		
United Kingdom	72.8	108.6
Continental Europe	119.1	80.3
United States of America	45.2	45.5
Australasia and the Far East	19.3	23.2
Other	0.6	1.3
Total	257.0	259.9

Consolidated balance sheet

	As at 31 December 1990 (£m)	As at 31 December 1989 (£m)
Fixed assets		
Tangible assets	1,138.1	1,061.5
Investments	148.5	123.4
	1,286.6	1,184.9
Current assets		
Stocks	189.8	196.3
Debtors	321.7	313.8
Short-term investments	232.8	249.9
	744.3	760.0
Creditors – due within one year		
Bank loans and overdrafts	(35.2)	(29.0)
Trade and other creditors	(277.4)	(270.1)
Corporate taxation	(32.6)	(85.2)
Dividends	(47.1)	(43.7)
	(392.3)	(428.9)
Net current assets	352.0	332.0
Total assets less current liabilities	1,638.6	1,516.9
Creditors – due after one year		
Loans	(482.9)	(413.2)
Convertible bonds – subordinated	(60.0)	(60.0)
Provisions for liabilities and charges	(68.5)	(67.8)
	1,027.2	975.9
Shareholders' funds		
Capital and reserves		
Called-up ordinary share capital	69.0	68.8
Share premium account	245.5	242.0
Revaluation reserve	167.9	94.6
Profit and loss account	294.9	326.4
Ordinary shareholders' funds	777.3	731.8
Preference stock	129.5	93.2
Minority interests	120.4	150.9
Total shareholders' funds	1,027.2	975.9

Five-year financial summary

	1985/86 £m	1986/87 £m	1987/88 £m	1988 £m	1989 £m
Sales – building materials					
United Kingdom	285.8	328.2	358.6	456.0	470.1
Overseas	355.3	417.1	623.4	809.2	839.7
Group share of associates	291.2	288.6	290.6	128.3	237.7
	932.3	1,033.9	1,272.6	1,393.5	1,547.5
Sales – fuel distribution	359.3	266.1	527.4	505.6	—
Total sales	1,291.6	1,300.0	1,800.0	1,899.1	1,547.5
Profit					
United Kingdom	60.6	68.7	88.8	104.8	107.4
Overseas	40.3	51.7	89.1	115.6	119.8
Group share of associates	23.8	23.4	18.3	10.7	32.7
Operating profit	124.7	143.8	196.2	231.1	259.9
Interest payable, net	(11.9)	(13.1)	(11.1)	(9.6)	(9.7)
Profit before taxation	112.8	130.7	185.1	221.5	250.2
Tax	(35.5)	(36.3)	(50.5)	(59.7)	(65.1)
Minority interests	(9.1)	(13.8)	(17.8)	(19.5)	(17.1)
Profit attributable to Redland Plc	68.2	80.6	116.8	142.3	168.0
Capital					
Net assets employed	554.5	888.7	902.5	1,000.8	1,516.9
Return on capital (%)	26.0	25.5	24.6	27.3	23.6
Shares					
Earnings per share (pence)	31.1	36.0	43.2	52.3	61.2
Dividends per share – net (pence)	11.30	13.00	15.85	19.80	23.35

Notes:
- In 1988, the financial year-end was changed to the end of December from the end of March.
- The return on capital employed is calculated as the ratio of operating to average total assets less current liabilities excluding cash, deposits and short-term investments and bank loans and overdrafts.
- Earnings and dividends per share for 1985/6 have been adjusted for the rights issue in 1986.
- The fuel distribution business was sold in December 1988.

ICI and Hanson – a contrast in styles

J.R. Anchor

INTRODUCTION

This case study tracks the evolution of ICI plc between late 1990 and the end of February 1992. The case focuses in particular upon the events surrounding the acquisition of a 2.8 per cent stake in the company by Hanson plc in May 1991. The subsequent demerger of ICI, which involved the flotation of its pharmaceutical division as a separate entity, Zeneca, is not covered by the case study. This seminal event in the history of the organization inevitably brought about major changes in ICI's operating procedures, as well as its structure. These are not reflected in the case study either.

ICI IN THE EARLY 1990s: BACKGROUND TO THE STAKE

In late 1990, ICI was being badly hit by the economic recession. Costs were rising but the company was unable to raise prices because demand was weak. This led ICI to announce plans to cut at least £100m off planned capital spending of £1bn in 1991. Current costs were also being monitored increasingly strictly. These cuts mirrored action which had been taken during the recession of the early 1980s. The difficulty for the company in 1990 was that the severity of the early 1980s round of reductions and the growing need to satisfy safety, health and environmental requirements meant that there was an ever upward pressure on its capital expenditure.

On 28 February 1991, ICI reported pre-tax profits of £977m in 1990, down from £1,527m in 1989. The company said that the 36 per cent fall was 'due both to the impact of recession in most major economies and to the effects of the Gulf crisis' of that year. In spite of this significant decline in profitability, ICI held its dividend at the previous year's level of 55p per share. Its dividend cut in 1980 – the first time in its history – had produced such an adverse market reaction that the company was determined not to repeat the exercise.

One significant feature of the 1990 accounts was an extraordinary charge of £300m for 'reshaping the ICI Group business portfolio, comprising withdrawals through business divestments, closures and other restructuring measures'. This was to back up its new corporate strategy which would concentrate the group's resources 'even more selectively' on 'strong businesses which can play a truly global role'. Sir Denys Henderson, ICI's chairman, said that other parts of the company would generally be viewed either as cash generators or as candidates for divestment. This statement of strategic intent was one which was to become a feature of the subsequent public debate between ICI and Hanson in relation to the future direction of the former.

ICI summarized its new posture by stating that its strategic objective was 'to increase shareholder value by focusing resources so as to exploit fully the profitable growth potential of those businesses where ICI already has or can develop strong global positions encompassing the major markets of Europe, North America and Asia Pacific'.

The company would also be reshaped organizationally into seven international business groupings: pharmaceuticals, agrochemicals and seeds, specialities, paints, industrial chemicals, explosives and materials. These businesses would have a pre-eminent position over the ICI territories (national companies and regional organizations).

In spite of these changes, a number of analysts continued to criticize ICI's performance, believing that not all of it could be laid at the door of the recession. The criticisms of ICI, which Hanson was to make subsequently, therefore fell upon fertile soil.

HANSON'S 2.8 PER CENT STAKE

On 15 May 1991 Hanson bought a 2.8 per cent stake in ICI. This prompted intense speculation that a full-blooded takeover attempt might eventually result. ICI's merchant bankers were called in to advise on the company's value and its tactics in the event that a bid was launched. Divisions also emerged on the government's backbenches between those who preferred to leave any possible bid to the market and those, some of whom had ICI plants in their constituencies, who feared that a damaging industrial war was about to break out. Discussion also took place regarding the respective roles of the European Commission and the UK's Monopolies and Mergers Commission in the event of a possible bid. It was eventually accepted that the European Commission would have jurisdiction over any bid.

ICI'S RESPONSE

Although there was considerable uncertainty about the eventual outcome of Hanson's stake in ICI, what was clear was that ICI was about to undergo fundamental changes. In effect, defending ICI from Hanson and restructuring the chemical company to make it more profitable became one and the same goal. Essentially ICI was faced with two, related decisions. The first was whether it should spin off or demerge a large chunk of the company or whether it should pursue evolutionary change through selling smaller bits of several divisions. If the company decided to opt for revolutionary change it would have to choose what to spin off: one of its star-performers, such as pharmaceuticals, or the cyclically performing bulk chemical businesses.

In relation to the pharmaceuticals division, there were three main options available. First of all, there was outright sale, although the large price-tag might make such an option non-viable in practice. Secondly, there was floating the division as a separate company. The main objection in this case was the loss of control which would result. The third alternative was a joint venture with one of the world's top twenty pharmaceutical groups, outside of the top five. The main difficulty with a demerger or joint venture is that it could well foil any bid from Hanson, but it would also leave ICI more dependent on cyclical businesses.

It was this risk which had led ICI in the mid 1980s to consider floating its bulk chemicals and polymers division. By detaching bulk chemicals, the value of the rest of the group might be enhanced. The recovery of the division between 1986 and 1989 led to a decision to keep it largely intact. By early 1991, however, bulk chemicals were only just breaking even and demand was still falling.

Incremental changes were alternatives to these radical moves. Among the alternatives which were put forward were joint ventures with other European and international petrochemicals groups for products such as soda ash, salt, chloralkali and limestone where ICI felt that it did not enjoy a technological edge; sale of its polypropylene production facilities; sale of Tioxide, the pigment maker, which was a distinct ICI company; disposal of its loss-making advanced materials businesses; withdrawal from film production; completion of its withdrawal from fertilizers. The explosives division would probably be retained intact, although it would not be top of the list for investment. It was unlikely that ICI would try to get out of bulk chemicals areas in which it had a strong market position. Such a programme of divestment and joint ventures would make ICI a very different company. As one commentator noted, 'in normal times, such a programme might be sufficient to satisfy investors. But since Hanson started breathing down the chemical group's neck, normal times have been a luxury at ICI.'

In the event public relations, as much as strategic considerations, were to influence the course of the relationship between the two companies during the remainder of 1991. ICI succeeded in gaining the support of its employees, former employees and opinion formers in areas in which it had a physical presence, in its attempt to ward off the attentions of Hanson. On Teesside, for instance, it was a case of 'better the devil you know' in spite of the fact that ICI had offloaded 20,000 workers during the preceding 20 years and that it was facing legal action from local residents over air pollution. As the chief executive of the local chamber of commerce put it, 'there is a lot of loyalty to ICI on Teesside because ICI has itself shown a lot of loyalty to the area.'

Amongst MPs there was a cross-party groundswell of opinion against Hanson. At one point this led Hanson to write to a number of MPs complaining that they had made unflattering comments about Hanson 'based on inaccurate information'. Indeed by early July Hanson was on the defensive – almost for the first time in its 30 year history. Since it took its stake in ICI, the ratio of the company's share price to the market average had fallen by almost 10 per cent.

On the day on which Hanson, Britain's most feared corporate raider, had taken its stake in ICI most City analysts had expected that ICI would be outdone by Hanson in the public relations contest between the two groups. In fact, ICI fought a surprisingly aggressive and effective campaign against Hanson. In the early weeks of the battle, Hanson had been able to capitalize on the City's disappointment with ICI's recent financial performance. Subsequently, however, ICI was able to engineer a debate about the quality of Hanson's profits and its style of management and to deflect attention from its own need to reorganize.

Hanson's success at financial manipulation had enabled it to pay tax at a rate well below the UK corporate average. The fact that the methods used to achieve this feat had never been public knowledge – perhaps understandably – focused attention on Hanson's style of management. The latter was essentially a centralized one. Only one non-executive member of Hanson's board had never held an executive post in the group. The role of executive directors on the board was also limited. Strategic decisions were not discussed at quarterly board meetings, the main purpose of which was to review the group's financial performance. The full board was not informed when Hanson made its investment in ICI, even though it was meeting while the shares were being bought. Strategy was determined by Lords Hanson and White, even though the latter was not a director of the UK holding company. A loss-making investment in the horse-racing industry added to public questioning about Lord White's role in the company – Lord White has a passion for horse racing. All this led one commentator to state that 'when Hanson took the stake in ICI, the reaction of most analysts was that ICI would be changed beyond recognition, whether or not it eventually faced a formal bid ... Less expected, but increasingly likely, is that Hanson too will never be the same again.'

In an attempt to regain the public relations initiative, Hanson announced on 15 July that it would like to acquire a 40 per cent stake in ICI's pharmaceutical subsidiary. Hanson argued that this would increase the stock market value of ICI and would also guarantee sufficient financial backing to ICI pharmaceuticals to turn it into a world leader, especially if another pharmaceutical company was invited to join the joint venture to increase its scientific and marketing resources.

Perhaps inadvertently, this also reinforced attention on another issue from which ICI was able to reap a propaganda advantage in the war of words between the two companies. This was their respective spending on research and development (R&D). ICI was one of the leading UK investors in research and development: in 1990 it had spent £679m. Historically it had an outstanding record as an innovator – polyester, polyethylene, Perspex and beta blocker heart drugs were among its 'successes'. It was estimated that between 1985 and 1989 ICI's spending on R&D rose by 70 per cent in real terms compared with a 40 per cent increase for the rest of the UK chemicals industry and a decrease of 8.4 per cent for manufacturing industry as a whole. An analysis of US patents by the Science Policy Research Unit at the University of Sussex found that ICI was the most innovative British company by a long way. One study also found evidence that ICI's R&D was targeted quite effectively at growing product areas by comparison with a number of its leading competitors worldwide. The company's performance as an innovator was central to its defence against Hanson. Critics of Hanson alleged that it would slash ICI's R&D budget. Indeed Hanson was accused of being a 'short-termist' company par excellence.

ICI'S 1991 HALF YEAR RESULTS

ICI became less vulnerable to a hostile takeover bid, in analysts' eyes, following the announcement of its 1991 half year results which were above City expectations. The profit figure of £507m was 31 per cent below the previous year's result but significantly above most forecasts. ICI also said that measures which it was taking to cut costs and close loss-making businesses would add £450m to annual pre-tax profits by the middle of 1993. Although no details were given about how this would be achieved, it was clear that significant job losses would be involved, either through disposal of businesses or via redundancies. Three divisions had been selected for the most significant cost-cutting measures: specialities, which makes dyes and ingredients for detergents; materials, which manufactures advanced plastics and acrylics;

and industrial chemicals, which groups together ICI's oldest businesses in bulk chemicals. The emphasis in the other four divisions would be upon more gradual efficiency gains.

Analysts were divided about the extent to which the results represented a significant improvement in ICI's underlying trading performance. Sir Denys Henderson, the company's chairman, said that ICI had not sped up plans to cut costs to ward off the threat of a hostile takeover bid. He admitted, however, that Hanson's presence, as a 2.8 per cent shareholder, had 'concentrated minds'. One analyst was somewhat more direct: 'ICI needs the pressure from Hanson and I hope that pressure continues for sometime', he said. Yet another opined: 'We have seen it before. A cyclical company, which is under pressure from a predator, delivers great results, despite a severe recession. This was par for the course as an image-building exercise.'

HANSON'S RESPONSE

Hanson's response to ICI's results was initially cautious. On the day of their announcement, Mr Martin Taylor, Hanson's vice-chairman, stated that his company would analyse the results and might then subsequently issue a statement on ICI's performance. Two days later, however, Lord Hanson himself publicly criticized ICI for the first time. He said that shareholders needed more real evidence that ICI's management was fully addressing the ways in which shareholder value could be maximized. More explicitly, he suggested that ICI was 'underperforming' and 'over-managed' and that there was 'significant scope for enhancing shareholder value'. He also complained that ICI had only given 'limited' information on how it intended to reshape the company. In a sense. Lord Hanson's comments may be seen, at least partly, in the context of the pressure which his company had been put under by ICI in relation to its own financial performance. As a Hanson adviser admitted, Hanson's motive for publishing its chairman's statement was to reassure its own shareholders that it had their interests at heart in making the investment in ICI. 'Our first objective is to create value for our shareholders', Lord Hanson said. Somewhat ironically, Hanson's third quarter results, which were unveiled in August, revealed that its own performance had been significantly affected by the recession. Indeed the results left analysts and investors wondering where further growth would come from since the company was overdue for an acquisition – it had been Hanson's policy since 1964 to increase profits and pursue 'interesting' acquisitions on an annual basis. The pressure for an acquisition is one reason why Hanson looked at the possibility of merging with ICI in the first place.

On 16 September, Hanson announced an agreed bid for Beazer, the Anglo-American building group, its first substantial acquisition for two years. For the first fifteen years of its corporate life, Hanson had been involved mainly with a series of small-scale acquisitions and divestments. During the 1980s it had engaged in a number of big deals, such as its acquisition of the Imperial Group, Smith Corona, Peabody and Consolidated Goldfields. The key to Hanson's strategy to date had been its decision to avoid businesses which were heavily capital-intensive, such as steel, shipbuilding, nuclear power, oil and gas. This explains why many observers suggested that any acquisition of ICI by Hanson would lead to the sale of ICI pharmaceuticals. These sorts of businesses, Lord Hanson said in 1987, 'rely on huge and expensive research with a prospect of a return sometime or never'.

Hanson's management structures are contained within geographical frontiers. Both the US and UK halves of Hanson reported to management which is resident in either New York or London. In only one product line did Hanson own significant assets which crossed frontiers. Lord Hanson summarized the situation by stating that the company concentrated on only two markets – what he termed 'over here and over there' (i.e. the UK and the USA). The companies (or 'profit centres' in Hanson-speak) which were kept typically had three attributes. First of all, they usually operated in a mature low technology sector in which they had a dominant or near dominant market share; secondly, they had a strong cash flow; finally they had a capable middle management. The latter were usually the beneficiaries of a process known as 'Hansonization'. This is a rigorous cost-cutting exercise which results in job losses for senior managers, but job opportunities for less senior ones, and cutbacks in capital investment and R&D spending. This emphasis on management percolated through Hanson's philosophy. As Lord Hanson put it, 'we are an industrial management company ... management .. is our greatest asset.' While the process of 'Hansonization' may raise an acquired company's efficiency and profitability to a higher level in the short to medium term, the long-term growth that these companies – low technology, mature market, large market share – achieve tends to track general economic conditions.

HANSON COMES UNDER THE MICROSCOPE

In an attempt to head off criticisms of its corporate governance Hanson announced the appointment of three new non-executive directors on 18 September. The head of the search committee suggested that the appointments could change the way that the company was run, and would bring about a stronger mechanism of communication between executive and non-executive directors. The reaction of institutional shareholders, however, was to voice their surprise that the three new non-executive directors were not of a higher calibre.

During the following week, ICI announced changes to the responsibilities of its executive directors. The most noteworthy change was the splitting of the chairman's job into two. Sir Denys Henderson would retain his title of Chairman and Chief Executive Officer but would concentrate on strategy and projecting ICI's image. Mr Ronnie Hampel would become Chief Operating Officer, responsible for day-to-day operations and for the implementation of the company's reconstruction plan. The chief operating officers of ICI's seven divisions would report to Mr Hampel, who would also be in charge of the company's acquisitions and divestments.

Hanson's fortunes in its propaganda battle with ICI took a turn for the worse when a letter which had been sent by Lord Hanson to his senior public relations adviser on 26 August was published in *The Observer* newspaper on 13 October. The letter had been provoked by an article in another newspaper which had attacked Lord Hanson for investing shareholders' money in a bloodstock partnership in which Lord White also held a personal stake. The letter stated Lord Hanson's belief that his company had lost the undeclared public relations war with ICI over the summer.

Hanson's institutional investors responded to this publicity by stating that the company must change its own managerial style and take account of criticisms over its corporate governance instead of simply blaming its public relations advisers for not getting its message across. Hanson's own advisers did in fact agree with many of these criticisms. Against their recommendations, Lord Hanson had scrapped his weekly meetings with his public relations advisers and senior directors; he had refused to attack ICI's environmental record; and he had not appointed 'heavyweight' non-executive directors to the board. The company's institutional investors suggested, *inter alia*, that Hanson should appoint a strong chief executive to counter the charge that it was really a 'two-man band' (i.e. Lords Hanson and White). More seriously still, they had begun to question whether Hanson's assets could be worth more if the conglomerate was broken up, i.e. if Hanson was itself subject to 'Hansonization'.

Within days, it was announced that Hanson was taking the unprecedented step of writing to its big shareholders outlining group strategy. Shareholders were promised a series of meetings after Hanson's full-year results were announced in December. Hanson's formal offer document for Beazer, which was published at the same time, revealed that Hanson had classified its 2.8 per cent stake in ICI as a fixed asset. This tended to suggest that Hanson intended to hold onto its stake for the foreseeable future.

'NO BID FOR THE MOMENT'

On 28 January 1992, at Hanson's Annual General Meeting, Lord Hanson announced that the company had no plans to bid for ICI. Indeed he stated that there had never been any public statement to the contrary – 'that was all media speculation and market rumour', he said. The City's Takeover Panel on mergers and acquisitions said that Lord Hanson's statement was 'unambiguous' and therefore prevented the conglomerate from making a bid for a 'considerable period of time'. Only a 'material change' in ICI's circumstances would give Hanson the right to try to acquire the chemicals company. A spokesman for the panel added that even if there was a significant fall in ICI's 1991 profit – to be announced on 27 February – this would not constitute a material change in circumstances. Lord Hanson told his shareholders that he believed that ICI had 'lost a great opportunity' by refusing to talk with him and that as ICI's second biggest shareholder Hanson would 'continue to watch its progress with great interest and affection'.

ICI's 1991 results, which were duly announced on 27 February, revealed a patchy performance. While pharmaceuticals and paints achieved record profits, the performance of the core specialty chemical operations were poor, with the materials division sustaining its second consecutive loss.

APPENDIX 19.1
ICI: BACKGROUND AND FINANCIAL INFORMATION

Strategy, structure and style

The corporate centre in ICI is concerned with business unit planning, but it believes in the company devolving decisions to its business units as much as possible. It, therefore, concentrates on planning processes and on the review of specific proposals. Control is exercised in the light of results achieved, against both financial and strategic objectives.

ICI has a number of independent – in both an operating and financial sense – divisions which are each held accountable for their results. Within each of these divisions, however, there are a number of businesses which require coordinated strategies. This coordination is brought about by divisional management. There is, in any case, a considerable degree of overlap between the businesses within ICI's divisions.

ICI is structured around a number of product based divisions in the UK, a number of overseas regions and a few worldwide product businesses. The latter include pharmaceuticals where a globally integrated strategy is seen to be important. The plastics and petrochemicals divisions were merged in 1987 due to their heavy mutual inter-dependence.

Divisional chairmen report to main board executive directors and for this purpose the divisions were aggregated into a number of groups. The main board director is intended to be a corporate representative rather than a representative of the division in question. This type of arrangement aims to keep the mind of the main board director focused on the aims and objectives of the company as a whole rather than on the activities and performance of the divisions.

In ICI, there is a commitment to a corporate review process that requires long-term strategic thinking to be laid out and linked to specific plans and budgets. The company's 'strategic' plan and its 'business' plan reviews take place at the same time every two years while its 'operating' plan review takes place annually. The centre's role in the review process involves a probing of the commercial logic and the consistency of the plans proposed – a sort of 'quality control' role. (The size of its head office staff fell from around 1,300 people in the early 1980s to no more than 300 by 1986.) In a strategic control company like ICI the review process is one of questioning and probing. If there are major concerns about a particular business strategy, independent consultants would usually be employed to provide a view on the matter.

Sir John Harvey-Jones, ICI's chairman from 1982 to 1987, saw the strategic development of the company as primarily a divisional role with the centre in a largely reactive mode. Nevertheless, there was (and is) a corporate level preference for shifting the company's portfolio towards higher value added 'effect' chemicals and towards a greater internationalization of its business. Specific initiatives to achieve these ends have been sponsored by corporate management in specialty chemicals, advanced materials and electronics. In spite of these recent cross divisional initiatives, ICI has usually insisted that where divisions trade with each other, transfer prices are set as far as possible at open market rates and that the relationship is an arm's length one.

Strategic control companies such as ICI generally avoid the need to manage interdependencies by their emphasis upon the separateness of divisions from a financial performance perspective. This style does, however, create coordination problems in some circumstances. (Similar difficulties arise for financial control companies such as Hanson plc.)

The allocation of resources is seen as a function of the corporate centre. It includes the sanctioning of capital investment, the closure or divestiture of businesses, acquisitions or new business ventures and senior management appointments within the divisions.

The approach to capital investment is particularly significant. Investment proposals may be initiated by the company's divisions, but the centre retains the right to review and sanction investments above a certain level. Below that level the divisions and business units are allowed to spend money at their own discretion. For capital expenditures above the divisional authorization limit, a formal capital appropriation system exists.

Capital expenditure which has previously been agreed in the company's corporate plan will meet with little or no opposition. On the other hand, new items will be more closely scrutinized. It is rare, however, for capital expenditure to be rejected by the corporate centre at the final stages of a review process. The centre's influence is felt at an earlier stage via informal discussions. Once a project has received a significant degree of business and divisional level sponsorship, however, it is unlikely to be rejected.

Although the initiative for capital investment normally comes from the business or divisional level, there are also important central inputs to the resource allocation process. The corporate centre can ultimately block business strategies by its power of veto over the sanctioning of important items of capital expenditure. It is this power which provides the centre with one means of shaping the company's portfolio.

In ICI the divisional authorization limit for capital expenditure proposals which had featured in a previous strategic plan was £50 million in 1986. For items which have not appeared in an earlier strategic plan, the limit was reduced to £200,000.

Capital expenditure decisions are not the only types of resource allocation which the corporate centre may be involved in. Business units and divisions are quite likely to put forward proposals for acquisitions or new business ventures which they believe will fit in with and strengthen their existing strategies, but they are unlikely to suggest close decisions or radical departures from existing practices. The latter areas, therefore, tend to become the prerogative of the corporate centre.

ICI makes only informal use of portfolio planning techniques when reviewing resource allocation decisions and questions of portfolio balance. This has not prevented the company, however, from identifying electronics and specialty chemicals as areas of potential growth.

The allocation of management resources is another area of decision-making in which the corporate centre plays a crucial role. Indeed, in ICI, the main board directors each have the responsibility for overseeing one of the company's divisions and one of their main tasks concerns management appointments, appraisal and succession.

Strategic control within ICI is exercised not just in terms of an appraisal of proposals for corporate development but also in terms of the setting of benchmarks against which future performance can be controlled.

The planning process is designed to generate both long-term plans and objectives and also short-term budgets and programmes which are consistent with the company's agreed long-term strategy. In practice, however, ICI has often found it difficult to specify non-financial, strategic objectives which are as tangible and credible as financial objectives. It has, therefore, tended to make statements such as 'our objectives are to gain share relative to buyer while remaining profitable'. Partly for this reason, ICI has moved away from using a very detailed set of controls and has, instead, begun to focus on a small number of key targets such as profits and cash flow. Moreover, these variables are increasingly measured at a divisional, rather than individual business unit, level. This provides greater discretion to the divisions to manage the individual business units in a flexible manner.

ICI has a monthly and quarterly reporting system to track actual results against its agreed plans. The company's move to fewer and more aggregated objectives has reduced the amount of detailed reporting required – a fact which has been welcomed within its divisions. The reporting system – such as it is – is based on written reports, rather than face-to-face meetings. It is only the annual planning exercise which involves a corporate review process. It is clear, therefore, that the monitoring of actual performance against plan takes place on a management by exception basis. This is in complete contrast to the situation which prevails in financial control companies, such as Hanson, where regular reviews of actual results versus plan are an important part of the management process.

Although control objectives have proved difficult to define within ICI, those which have been agreed have been enforced tightly since the reorientation of the company which began during the early 1980s. As the chairman of one of ICI's divisions put it in the mid 1980s, 'in the past, if you came in halfway through the year and said you would be £5 million down, the response would be "that's too bad". And if in the event you were £15 million down, the response would again be "that's too bad". Now all that has changed, and targets really matter.'

This attempt to attain performance targets has both a stick and a carrot element to it. In ICI, incentive bonuses can contribute up to 10 per cent of a manager's salary – a relatively low proportion compared to other strategic control type companies. ICI, like other companies, achieves 'control' by comparing outcomes with its budgeted financial results for the coming year. Inevitably this may lead to managerial behaviour in the short-term which is inimical to longer-term strategic objectives, although the budget is set in the light of the strategy. In ICI, chairmen of divisions are expected to take whatever action is necessary to achieve their budgeted profit and cash flow targets, but only provided this does not jeopardize their long-term strategy. In the event that they feel compelled to take action which could alter their agreed strategy, they are formally required to refer back the matter to the centre for a decision.

Financial information

A variety of group accounts and financial statistics for ICI Plc is provided in Tables 19.1 to 19.5.

Table 19.1 ICI Plc: Group profit and loss account (for the year ended 31 December)

	1991 £m	1990* £m
Turnover	12,488	12,906
Operating costs	(11,591)	(12,057)
Other operating income	136	180
Trading profit	1,033	1,029
Share of profits less losses of associated undertakings		
As published in the 1990 accounts		154
Extraordinary item restated as exceptional		(41)
	30	113
Net interest payable	(220)	(206)
Profit on ordinary activities before taxation	843	936
Tax on profit on ordinary activities	(279)	(336)
Profit on ordinary activities after taxation	564	600
Attributable to minorities	(22)	(22)
Net profit attributable to parent company	542	578
Extraordinary items	—	92
Net profit for the financial year	542	670
Dividends	(391)	(389)
Profit retained for year	151	281
Earnings before extraordinary items per £1 ordinary share	76.4p	82.3p
Group reserves attributable to parent company		
At beginning of year	3,963	4,320
Profit retained for year		
Company	13	381
Subsidiary undertakings	178	(53)
Associated undertakings	(40)	(47)
	151	281
Amounts taken direct to reserves	(33)	(638)
At end of year	4,081	3,963

£m means millions of pounds sterling.
Source: ICI Accounts, 1991, pp. 34–6.

Table 9.2 ICI Plc: Balance sheets (as at 31 December)

	Group		Company	
	1991 £m	1990 £m	1991 £m	1990 £m
ASSETS EMPLOYED				
Fixed assets				
Tangible assets	**5,128**	4,947	**1,079**	1,074
Investments				
Subsidiary undertakings			**4,347**	4,189
Participating interests	**421**	483	**222**	220
	5549	5,430	**5,648**	5,483
Current assets				
Stocks	**2,025**	2,214	**379**	395
Debtors	**2,636**	2,590	**815**	1,301
Investments and short-term deposits	**608**	388	—	—
Cash	**197**	177	**8**	7
	5,466	5,369	**1,202**	1,703
Total assets	**11,015**	10,799	**6,850**	7,186
Creditors due within one year				
Short-term borrowings	**(296)**	(447)	**(10)**	(5)
Current instalments of loans	**(220)**	(78)	**(156)**	—
Other creditors	**(2,894)**	(2,881)	**(1,281)**	(814)
	(3,410)	(3,406)	**(1,447)**	(819)
Net current assets (liabilities)	**2,056**	1,963	**(245)**	884
Total assets less current liabilities	**7,605**	7,393	**5,403**	6,367
FINANCED BY				
Creditors due after more than one year				
Loans	**1,788**	1,670	**400**	555
Other creditors	**159**	154	**1,053**	1,698
	1,947	1,824	**1,453**	2,253
Provisions for liabilities and charges	**526**	549	**14**	119
Deferred income: Grants not yet credited				
to profit	**52**	63	**5**	6
Minority interests	**288**	286		
Capital and reserves attributable to parent company				
Called-up share capital	**711**	708	**711**	708
Reserves				
Share premium account	**469**	446	**469**	446
Revaluation reserve	**56**	50	—	—
Profit and loss account	**3,131**	3,014	**2,315**	2,302
Associated undertakings' reserves	**26**	72		
Total reserves	**4,081**	3,963	**3,220**	3,281
Total capital and reserves				
attributable to parent company	**4,792**	4,671	**3,931**	3,989
	7,605	7,393	**5,403**	6,367

Table 19.3 ICI Plc: Statement of group cash flow (for the year ended 31 December)

	1991 £m	1990 £m
Cash inflow from operating activities		
Net cash inflow from trading operations	1,651	1,735
Outflow related to extraordinary provisions	(193)	(7)
Net cash inflow from operating activities	1,458	1,728
Returns on investments and servicing of finance		
Interest and dividends received	97	142
Interest paid	(294)	(278)
Dividends paid by parent company	(390)	(384)
Dividends paid by subsidiary undertakings to minority interests	(7)	(44)
Net cash outflow from returns on investments and servicing of finance	(594)	(564)
Tax paid	(286)	(412)
Investing activities		
Cash expenditure on tangible fixed assets	(896)	(1,019)
Acquisitions and new fixed asset investments	(57)	(480)
Disposals accounted for as extraordinary items	372	918
Other disposals	142	229
Realization of short-term investments and deposits	5	7
Net cash outflow from investing activities	(434)	(345)
Net cash inflow before financing	144	407
Financing		
Issues of ICI ordinary shares	19	56
Net increase in loans	251	31
Net decrease in lease finance (1990 increase)	(10)	(75)
Net decrease in short-term borrowings	(71)	(5)
Net cash inflow from financing	189	157
Increase in cash and cash equivalents	333	564

Table 19.4 ICI Plc Key ratios 1986–90

	31/12/86	31/12/87	31/12/88	31/12/89	31/12/90
Return on shareholders' equity (%)	15.37	21.04	21.66	16.73	12.63
Return on capital employed (%)	18.26	23.75	25.20	20.56	15.68
Operating profit margin (%)	10.02	11.38	12.32	10.93	7.74
Pre-tax profit margin (%)	9.04	10.30	11.14	9.45	6.37
Net profit margin (%)	6.32	7.61	8.07	7.24	4.82
Income gearing (%)	18.07	15.49	14.73	18.73	25.41
Borrowing ratio	0.54	0.59	0.50	0.49	0.49
Stock ratio (days)	62.44	59.46	62.52	65.96	62.62
Debtors ratio (days)	72.56	70.95	72.51	79.04	71.86
Creditors ratio (days)	63.83	67.19	74.02	70.62	76.45
Working capital ratio	1.71	1.53	1.55	1.55	1.54
Sales per employee	83,218	87,034	89,716	98,438	97,699
Operating profit per employee	8,342	9,906	11,051	10,762	7,562
Capital employed per employee	54,261	49,820	51,028	63,797	59,727
Tax ratio	36.22	35.02	34.99	35.01	35.01
Cash earnings per share	162.22	182.66	201.47	210.16	165.67

Source: Datastream.

Table 19.5 Key ratios for UK chemicals sector, 1987–91

	2/3/87	28/2/88	15/2/89	15/2/90	19/2/91
Return on shareholders' equity (%)	16.54	20.93	20.69	19.52	15.94
Return on capital employed(%)	19.23	23.12	23.20	21.80	18.06
Operating profit margin (%)	10.44	11.43	11.72	10.81	9.04
Pre-tax profit margin (%)	9.42	10.40	10.60	9.41	7.60
Net profit margin (%)	6.49	7.60	7.59	6.90	5.52
Income gearing (%)	17.80	15.29	15.75	20.47	24.49
Borrowing ratio	0.51	0.57	0.53	0.59	0.59
Stock ratio (days)	60.57	57.82	58.61	56.46	54.83
Debtors ratio (days)	72.91	72.22	73.38	76.69	75.29
Creditors ratio (days)	70.97	73.92	79.77	76.12	81.74
Working capital ratio	1.65	1.48	1.44	1.36	1.40
Sales per employee	63,213	66,025	71,558	83,318	75,235
Operating profit per employee	6,597	7,544	8,386	9,003	6,804
Capital employed per employee	40,783	38,752	42,514	50,366	45,774
Tax ratio	37.41	34.98	35.73	35.88	35.28

Source: Datastream

APPENDIX 19.2
HANSON: BACKGROUND AND FINANCIAL INFORMATION

Strategy, structure and style

Introduction

Hanson Plc, a leading UK conglomerate, traces its existence back to 1964 when its eponymous founder went into partnership with Gordon White, a businessman, who like Hanson came from Yorkshire. The two men merged their transport and printing services businesses to create a mini conglomerate. From the start they aimed to create a vehicle for buying, selling and building up basic businesses which they perceived were badly managed and run.

By 1991 Hanson Plc had become the sixth largest UK company by market capitalization. In contrast, it took J. Sainsbury Plc, the UK supermarket operator, the best part of one hundred years to become the largest food retailer in the UK. Furthermore, Hanson Industries, Hanson Plc's US operating arm, was among the top 50 US corporations by the end of the 1980s.

The basic guiding principles first articulated in 1964 were still at the forefront of the Hanson strategy in the 1990s. Hanson Plc had grown by the acquisition of businesses with mature technologies and strong market positions which were not threatened by technological change and competition. This acquisition-led growth was balanced with appropriate divestments of businesses that did not fit into the Hanson mainstream business definition. Furthermore, the nature of the deal-making expertise built up over the years had meant that business disposals after an acquisition frequently reduced considerably the real cost of the acquisition.

In 1973, Hanson Plc, then known as Hanson Trust, incorporated a US company called Hanson Industries Inc. under the chairmanship of Gordon White. It is from this point that the bi-national character of the company began to develop. Gordon White and James Hanson together built the Hanson empire on both sides of the Atlantic, with White being responsible for the US and Hanson for the UK. There followed in the 1970s and 1980s a string of major acquisitions, from bricks to batteries, which fulfilled the strategic aim of the group.

Hanson Plc's best decade for growth was the 1980s, when stock markets soared and a merger wave on both sides of the Atlantic occurred. Hanson and White concluded a number of major acquisitions that included SCM, a US conglomerate, Imperial Group, the UK food and tobacco products company, Consolidated Goldfields, a gold and mining group, and Peabody, a major US coalmining concern.

In the early 1990s, two deals further strengthened the Hanson group – Cavenham, a forest and timberlands operator in the US, and Beazer, an Anglo-American house builder and quarry operator.

Table 19.6 gives a five-year financial summary of Hanson Plc with a comparative column showing the group's position in 1980.

Table 19.6 Hanson Plc: Five-year financial summary and 1980 comparison[1]

£m except per share data	1991	1990	1989	1988	1987	1980
PROFIT AND LOSS ACCOUNT[2]						
Sales turnover	7,691	7,153	6,998	7,396	6,682	684
Profit before taxation	1,319	1,285	1,064	880	741	39
Taxation	284	314	251	204	169	14
Profit after taxation	1,035	971	813	676	572	25
Extraordinary items	71	29	288	445	—	—
Profit for the year	1,106	1,000	1,101	1,121	572	25
Earnings per share						
– diluted	21.2p	19.9p	18.4p	15.9p	14.0p	1.9p
Dividends per share	11.0p	10.4p	8.5p	6.8p	4.4p	0.7p
BALANCE SHEET[2]						
Assets less liabilities						
Tangible assets	6,199	5,057	2,414	1,476	1,183	92
Investments	429	704	957	178	178	6
Current assets	9,955	8,993	7,454	6,158	5,014	216
	16,583	14,754	10,825	7,812	6,375	314
Less creditors – due within one year	4,751	4,226	3,269	2,463	2,083	142
	11,832	10,528	7,556	5,349	4,292	172
Financed by						
Share capital	1,202	1,199	1,024	1,104	1,043	27
Reserves	2,123	1,635	62	1,235	836	94
Shareholders' interests	3,325	2,834	1,086	2,339	1,879	121
Creditors – due after one year	4,880	4,258	4,971	2,124	1,727	42
Provisions for liabilities	3,627	3,436	1,499	886	686	9
	11,832	10,528	7,556	5,349	4,292	172
Net assets per share	69p	59p	27p	57p	48p	9p

1. The key ratios for Hanson Plc are given in Table 19.10.
2. More detailed consolidated profit and loss accounts and balance sheets covering the years 1989–91 for the Hanson Group are contained in Tables 19.7 and 19.8.

Source: Company Accounts 1990 and 1991.

Strategy, structure and style

Corporate strategy at Hanson Plc involved more than just the acquisitions of businesses in the right industries. It also involved finding businesses that were undervalued due to poor management or with poor relationships with the financial community and where, in Hanson's view, their management style and disciplines could be made to obtain more surplus value out of the assets than the current management was capable of. This notion of 'releasing shareholder value' was an important motivational issue in the strategy of Hanson. The acquisitions of SCM corporation in the USA and Imperial Group in the UK underline this point clearly. At SCM, some 70 per cent of the company was disposed of and, in so doing, Hanson Industries recouped its entire investment in the acquisition and retained a section of the original business that made a profit of $160m in 1986. At Imperial in the UK a similar situation occurred. The disposals of non-core businesses meant that Hanson Plc controlled the highly profitable and cash generative cigarettes and tobacco products SBUs from the original Imperial Group at a fraction of their worth. This strengthened Hanson Plc's growing consumer business division in the UK.

Three examples from the acquisitions of SCM, Imperial Group and Kidde demonstrate how Hanson obtains more surplus value from a firm's operating assets. At SCM some $8m was saved by the elimination of the data services centre. Next to go was the management training centre and the company's strategic planners. At Imperial, three weeks after the takeover, some 250 headquarters staff were made redundant and the internal telephone exchange was reprogrammed. At Kidde, an acquisition made in 1987, an extra $100m was earned by the business by introducing better credit controls. The other aspect of this notion, was that parts of a company which had been newly acquired and which may have value to someone else meant that the potential for a deal was always present. For example, Hanson Industries sold Glidden Paints, a subsidiary of SCM, to ICI for $580m. Indeed, one former senior manager at Hanson Plc had commented:

> All our businesses are for sale, all of the time. If we think we can get more for them than they are worth to us, we will sell.

Hanson Plc has always stressed that its success was predicated by producing maximum financial performance. Individual businesses seek high margins, often in protected niches, or through cost reduction programmes. Such businesses are unwilling to sacrifice margins, or risk long-term paybacks in defence of their competitive advantage. They are concerned with finding opportunities for growth in sales and profits through the acquisition process as well as from internal growth. Hanson's corporate portfolio had been built up with such a strategy in mind. Furthermore, the acquisitions were intended to spread the risk across industries and between countries, concentrated as they were in predominantly mature markets, contrary to the conventional lifecycle theory of balanced portfolios.

Insights into the strategy, style and structure practised at Hanson Plc can be seen from a number of viewpoints, as this aspect of the management of the company is well documented. For example, to quote from the 1978 annual report to shareholders where Hanson himself described the way the business operates:

> We believe in exercising business leadership and it has worked well for us. Our decentralized system of management control makes each manager the boss of his own business 90 per cent of the time. The other 10 per cent is the financial control exercised by Hanson Trust, but this does not inhibit management throughout your very large company from making individual decisions daily and, we believe, builds more leaders for the future strength of Hanson Trust. We have a company which can produce an increasing return and growth in earnings annually, but is not afraid to take bold and imaginative steps.

The corporate strategy followed at Hanson Plc can be clearly seen from the acquisitions that the company had made over the years. This acquisition strategy was always coupled with a very disciplined approach to the management of the acquired businesses and is best articulated by Lord Hanson himself in the following way:

> We aim to invest in good basic businesses, producing essential products for which there is a clear and continuing demand. We avoid areas of high technology. We do not want to be involved in businesses that are capital intensive and where decision-making is centralized. We want to be involved in businesses where our 'free form' management approach is appropriate.

The decentralized nature of the company meant that operating units traded under their own names and no mention was made of the association with the parent company – Hanson Plc or Hanson Industries Inc. Each SBU was a profit centre where strategy was conceived and implemented. The system of organization discouraged overlap between different business units. This has meant that while Hanson can be seen as an international company, it really operated its businesses in separate national markets with little international overlap. Financial control of the SBU was carried out through the budgeting process and it was through this process that the wider aspects of strategy were developed. The two sides of the company – UK and US – were operated as separate entities each with its own holding company and subsidiaries reporting to it. The US operation was incorporated into the Hanson Plc master company registered in the UK. It is this structure that leads to Hanson Plc being described as a 'bi-national' company.

Control of the business was centred around financial results, with each project taken on its merits. Financial manageability was more important than strategic fit between businesses. Centre and operating businesses were actively seeking what Lord White described in the 1991 reports as 'bolt on' acquisitions to help build up existing SBUs. As a general rule, in such organizations, diversification at the business level is discouraged, Hanson is no exception. All unit managers are under strong pressure to meet short-term targets and to get 'results'. This accountability at Hanson applies to all levels of the company. The company sets great store on being able to react quickly to poor results.

At the business unit level, there is no apparent formula for a winning strategy. Each business makes its own strategy guided by ROI and profitability objectives set by the centre. Pressure is placed on SBU managers to search for and to eliminate under-utilized assets and loss-making operations. There is a strong focus at the SBU level on the control of costs and the constant raising of efficiency levels. Newly acquired companies go through a retrenchment phase followed by an efficiency drive that could last a number of years. But once the cost base is secured, different business unit strategies could be deployed depending upon the situation which each business unit is faced with in its own market. A form of a market leadership strategy is attempted by the many SBUs that Hanson Plc controls in the US and the UK. In the consumer goods area Hanson Plc has followed a strategy of brand identification supported by heavy advertising and cost reduction strategies. The battery division under the EverReady brand had to contain the advance made by Duracell in the UK dry cell market. This it achieved by cost efficiencies and heavy consumer advertising. In cigarettes and tobacco products, brand identification is a key to consumer loyalty, particularly as that sector has been under increasing regulation by government bans and regulations in the EC markets. This has meant that Hanson spends considerable sums of money on sports promotion and sponsorship. By contrast, at Butterley Bricks, part of the Industrial Products division, the emphasis on cost advantage and product quality has been the key operating strategy to allow Butterley to exploit the advantages of its specialist products. At Peabody Mining, the accent is on cost efficiency in extraction and distribution.

Hanson Plc's strategy is not without its critics. This criticism is centred around two key issues: firstly, its portfolio mix and its acquisition-led growth, and secondly, the lack of synergy in its businesses based as they are on decentralization and lack of international linkage.

The issues of portfolio mix and acquisition-led growth have followed the company for many years. The Lex Column in the *Financial Times* of 22 January 1985 summarized them effectively:

> The problem is that mature businesses (bricks and batteries to name but two) tend to stay mature, so that the acquirer has to buy more and bigger businesses in order to sustain the growth rating of the share price which makes the whole process possible in the first place. The logical conclusion of this argument is that the likes of ICI must be eventually swallowed up if the momentum is to be sustained.

The issues of synergy and international linkage may be addressed as follows. The nature of the strategy at Hanson Plc was described earlier as bi-national in outlook in that each business is run independently. The other way of looking at Hanson's operations is to describe them as 'multi-local'. That is the company owns businesses whose economics do not require them to operate across international boundaries. Hanson Plc has great management in depth in running its own form of organizational strategy and it has studiously avoided international linkage, even when such linkage may be possible or even desirable. The query, then, is about Hanson Plc's ability to run the international strategy that would inevitably be required if the takeover or merger of ICI Plc had proceeded.

Financial information

Further financial information on Hanson Plc is provided in Tables 19.7 to 19.10.

Table 19.7 Hanson: Consolidated profit and loss accounts (for the year ended 30 September)

	1991 £m	1990 £m	1989 £m
Sales turnover	7,691	7,153	6,998
Costs and overheads less other income	6,372	5,868	5,934
Profit on ordinary activities	1,319	1,285	1,064
Taxation	264	314	251
Profit after taxation	1,035	971	813
Extraordinary items	71	29	288
Profit available for appropriation	1,106	1,000	1,101
Dividends:			
Ordinary : interim	152	144	98
: proposed final	377	355	237
: preference	—	—	2
	529	499	337
Profit retained	577	501	764

Table 19.8 Hanson: consolidated balance sheets (as at 30 September)

	1991 £m	1990 £m	1989 £m
Fixed assets			
Tangible	6,199	5,057	2,414
Investments	429	704	957
	6,628	5,761	3,371
Current assets			
Stocks	992	984	988
Debtors	1,192	1,126	1,157
Listed investments	6	5	43
Cash at bank	7,765	6,878	5,266
	9,955	8,993	7,454
Creditors – due within one year			
Debenture loans	1,725	20	23
Bank loans & overdrafts	810	2,041	1,121
Trade creditors	507	501	508
Other creditors	1,332	1,309	1,379
Dividend	377	355	238
	4,751	4,226	3,269
Net current assets	5,204	4,767	4,185
Total assets less current liabilities	11,832	10,528	7,556
Creditors – due after one year			
Convertible loans	500	—	976
Debenture loans	579	420	651
Bank loans	3,801	3,838	3,344
	4,880	4,258	4,971
Provisions for liabilities	3,627	3,436	1,499
Capital and reserves			
Called-up share capital	1,202	1,199	1,024
Share premium account	1,153	1,155	256
Revaluation reserve	163	163	165
Profit and loss account	807	317	(359)
	3,325	2,834	1,086
Total capital employed	11,832	10,528	7,556

Table 19.9 Hanson: profit, sales turnover and capital employed 1990–91

	1991			1990		
	Profit £m	Sales turnover £m	Capital employed £m	Profit £m	Sales turnover £m	Capital employed £m
Industrial						
Coal mining	170	1,099	3,316	59	521	2,976
Chemicals	136	563	370	187	608	346
Materials handling	49	276	97	53	309	76
Gold mining	38	98	141	31	81	120
Other	57	800	209	73	763	263
Total	450	2,836	4,133	403	2,282	3,781
Consumer						
Tobacco products	240	2,670	(7)	225	2,449	32
Other	107	702	275	83	672	290
Total	347	3,372	268	308	3,121	322
Building products						
Aggregates	69	573	721	102	677	763
Forestry & lumber	44	178	930	2	54	10
Other	65	732	773	108	759	731
Total	178	1,483	2,424	212	1,490	1,504
Trading operations	975	7,691	6,825	923	6,893	5,607
Associated businesses	20	—	152	43	—	140
Discontinued operations	—	—	—	8	260	106
Total	995	7,691	6,977	974	7,153	5,853
Profit on disposal of natural resource assets	170			101		
Net interest income	188			186		
Central expenses less other income	(34)			24		
Total	1,319			1,285		
Geographical location						
UK	424	3,858	1,423	474	3,816	1,483
USA	493	3,506	5,368	382	2,743	4,036
Other	78	327	186	110	334	228
Discontinued	—	—	—	8	260	106
Total from operations	995	7,691	6,977	974	7,153	5,853

Source: Note 1, p. 27, *Company Accounts* 1991.

Note: Capital employed is defined by Hanson Plc as follows:

Shareholders' Funds, Provisions for Liabilities, Tax & Dividends, Net Cash, Investments and Non-operating Assets (Note 2, p. 28, 1991 Company Accounts).

Table 19.10 Hanson: key ratios, 1987–91

	30/9/87	30/9/88	30/9/89	30/9/90	30/9/91
Return on shareholders' equity (%)	30.12	27.97	72.28	32.76	24.92
Return on capital employed (%)	20.92	18.75	16.02	15.28	13.16
Operating profit margin (%)	9.58	10.65	12.13	14.32	12.08
Pre-tax profit margin (%)	10.98	11.82	15.00	17.36	14.68
Net profit margin (%)	7.21	7.73	9.89	11.67	9.93
Income gearing (%)	29.01	24.72	23.91	33.94	39.63
Borrowing ratio	1.29	1.26	5.45	2.13	2.14
Stock ratio (days)	45.45	52.85	51.53	50.21	47.08
Debtors ratio (days)	61.34	60.55	60.35	57.46	56.57
Creditors ratio (days)	46.29	51.87	77.85	71.10	59.74
Working capital ratio	2.41	2.50	2.28	2.13	2.10
Sales per employee	75,932	70,438	78,629	89,413	109,871
Operating profit per employee	7,273	7,505	9,539	12,800	13,271
Capital employed per employee	56,534	59,286	97,753	157,363	205,243
Tax ratio	34.95	35.00	34.96	35.02	33.51
Cash earnings per share	19.12	21.74	24.50	24.96	22.17

Source: Datastream.

SECTION 7

Transport and distribution

Case 20   Stagecoach Holdings Plc
G.M. Sharkey and J.G. Gallagher, Napier University

Case 21   Christian Salvesen Plc
C.M. Clarke-Hill, University of Huddersfield

Case 22   Virgin Atlantic Airways
K.W. Glaister, University of Leeds

Case 23   NFC Plc
C.M. Clarke-Hill, University of Huddersfield

Case 24   Distribution in the UK: an industry note
A.E. Whiteing and C.G. Bamford, University of Huddersfield

Stagecoach Holdings Plc

G.M. Sharkey and J.G. Gallagher

On Thursday 11 October 1980 the 'Stage Coach' made its first trip. It needed 25 passengers to break even; 35 turned up to travel on the second-hand bus between Dundee, Scotland and London. Today the company is the largest independent bus operator in Europe. It has approximately 6 per cent of the total local[1] bus market in the UK and invests around £23 million per year in its vehicle fleet. It employs around 15,000 staff worldwide with operations also in Kenya, Malawi, and New Zealand.

THE BEGINNING – A FAMILY AFFAIR

The Transport Act 1980[2] which deregulated express, excursion and tour services offered Stagecoach its first major business opportunity. Before the launch of their Anglo-Scottish service in October 1980, Brian Souter[3] and sister Ann Gloag pooled the family capital, including redundancy monies belonging to father – Iain Souter, a bus driver for 40 years – to purchase two second-hand buses. Headquarters and hub of catering operations was the home of Ann Gloag and on the first trip south, snacks were provided by courtesy of the home cooking of mother, Mrs Cathy Souter. At the end of that first week the company ran two full buses to London and the name Stagecoach, suggested by brother David, was adopted as the trading name for express services.

The primary aim of the company was to provide a cheap overnight Anglo-Scottish service. Coach competitors provided luxurious coaches (with toilets and reclining seats) at a single fare of about £11.50. For a charge of £6.75 Stagecoach passengers could travel from Glasgow to London and get food and beverages as well. Although these early Stagecoach buses were spartan, the services competed on efficiency and friendliness with concessionary travel for groups such as students. Efforts were made also to differentiate Stagecoach travel as a 'fun' experience with staff serving snacks wearing 'wild west' costume and this emphasis still pervades company philosophy to the extent that enthusiasm for new challenges and opportunities still provides a compelling motivation for the founders.

In 1981/82 the company began to invest in their vehicle fleet as a means to establish

---

1. A 'local' service (sometimes called a stage carriage service) involves the transport of passengers on a journey of less than 15 miles using a public service vehicle (psv).
2. The Transport Act 1980 came into effect on 9 October of that year and changed the system of strictly regulated route monopolies which had prevailed in the bus industry for over 50 years. Road service licences (RSLs) for each route were abolished for express, excursion and tour operations, express operations being those with over thirty miles between picking up and setting down points.
3. See Appendix 20.1 for management team.

a brand image. Funds for this investment came partly from an uncle, Fraser McColl, a millionaire domiciled in Canada who took a £25,000 stake in the company. As the 1980s progressed efforts were concentrated on express (rather than local) services and competition on fares and frequency was fierce. With an expanding fleet the acquisition of depots and facilities for vehicle maintenance and care became important.

GROWTH THROUGH ACQUISITION – UNITED KINGDOM

New opportunities – this time in the realm of local bus services – were provided by the Transport Act 1985.[4] In addition to deregulation the Act required all public bus companies in the UK (outwith Greater London) to privatize. In preparation Stagecoach (Holdings) Limited was formed on 4 September 1986 and a number of services were registered to begin in Scotland on 26 October 1986 or 'D-Day' as it became known. 'D-Day' generated a good deal of press and TV coverage and, in Scotland, much of this was monopolized by Brian Souter who adopted fancy dress to attract passengers to Stagecoach buses.

In 1986/87 the company shifted its effort from express operations to local bus companies. The sale in 1989 to National Express of Anglo-Scottish express operations – a relatively low profit earner and amounting at the time to around 10 per cent of the group's turnover – confirmed the decision to concentrate on local bus services.

A focus on growth by acquisition was adopted and the results of the acquisitions strategy can be found in Table 20.1. The majority of earlier acquisitions were in England – one-time subsidiaries of the National Bus Company (NBC) – and in the early 1990s acquisitions were from the Scottish Bus Group (SBG). In England, one bidder was allowed a maximum of three acquisitions and Hampshire Bus, Cumberland and United Counties were purchased by Stagecoach on their privatization. In Scotland no one operator was permitted to buy more than two companies which could not be in adjoining areas and Fife Scottish and Northern Scottish Omnibuses Ltd (now Bluebird Buses Ltd) were purchased on privatization. The remaining companies in the table were purchased from teams of managers who staged management buy-outs at initial privatization. These buy-out teams received a price preference of 5 per cent compared with other bids. Within regions, the geographic proximity of operating territory has led to investigation and action by the Office of Fair Trading and the Monopolies and Mergers Commission (see section 'Competition and Regulation').

These acquisitions, in combination with the increasing number of vehicles in the group fleet, made it essential to establish a clear corporate identity. The striking Stagecoach colours of a white background with red, blue and orange stripes and chevrons were employed as standardized livery to build public recognition of the group and allow vehicles to be quickly switched to different parts of the expanding Stagecoach territory.

---

4. The Transport Act 1985: provided for (a) the deregulation of the local bus industry – with the exception of London. Dispensing with RSLs removed the restriction on the quantity of services supplied, giving any qualified operator an unrestricted right to provide bus services on a commercial basis; (b) splitting up and privatizing the National Bus Company (NBC) and local authority and municipal bus operations; (c) obligatory competitive tendering; and (d) subsidy reductions.

Table 20.1 Acquisitions 1987–93: United Kingdom

	Name	Geographical area/ area of operation	Date	Price £m	Vehicles (no.)
1	Hampshire Bus	Hampshire	1987	2.2	240
2	Cumberland	Cumbria	1987	2.8	260
3	United Counties	Northants, Beds, Cambs	1987	4.0	250
4	East Midland	Derbyshire, Notts	1989	4.5	300
5	Ribble Motor Services Ltd	Lancashire	1989	6.3	830
6	Southdown Motor Services Ltd[1]	Hamps, W. Sussex, Portsmouth	1989	6.3	300
7	Portsmouth Citybus*	Portsmouth	1989	0.7	70
8	Inverness Traction*	Highland Region	1989	0.1	Nil
9	Hastings & District Transport Ltd*[2]	Hastings	1989	1.2	100
10	Northern Scottish Omnibuses Ltd[3]	Grampian Region	1991	5.8	200
11	Fife Scottish	Fife	1991	9.2	300
12	Alder Valley[4]	Hants & Surrey	1992	1.3	80
13	National Transport Tokens Ltd	Preston	1992	2.1	N/a
14	Lancaster City Transport	Lancashire	1993	1.0	78
15	East Kent Travel Ltd	Kent	1993	4.78	240
16	Grimsby-Cleethorpes Transport Ltd	Lincolnshire	1993	4.4	100
17	Western Travel Subsidiaries: (a) C&G; (b) Midland Red (South); (c) Red & White Services	(a) Cheltenham, Gloucester Swindon and Stroud; (b) Warwickshire and north Oxfordshire; (c) rural South Wales	1993	9.25	650

* Purchased by subsidiaries.

1. Southdown was purchased as part of a deal to acquire its holding company Sharpton. Southdown itself has been split, and is part of both Coastline and of South Coast Buses.
2. Hastings & District was purchased as part of a deal to acquire its holding company, the Formia Group.
3. NSO Limited is now called Bluebird Buses.
4. Alder Valley is now called Hants & Surrey.

A number of other, minor, acquisitions were also made during this period – sometimes to acquire depots in a particular area, sometimes to eliminate competition on specific routes – enabling a rationalized route network and savings in mileage. Non-bus company interests are Transmedia Advertising Limited (50 per cent owned by Stagecoach) and National Transport Tokens Ltd (NTT) – 99.9 per cent interest. The former sells advertising space on group vehicles, the latter redeems concessionary and other tokens. The tokens act as a medium of exchange in the transport market and NTT sells around £14m worth of tokens each year, on which interest is earned until they are redeemed by operators.

THE ACQUISITION PROCESS

The importance of acquisitions to the Group is reflected in their corporate objectives.[5] They aim:

- to maximize profit margins at all existing operations and
- to acquire undervalued or underperforming companies where they can identify the potential to improve operating margins to at least 15 per cent of turnover.

The identification of acquisition targets – those with profit growth potential and sound property assets – is led by Brian Souter. The group attempts to maintain continuous and detailed surveillance of acquisition and other opportunities – whether in the United Kingdom or globally. Where opportunities are identified the target business is further analysed to determine such factors as how much of the business is supported by commercial and how much by government subsidized activities, its property portfolio and its future prospects. Initial prospecting can sometimes take place a considerable time before opportunities crystallize and contracts are signed but this industry intelligence, combined with access to finance, allows Stagecoach to close a deal in a short time.

Once companies are acquired, a pattern for their integration has been established. In the early stages senior Stagecoach group director(s) are appointed as managing director(s) and their task is to restructure to quickly enhance profitability and efficiency. An early example of this process of integration was provided in 1987 when the Stagecoach Group, through Skipburn,[6] became the first successful private bidder to acquire an ex-NBC unit, Hampshire Bus Company. After the acquisition, 40 per cent of the vehicles were transferred as part of a deal to sell the Southampton operations and, in a move which was to create controversy, the Southampton bus station was sold for more than it cost to buy the company. On the one hand this enhanced the reputation of Stagecoach as a company able to do a good deal while on the other, the event proved politically embarrassing for a government sensitive to accusations of asset stripping. Other site sales have also been controversial, involving House of Commons discussion and Parliamentary Questions.[7] During the period 1 May 1989 to 9 January 1993 a profit of £2.7m was made from property sales with total cash proceeds of £10.9m.

An important aspect of the acquisition process is the identification of key managers – those with the potential of adding value to the integrated units – and substantial efforts are made to retain such individuals. In the initial stages, senior Stagecoach personnel take care to get to know employees of the acquired unit and whereas their

5. Executive Chairman, Stagecoach (Holdings) plc, Annual Report 1993.
6. Skipburn Limited was a holding company set up with the aim of bidding for several English National Bus Company (NBC) units. The directors of Skipburn included Fraser McColl, Ann Gloag and Brian Souter. Skipburn was absorbed in late 1987 after the departure of Fraser McColl to Canada.
7. The sale of Keswick bus station for £705,000 and the offer for sale of land at Workington caused the local Member of Parliament to table a Parliamentary question about the property valuation methods used by the NBC in the sale of Cumberland Motor Services.

Table 20.2 Disposals 1987–93 (UK)

Unit	Description	Date	Price £m
Hampshire Bus	Sale of Southampton operations	1987	4.2
Stagecoach Ltd	Sale of inter-urban express operations vehicles and property	1989	1.1
Ribble Motor Services Ltd/ East Midland	Sale of Manchester operations	1989	0.8
East Midland	Sale of London operations	1989	0.8
Portsmouth City Bus Ltd/ Southdown Motor Services Ltd	Sale of certain of the trading operations of both units	1991	3.7
Stagecoach (Scotland) Ltd	Sale of certain of the assets and trading operation (Magicbus) in Glasgow and Strathclyde Region	1992	0.9

competence is paramount, their ability to become a productive team player is also stressed. Sometimes such managers are placed with a team elsewhere in the company, something made possible by the different management cultures prevailing at subsidiary level. Incentives such as the opportunity to buy into stock options and other profit-related pay and incentive bonus schemes encourage key managers to further identify with the group.

Disposals since 1987 of UK subsidiaries or operating units are noted in Table 20.2.

MANAGEMENT TEAM, ORGANIZATION STRUCTURE AND COMPANY STYLE

The senior management team (see Appendix 20.1) is led by five executive and three non-executive directors. The executive chairman is Brian Souter (39), a qualified chartered accountant who, after graduating, held down two jobs – a day job with a major accountancy firm and another job – working on the buses in and around Glasgow. After incurring cuts and bruises in a fight among passengers, he then gave up the day job and built a career on the buses. Managing director Ann Gloag (51) worked in the Health Service as a theatre sister before forming Stagecoach, and group finance director Derek Scott (40) was formerly one of the company's auditors and advised on potential acquisitions during the 1986/87 NBC privatization. Both Brian Cox (46) and Barry Hinkley (44) had established careers in the bus passenger transport industry as, respectively, a general manager of an SBG subsidiary and an NBC bus company chief engineer before joining Stagecoach. Of the three non-executive directors Ewan Brown (52) is the longest serving – having been on the board since December 1988. Both Muir Russell (45), an Under Secretary in the Scottish Office Environment Department and Barry Sealey (58), an independent director on a number of boards, joined the Stagecoach board in December 1992.

Teamworking and being a 'team player' is considered an important feature of the company and the sharing of specialist skills and knowledge within the team is exemplified also at board level. As well as taking major responsibility for operations in Africa and China, Ann Gloag specializes in properties and insurance, Derek Scott in pensions, Barry Hinkley in the engineering aspects of the business and purchasing and Brian Cox specializes in traffic schemes. Brian Souter specializes in business development and in the architecture and structure of the business. At one time he was personally involved with reorganizing acquired companies, appointing himself as MD and taking the initial decisions about their development and operation, but other board members are now involved in this task although the executive chairman maintains a close interest in developments.

Brian Souter believes that Stagecoach has the 'best bus management team in the UK, and the leanest'. There are four levels in the hierarchy: bus drivers, depot managers, the team at subsidiary company level and the main board. As a consequence there are very short lines of communication and communication itself tends to be direct and informal – often taking place by telephone rather than by written means.

The geographic dispersion of UK subsidiary companies is illustrated in Fig. 20.1. These subsidiary companies are established as profit units and are led by a managing

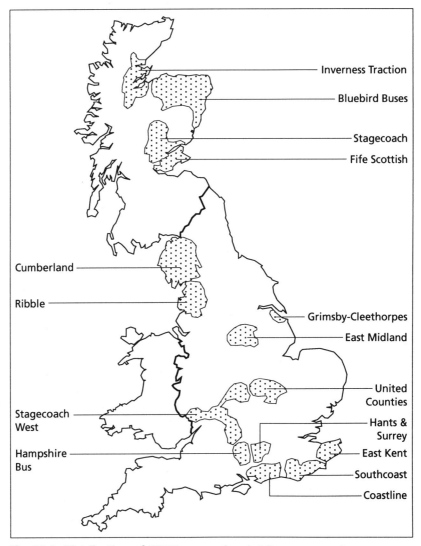

Fig. 20.1 Distribution of UK Stagecoach subsidiary companies.

director, reporting to an area chairman who is a board member. Profit centres are also established within subsidiary companies so that, for example, Ribble has eight depots which are profit centres with their own agreed budgets. Policy decisions are taken at headquarters while day-to-day responsibility for financial performance to meet predetermined targets is devolved to the managing director of each unit.

Incentive schemes are operated at all levels and in 1992 a number of schemes – Inland Revenue approved schemes for key executives and Inland Revenue registered profit-related pay schemes – were introduced in four locations. It is likely that similar schemes will be implemented as part of the local wage negotiation process in other UK companies in the group. The group-determined employee share ownership plan (ESOP) and pension schemes have worker directors/trustees and provide a framework to motivate geographically dispersed point-of-sale staff who crucially affect the quality of service delivery. Stagecoach Malawi have a separate scheme allowing employees to buy 15 per cent of the shares formerly held by the government and local arrangements are also in force in Kenya and New Zealand.

Headquarters control is undertaken through a review function. This requires managers within subsidiary companies, with their managing directors and with group executives, to undertake a regular review of operations using a variety of performance measures such as operating margins and cash flow. The senior management team view site visits as an important element in the motivation and control process and undertake regular visits to subsidiaries – since 1989 Ann Gloag has visited the African operations about 30 times. The other aspect of control of the business relates to the design of the subsidiary companies themselves. These have been structured to be all of a similar size – what is considered the optimum size for a bus company – a size which is sufficiently large to allow economies of scale but not too large to allow diseconomies to become apparent. This concept of an economic unit is considered an important aspect in retaining effective management and control of a growth organization.

Care is taken to balance headquarters expertise with the devolution of authority to subsidiary company level. In this way local management is given access to headquarters functions such as insurance, purchasing and pensions while company-level and depot-level managers are encouraged to take whatever local action is necessary to reach targets. Group-level policy, for example the ESOP scheme, provides a framework for company initiatives and subsidiary company initiatives can also reinforce group philosophy. For example, a pilot National Vocational Qualification (NVQ) programme for bus and coach drivers which develops and assesses practical skills such as driving ability and customer care has been tested at company level. Feedback is made available via group management conferences which discuss strategic and operational issues and which are held three times a year, and through a quarterly magazine *On Stage* which provides staff with news on commercial and other activities throughout the group.

The amount of freedom of choice afforded to local managers is regarded as important because of the dispersed nature of operations but also because it reflects Stagecoach philosophy in freeing up managers to use their own initiative. One outcome of this is that there exists a wide range of management styles and cultures at subsidiary level. The development of a shared Stagecoach philosophy is seen as the 'gel' which secures action in the group's interests and which allows managers to be left to get on with running the business.

The growth orientation and opportunistic nature of Stagecoach group development has meant that they have made mistakes. However, they believe they have learned from these mistakes and their ability to recognize difficult trading conditions and act quickly in the interests of the group has much to do with their being willing to objectively self-review their decisions:

> The important thing is to recognize where you've gone wrong and to be able to identify your fire escape and get your sannys[8] on and get down it as quick as you can and I think Stagecoach have managed to do that ... Tunnel vision is a great disaster for businesses and often inventors are the worst people to admit that their inventions aren't working.

While Stagecoach was still a private company, Ann Gloag and Brian Souter established charitable trusts to fund a number of projects including the despatch of buses laden with food, medicine and supplies to communities affected by war or famine. In 1993 the trusts funded the construction and ongoing operation of a 26-bed hospital unit for burns victims in Malawi which has an operating theatre, physiotherapy facilities and 25 staff. Future projects include an orphanage for the street children of Nairobi, Kenya.

BUS OPERATIONS – THE NATURE OF COMPETITION

Costs

Since privatization the ability to compete on cost has been a significant feature of the successful operator in the bus industry. The maximization of profit margins is a primary corporate objective of Stagecoach and there is a very high priority on tight cost controls throughout the group. In an industry where wage costs can contribute up to 60–70 per cent of total costs, staff productivity is particularly important. Stagecoach favour individual wage negotiations at each local company and the cost of platform staff is controlled by efficient work practices and close supervision to achieve planned schedules. Strict controls are also operated over cash receipts from buses and engineering wage costs are tied to staff/vehicle ratios and supervision of overtime.

Non-labour costs can amount to 30 per cent of total operating costs. A centralized purchasing programme allows Stagecoach to achieve considerable scale economies and cost reductions are also made possible by standardizing on a range of three or four different vehicle types with features designed to simplify maintenance. Stagecoach's fleet investment programme has been credited with 'sustaining the domestic bus manufacturing market during the recent recession'.[9] The company's five-year UK vehicle investment plan (1990–95) required expenditure of £53m, equivalent to 30 per cent of the UK fleet. New vehicles create a positive image for the company, and meet the most modern emission control standards, with vehicles for medium distance routes being equipped with lap seat belts. Maintenance costs can also be reduced by, for example, providing for better fuel efficiency and by making good use of warranty periods.

The location of maintenance and other depots can also substantially affect operating costs. The Stagecoach group has a policy of closing acquired central mainten-

---

8. Trainers.
9. View of Bus & Coach Council at Monopolies & Mergers Commission hearing on Stagecoach Holdings plc and Lancaster City Transport Ltd, CM 2423, London, HMSO, December 93.

ance workshops and opening purpose-built units. These depots have state-of-the-art cost-saving features such as, for example, sensor switch floodlights and water recycling units which can reprocess 95 per cent of the water used by a bus wash.

Competitors – bus companies

On particular routes or in local geographical pockets, competition between providers of bus services can be intense and there is a very real sense of territory being invaded where a new service is launched. Time honoured tactics include duplication of departures, use of the same service number and blocking of bus stops and termini. Competitive bouts can involve complaints to and investigation by the Office of Fair Trading (OFT), OFT registered agreements between the parties and sometimes, in the long run, the withdrawal of one of the combatants.

Although intense competition can be used to exert considerable financial pressure on others, in the interim both parties are inevitably damaged as these periods rarely allow for a commercial return to be made. It is desirable then that competitive bouts are kept as short as possible and that short-term losses are monitored closely and set against medium- to long-term potential benefits. For this to work the exercise of market power – based on a substantial resource base and experience gained in similar episodes elsewhere – is important. The reputation of Stagecoach has been considered by the MMC:

> Stagecoach appears to be generally perceived as an 'aggressive' operator with a reputation for 'seeing off' the competition ...[10]

A competitive instance in the Tayside area of Scotland began in 1989 when an operating unit – Perth Panther – was established to compete with the incumbent operator Strathtay Scottish – a publicly owned bus company which, at the time, was expected to be one of the first offered for sale in the forthcoming SBG privatization. In May 1991, Stagecoach was advised by the OFT to withdraw from bidding for Strathtay Scottish and the company was sold to Barnsley-based Yorkshire Traction. In August 1993, as a consequence of poor returns, Strathtay Scottish closed their depot in Perth and withdrew commercial and other services from the city – leaving the way open for Stagecoach's service provision.

Competition – private modes of transport

Private transport, in the form of either cars or taxis, represents the major competition for all bus operators. Despite deregulation being viewed as a means to arrest the long-term decline in bus passenger transport, some believe that the instability in service and operator provision and resulting passenger confusion has helped reinforce the trend. There are instances, however, where bus operators have been successful and this is where they have imitated the qualities of private transport, as illustrated by a Stagecoach experiment in United Counties territory. In Corby, taxis had dominated passenger transport but after close monitoring and analysis of taxi movements, the chairman Brian Souter recommended that 'Magic Minis' be

---

10. *Stagecoach (Holdings) Ltd and Formia Ltd: A report on the acquisition by Stagecoach (Holdings) Ltd of Formia Ltd*, Monopolies & Mergers Commission, Cm 1382, London, HMSO, December 1990 – p. 30.

introduced. These minibuses had six seats removed and luggage racks installed to enable easier customer access and accommodation for push-chairs/shopping trolleys. The hybrids combined the best features of taxis with those of conventional minibuses and substantially increased bus patronage, something which was consolidated by fare offers, route analysis and timetable revisions.

On the supply side the provision of high quality services and good marketing are seen as means to prevent further bus industry decline. Recent examples of the design of bus services are the Ribble 'Network 2000' services where passenger requirements were identified from research data. Consequent work involved redesigning timetables, providing higher standards of vehicle cleanliness, operating new fare structures and providing direct debit facilities for regular commuters. Care is taken to monitor quality attributes such as frequency and the reliability of commercial and tendered services; attributes such as vehicle and driver presentation are also monitored and the Bus & Coach Council (B&CC) code of practice on complaints handling has been implemented. On the demand side, local authority transport policies which involve banning of cars from town centres and park-and-ride schemes have increased local demand for buses.

Stagecoach is also involved with the B&CC in attempts to promote the industry itself. The B&CC have adopted the Stagecoach slogan 'Buses Mean Business' in a campaign to promote the bus as a solution rather than a problem, particularly in terms of city congestion.

COMPETITION AND REGULATION

The deregulation of bus transport removed the industry's previous exemption from UK competition laws. Acquisitions can be referred to the MMC if a company supplies over 25 per cent of local bus services in a 'substantial part of the United Kingdom'. In common with an increasing number of companies in the industry, Stagecoach has been investigated a number of times by the Office of Fair Trading (OFT) and undergone a number of investigations by the Monopolies and Mergers Commission (MMC). Table 20.3 provides information on MMC investigations into Stagecoach group units.

Although deregulation occurred in 1986 it remains the case that some of the legal aspects of how the industry can lawfully conduct itself – and how much of a network a company can own – still require to be clarified. The number of companies seeking legal remedies through the courts is a reflection of this.

STAGECOACH RAIL LIMITED

On 11 May 1992 the Stagecoach Group made history when it broke British Rail's (BR) 44 year monopoly by carrying its own passengers on chartered, refurbished carriages on the Aberdeen to London overnight train. Brian Souter had approached BR five years previously about running rail services in Scotland. Stagecoach's next approach in 1992 was taken more seriously because BR had been planning to franchise passenger rail services and to sell off freight and parcels operations. In securing the franchise with BR, Stagecoach Rail gained considerable initial spin-off from the free publicity for the Stagecoach brand. The joint venture was part of a three-year £1.5m contract to lease BR carriages, plus maintenance and staffing costs.

Table 20.3 MMC investigations into Stagecoach group units

Date	Unit	Area	Outcome
1990	Portsmouth City Bus	West Sussex	After acquisition Portsmouth City Bus (PCB), considered by Stagecoach to be on the verge of insolvency following intense competition in the area, was merged with Hampshire Bus and with Southdown Motors. The MMC, finding that the merger was potentially anti-competitive, recommended that undertakings be sought from Stagecoach to prevent their acting unfairly against potential competitors and that conditions be imposed preventing their exploitation of the merger situation. Despite the ruling the then Trade & Industry Secretary, Nicholas Ridley, directed that discussions take place about the disposal of PCB and the routes and assets were sold in 1991.[1]
1991	Hastings & District	East Sussex	After acquisition the unit was merged with Hastings Topline Buses, itself purchased as part of a deal acquiring the subsidiary Southdown. The MMC recommended that Stagecoach be asked to provide undertakings designed to prevent predatory behaviour. Peter Lilley, Trade & Industry Secretary, instructed the OFT to hold further talks with the company about the divestment of part of the Hastings operation to stimulate competition. Implementation of the order was postponed to the end of 1992 pending the outcome of a High Court legal challenge taken by another company relating to the jurisdiction of the MMC. By August 1993 the Trade & Industry Secretary, Tim Sainsbury, allowed the divestment order to be dropped in favour of undertakings.
1992	Coastline	West Sussex	Coastline, at one time part of Southdown, was referred to the MMC after they refused to give acceptable undertakings over future behaviour in relation to the charging of uneconomic fares on a route in Bognor Regis. The MMC concluded that the company's behaviour was anti-competitive and the Director General of Fair Trading will seek undertakings on a number of criteria including limiting fare increases and maintaining service levels. Stagecoach took successful legal action on the OFT referral to prevent the MMC widening its remit to the whole of the Coastline network.
1993	Lancaster City	Lancaster	Intense competition between Ribble and LCT concluded, after allegations of anti-competitive behaviour by Stagecoach, in an OFT registered agreement in 1989. In 1993 Lancaster County Council sought bids for the privatization of LCT. Stagecoach reduced fares on several corridors and announced plans to start competing services. Despite announcing initially that they would not bid, they offered a price of £1m for certain of the assets of LCT. The bid was comfortably in excess of other bids for the unit as a going concern and Lancaster City Council closed down the bus company and sold the assets to Stagecoach. MMC recommendation – to seek undertakings on fares and frequency which limit Stagecoach's ability to retaliate against new entrants and the publication of financial information on operations in the Lancaster district. These undertakings are preferred to the alternative – the divestment of a central bus depot of local strategic importance.

1. This unit, now called Portsmouth Transit, has the worst performance of all ex-NBC units with a loss of 30.8%. Bus Industry Monitor 1993.

The Stagecoach package involved the combination of a cheap fare with high service level and the objective was to build a new market from people who would not normally travel by InterCity trains and to encourage existing customers to travel more. However, by the autumn of 1992, the service had not attracted a 70 per cent capacity target although passenger levels had gradually built up, and in November 1992 a new arrangement, which substantially reduced Stagecoach costs, was implemented. By November 1993, half a million pound losses encouraged the company to withdraw from the rail market.

GROWTH THROUGH ACQUISITION – INTERNATIONAL

By 1993 the Stagecoach group generated around 20 per cent of its turnover from overseas with each acquisition expected to meet a number of requirements:

- finance for new vehicles and vehicle replacement should be available locally;
- the company should be able to repatriate acceptable levels of cash to the UK; and
- there should be a low purchase price and a strong private sector market.

Table 20.4 indicates international acquisitions to date and the group is continuing to look at worldwide opportunities, particularly in those countries which have deregulated passenger transport as the UK has done, in order to apply private-sector practices to the situation.

Hong Kong/China

In 1988 the Stagecoach group purchased 50 per cent of Speedybus Enterprises Limited, with first refusal on all surplus vehicles of the Kowloon Motor Bus Company. The buses, repainted in all-over advertising liveries, were supplied free on three-

Table 20.4 Acquisitions 1987–93: international

Name	Geographical area/ area of operation	Date	Vehicles purchased	Vehicle stock 1993	Staff	Depots
Speedybus Enterprises Ltd	Hong Kong/ China	1988	N/a	N/a	—	—
Stagecoach Malawi Ltd	Malawi	1989	260	343	2,829	7
Kenya Bus Services Ltd, Nairobi	Kenya	1991	250	} 337	} 2,628	} 2
Kenys Bus Service (Mombasa) Ltd)	Kenya	1991	80			
Gray Coach Lines Inc, Ontario	Eastern Canada, NE USA	1990	90	—	—	—
Wellington City Transport	New Zealand	1992	300	358	477	4

year contracts in several Chinese cities in return for the rental income from advertisers and by the start of 1991, 42 buses were provided in this way in the People's Republic of China. In 1993 Stagecoach sold their 50 per cent stake and now operate five new vehicles in Hong Kong as Stagecoach International (Hong Kong) Limited.

In the latter half of 1992, the group was unsuccessful in tendering for the first new franchise to be offered in Hong Kong. The company still maintains an interest in any potential businesses which may become available in the region.

Malawi

Stagecoach International Limited own a 51 per cent stake[11] in Malawi's national transport company purchased for £0.8m, the other shares being held by the Malawi government (34 per cent) and by employees (15 per cent) through an employee share ownership plan. In a country the size of England and Scotland together the company is split into eight operating divisions and is effectively the national carrier, operating in all areas and having some 90 per cent of the passenger market. Competition from smaller Malawian operators takes place largely on the profitable long-distance tar routes and passenger volume on Stagecoach group vehicles has increased by approximately 20 per cent since acquisition. Fares, regulated by government, are very low compared to UK levels and labour costs are also low (an average driver earns some £70 per month).

Vehicle maintenance is made more difficult for the chief engineer by the fact that depots can be up to 700 miles from the head office in Blantyre. Spares, most of which have to be shipped from the UK, are expensive due to high import duty and surtax and freight costs. The company has imported a considerable number of ex-Kowloon Motor Bus Company double deckers from Hong Kong which has increased passenger loadings by nearly 50 per cent and it is intended to replace the entire ageing Malawian fleet by 1996. The finance for this bus replacement programme is being sourced from local banks and the Commonwealth Development Corporation – a UK aid agency.

Kenya

A majority stake is held in the two largest municipal bus companies in Kenya: 75 per cent in Kenya Bus Services Ltd Nairobi and 51 per cent in Kenya Bus Services (Mombasa) Ltd, the remaining shares being held by the municipal authorities in these areas.

The companies, purchased for £0.4m, suffered from lack of investment in new rolling stock and a bus investment programme has been implemented. Numbers of employees have been reduced by 400 primarily among administrative support grades. Investment has included monies spent on renovation of staff houses and their supply with electricity and the drilling of a borehole to guarantee water supplies. The companies are facing intense competition in local markets to the extent that their vehicles are outnumbered by over 12 to 1. Competition comes in the form of nearly 4,000 'Manyanga Matatus': 25-seater minibuses that carry loads of up to 50 and run on an informal and unregulated basis, and from 100 buses run by the government-owned Nyayo Bus Service.

---

11. Initially the Malawian government owned 49 per cent of the company. The Stagecoach group organized an ESOP to take 15 per cent of the government's equity for bus company employees.

Canada

In one of the first major privatization moves for the Canadian transit industry, Stagecoach spent Can$16m purchasing 90 per cent of Gray Coach Lines Incorporated, Ontario in 1990 from its municipal owner, the Toronto Transit Commission. In November 1992, Northern routes were sold for Can$7m. In January 1993 the rest of the company was sold for Can$9m. The sale was a consequence of the combined effect of a severe economic recession and a dispute with the vendor which led to Stagecoach seeking protection under the Companies Creditors Arrangements Act, placing Gray Coach Lines in the Canadian equivalent of administration.

New Zealand

In 1989 New Zealand passed legislation similar to the UK's to privatize its bus services and in October 1992 Stagecoach purchased Wellington City Transport Limited for £2m. The company and its subsidiary, Cityline (NZ) Ltd, is the second largest urban bus operator in New Zealand and as part of the acquisition 90 electrically operated trolley buses were acquired as was management of the joint operation of Wellington's funicular railway service, one of the world's few remaining cable car systems. Given the growing support in Europe for electric transport as a quiet, efficient and environmentally friendly mode of transport, practical experience of this is seen as useful. Staffing levels are similar to those among privatized UK bus operations. More recently an additional number of small acquisitions have been made as has new vehicle investment.

FINANCE

For much of its life the growth of the Stagecoach group has been financed principally through family capital and bank facilities. In 1988 with the privatization of the Scottish Bus Group on the horizon, additional capital was raised by a private placing. The issue was over-subscribed by seven Scottish financial companies[12] underwriting £5m of new equity capital. The consequent financial boost, helped by £50m of bank facilities which were also made available, aided plans for massive expansion during 1989. By 1989 the share capital of Stagecoach Holdings had increased to 2,000,000 ordinary shares, of which Brian Souter and Anne Gloag owned 1,997,600, and 5,000,000 partly convertible preference shares which were owned by Scottish financial institutions.

In 1993, the group announced that it was to go public with a flotation in April. The aim was to raise around £20.6m of new capital, after expenses, to assist with expansion plans both in the UK and overseas. The 33.5 million shares making up the issue comprise 13.8 million from the selling shareholders and 19.7 million being issued by the company. The shares were 6.9 times over-subscribed and whereas the flotation had put the firm's value at £134m, by early 1994 market capitalization was around £240m. Performance over the previous years is shown in Fig. 20.2.

The group ended April 1993 with reduced net borrowings of £26.3m giving a

12. TSB Scotland plc; Murray Ventures plc; Noble Grossart Investments Ltd; The Standard Life Assurance Co; Scottish Enterprise; Scottish Investment Trust plc; Scottish Eastern Investment Trust plc.

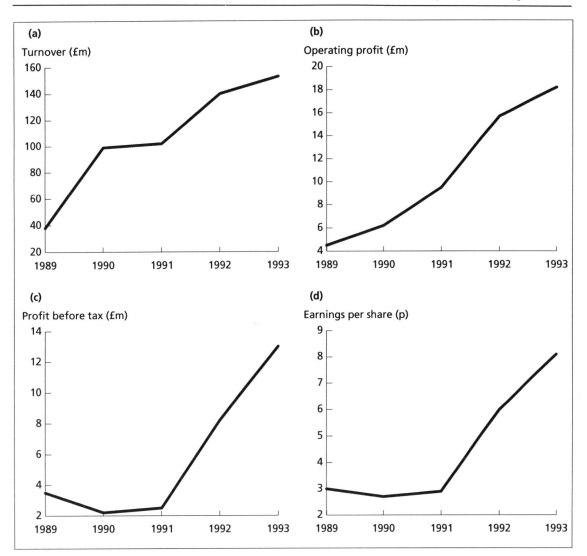

Fig. 20.2 Stagecoach Holdings Plc: performance 1989–93: (a) turnover; (b) operating profit; (c) profit before tax; (d) earnings per share.

gearing of 58 per cent – down from 243 per cent a year earlier. Before the flotation, Brian Souter and Ann Gloag owned between them around 90 per cent of the company. The flotation also allowed these two principal shareholders to realize part of their investment, with Ann Gloag holding 22.2 per cent and Brian Souter 26.8 per cent of ordinary shares following the issue. In total, family interests will hold about 55 per cent of the equity following the listing.

Appendix 20.2 contains recent financial data on the company.

THE FUTURE

Brian Souter is optimistic about UK and overseas prospects. In UK local bus markets, business is expected to benefit from environmental initiatives and bus priority schemes such as 'park and ride' – designed to keep the car out of town centres. Development of overseas business is initially focused on Commonwealth countries and increases in disposable income are expected to move these geographic markets into a growth phase in their lifecycle creating opportunities for bus transport. The executive chairman also believes that bus privatization opportunities are now being played out on a global scale and will provide substantial means for company growth over the next ten years. Expected developments of this nature will facilitate achievement of the Stagecoach vision:

> ... provision of land-based quality bus services at affordable prices and during a 10 year period Stagecoach can generate a billion in turnover: £400–500m of this from United Kingdom markets, £200–250m from the Pacific Basin and the remainder from the rest of the world, with the possibility of railways included.[13]

---

13. Interview – Brian Souter, Stagecoach Group headquarters, October 1993.

APPENDIX 20.1
THE MANAGEMENT TEAM

The composition of the board of directors of Stagecoach Holdings Plc is given in Table 20.5.

Table 20.5 The board

Executive directors	Interest	No. of ordinary shares held following the issue	% of issued share capital following the issue
Brian Souter (39) Executive Chairman responsible for business development and group strategy worldwide, for management philosophy and structure and for operations in the UK. Winner of Scottish Business Achievement Trust Award 1990.	Beneficial Non-beneficial	32,125,300 2,833,572	26.77 3.52
Ann Gloag (51) Managing Director, is responsible for group purchasing, insurance and property management. Also takes major responsibility for operations in Africa and China. One of three European Women of Achievement 1992 and Veuve Cliquot/ Institute of Directors Businesswoman of the Year 1990.	Beneficial Non-beneficial	26,652,894 2,600,000	22.21 3.83
Derek Scott (40) Group Finance Director, a chartered accountant responsible for the group's financial policy and cash management and also acts as Chairman of the Trustees of the Stagecoach pension schemes with assets of over £60m in the UK alone.	Beneficial	280,000	0.23
Brian Cox (46) Executive Director since October 1992, Chairman of Stagecoach (South) Limited, is responsible for Stagecoach Rail and also supports the Executive Chairman on transport policy and commercial development issues.	Beneficial	119,200	0.09
Barry Hinkley (44) joined the Board as an Executive Director in October 1992. Chairman of CMS Cumberland, Ribble Buses, East Midland and United Counties. Supports the Executive Chairman in reorganizing newly acquired group companies and assists the Managing Director with purchasing.	Beneficial	102,400	0.08
Ewan Brown (52). Professor Brown is a chartered accountant, an executive director of Noble Grossart and a non-executive director of a number of companies including Amicable Smaller Enterprises Trust plc, John Wood Group PLC. He was previously a non-executive director of the Scottish Transport Group and played a central role in the Scottish Power flotation and the reconstruction of the Stakis leisure group.	Beneficial	—	—
Muir Russell (45), Under Secretary in charge of housing in The Scottish Office Environment Department. Has been with the Scottish Office since 1970 and was seconded to the Scottish Development Agency (Scottish Enterprise) in 1975 and to the Cabinet Office Secretariat from 1990 to 1992. From 1981 to 1983 he was Principal Private Secretary to the Secretary of State for Scotland.	Beneficial	—	—
Barry Sealey CBE (58), Managing Director of Christian Salvesen plc from 1981 to 1989 and director of the Scottish Transport Group from 1986 to 1990. Currently an independent director serving on the boards of Scottish Equitable Life Assurance Society, Scottish American Investment Company plc, Wilson Byard PLC and other companies.	Beneficial	25,000	0.02

APPENDIX 20.2
RECENT FINANCIAL DATA

Tables 20.6 to 20.9 provide a range of further recent financial data on Stagecoach Holdings Plc.

Table 20.6 Consolidated profit and loss account (for the year ended 30 April 1993), Stagecoach Holdings plc and subsidiary undertakings

	1993 £000	1992 £000	1991 £000	1990 £000
Turnover				
Continuing operations	148,108	131,461	101,315	97,255
Acquisitions during the current year	4,385	0	0	0
	152,493	131,461	101,315	97,255
Discontinued operations	1,818	9,211	2,039	1,126
	154,311	140,672	103,354	98,381
Operating costs	(137,977)	(126,083)	(95,660)	(92,935)
Group overheads	(345)	(1,264)	(1,082)	(937)
Other operating income	3,212	2,459	3,021	1,917
Operating profit	18,328	15,784	9,633	6,426
Represented by:				
Continuing operations	17,553	15,173	9,452	6,426
Acquisitions during the current year	679	0	0	0
	18,232	15,173	9,452	6,426
Discontinued operations	96	611	181	0
Total operating profit	18,328	15,784	9,633	6,426
Profit on sale of properties – continuing operations	219	244	1,009	816
Profit/Loss on sales of discontinued operations	(434)	(353)	—	332
Profit on ordinary activities before interest and taxation	18,113	15,675	10,642	7,999
Interest payable (net)	(5,159)	7,434	(8,140)	(5,724)
Profit on ordinary activities before taxation	12,954	8,241	2,502	2,275
Taxation on profit on ordinary activities	(3,433)	(1,533)	497	778
Profit on ordinary activities after taxation	9,521	6,708	2,999	3,053
Minority interests	(944)	(477)	(37)	(432)
Profit for the financial year	8,577	6,231	2,962	2,621
Dividends	(561)	(1,862)	(453)	(235)
Retained profit for the year	8,016	4,369	2,509	2,386
Earnings per share	8.3p	6.0p	2.9p	2.6p

Table 20.7 Consolidated balance sheet (as at 30 April 1993), Stagecoach Holdings plc and subsidiary undertakings

	1993 £000	1992 £000	1991 £000	1990 £000
Fixed assets				
Intangible assets	0	1,078	1,339	0
Tangible assets	100,252	88,162	74,728	66,084
Investments	512	888	1,797	663
	100,764	90,128	77,864	66,747
Current assets				
Debtors and prepaid charges	20,792	21,189	15,079	14,002
Investments	0	1,417	4,757	1,602
Cash at bank and in hand	1,441	3,316	1,040	1,505
	22,233	25,922	20,876	17,109
Creditors: Amounts falling due within one year	(53,010)	(53,921)	(43,526)	(39,191)
Net current liabilities	(30,777)	(27,999)	(22,650)	(22,082)
Total assets less current liabilities	69,987	62,129	55,214	44,665
Creditors: Amounts falling due after more than one year	(14,058)	(31,218)	(37,748)	(29,801)
Provisions for liabilities and charges	(10,587)	(11,619)	(1,699)	(1,267)
Net assets	45,342	19,292	18,767	13,597
Capital and reserves				
Called-up share capital	5,004	7,107	7,000	7,000
Share premium account	23,513	617	923	923
Profit and loss account	23,317	15,753	12,050	9,255
Revaluation reserve	(602)	2,274		
Other reserves	(8,933)	(9,098)	(3,422)	(4,962)
Shareholders' funds	42,299	16,653	16,551	12,216
Minority interests	3,043	2,639	2,216	1,381
Total capital employed	45,342	19,292	18,767	13,597

Table 20.8 Consolidated cash flow statement (for the year ended 30 April 1993), Stagecoach Holdings plc and subsidiary undertakings

	1993 £000	1992 £000	1991 £000	1990 £000
Net cash inflow from operating activities	26,164	17,634	15,894	4,972
Returns on investments and servicing of finance				
Interests received	185	147	18	99
Interests paid	(3,512)	(5,866)	(6,229)	(4,716)
Interest element of hire purchase and lease finance	(1,832)	(1,715)	(1,929)	(1,107)
Dividends paid	(561)	(1,862)	(453)	(335)
Net cash outflow from returns on investments and servicing of finance	(5,720)	(9,296)	(8,593)	(6,059)
Taxation paid	(2,267)	(57)	(286)	(434)
Investing activities				
Purchase of tangible fixed assets	(26,126)	(13,745)	(7,451)	(15,122)
New hire purchase and lease finance	12,281	9,589	5,169	2,400
Purchase of subsidiary undertakings	(2,018)	(11,138)	(5,812)	(8,154)
Purchase of goodwill	(1,143)	0	(9)	(216)
Sales of fixed asset investments	208	0		
Sales of tangible fixed assets	1,925	6,635	(396)	(563)
Funds held in trust	3,386	(3,386)	—	—
Net cash outflow from investing activities	(11,487)	(12,045)	(4,302)	(9,371)
Net cash inflow/(outflow) before financing	6,690	(3,764)	2,713	(10,892)
Financing				
Sales of tokens	15,410	7,694	—	—
Redemption of tokens	(11,787)	(5,077)	—	—
Issue of share capital	22,025	107	—	2,500
Cost of issuing new shares	(750)	—		
Increase/(decrease) in overseas borrowings	3,587	(1,228)	1,550	725
Repayments of UK bank borrowings	(19,958)	(2,965)	(1,108)	4,378
Cash and cash equivalents of acquired subsidiary undertakings	292	19,112	—	—
Repayments of hire purchase and lease finance	(7,943)	(5,897)	(5,630)	(2,645)
Net cash inflow from financing	813	11,746	(5,188)	(4,958)
Increase in cash and cash equivalents	7,503	7,982	(2,475)	(5,934)

Table 20.9 Segment information (for the year ended 30 April 1993), Stagecoach Holdings plc and subsidiary undertakings

	1993 £000	1992 £000	1991 £000	1990 £000
Turnover:				
Scotland	35,625	28,416	5,158	3,335
North West Of England	33,249	32,607	34,842	33,935
Midlands	31,470	30,980	29,735	30,499
South Of England	23,675	19,888	17,848	17,745
United Kingdom – total	124,019	111,891	87,583	85,514
Overseas operations – Africa	24,089	19,570	13,732	11,741
Total continuing operations excluding acquisitions	148,108	131,461	101,315	97,255
Acquisition – New Zealand	4,385	—	—	—
Turnover continuing operations	152,493	131,461	101,315	97,255
Turnover – discontinued operations	1,818	9,211	2,039	1,126
Total turnover	154,311	140,672	103,354	98,381
Operating profit:				
Scotland	4,363	5,054	581	(244)
North West of England	4,568	4,003	3,994	2,307
Midlands	4,416	4,693	3,725	2,188
South of England	2,801	1,555	2,093	1,608
United Kingdom – total	16,148	15,305	10,393	5,859
Overseas operations – Africa	3,207	1,838	722	1,504
Total continuing operations excluding acquisitions	19,355	17,143	11,115	7,363
Acquisition – New Zealand	679	—	—	—
	20,034	17,143	11,115	7,363
Group overheads	(1,218)	(1,264)	(1,082)	(937)
Prior year rates rebate	600	—	—	—
Redundancy costs	(1,184)	(706)	(981)	—
Operating profit continuing operations	18,232	15,173	9,452	6,426
Operating profit – discontinued operations	96	611	181	—
Total operating profit	18,328	15,784	9,633	6,426
Net assets:				
United Kingdom	36,901	13,697	12,768	10,779
Africa excluding minority interests	3,355	2,956	2,031	1,437
New Zealand	2,043	—	—	—
Total shareholders' funds	42,299	16,653	16,551	12,216
Minority interests	3,043	2,639	2,216	1,381
Total net assets	45,342	19,292	18,767	13,597

Christian Salvesen Plc

C.M. Clarke-Hill

INTRODUCTION

The Christian Salvesen Company was founded by a Norwegian in Scotland in the 1850s, when its eponymous founder left his brother's shipping and ship agent business to form his own enterprise. Christian Salvesen first formed a partnership with others in 1853, and later in 1872 set up a joint stock company bearing his own name. During those twenty years of partnership, the firm had become a significant force in ship-owning, timber and coal-broking as well as operating a basic agency business. The firm attempted to enter the paraffin refining trade with disastrous results.

In the 1890s the firm went into the whaling business. Some years previously, the company had acted as UK agents for a number of Norwegian whaling concerns and saw an opportunity in that business for itself. By the turn of the century the group had become one of the largest whaling companies with fleets operating in the Arctic and Antarctic waters. The company also operated a permanent whaling station on South Georgia. Between the two world wars there was further expansion of the fleet, but during the Second World War, virtually the entire fleet was sunk by enemy action and had to be replaced.

The period soon after the Second World War saw the demise of the firm's coal and timber trade, and following a sharp downturn in whale stocks and the political climate that was soon to prevail in this industry, the company left the whaling business in the late 1950s and sold its fleet, mainly to the Japanese, and invested its money elsewhere. The 1960s was to see a period of rapid diversification and the emergence of the modern company.

It was during this early period of diversification that the company became involved with deep-sea fishing – including the development of one of the earliest freeze-at-sea factory fleets – fish processing and distribution, and the construction of a large cold store dedicated to its fishing businesses on Grimsby docks.

However, it was this base that allowed Christian Salvesen to move into the rapidly expanding market for frozen and chilled food, supplying customers like J. Sainsbury and Marks & Spencer. It later invested in food processing and packing factories and began to expand its operations in Europe and the USA.

Although this diversification looked logical, it was far from smooth in its implementation. During this early period, the company, forced by heavy losses, pulled out of deep-sea fishing, cut back its fish processing business, set up and failed in a fresh food distribution venture, and the operation of a North Sea drilling ship proved unprofitable for many years.

The early 1970s saw further diversification for the company. It entered the house building market and expanding quickly, and after purchasing a large land bank accumulated heavy debts before the land prices crashed in 1974. The business was scaled down and gradually returned to profitability. Also in this period, Christian Salvesen acquired a brick company that was added to in 1985 by the purchase of W.H. Collier, a high-quality traditional hand-made brick-maker that operated in the restoration and prestigious buildings market.

The early to mid 1980s saw Christian Salvesen build its overseas operations, particularly in food distribution, by a mixed policy of acquisition and organic development. In 1981, it acquired Merchants Refrigeration Company in the USA, and continually expanded its operations in continental Europe. Meanwhile in the UK it added to its cold and frozen food distribution business, by expanding into related non-food markets, contract distribution and third-party warehousing. In 1984, Christian Salvesen added heavy electrical plant hire (portable generators), and a company that produced and operated oil pollution equipment to its portfolio, and further added to its North Sea oil business.

The year 1985 was an important one for the company. Up until then it was one of the UK's largest private companies. Salvesen decided to go public in the summer of that year. This was partly due to a pressure from its shareholders wishing to create a market for their shares and partly due to the buoyancy of the stock market. Three-quarters of the 1,000 shareholders in the private company were members of the family, the rest were employees, institutions and the Church of Scotland (the beneficiary of Salvesen shares from a family bequest). The money raised in the flotation would be used for the company's own needs and the surplus funds were not, at the time, earmarked for any particular development. Mr Gerald Elliot, the then chairman and great grandson of the founder, said at the time that: 'We have built our business ourselves. We prefer internal growth to acquisition.'

The public flotation was a success and 57.1 million shares were placed on the market at 115 pence a share, valuing the company at £315 million. The flotation raised £66 million of which £21.4 million went directly to the company leaving it very positively cash rich and clearly in a position to fund further capital development or acquisitions. Mr Barry Sealey, managing director at that time, said: 'We see prospects of expansion in almost all our business areas.'

THE MODERN COMPANY

The period 1985/6 to 1991 saw the consolidation and growth of the group. This period was characterized by subtle changes in strategic direction, reorganization of the operating structure and the development of a clear future strategic vision.

The character of the modern company owed much to its early whaling days, in that it fostered a very close relationship with its employees when every whaler and his family was known by name by the founder, and this was reflected in the company's attitude to people and its employment policies.

By 1991, the company was now established in temperature controlled storage, processing and distribution of ambient food and non-food products; supplied portable diesel powered electric generators and transformers; oil drilling and production services in the North Sea; pollution control equipment; and manufactured high-quality facing bricks. The company was divided into three strategic units – Distribution, Manufacturing and Specialist Hire. Each division had its own clear operating structure. Table 21.1 gives summary financial highlights of the group.

Table 21.1 Group financial highlights 1987–91

	1991 £m	1990 £m	1989 £m	1988 £m	1987 £m
Profit and loss account					
Turnover	422.7	380.7	312.0	250.1	200.1
Operating profits	67.8	63.8	54.7	48.8	42.6
Profits before taxation	66.6	62.1	52.4	46.6	42.0
Retained profits	14.8	24.3	11.7	18.6	18.8
Balance Sheet					
Tangible assets	333.3	290.0	243.0	217.6	167.7
Working capital	16.5	5.3	2.9	11.3	11.2
Investments	0.2	4.6	10.4	15.4	38.2
Taxes and dividends	30.8	30.7	24.1	21.2	19.8
	319.2	269.2	232.2	223.1	197.4
Financed by					
Shareholders' funds	224.7	211.5	189.6	179.4	174.1
Provisions	32.0	23.2	22.0	20.3	20.2
Borrowings (net of cash)	62.5	34.5	20.6	23.4	3.1
Shareholders' funds employed	319.2	269.2	232.2	233.1	197.4
Year-end ratios					
Operating profit as a % of funds employed	21.2	23.7	23.6	21.9	21.6
Dividend per share (p)	6.6	6.0	4.8	4.1	3.6
Earnings per share (p)	16.6	15.0	12.0	10.8	9.7
Operating profit margin (%)	16.0	16.3	16.8	18.6	20.9

Source: Company reports.

STRATEGY AND STRUCTURE

Most Christian Salvesen operating companies had common features that would have been understood by its founder. They were capital-intensive operations, fairly low technology, basic businesses that respond to high-quality management. Almost all operated in the service sector, and wherever possible the company did not own the product.

While the company avowed a preference for direct investment rather than growth by acquisition, it had, nevertheless, built up an expertise of entering and leaving markets and changing strategic direction, using acquisition and divestment as a strategic means. In Christian Salvesen's managing director Mr Barry Sealey's words in 1985:

> We've had businesses die on us, like whaling...but we have got on our bikes, as Norman Tebbit said we should, and gone out and tried other things.

While this was true for some of the early ventures of the company, in other instances projects and strategic decisions were poorly conceived and implemented. One example was Christian Salvesen's attempt to operate in the house building market. A series of poor decisions compounded by falling and then later rising land values left the group with considerable debts. While this was to an extent turned around in the early 1980s, the company did not have the resources to capitalize on the housing boom of the 1980s in the South East of England. It eventually left the house building market by selling its division in 1986, netting some £30m, which it then spent on its existing operations.

Another example of this strategy can be witnessed by Christian Salvesen's expansion programme in the USA. In the early 1980s, the company acquired the Merchants Refrigeration Company on the West Coast of America. It added to its American operation by a further acquisition in late 1985 when it bought the United Packaging Company of California. United Packaging operated a fruit packing station and selling service. To help service this investment Christian Salvesen took a 33 per cent interest in United California Farms which supplied part of its output to the packing station. This operation was a disappointment to the company, and in 1989, it sold its food and fruit operations in California, arguing that continued management time and resources needed to be invested in the operation were not justified. They were to concentrate instead in building up the transportation and distribution operation in the US instead.

Although acquisition was seen as an important part of Salvesen's strategy, much of its acquisitions had been modest in size and often implemented without a public battle. Organic growth and direct investment was a more favoured policy, as Barry Sealey noted in 1988:

> We are not in the business of buying massive, public quoted companies, though we are not afraid of doing so... But we avoid doing anything which would change the flavour of the company and we have a preference for direct investment rather than acquisition.

Christian Salvesen had, for a number of years spent a considerable portion of its cash flow on internal investment, upgrading facilities, investing in new plant, building new depots and warehouses, and investing in systems technology to improve the efficiency of its operations. Much of this investment was focused on its Distribution division as it sought to expand geographically and increasingly penetrate the growing third-party dedicated transport operations that serviced the major retailers in the UK and Europe.

Christian Salvesen had always been a company that operated in more than one country. This international outlook was a cornerstone to its development strategy. Expansion in the USA, continental Europe and elsewhere was not something new to this group. It employed both internal as well as external means to achieve this territorial expansion, building greenfield sites in France, Belgium, the Netherlands and growing its business organically by extending its operating formats and transferring its technological expertise in transport and distribution systems into these new markets. It employed acquisition as a means of securing a German presence in the cold and frozen distribution markets. It was the company's view that 'given time, we would be interested in having a presence throughout Europe'. The management of the company believed that the 1992 Single Market would have a number of key effects on food distribution. Permitted product recipes would become increasingly standardized and that regulations on transport would become more uniform. The company's view on these likely trends was that although there was strong local competition in many of Salvesen's European markets, there was no competitor that was represented across all areas. It was Salvesen's objective to create a network and a unified service that covered all the main EC markets, and later expand east into the former Eastern bloc countries.

By the 1990s all of Christian Salvesen's businesses – with the exception of bricks – were international businesses.

October 1989 was an important point in the development of the Christian Salvesen company. Mr Barry Sealey, Salvesen's long-serving managing director, retired and was replaced by the internal appointment of Dr Chris Masters as Salvesen's new chief executive. Masters was a Yorkshireman whose early career was with Shell Chemicals and later had spent a number of years with the company the last four of which as managing director of the (former) Industrial Services Division. Within weeks of taking up the appointment, Masters had began a review of Salvesen's strategy and the ship agency business based in Aberdeen was sold, netting the company some £8.5 million. The operating structure of the business based on four divisions was rationalized into three, and the reporting structure was flattened by delayering. The new divisional structure resembled a classic multi-divisional organization. Masters also set up a small executive committee of eight people responsible for strategy. Each divisional unit was now made more directly accountable for their own activities.

Masters articulated his new approach at Salvesen as follows:

> I strongly believe that the key to increasing both the quality and magnitude of our earnings is to concentrate on activities where we have a real, demonstrable and maintainable competitive edge and then to structure the the company in such a way that the business sectors are clearly identified, accountabilities are unambiguous, and our people have the freedom to develop the operations within an agreed and well communicated strategy.

The reorganisation in 1989–90 led to the relocation of the headquarters of the Distribution Division from Edinburgh to the English Midlands, and by 1991 was seen to be working smoothly with the anticipated cost savings beginning to show through into the profit and loss account.

The traditional values of the company, particularly in its cautious financial management and borrowing policy, was to be left unaltered by the new strategic approach brought in by Masters, in other words: 'strong cash flow from aggressive but selective investment in the core business without significantly affecting borrowing' would continue under Masters' leadership as it had under Sealey's.

Masters' strategic outlook for Christian Salvesen did not, however, alter the fundamental values of the company. Masters was quick to recognize the traditional values of the firm and the culture which it had developed over the decades. Masters conceded that:

> All companies have a culture and you value it and safeguard it as an asset. We operate in a tough competitive world and have to grow earnings constantly year by year, so we need a sound strategy that everybody understands.

Masters was keen to develop a more clearly defined corporate culture in Salvesen and conceded that this would be a difficult task, but the process of decentralization that he started in 1989 would help to alter the culture more towards what he believed in – accountability and control while maintaining strict fiscal policy at the centre. The divisional operating strategy also had to fit into the overall strategy of the group.

The Masters approach was to articulate the overall strategy of the group and to give the divisional teams clear guidance on how they were to develop their response within the overall plan.

Masters' *raison d'être* for the company's strategy was very straightforward:

> Either we have technical leadership or market leadership, in other words something that

is measurable. Corporate culture and all those things are important but fundamentally, that's the strategy of looking at our businesses.

This view would soon become the guiding principle behind any future strategic review of the business. This philosophy was translated into a mission statement for the company, part of which reads as follows:

> Our strategy is to concentrate on a limited number of activities where we have a demonstrable and maintainable competitive edge, based on market leadership or technological superiority. We invest for organic growth with strong cash generation enabling us to fund high levels of capital expenditure in growth markets.
>
> ... Our strategy aims to ensure consistent growth in high quality earnings for the benefits of shareholders, employees and the communities in which we operate.

Masters had strong views about training and human resource management as having key roles to play in the success of the strategy. Salvesen in 1990–91 spent about £2 million on training. Masters' view of this investment in people was simple:

> We spend an incredible amount of money – and rightly so – training people. We doubled the amount we spent on training last year. Not because it made us feel good, but because it's something which can actually give you an edge in the future.

This commitment to training was also articulated strongly in other aspects of the company mission statement, in terms of seeing people as the key to success, especially in a service-orientated business.

Any company that had operations in a number of diverse areas such as manufacturing bricks, freezing vegetables, hiring out power plant, operating a North Sea drilling company and managing third-party distribution systems would be classified as a conglomerate. But Christian Salvesen did not see itself in such a way, and referred to itself instead as a 'technology-driven service company specializing in markets which it can afford to dominate.'

Masters did not agree with the conglomerate definition of his company and said:

> I don't like the word conglomerate. To my mind that's an organization which trades in other companies – one which buys a company, keeps it for a bit and then flogs it. That's what Hanson, Grampian and any of these companies does. I am not knocking it at all but we are not in that business. We'll sell a company when it no longer meets our requirements – but we don't buy and sell companies.

Although Masters may not have viewed the company in such a way, nevertheless in many other respects Christian Salvesen could be seen as representing the classic virtues of a conglomerate – in terms of cash generation, with high growth businesses in areas like power plant hire being financed by low growth traditional businesses like distribution. In many ways Christian Salvesen could be said to operate a balanced portfolio of activities.

Finally, to sum up, Masters believed that there were three key things in a business: the strategy, the people and the finance. In Masters' own words:

> Probably in that order. If you don't have the strategy you're dead. If you don't have the people, you're dead. And the finance I would place as secondary to the people because if you have a good organization you can always get the finance.

CHRISTIAN SALVESEN'S OPERATIONS

Tables 21.2 and 21.3 set out Christian Salvensen's divisional performance and the geographical spread of its businesses.

Table 21.2 Christian Salvesen sector analysis 1989–91

	Turnover			Trading profit			Capital expenditure		
	1991 £m	1990 £m	1989 £m	1991 £m	1990 £m	1989 £m	1991 £m	1990 £m	1989 £m
Distribution	248.4	222.8	179.4	27.5	27.6	25.2	33.0	34.4	29.1
Manufacturing	91.9	87.6	78.7	18.2	20.2	17.0	14.0	10.5	13.5
Specialist Hire	82.4	66.2	40.8	21.8	15.8	9.7	55.1	44.5	19.6
Reorganization costs					(2.2)				
Totals									
Continuing activities	422.7	376.6	298.9	67.5	61.4	51.9			
Discontinued activities	—	4.1	13.1	—	0.9	2.0			
Total for year	422.7	380.7	312.0	67.5	62.3	53.9	102.1	89.2	62.2

Table 21.3 Christian Salvesen geographical analysis 1989–91

	Turnover			Trading profit		
	1991 £m	1990 £m	1989 £m	1991 £m	1990 £m	1989 £m
United Kingdom	238.8	214.2	186.7	42.2	41.4	37.8
North America	64.8	60.1	45.8	13.8	10.8	7.2
Germany	54.6	50.4	39.7			
France	21.6	20.0	16.1			
Holland	18.6	16.1	14.2	10.4	9.7	8.9
Belgium	11.2	10.1	6.5			
Other Europe	4.8	5.4	2.9			
Rest of World	8.3	4.4	—	1.1	0.4	—
Totals	422.7	380.7	312.0	67.5	62.3	53.9

Distribution

Christian Salvesen's distribution business operated in six countries of the EC and in the USA. Its strategic mission was described by the company as:

> We aim to sustain our competitive edge by developing added-value logistic services for retailers and manufacturers, and offering the highest standards of contract management and customer service.

The division was split into three operating sub-units based on geographical location; UK, Continental Europe and the USA.

UK Distribution The UK Distribution operation provided contract distribution services to many of the UK's leading high street retailers, with some 85 per cent of distribution volumes in 1990 being in the food related sectors. A number of new management contracts had been added to service the Asda and Safeway food stores groups in 1990. It had always been the policy of the division to expand their trading base into the non-food sectors. The continuing recession in the UK, with its corresponding effect on retail sales, had hampered this objective.

The UK division operated two companies for the exclusive contract business for the Marks & Spencer's retail business. Salserve and Salstream serviced all Marks & Spencer's chilled and frozen food ranges and new depots in North London and in the Midlands were created to service Marks & Spencer stores with garments and other non-food items. Further expansion of this business was planned with new depot and warehouse openings in Yorkshire and elsewhere in the UK.

The market for third-party distribution in the UK was rapidly turning into a mature market. By 1991, less than 10 per cent of the UK distribution business was now in the non-contract hire sector. The UK was seen as having the most advanced market in the world for contract distribution, with many large firms operating in this sector – Tibbett & Britten, Transport Development Group, National Freight Corporation, and the Australian group TNT being among the biggest. (Appendix 21.3 shows brief operating ratios for UK registered operators.)

Continental Distribution

The Continental Distribution division served both retailers and manufacturers and operated from 31 sites on mainland Europe spread among five nations. In a number of these markets, Salvesen claimed market leadership. However, the early 1990s saw a mixed set of results for its European operations, particularly in France and in the Netherlands, even though Salvesen had signed contracts with Unilever to supply all its frozen foods in Holland. These poor trading conditions were partially offset by meeting financial targets in the Belgian market. It was in this geographic market where Salvesen had market leadership in frozen food and where the company saw future expansion into non-food sectors. Prospects in France were to improve by late 1991 when new contracts were signed by Salvesen with Euromarché and Carrefour, two large French hypermarket retailers, and with the Mars Group's petfood division. Certain sites in France and the Netherlands were sold, reducing Salvesen's exposure to commodity storage of frozen foods in Europe. The Spanish operation, although small, was to continue to be grown with new facilities being commissioned in Seville to meet new contracts that were signed by Salvesen for contract services to two Spanish supermarket groups.

The German market was to prove the most difficult for the company to operate in with the contract business in that country developing more slowly than was predicted by Salvesen. By 1990, Salvesen had built up a 30 per cent share of the deep-frozen food distribution market through speculative acquisition. Catering accounted for 13 per cent of this business, restaurants for 21 per cent, home deliveries for 10 per cent and traditional retailing for 7 per cent. The company believed that some rationalization had to take place and a review of the whole German operation was to be undertaken. Part of the reasoning behind this was that the company had to keep pace with rationalization in the German food industry. Some 20,000 of the existing 70,000 stores are expected to disappear by the year 2000. Experts believed that around 40 per cent of the deep-frozen food market was shared by three large retailers – Aldi, Leibbrand and Tengleman, while producers like Oetker, Schoeller and Langese-Iglo have between them a 60–70 per cent market share. The prospect of Salvesen going east was still a strategic possibility. This was likely to offset, in part, the forecast changes in the German retail market as the top German retailers expanded east during the early part of the 1990s. These German retailers would have to build logistic infrastructures if they were to operate in the east in the same way as they trade in the west of Germany. Salvesen saw this trend as positive for their company.

US Distribution

Salvesen operated from three regions in the USA covering nine US states. Salvesen's development strategy of added value distribution services was most advanced on the East Coast of the US, where the company continued to sign new contracts with retailers and manufacturers. Structural changes taking place in the retailing sector in the USA increased the confidence of the company that it could grow the third-party concepts used successfully in the UK in the changing US retailing industry. Salvesen's operation on the West Coast still proved problematical for the company. The West Coast operations continued to be beset by over capacity in the cold storage businesses and the third-party concept was still slow to be adopted. Salvesen's Central Region operations, centred around Denver and St Louis, were regarded as having good prospects and met their operating targets in both 1990 and 1991.

Manufacturing

The Manufacturing Division was made up of three key sub-units – Food Services, Bricks and Oil Pollution. These manufacturing businesses each serve very different markets and in each of these markets, Salvesen was a leader in its field.

Salvesen Brick

Salvesen Brick was one of the most efficient brick-makers in the UK. The strategy of continual investment in automation and flexible manufacturing systems allowed Salvesen Brick to strengthen its market position in the UK mass market, even though the industry had experienced dramatic falls in demand due to the prolonged recession in the UK housing market. Figures for 1988/89 were estimated to be down by some 30 per cent and a further 12 per cent fall was recorded for demand in 1989/90. Trading volumes, however, at Salvesen Brick fell only some 2 per cent in 1990 on an output of some 15 million bricks in 1989/90. Added to the investment strategy on the production side, improvements in marketing and sales strategies allowed Salvesen Brick to raise market share from 3.5 per cent to 5.5 per cent in the UK market for bricks. This market share rise was coupled with improvements in ROCE and cash flow. Flexibility and continual innovation had created a competitive advantage for Salvesen Brick in the UK brick market.

Food Services

Christian Salvesen's Food Services Division was one of the UK's largest processors of frozen vegetables, with thirteen plants servicing all the main east coast growing areas. Its services include freezing, storing, optical colour sorting, quality grading and packaging for retail sale by supermarkets and other food groups. The food market could be seen as stable – people have to eat. The market was also changing – quick chill and convenience foods were increasing in popularity, quality at the supermarket counter was a key buying factor with the customer along with packaging and design. Many retailers required a complete service package, and Salvesen was able to provide this value added service to its customers. A few statistics give some idea of the scope of Salvesen's food interests. The company froze 80,000 tonnes of peas in 1990, 120,000 tonnes of green vegetables and root crops and around 33,000 tonnes of fish. The strategy of value added services and the accent on quality was reinforced by continual new investment to improve the efficiency of the operation and was seen as important to the division so that its position in the market was preserved. One of its main competitors in this area was Albert Fisher, which also packed and distributed vegetables and fruit to retailers and institutional caterers. (Albert Fisher's key ratios are shown in Appendix 21.3.)

Vikoma

Vikoma was Salvesen's operating company that was a world leader in the design and manufacture of specialized equipment such as booms and skimmers used in the control of oil pollution at sea and on rivers. Its business in this field was enhanced by a number of ecological disasters, namely the sinking of the *Exxon Valdez* supertanker in Prince William Sound in Alaska in 1989 and the considerable oil pollution caused during the Gulf War of 1991. Other oil pollution incidents off the Italian coast and in the Gulf of Mexico meant that Vikoma's services were in constant demand. A number of small acquisitions in 1990 were made to increase Vikoma's production capacity and to ensure its premier position in the international oil pollution control market. In addition to equipment, Vikoma also offered training and consultancy services in pollution control.

Specialist Hire

Christian Salvesen had two distinct businesses in the Specialist Hire Division – Aggreko and Salvesen Oilfield Technology. Both shared a common commitment to quality and service.

Aggreko

Aggreko's business was the provision of mobile power generators to customers as diverse as pop concert producers and North Sea oil platform operators. Many of the generator sets hired from Aggreko were on long-term lease or charter. The company has production facilities in the UK, the Netherlands and Singapore and assembled temperature control equipment in the USA. The Aggreko business was an expanding international business in both the European market and increasingly in the USA. A few selected acquisitions, particularly in the USA, had strengthened Aggreko's market base in the USA. A number of related business areas were added to the US operation strengthening the core business and allowing Aggreko to branch out into the new business area of live TV transmissions of major US sporting events. An acquisition in Singapore allowed Aggreko to enter the Australian market with another acquisition of a company based in Sydney and Newcastle. New investment was put into the Australian market with the commissioning of new depot facilities in Melbourne and Perth. By 1991, Aggreko had coverage of the main Australian markets and had equipment on hire in every Australian state.

The geographical expansion was strengthened in 1991 by selected investment and the purchase of depot facilities in Antwerp and new investment in the German operation in Mulhiem and Berlin. The objective behind this was to further expand into the eastern part of Germany. The company had also opened new facilities in Barcelona, Seville and Bilbao.

Aggreko's competitive advantage over other traditional hire companies was the fact that Aggreko designs and, in most cases, assembles its own equipment specially for the international hire market. The strategy at Aggreko was one of aggressive sales growth led from a position of technical leadership and the creation of a related diversity of products and an international customer base.

Salvesen Oilfield
Technology

The Oilfield Technology Division provided three highly specialized but related service businesses to the oil and gas industry throughout Europe, both on and off shore.

- *Tubular Services* involved the installation and testing of lining for both exploration and production wells. The division claimed a 50 per cent market share in this specialist business market.
- *Completion Services* provided a specialist 'down-hole' component assembly facility from its on-shore base in Scotland.
- *The Well Services* business provided sophisticated and cost effective maintenance service packages to oil well operators.

The services provided by the Division were targeted mainly at the Northern European market and are to an extent protected from the fluctuations of international oil prices although the marker price for Brent Crude does have an effect on North Sea oil activity.

PROSPECTS

As a final section to this case study, consider the following quotations taken from Christian Salvesen's chief executive's statement to the company's shareholders.

> Our strategy is to concentrate on business areas where we have a demonstrable, measurable and maintainable competitive edge. In pursuit of this, we have withdrawn from some businesses, focused on others and aggressively developed those which offer the best market opportunities within our three core activities of Distribution, Manufacturing and Specialist Hire.

> We have a range of high quality businesses, growing at different rate and with different – though largely complementary – cash flow characteristics. Taken together they represent an excellent portfolio which will ensure Christian Salvesen's prosperity in the years ahead.

APPENDIX 21.1
CHRISTIAN SALVESEN PLC: GROUP ACCOUNTS

Table 21.4 Group profit and loss account (for the year ended 31 March)

	1991 £m	1990 £m	1989 £m
Turnover	422.7	380.7	312.0
Cost of sales	310.9	277.5	227.0
Gross profit	111.8	103.2	85.0
Other operating expenses	44.3	40.9	31.1
Trading profit	67.5	62.3	53.9
Income from associated undertakings	0.1	0.1	-
Other income	0.2	1.4	0.8
Operating profit	67.8	63.8	54.7
Net interest payable	1.2	1.7	2.3
Profit on ordinary activities before taxation	66.6	62.1	52.4
Taxation	19.5	20.0	18.7
Profit on ordinary activities after taxation	47.1	42.1	33.7
Extraordinary items	13.3	0.8	8.4
Profit for the year	33.8	41.3	25.3
Dividends	19.0	17.0	13.6
Retained profit	14.8	24.3	11.7

Table 21.5 Group balance sheets (for the year ended March 31)

	1991 £m	1990 £m	1989 £m
Fixed assets			
Tangible assets	333.3	290.0	243.0
Investments in associated companies	0.1	0.5	0.8
	333.4	290.5	243.8
Current assets			
Stocks	28.6	21.8	16.2
Debtors	108.3	93.0	63.5
Investments	0.1	4.1	9.6
Cash	8.4	27.2	8.2
	145.4	146.1	97.5
Current liabilities			
Creditors: amounts falling due within one year			
Borrowings	10.5	11.6	9.9
Corporation tax	19.7	20.8	15.4
Ordinary dividends	11.1	9.9	8.7
Other creditors	102.9	95.0	72.8
Net current assets/(liabilities)	1.2	8.8	(9.3)
Total assets less current liabilities	334.6	299.3	234.5
Long-term liabilities			
Creditors: Amounts falling due beyond one year			
Borrowings	60.4	50.1	18.9
Other creditors	17.5	14.5	4.0
Provisions for liabilities and charges	32.0	23.2	22.0
Net worth	224.7	211.5	189.6
Capital and reserves			
Share capital	74.6	73.7	73.3
Share premium account	23.7	22.0	21.1
Profit and loss account	126.3	115.7	95.1
Shareholders' funds	224.6	211.4	189.5
Minority interests	0.1	0.1	0.1
Total shareholders' funds	224.7	211.5	189.6

APPENDIX 21.2
FINANCIAL RATIOS OF KEY ITEMS

Table 21.6 Christian Salvesen Plc

No.	Description	31/3/87	31/3/88	31/3/89	31/3/90	31/3/91
701	Return on Shareholders' equity (%)	14.12	15.51	16.72	19.34	19.01
707	Return on capital employed (%)	19.49	21.42	23.47	22.97	21.19
713	Operating profit margin (%)	20.02	15.00	17.71	17.05	15.83
716	Pre-tax profit margin (%)	20.26	15.89	17.25	16.94	15.78
717	Net profit margin (%)	13.20	10.23	11.21	11.79	10.98
732	Income gearing (%)	4.71	5.94	5.23	8.90	7.62
733	Borrowing ratio	0.15	0.17	0.14	0.27	0.29
725	Stock ratio (days)	16.45	16.94	18.90	20.90	24.70
727	Debtors ratio (days)	69.36	61.29	74.29	89.16	93.52
729	Creditors ratio (days)	94.41	80.60	122.06	126.57	123.67
741	Working capital ratio	1.64	1.12	0.89	1.05	0.98
762	Sales per employee	34,983	43,209	35,453	38,358	41,275
763	Operating profit per employee	7,002	6,482	6,278	6,539	6,533
764	Capital employed/ employee	38,250	33,964	27,501	31,093	33,317
761	Tax ratio	34.99	35.39	35.01	30.50	30.54
792	Cash earnings per share	18.00	19.26	25.17	28.78	30.69

Source: Datastream Output from Program 190D.

Table 21.7 Transport sector UK

No.	Description	9/11/86	9/11/87	6/11/88	3/11/89	4/11/90
701	Return on shareholders' equity (%)	13.71	11.10	11.25	12.96	9.97
707	Return on capital employed (%)	15.27	13.18	12.47	12.83	10.21
713	Operating profit margin (%)	6.92	9.05	9.73	10.59	9.61
716	Pre-tax profit margin (%)	6.14	8.40	8.74	9.10	6.89
717	Net profit margin (%)	4.13	5.43	5.57	5.81	4.61
732	Income gearing (%)	19.52	14.28	18.12	21.84	35.72
733	Borrowing ratio	0.47	0.45	0.58	0.76	1.03
725	Stock ratio (days)	15.87	19.18	27.12	27.20	24.81
727	Debtors ratio (days)	69.38	68.64	68.39	75.88	69.21
729	Creditors ratio (days)	103.36	113.11	121.14	119.14	109.89
741	Working capital ratio	0.93	1.02	0.85	0.85	0.96
762	Sales per employee	64,484	71,473	70,261	72,399	71,812
763	Operating profit per employee	4,462	6,466	6,837	7,668	6,902
764	Capital employed/ employee	34,371	55,199	61,573	65,783	75,751
761	Tax ratio	37.80	38.11	38.08	36.25	33.64

Source: Datastream Output from Program 190D.

APPENDIX 21.3
KEY RATIOS OF CHRISTIAN SALVESEN'S LEADING COMPETITORS

Table 21.8 Transport development

No.	Description	31/12/86	31/12/87	31/12/88	31/12/89	31/12/90
701	Return on shareholders' equity (%)	14.33	15.84	13.58	10.21	9.60
707	Return on capital employed (%)	18.96	19.78	17.47	14.17	12.96
713	Operating profit margin (%)	8.82	9.32	8.91	7.87	7.50
716	Pre-tax profit margin (%)	7.30	8.01	7.71	7.22	6.79
717	Net profit margin (%)	4.67	5.35	5.09	4.83	4.57
733	Borrowing ratio	0.43	0.38	0.38	0.29	0.31
762	Sales per employee	42,345	41,012	44,553	45,225	46,357
763	Operating profit per employee	3,737	3,822	3,969	3,560	3,478
764	Capital employed/ employee	20,187	19,899	23,284	27,801	30,003
792	Cash earnings	38.42	41.06	46.47	49.48	50.46

Source: Datastream Output from Program 190D.

Table 21.9 Albert Fisher

No.	Description	31/8/86	31/8/87	31/8/88	31/8/89	31/8/90
701	Return on shareholders' equity (%)	26.57	9.95	22.67	27.58	18.20
707	Return on capital employed (%)	25.47	14.08	21.01	22.49	20.86
713	Operating profit margin (%)	7.22	7.21	5.81	5.90	6.60
716	Pre-tax profit margin (%)	7.20	7.48	6.23	5.44	7.18
717	Net profit margin (%)	4.47	4.86	4.05	3.54	4.66
733	Borrowing ratio	0.65	0.16	0.83	0.92	0.42
762	Sales per employee	141,142	131,617	141,485	162,855	163,716
763	Operating profit per employee	10,196	9,488	8,225	9,611	10,800
764	Capital employed/ employee	46,247	78,951	48,150	48,758	66,846
792	Cash earnings per share	4.16	5.70	7.65	10.49	12.27

Source: Datastream Output from Program 190D.

Table 21.10 NFC

No.	Description	31/9/89	6/10/90
701	Return on shareholders' equity (%)	16.50	17.45
707	Return on capital employed (%)	20.58	20.40
713	Operating profit margin (%)	5.54	5.11
716	Pre-tax profit margin (%)	5.23	5.10
717	Net profit margin (%)	3.48	3.34
733	Borrowing ratio	0.15	0.30
762	Sales per employee	47,030	48,189
763	Operating profit per employee	2,604	2,464
764	Capital employed/ employee	13,352	13,708
792	Cash earnings per share	17.04	16.56

Source: Datastream Output from Program 190D.

Table 21.11 Tibbett & Britten

No.	Description	31/12/86	31/12/87	31/12/88	31/12/89	31/12/90
701	Return on shareholders' equity (%)	15.37	19.38	21.34	12.77	16.28
707	Return on capital employed (%)	20.15	24.80	25.78	18.22	25.42
713	Operating profit margin (%)	8.47	9.36	10.19	8.98	7.26
716	Pre-tax profit margin (%)	9.73	9.39	9.20	8.93	7.52
717	Net profit margin (%)	6.13	6.10	5.95	5.77	4.89
733	Borrowing ratio	0.12	0.11	0.43	0.23	0.12
762	Sales per employee	22,601	24,635	26,160	26,453	28,694
763	Operating profit per employee	1,914	2,305	2,666	2,375	2,083
764	Capital employed/ employee	11,658	9,784	10,437	14,695	9,696
792	Cash earnings per share	15.94	19.94	30.77	37.41	45.16

Source: Datastream Output from Program 190D.

Virgin Atlantic Airways[1]

Keith W. Glaister

INTRODUCTION

Virgin was founded in 1970 when Richard Branson established a business selling popular records by mail order. The first Virgin shop was opened in Oxford Street, London, in 1971. By the end of 1973, a record company, a music publishing company, a recording studio operation and an export company had been added. By the end of 1979, the Virgin record company had a growing presence in the UK and, predominantly on a licensing basis, in overseas markets. In 1984 Branson established his fledgling airline when Virgin Atlantic Airways and Virgin Cargo were launched. In 1985 Virgin Holidays, a long-haul tour operator, was formed. In November 1986 the Virgin Group comprising the Music, Retail and Property and Communications divisions, was floated on the London stock exchange. The airline, clubs, holidays and aviation services remained part of a privately owned company called Voyager Group Limited. Branson was advised to keep the airline out of the float because of worries in the City that it was too risky a business and could endanger the success of the flotation. The share price performed badly, however, drifting from the 140p issue price to below 90p, and Virgin's stay on the stock market was short lived. In October 1988 Branson organized a management buy-out and the Virgin Group rejoined the Voyager Group as a privately owned company. Branson bought the shares back at the same price at which he originally floated the company. The main reason given by Branson for taking Virgin back into private ownership was that the City was undervaluing the share price. There were also differences between Virgin and some of the institutional shareholders over the company's plans to invest in long-term projects, with Branson taking the view that the City was too focused on the short run. Branson's concern for the long term is reflected in his vision for Virgin Atlantic: 'We aim to be the best airline in the world by the year 2000, and we will sacrifice short-term profits to make sure we will.'

In 1989 Voyager Travel Holdings, the holding company for Virgin Atlantic Airways, sold 10 per cent of its equity to Seibu Saison International, one of Japan's largest retail and travel groups, in return for an injection of £36m of equity and convertible loan capital. In 1992 the Virgin Music Group, at that time the world's largest independent music business, was sold to Thorn-EMI for £560m. The money was earmarked for investment in other Virgin businesses such as the airline and Virgin record shops.

---

1. I would like to thank Amanda Donaldson-Briggs for her assistance in helping to prepare material for this case.

By 1993 the Virgin Group consisted of three wholly owned separate holding companies:

- Virgin Retail Group – operating a chain of megastores in the UK, continental Europe, Australia and the Pacific, selling music, videos, games and other entertainment products;
- Virgin Communications – controlling film, video and commercial radio investments; production services to the television industry; publishing, including books and computer games software;
- Virgin Holdings and Virgin Travel group – consisting of airline and other travel activities; clubs and hotels. Virgin Atlantic Airways is the main operating subsidiary of Voyager Travel Holdings, an intermediary holding company for a number of travel and leisure businesses.

There were over 100 operating companies controlled by the three holding companies doing business in 12 countries worldwide.

RICHARD BRANSON

Richard Branson was born in 1950, and educated at Stowe School, where he established a national magazine called *Student* at the age of sixteen. In 1970 he started selling LPs by mail order, choosing 'Virgin' as the name for the company in order to reflect his innocence of the ways of business. Branson eventually established a record company, the first release being Mike Oldfield's *Tubular Bells*, which sold millions of copies. Over the years many top-rated artists joined the Virgin label, to help make Virgin one of the top six record companies in the world.

Although never a member of the British business establishment, Branson became one of Britain's best known entrepreneurs. This was in large measure due to his skills at self-promotion, for example being photographed sitting in the bath playing with a model aircraft at the time of the launch of Virgin Atlantic, and arriving at the inaugural press conference for the airline wearing a brown leather aviator's jacket with matching helmet and goggles in the style of Biggles. He also gained much publicity from various world record breaking attempts. In 1986 his boat crossed the Atlantic in the fastest ever recorded time. A year later he made the fastest ever hot-air balloon crossing of the Atlantic. It was estimated that Virgin obtained £20m worth of exposure from this endeavour at a total cost of £500,000. In 1991 he made the fastest ever crossing of the Pacific Ocean, from Japan to Arctic Canada, in a hot-air balloon.

Branson has been described by critics as the archetypal 'hippy capitalist', summarized by one journalist as 'sowing the seeds of his fortune in a shrewd understanding of the mores and tastes of a hazy era of libertarian-idealism, and reaping the fruits in an era of pragmatic commercialism' (Mick Brown, *The Sunday Times*, 8 June 1986). It is probably the case that Branson has always equally enjoyed eschewing convention (for instance he appears only rarely in a suit preferring instead to wear a woolly jumper) and making money. Branson has a personal fortune in excess of £800m with *The Sunday Times* ranking him as the eleventh richest person in Britain. Despite his apparent casual approach to business, Branson is a great believer in 'protecting the downside'. He says: 'An entrepreneur has also got to accept failure. If it works, great; if not, cut your losses quickly and move on to the next thing.' But one man's loss-maker can be somebody else's success. 'That's the most important thing as an entrepreneur. Just because somebody has failed at something – like Freddie Laker – it doesn't mean you should avoid it. If somebody else has been a pioneer, you can learn from their mistakes' (*The Sunday Telegraph*, 19 November 1989). Branson has also recognized that 'There is an element of luck as to whether you succeed at the end. But I've never been afraid of failure. If you don't accept you may fail, you'll never take any risks' (*Investors Chronicle*, 9 March 1990). Branson puts a premium on conservative risk management. In a 1989 interview, he put his cautionary philosophy this way: 'We go into each venture watching the downside very carefully; a key principle is to arrange the financing of group activities so that borrowings and liabilities are without recourse to group funds.'

While the Virgin name is almost synonymous with Richard Branson, he has maintained that the company could exist without him. 'Virgin is one of the best delegated companies you could come across ... of the 35 managing directors, only one has ever left. They all have an enormous amount of freedom' (*Investors Chronicle*, 9 March 1990). In fact, on a day-to-day basis Branson has little involvement in Virgin's other businesses, but concentrates on the airline, not having been involved in running the music company since 1978.

THE DEVELOPMENT OF VIRGIN ATLANTIC AIRWAYS[2]

It was not Richard Branson's idea that he should own an airline. The idea was brought to him by Randolph Fields, a 31-year-old barrister, who owned a 'paper' airline, British Atlantic, which had applied for a licence to fly from Gatwick to Newark airport in New Jersey, which is close to New York City. Fields had applied for the right to fly on a route that had been vacant since the collapse of Laker Airways two years previously. Fields had examined the feasibility of a new transatlantic airline and had made enquiries about purchasing aircraft. However, he had no money to establish the airline.

For Virgin to move into the airline business did not make sense. Branson knew nothing about airlines. All of the expertise at Virgin was based generally on the entertainment business and specifically the record industry. Virgin had grown by a process of related diversification and so a move into airlines would be a radical departure. There was also the risk that the large investments needed to establish a presence in the airline business could ultimately force Virgin to bankruptcy. Nevertheless, Branson was persuaded of the attractiveness of the proposition and within a week of meeting, Branson and Fields agreed to be partners.

Fields's original concept had been of a dedicated business-class service between London and New York. But Branson was uneasy with the notion believing that it did not have the right image from Virgin's point of view. Instead he preferred the idea of a cut-price airline, partly because discounting was what Virgin had been built on. The American cut-price airline People Express had recently become successfully established as a transatlantic carrier and research convinced Branson that the market was big enough to support two cut-price carriers. Also Branson came to believe that

2. Much of this section is drawn from Chapter 10: 'Virgin Atlantic', in Mick Brown, *Richard Branson: The Inside Story*. Michael Joseph, London, 1988.

an airline was not that far removed from the principle of expanding into related businesses. In running a cut-price operation the potential customers would be the same people – young, mobile, relatively affluent – who for years had been buying records by Virgin artists in Virgin record shops. More recently they would have been buying Virgin books and videos and watching Virgin films.

While Branson was sold on the idea that Virgin should establish a cut-price airline his senior colleagues in the company were extremely hostile to the scheme. As the owner of 85 per cent of the shares in Virgin, however, they were powerless to stop Branson and he set out to establish an airline from scratch in the space of three to four months. Between March and June 1984, Branson worked harder than he had ever worked in his life before in order to get the airline up and flying.

Branson sought to avoid the mistakes made by Freddie Laker whose Laker Airways had gone out of business in late 1981. Laker had over-extended himself by buying a relatively large number of aircraft with borrowed money. With very low profit margins Laker had to keep the planes flying to capacity in order to be able to meet the interest payments and repay the principal. This proved difficult to do. Laker was finally put out of business when the major transatlantic airlines, including British Airways, slashed their fares to match Laker's. In October 1981, BA, PanAm and TWA agreed to cut their transatlantic fares by 66 per cent. It drove Laker out of business. Three months later they put them up again. Subsequently Laker sued the big airlines in the American courts under the anti-trust laws for driving him out of business.

Very quickly Branson came to some firm decisions: the airline would combine an economy section with a first-class section at business-class prices; in order to carry freight as well as passengers the aircraft would be a 747; the aircraft should be leased; the leasing agreement should be protected against currency fluctuations.

In April 1984 the Civil Aviation Authority (CAA) granted Virgin the licence to fly the Gatwick–Newark route, and in June the American regulatory bodies granted permission to fly into the USA. The plane Virgin bought was a 747-200 series, with one previous owner, and only 19,000 recorded flying hours. On 22 June 1984 the inaugural flight of Virgin Atlantic's Gatwick–Newark flight took off. The plane had only a few paying passengers, but was loaded with journalists, television crews, several celebrities and seventy crates of champagne. The maiden flight was warmly and comprehensively reported in the national press.

The agreement between Branson and Fields, drawn up in April 1984, gave Fields responsibility for the day-to-day running of the airline, while Branson considered the broader picture. Branson soon became disillusioned with Fields's ability to run his side of the operation and in September 1984, Virgin and Fields agreed that his contract should be terminated, with a sum of £125,000 paid in compensation. Fields remained a director and shareholder in Virgin Atlantic until an agreement was reached in 1985 to buy out his shareholding for £1m and unlimited free travel on Virgin Atlantic. Branson now had total control of the airline.

Branson anticipated he would eventually face a price war with the major transatlantic carriers and in October 1984 his expectations were fulfilled when British Airways indicated their intention (which had to be approved by the government because BA was at that time in public ownership) to drop the price of their cheapest return ticket on the London–New York route to only £1 more than Virgin's price. The same day, the other major transatlantic carriers, PanAm and TWA, announced that they would match the lower prices. Branson argued that while the Virgin price reflected his airline's lower costs, the new fares proposed by the big airlines were not realistic, but predatory in nature and designed to put Virgin out of business. Branson's attack on predatory pricing with the implied threat of suing BA under anti-trust laws in the US courts was profoundly worrying for the UK government in the run up to the privatization of BA. The British government turned down the new fare proposals from the American operators, while the CAA rejected BA's request. In the event this was not an effective measure. BA was allowed by the CAA to introduce a low-cost fare on the London–Boston route. PanAm, which did not serve Boston, introduced a London–New York–Boston ticket, in order to fly to New York on the lower Boston fare. The result was that all New York fares could now be reduced, bringing them to a level only slightly above that of Virgin's competing New York fare, and fares on the Boston route were adjusted to match the New York level. Branson learned quickly that the international airline business is a fiercely competitive arena. Branson also learned that big business and politics were intimately related.

By the end of 1984, Virgin Atlantic had withstood the predatory pricing moves of its competitors and had overcome an early loss. It had been running at over 90 per cent capacity through the peak season, and weathered the slow winter months to reach a profit of over £250,000. (The financial performance of Virgin Atlantic from 1985 to 1992 is shown in Appendix 22.1.) Encouraged by the success of the transatlantic venture, Virgin next introduced a short-haul service to Maastricht in Holland, using a plane leased from British Island Airways. This also proved a success and Branson began to explore the possibility of flying to Dublin and Miami.

In the year to July 1988, Virgin Atlantic made record profits of £10m, a 104 per cent increase on the previous year. The success story had been achieved in little over four years. Virgin now had six 747s and expected the size of the fleet to double in the following two years, aiming to fly to 12 major cities around the world. In 1989 Virgin Atlantic Airways was named the third most profitable airline in the world by *Airline World*. Asked how this success had been achieved Branson said, 'It's easier to follow a pioneer than be a pioneer. We learned from Freddie Laker's mistakes. He created an airline just based on price, not quality. And he expanded too fast, and didn't protect himself on currencies. So we decided to create the best airline in the world, not the biggest.' Branson also indicated that he did not want to expand the airline too much, 'As far as I am concerned in the airline business small is beautiful. Man's instinct to expand and grow must be taken out on the other businesses' (*Investors Chronicle*, 9 March 1990). Branson stresses: 'Airlines should be kept small and personal. They should be run like private clubs. We try to manage ours from the bottom up' (*The Observer*, 21 May 1989).

COMPETITIVE DEVELOPMENTS

A chronology of developments at Virgin Atlantic is set out in Table 22.1. The Virgin Atlantic route structure, as of 1994, is shown in Fig. 22.1. Originally Virgin Atlantic offered two classes of service, Upper Class and Economy Class, in order to attract two kinds of customers: those in search of cheap flights, and businessmen with large expense accounts. Business travellers are notoriously indifferent to bargain fares. Surveys show that they are swayed much more in their choice of airline and flight by brand awareness, speed, safety and the timings of flights. They also have a surprising

Table 22.1 Chronology of main developments at Virgin Atlantic

1984	February	The concept of a high quality, value for money airline is first developed.
	March	Licence granted for London (Gatwick) to New York (Newark).
	May	Lease purchase for the first aircraft, a Boeing 747, successfully negotiated.
	June	Virgin takes off from Gatwick starting a regular connection to New York (Newark).
1985	October	Virgin Cargo and Virgin Holidays are established.
	November	Licence granted for London (Gatwick) to Miami.
1986	April	The Miami service takes off.
	April	Virgin Mailing and Distribution is established.
	June	Virgin takes delivery of a second B747 and the Miami flights are increased to four a week.
1987	July	UK licence granted for the Boston route.
	September	Virgin's one millionth transatlantic passenger takes to the air.
1988	March	Licence granted for the Los Angeles and New York (JFK) routes.
	May	Virgin commences charter services to Orlando, Florida.
	July	Licence granted for the Tokyo route.
	September	Lease agreements entered into for the third and fourth 747.
1989	May	Virgin commences its three flights a week service to Tokyo.
	May	Virgin established aircraft maintenance facilities for its own aircraft and to provide a service to other airlines.
	July	UK licence granted for the Singapore route.
	August	Virgin doubles its capacity to New York with seven flights a week to JFK.
	August	Cargo opens terminal at JFK airport.
	September	Fourth frequency to Tokyo commences.
	October	Negotiations concluded in respect of Virgin's fifth and sixth Boeing 747.
1990	May	Virgin commences its service to Los Angeles.
1991	Jan	Civil Aviation Authority opens the door to Heathrow for Virgin's award winning operations.
	April	Service to Tokyo increases to six flights a week.
	May	Daily service from London Gatwick to Boston commences.
	May	Virgin obtains seventh and eighth 747.
	July	Virgin commences services from Heathrow to Los Angeles, New York JFK, and Tokyo.
	July	UK licence granted for Johannesburg.
	August	Virgin starts its own on-board courier service.
	October	Cargo opens its own terminal in Miami.
	November	Cargo opens its own terminal in Los Angeles.
1992	May	Orlando scheduled service starts.
	July	Launch of Mid Class.
1993	July	Virgin Atlantic wins libel settlement of £610,000 plus costs from British Airways.
1994	February	Virgin begins operating a daily flight to Hong Kong.
	March	New scheduled flight from Gatwick to Athens introduced in collaboration with Hermes.
	May	Virgin launches new daily non-stop service to San Francisco.

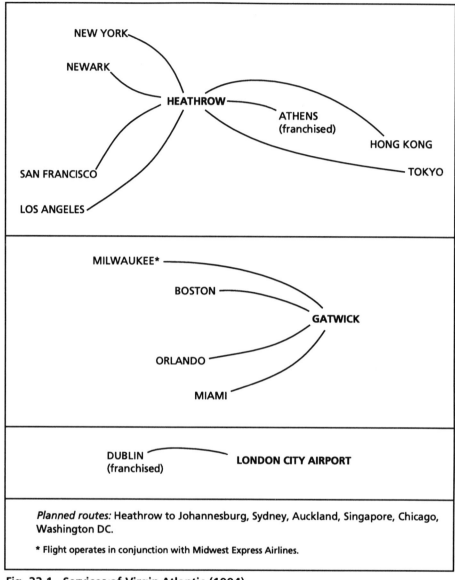

Fig. 22.1 Services of Virgin Atlantic (1994)

Table 22.2 Some of Virgin Atlantic's industry awards

Executive Travel Magazine
- Airline of the Year (1990/91–92/93)
- Best Transatlantic Carrier (1989/90/91–92/93/94)
- Best In-Flight Entertainment (1989/90/91–92/93)
- Best Business Class (1989/92/93/94)
- Best In-Flight Food (1992/93)
- Best Cabin Staff (1993)
- Best Airport Lounges (1993)
- Best In-Flight Magazine (1993/94)
- Best Ground/Check-in Staff (1992/93)

Travel Weekly
- Best Transatlantic Airline (1992)

Business Traveller Magazine
- Best Business Class Long Haul (1988/89/90/91/92)

Travel Trade Gazette
- Best Transatlantic Airline (1990/91/92/93)
- Most Attentive Staff (1991)

amount of freedom in choosing an airline, with most being unfettered by corporate travel policies. Virgin boasted an 'upper class' (rather than a first class) which won a large number of awards. Some of the 'best' categories of award won by Virgin are shown in Table 22.2. During 1993, Virgin introduced its own answer to pressure on business travel budgets – Mid Class, which offers a separate cabin for full-fare economy passengers, with bigger seats and better check-in facilities, and which straddles First and Business. The nature of the services offered in each class is listed in Appendix 22.2.

Virgin's two short-haul routes, from London to Maastricht and from London to Dublin, were abandoned a few years after being established. The withdrawal was not because of failure, but because Virgin decided as a matter of group policy that they had to either concentrate on short haul or long haul. In the end Virgin decided to become the alternative long-haul airline to British Airways . Apart from the short-haul business being quite marginal – with strong competition from other domestic airlines profits were never going to be great – it was also somewhat muddling from an image point of view. While flying 747 jets on the long-haul routes, Virgin were at the same time flying a propeller craft to Ireland or Holland. Virgin therefore decided to fly long haul and to have no short haul at all.

In March 1990, Virgin announced a 'frequent flier' bonus campaign, whereby free flights were offered on Virgin Atlantic to buyers of certain products and services who built up points depending on the size and frequency of the purchase. The save and collect scheme, called Virgin Freeway, was launched in response to British Airways' Air Miles initiative started 16 months previously.

In the summer of 1991, following the success of Virgin in winning the right to fly into Heathrow and add routes to the Tokyo service, Virgin applied for permission to fly from London to Johannesburg. The route was reportedly a very profitable one for BA and South African Airlines who shared it. Lord King, the chairman of BA, was reported as being vexed, and amused, by Branson's ability to convince the authorities that his company deserved the right to challenge BA in its heartland. 'Richard Branson is a pirate – and good luck to him' Lord King (*Evening Standard*, 12 July 1991). BA's supporters were reported as saying that Branson could fail by over-expanding and would need better quality computer systems to handle larger numbers of reservations. Branson countered by stating that Virgin would not expand its services beyond long-haul flights to 12 cities serviced by 20 Boeing 747s, that Virgin had perfectly good computers, and chose to put emphasis on quality of service, adding 'Anyone who counts the number of passengers on BA and calls it "the world's favourite airline" presumably rates the M25 Britain's favourite motorway' (*Evening Standard*, 12 July 1991).

In an interview in July 1991, Branson said that Virgin wanted to fly long haul to the 12 most exciting cities in the world: Los Angeles, Miami, Orlando, New York, Boston, Tokyo, San Francisco, Johannesburg, Singapore, Sydney, Washington and Chicago. Branson also emphasized that Virgin put service first, rather than computerized operations. 'Staff loyalty can only be guaranteed for an airline operation up to a certain size' (*Evening Standard*, 15 July 1991). Branson also outlined his opposition to mega-leaps and belief in organic growth. Indicating that he was glad he parted company with the City, Branson said that the attitudes of Japanese investors are more to his taste – 'They invest for the long haul and really care for the attitudes of employees.' From this position Branson claims to have taken a very Japanese approach to doing business: going for growth, quality and creating valuable assets.

And doing it if necessary at the expense of short-term profits. For example, in 1990 Virgin decided to take 50 seats out of every aircraft to give passengers much more leg-room than they get with any of the competitors. This decision was made although it was known it would cost the airline up to £12 million of short-term profits. It was done, however, because it was felt that in the long term, the airline would gain business by giving the best service. Branson has repeatedly emphasized that the luxury of being private is that long-term thinking overrules short-termism.

Although Virgin makes great play of having the second largest long-haul airline in the UK, there are only two long-haul airlines in the UK, and for all the publicity it attracts, by size, Virgin is tiny beside the giant BA. It has just sixteen aircraft to BA's 230, and flies 144 fewer routes than 'the world's favourite airline'. That makes it no less of a threat, however, to BA's profitability. Airline profits are made at the margin: the income from most of the seats that fill an aircraft goes towards covering the immense costs of running a network, but it is the last few seats sold that produce all the profit. Also a few popular routes, such as London to New York, subsidize many others. Hence Virgin's tactic of plying the most profitable routes between big cities costs BA a lot of money. Analysts calculate that if Virgin were to go out of business, and its customers split between remaining airlines on the basis of market share, BA would make £150m extra profit. As Virgin expands, it also faces the challenge of setting up more of its own service operations, adding to its fixed cost base, making it even more important to fill its planes with revenue-earning passengers. Virgin therefore remains highly exposed.

The big question is whether Branson can transform Virgin from a transatlantic niche airline into a global player, albeit with only 16 or so aircraft. In a way Branson has had it easy so far. The airline business has changed beyond recognition since 1984 and is likely to go on changing. Deregulation in America and Britain has hit hard – increased competition means there are now too many carriers chasing too few passengers. Airline analysts believe power could polarize into the hands of seven or eight 'mega-carriers'. The changes affected Britain with the arrival of American and United, the world's biggest airlines, at Heathrow, driving down transatlantic fares to an all-time low. Return tickets between London and New York could be picked up for less than in Freddie Laker's day. For a small airline like Virgin, it is likely to be a very tough fight. While the bigger airlines give a niche player like Virgin Atlantic more scope and are perhaps more clumsy, they are also powerful and have deep pockets.

The cost of acquiring aircraft is hefty. It would cost about $1m a month to buy a new plane at the top end of Boeing's range. With a depressed market Virgin could pick up a second-hand aircraft, but this would still cost about $500,000 a month even before it got into the air. Virgin's cost levels are extremely competitive and estimates indicate that they are below BA's across the Atlantic, with BA's being below American and United. Virgin's low costs make the airline a sharp competitor. Virgin's wages are relatively low but nevertheless the airline is inundated by people wanting to work for it. Branson flies with the airline at least once a month, working with the cabin crew, and believes in making the work fun, in the belief that high staff morale produces good service. This is confirmed in independent surveys of service quality which give Virgin top ratings.

Apart from a competitive cost structure Virgin's principal strength – and a major reason why he should not be compared with Laker – is that he has built up a loyal following among business flyers for Virgin's 'Upper Class' service. Virgin prides itself on providing a first-class service for a business-class fare. That makes it a bigger threat than its size would suggest.

In April 1989 Virgin obtained a licence to fly the London–Tokyo route. For 40 years this route had been operated only by Japan Air Lines (JAL) and BA, interrupted briefly by British Caledonian, which served the route for a year before its demise. BA, which opposed the Virgin application, was as nervous as JAL about Branson getting the Tokyo route – the 6,218 flight miles between the two capitals are amongst the most profitable in the world. Branson said 'It's not right that JAL and BA have been able to fix prices against the interests of the public' (*Daily Telegraph*, 10 April 1989). Branson appointed Akira Nakamura, formerly with Japan Air Lines, to head the Tokyo operation. On the inaugural flight from Gatwick to Tokyo Branson commented on his publicity stunts: 'I am competing with the likes of TWA, PanAm and BA. They can afford to spend millions on advertising. I compete by getting my product across to the public via as much publicity as possible.' According to Branson 'British Airways forcefully opposed Virgin's application to fly to Tokyo for a full 10 months. We were forced to delay our original plans as a result and to go through all the preliminary procedures for an opposed public hearing at the CAA. British Airways only withdrew their objection at the last minute and in the face of almost certain defeat at the public hearing' (*The Observer*, 4 June 1989).

In January 1991 the Civil Aviation Authority stripped BA of four of its take-off and landing rights at Tokyo's Narita airport and handed them to Virgin Atlantic. The CAA said it had decided to award Virgin Atlantic extra services to the airport at the expense of BA to safeguard competition and consumer choice. The decision meant that BA was allowed only 26 flights a week in and out of Tokyo against the 30 it previously held. The four extra flights given to Virgin Atlantic enabled it to increase its Gatwick–Narita round trips from four to six a week.

In April 1993, Virgin Atlantic launched its first European route with a daily scheduled service from Gatwick to Athens. This undercut the BA–Olympus duopoly out of Heathrow with lower economy and business fares. This was just the first of many new ventures the airline was planning, with Virgin being poised to double its fleet and its routes over the following two to three years. Virgin's aim was to fly all the main 12 long-haul business routes from London including San Francisco, Singapore, Johannesburg, Sydney, Washington, Chicago and Hong Kong. While it already had licences for those routes, it did not have the slots out of Heathrow. While Virgin did not believe Stanstead and Gatwick airports were options for long-haul routes, it was happy to use Gatwick for its new European network, which it regarded as a separate development from Virgin Atlantic, to be managed in joint partnership with local European partners. Virgin launched the Athens route with the private Greek airline South East European Airlines, applied for more Gatwick slots and held discussions with potential French partners about the chances of invading that two-airline market. Branson believes in different brands, and the colour scheme of Virgin Europe was to be different from Virgin Atlantic's.

In October 1993, Branson announced that he had completed a private deal to buy out Virgin Atlantic's only outside shareholder as part of a plan to expand the company. Branson's decision to spend about £45m to buy back the 10 per cent shareholding held by the Japanese group Seibu Saison gave him total control. Branson decided to buy them out after the group sought to exercise its option to increase its stake to 20 per cent. The buy-out was the first significant deal Branson had financed from the £560m he received for the sale of Virgin's music arm to Thorn-EMI in 1992. Branson indicated that the remainder of a £115m expansion package would be used to recruit 500 new staff and equip six aircraft for the airline's new long-distance routes, beginning in early 1994 with Hong Kong and San Francisco.

In January 1994 Virgin began to operate a new jet passenger service to Dublin from London's City airport. Virgin teamed up with Cityjet, a new company based in Dublin, to offer flights using the Virgin name and livery under a franchise agreement. The London-to-Dublin route, which attracts 2.5m passengers a year, is the busiest European route after London-to-Paris, which has 3.1m passengers. Branson said that if the service was successful he would consider offering flights to other European cities, such as Paris and Brussels.

In April 1994, Virgin raised the stakes in the battle for transatlantic passengers by announcing a link-up with the third largest US carrier, Delta Air Lines. The deal, which gave Virgin access to 200 US cities and gave Delta an entry to London's Heathrow Airport, stepped up the pressure on BA, the largest transatlantic carrier. The Virgin–Delta deal could lead to a long-term shareholding alliance between the two companies. The main terms of the deal involve 'code sharing' (through-ticketing) arrangements between the two airlines on some Virgin flights from eight US airports and London, and the purchase of 'blocked space' by Delta on those flights. (BA already had its own code-sharing arrangement with American carrier USAir.) It was anticipated that Virgin would benefit by around £100m per year from the blocked space arrangements. In return Virgin would be able to sell tickets at cheap rates to passengers wishing to travel on Delta within the US from flights originating in London, and would share Delta terminals and other ground facilities. Branson said the deal would enable Virgin to remain independent and competitive in the face of an increasing number of global alliances in the airline industry. The deal provided Delta with access to Heathrow airport for the first time and teamed Virgin with a major US carrier, which already had partnerships with two other niche players, Swissair and Singapore Airlines. Industry analysts said the deal was good for Virgin. 'It gets greater access to the US, while Delta pays for access to Heathrow. BA should be worried because Virgin has not made the mistakes that so many small British airlines have made,' one commented. The shares of the UK/US air market are shown in Table 22.3.

During the recession at the beginning of the 1990s, Branson took advantage of the depressed state of the market to buy new Airbus A340s (a 282-seat long-range four-engine jet) and Boeing 747-400s at lower prices than airlines were paying towards the end of the 1980s. Both types will have every seat equipped with Virgin's interactive 14-channel in-flight entertainment system. The two plane types enhance Virgin's flexibility. The airline's basic strategy is to fly on those routes out of London where the traffic would support an extra daily 747 service. However, this would confine Virgin's future growth to 15 or 16 routes. The smaller A340 opens up a much wider world and is useful, for instance, in developing a new route such as that to Hong Kong. Branson has identified China and Hong Kong as high growth points over the next 20 years and is keen for Virgin to have a presence there. He has indicated

Table 22.3 Share of the UK/US air market

UK/US air market	% share
British Airways	42
American	15
Virgin	14
United	10
Delta	6
Northwest	5
Continental	5
Others	3

Source: Industry estimates (*The Guardian*, 13 April 1994).

that he wants Virgin to fly to Shanghai as soon as possible and is hoping for airport slots in Malaysia and Thailand by 1996. Branson has admitted that expansion on this scale is a challenge to his determination to stop Virgin becoming too big. So in a bid to maintain the 'small and friendly' style, Branson says Virgin's 2,000 plus cabin staff are to be divided into 15 teams of 150, with each team flying regularly with each other. Furthermore, if the plans for Far Eastern expansion are fulfilled Branson is prepared to hive off another airline, Virgin Pacific, from Virgin Atlantic and manage it separately. This fear of organizational obesity has largely kept Branson clear of labour-intensive short-haul flying in Europe, but franchising routes, as with the Athens and Dublin services, may be the way to opening more of them than the creation of Virgin Europe. However, cracking the BA–Cathay Pacific duopoly that dominates London to Hong Kong is the current prime target. The fact that the opposition is so well entrenched, and perhaps rather complacent, encourages Branson. 'You have had identical fares throughout for a number of years. The competition will be good for the consumer,' he says (*The Sunday Times*, 6 February 1994).

DIRTY TRICKS

In January 1991, Branson accused BA of behaving uncompetitively by trying to damage his airline's long-distance services from London Gatwick. Virgin filed a formal complaint against BA with the European Commission, and indicated that it was considering launching an anti-trust claim in the USA against BA. Branson accused BA of operating 'a predatory pricing policy' on transatlantic routes from Gatwick, and claimed that BA was breaching article 86 of the Treaty of Rome by loading thousands of tickets for Gatwick flights into bucket shops at loss-making prices. Citing this as an example of BA's deliberate predatory action Branson argued that Virgin was not scared of competition but that it must be fair. BA rejected Branson's allegations, arguing that it was operating in a deregulated market. A spokesperson for BA said, 'Our fares policy is designed for the comfort of consumers and not competitors', adding: 'We do not adopt predatory pricing. We have special offers at certain times. Branson's allegations are, as usual, over the top to attract publicity. If he chooses to take legal action we shall defend ourselves vigorously. Mr Branson would do better to run his own business efficiently rather than attack the competition.'

Also in January 1991, Branson started libel proceedings against BA over allegations about Virgin's 'reliability record'. The remarks were made in an official BA press statement responding to the moves by Branson making a formal complaint of unfair competition to the European Commission. A Virgin spokesperson said they would be surprised if the statement had been issued without prior consultation with Lord King, BA's 73-year-old chairman.

The issue that really set Virgin Atlantic and BA against each other was about who should fly from Heathrow, the businessman's airport, the international hub, and the money spinner for airlines. On 22 January 1991, the Civil Aviation Authority did what BA had long dreaded, and Virgin Atlantic saw as the first step towards an era of true competition and the end of monopoly, advising the Transport Secretary to change traffic distribution rights at Heathrow. The theory ran that by allowing Virgin Atlantic to run its services to the US from there, dominant BA would be subjected to genuine competition, bringing higher quality, competitive fares and a better deal for consumers. The CAA's move, which came less than a fortnight after it had stripped BA of four weekly slots for landing and take-off at Tokyo, emphasized that, in the CAA's view, slots belonged to Britain, not any one British airline. While the news delighted Virgin, BA which controlled 39 per cent of slots at Heathrow and saw the extent of its historic dominance threatened, was outraged. Flying from Heathrow, with the advantages over Gatwick of being nearer central London and of longer runways allowing heavier loads, would mean a 15 per cent increase in yield for Virgin, which Branson promised to pass on in cheaper fares.

BA argued that to change the regulatory framework and allow Virgin to muscle in on its routes would be to change the rules under which BA was privatized and, therefore, the understanding on which shareholders invested. Only by protecting BA's rights could it compete with giant counterparts in the US and across the world. Lord King also stressed that the likes of Virgin were not competitors but poor substitutes.

In the event Heathrow was opened to all airlines from July 1991 and Virgin was given 40 slots. On the morning of by 1 July 1991, Branson dressed as a pirate was photographed at the entrance to Heathrow airport beside a huge model of Concorde – the symbol that tells everyone arriving at Heathrow that the busiest airport in the world is the home of BA – after having had the tail-fin of the aircraft covered with the Virgin logo, together with hastily erected signboards proclaiming Heathrow as 'Virgin Territory' and obscuring BA's logo. While designed to annoy BA executives the stunt also generated a great deal of publicity for Virgin. Branson said, 'Today is the second most exciting day in the history of Virgin. The first was when we launched the airline in 1984' (*Financial Times*, 2 July 1991).

The arrival of Virgin and other international carriers at Heathrow intensified competition for BA at its home base. BA operated about 150 weekly flights from the UK to the US with the North Atlantic accounting for around one third of BA's revenues. The UK government's decision to abolish the regulations limiting the number of carriers at Heathrow enabled several airlines, previously forced to fly out of Gatwick, to switch some of their services to Heathrow. The negotiation of a bilateral aviation agreement between the UK and the US in 1991 also cleared the way for American Airlines and United Airlines, two of the strongest US carriers, to replace TWA and Pan American, two of the weakest, at Heathrow. The opening of Heathrow clearly angered Lord King. In an interview in *The Observer*, he accused the Conservative government of betraying its principles and the thousands of investors whom Margaret Thatcher had encouraged to buy BA shares at the time of privatization. He claimed that '£250m of the revenue lost to our public shareholders will go straight into Richard Branson's private pocket.' In his diary Branson noted that BA appeared to have something in common with the Soviet Union: 'Both seem to be having problems adjusting to a free market economy.'[3]

In November 1991, Virgin Atlantic announced it was preparing a list of complaints alleging anti-competitive behaviour by BA, which Branson intended sending to the European Commission, the Civil Aviation Authority and the Department of Transport. Branson accused BA of a 'dirty tricks campaign', orchestrated to discredit Virgin's public standing. The claims were denied by BA, which insisted that it was too busy coping with the giant US airlines and that Branson, who had only a handful of routes, was little more than a mere irritation.

Documents setting out the complaints and lodged with the European Commission were the culmination of seven years' sniping between BA and Virgin, during which time Virgin repeatedly claimed that BA was undermining its position. In its dossier to the EC, Virgin claimed that BA was abusing its position as a majority carrier, potentially undermining the EC's objective of building up airline competition. Virgin claimed that BA had been trying to squeeze it out of the market 'through predatory pricing together with its other exclusionary and abusive conduct'. BA was alleged to have taken a series of steps in the provision of air transport and maintenance services aimed at strengthening its dominant position. According to the documents BA established a special committee early in 1990 as it became clear Virgin was becoming a commercial threat. In the autumn of the same year, the committee, it was claimed, was operating in such secrecy that 'instructions were issued within BA for documentation relating to the committee to be destroyed.' Virgin also claimed BA flouted aviation industry conventions by 'acting in an abusive and exclusionary manner', denying it full access to maintenance facilities, which was 'a further breach of a dominant position in breach of article 86 of the Treaty of Rome'. Prior to BA's merger with British Caledonian in early 1988, BCal helped maintain Virgin aircraft. According to Virgin immediately following the BA/BCal merger, BA reviewed its combined maintenance services and introduced various new policies including higher levels of charges that Virgin now had to pay. The Virgin document claimed that 'the terms of BA's proposals for maintenance to Virgin were tantamount to a refusal to continue to supply such services in view of the unjustified increase in BA's proposed charges for the provision of more limited maintenance services than those previously supplied by BCal.' Virgin considered BA's effective refusal to supply was an abuse of BA's dominant position on the market. The Virgin document also added that fare levels set by BA 'appears to be selectively aimed at Virgin, which would constitute an unfair commercial practice by a dominant undertaking intended to eliminate or at least discipline Virgin, which is a much smaller competitor. Such action is prohibited by article 86 as an abuse of a dominant market position.' BA denied any unfair campaign against its rivals.

In December 1991, in an appeal over the head of BA chairman Lord King, Branson wrote directly to the group's non-executive directors demanding an investigation into the allegations that BA had set up an internal task force specifically to 'discredit

---

3. From *Dirty Tricks* by Martyn Gregory, published by Little, Brown & Co., 1994.

Virgin Atlantic and damage its business'. Branson was reported as saying that he compared the BA campaign with the one which allegedly contributed to the collapse of Sir Freddie Laker's airline business some ten years previously. Adding that 'BA would like there to be only one long-haul carrier in this country' (*Evening Standard*, 12 December 1991). Branson said that he had written to the non-executive directors because previous contacts had convinced him that writing to Lord King would not have achieved anything. Branson's letter to the non-executive directors stated: 'It is as if these decisions by regulators, to enable Virgin to expand, have engendered such fear and anger, that normal and acceptable standards of commercial behaviour have been abandoned by BA.' In an appendix to the letter Branson highlighted the way BA allegedly manipulated the press to damage Virgin's image. Branson claimed that Brian Basham, a well-known City public relations man, 'has been given a brief to try to discredit both the Virgin group of companies and myself'. According to the Virgin allegations, Basham had been telephoning journalists and 'seeking to circulate misleading, false and damaging information'. It transpired that the strategy of the press campaign against Branson was to paint Virgin as a dangerously over-stretched airline, headed by an irrational eccentric who indulged in a range of physically and morally dangerous pursuits. This combination of defects could cause investors to lose confidence in Branson. By discrediting him in this way, they would prevent him from expanding his airline and taking more of BA's profits.[4]

Branson also claimed that he had been told by two separate sources that BA had employed private investigators to tail him and that the cars of Virgin Atlantic's managing director and chief press officer had been broken into five times. Branson called on BA to confirm that it was not behind such conduct. Sir Michael Angus, chairman of Unilever and non-executive deputy chairman of BA, replied that it would be 'wholly inappropriate' for the non-executive directors to respond to the allegations and that they should be directed to the company itself.

In January 1993, Branson successfully sued BA for libel over an alleged smear campaign. Virgin argued that Lord King had accused Branson of fabricating details of a dirty tricks war waged against Virgin by BA in an attempt to gain publicity. Virgin's victory in the High Court marked an embarrassing climb down for Lord King. Legal documents showed that BA obtained confidential computer information about Virgin passengers and flights and mounted a massive counter-espionage operation because they feared Branson was spying on them. Branson also claimed that BA poached passengers, sometimes as they queued to buy Virgin Atlantic tickets at New York's JFK airport.

BA was forced to make a humbling, unqualified apology to Virgin as part of a High Court settlement that included the payment of £610,000 in damages (£500,000 to Branson and £110,000 to the airline – subsequently Branson used the £500,000 to pay staff a bonus for their support, the 2,800 employees receiving about £178.50 each), and about £3m in costs. BA admitted and apologized for libel against Richard Branson, and described some of the 'dirty tricks' perpetuated by its employees against Virgin as 'regrettable'. 'Both British Airways and Lord King apologized unreservedly for the injury caused to the reputation and feelings of Richard Branson and Virgin Atlantic by the articles and letters which they published,' the BA statement said in part.

---

4. From Gregory, *Dirty Tricks*.

There appeared to be extraordinary corporate paranoia at the top of BA. Press investigations revealed that:

- BA obtained confidential computer information about Virgin passengers and flights. In autumn 1990, during the lean months for the air travel industry of the Gulf Crisis and the start of the recession, a team of BA computer operators was told to access information on Virgin's passengers and flights. The commercially confidential information, obtained via the BA booking system (BABS), allowed BA to monitor the number of passengers on each Virgin flight, their class of seat and details of lucrative corporate accounts. BA staff were able to acquire detailed information on which of Virgin's transatlantic routes were profitable, how many passengers they were carrying and what class they flew in. Disguised by the name Helpline, the Gatwick operation was shrouded in secrecy. Special combination locks were fitted to the Helpline office. Information on Virgin was logged at the end of each shift and sent in sealed envelopes to a BA manager. Soon after the secret operation was set up, Virgin passengers were cold-called at home. They were offered free supplementary tickets, flights on Concorde and even triple air miles to switch to BA flights. BA staff were instructed to impersonate Virgin employees to obtain more detailed data on their rivals' flights. Some solicited Virgin passengers in Gatwick's south terminal where BA does not operate persuading them to switch to BA flights. A similar team, nicknamed The Hunters, operated from BA's offices at Heathrow.
- Lord King and Sir Colin Marshall BA's chief executive, sanctioned an aggressive counter-espionage operation because they feared Branson was spying on them.
- BA paid security advisors more than £200,000 for the counter-espionage campaign, code named Covent Garden.
- At the operational level the counter-espionage campaign involved the theft of documents and snooping on journalists and BA's own senior staff.
- Brian Basham, a top City public affairs consultant, was hired by BA to run a negative press campaign against Branson, code named 'Operation Barbara'. Basham briefed journalists, wrongly, that Virgin's problems were so acute that the smaller airline had been refused credit by Shell Petroleum to buy its aviation fuel. Documents were also leaked to journalists that described Branson as 'irrational and experimental' in business and made disparaging links with his ownership of a London gay club. When Basham's PR campaign was disclosed to be false in the press in November 1991, BA became convinced it was the victim of a hostile media campaign orchestrated by Branson. In late 1991, BA asked a firm of security consultants to assemble a private team to find out who was manipulating the media and whether there was a 'mole' among its staff. During the following months, tens of thousands of pounds of BA money was spent searching personnel files of airline staff, following suspects, searching for phone taps and bugs, and spying on other investigation agencies. Despite the huge sums BA was paying for the operation, it yielded nothing. No BA mole was ever unearthed.

After the High Court apology Branson said that unless action was taken by BA to compensate Virgin for the 'incalculable damage' that had been done to Virgin Atlantic, he would instigate anti-trust proceedings and investigations against senior BA executives in the USA. Such action would mean that his £3.6m libel win over BA would be only the beginning. Only BA's sacrifice of lucrative take-off slots to prime international destinations such as San Francisco, Johannesburg and Tokyo would prevent a renewed legal attack. BA had offered to pay Virgin £9m in compensation on the understanding that neither side referred to the dirty tricks saga in the future, Branson rejected this, claiming that it amounted to a gagging order on him and his airline.

At the beginning of March 1993, Virgin Atlantic Airways launched High Court proceedings against BA following the failure of the two airlines to settle their long-running 'dirty tricks' dispute. Branson declared that the airlines were now 'at war'. Virgin's writ against BA alleged copyright infringement, breach of confidence and misuse of confidential information. The High Court action related to Virgin's allegations that BA accessed Virgin passenger details and information as well as data concerning aircraft and load factors relating to flights and associated passenger travel services. Virgin said the proceedings were only the first of several other legal and regulatory steps it proposed taking against BA in various jurisdictions including the US and the European Community.

In April 1993, the battle between BA and Virgin Atlantic flared up again with Branson challenging the highest level of BA management to resign after renewed allegations in a television documentary that top BA directors were aware of their airline's 'dirty tricks' campaign against Virgin. 'They should either test the programme in court or they should consider their position,' Branson said (*Financial Times*, 28 April 1993).

In October 1993, Virgin announced its decision to file an anti-trust action in the US courts against BA, alleging that the rival airline was distorting competition on transatlantic flights by abusing its position at Heathrow airport. Virgin Atlantic was seeking compensation of up to $975m through the US lawsuit. The case was likely to take at least three and a half years to get to court. The law suit alleges that BA had abused and continued to abuse the monopoly power which it acquired while still in state ownership.

Two other actions were launched during 1993. One, relating to breach of copyright and misuse of Virgin's computer-held passenger lists, was expected to go to the High Court in May 1995. The second complaint, to the European Union, centres on the financial incentives and discounts offered by BA to travel agents and large companies. It is being examined by competition authorities in Brussels.

Lord King suffered a bitter blow to his reputation in the twilight of an exceptional career. He was set to retire in June 1993, but did so shortly after the libel settlement of February 1993, moving to the honorary post of president of BA. This produced a succession of other changes, with Sir Colin Marshall succeeding King as chairman of BA, and Robert Ayling becoming managing director. King's resignation marked an inglorious end to one of the most remarkable corporate success stories of the 1980s. Lord King had transformed BA from a loss-making nationalized flag carrier into the world's most profitable airline, employing 50,000 people across the globe. King later admitted that Branson's appearance had blinded him to the threat. He confided to a friend: 'If Richard Branson had worn a pair of steel-rimmed glasses, a double-breasted suit and shaved off his beard, I would have taken him seriously. As it was, I couldn't.'

APPENDIX 22.1
VIRGIN ATLANTIC AIRWAYS LTD – FINANCIAL INFORMATION

Tables 22.4 and 22.5 provide details of the main accounts of Virgin Atlantic Airways for the period 1985 to 1992.

Table 22.4 Profit and loss accounts 1985–92 (£000)

	Year to 31 Jan. 1985	18 months to 31 Jul. 1986	Year to 31 Jul. 1987	Year to 31 Jul. 1988	Year to 31 Jul. 1989	Year to 31 Jul. 1990	15 months to 31 Oct. 1991	Year to 31 Oct. 1992
Turnover	19,321	51,021	59,999	75,387	92,293	180,544	336,678	303,480
Cost of sales	16,647	36,227	39,127	49,272	64,864	137,570	281,047	264,282
Gross profit	2,673	14,794	20,872	26,115	27,429	42,974	55,631	39,198
Administrative expenses	2,099	13,180	12,749	14,075	18,896	33,356	56,969	55,811
Other operating (cost)/ income	—	—	40	—	—	—	6,417	(177)
Interest receivable	37	176	561	123	1,490	1,305	1,258	838
Interest payable	1,150	3,082	3,757	2,025	2,833	3,584	5,603	5,087
Profit/(loss) on ordinary activities before tax	(539)	(1,292)	4,967	10,138	7,190	7,339	734	(21,039)
Tax on profit/(loss) on ordinary activities	(329)	517	(1,774)	1,868	136	(1,515)	873	2,611
Extraordinary charge	1,287	—	—	—	—	—	—	—
Profit attributable to shareholders	—	—	3,193	12,006	7,326	5,824	—	—
Dividends	—	—	—	2,000	5,000	—	—	—
Retained profit/(loss) for the financial period	(1,497)	(775)	3,193	12,006	2,326	5,824	1,607	(18,428)

Table 22.5 Balance sheets 1985–92 (£000)

	31 Jul. 1985	31 Jul. 1986	31 Jul. 1987	31 Jul. 1988	31 Jul. 1989	31 Jul. 1990	31 Oct. 1991	31 Oct. 1992
Fixed assets								
Intangible assets	—	—	—	—	3,050	6,502	9,246	8,390
Tangible assets	24,760	44,460	49,019	46,276	56,568	74,696	70,545	74,170
Current assets								
Stocks	3	21	30	38	360	3,337	4,850	5,050
Debtors	5,381	8,794	12,978	15,857	30,791	41,014	67,902	74,711
Assets held for resale	—	1,025	1,000	540	—	—	—	—
Cash	797	1,497	2,972	7,307	17,846	16,843	36,630	33,770
	6,181	11,338	16,980	23,742	48,997	66,194	109,382	113,531
Creditors: amounts falling due within one year	14,544	16,822	18,278	23,626	40,724	60,636	97,199	125,350
Net current assets/(liabilities)	(8,362)	(5,484)	1,298	116	8,273	5,558	12,183	(11,819)
Total assets less current liabilities	16,397	38,976	47,721	46,392	67,891	86,756	91,974	70,741
Creditors: amounts falling due after one year	18,092	38,069	36,513	27,805	39,064	51,481	53,134	51,314
Provisions for liabilities and charges	464	3,254	5,225	2,598	5,512	6,136	7,569	6,584
Capital and resources								
Called-up share capital	100	100	100	100	110	110	110	110
Share premium account	—	—	—	—	4,990	4,990	4,990	4,990
Revaluation reserve	(588)	—	5,137	5,137	5,137	5,137	4,537	3,834
Profit and loss account	(1,671)	(2,447)	746	10,752	13,078	18,902	21,634	3,909
	(2,159)	(2,347)	5,983	15,989	23,315	29,139	31,271	12,843

APPENDIX 22.2
CLASS OF SERVICE OFFERED

Tables 22.6 to 22.8 provide details of the classes of service offered by Virgin Atlantic.

Table 22.6 Upper Class

The unique range of services offered in Virgin's Upper Class sets it apart from any other business class in the air. They are normally only found in the first-class cabins of other carriers.

When you book
- Advance seat selection

Getting to the airport
- Complimentary chauffeur-driven car to and from anywhere in the Home Counties.
- For Garwick departures free First Class Gatwick Express Tickets.
- Free car parking to the value of £28.00 at Gatwick or £36.00 at Heathrow.
- Or Taxijet bike – fast transfer option to and from Heathrow and Gatwick.

At the airport
- Separate Upper Class check-in.
- First Class baggage allowance.
- Upper Class lounge facilities with Business Centres to use on departure and arrival including The Virgin Clubhouse and the Arrivals Clubhouse at Heathrow.
- Priority boarding, baggage handling and disembarkation.

On board
- First Class sleeper seat with 55" legroom, giving 80% more legroom than most other business classes.
- Cabin crew to Passenger ratio 1–7.
- On-board lounge and bar (on most aircraft).
- Complimentary award winning entertainment. With 32 channel Arcadia system featuring movies, sports, news and games, as well as CD audio sound on personal armrest. TV screens at each seat being introduced on all routes.
- Choice of gourmet entrees including Raymond Blanc speciality.
- Complimentary beverage service.
- Beauty Therapist on selected flights.
- Complimentary Upper Class amenity kit.
- Snoozzone service giving duvet, pillow, snoozesuit and eyeshades on all night flights.

Complimentary transfer options in the US & Tokyo
- Complimentary chauffeur-driven limousine service to selected Counties within each US gateway State.
- Free Avis car hire for four days (round trip passengers) or two days (one way passengers).
- Boston via the airport water shuttle to Rowes Wharf.
- Limousine Bus to Tokyo City Centre or Haneda Airport.
- Free porter service to and from Narita and any city in Japan.
- First Class rail travel on the Narita Express to Tokyo City Centre.

Added value benefits
- Complimentary membership of Virgin Freeway, Virgin Atlantic's frequent flyer programme.
- Earn 40,000 miles for your first Upper Class transatlantic round trip as a Virgin Freeway member (60,000 miles for Tokyo and Hong Kong).
- For each subsequent Upper Class flight made you will earn twice the miles you fly, allowing you to earn a standby economy class ticket every time you fly!

Source: Virgin Atlantic Airways.

Table 22.7 Mid Class

The best Economy Class seat in the world

When you book
- Advance seat selection.

At the airport
- Separate Mid Class check-in.
- Express baggage reclaim.

Added value benefit
- Complimentary membership of Virgin Freeway, Virgin Atlantic's frequent flyer programme which enables clients to earn unique awards.

On board
- Separate Mid Class cabin.
- Most comfortable economy class seats in the world with up to 38" of legroom.
- Award winning 14 channel video entertainment including 8 movie channels, 10 Super Nintendo games, 16 CD audio channels on personal In-seat TV's being introduced on all routes (currently 6 channels available). A small charge for some channels will apply.

- Pre take off drinks.
- Complimentary drinks served throughout the flight.
- Priority meal service.
- Choice of meals.
- Priority selection from a wide range of duty free items.
- Complimentary amenity kit.
- Selection of newspapers.

Source: Virgin Atlantic Airways.

Table 22.8 Economy Class

Economy – Good value – Great fun

When you book
- Advanced seat selection.

On board
- Award winning 14 channel video entertainment including 8 movie channels, 10 Super Nintendo games, 16 CD audio channels on personal in-seat TVs being introduced on all routes (currently 6 channels available) a small charge for some channels will apply.
- Comfortable seats.
- Complimentary drinks served throughout the flight.
- Choice of meals.
- Free fun pack for children.
- Children's meal.
- Complimentary amenity kit.
- Complimentary *Hot Air,* our very own inflight magazine.

For groups of over ten adults
- Group check-in at Gatwick only.
- Off-airport check-in.*
- Printed headrest covers in Economy, Mid and Upper Class.*
- Welcome on board message.
- Advances seat assignment.
- Upper Class amenity packs to Economy passengers.*
- Use of Heathrow lounge.*

* A minimum charge will apply.
Source: Virgin Atlantic Airways.

NFC Plc

C.M. Clarke-Hill

INTRODUCTION

All long-distance road haulage companies were nationalized by the post-war Labour government. The Conservative government of 1953–56 partially denationalized the transport sector. The Transport Act of 1968 formed all the remaining state-owned road transport businesses into one corporation – The National Freight Corporation. To this was added the road haulage interests of British Railways, which became National Carriers.

The Conservative government of 1979 began a policy of privatization of state-owned corporations. It was the intention of the government to float the National Freight Corporation on the London stock exchange. The assets of the corporation were held by 40 subsidiary limited companies and this was rationalized into one newly created entity called the National Freight Company Ltd. The government, following advice from its merchant bank advisors, postponed the launch of the company on the stock exchange.

After some restructuring of the business that included 5,000 redundancies in 1980–81, the management considered that the business probably would not be floated but would be sold to another group. It was at this point that Peter Thompson, the then head of the business, along with a number of senior managers, considered and later effected an employee buy-out.

In 1982 the National Freight Company was purchased from the government for £53m by 10,300 NFC employees, their families and NFC pensioners, who held some 83 per cent of the share capital of the business – the remaining equity was held by a syndicate of banks who lent the consortium the money to facilitate the buy-out of the company. The name of the company was changed to the National Freight Consortium (NFC), to reflect the new nature of its shareholding.[1] The successful employee buy-out was followed in 1989 with the public flotation of the firm on the London stock exchange and the company became incorporated as NFC Plc.

During the seven years between the employee buy-out and the public flotation, employees, their families, pensioners and former employees owned around 80 per cent of the equity, but this percentage was to be considerably diluted as a result of flotation to the 55 per cent it stood at in 1992. Employee shareholder rights were protected by the granting of a double voting right, a right which was retained after flotation. This double voting right would disappear once the employee shareholding

1. An excellent account of the buy-out is given by Sir Peter Thompson in *Long Range Planning*, Vol. 18, October 1985, pp. 19–27.

Table 23.1 NFC plc: Trading record 1989–93[1]

	1989 £m	1990 £m	1991 £m	1992 £m	1993 £m
Turnover	1,493.8	1,626.9	1,663.7	1,723.8	1,901.6
Operating profit	94.1	82.3	87.8	97.1	116.7
Interest	8.3	5.9	5.0	8.4	18.1
Profit sharing	15.9	5.1	3.4	3.3	3.5
Pre-tax profit[2]	78.4	81.9	64.6	89.9	104.9
Taxation	24.4	21.6	20.8	24.1	16.9
Net earnings	53.0	60.2	43.8	65.7	87.8
Tangible fixed assets	408.0	459.4	480.7	550.7	542.0
Shareholders' funds[3]	325.9	328.8	331.8	321.5	321.9
	pence	pence	pence	pence	pence
Earning per share (EPS)	10.0	11.0	8.0	11.9	15.9
EPS before exceptional items	8.8	9.6	11.0	10.7	13.1
Dividends per share	4.95	5.65	6.25	6.55	7.0
Average employees	31,763	33,761	33,861	33,850	32,955

1. Historical figures have been restated to comply with Financial Reporting Standard No 3. The EPS and DPS have been adjusted to reflect the capitalization issue in April 1990.
2. Pre-tax profits are profits after exceptional items.
3. Shareholders' funds taken before minority interests.

Source: Company Accounts 1993.

aggregate fell to 10 per cent or less. The firm had an active profit-sharing scheme to encourage more employee shareholding and to protect their rights to decide who should run the business in which both their livelihood and savings were invested. By 1993, the employee shareholding figure had further fallen to just under 14 per cent of the allotted share capital. (Employee shareholding at flotation stood at 31 per cent, and employee family holdings in 1994 stood at 45 per cent.)

On 11 January 1994, NFC had a market capitalization of £1.74 billion with its shares being traded on both the London and American stock exchanges. The company's sales stood at £1.9bn with pre-tax profits of £105m in 1993 making it the largest UK transport services company. Table 23.1 shows the five-year trading record of NFC.

Through a series of astute acquisitions and well managed organic growth, the company became a geographically and product diversified international logistics and moving services enterprise. NFC could be described as being a successful business that has grown out of a previously unsuccessful state-controlled parent. Appendix 23.1 shows the geographical and divisional segment analysis for NFC between 1990 and 1993, and Appendix 23.2 shows NFC's profit and loss account and balance sheet for the period 1992–93.

CULTURE AND STYLE

Success at NFC owed as much to the skilful strategic development of the business as it was based on what Sir Peter Thompson described as 'the hidden plus factor'. This 'hidden plus factor' was the culture of the company centred around employee ownership. Sir Peter Thompson, and his successor James Watson, both agreed that it was this factor that made a significant contribution to the competitive advantage of the company. It was unusual in the 1990s to find that around 45 per cent of the equity of a firm as large as NFC still remained in private hands. An employee who invested £1 in the buy-out in 1982 saw that stake worth £100 in 1990. The double voting rights for employee-shareholders (in 1993, 85 per cent of employees were shareholders), along with the high percentage of shares held by employees' families and NFC pensioners, effectively block any likely predatory bid. The worker shareholder and the attendant employee participation systems that operated at NFC in the UK have been replicated elsewhere as the firm expanded geographically, and helped build morale and make for a unified company.

Sir Peter's 1980s vision of a 'share-owning democracy' was translated into a real commitment to employees and obligations to shareholders. Sir Peter was of the belief that 'business is not about making profits, it is about how you share them and who does well out of them.' The employee-shareholder clearly had gained from the structure of the business. However, during the period 1990 to 1993, the money available for profit-sharing saw sharp falls from the previous years, while ordinary shareholders had seen their shares rise sharply over the same period. Sir Peter was 'embarrassed' by this state of affairs when he announced the 1990 figures before he was due to retire and welcome to his chair his deputy James Watson. NFC made Sir Peter president of the company, but in 1993 Sir Peter Thompson retired from this post.

Certain changes made by James Watson during the last two years have seen a partial break from the past – strategic withdrawal from key business areas, and the introduction of share option schemes and profit-sharing schemes for senior executives, a thing that Sir Peter was always opposed to.

As employee control of the equity of the company fell as a percentage of total shares in issue, NFC would gradually become a more conventionally controlled and run business. However, James Watson was still as firmly committed to the core values of the company as chairman as he was as deputy chairman, in particular to the core value of employee shareholding. James Watson believed that it was the percentage of employees who held shares that was more important than the percentage of shares that they held.

The culture at NFC was defined in the statement of the core values of the company – employee ownership, quality, internationalism, people development, social responsibility and premium performance. Appendix 23.3 sets out these core values in detail as they applied in 1991. The same core values were articulated somewhat differently and more concisely in the directors' report in 1992, as follows:

> *Quality* is inherent in the way we run the business and in the service we provide to our customers. *Internationalism* is the essence of our ambition to become one of the world's foremost international businesses. *Employee Ownership* gives us a competitive edge and benefits the company, its employees and its shareholders. *People Development* means we have a commitment to invest in our employees to enable them to realize their full potential. *Social Responsibilities* reflect our resolve to contribute to the communities and the environments in which we operate. *Premium Performance* only comes from living and working by our core values which aim to deliver the best results for all our shareholders.

Although NFC had a clearly stated policy of maintaining the employee-shareholder interest and participative decision-making, the role of the management to manage the business was never compromised. Decisions on investment, divestment and restructuring still remained firmly in the management's domain. In James Watson's words:

> If a business does not fit strategically and the board and management do not want to put money into it and develop it then I do not think that is a decision that employees can make.

Key restructuring in 1991 at NFC saw the retirement of around 10 per cent or 1,706 of its commercial vehicle fleet and a 4.8 per cent reduction in staff through redundancy at a cost to the business of £9.3 m. NFC argued that change and restructuring was achieved smoothly as a direct result of its employee policy and the commitment NFC had to training and its wider human resource management policies. The creation of an internal employment exchange allowed staff to be redeployed within NFC reducing the numbers of staff that had to be released. In James Watson's words:

> You can carry people with you if you communicate and explain. We don't link shareholding with redundancy. Most people go quietly if it's done reasonably and they are kept informed. We try to deal with people decently – to explain and go through things as much as possible.

Social responsibility as a core value at NFC had always been taken seriously. The company diverted one per cent of its pre-tax profits to a charitable foundation – the NFC Foundation, that was set up by the employee-shareholders in 1988. The NFC Foundation had an income of some £1.3m in 1992 from dividends received from shares that it holds in NFC Plc and from the one per cent pre-tax earnings that the company donated to it specifically for charitable donations.

The role of the NFC Foundation was to enable NFC Plc to participate in the communities that it operated in as a good corporate citizen. The Foundation helped charitable causes, provided financial assistance and relief to NFC pensioners through its benevolent fund and helped fund and sponsor charitable events and institutions in the community. Furthermore, the NFC Foundation was also involved in youth and community projects in the UK and elsewhere as NFC Plc widened its geographic presence in overseas markets. Furthermore, the company through the Foundation was wholly committed to furthering the cause of business education in the communities and around the country where its subsidiaries operate. In 1992, the company created a new management post in the United States to help coordinate the NFC Foundation activities in America.

STRUCTURE AND GOVERNANCE

Structure

The company's structure is fairly complicated, in that it incorporates special features from its buy-out roots and employee participation systems that operated in the company. At the operating end of the firm, NFC is a multi-divisionalized company comprising three main operating divisions – Logistics, Home Services and Transport. Each division is controlled by an overall master company – Exel Logistics, Allied Pickfords and BRS respectively. These 'master' groups trade through a number of other companies in a variety of related sectors and geographical areas, thus forming a matrix organizational form. Figure 23.1 shows the company structure as at October 1993, and before the Sherlock reorganization.

Fig. 23.1 NFC Plc: operating structure as at October 1993.

Governance

At NFC, the board of directors is responsible for the corporate strategy, culture and core values of the company. It approves the annual corporate plan, the company budget and financial plans for the group along with all investment and planning issues that relate to the company. The board comprises of seven executive directors and four non-executive directors who are appointed by the board, and a shareholder director who is elected through a postal ballot of shareholders every two years.

The board has four standing committees consisting of certain directors and senior company executives:

- *The Audit Committee*, which meets at least three times a year to review financial statements, internal controls, accounting policy and other financial matters affecting the group.
- *The Chairman's Committee*, consisting of the chairman, deputy chairman chief executive and the finance director. This committee is responsible for coordinating the strategic review and the corporate plan, reviewing new investment and developing acquisition proposals before submission to the full board for approval.
- *The Chief Executive's Committee*, chaired by the CEO, consists of the group financial director and the three divisional directors, the directors for human resources, corporate planning, communications and the company secretary. This committee is responsible for the day-to-day operations of the group.
- *The Board Remuneration Committee*, consisting of the chairman and the four non-executive directors, is responsible for the determination of the salaries and bonuses of the executive directors, the chief executive and other senior executives. External advice is often sought when pay and salary levels are being set. The chairman is never present when his own remuneration is discussed.

At NFC, directors' remuneration consists of a salary component, based on individual performance and market position, along with an annual performance bonus. In the case of the divisional managing directors, half of any bonus is based on corporate performance and half on the divisional profit performance against budget. For all other executive directors, the bonus component is based on the performance of

NFC Plc measured by growth in annual earnings per share. In the two financial years, 1990–91 and 1991–92, no such bonuses were paid out.

STRATEGY

The strategy that NFC have followed was in part guided by the vision of Sir Peter Thompson, who passionately believed that 'business is not just about making profits'. The Thompson vision had been continued by the company's new chairman, James Watson, and reinterpreted for the 1990s. James Watson's vision for NFC was to follow objectives that would result in 40 per cent of NFC's profits coming from overseas operations by 1995 and, furthermore, that:

> NFC will invest about £500m over the next five years with a view to achieve annual profits of £250m by the end of the decade.

In 1993, NFC published its new mission statement that reflected this international perspective, and stated that NFC aspired to being one of the leading international logistics and moving services companies in the world. It would achieve this by:

- creating customer value;
- achieving market leadership and sustainable competitive advantage;
- increasing innovation, learning and core skills;
- optimizing the utilization of tangible assets, skills and experience throughout NFC;
- encouraging people collectively to exceed their own and customers' expectations;
- growing shareholder value.

Unlike Thompson, Watson followed both an acquisition and a disposal strategy – to strengthen NFC in chosen sectors where the company wished to compete in, and to withdraw from those operations where, in Watson's view, NFC saw few operational synergies. It was Watson's view that for NFC to compete in the 1990s, management needed;

> Rigorous cost controls and to be decisive with under-performing sectors. Costs need to be cut, peripheral businesses sold and NFC needs to focus on three sectors – Logistics, Transport and Home Services.

Two major disposals in the period 1991–93 were the sale of NFC's waste management business to Wessex Waste Management Ltd and Pickfords Travel Services division to Airtours Plc.

Although acquisitions and disposals have been a keystone to the NFC strategy, attention to detail and operational management of the business have not been neglected. This has meant that NFC have built their business from within, by investing in people and systems infrastructure. The aim was to drive down costs and bring NFC closer to their customers through partnerships and to focus on quality.

Watson's objective of making 40 per cent of NFC's profits from overseas operations has meant that NFC have concentrated on internationalizing their businesses by expanding geographically, notably into the USA, Canada and Europe. This strategy was succinctly articulated by Jack Mather, NFC's chief executive, in 1992 as follows:

NFC's strategy is to make the company a fully international organization by using its skills and expertise to extend into new geographical areas and to respond to the growing demand for more sophisticated logistics and transport systems. This international development will compensate for the lower growth expected in the UK.

NFC executives firmly believe that the firm's considerable skills and resources can be transferred into new geographical markets, provided that NFC stays in its own business areas. This would enable NFC to develop its product range across global markets. In the case of France, for example, Watson believed that:

> The operation to take what we have in the UK and put it into France is very significant. The French market is very unsophisticated, it is mainly a financial operation rather than a value adding one.

The acquisition strategy had been a very carefully thought out policy. It allowed entry into foreign markets by sidestepping potential entry barriers, it allowed NFC to service customers who themselves were often following international strategies and it permitted NFC to augment an existing small operation and move it more towards critical mass. For example, fourteen of NFC's top fifty customers are based in North America, and one third are American owned. A number of NFC's European and American customers operate on an increasing pan-European level. NFC's chief executive, Jack Mather believed that:

> We (NFC) have proved that we can work with customers in partnership across national boundaries, taking responsibility for the logistics operations and enabling our customers to concentrate on exploiting their own areas of expertise.

Jack Mather, NFC's chief executive who had been with the company for 25 years, retired in 1993, and a new chief executive, Peter Sherlock, was appointed to replace him. One of Sherlock's first tasks was to conduct a full review of the NFC strategy, the outcome of which reaffirmed the group's commitment to two broad areas of development – logistics and moving services. In both these areas NFC has considerable skills, expertise and in-depth strength, and furthermore both these areas offer long-term opportunity for the group. Sherlock rewrote the mission statement to encapsulate an international dimension and to recognize the strengths of the company. (The 1993 mission statement has been quoted above.)

Sherlock's strategic aims for the mid to late 1990s are summed up in his own words:

> Our goal is to become the leading international provider of value added logistics solutions for customers. To achieve this goal we are focusing on enhancing our leading position in UK logistics; extending our range of skills in North America in attractive key market segments; developing a pan-European capability in selected markets; and preparing for expansion in Asia and the Pacific Rim.

The Sherlock review reorganized the divisions to take into account the strength of the NFC 'brands', under which a number of its companies operate. The logistics division was renamed Exel Logistics, the transport division was to be called BRS, and what was 'moving services' became Allied, Pickfords, Merchants. The parcel service company, Lynx, part of the old transport division, became an SBU in its own right. At NFC it was clear that:

The brands are, however, brands, not companies in their own right ... The object in our branding is to ensure that careful product differentiation captures a premium return to the shareholder by providing a premium service to the customer.

To obtain this premium performance and to justify this branding strategy, NFC intended to operate in a 'unified way' across the whole business, so that customers received a 'combined solution' to their problems. Often this would mean that logistics and transport services would be integrated either in a domestic market or on an international scale. In the UK, Exel Logistics and BRS were unified into a single team.

ACQUISITIONS AND DISPOSALS

The acquisition and disposal strategy had been a central part of Watson's NFC business policy. Many of the acquisitions have been relatively small in scale (in comparative terms), but nevertheless significant for NFC. Some £75m was spent on acquisitions in 1992, notably in North America, where Trammell Crow Distribution Corporation and J.H. Coffman were acquired giving NFC a network of 44 warehouses, six million square feet of warehousing capacity and a number of important clients to add to its product mix and customer list. Further acquisitions in Canada and the USA during the period 1991–93 strengthened NFC's Logistics division in the North American region. A number of minor acquisitions were also made in North America to augment NFC's Home Services division in that region.

In Europe, the acquisition of BOS Finances, a French company specializing in frozen and chilled foods distribution gave NFC coverage of one third of France in the West, North West and Central regions. Further acquisitions in France, the Netherlands and Germany in the period 1991–93 increased the scale and scope of the Logistics division in Europe. Other acquisitions, notably in Belgium and the UK, were made and integrated into the Home Services division, the biggest being that of Bullens and GB Crate Hire.

Two major disposals occurred during the 1991–93 period. Pickfords Travel Services was sold to Airtours, Pickfords Business Travel was acquired by the Belgian firm Compagnie International Wagon-Lits and Waste Management Ltd, a subsidiary operating in the Transport division, was acquired by Wessex Water and Waste Management International that operated an international joint venture. The reasons behind each of these major disposals were stated by the company as follows:

Pickfords Travel:

The travel operation was a peripheral activity to the NFC group and for that reason was not a primary target for development. I am delighted, therefore that, that the buyer is committed to developing and expanding the business.

(James Watson's words)

Waste Management:

NFC has recognized the increasing level of specialist resources and investment which would be needed if NFC were to continue the development of Waste Management Ltd into one of the industry's leading players.

In recent years NFC has focused increasingly on the UK and international development of its core businesses of transport, logistics and home services. The NFC Board acknowledged that the purchaser's terms for Waste Management would meet the need for Waste

Table 23.2 Recent acquisitions and disposals 1991–93

	Country	£m	Division
Acquisitions 1991			
Hellweg Tiefkühl-Logistik GmbH	Germany	8.9	Logistics
Universal Terminal Warehouse	USA	2.8	Logistics
Food Express Holding BV	Netherlands	1.5	Logistics
Hellweg Tiefkühl-Logistik Restaurant Service GmbH	Germany	1.3	Logistics
Ofsite Records Systems Inc.	Canada	1.2	Home Services
Other companies and businesses	Various	2.6	Not disclosed
		18.3	

Disposals 1991

Pickfords Business Travel – Sold to the Belgian company Compagnie International Wagon Lits-Lits et du Tourisme for an undisclosed sum.

AA-BRS Services Ltd – A joint venture with the Automobile Association (AA) sold to the AA for a undisclosed sum.

	Country	£m	Division
Acquisitions 1992			
Trammell Crow Distribution Corp.	USA	13.4	Logistics
BOS Finances SA & Subsidiaries	France	13.0	Logistics
Bullens & GB Crate Hire	UK	4.7	Home Services
Distribution Centres Inc.	USA	3.4	
J.H. Coffman & Sons	USA	1.9	Logistics
Trans International	Aust/NZ	1.3	
Service Furniture Delivery	USA	0.9	
Other companies and businesses	Various	2.7	
		41.3	

Disposals 1992

Pickfords Travel – The main operating company in the Travel Division, sold to Airtours Plc for £16m.

	Country	£m	Division
Acquisitions 1992–1993			
Arthur Pierre Group	Belgium	11.4	Home Services
Theo Macke und Sohn	Germany	5.6	Logistics
Record Centre	USA	4.5	Not disclosed
Transports Pujos	France	4.0	Logistics
Transports Martin	France	2.3	Logistics
J. Tomlinson	UK	1.3	Not disclosed
Others	Various	2.2	Not disclosed
		31.3	

Disposals 1993

Waste Management Ltd – An operating company in the Transport Division, sold to Wessex Waste Management Ltd, a joint venture between Wessex Water Plc and Waste Management International Inc. for £113m.

Source: Company Accounts 1991–93 and press releases.

Management to develop within a major international business dedicated to the waste industry while enabling NFC to concentrate its investments and strategic growth into its core businesses.

(NFC press release)

Table 23.2 sets out a list of NFC's major acquisitions and disposals for the period 1991–93.

NFC'S OPERATIONS

The financial performance of the three operating divisions of NFC is given in Appendix 23.1.

A number of NFC's activities in 1991–92 experienced difficulties as the UK and the world recession continued. In the UK, BRS saw its profits turn down in its contract

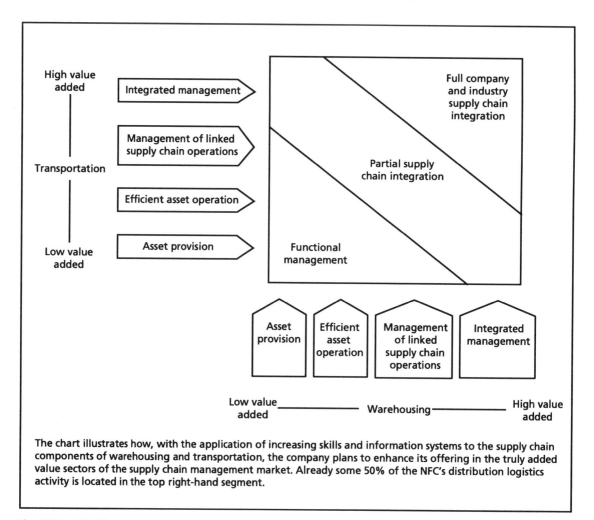

The chart illustrates how, with the application of increasing skills and information systems to the supply chain components of warehousing and transportation, the company plans to enhance its offering in the truly added value sectors of the supply chain management market. Already some 50% of the NFC's distribution logistics activity is located in the top right-hand segment.

Fig. 23.2 NFC Plc: transportation/warehousing value added matrix.

Source: NFC Annual Report 1993, p. 10.

hire activities, as did the parcel service, Lynx. The parcel business in the UK was particularly hit by a recession that saw large companies like Federal Express scale down their operations. Volume declined as the market contracted. This was to continue into 1993, with Lynx posting an operating loss of £10m. Some of this loss could be explained by operational difficulties following the acquisition of Federal Express's Central England sorting facility. The loss at Lynx was expected to be turned around in 1994.

UK transport activities, principally through BRS, experienced significant gains in 1993 after a difficult year in 1992 that saw turnover fall as volume-related activity struggled. Project United, intended to reorganize BRS with a view to reducing overheads through branch reorganization into hub and spoke systems, was accelerated. This was designed to offset the effects of the continuing recession in the UK.

Exel Logistics, the jewel in the NFC crown, continued to sustain year-on-year profit increases. The investments in America, Europe and Canada extended its operations worldwide. In 1993, following the Sherlock strategic review, Exel Logistics and BRS in the UK were brought together as a single unified team. NFC's strategy was designed to increase the value-added business that both brands enjoyed. Relationships, operating skills, integration of systems and service quality would become the key success factors to create the competitive edge in the mid-to-late 1990s. Integrated logistics and total supply chain management would become more firmly established as new operating systems like Quick Response would be increasingly demanded by customers. Figure 23.2 shows how NFC conceptualized this strategy.

Home Services maintained a strong cash generating profile by targeting expansion into areas of the market still capable of producing profits through keeping costs down. A series of astute acquisitions in overseas markets extended this division geographically and internationalized its operations.

Appendix 23.4 gives a review of the divisional operations over the period 1991–92 and Appendix 23.5 gives the chief executive's review for 1993, providing information on NFC's operations for that year.

THE RIGHTS ISSUE

In December 1993, NFC announced a 1 for 4 rights issue of 138.6 million shares at 195 pence a share. This was designed to raise £263 million. After the issue, NFC would be left with net cash of £89.4m, a significant turnaround from the 53 per cent gearing shown in the 1993 accounts. The rights issue reflected the unique character of the company's share structure, with about 45 per cent of the stock held in private hands, and some 85 per cent of its 32,000 employees being shareholders. The small shareholder who did not wish to participate in the rights issue was offered 14 pence per new share in cash.

The rights issue would increase the number of shares held by institutional shareholders, but Peter Sherlock said that:

> He did not want to lose NFC's distinctive culture ... [but] it is much easier to articulate a philosophy of increasing shareholder value if 85 per cent of the employees are shareholders. But we must not let it act as a restraint on the business, which the employees understand.

It was estimated that the rights issue would dilute the employee shareholder aggregate from the 14 per cent level that it was in 1993 to around 11 per cent when the issue was fully taken up by the end of January 1994. Although this new expected level was lower than before, it was still sufficient to protect the double voting rights for employee shareholders allowed in the NFC constitution.

The rights issue would allow NFC to further develop its business and to continue with its expansion strategy.

On Saturday 29 January 1994, NFC held its annual general meeting attended by over 4,000 of its shareholders. At that meeting Sir Peter Thompson accused his successor, James Watson, of placing the group's traditional values at risk. He was particularly critical of the board for not seeking permission from the shareholders before organizing the rights issue. Furthermore, Sir Peter was concerned that a number of recent developments at NFC threatened the core values of the company, arguing that 'we used to be non-elitist – and I now see executive share options creeping in all over the place'. The policy of the NFC board was robustly defended by James Watson who said that 'he resented the suggestion that I don't share these values'. James Watson argued that the rights issue was necessary to develop NFC, and that it was essential to have a pattern of shareholding that worked for the company in the 1990s. 'We can't always look back to the 1980s', he said.

The meeting overwhelmingly approved all the resolutions before it and indicated its strong support for the board.

APPENDIX 23.1
GEOGRAPHICAL AND SEGMENTAL ANALYSIS 1990–92

Table 23.3 Geographical analysis

	External turnover			Operating profit			Net assets		
	1990 £m	1991 £m	1992 £m	1990 £m	1991 £m	1992 £m	1990 £m	1991 £m	1992 £m
UK and Ireland	1,097.1	1,122.3	1,083.2	76.2	71.6	72.7	373.0	367.0	373.3
Rest of Europe	11.0	31.2	103.0	0.9	1.0	3.0	3.3	18.5	58.9
North America	494.1	486.7	515.2	30.0	27.5	26.0	55.1	82.1	115.6
Australasia & Far East	24.7	23.5	22.4	1.6	2.0	1.0	7.0	8.7	6.4
Total	1,626.9	1,663.7	1,723.8	108.7	102.1	102.7	438.4	476.3	554.2
Less non-operating liabilities							105.7	138.7	221.2
Total net assets							332.7	337.6	333.0

Table 23.4 Segmental information 1990

	Turnover 1990 £m	Operating profit 1990 £m	Operating assets 1990 £m	Employees year end 1990
Transport	544.3	27.3	166.2	14,704
Logistics	411.7	31.5	160.5	12,774
Home Services	557.0	25.5	50.4	4,318
	1,513.0	84.3	377.1	31,796
Property	35.7	26.8	47.9	89
Travel	76.2	(2.7)	(30.8)	2,623
Other	2.0	0.3	44.2	289
Total	1,626.9	108.7	438.4	34,797

Table 23.5 Segmental information 1991–92

	Turnover		Operating profit		Operating assets		Employees year end	
	1991 £m	1992 £m	1991 £m	1992 £m	1991 £m	1992 £m	1991	1992
Transport	562.2	531.8	32.6	26.8	224.2	228.3	12,966	11,981
Logistics	501.1	590.5	38.2	46.8	176.6	222.4	13,910	15,444
Home Services	524.8	544.4	23.1	23.4	63.8	58.0	4,121	4,342
	1,588.1	1,666.7	93.9	96.8	464.6	508.7	30,997	31,767
Property	5.7	0.8	6.9	5.3	25.7	28.2	77	73
Other	1.2	1.2	1.3	0.6	6.3	17.3	241	232
Discontinued	68.7	55.1	—	—	(20.3)	—	1,837	—
Total	1,663.7	1,723.8	102.1	102.7	476.3	554.2	33,152	32,072

Table 23.6 Geographical analysis (1992 restated)

	External turnover		Operating profit		Net assets	
	1993 £m	1992 £m	1993 £m	1992 £m	1993 £m	1992 £m
UK and Ireland	991.3	997.8	80.2	64.4	345.2	331.8
Rest of Europe	171.6	103.0	4.8	2.7	62.7	58.9
North America	700.8	515.2	29.4	24.6	116.2	115.6
Australasia & Far East	28.7	22.4	1.5	1.0	7.7	6.4
	1,892.4	1,638.4	115.9	92.7	531.8	512.7
Discontinued Operations	9.2	85.4	0.8	4.4	—	41.5
Total	1,901.6	1,723.8	116.7	97.1		
Less non-operating liabilities					217.6	231.2
Total net assets					314.2	323.0

Table 23.7 Segmental information 1992–93 (1992 restated[1])

	External turnover		Operating profit		Operating assets		Employees average for year	
	1993 £m	1992 £m	1993 £m	1992 £m	1993 £m	1992 £m	1993	1992
Continuing operations								
Exel Logistics	713.2	590.5	64.9	46.8	233.9	222.4	16,611	15,267
BRS	411.4	421.4	32.6	23.9	172.1	151.9	7,969	8,079
Allied Pickfords and Merchants	683.6	544.4	28.8	23.2	63.4	58.0	4,514	4,267
	1,808.2	1,556.3	126.3	93.9	469.4	432.3	29,093	27,613
Lynx	73.5	80.1	(10.1)	(1.5)	34.8	34.9	3,404	3,852
Property	9.6	0.8	(0.9)	(0.3)	18.7	28.2	72	75
Other	1.1	1.2	0.6	0.6	8.9	17.3	211	226
	1,892.4	1,638.4	115.9	92.7	531.8	512.7	32,780	31,496
Discontinued	9.2	85.4	0.8	4.4	—	41.5	175	2,354
Total	1,901.6	1,723.8	116.7	97.1	531.8	554.2	32,955	33,850

1. In 1993 the three main divisions – Logistics, Transport and Home Services – were reorganized and the key operating brands controlled by NFC became the operating titles for the new divisions. The NFC parcel and courier service, Lynx, formerly in the Transport Division, was placed under its own brand name as a separate heading. This meant that for 1993–92 comparison purposes, the 1992 figures have had to be rebased.

Source: Company Accounts 1993.

APPENDIX 23.2
NFC: PROFIT AND LOSS ACCOUNT AND BALANCE SHEETS 1992–93

Table 23.8 Consolidated profit and loss account (for the year ended 3 October 1993)

	1993 £m	1992 As restated £m
Turnover		
Continuing operations	1,834.4	1,638.4
Acquisitions	58.0	—
	1,892.4	1,638.4
Discontinued operations	9.2	85.4
	1,901.6	1,723.8
Operating profit		
Continuing operations	110.6	92.7
Acquisitions	5.3	—
	115.9	92.7
Discontinued operations	0.8	4.4
Operating profit	116.7	97.1
Profit/(loss) on disposals of properties in continuing operations	3.3	(1.5)
Provision for reorganization in continuing operations	(45.0)	—
Profit on disposals of discontinued operations	51.5	6.0
Profit before interest	126.5	101.6
Interest	(18.1)	(8.4)
Profit before profit-sharing	108.4	93.2
Profit sharing	(3.5)	(3.3)
Profit on ordinary activities before taxation	104.9	89.9
Taxation on ordinary activities	(16.9)	(24.1)
Profit on ordinary activities after taxation	88.0	65.8
Minority interest	(0.2)	(0.1)
Profit for the financial year	87.8	65.7
Dividends	(35.9)	(33.2)
Retained profit for the year	51.9	32.5
	Pence	Pence
Earnings per share	15.9	11.9
Earnings per share after exceptional items	13.1	10.7
Dividends per share	7.0	6.55

Source: Company accounts 1993.

Table 23.9 NFC Consolidated balance sheets (for the year ended 2 October 1993)

	1993 £m	1992 As restated £m
Fixed assets		
Tangible assets	542.0	550.7
Investments	27.5	20.7
	569.5	571.4
Current assets		
Stocks	18.2	27.0
Debtors: Amounts falling due within one year	337.6	341.7
Debtors: Amounts falling due after one year	81.1	44.1
Cash in hand and in bank	47.0	31.1
	483.9	443.9
Creditors		
Amounts falling due within one year	(468.4)	(517.4)
Net current (liabilities)/assets	15.5	(73.5)
Total assets less current liabilities	585.0	497.9
Creditors: amounts due after one year	(180.7)	(125.3)
Provisions for liabilities and charges	(90.1)	(49.6)
	314.2	323.0
Capital and reserves		
Called-up share capital	27.6	27.6
Share premium account	57.5	60.4
Revaluation reserve	83.5	95.7
Profit and loss account	144.2	137.8
Shareholders' funds	312.9	321.5
Minority interests	1.3	1.5
	314.2	323.0

Source: Company Accounts 1993.

APPENDIX 23.3
STATEMENT OF NFC PLC'S CORE VALUES

Table 23.10 NFC: Core values (1991)

NFC's beliefs and culture, as expressed in its core values, are fundamental to the way the business is run. These core values are expressed as follows:

EMPLOYEE OWNERSHIP

The essence of NFC's culture, employee ownership reflects our belief that the people who work in the business should have the opportunity to own a stake in it, to share in the wealth created and to take part in the strategic decision process which determines its future.

QUALITY

Fundamental to our culture, quality stems from the commitment of the employees to NFC's success through the provision of the highest level of service to our customers. It is inherent in the way we think, behave and run our business.

INTERNATIONALISM

NFC's culture and policies have to develop alongside the physical growth of the business in international markets. Internationalism as a core value links our culture with our ability to develop indigenous businesses and to provide international services to our customers.

PEOPLE DEVELOPMENT

Our employees are our greatest asset. The benefits which we can provide for them through training and development as they progress through their employment in the business are equally important to us as the benefits we seek to achieve for them as shareholders.

SOCIAL RESPONSIBILITY

NFC acknowledges that its social responsibilities extend to the welfare of the communities in which it operates and allocates one per cent of its profits to the fulfilment of those responsibilities.

PREMIUM PERFORMANCE

The ultimate measure of NFC's success, premium performance is our prime objective. It is therefore first on our list of core values but also last in that it flows out of the values by which the business is run.

Source: 1991 Annual Review and Summary Financial Statement.

APPENDIX 23.4
OPERATIONAL REPORT 1992

Logistics Division

'Our chief successes this year were in sustaining year-on-year profit improvement, making further progress towards our long-term strategic goals and protecting our market share. We also significantly expanded our operations in North America.'

Two new acquisitions, JH Coffman and Trammel Crow Distribution Corporation, added six million square feet to warehousing capacity and gave us entry into the new and important regional markets of the West Coast and Mid West. The purchase of Trammell Crow also gave us access to the petrochemicals sector. The South East, a third new region, was penetrated by the development of a new operation for an existing customer in Atlanta, Georgia, so we now operate in thirty states. We also gained access to the Canadian market with the opening of a warehouse for a worldwide customer and to Mexico with the establishment of a warehouse for an existing and important US customer.

In Europe, the acquisition of BOS Finances, a specialist frozen and chilled food transport and distribution group, gives us coverage of around one third of France in the West, North West and North Central regions. Further progress was made in central France through the acquisition from Sodiaal of the temperature controlled warehousing and distribution activities of its dairy product co-operative. Customers in Britain who awarded us new contracts in the year include Mercona, 7-Eleven, John West, Heinz, Bass, Kwiksave, Budgens, DuPont, SmithKline Beecham, New England Foods, Disney Stores, IMI Cornelius, ICL Worldwide Spares, Courtaulds Packaging, ARM Construction, Autotrader and Lochar Publishing. In North America, we won contracts with Adolph Coors, PPG and Honeywell.

In mainland Europe, we signed new business with Olympus Sports, Pizza Hut, Apple Computers and Texas Instruments. Existing customers who awarded us additional business include Golden Wonder, Woolworths, Kimberly-Clark, Superdrug, BHS, Pepe Jeans, London Underground and Mander Brothers. We also opened a distribution centre for Marks & Spencer in Guadalajara to serve their stores in Spain.

Transport Division

'Project United, the reorganization of BRS, has been the key component of the division's strategy to reduce overheads and provide a platform for future profitable growth. As the economy worsened, we accelerated the reorganization of the branches into the hub and spoke system to bring forward anticipated cost savings.'

Volume-related activities continued to struggle although there were encouraging year-on-year profit improvements from truck rental, bulk distribution and car delivery, reflecting the management action taken last year to reduce resources. BRS Car Lease and Mastershire, a joint venture with Vauxhall Motors, had a successful year with strong revenue and profit growth in a highly competitive market sector. The newly-created industry sector management teams confirmed the validity of adopting a sectored approach by securing major new business with Rover, Ford and Walker UK in the automotive industry, Albright and Wilson in chemicals, RHM, Kelloggs, Hoover and Candy in manufacturing and Safeway in grocery retailing. BRS Taskforce, the premium driver agency launched in 1990, enjoyed strong growth in line with development plans.

Lynx Express Delivery Network continued to gain new business offsetting reductions in volume from existing customers and some shedding of unprofitable business. Fierce price competition in the express delivery market was mitigated by a continued move towards contract-backed business in selected market sectors. The acquisition of the Midlands hub of the former Federal Express parcels operation, completed in September 1992, will enable the company to improve service standards and significantly reduce handling and trunking costs.

Waste Management performed well despite the reduction in volume of industrial waste and the severe margin pressure on new business. Development work continued strongly on sites in the Wirral and on Humberside. Warnham, a major landfill site in Sussex, is due to commence operation in January 1993. Several new waste collection contracts were secured and the company's largest contract, with the Wirral District Council, was successfully renewed with an innovative new working methodology.

While economic forecasts remain bleak, we are confident the reorganization implemented this year, together with strong cash and cost control, will underpin trading in the coming year.

Home Services Division

'We maintained a strong cash-generating profile by targeting only those areas of the market still capable of producing profit and by keeping a tight rein on costs. At the same time, we continued to invest significant sums in information technology development and in sustainable quality initiatives.'

The most significant event of the year was the launch of Allied Pickfords as a global brand with all companies in the worldwide network rebranded under a unified identity. As well as the rebranding, all companies participated in Project World Class, an initiative that brought our international moving operations within one consistent set of procedures and standards. Allied Pickfords is now the world's largest and most cohesive international moving network, offering multi-national companies and their employees a reliable standard of service in each city and at each country of access. The market response has been most encouraging.

We secured the full ownership of Allied Van Lines in Canada to revitalize that network for the benefit of the company and other independent Canadian agents. We also acquired a number of small, specialist businesses to build our credibility and our share of the records management market. We now have dedicated records management activities in Australia, New Zealand, the United Kingdom, Ireland and Canada, all of which are making sound contributions to profits. Major account gains in this market included a contract in Canada to manage the records of Royal Trust of Toronto and a five year contract in Australia with AMP, the country's largest insurance company.

Within Allied Van Lines, the consistently high standard of service given to its customers led IBM to more than double the volume of business placed with the company and the level of relocation contract business signed increased by 20% over the previous year. The new contracts involve employee moves for leading corporations such as Walmart, Alamo Car Rental, Pizza Hut and McDonnell Douglas. In the home delivery market, Merchants Home Delivery Service renewed its substantial contract with the Levitz furniture chain and brought 100 new trucks on stream to service new business for Montgomery Ward.

APPENDIX 23.5
CHIEF EXECUTIVE'S REVIEW 1993

Our UK transport activities, trading as BRS, increased operating profit by 36% to £32.6m. This reflected the benefits of reorganization and tight cost control. While revenue overall was flat BRS achieved significant new business gains and several important renewals were signed with key accounts.

Our UK parcels company, Lynx, encountered operational difficulties following the acquisition of a central sortation facility in August 1992, the costs and timing of which materially contributed to the year's losses of £10.1m. A new management team was installed in the middle of the financial year and has made considerable progress in reducing the rate of loss. However, the company is not yet profitable and the management continue to pursue appropriate corrective action.

Exel Logistics performed well, particularly in the UK, with operating profit up 39% at £64.9m. In the UK, Exel Logistics won new business from several sources in the grocery sector and from other large high street customers. The industrial sector was less buoyant, but additional business was secured from existing customers and important new customers signed. Three major distribution contracts for national newspapers, worth in excess of £30m in total over a four year period, were renewed in the year.

In mainland Europe, Exel Logistics expanded its operations in France in the chill and frozen sectors and in textiles, building on the success of its work for Marks & Spencer. The launch of Exel Logistics in Belgium provided entry into the grocery retail and petroleum and lubricants sectors. Important business in the Netherlands was won in the frozen, grocery and electronics markets, and in the clothing sector. In Germany the new management team successfully restructured the companies previously acquired to create a unified business. Good progress has been made in several important markets, including fast and frozen food and the grocery sector. In Spain, the 14 Exel Logistics Iberica sites have been consolidated to form a long-distance national network. Major new contracts gained include Pirelli in tyres and Tudor in car batteries.

Exel Logistics North America continued to invest in further growth despite a flat economy and competitive pressure on margins, pursuing its mission of achieving clear and acknowledged market leadership. Substantial new revenue was gained, mostly through long-term contracts. Lead logistics provider status was attained with all our current key accounts in consumer goods. In this sector, development of a strategic alliance with Schneider National (the largest truck load carrier in the USA) has positioned the company to offer an integrated logistics service package to key accounts in the consumer products sector.

There were difficult trading conditions in all the major markets served by the companies in the former Home Services Division. Despite this, operating profit in Allied, Pickfords and Merchants was up 24% at £28.8m. The Pickfords Group achieved further growth in international home moving, following the acquisition of the Arthur Pierre Group in November 1992 which secured the company's market leadership in Belgium and the Netherlands. The benefits from the combined operations include improved utilization of resources and pan-European coordination of traffic control.

For the first time in several years, market share gains were achieved in the US moving services business. Allied Van Lines achieved its highest gains in home moving, with corporate moving and military moves also showing improvement. In the trade show market, Allied significantly out-performed the rest of the industry. It was generally a poor year for the relocation industry in Canada. However, substantial progress was made in quality, marketing and operations in the first full year of owning Allied Van Lines Ltd, which now operates in concert with the owned branch network far better than in the past.

Development at Merchants Home Delivery Service featured its entry into the 'vendor direct' market and a major contract with the Bloomingdales store group which came on stream following the acquisition of SFD in the previous financial year. Three branches were opened for another new market entry, 'In-Home Services'. Merchants is leading the combined NFC operation to provide a fully integrated logistics service for catalogue sales of office furniture to small businesses throughout the USA. The new IT system known as CARMS (Computer Aided Routing and Management System), now in use on 25% of Merchants' business, links into in-cab systems for real-time updates on delivery performance.

At the third quarter we announced the new responsibilities which were being assigned to the three Divisional Managing Directors in order to lead and manage the restructuring and development process. Robbie Burns, Managing Director, UK Transport and Logistics, is leading the integration of BRS and Exel Logistics into a single team process. Graham Roberts' role as Managing Director, Operations Europe, is to provide the important focus on improving our asset and operational infrastructure management. Denis Olliver, Managing Director, International Projects, is leading the development of the Allied International Moving Network in addition to his responsibilities for Lynx. I have found their support and commitment and that of their colleagues on the Board, Trevor Larman and Ian Barr, invaluable. That commitment has been matched by management at all levels. It is this resource of people with skills and experience but above all commitment, determination and enthusiasm that is one of our greatest assets.

Strategy for the future

The past year has seen NFC embark on fundamental change. A far reaching strategic review has enabled management to reassess the group's current business and to position NFC in order to capitalize on its long-term prospects for growth.

The review has reaffirmed the group's commitment to two broad areas of development – distribution logistics and moving services. Both these areas offer the scale and opportunities which match the company's strengths. We aspire to be one of the leading international companies in these markets.

We intend to achieve this by:

- creating customer value
- achieving market leadership and sustainable competitive advantage
- increasing innovation, learning and core skills
- optimizing the utilization of our tangible assets, skills and experience throughout NFC
- encouraging our people collectively to exceed their own and our customers' expectations
- growing shareholder value.

Distribution logistics

The world market for third party distribution logistics services is estimated to exceed £100 billion and is forecast to show strong long-term growth. Our goal is to become the leading international provider of value added logistics solutions for customers. To achieve this goal we are focusing on enhancing our leading position in UK logistics; extending our range of skills in North America in attractive key market segments; developing a pan-European capability in selected markets; and preparing for expansion in Asia and the Pacific Rim.

The emerging conclusions of our strategic review led to the announcement with the third quarter's results of the:

- integration of BRS and Exel Logistics into a single UK team
- major focus on asset and operational infrastructure management
- enhancement of our international key account management process
- further development of international logistics support capability
- the appointment of a director of information services to lead the development of IT throughout the group.

All operations will benefit from improved infrastructure management. Horizontal processes are being developed across the business to use our assets at the most intensive level possible and to enhance efficiency for the benefit of our customers and ourselves. New monitoring systems will help to measure and improve effectiveness and ensure the transfer of best practice between operations across the group.

The anticipated future needs of our customers for pan-European capability will require the strengthening of our asset and operational base in the key markets of France, Germany, Spain and the Benelux countries. We are giving priority to building on relationships with existing customers such as Marks & Spencer and Apple to help provide them with new and extended solutions. This priority has been recognized by the appointment of a director for mainland European logistics.

In the USA both Exel Logistics and Merchants Home Delivery Service provide distribution logistics services although they have somewhat different portfolios. Merchants is especially strong in the furniture and appliance industries while Exel Logistics, with its highly successful TOPEX warehouse management system, is based on the consumer markets. However, we recognize that benefits can flow from their working more closely together, especially at a time when customers are demanding more complex, integrated services.

Merchants has achieved outstanding results with its self-employed owner-driver philosophy and its application of Total Quality Management, where it ranks among the leaders in US service industries. Substantial benefits will be won from efficient capitalization on the available synergies of this and our other US businesses.

A further important leg of our strategy is to develop and subsequently implement plans to meet the needs of existing customers in the Asia Pacific region to further the group's logistics capability worldwide.

Moving services

In moving services, we aim to capitalize on the strength of our brands. In the UK, for instance, we lead the market with a share of over 20% in aggregate while in North America Allied is one of the leading van lines serving the domestic, international and business moving markets. We aim to build a leading position in worldwide international moving services by enhancing customer value, implementing global operating procedures and systems and capitalizing on our excellent brand names of Allied and Pickfords.

We are targeting the moving market, based on business relocation and domestic household goods moving in North America, the UK, mainland Europe and Australia, and worldwide international moving services. This market is estimated to exceed £12 billion. NFC is committed to a business development plan that will establish appropriate representation in all key areas, either through our own facilities or through franchising, to build an international network of coordinated and integrated franchisees and agents and wholly owned operations capable of meeting the needs of the most exacting customers.

Part of the thrust to create a global network is to re-establish Allied Van Lines as the leader in the US market.

A unified approach

NFC is providing the focus for a unified team process across the whole of the business. We can draw on our many and varied skills which are contained within our product brands – but what the customer receives is a combined solution. We will operate in a much more integrated way, using the logistics and international moving network to provide integrate solutions for major organizations to meet their exacting international requirements.

Branding across the whole range of group services is an important factor in the development. The brands are, however, brands, not companies in their own right. That a clear consequence of the business restructuring that is flowing from the strategic review. The new structure recognizes that NFC is an integrated entity whose whole is greater than the sum of its parts. The object in our branding is to ensure that careful product differentiation captures a premium return to the shareholder by providing a premium service to the customer.

Growth will come in part from continuing to support the existing customer base and seeking to match customer requirements to the geographic extension of our services. We will continue to pursue organic growth using existing skills and assets, backed by appropriate capital investment. The sheer scale of the international challenge makes it necessary and desirable to enter into strategic alliances, joint ventures and franchises as the means of serving international clients.

The company's commitment to employee share ownership, and the enthusiasm, determination and commitment of employees to the company, are fundamental to long-term success. We will continue to encourage all employees to hold shares, which provides a tangible commitment to our objective of growing shareholder value.

Creating customer value

Our leadership goals are not based on market share alone, for that does not necessarily qualify a company as a leader. We are committed to investment to achieve the most advanced capabilities in the areas of logistics and moving services.

Our goals, moreover, reinforce each other. For instance, full utilization of the asset base has a direct link with customer value. NFC's efficiency improves customer asset utilization as well as our own, freeing warehouse, factory and retail space, reducing the need for working capital and shortening lead-times. Much can be achieved by optimizing the availability of trucks and the use of warehouse capacity and by having goods in transit in vehicles, rather than stored in warehouses or stockrooms.

The compelling obligation on any third party provider is to ensure that efficiency and value exceed those available to customers in-house. For NFC, logistics and moving services are core activities: they rarely are for our customers. That is our virtue and our strength.

For many customers, that involves building long-term relationships with NFC – for instance, by forming dedicated partnerships whose terms recognize the importance of sharing risk and reward by performance-related agreements and 'rolling, evergreen' contracts. In other cases, the need to reduce costs will lead customers to share their transport and logistics arrangements. Either way, the skills of the third party provider are essential.

Flexibility and responsiveness are the key to future relationships with customers. To provide flexible, responsive solutions for customers, we are seeking to develop a culture that can anticipate and create change. We will seek to encourage creativity and innovation, to find better ways of doing everything. The year has provided encouraging evidence that good progress is being achieved towards this aim and that further benefits will flow in the years ahead.

Peter Sherlock
Chief Executive

APPENDIX 23.6
KEY FINANCIAL RATIOS FOR NFC PLC AND ITS MAIN COMPETITORS

Table 23.11 NFC Plc 1989–93

No.	Description	30/9/89	6/10/90	5/10/91	3/10/92	2/10/93
701	Return on shareholders' equity (%)	16.50	17.45	18.68	22.93	25.14
707	Return on capital employed (%)	20.58	20.40	17.62	19.43	21.34
713	Operating profit margin (%)	5.54	5.11	5.43	6.15	6.47
716	Pre-tax profit margin (%)	5.23	5.10	5.30	5.66	5.52
717	Net profit margin (%)	3.48	3.34	3.54	3.78	3.98
732	Income gearing (%)	8.55	11.53	9.35	13.01	18.29
733	Borrowing ratio	0.15	0.30	0.53	0.67	0.71
725	Stock ratio (days)	9.72	4.42	5.35	5.72	3.49
727	Debtors ratio (days)	69.66	67.71	83.21	73.11	67.01
729	Creditors ratio (days)	81.31	71.14	76.80	73.86	76.81
762	Sales per employee	47,030	48,189	49,133	50,925	58,011
763	Operating profit per employee	2,604	2,464	2,670	3,131	3,755
764	Capital employed /employee	13,352	13,708	16,376	16,981	18,368
792	Cash earnings per share	16.32	15.86	16.39	20.31	22.59

Source: Output taken from Datastream Program 190D.

Table 23.12 Christian Salvesen Plc 1989–93

No.	Description	31/3/89	31/3/90	31/3/91	31/3/92	31/3/93
701	Return on shareholders' equity (%)	16.72	19.34	19.01	19.63	17.78
707	Return on capital employed (%)	23.47	22.97	21.19	18.92	19.85
713	Operating profit margin (%)	17.71	17.05	15.83	14.95	14.83
716	Pre-tax profit margin (%)	17.25	16.94	15.78	13.86	14.15
717	Net profit margin (%)	11.21	11.79	10.98	9.31	9.49
732	Income gearing (%)	5.23	8.90	7.62	10.53	10.32
733	Borrowing ratio	0.14	0.27	0.29	0.45	0.31
725	Stock ratio (days)	18.90	20.90	24.70	23.59	29.73
727	Debtors ratio (days)	74.29	89.16	93.52	89.69	95.40
729	Creditors ratio (days)	122.06	126.57	123.67	124.18	148.36
762	Sales per employee	35,453	38,358	41,275	42,139	47,576
763	Operating profit per employee	6,277	6,539	6,533	6,299	7,055
764	Capital employed /employee	27,501	31,093	33,317	34,543	37,863
792	Cash earnings per share	25.17	28.78	30.69	33.46	37.52

Source: Output taken from Datastream Program 190D.

Table 23.13 Transport Development Group Plc 1988–92

No.	Description	31/12/88	31/12/89	31/12/90	31/12/91	31/12/92
701	Return on shareholders'equity (%)	13.58	10.21	9.60	10.20	8.92
707	Return on capital employed (%)	17.47	14.17	12.96	13.76	13.55
713	Operating profit margin (%)	8.91	7.87	7.50	7.66	6.95
716	Pre-tax profit margin (%)	7.71	7.22	6.79	6.96	6.32
717	Net profit margin (%)	5.09	4.83	4.57	4.55	4.34
732	Income gearing (%)	15.20	17.51	19.25	20.03	21.24
733	Borrowing ratio	0.38	0.29	0.31	0.37	0.36
725	Stock ratio (days)	11.67	4.45	4.48	3.98	2.75
727	Debtors ratio (days)	78.88	73.01	75.19	80.51	84.65
729	Creditors ratio (days)	72.78	65.67	67.99	80.75	79.44
762	Sales per employee	44,553	45,225	46,357	50,565	55,462
763	Operating profit per employee	3,969	3,560	3,478	3,872	3,854
764	Capital employed /employee	23,284	27,801	30,003	32,190	33,465
792	Cash earnings per share	46.47	49.48	50.46	47.05	49.72

Source: Output taken from Datastream Program 190D.

Table 23.14 Tibbett & Britten Group Plc 1988–92

No.	Description	31/12/88	31/12/89	31/12/90	31/12/91	31/12/92
701	Return on shareholders' equity (%)	21.34	12.77	16.28	16.66	13.46
707	Return on capital employed (%)	25.78	18.22	25.42	22.57	16.25
713	Operating profit margin (%)	10.19	8.98	7.26	6.86	6.31
716	Pre-tax profit margin (%)	9.20	8.93	7.52	7.43	6.37
717	Net profit margin (%)	5.95	5.77	4.89	4.91	4.19
732	Income gearing (%)	10.49	11.76	12.46	5.01	7.83
733	Borrowing ratio	0.43	0.23	0.12	0.16	0.30
725	Stock ratio (days)	2.25	2.41	2.35	5.19	3.27
727	Debtors ratio (days)	51.77	63.25	39.52	41.20	67.11
729	Creditors ratio (days)	97.57	102.34	86.83	90.66	129.39
762	Sales per employee	26,160	26,453	28,694	29,296	32,196
763	Operating profit per employee	2,666	2,375	2,083	2,009	2,031
764	Capital employed /employee	10,437	14,695	9,696	10,147	13,662
792	Cash earnings per share	29.60	35.99	43.45	47.62	54.92

Source: Output taken from Datastream Program 190D.

Distribution in the UK: an industry note

A.E. Whiteing and C.G. Bamford

DISTRIBUTION MANAGEMENT, LOGISTICS MANAGEMENT AND SUPPLY CHAIN MANAGEMENT

A popular definition of *physical distribution management*, and one which has stood the test of time, is that it involves getting the right goods to the right place at the right time and at the right cost.

During the 1960s and 1970s the 'distribution mix' expanded to cover a range of separate but related management activities, which would typically include:

- the transport of goods by various modes (e.g. road, rail, sea, air), both within the company and to its customers;
- the holding of stock or inventory;
- provision and operation of facilities such as depots and warehouses for the storage of inventory;
- the handling of finished products and any packaging requirements;
- processing of orders and maintenance of all information relating to customer requirements and to stockholding.

Progressive companies no longer viewed these activities in isolation as individual tasks that had to be performed. The 'Total Distribution' philosophy, as advocated by many American writers and notably in the British situation by Christopher, was that the overall costs and benefits of all these distribution-related activities should be established. The preferred distribution strategy therefore combined the various activities in such a way as to minimize the total costs of the distribution operation without detriment to desired levels of customer service. It was also acknowledged that it may be necessary to raise expenditure on certain individual activities in order to reap greater savings elsewhere in the distribution network. This concept of 'trade-off' became central to thinking on distribution management, and led to fundamental changes in attitude towards transport and distribution management in many companies (Bowersox *et al.*, 1986; Christopher, 1971, 1985).

In the early 1980s a small number of companies started to regard their systems for product distribution as merely one component of their overall *logistics* system. As this view started to gain acceptance, emphasis switched to designing frameworks for fully integrated logistics management. The scope for such integration was seen to vary from company to company, but the underlying aim was to exploit synergy potential through the total coordination of systems for the management of inbound materials and the operation of internal logistical support systems for manufacturing facilities, as well as the efficient management of outbound product movements through effective channels of distribution (Bowersox *et al.*, 1986). The objective of the logistics manager came to be the development of effective interfaces between these different business activities within the organization (Christopher, 1985). As a result, the scope of the logistics manager's job, and the responsibilities to be borne, have both increased steadily, and this has been reflected in improved status and remuneration for those involved.

The state of the art in the 1990s is *supply chain management.* This is a further widening of the management net, in order to identify the position and role of the company along the entire chain of supply, stretching all the way from raw materials sources to receipt by the final consumer. Supply chain management is concerned with the development, implementation and operation of the interfaces between all organizations along the chain, in order to provide appropriate service levels at acceptable cost. The emphasis has changed from adversarial interfaces – common in traditional purchasing strategies for example – towards a partnership approach in which companies accept that there are mutual benefits to be gained from cooperation.

These most recent developments should be seen against the background of increasing adoption of 'Just-in-Time' techniques for production and distribution. Historically, high capital costs have forced industry to identify ways to reduce inventory levels. Many firms, both in manufacturing and retail environments, have implemented systems whereby goods are procured or produced and passed down the channels of distribution to their customers in close coordination with the final demand for those goods, thereby eliminating costly stockholding at all points in the supply chain.

Retailers often refer to 'Quick Response' rather than 'Just-in-Time' techniques, and place the emphasis on minimal stockholding at retail stores, which are serviced at frequent intervals from large centralized or regional depots, designed for rapid stockturn and regular scheduled replenishment from suppliers.

Consumer goods manufacturers facing increased pressure from major retailers, and increasingly supplying into those retailers' depots rather than their stores, have tended to centralize stockholding at or near the factory, rather than persist with hierarchical storage networks. A growing trend is for communications between retailers and their suppliers to be aided and accelerated by the use of Electronic Data Interchange (EDI) systems.

In manufacturing industry more generally, there has been considerable pressure for greater flexibility and a new philosophy towards production scheduling. Materials Requirements Planning (MRP), Manufacturing Resources Planning (MRP II) and Distribution Requirements Planning (DRP) are techniques that have come to be used increasingly for the coordination and fine-tuning of procurement, production and distribution operations (McClelland, 1989; Lee and Ebrahimpour, 1987; Sohal, Keller and Fouad, 1989).

Companies that have adopted 'Just-in-Time' and 'Quick Response' techniques have had to consider many complex implications for their use of transport and distribution services. Their key requirements are flexibility, reliability and dependability. The successful suppliers of such services are those that have had the resources to provide high-quality performance and have been flexible enough to produce innovative solutions to their clients' needs.

The changes that have occurred in the supply of freight transport and distribution services therefore need to be studied in the light of the changing nature of the demand for those services from industrial users who, as explained above, have undergone major changes in outlook, and have learned to manage their businesses in increasingly sophisticated ways.

FREIGHT TRANSPORT IN THE LOGISTICS MIX

With over 85 per cent of the domestic market, road freight dominates the transport aspect of the provision of logistics services. Rail does have a part to play, for example in the distribution of chemicals, fuel oils, building products, iron and steel and similar products which are bulky and can be carried in train load units, but many of these products have declined in importance as the emphasis in the UK economy has moved away from heavy industry towards the service sector. In such circumstances, the decline of rail freight has been inevitable. Recent government statements have been supportive of rail freight, but the reality is that the uncertainties surrounding the privatization of rail freight have accelerated the switch of freight from rail to road.

Traditionally, there have been two main types of operator in road freight transport:

- *haulage companies operating for hire or reward*, including specialist logistics/distribution contractors;
- *'own-account' operators*, which, as the name suggests, move goods and/or assemble raw materials primarily in connection with their own core business activity.

There have, however, been big structural changes in the industry over the last decade or so, notably the relative decline of own-account operations and the spectacular growth of the specialist logistics/distribution contractors.

These trends are summarized in Table 24.1, which highlights the substantial market growth, particularly in terms of tonne kilometres moved. The reasons for this include some transport factors (e.g. 38-tonne articulated vehicles which were introduced in 1983), but other causes such as the trend towards centralization in logistics systems referred to earlier have also been important. The relative decline of own-account operations is also clearly shown in this table, and is due in no small part to the growing use of contract distribution and logistics services.

Table 24.1 Road freight in UK, by mode of working

		1980	1985	1991
(a)	*Millions of tonnes lifted*			
	For hire or reward	658	748	976
	Own account	659	619	670
	Total	1,317	1,367	1,646
(b)	*Billion tonne-kilometres moved*			
	For hire or reward	54.7	66.6	98.8
	Own account	35.0	32.5	34.0
	Total	89.7	99.1	132.8

Source: Transport Statistics, Great Britain (various years).

Table 24.2 shows a profile of the top UK transport and distribution companies in 1990. In European terms, UK companies in general are large, although NFC plc is less than half the size of Danzas, the Swiss-owned European transport business. All the top eleven companies shown have experienced considerable growth and a reorientation in their business since 1980, and significantly the majority are heavily committed to the provision of contract distribution/logistics services.

Table 24.3, which is an alphabetical list of the leading providers of contract distribution services, was obtained from a trade magazine and shows the top thirty businesses in this growing sector.

THE NATURE OF THE MARKET FOR CONTRACT LOGISTICS/DISTRIBUTION SERVICES

The growing use of contract logistics/distribution services is in part a consequence of broader trends affecting British business, and as with many developments in logistics, major retailers have led the way. For a number of reasons such retailers have wished to divest themselves of distribution in order to focus attention on their core business.

Various degrees of divestment are possible, and for many users of contract distribution services, the contractor provides transport services alone. This is where the contractual commitment starts and finishes for many retail and manufacturing customers. For an increasing number of users, however, the contractor provides a package of supply chain or logistics management services covering:

- storage and warehousing;
- transport;
- assembly of stock and/or raw materials;
- information management, especially on inventory.

To go so far involves a clear recognition of partnership and mutual dependence. In other words, the business well-being of customer and provider becomes inextricably linked. Often, 'open book' accounting procedures subject to two-way scrutiny are employed. Major operators such as Exel Logistics, Federal Express and Tibbett & Britten openly offer such a full logistics service to their clients.

Table 24.2 Top UK transport and distribution companies in 1990

	Turnover (£m)	Employees	Vehicles
NFC plc	1,627	34,000	21,600
Lep	1,390	10,400	—
Ocean Group	1,101	10,500	—
Wincanton Group	698	9,800	26,000
Transport Development Group	581	12,600	6,700
POETS	557	6,300	—
Securicor	532	41,000	6,500
Hays Distribution Services	523	4,000	650
United Transport	459	12,900	13,100
Christian Salvesen	381	9,925	900
Tibbett & Britten Group	156	5,400	575

Source: Key Note Publications, 1992.

Table 24.3 The contract distribution market: thirty top contenders in 1993

(a)	*Annual turnover exceeding £50 million*
1	BOC Distribution Services
2	BRS (part of NFC)
3	Christian Salvesen
4	Exel Logistics (part of NFC)
5	Federal Express Business Logistics
6	Hays Distribution Services
7	McGregor Cory
8	NFT Distribution
9	Swift Transport Services
10	Tibbett & Britten Group
11	TNT Contract Distribution
12	Transport Development Group
13	Wincanton
(b)	*Annual turnover exceeding £12 million*
14	AAH Distribution
15	Applied Distribution
16	Bibby Distribution
17	Cert
18	Eleco Distribution Services
19	Frigoscandia
20	Heron Distribution
21	Lane Group
22	P & O Distribution
23	Potter Group
24	Russell Davies Distribution
25	Ryder Distribution Services
26	Taylor Barnard Distribution
27	Transfleet Services
28	UCI Logistics
29	United Transport Logistics
30	Vangen Services

Source: Distribution Business, No. 3, 1993.

Two other important points of perspective must also be made;

- Many users of contract distribution services are also own-account operators. Amongst the major retailers, J. Sainsbury, Tesco and Asda operate some of their own depots and transport services within their distribution networks. There is strategic value in a 'mix and match' approach to the provision of distribution/logistics services and the performance of the contractor can be used as a benchmark to assess own-account operations. In brewing also, the 'take-home' side of most brewers' operations is contracted out while the more specialist trade deliveries are retained as in-house operations.
- Many large users of contract distribution services use more than one contractor. This again offers certain strategic advantages and allows inter-contractor benchmarking to take place.

As the market for contract distribution services has grown, then so it has become more segmented. Various segments can be identified including:

- ambient temperature products;
- chilled goods;
- frozen goods;
- bulk liquids;
- fuel oil and chemicals;
- garments, hanging and boxed;
- leisure products including compact discs and videotapes;
- household products;
- express services such as document distribution and parcels;
- vehicle spares and parts.

The largest operators such as NFC plc and the Transport Development Group are in most if not all of the above segments; others tend to specialize in one or a small number of segments. Grocery distribution offers relatively little scope for further growth in contract distribution/logistics, and this adds to the pressure to diversify into new market segments (Milburn and Murray, 1993).

A final and in many respects very significant trend is that as the market has grown, so too has the level of industrial concentration. Although concentration is still low compared with many other industries, the largest companies have gained in strength and fight keenly for the key client accounts. Growth has frequently been through acquisition. Smaller players are less likely to win significant business, and economic recession has resulted in bankruptcies amongst the weaker competitors.

IN OR OUT? A KEY LOGISTICS DECISION

It is fair to say that whether or not to contract out some or all logistics services is one of the key decisions facing logistics managers today (Walters, 1993). The arguments on both sides have been widely debated by all concerned. The emphasis and outcome of the respective arguments depend in most businesses on particular circumstances and, in some cases, precedent. There is therefore no hard and fast set of rules which can be applied, but in general the following arguments for contracting out logistics services have been used, particularly by the operators of such services:

- contracting out allows a customer to concentrate upon the core business;
- contractors have substantial experience in many fields which they can transfer to their clients' businesses;
- customers can divest out of distribution and use the proceeds of divestment to retain or enhance their competitive position;
- contractors possess leading-edge expertise, particularly in logistics systems and technology;
- costs are known and stated in the contract;
- the contractor has to deal with any labour or industrial relations problems;
- the normally short length of contract provides an incentive for contractors to meet client needs and expectations;
- contracting out can be used as a benchmark for the assessment of own-account operations.

These are very powerful arguments and have clearly persuaded many companies to use contract logistics specialists. Equally, in many types of business, the decision has been made to retain in-house operations. Reasons put forward for the operation of own account services include:

- customer service advantages, particularly where deliveries are not within the same company or organization;
- outside hire can be used at peak periods to supplement a core own-account operation;
- marketing and/or image arguments which favour the retention of in-house services;
- no surrender of control to other parties;
- retention of core skills within the business.

Precise cost differentials between own-account and contract distribution are hard to determine and are probably very small for many businesses. There will be examples where own account distribution is the cheaper option as long as high levels of efficiency can be maintained, but many firms will find this hard to achieve. Similarly, there will be firms who have not realized that divestment will allow reductions in costs long considered to be fixed or overhead in nature. The key point is to weigh up all the above issues before making a decision. A realistic compromise, employed by many firms, is to use a mix of own-account and contracted-out provision. In this way, benchmarks can be established and there are built-in competitive elements in the logistics system to ensure that both parties strive to reduce their respective costs of operation.

PROSPECTS FOR THE FUTURE

The market for logistics services is undoubtedly affected by the state of the economy generally, although the precise nature of the relationship is by no means clear. As a service sector activity closely linked to the fortunes of retailing, the distribution industry escaped the worst of the recent UK recession. However, the simple fact that distribution involves handling manufactured goods means that some downturn is inevitable when manufacturing industry is in recession.

Assuming that economic recovery can be sustained, it seems likely that providers of contract distribution/logistics services will continue to gain business. Economic upturn will increase the demand for distribution services in general, and some firms will decide to employ contract distributors in order to concentrate on their core businesses. At present, only about 1 in 5 companies who *could* use contract carriers actually do so, suggesting that there is a large pool of companies and clients ready to be targeted by contractors. The growing client requirement for a full logistics service, rather than simply transport provision, will reinforce this trend. There would seem therefore to be every indication that contract logistics/distribution services will continue to increase in importance.

On the other hand, warning notes have been consistently sounded by P-E's quality surveys (P-E International, 1994; Meredith and O'Sullivan, 1991; Szymankiewicz, 1993). These indicate that many users of contract services are not satisfied with the level of service being provided and that customer service remains a major obstacle to further generic growth. As a result, a small number of companies have reverted to own-account operation.

These cautionary notes reinforce the need for contract providers to ensure that their services are precisely in line with their clients' requirements. The key need is for both parties to consider very carefully the exact specification of the contract, and particularly to avoid over-specification which will inflate the cost to the client. Contractors must then deliver their claim that they are adding value to their clients' market offering, rather than simply replacing an earlier own-account operation for an agreed price.

Against this background, there is some justification for the views put forward by Walters (1993) to the effect that:

● contractors will become more specialized, for example in a particular industrial sector;
● there is room for niche operators, operating successfully alongside the large players such as NFC, Transport Development Group and Wincanton.

Walters also points out that UK operators face a growing real threat from other European and Japanese competitors, and strategies to fight such competition will need to be developed.

REFERENCES

Bowersox, D.J., D.J. Closs and O.K. Helferich (1986) *Logistical Management*, 3rd ed. London, Macmillan.

Buck, D. (1988) 'Changing to contract distribution', *Management Decision*, Vol. 26, No 5, pp. 42–7.

Christopher, M.J. (1971) *Total Distribution*. London, Gower.

Christopher, M.J. (1985) *The Strategy of Distribution Management*. Aldershot, Gower.

Corporate Development Consultants Limited (1988). Consultancy Report on *UK market for contract distribution*.

Department of Transport (1993) *Transport Statistics, Great Britain, 1982–1992*. London, CSO.

Distribution Business (1993) 'The 1993 contract distribution profiles', *Distribution Business*, No. 3, pp. 17–56.

Drucker, P.F. (1962) 'The economy's dark continent', *Fortune*, April, pp. 103, 265, 268, 270.

Key Note Publications Ltd (1992) *Market Review: Industry Trends and Forecasts – UK Distribution*.

Lawrence, J. (1988) 'Going places', *Commercial Motor*, 29 September, pp. 47–8.

Lee, S.M. and M. Ebrahimpour (1987) 'Just-in-time', *Management Decision*, Vol. 25, No. 6, pp. 50–4.

McClelland, S. (1989) 'Just-in-time for world class', *Logistics World*, September, pp. 161–4.

McKinnon, A.C. (1989) *Physical Distribution Systems*. London, Routledge.

Meredith, C. and D. O'Sullivan (1991) 'Contract distribution in the UK: what the customer really thinks', *Logistics Today*, Vol. 10, No. 2, March/April, pp. 15–18.

Milburn, A. and W. Murray (1993) 'Saturation in the market for dedicated contract distribution?', *Logistics Focus*, Vol. 1, No. 5, December, pp. 6–8.

P-E International (1994) 'More than cash to third party move', *MT Logistica*, February, p. 4.

Sohal, A.S., A.Z. Keller and R.H. Fouad (1989) 'A review of literature relating to JIT', *International Journal of Operations and Production Management*, Vol. 9, No. 3, pp. 15–25.

Szymankiewicz, J. (1993) 'Contracting out or selling out?' *Logistics Focus*, Vol. 1, No. 5, December, pp. 2–5.

Walters, P.J. (1993) *In or Out? The Contract Distribution Dilemma*. Sevenoaks, Distribution Dynamics.

QUESTIONS RELATING TO THE CASES

CASE 1 ASDA GROUP PLC (A)

Indicative questions

1. Critically appraise the merger between Asda and MFI.

2. Appraise the strategic management of the Asda Group in the ten years to the departure of John Hardman.

3. Provide a SWOT analysis for the Asda Group as at the end of 1991. Assume that you have been appointed as the new chief executive of the Asda Group: what short-term and long-term strategic actions would you undertake to improve Asda's competitive position?

CASE 2 ASDA GROUP PLC (B)

Indicative questions

1. Identify and discuss the generic turnaround strategies used at Asda.

2. Archie Norman's strategy for Asda is one of 'back to basics'. Is this enough to ensure recovery and to meet the objective of sustainable increases in shareholder value?

CASE 3 ARGYLL GROUP PLC

Indicative questions

1. Provide a full strategic appraisal of the Argyll Group as at the end of December 1992.

2. Identify and evaluate the key success factors in UK grocery retailing. To what extent are these factors transferable to the European market? Does the Argyll Group possess these skills and resources to compete effectively in Europe?

3. Assume that Argyll in 1993/94 is considering a strategic move into Europe. Outline and discuss the various entry strategies open to the company, particularly highlighting the following factors: risk, profitability and commitment.

4. Critically compare and contrast a standard global approach to marketing strategy with that of a more nationally segmented approach in international markets. Which would be more/less applicable for grocery retailers like Argyll?

CASE 4   BURTON AND NEXT – THE CHANGING HIGH STREET

Indicative questions

1. Using appropriate frameworks, critically appraise the strategic positions of Burton and Next as at April 1994. In your analysis compare and contrast the financial performances of the two companies.

2. What aspects of turnaround theory are evident in the strategic approaches taken at both Burton and Next in the early 1990s? To what extent were they successful?

3. Identify and discuss the strategic options open to both companies for the period 1995–96.

CASE 5   CROMARTY COURTHOUSE MUSEUM

Indicative questions

1. Determine the stakeholders in the success of Cromarty Courthouse and the conflicting pressures they might put on the organization.

2. How might the use of a strategic planning framework assist not-for-profit organizations balance core values, multiple objectives and income generation?

3. Are the Courthouse Trustees correct to assume that the organization has completed the start-up phase of its business lifecycle? Based on your premise, how might the Trustees evaluate the success of their strategy?

CASE 6   LONDON ZOO

Indicative questions

General

1. What are the arguments for and against subsidizing national zoos like London Zoo? Do you believe that the UK government should provide a public subsidy for the London Zoo? Why or why not?

2. How do you think the different stakeholders would interpret the statement of purpose of the Zoological Society of London with respect to London Zoo?

Part A

3. Identify the strategic problems faced by London Zoo during the late 1980s.

4. If you had been in charge, what strategies would you have sought to follow?

Part B

5. Evaluate the Peat Marwick McClintock recommendations and the subsequent actions taken to try to overcome the strategic problems of the zoo.

6. Are the changes suggested during 1992 likely to prove adequate for the long-term survival of the zoo?

Optional updating question

7. Which (if any) of these proposals have been implemented, and how successful have they proved?

CASE 7 THE NATIONAL TRUST

Indicative questions

1. What are the objectives of the National Trust? What are the inherent conflicts? How do you feel the objectives would be prioritized by the major stakeholders?

2. Do you think the performance measures used by the National Trust are wholly appropriate? If not, what measures should be adopted either instead of, or in addition to, those used?

3. Assess the National Trust in respect of Environment–Values–Resources (E–V–R) congruence. What, if any, changes are required if the National Trust is to enjoy congruence in its centenary year (1995)?

4. What opportunities for change are available to the National Trust? What would constitute appropriate change? Do other charities pose any threats to the National Trust? Where are the main constraints to change?

CASE 8 KIRKLEES METROPOLITAN COUNCIL: CORPORATE STRATEGY IN A LOCAL AUTHORITY

Indicative questions

1. Carry out a stakeholder analysis of Kirklees Metropolitan Council and comment on its implications for the strategic management of this local authority.

2. How important are Harman and Hughes in establishing Kirklees Metropolitan Council's strategic direction?

3. Describe the culture of Kirklees Metropolitan Council and discuss the implications for strategic management.

4. How appropriate are rational theories of strategic management in explaining Kirklees Metropolitan Council's development in the period covered by this case study?

CASE 9 ABBEY NATIONAL PLC

Indicative questions

1. Evaluate the changing nature of the external environment facing the Abbey

National and other building societies in the late 1980s. What impact will these factors have on strategy formulation?

2. Consider the nature of Abbey National's culture and its influence on the decision to convert to a plc.

3. Evaluate the appropriateness of the post-flotation and diversification activities of Abbey National.

4. What interest rate and housing market scenario could encourage other building societies to convert to a plc?

5. There are approximately 80 building societies operating in the UK. Is this number realistic given the nature of financial service provision?

Optional question

6. What part does managerial perception play in environment analysis and in what ways can managerial perception be improved?

CASE 10 THE CAISSES D'EPARGNE (FRENCH SAVINGS BANKS)

Indicative questions

1. Conduct a SWOT analysis for the *caisses d'épargne*.

2. Identify the problems that were caused as a result of reorganization (in this case the setting up of the Caisse d' Epargne of Frenche-Comté).

3. 'Identity is what helps to define an organization's specificity, stability and coherence. It can be at the same time an action strength and an inertia strength.' Discuss this statement with reference to the case organization. (Your analysis may consider the relationship between strategy, structure and culture.)

4. What measures would you suggest the company consider taking to manage its corporate identity?

CASE 11 CORPORATE STRATEGIES WITHIN THE NEWLY PRIVATIZED WATER PLCS

Indicative questions

1. What were the strategies pursued by the water plcs, and how suitable do you think they were in terms of their strategic logic?

2. How would you assess whether waste management was a suitable market for the water plcs to enter? What other markets do you think would be suitable?

CASE 12   THE EUROPEAN FOOD INDUSTRY AND GROUPE BSN

Indicative questions

1. Compare and contrast the four cross-border acquisition strategies referred to in the case with Porter's three generic strategies of cost leadership, differentiation and focus.

2. Bearing in mind trends in the European food industry and its markets, assess the view of the industry experts referred to on pages 252–3 that opportunities for 'remargining' and 'pan-European distribution' will increase at the expense of 'consolidation' and 'growth engineering'.

3. Critically appraise Groupe BSN's historic strategy and performance within the European food industry.

CASE 13   GLAXO HOLDINGS PLC

Indicative questions

1. Identify the key success factors that are seen to operate in the pharmaceutical industry and evaluate Glaxo's strategic success in that industry during the 1980s and early 1990s.

2. Assess Glaxo's product portfolio as at the case date.

3. As health care costs rise and government health budgets are under pressure, physicians are being asked to prescribe generic drugs wherever possible, and former prescription drugs are being made available 'over the counter'. How does Glaxo compete in this new environment?

CASE 14   KWIK-FIT HOLDINGS

Indicative questions

1. 'Kwik-Fit is Tom Farmer – it is his stamp that has marked the structural development of the organization.' Discuss.

2. Evaluate the proposition that 'an investment in Kwik-Fit is merely an investment in Tom Farmer'.

3. 'Kwik-Fit's success owes more to luck than to strategic planning.' In light of this statement assess the strategic development pursued by Kwik-Fit.

4. 'The key to Kwik-Fit's success lies in its control systems, especially its computer system.' Discuss.

5. Critically assess Kwik-Fit's strategic position for meeting the challenges of the future.

CASE 15   CHRYSALIS GROUP

Indicative questions

1. In order to form a successful strategy companies need to have congruence between their available resources, their culture and values, and the opportunities and threats posed by the environment within which they are operating. To what degree has Chrysalis found a satisfactory congruence?

2. How has the music industry changed over the last 20 years, and what implications does this have for the new Chrysalis label, Echo?

3. Has Chris Wright been proactive or reactive to the opportunities in his industry?

4. Using appropriate company financial databases, select three other record companies and compare and contrast their relative financial positions. Identify the problems that exist in selecting and comparing your sample.

5. To what extent have prices at which Chrysalis shares have traded over the last five years been a fair representation of the viability of the business?

6. Draw up a SWOT analysis in respect of music 'hardware' and discuss the implications for the providers of music 'software'.

7. Why have some record companies sought to become vertically and horizontally integrated providers of both music 'software' and music 'hardware'?

8. Given that musical taste is very much bound up in the particular culture of a country or segment of its population, what are the real advantages to be realized from the increasing internationalization of record companies?

CASE 16   VOLKSWAGEN GROUP

Indicative questions

1. Analyse the strategic position of the VW group in 1994.

2. Analyse and evaluate the strategic options open to the VW group in 1994.

3. What steps would VW have to take to become a 'lean' manufacturer like Toyota or Mazda? What are the main obstacles and how could they be overcome?

CASE 17   FISONS PLC

Indicative questions

1. With reference to theories of entry and exit, critically appraise Fisons' decision to divest its fertilizer business in 1982.

2. Advance reasons for Fisons' failure to sustain the improved performance which was evidenced during the mid 1980s.

3. On the basis of the company's position at the end of 1993, formulate a strategy for Fisons to pursue to the end of the decade.

CASE 18   REDLAND PLC

Indicative questions

1. Assess the financial performance of Redland Plc as at the case date.

2. Identify and discuss the recurrent themes running through Redland's joint ventures and consider the rationale behind this.

3. In the light of the discussion on questions 1 and 2, consider how effective Redland's strategy has been.

4. What factors constitute a major opportunity in Eastern Europe in the early 1990s?

5. Which country (in Eastern Europe) would you select for Redland's next expansion move and what factors should be considered in making such a choice? How should such factors be evaluated?

CASE 19   ICI AND HANSON – A CONTRAST IN STYLES

Indicative questions

1. Critically evaluate the usefulness of portfolio planning theory for the process of strategy formulation. Compare and contrast ICI's portfolio with that of Hanson Plc.

2. 'The key issue in the Hanson–ICI debate is not the need for tighter financial control. It is that a takeover or merger would not only be merely inappropriate, but dangerous to both sides.' Discuss.

3. Suggest a strategic way forward for ICI to help it overcome some of the weaknesses which were highlighted by the events of 1991–92.

CASE 21   STAGECOACH HOLDINGS PLC

Indicative questions

1. Examine the reasons which underpin the growth and survival of Stagecoach in an industry which shows such obvious signs of decline.

2. Evaluate the contributions that Ann Gloag and Brian Souter make to the success of Stagecoach.

3. Critically assess Stagecoach's strategic position for meeting the challenges of the future.

4. Examine the relationship between strategy, structure and performance and evaluate any dysfunctional elements you perceive in the case which may influence such a relationship.

5. 'The key to Stagecoach's success lies in its ability to identify and aggressively implement a policy of acquisition against a potential takeover target.' To what extent would you agree or disagree with this view?

6. 'For Stagecoach, finance has been a competitive tool which they have used to great effect in building the fortunes of the company.' In the light of this statement examine the factors which have led to the current financial position of Stagecoach.

CASE 21   CHRISTIAN SALVESEN PLC

Indicative questions

1. Using a model of your choice, evaluate the usefulness of portfolio planning theory for strategy evaluation for Christian Salvesen.

2. Conduct a full strategic appraisal of Christian Salvesen Plc as at the end of 1991. Include in your appraisal a detailed comment on the company's financial performance.

3. If we assume that the current economic climate of recession is likely to continue in the near term, identify and assess possible strategy options open to Christian Salvesen that will enable it to continue to 'enhance the quality of its earnings'.

CASE 22   VIRGIN ATLANTIC AIRWAYS

Indicative questions

1. Argue the case for and against Richard Branson starting the airline in 1984.

2. Why has Virgin Atlantic Airways been successful so far, while similar airlines such as Laker Airways and People Express failed?'

3. How well do you think that (a) the non-executive directors of BA, (b) the institutional shareholders of BA, reacted to the 'dirty tricks' campaign against Virgin Atlantic? Should they have done anything differently? Should the top management of BA have resigned and left the company?

4. Assume that you were a middle manager with BA at the time of the 'dirty tricks' campaign against Virgin Atlantic, and that you had been asked to perform a task you believed to be ethically wrong. List the possible responses to this ethical dilemma and the pros and cons of the responses. How do you think that you would have actually responded?

CASE 23   NFC PLC

Indicative questions

1. Using frameworks of your choice, critically examine the growth strategy of NFC up to the case date. Suggest a strategy for NFC to follow for the remaining part of the decade.

2. Identify possible reasons that influence a firm's international strategic development and critically evaluate the international strategy of NFC. Comment on whether or not its strategy has been a financial success.

3. Are 'people' a key element to the success of corporate strategies in a service-orientated business? To what extent can NFC use this 'people' element to gain competitive advantage?

CASE 24 DISTRIBUTION IN THE UK: AN INDUSTRY NOTE

Indicative questions

1. Explain the differences between physical distribution management, logistics and supply chain management.

2. Discuss the main trade-offs which are present in a distribution system and examine their implications for managing a business.

3. Produce a customer profile of one of the top UK transport and distribution companies shown in Table 24.2 of the case.

4. Assess the arguments for contracting out distribution/logistics services in:
   (a) a large grocery retailer;
   (b) a brewing business;
   (c) a regional health authority or a former public utility.

INDEX

acid test   41–2
activity ratios   44–5
Ansoff, H.I.   16
average collection period   45

balance sheet   33, 35
bargaining power
   of buyers   10
   of suppliers   11

capital cost   10
capabilities   14
capital employed   45
cash flow statements   50
case analysis
   guidelines   27–9
   oral   29–30
   written   30–1
case studies   25–31
competitive forces   10, 12
competitive rivalry   11
consolidated accounts   33
corporate social responsibility   15
cost leadership   19–20
culture   14, 21
current ratio   39, 41

debtor turnover   45
debt ratio   43
debt-to-equity ratio   43
deliberate strategies   23
demographic factors   9
differentiation   10, 20
distinctive competence   14
diversification
   related   17
   unrelated   18
divestment   18

dividend cover   49–50
Drucker, P.   7

earnings per share (EPS)   49
economic forces   9
economies of scale   10
effectiveness   13
efficiency   13
entry barriers   10, 12
environment   4, 8–12
   broad   8–9
   competitive   8, 9–11
emergent strategies   23
exit-barriers   11, 12
external analysis   8–12

financial analysis   33–52
fixed asset turnover   44
focus strategy   20
functional policies   22

gearing ratios   42–4
generic strategies   19–20
global strategy   19
governmental factors   9
growth   16–18
   by acquisition   18
   international   19
   organic   18

harvesting strategy   18
holding strategy   18

industry analysis 10–12
inflation adjusted figures   34–6
integration
   backward   17
   forward   17
   horizontal   17–18

interest cover   43–4
internal analysis   12–14
internal audit 13

leadership style   21–2
liquidation strategy   18
liquidity ratios   39–42

management values   15–16
market
    development   16–17
    penetration   16
Mintzberg, H.   23
mission   4, 7
mobility barriers   12
multi-domestic strategy   19
multinational companies (MNCs)
    19

net asset turnover   44
net dividend yield   49
new entrants   10

objectives   4, 7–8
opportunity   4, 11, 12

political factors   9
Porter, M.E   10, 11, 12, 19
price/earnings (PE) ratio   49
product development   17
profit margin
    operating   46
    net   46
profitability ratios   45–6
profit and loss account   33, 34
pyramid of ratios   46–7

quick ratio   41–2

ratio analysis   37–50
resources   12–13, 14

retrenchment   18
return on capital employed   45
return on equity   46
reward systems   22

socio-cultural forces 9
stability   18
stakeholders   8
stock market ratios   47–50
stock turnover   44
strategic business unit (SBU)   5, 13
strategic groups   12
strategic management
    different perspectives   23
    model   5, 6
    position   8
    process   5
strategy
    alternatives   16
    business   4, 5, 19–20
    choice   20–1
    corporate   4 5, 16–19
    evaluation   22–3
    formulation   7
    functional   4, 5, 20
    implementation   21–2
    level and types   3, 4
strength   4, 14
structure   13, 21
substitutes   11
SWOT   6, 28
    matrix   14, 15

technological factors   9
threat   4, 11, 12
threat of entry   10
turnaround strategy   18

weakness   4, 14
working capital   47